W9-ANH-458

MASTERPLOTS II

AFRICAN AMERICAN
LITERATURE
SERIES

MASTERPLOTS II

AFRICAN AMERICAN LITERATURE SERIES

3

Po-Z

Indexes

Edited by

FRANK N. MAGILL

SALEM PRESS

Pasadena, California   Englewood Cliffs, New Jersey

∞ The paper used in these volumes conforms to the
American National Standard for Permanence of Paper
for Printed Library Materials, Z39.48-1984.

Library of Congress Cataloging-in-Publication Data
Masterplots II: African American literature series/edited
by Frank N. Magill
    p. cm.
    Includes bibliographical references and index.
       1. American literature—Afro-American authors—
Stories, plots, etc. 2. Afro-Americans in literature. I.
Magill, Frank Northen, 1907-   . II. Title: Master-
plots 2. III. Title: Masterplots two.
PS153.N5M2645 1994   93-33876
810.9'896073—dc20   CIP
ISBN 0-89356-594-6 (set)
ISBN 0-89356-597-0 (volume 3)

PRINTED IN THE UNITED STATES OF AMERICA

LIST OF TITLES IN VOLUME 3

LIST OF TITLES IN VOLUME 3

MASTERPLOTS II

AFRICAN AMERICAN
LITERATURE
SERIES

THE POETRY OF OWEN DODSON

Author: Owen Dodson (1914-1983)
Type of work: Poetry
First published: Powerful Long Ladder, 1946; *Cages,* 1953; *The Confession Stone: Song Cycles,* 1970, with James Van DerZee and Camille Billops; *The Harlem Book of the Dead,* 1978

One of nine children, Owen Dodson was born on November 28, 1914, in Brooklyn, New York, to Nathaniel Barnett Dodson, a free-lance journalist, and his wife, Sarah Elizabeth Goode Dodson. Owen grew up proud of his identity and of his lineage. He early knew of the social contributions of such black luminaries as Booker T. Washington, James Weldon Johnson, and W. E. B. Du Bois.

Fate conspired to turn the young Owen Dodson into the writer he became. He attended Thomas Jefferson High School; the school's principal, Elias Lieberman, was a poet. Lieberman encouraged the boy to enter contests that resulted in his winning medals for public recitations of verse. Owen was at this time also active in the Concord Baptist Church in Brooklyn, where he imbibed the cadences of black spirituals with which he was later to infuse his verse.

Upon graduation from high school, Dodson received a scholarship to Bates College in Lewiston, Maine, where he enrolled in a freshman course that John Berkelman taught. Dodson brashly told Berkelman that he had the capability to write sonnets as good as those of John Keats. Berkelman thereupon told Dodson to write a sonnet a week until graduation. Carrying out this assignment helped Dodson to perfect his craft and resulted in his publishing pieces in the *New York Herald Tribune,* in *Opportunity,* and in *Phylon* before he left Bates in 1936 to continue his studies at Yale University, where he received an M.F.A. degree in 1939.

Although Dodson was diverted from writing poetry first by the demands of his program in drama at Yale and later by his service in the United States Navy, where he was assigned to write dramas to boost the morale of black servicemen, a number of his poems appeared in such publications as *Common Ground, New Currents, Theatre Arts,* and *Harlem Quarterly* between 1942 and the publication of his first volume of verse, *Powerful Long Ladder,* in 1946. The poems Dodson published in these periodicals were incorporated into this first volume. During his time at Yale, Dodson also produced his verse play, *Divine Comedy* (pr. 1938), a portion of which appears in *Powerful Long Ladder* and which was awarded the Maxwell Anderson prize for verse drama. Although Dodson felt that his greatest poetic achievement was *The Confession Stone: Song Cycles,* which he first published in 1970, most critics have turned to the earlier work as best representing Dodson's poetry.

Powerful Long Ladder is concerned with human struggle, particularly with the struggle of blacks in a society that first enslaved and then simultaneously exploited and ignored them. At the time the book was published, segregation was widespread. Dodson had recently been discharged from the Navy, where he belonged to a segregated company at the Great Lakes Naval Training Station outside Chicago.

The book, divided into five sections, takes its title from the Dodson poem "Some-day We're Gonna Tear Them Pillars Down," a seven-page verse drama that uses dramatic technique to the utmost. The pillars are symbolically akin to the wall in Robert Frost's famous poem "Mending Wall"; they are barriers that serve as points of demarcation between people—in the Dodson poem, between blacks and the dominant society.

Dodson has often been compared to Frost. In a sense, however, this comparison may be misleading because of Dodson's deep personal involvement on a daily basis with the inequities of segregation and discrimination, which continually devoured his spirit. Robert Frost could afford a philosophical detachment that no black of Owen Dodson's period could reasonably enjoy.

The first section of *Powerful Long Ladder* contains a dozen poems of from two to six pages each. The range of these poems is remarkable. Some focus on individuals; others deal broadly with topics ranging from racial tension to death to the accomplishments of blacks. Many of them are dialect poems. The first poem, "Lament," which is not in dialect, is exceptionally interesting, beginning with an imperative to a dead boy to wake and tell how he died. What the poem essentially conveys is the hopelessness of trying fully to understand life's common abstractions—love, freedom, terror, death.

A more complicated view of human existence emanates from "Guitar," a ballad about a black jailed for hitting a white person. Society decrees that, without solid evidence, the black should be adjudged guilty. This poem has strong metrical overtones from "The Weary Blues" by Langston Hughes. The tone of the poem is one of despair tempered by resignation. The black man has no recourse as society is constituted.

Among the best-known Dodson poems is "Black Mother Praying," a war poem about a mother whose sons have left to defend their country. She compares her sacrifice to Christ's crucifixion, her sons to the son of Mary. The rub is that when her sons come home—if they come home—the freedom they fought to assure will, because of their color, extend neither to her nor to them. This poem is a precursor of Dodson's *The Confession Stone*, in which Dodson makes the Virgin Mary and her son quite ordinary people dealing with the details of daily life. Mary admonishes the young Jesus not to play with Judas when he goes out.

The second section of *Powerful Long Ladder* contains a substantial excerpt from Dodson's verse play, *Divine Comedy*, which is an ironic presentation of the kind of hope that the evangelist Father Divine offered his hapless followers, most of them black, for several decades. Dodson as a boy went to one of Father Divine's meetings with his brother Kenneth and never forgot the experience. Like Jesus feeding the five thousand, Father Divine fed his followers. He drew milk from a seemingly bottomless well. When the crowd had dispersed, however, Kenneth lifted the tablecloth to find that a black boy was underneath pumping milk into the vat from which Father Divine magically extracted it.

Surely this experience provided an initial stimulus for *Divine Comedy*, which also has many structural elements borrowed from Dante's masterpiece. Yet Dodson's verse drama provides, in essence, a startling insight into how black people, stripped of much of their hope, can be exploited and duped, as Father Divine's followers usually were, even by their fellow black people.

The other sections of *Powerful Long Ladder*, "Poems for My Brother Kenneth," "All This Review," and "Counterpoint," develop the racial themes that Dodson examines in the earlier sections. The latter sections, though, show a growing artistic maturity on the author's part, particularly in the lyricism with which he approaches his material.

The twenty-four-year hiatus between *Powerful Long Ladder* and *The Confession Stone* occurred because Dodson was serving as professor of drama at Howard University. During this period—1947 until 1969—Dodson concentrated primarily on writing plays, although he did write two novels, *The Boy in the Window*, published in 1951, and *A Bent House*, completed when a Guggenheim Fellowship in 1953 enabled Dodson to spend an extended period in Italy. This novel did not appear until 1977, re-titled *Come Home Early, Child*.

The thin poetry collection *Cages*, which Dodson also completed during his stay in Italy, explores essentially the same racial themes that are found in his first collection. *The Confession Stone* consists of seven brief sections, including comments by Mary on Jesus, letters from Joseph to Mary, journals of Mary Magdalene, songs from Judas to Jesus, songs by Jesus to God, songs by God to His son, and a final song by Mary to Jesus. The parallels between the biblical epic and the racial situation from which Dodson wrote are striking. An additional volume of Dodson's poems remained unpublished at his death.

Owen Dodson was caught between two compelling movements, a part of neither. The Harlem Renaissance had run its course by the time Dodson began to emerge as a literary figure. Ahead lay the black militancy of the 1960's and early 1970's.

When *Powerful Long Ladder* appeared in 1946, some critics considered it too much concerned with issues of race, although these critics, including John Holmes, who reviewed the book for *The New York Times*, found considerable promise in Dodson's writing. Alfred Kreymborg commented on the notable dramatic qualities in Dodson's poetry, observing that the poet could infuse old topics such as estranged love with "fire, wisdom, and dignity." Richard Eberhart, on the basis of this first volume, called Dodson the best black poet in the United States.

The poems in *Powerful Long Ladder* are largely concerned with the effects of continuing poverty and prejudice upon a race transplanted from its own continent, enslaved, and freed only to endure humiliation and repression from mainstream society. Obviously, in a poem such as "Autumn Chorus: After the Prophet Has Been Killed," the poet uses such dramatic devices as dialogue and a chorus to sustain a plaint that seems eerily prescient: Malcolm X and Martin Luther King, Jr., were alive but were scarcely known to the public at the time that this chilling poem was written.

To those nonblack critics who suggest that Dodson was too much concerned with race, one can only say that a cauldron of racial tension was simmering and was soon to boil over in America. Dodson was daily exposed to the tensions that within twenty years would result in the violence that darkened the 1960's. He could not ignore the strife he saw around him.

On the other hand, Dodson did not consciously fan the fires that were smoldering. He was being objective, but his objectivity was from the black rather than the white point of view. Therefore, his stance seemed to many whites to be more extreme than it was.

The most personal and, in some ways, the most deeply felt poems in *Powerful Long Ladder* are those contained in the section entitled "Poems for My Brother Kenneth," in which Dodson reflects on personal memories and relives portions of his youth. The racial tone in these poems is more subdued than in the other sections of this collection, although it necessarily intrudes even upon these poems.

Dodson resisted being identified with blacks who were grouped merely by their color. Invited to join Bates College's black alumni association, he declined, asking, "Did I learn black Latin?" His poems continually reflect a similar attitude. He suggests that if blacks are to become a part of mainstream American life, such organizations as black alumni associations must go.

In his poems, Dodson exudes energy. He does not shrink from the struggle in which his race, in his eyes, must participate actively—and he suggests that white people can help in this struggle. In "Miss Packard and Miss Giles," Dodson celebrates the two white women who founded Spelman College for Negro Women in Atlanta, where he taught from 1938 until 1941. He commends their stalwartness, their refusal to return to their native New England when things were not going well.

Similarly, in poems such as "Epitaph for a Negro Woman" and "Black Mother Praying," the suggestion is that people must keep moving forward, struggling hand over hand up the ladder that provides the title for Dodson's first volume of poetry. In small details of his later life, Dodson followed his own advice.

When, severely crippled by arthritis, Dodson went to an experimental theatrical production with James Hatch, he had to climb a long flight of stairs to reach the auditorium. Giving Hatch his canes, he grasped the railing and, quite painfully, pulled himself up the stairs, refusing help offered by passersby. In this act, Dodson was playing out the philosophy that many of his poems espouse.

Throughout his career, Dodson wrote poignant death poems, some celebrating the deaths of individuals, such as "Countee Cullen" in *Powerful Long Ladder*, others addressing the topic generally. He wrote the poems for *The Harlem Book of the Dead*, a collection of funeral photographs taken by James Van DerZee and assembled by Camille Billops.

Most of Dodson's death poems express the sentiment that death, the great equalizer, diminishes one's blackness. The earth consumes it, a thought which appears to be comforting for the poet. One of his last poems, "There Are No Tears" (1981), suggests that grief "photographs" all that has been. It is not accompanied by tears or the sounds of trombones, but the dead person's "heart is quiet;/ A grain of sand./

His beach is not afraid/ Of the ocean anymore."

Owen Dodson was an inheritor of the black poetic tradition established by Paul Laurence Dunbar, Langston Hughes, and Countée Cullen, to whom Dodson acknowledges his debt. He was also well acquainted with the writing of W. E. B. Du Bois and James Weldon Johnson, although his poetry seems less influenced by their work than by that of poets closer to him in time.

Dodson was different from most of the black poets before him because he had essentially been reared in a middle-class Northern black family that was not dysfunctional in the way that, for example, Langston Hughes's family was. Dodson's going to New England to attend a predominantly white college also set him apart, as did his further education at Yale University.

Although he knew what it was to feel discrimination and to be subjected to segregation, Dodson also knew what it was to be accepted and not to endure segregation. Perhaps this dichotomy made him feel more deeply than some earlier black poets the stings of racial prejudice when he encountered them. His was essentially a moderate voice bridging the period between the Harlem Renaissance, with its artistic promise, and the racial strife of the 1960's.

Bibliography

Hardy, Sallee W., ed. *Remembering Owen Dodson.* New York: Hatch-Billops Collection, 1984. This is a collection of reminiscences, poems, and other materials about Owen Dodson presented at his funeral. Among the contributors are Margaret Walker, David Abram, Amiri Baraka, and Joe Weixlmann.

Hatch, James V. "Remembering Owen Dodson." In *Artist and Influence, 1985.* New York: Hatch-Billops Collection, 1985. Hatch, who first met Dodson when he participated in a playwriting workshop at the University of Iowa while Hatch was a student there, provides warm reminiscences about an evening when he and Dodson, then badly crippled and barely mobile, went to see a new play written by one of Hatch's students.

O'Brien, John. "Owen Dodson." In *Interviews with Black Writers.* New York: Liveright, 1973. O'Brien conducted this hourlong interview in 1971. Dodson later supplemented it with written responses. It is revealing in that Dodson comments on other black writers and clearly distances himself from some who wrote in the turbulent 1960's. Dodson discusses the themes of religion and history in his work.

Peterson, Bernard L., Jr. "The Legendary Owen Dodson of Howard University." *Crisis* 86 (November, 1979): 373-374. Peterson, although not the most disinterested critic of Dodson, has, nevertheless, a good feeling for his writing and for its place in and relationship to black writing in the United States generally.

Schraufnagel, Noel. *From Apology to Protest: The Black American Novel.* Deland, Fla.: Everett/Edwards Press, 1973. Schraufnagel devotes only two pages to Dodson and concentrates essentially on his novels. Nevertheless, his comments help to place Dodson in a useful literary context.

R. Baird Shuman

THE POETRY OF RITA DOVE

Author: Rita Dove (1952-   )
Type of work: Poetry
First published: The Yellow House on the Corner, 1980; *Museum*, 1983; *Thomas and Beulah*, 1986; *Grace Notes*, 1989

With the publication of four volumes of poetry and one volume of short stories since 1980, and a Pulitzer Prize in 1987 for *Thomas and Beulah*, her third volume of poetry, Rita Dove has established herself as a major force in contemporary American poetry. Born August 28, 1952, in Akron, Ohio, Dove received her bachelor's degree from Miami University (Ohio) in 1973 and attended the University of Tübingen on a Fulbright fellowship to study modern European literature. She returned to the United States to attend the highly regarded University of Iowa Writers Workshop, earning a master of fine arts degree in 1977. Dove has held a number of teaching posts since that time, has traveled extensively in Europe and the Middle East, and has become a professor of English at the University of Virginia.

As an African American writer with strong European connections (in addition to her travels there, she is married to the German writer Fred Viebahn) and a sense of the past as well as the present, Rita Dove has claimed a vast world—full of mysteries, small objects, broken promises, desires, contradictions, cruelties, and strange weathers—for her subject matter. The particularities of race, gender, and culture are explored in the interstices of everything and everywhere.

In "Nexus," a poem in her first volume, *The Yellow House on the Corner*, the praying mantis and the poet merge to claim all, in the "formlessness," the "lapping darkness," for poetry:

> I wrote stubbornly into the evening.
> At the window, a giant praying mantis
> rubbed his monkey wrench head against the glass,
> begging vacantly with pale eyes;
>
> and the commas leapt at me like worms
> or miniature scythes blackened with age.
> The praying mantis screeched louder,
> his ragged jaws opening onto formlessness.
>
> I walked outside;
> the grass hissed at my heels.
> Up ahead in the lapping darkness
> he wobbled, magnified and absurdly green,
> a brontosaurus, a poet.

In this first book, the range of subject matter is extraordinary: from the depiction of a slave mutiny in "The Transport of Slaves from Maryland to Mississippi" to "Robert Schumann, Or: Musical Genius Begins with Affliction." The title poem and final entry in the volume, "The Yellow House on the Corner," depicts the yellow house as "a galleon stranded in flowers," and imagines that "if, one evening, the house on the corner/ took off over the marshland,/ neither I nor my neighbor/ would be amazed." Throughout these poems, connections are made between the homely and the exotic, the near and the far, the past, the present, and the future.

Dove's second book of poems, *Museum*, continues to range broadly through geography and history. Notes at the end of the book give information on a Chinese empress, on Saint Catherine of Alexandria and Saint Catherine of Siena, on Benjamin Banneker, and on Dominican Republic dictator Rafael Trujillo's murder of twenty thousand blacks for their inability to pronounce in Spanish the word for parsley. This last horror is presented coolly yet powerfully in the final poem, "Parsley." In addition to its sweep of history and geography, *Museum*, by its very title and several of its poems, also raises the issue of the role of the artist and of art in such a world. Implicit in the work are a critique of society and an obligation to witness through an art that is both passionate and detached.

Critics have praised Dove's ability to convey an international aesthetic vision. In an essay entitled "Rita Dove: Crossing Boundaries," Ekaterini Georgoudaki notes that Dove "speaks with the voice of a world citizen who places her personal, racial, and national experience within the context of the human experience as a whole." In addition to commenting on the historical richness of Dove's poetry and the journey motif that she finds in much of Dove's work, Georgoudaki also commends Dove's achievement of a uniquely feminine poetic. By claiming women of diverse racial and cultural backgrounds as her aesthetic ancestors, Georgoudaki argues, "Dove develops a more inclusive female voice," appropriating this rich cultural heritage "to renew and redefine her own."

Thomas and Beulah, Rita Dove's third collection of poems, won the Pulitzer Prize for poetry in 1987—making Dove only the second African American woman to receive this award. (In 1950, Gwendolyn Brooks was the first African American female recipient.) Unlike her previous two collections, this volume concentrates Dove's vast scope of awareness into the poetic exploration of the separate lives of a married couple. This couple, Thomas and Beulah, are based loosely on Dove's own grandparents—a connection suggested by the printing of her grandparents' photos on the cover and acknowledged by Dove in interviews, though not explicitly stated in the book. Their individual lives are shown obliquely in relation to larger social forces and events, such as the March on Washington in 1963 ("Last August she stood alone for hours/ in front of the T.V. set/ as a crow's wing moved slowly through/ the white streets of government").

The stories of Thomas and Beulah are told separately, from their separate youthful experiences (most poignantly, the drowning of Thomas' close friend Lem when the two young men are traveling together), through a long marriage, to age and death. Each member of the couple is presented as essentially alone, with his and her greatest pains, disappointments, and dreams kept private from others, but shared with the

reader in a cryptic and fragmented way. The effect is eerily intimate while at the
same time tragically distant. Thomas grieves (and perhaps carries a feeling of guilt)
throughout his life for his drowned friend Lem, and perhaps in consequence is slow
to find other sources of real meaning and affirmation. Late in his sequence, in "Roast
Possum," Thomas reveals a passionate desire to teach a manly kind of woods lore,
survival skills, and capacity for enjoyment to his one grandson, significantly named
Malcolm (the poem contains a pun on Malcolm X's original name, Malcolm Little):

> A granddaughter
> propped on each knee,
> Thomas went on with his tale—
>
> but it was for Malcolm, little
> Red Delicious, that he invented
> embellishments.

Beulah is given no single tragic incident to mourn, but rather evidences a subtle
movement from disappointment to fantasies to meditative resignation, or possibly
wisdom. In "Headdress," working as a milliner, Beulah lets the hat she creates for
some other woman become the image of her own dreams:

> The brim believes
> in itself, its
> double rose and feathers
> ashiver. Extravagance
> redeems. O
> intimate parasol
> that teaches to walk
> with grace along beauty's seam.

Among all her achievements in this prize-winning collection, Dove's handling of
narrative voice in *Thomas and Beulah* has generated the most commentary. Praising
the discipline and compression of *Thomas and Beulah*, Bonnie Costello analyzes
Dove's success in overcoming the problems of how to "get years of her grandparents' joy and anguish into spare lines without presuming to sum up for them; how
to telescope distances of place, background, dreams, without narrating," and pronounces Dove's solutions as brilliant. In his essay on *Thomas and Beulah*, John
Shoptaw alludes to Thomas' purchase of an incomplete set of encyclopedias "for
five bucks/ no zebras, no Virginia,/ no wars" in "One Volume Missing" as providing
a clue to understanding the "gaps, divisions, and deletions" to be found in Dove's
own collection. Dove's poetry is a "fragmentary alphabet," according to Shoptaw,
and "the never-never Volume that would integrate . . . the narrator and her stories,
must remain missing."

Dove's fourth volume of poetry was *Grace Notes*, about which she has commented,
"With *Grace Notes* I had several things in mind: every possible meaning of grace, and
of notes, and of grace notes, and also a little added riff," trying to counter "the heavy

weight of *Thomas and Beulah*, which had such a big scope." The collection marks Dove's return to a purely lyric mode, but an autobiographical impulse also dominates the work. More than in any of her previous collections, Dove can be seen as the actor in each vignette, whether as a young child learning a brutal lesson in the Southern black school of survival ("Crab-Boil") or as a mother groping for a way to reveal feminine mysteries to her own young daughter ("After Reading *Mickey in the Night Kitchen* for the Third Time Before Bed"). In the ironic "Ars Poetica," she places herself on the literary chain of being with what might pass for self-deprecation. Her ambition is to make a small poem, like a ghost town, a minute speck on the "larger map of wills." "Then you can pencil me in as a hawk:/ a traveling x-marks-the-spot." In her assessment of *Grace Notes*, Bonnie Costello finds that the literary features readers have grown to appreciate in Dove "arise here in their finest form: descriptive precision, tonal control, metaphoric reach within uncompromising realism. Moreover, she has brought these talents to bear upon a new intimacy and moral depth, served by memory and imagination working together."

Accomplished though she is as a poet, Rita Dove is also a fiction writer, and discussion of her poetry can benefit by an awareness of her talent for fiction. Her volume of short stories, *Fifth Sunday*, was published in 1985, and her novel *Through the Ivory Gate* was published in 1991. Her stories convey some of the same qualities of compression and understatement that are found in her poetry, and a similar range of locations between Europe and America. Included among the eight stories in *Fifth Sunday* are "Zulus," about an American motorcycle gang crashing the wedding of one of its own; "Vibraphone," about a woman music student who follows one of her musical heroes to a revealing and disappointing meeting in Italy; and "The Spray Paint King," a moving story about an outlaw graffiti artist.

Rita Dove has made herself available to interviewers, with the result that a number of her ideas about her own writing, about the craft of poetry, and about a variety of other concerns such as feminism, race, politics, and human values are available in published interviews. In an interview in *Callaloo*, she says that in her poems, she tries "very hard to create characters who are seen as individuals—not only as Blacks or as women, or whatever, but as a Black woman with her own particular problems, or one White bum struggling in a specific predicament." Dove considers herself to be a feminist, but notes that "when I walk into my room to write, I don't think of myself in political terms. I approach that piece of paper or the computer screen to search for . . . truth and beauty through language."

There is a growing body of critical discussion of Rita Dove's work, and most of it recognizes her as a major talent. In his 1986 review of *Thomas and Beulah*, Peter Stitt remarks on the powerful sense of community, family, and place that lies at the heart of the collection and calls for Dove's recognition "as among the best young poets in the country today." Helen Vendler, writing in *The New York Review of Books*, notes that Dove is principally "a poet of dramatic force—a quality found relatively rarely in lyric, a genre by its nature reflective, circling, and static." Robert McDowell, commenting on Dove's poetry, praises her storyteller's instinct, an instinct that "has found expression in a synthesis of striking imagery, myth, magic, fable, with humor, political comment, and a sure knowledge of history." One might add to that catalog of Rita Dove's strengths these two essential poetic powers, which her work consistently displays: the poet's gift for language and the poet's gift for elision and condensation.

Bibliography

McDowell, Robert. "The Assembling Vision of Rita Dove." In *Conversant Essays: Contemporary Poets on Poetry*, edited by James McCorkle. Detroit: Wayne State University Press, 1990. Overview of Dove's *Yellow House on the Corner* (1980), *Museum* (1983), and *Thomas and Beulah* (1986). Regards Dove as a storyteller who "tells all sides of the story" from different perspectives. Stresses her use of myth, which she distorts and revises along gender lines, and her relating public and private events as in "Parsley."

Rubin, Stan Sanvel, Earl G. Ingersoll, and Judith Kitchen. "A Conversation with Rita Dove." *Black American Literature Forum* 20 (Fall, 1986): 227-240. Dove discusses how "Parsley," a poem about Dominican dictator Rafael Trujillo, was composed. She focuses on the sounds in the poem. Most of the article concerns poems from *Museum* (1983), which was influenced by her stay in Europe, though "Dusting" from *Thomas and Beulah* (1986) also receives some attention.

Shoptaw, John. "Segregated Lives: Rita Dove's *Thomas and Beulah*." In *Reading Black, Reading Feminist: A Critical Anthology*, edited by Henry L. Gates, Jr. New York: Meridian Book, 1990. Believes that *Thomas and Beulah* resembles fiction more than it does "a poetic sequence." Outlines the chronology of the poem, finding that the couple "rarely intersect" and remain separate. Focuses on the lasting impact of Lem's death on Thomas and on the unfulfilled promises in Beulah's life. Concludes with an analysis of the biblical/religious use of "Beulah."

Taleb-Khyar, Mohamed B. "An Interview with Maryse Condé and Rita Dove." *Callaloo* 14 (Spring, 1991): 347-366. Contains many biographical details about Dove's family and growing up in Akron, Ohio. Dove comments on how language can change perceptions and on how people caught in the "web of history" fascinate her. Although she is a feminist, she resists the urge to politicize her poetry and claims that she creates individual characters rather than symbolic black women characters. She comments on her feelings about her books of poetry.

Vendler, Helen. "An Interview with Rita Dove." In *Reading Black, Reading Feminist: A Critical Anthology*, edited by Henry L. Gates, Jr. New York: Meridian Book, 1990. Begins with biographical information, including information on Dove's visit to Germany, and proceeds to a discussion of some particularly arresting images (the parrot in "Parsley," the mandolin in *Thomas and Beulah)*. Dove acknowledges the domesticity of her first volume of poetry, which she says was followed by a "counter impulse." In her later poems, she notes, she is concerned with children and motherhood.

                                                                                              Thomas L. Erskine

THE POETRY OF PAUL LAURENCE DUNBAR

Author: Paul Laurence Dunbar (1872-1906)
Type of work: Poetry
First published: Oak and Ivy, 1893; *Majors and Minors,* 1895; *Lyrics of Lowly Life,*
1896; *Lyrics of the Hearthside,* 1899; *Lyrics of Love and Laughter,* 1903; *Lyrics of
Sunshine and Shadow,* 1905; *The Complete Poems of Paul Laurence Dunbar,* 1913

Though he lived a mere thirty-three years, Paul Laurence Dunbar wrote six published volumes of poetry, four novels, and quite a few volumes of short stories.
Altogether, he authored no fewer than twenty books. Yet for all this prodigious productivity and in spite of his widespread reputation as the first African American to
master the art of writing poetry, Dunbar, a lyricist of tremendous ability, has come
down to modern readers primarily as a poet of "Negro" dialect. In the process, he
also acquired the reputation of being a superb reader of his own poetry. As poet and
reader, he was eagerly sought after, and whether it was in London, New York, Washington, the South, or his birthplace, Dayton, Ohio, his soft, musical voice induced
his listeners to take note of his poetic abilities, his devotion to his art, and his
determination to live as a professional artist.

Encumbered by sorrow, ill-health, frequent financial difficulties, unfulfilled love,
and an unhappy marriage, he persevered; with a heroic resilience, Dunbar composed
throughout his entire life, each composition showing promise of greater literary
achievement than the one before. Even in the midst of failing health and a crushed
spirit, he could produce poetry full of love, laughter, and sunshine. From all accounts, his untiring devotion to his mother, and hers to him, must have gone a long
way in maintaining this equanimity in the midst of trying times.

Though more than two-thirds of Dunbar's poems are written in standard English,
these are not the works that made him famous, nor are they the ones that have
secured him a place in the history of American literature. The qualities that he
displays in his standard poetry—such as the detailed attention to nature, the skillful
manipulation of imagery, the masterful experimentation with rhyme and meter, and
the controlled handling of serious philosophical themes—have traditionally been
ignored in favor of the rhythmic, narrative, and pleasing delineation of black peasant
life that characterizes much of his dialect poetry.

Little did Dunbar know that when one of America's most influential literary critics—William Dean Howells—favorably reviewed *Oak and Ivy* and *Majors and Minors,* it would not only bring the poet instant fame, but it would also place severe
limitations on him as an artist. Scarcely twenty years old, Dunbar had written *Oak
and Ivy* in 1892 and followed this collection of poetry with another in 1895, *Majors
and Minors.* Being very poor, he found himself reduced to selling copies of these
collections himself; the favorable review of these volumes by Howells in *Harper's
Weekly* was more than welcome news to Dunbar at the time.

Howells not only arranged for the publication of *Lyrics of Lowly Life* in 1896 but also wrote an introduction to the volume, describing Dunbar as "the first instance of an American negro who had evinced innate distinction in literature." Howells proceeded to characterize him as "The only man of pure African blood and of American civilization to feel the negro life aesthetically and express it lyrically." Though Howells admitted that some of Dunbar's poetry in literary English was quite good, he was emphasizing that these were not "distinctively his contribution to the body of American poetry." For him, that distinction belonged to the dialect pieces, in which he saw the poet presenting black life with a humor and sympathy as had never been done before.

While Dunbar must have initially felt honored by Howells' promises, he soon came to regard them as a mixed blessing. One year later, Dunbar wrote a friend with the complaint that "Mr. Howells has done me irrevocable harm in the dictum he laid down regarding my dialect verse." This dictum made it difficult for the young poet from Ohio to be accepted as a serious artist.

After *Lyrics of Lowly Life*, Dunbar published his *Lyrics of the Hearthside* in 1899, followed by *Lyrics of Love and Laughter* in 1903 and *Lyrics of Sunshine and Shadow* in 1905, thus clearly demonstrating a preference for the lyrical mode. The volume of Dunbar's literary output during these years suggests a frantic race with time, since the poet knew as early as 1899 that he was suffering from an incurable illness, to which he finally succumbed in 1906. Seven years after his death, all of his poems were assembled in one volume, *The Complete Poems of Paul Laurence Dunbar.*

Dunbar provides the key to evaluating his work in "The Poet":

> He sang of life, serenely sweet,
>   With, now and then, a deeper note.
>   From some high peak, nigh yet remote,
> He voiced the world's absorbing beat.
>
> He sang of love when earth was young,
> And Love, itself, was in his lays.
> But ah, the world, it turned to praise
> A jingle in a broken tongue.

With more than two-thirds of Dunbar's poetry focused on "life, serenely sweet," the public saw fit to praise his "jingle in a broken tongue." Therein lay the basis for Dunbar's discontent.

As soon as one approaches the dialect poetry, one understands why the white literary public at the time praised his poetry, why he himself rejected the dialect poems, and why subsequently many critics, particularly black ones, would be harsh in their judgment of Dunbar. As "jingles," they are not on the level of serious poems, jingles being no more than short, catchy songs. Moreover, to characterize their language as that of a "broken tongue" is to diminish the very medium of those poems. An examination of the content and language of the dialect poems substantiates Dunbar's assertion to some degree.

Generally speaking, Dunbar's dialect poetry presents an idealized, and therefore unrealistic, picture of black peasant life in the South. This life is characterized by a plenitude of good living. There is an abundance of food of all descriptions, as in "The Party":

> Well, we eat and drunk ouah po'tion, 'twell dah
> wasn't nothin lef,
> An' we felt jes' like new sausage, we was mos'
> nigh stuffed to def!

The people are always ready to "Feed you tell you hear the buttons/ Crackin' on yore Sunday vest" ("After a Visit"). There is always something to eat, even if it is merely a hot "co'n pone" ("When de Co'n Pone's Hot"). Here no one goes hungry. In fact, Dunbar's characters often seem to be celebrating a holiday, as in "Chrismus Is A-Comin'," "Dey'll be lots o' chicken/ Plenty tukky, too."

Constant merrymaking seems to be the order of the day. There is frequent dancing, sometimes "all night th'oo," and youngsters are always "A-singin' o' the ol' tunes/ In the ol'-fashioned way"; there is always someone to play the "real ol'-fashioned banjo" ("A Banjo Song") or the fiddle, and there are those who are at all times ready "to give dheir feet a fling" as they dance "Jigs, cotillions, reels an' break-downs, cordrills an' a waltz er two" ("The Party"). There is a good time to be had by one and all.

It stands to reason that if dancing and singing and, in general, merrymaking are associated with the slave plantation, then the old slaves would be distressed over the abolition of slavery. There are fond memories of "de happy days gone by," for the slave sees in the deserted plantation "All dat loved me an' dat I loved in de pas'" ("The Deserted Plantation"). So tied to his slave past is the slave that he decides to "stay an' watch de deah ole place an' tend it" until death. The slaves' gratitude to their master reaches beyond the grave to heaven, where they hope to continue serving their old master; faced with the prospect of being released from slavery, men and women begin crying and are ready to "tell Mistah Lincum fu' to tek his freedom back" ("Chrismus on the Plantation").

When the black peasants in Dunbar's idyllic world are not having a joyous time, singing and dancing, they are hunting "fu' coon an' fu' 'possum" ("Hunting Song"), fishing without a care in the world ("Fishing"), or courting ("A Spring Wooing," "The Old Front Gate"). There is very little notion of the turbulence taking place in black people's life at the time. Living and writing in a period when black people were increasingly being disenfranchised, when the country was rapidly being segregated, when the lynching of a black man was fast becoming the pastime of white hate groups, and when terror was being generally directed at the black community, this son of ex-slaves chose to ignore the essential factors that helped to shape the lives of the very people his dialect poetry purported to reflect.

There are times, however, when Dunbar suggests in his dialect poetry that all is not quite well. From time to time, there is a muted sense of protest. The maid in

"When Dey 'Listed Colored Soldiers" is proud that her man has gone to fight for his freedom on the side of the North, but this sentiment is undercut by the fact that she can be equally touched by the death of her two "mastahs . . . in gray suits." There is also a distinct sense of freedom permeating "An Ante-Bellum Sermon," but the seriousness of the poem is undermined by the humor that crops up from time to time. In the very last paragraph of "A Banjo Song," there is a hint that all is not right. The music of the banjo is important because it is "de greates' joy an' solace/ Dat a weary slave kin know!" and because it is one of the few pleasures "O' dis life." When the slave finally begins to think of "de days w'en slavery helt me/ In my mis'ry—ha'd an' fas'," and acknowledges the cruelty of slavery, he is very quick to forget "de whuppins" and the terror of the "block an' lash" ("The Old Cabin"). These sentiments of the slave on the plantation may be accounted for or explained away in the poem "We Wear the Mask." It is significant that the "mask" not only "grins," but it "lies" as well. This mask hides "tears and sighs," "torn and bleeding hearts," and even "tortured souls." All this is achieved while "We smile" and while "We sing."

Among Dunbar's dialect poems, there is only one that comes close to questioning the plantation stereotype, to challenging the necessity to "wear the mask." In "Philosophy," the poet announces:

> But you don't ketch folks a-grinnin' wid a
>   misery in de back;
> An' you don't fin' dem a-smilin' w'en dey's
>   hongry ez kin be.

The poet does seem somewhat appalled at the idea of having to "grin/ W'en we knows dat in ouah innards we is p'intly mad ez sin." This is not a very strong protest, however, nor is it sustained in any way; it certainly is not sufficient to erase or invalidate the prevailing posture of the rest of his dialect poems.

It is not only the distorted picture of life and the philosophy of the dialect poems that have irritated many critics; the language of the poems has been a sore point as well. It is by no means an accurate representation of folk speech. It is rather a highly conventionalized literary speech that seeks to achieve its objective by means of exaggeration and deliberate truncation of standard English. Dunbar himself refers to it merely as a "broken tongue," suggesting that it does not have the integrity of a separate language and that it is not worthy of being considered valid. The white literary public at the time, however, viewed it as a failed attempt to speak "proper" English on the part of the black folk.

For all of the objection that one may have to Dunbar's dialect poetry, one must still acknowledge and admire the strong rhythmic and narrative qualities of the dialect poems. Poems like "Dat Ol' Mare o' Mine," "The Old Front Gate," and "Lullaby" charm with their tale and music. Moreover, Dunbar humanizes his characters and makes them likable to some degree. This in itself is an achievement of considerable importance, even if Dunbar himself may not have thought so.

Not attaching much significance to his dialect poetry, the poet seems to have re-served for his poetry in Standard English his most serious themes. These are the poems in which his philosophy of life is most consistently articulated. In these po-ems, he exhibits the true breadth of his interest as a man and a poet; in them, he is able to demonstrate his mastery of conventional literary forms. In fact, these poems suggest an attitude of mind that is not only different from but also contradictory to that which emerges in his dialect poetry.

Dunbar's poetry in Standard English reveals a Romantic in the vein of John Keats, who, like Dunbar, died an early death. His "Ere Sleep Comes Down to Soothe the Weary Eyes" is worthy of the best in the tradition. In the tradition of the Romantic poet, Dunbar has an affinity to and a fascination for nature. He loves to "walk with nature heart by heart" ("In Summer Time") and wishes "Dame Nature were [his] mate" ("Nutting Song"). The poet responds to nature in its myriad manifestations. Nature in its wild, luxuriant state provides the atmosphere for the subjective experi-ence of Dunbar. As such, every season of the year, every segment of the day, every flower and bird known to the poet, every natural phenomenon meet with extensive treatment. His commitment to nature is summed up in the skillfully wrought poem "Nature and Art," in which he pronounces the marriage between the two: "And at the morrow's dawning they were wed."

Dunbar also uses his standard poetry to articulate philosophical positions, most noteworthy of which are his deliberations on life itself. For the poet, life is a con-stant struggle, for his "days are never days of ease." Life is sad and "cheerless," since "Life's music beats for me/ A melancholy strain" ("Worn Out"). Elsewhere, life is an "arduous" journey beset by "cruel thorns," "detaining hands," and "frown-ing skies" ("By Rugged Ways"); at its worst, it becomes a prison for the poet—a prison in which he feels trapped much as the "caged bird" who beats his wing on cruel bars in the poem "Sympathy." Still, life is more than mere pain. In one of his more famous and popular poems, "Life," the poet speaks of life in all of its essential contradictions. It is:

> A minute to smile and an hour to weep in,
> A pint of joy to a peck of trouble,
> And never a laugh but the moans come double.

Believing that each thing is an interpenetration of opposites, so that if life grants "the smile to warm" it must also grant "the tears to refresh," the poet consoles himself with the thought that "joy seems sweeter when cares come after,/ And a moan is the finest of foils for laughter."

Those who from reading his dialect poetry are quick to assert that Dunbar is "brainwashed" and has no sense of racial consciousness would do well to pay close at-tention to some of his standard poems. Poems such as "Frederick Douglass," "Ode to Ethiopia," "The Colored Soldiers," "Black Samson of Brandywine," "Harriet Beecher Stowe," "Robert Gould Shaw," and "We Wear the Mask" project one who is not only conscious but also committed. Occasionally, he can even produce a militant tone, as when he condemns "grim Oppression" in "Frederick Douglass" and insists in "The Colored Soldiers" that "the Blacks enjoy their freedom" because they won it dearly. He is not unmindful of the damaging effects of racism on blacks. In an act of total identification, the pain of the lynched victim becomes his own pain, and the "curse of a guiltless man" against the oak tree on which he has been lynched becomes the poet's curse as well in "The Haunted Oak." Such attitudes signal a clear departure from the world that Dunbar presents in his dialect poetry.

His standard poetry is also reserved for his comments on the critical issue of his concept of his art and his feelings about his career as a poet, the joy that his art brings him and the simultaneous feelings of bitter disappointment over the fact that his dialect poetry has been praised and preferred while his standard poetry has been overlooked and disregarded. He is terribly bothered by people's expectations of him as a poet. In "Misapprehension," he speaks of having written a very serious and emotionally charged poem; one who claimed to have loved it, "read and considered it," and said: "Ay, brother,—'t is well writ,/ But where's the joke?" It is obvious that this person has come to expect and prefer the qualities of the dialect poetry.

Haunted by these expectations, and considering himself a failure for not having achieved fame for his standard poetry, Dunbar despairs in the end and writes what seems to be his own obituary. Affirming that he has not properly used "the gift of song" that "God in His great compassion" gave him, the poet is convinced that the "Master in infinite mercy" now rewards him with death ("Compensation"). The critic need not accept this self-assessment. In fact, Dunbar himself would be forced to reassess his self-evaluation were he alive today, for his reputation now stands more on his poetry written in standard English than on his "jingle in a broken tongue." One need only read Dunbar's more serious poetry to agree with him that "I sing my song, and all is well."

Bibliography
Baker Jr., Houston A. "Paul Laurence Dunbar, an Evaluation." In *Singers of Daybreak*. Washington, D.C.: Howard University Press, 1974. Examines the tremendous sociohistorical and psychological odds against which the poet had to struggle. Notes the literary framework with which Dunbar had been burdened and within which he had to write. Applauds the limited success the poet achieved in his "skillful blending of southern folk regionalism with a conscious literary tradition."
Brawley, Benjamin. *Paul Laurence Dunbar: Poet of His People.* Chapel Hill: University of North Carolina Press, 1936. A biography and a critical analysis. Highlights some of Dunbar's earliest works in tracing his pursuit of his aspiration and the development of his career. Deplores the "slavish" adherence by some critics to Howell's review of Dunbar's poetry. Ends with an impressive bibliography of Dunbar's works, both primary and secondary.
Brown, Sterling. "Dunbar and Traditional Dialect" and "Dunbar and the Romantic Tradition." In *Negro Poetry and Drama and the Negro in American Fiction.* New

York: Atheneum, 1969. Gives Dunbar credit for humanizing, to some degree, black folk life; notes with regret, however, the many omissions in his portrayal of that life. Observes that Dunbar reserved most of his serious issues for his poetry in Standard English, but that these are largely imitative.

Cunningham, Virginia. *Paul Laurence Dunbar and His Song.* New York: Dodd, Mead, 1947. Literary biography based on scrapbooks and on documents written by and to Dunbar and his mother. Contains valuable explanations of and background to many of the poet's works.

Gayle, Addison G. *Oak and Ivy: A Biography of Paul Laurence Dunbar.* Garden City, N.Y.: Doubleday, 1971. Argues that Dunbar was forced to sell his soul in order to survive in a country that constantly deemed him unworthy. Makes the point that Dunbar knew that very little of what he wrote in dialect was true.

Revell, Peter. *Paul Laurence Dunbar.* Boston: Twayne, 1979. Analyzes Dunbar's work, paying special attention to his treatment of themes from African American life and history. Contains a biographical summary along with an analysis of the problems faced by black writers at the time. Examines the poetry in literary English and that in dialect separately.

Roosevelt J. Williams

THE POETRY OF MARI EVANS

Author: Mari Evans (1923-   )
Type of work: Poetry
First published: Where Is All the Music?, 1968; *I Am a Black Woman*, 1970; *Night-star, 1973-1978*, 1981; *A Dark and Splendid Mass*, 1992

Mari Evans' work in the last decade of the twentieth century remains as original and striking as it did when she published her first poetry in the initial stages of the emerging social revolution in black consciousness in the mid-1960's. The title of her second collection, *I Am a Black Woman*, became a signature statement for a genera-tion of African American women, proclaiming in unapologetic, forceful terms the fundamental facts of existence for a hitherto nearly invisible, effectively silenced people. Her poetry, like that of Sonia Sanchez, Nikki Giovanni, and Carolyn Rogers, was a profound demonstration of the aptness of Robert Frost's claim that poetry should be "common to experience but uncommon to expression"; the work of Evans and others provided, for the first time in American literary history, the vernacular language, particular rhythms, and psychological perspective of African American women in published form. In addition, she shared the political awareness of such poets as Amiri Baraka (then writing as LeRoi Jones) and Haki Madhubuti (then writing as Don L. Lee), who insisted on the obligation of the poet to speak as the forceful voice of a suppressed segment of the population that had been victimized—or terrorized—by racist society.

While poetry has always existed in an oral form in the African American commu-nity, very few black men, and even fewer black women, were able to break into print during the nineteenth and early twentieth centuries. As the critic Barbara Christian has pointed out, the "rich, oral tradition" of African American culture ran "counter to the accepted norms of European poetry," so that the highly gifted Phillis Wheat-ley, for example, fashioned herself into a convincing replica of an eighteenth century English poet in her published work. Moreover, anthologies of black poetry present little work by women of measurable poetic accomplishment before Margaret Walker (born in 1915) and Gwendolyn Brooks (born in 1917). The implication of this appar-ent dearth of preservable poetry was that poets such as Wheatley seemed like un-usual exceptions rather than the voices of a neglected mass; when Evans, among others, found the means to get her work into print, its first appearance had the exhilarating effect of opening a huge field, introducing a voice largely unfamiliar to most readers or listeners.

The pioneering aspects of Evans' work are undeniably significant, but they may have tended to obscure other elements that are equally important in terms of her achievements and that are an integral aspect of her continuing poetic interest. Like Brooks, Evans has worked from a thorough familiarity with the traditions of English poetry and with the dedication to craft that is the mark of the serious artist. As she mentions in the essay "My Father's Passage," she learned from Langston Hughes the necessity for a commitment to writing as a way of living, and this led her to a definition of writing as craft, "a rigorous, demanding occupation, to be treated as such." She worked as an assistant editor at a chain-manufacturing plant, the "first Black employee to work anywhere in the company other than the foundry or delivery," and for three years apprenticed, in a sense, with a skilled professional writer whose demands for revision were not initially welcomed but who gave her the basis for her command of style and form. At the same time, the openly racist arrangements of the company led her toward the position taken by many other members of her generation who saw themselves as the vanguard of the Black Arts movement. Consequently, Evans has combined her mastery of traditional English with a sensitivity to the particulars of what Madhubuti has called a "blackening" of the language, insisting on an awareness of how writers working within the African American tradition have used language devices in unconventional fashion.

This widening was a part of a post-World War II embrace of the concept of the poet who could incorporate into poetry the language of citizens without literary training, as Walt Whitman proposed to do, and who could use the "healthy speech" (as Henry David Thoreau defined poetry) of people with no conscious literary ambition in a poetic form. Evans shared with poets such as Allen Ginsberg, Gary Snyder, and Robert Creeley the feeling that a poem was not meant to be a rigid container for one's ideas or emotions but rather a supple, flexible construct that developed in accordance with the demands of the subject and mood. Her first published poems appeared in periodicals such as *Negro Digest* and in the landmark collection *Black Voices* (1968), edited by Abraham Chapman; some of these were gathered into Evans' initial volume, *Where Is All the Music?* Among these early poems, the often-anthologized "Black Jam for Dr. Negro" expresses the same attitude of disgust or contempt as Baraka's "Black Bourgeoisie" and Madhubuti's "But He Was Cool or: he even stopped for green lights," which are extremely critical of the accommodationist stance taken by some African Americans who "accepted" white ideas of beauty and behavior. Evans uses the robust vernacular of the plain speech she heard around her to resist the bogus manners of the officially credentialed "Dr. Negro.": "my ancient/ eyes/ see your thang/ baby/ an it aint/ shit" she asserts, enraged that someone has decided to "cut my afro turn/ my collar/ down" and commit other acts of cultural suppression.

Evans' first collection is more the product of an artist in a stage of development than of one who is fully prepared to set out the dimensions of a vision. In 1970, six years after her first poems were published in journals, Evans collected some of her earlier work in *I Am a Black Woman*. The volume moved beyond expressions of resistance to a directly political, defiantly feminist, conspicuously blackened poetics that conveyed the mood, contributed to the tone, and cast the die for a mode of discourse that has come to seem the dominant female poetic voice of its time. Her title is both an echo of and a contemporary response to Sojourner Truth's famous "Ain't I a woman?" demand that her gender be recognized. More than a century later, Evans has removed the interrogative doubt to proclaim her race and gender with pride, reiterating her identity by placing the poem at the beginning of the collection and then repeating the last part at the book's close.

The feeling of assurance, the emphasis on the "I" observer as a seer, and the willingness to exhibit and share strength are characteristic of Evans' subsequent poetry. To combat the enforced impression that there is something inferior about being black and a woman, Evans creates an initial image of a soulful beauty enduring through centuries of tribulation, "the music of my song/ some sweet arpeggio of tears/ is written in a minor key." This introduction leads to a compressed historical survey, moving from the agony of the middle passage ("I saw my mate leap screaming to the sea"), through the pain of slavery ("I lost Nat's swinging body in a rain of tears"), when rebellion usually ended in death, to the sacrifice of African American soldiers at Anzio, Da Nang, and Pork Chop Hill in wars fought for a democratic ideal unavailable to African Americans. Bringing the poem to the present, Evans shifts from mourning fallen warriors to active involvement in political action ("Now my nostrils know the gas"). In a second section, she acknowledges the protean, mythic quality she embodies and connects her existence to the cosmos, claiming an eternal, life-affirming essence previously denied:

> I
> am a black woman
> tall as cypress
> strong
> beyond all definition still
> defying place
> and time
> and circumstance
>   assailed
>   impervious
>   indestructible

In a summary statement of unquenchable optimism, speaking like a prophet in a voice that encompasses historical epochs, she counsels, "Look/ on me and be/ renewed."

The strength of Evans' voice in this poem is built on a historical foundation of silent yearning. The unspoken heritage of black experience is expressed in language that is both contemporary and biblical. Because of its assurance, there is no dramatic sense of a poet progressively gaining control of means and material; instead, from the start the work gives the impression of a mature style that gradually ripens and becomes somewhat more reflective. Although she declares that "a black woman" is "beyond all definition," the unspoken assumption of the poems that follow is that Evans will be able to offer some sense of how she has been formed, of what matters to her, and of how she lives. The example of her spiritual mentor Langston Hughes, who "sang the shimmering depths of Blkactions," gives her a strategy that depends on the conviction that the richness of the culture she expresses can be captured and conveyed in poetry and the belief that this poetry is a vital contribution to "an evolving Family/ Nation." The subjects that engaged Evans in her first book remain the ones that continue to interest her, as well as to extend—in her responses—the "definition" of black womanhood. Their treatment across her three major collections is a more effective method of considering her work than a division within each volume.

A crucial component of the cultural vitality she considers and celebrates is the figure of the hero, sometimes seen in the form of a legendary giant such as Malcolm X or Martin Luther King, Jr., but also regarded for the potentially heroic act of an unknown citizen or even a social renegade. The poem that honors Malcolm X, "El Hajj Malik Shabazz," is a tribute to the continuing impact of the man, written in dense, charged language that projects a troubling, inspiring presence (". . . and we/ inbreathed him and he became a part of me/ and you/ carry him in you/ and he is restless and demands/ Demands an action"). The poetic reflection on King never mentions his name but uses the reaction of the American media ("a million hard white eyes/ swung impiously heavenward") to indict a social policy that has been responsible for "quiet" assassinations that "occupy the heart/ four hundred/ years." The unnamed, indefatigable old people in "The Elders" are a symbol of black endurance, "bony symbols of indomitable will" who "survived cotton and cane/ branding iron and bull whip" and continue on into the turmoil of the present smiling "through smoking Watts." In an appropriate use of a vernacular that conveys the immediacy and enthusiasm of a living language, Evans says "they be our national treasure." The activist Hoyt Fuller is remembered in a personal eulogy, "Brother, Comrade, Confidant." Horn player Lee Morgan and other great jazz musicians and artists who kept the soul and spirit of African American life vibrant in their art are presented in poetry that attempts to use the rhythmic structures of jazz to capture the moods of the music in verbal arrangements.

Evans' recognition of the central place of music in African American life is also evident in her use of the blues tradition to show how a folk-centered form of expression can be updated to carry a contemporary feminist philosophy (as in "Liberation Blues"). She also demonstrates how the blues form has survived because its archetypal complaint about careless love ("Blues in B♭") still applies. The blues' ability to carry a message of pain and remorse ("Cellblock Blues") in an almost prearticulate language ("Doin black/ time by the hour/ don eeeven be about no days") appeals to an instinctive feeling for almost metaverbal communication. Similarly, the cumulative power of the biblical cadences of the sermon of exhortation are used in musically inclined, stirring poems delivered as if from a pulpit or a platform to an audience hungry for affirmation and direction. "If we would rise/ O brethren/ first/ we stand/ At one with time," she says in "The Time Is Now." "Touch Your Finger to the Wind," her address to her "Kinsmen," challenges them to "peel the opaque from your eyes/ denounce the scented blossoms what/ bouquet more delicate and deadly/ Ours to be plucked and savored, what/ delusive dreams"; here, Evans uses vivid, flamboyant language to redirect sensual passion toward productive social activity.

The need to identify heroic figures, to invoke the force of the black arts, and to deliver sermons of hope stems from the necessity to preserve African American traditions in the face of racist pressures that are designed to degrade or dissolve those traditions. The social situation in which this has been happening for four centuries has moved Evans to comment that "I think of myself as a political writer"; while this is not the dominant thrust of her work, poems such as "Vive Noir!," with emphatic assertions such as "i'm/ gonna spread out/ over America/ intrude/ my proud blackness/ all/ over the place" have left the impression, especially in earlier critical commentary, that she is basically a political poet. Actually, her more specifically political poems are versions of social commentary in which the political content is implied more than instructed, as in "The Friday Ladies of the Pay Envelope," which describes prostitutes "in the broken doorways" accepting payment with "their drydamp/ limpworn hands." "When in Rome" is written from the point of view of a rich woman's servant who is the dubious recipient of largesse. Even the most overtly political poems, including "Alabama Landscape" and "The Great Civil Rights Law (A.D. 1964)," are cast in the form of historic recollection so that the lessons of history grow from the angle of vision and the context.

Like Nikki Giovanni and Sonia Sanchez, who have also written some powerful, angry, even violent political poems, Evans has a lyric ability that she has employed throughout her poetry. There are many examples of what can be called love poetry, including the poignant, plaintive "I Have Not Ceased to Love You," which has a lyrical conclusion:

> I have not ceased to love you
> Nor have I ceased
> to care

This is quite a linguistic distance from "III Entitlement," which begins "them muthuhfuhyuhs think they baddd"; the contrast serves to suggest the limits of any attempt to categorize so accomplished a poet.

All the poetry Mari Evans has written since her work began to appear in journals in the early 1960's has been a continuation of the poetic persona who introduced herself by saying, "I am a black woman," the singular expression of a strong, confident, evolving artist, teacher, and political activist. A poet working in the oral African American tradition, an honors graduate of Howard University, a professional writer with a command of her craft that is evident in the range of her subjects and her language, Evans has joined and directed a cultural legacy that is enriched by her participation.

Bibliography
Christian, Barbara. *Black Feminist Criticism: Perspectives on Black Women Writers.* New York: Pergamon Press, 1985. Offers a context for understanding Evans' writing. Particularly helpful is the chapter entitled "Afro-American Women Poets: A Historical Introduction."

Cook, Mercer, and Stephen E. Henderson. *The Militant Black Writer in Africa and the United States.* Madison: University of Wisconsin Press, 1969. An examination of the mood of the 1960's, when a great deal of poetry designed as political protest was written. Evans is covered briefly but as a significant figure.

Evans, Mari, ed. *Black Women Writers, 1950-1980: A Critical Evaluation.* Garden City, N.Y.: Anchor Press/Doubleday, 1983. Includes Evans' important essay "My Father's Passage," in which she describes her philosophy of composition. Contains considerable additional information about Evans and two critical essays on her poetry.

Keys, Romey T. Foreword to *Nightstar,* by Mari Evans. Los Angeles: Center for Afro-American Studies, University of California, 1981. A brief but incisive introduction to the second major volume of Evans' poetry.

Melhem, D. H. *Heroism in the New Black Poetry.* Lexington: University Press of Kentucky, 1990. Refers to and discusses Evans' work in the course of interviews with Sonia Sanchez, Jayne Cortez, and Gwendolyn Brooks.

Russell, Sandi. *Render Me My Song: African-American Women Writers from Slavery to the Present.* New York: St. Martin's Press, 1990. An overview that does not go much below the surface but that provides a historical perspective from a transatlantic point of view. Evans is mentioned only in passing.

Leon Lewis

THE POETRY OF NIKKI GIOVANNI

Author: Nikki Giovanni (1943-   )

Type of work: Poetry

First published: Black Feeling, Black Talk, 1968; *Black Judgement,* 1968; *Black Feeling, Black Talk, Black Judgement,* 1970; *Re: Creation,* 1970; *Poem of Angela Yvonne Davis,* 1970; *Spin a Soft Black Song: Poems for Children,* 1971; *My House,* 1972; *Ego-Tripping and Other Poems for Young People,* 1973; *The Women and the Men,* 1975; *Cotton Candy on a Rainy Day,* 1978; *Vacation Time: Poems for Children,* 1980; *Those Who Ride the Night Winds,* 1983

Born Yolande Cornelia Giovanni on June 7, 1943, in Knoxville, Tennessee, Nikki Giovanni grew up in the suburbs of Cincinnati. At the age of sixteen, she entered Fisk University; she was graduated *magna cum laude* with a degree in history in 1967. Her political involvement at the university in the early 1960's, combined with her increasing interest in writing, led to her obtaining a Ford Foundation grant in 1967 that aided her in the publication of her first book of poetry, *Black Feeling, Black Talk.* She quickly gained popularity for her first collection and followed in the same year with the publication of *Black Judgement.* The unifying themes of the work are the black struggle and the role she sees for herself as both a participant in and a witness to the historic events of the Civil Rights movement.

Giving a glimpse into the childhood of the poet is the poem "Nikki-Rosa," which highlights a happy childhood: "everybody is together and you/ and your sister have happy birthdays and very good/ Christmases." In addition to writing about her sister, Gary, in many of her works, Giovanni describes her close relationship with her mother, Yolande, her father, Gus, and her maternal grandparents, John and Louvenia Brown. Later, with the birth of her son, Tommy, in 1969, Giovanni began writing children's poetry, including *Spin a Soft Black Song: Poems for Children, Ego-Tripping and Other Poems for Young People,* and *Vacation Time: Poems for Children.* In addition to her strong pride in herself as an African American came the pride of a mother; she tried to transmit her values of black aestheticism to children through her poetry, as in the following: "i wish i were/ a shadow/ oh wow! when they put/ the light on/ me i'd grow/ longer and taller and/ BLACKER."

The social and political changes that Giovanni has witnessed have affected the tone of her works. Chronicling the changes are her autobiography, entitled *Gemini: An Extended Autobiographical Statement on My First Twenty-Five Years of Being a Black Poet* (1971), and her collection of essays *Sacred Cows—And Other Edibles* (1988).

Pulling the tenets of her life together, Giovanni faces, as do her readers, contradictions in her poetry. Many of these seeming contradictions are the result of the changes that have taken place on the "rooms outside" (society) and on the "rooms inside" (the individual), which are major themes in her poetry. In an interview with Claudia Tate, the poet addresses these contradictions:

If I never contradict myself then I'm either not thinking or I'm conciliating positions and, therefore, not growing. There has to be a contradiction. There would be no point to having me go three-fourths of the way around the world if I couldn't create an inconsistency, if I hadn't learned anything. If I ever get to the moon, it would be absolutely pointless to have gone to the moon and come back with the same position.

Beginning with *My House*, Giovanni attempts to put into perspective the truth for herself and many other black women, identifying the "inner self" and the "outer self." These personas are, in part, the result of the tumultuous 1960's; the poet must reconcile her role in speaking for the many and her responsibility to verbalize her own unique, individual experiences. Introduced as the "Princess of Black Poetry" in the volume's foreword by Ida Lewis, a close friend, Giovanni describes in *My House* the drama that is taking place in her mind. Divided into two sections, "The Rooms Inside" and "The Rooms Outside," the collection mirrors the conflict between the individual's desire to assert herself and her uniqueness and the altruistic desire to help others. For example, in the poem "The Only Song I'm Singing," from "The Rooms Inside," she focuses on this conflict: "in fact the truth is true/ the only song i'm singing now is my song/ of you." The persona then asks: "baby please/ please somehow show me what i need/ to know so i can love you right/ now." Inherent in the poem is its pleading tone, as the individual struggles to define herself in relationship to others.

In the world outside, however, "Nothing Makes Sense," as Giovanni notes in the title of a poem in "The Rooms Outside." An image of destruction amplifies the conflict: "the blinding light . . . quickly swept up to my house melting my flesh." Therefore, the theme of self-sacrifice is in direct conflict with the theme of self-actualization. Moreover, the house of the book's title becomes a symbol for Giovanni's art; the house is a place both to create in and to retreat into domesticity. In "My House," the concluding poem, she states:

> i'm saying it's my house
> and i'll make fudge and call
> it love and touch my lips
> to the chocolate warmth
> and smile at old men and call
> it revolution. . . .

In an interview, Giovanni has stated that "literature is only as useful as it reflects reality." Therefore, the African American woman in the early 1970's is portrayed as trying to put her house in order to keep outside atrocities ("in a day where the c.i.a. could hire Black hands to pull/ the trigger on malcolm") from tearing down her house, which is built on both the reality of "baby/ clothes to be washed . . . loneliness to be borne" and dreams of revolution, which is "screeeeeeeeeeeching to a halt." As the model for this both personal and public struggle, Giovanni uses her strength through language to describe "that a change had come."

In *The Women and the Men*, the theme of revolution is redefined to mean "that if i dreamed/ natural dreams of being a natural/ woman doing what a woman/ does when she's natural/ i would have a revolution." Soul singer Aretha Franklin is the subject of "Poem for Aretha," in which the poet examines the need to deal with Franklin as "a mother with four children," not as a talented singer to use and to exploit, "to relive billie holiday's life."

The emerging natural woman, who derives pleasure from her children and her man, whom she seems unable to hold on to, also sits by the typewriter, but instead of writing, questions its value: "and i think/ not of someone/ cause there isn't any-one/ to think/ about and i wonder/ is it worth it." In her poetry included in the section entitled "The Men," which is the second division of the collection, the po-ems wrap around the theme of love—a satisfying, rich love: "i'm gonna grab your love/ and you'll be satisfied." Ultimately, the natural woman finds satisfaction in her devotion to her man's love, and Giovanni's poetry is a reference for the black woman in which her role is described and reaffirmed: "the heat/ you left with me/ last night/ still smolders." Yet she adds, "i am a leaf/ falling from your tree/ upon which i was/ impaled." Although the love is satisfying, it may also be destructive for the artist, the individual.

Ironically, the third division of the collection, entitled "And Some Places," is not part of the main title of the book, but it is the section that unifies the private, person-alized poetic journey with the more public, political one. For example, the poems "Africa," "Night," and "Poetry" provide a link between the two aspects of truth— the inner and outer self—for the African American poet, as exemplified in the fol-lowing:

> it [poetry] never says "love me" for poets are
> beyond love
> it never says "accept me" for poems seek not
> acceptance but controversy
> it only says "i am". . . .

The individualistic spirit of Giovanni's voice reasserts itself in this concluding sec-tion, but it is much softer and less strident than in earlier works.

In *Cotton Candy on a Rainy Day*, the poet's tone is compromising; the spirit is dampened. She confronts the themes of loneliness and disillusionment. In her poem "The Rose Bush," her sense of isolation is reflected: "Now I don't fit beneath the rose bushes anymore." The theme of homelessness permeates the poetry and drama-tizes the poet's conflict: She can no longer keep her private, inner world of art separate from the more public outer world and its demands. In an attempt to define her position, she appears lost in thought on a rainy day; the theme is introspection. Not retreat but the reexamining of one's goals defines the collection.

In general, Giovanni's poetry is rhythmic and replete with arbitrary, yet universal, imagery. In her earlier works, however, a simple, repetitive rhythm is striking and resonant, as in the poem "The True Import of Present Dialogue: Black vs. Negro," in which she asks "Nigger/ Can you kill" over and over again. The harmonious blending of the lines stands in stark contrast to the tone of rage. The poet uses this unique combination to emphasize the harshness of the theme. In addition, she frequently uses alliteration, as in "Poem (No name No. 2): "Bitter Black Get/ Blacker Get Bitter/ Get Black Bitterness/ NOW."

Her poetry in later volumes focuses on the use of more personal imagery associated with family, domesticity, and everyday life. Although the poems are rhythmic, they rely more on descriptions that create common, natural visual images, as in the poem "The Butterfly," which describes hands as "butterflies fluttering/ across the pleasure/ they give/ my body." In "The December of My Springs," the rhythmic pattern reinforces the universal theme of aging: "that pitter-patter rhythm of rain/ sliding on city streets is as satisfying/ to me as this quiet has become." Ultimately, the past language she has used to describe the black experience does not offer her the dimension she needs to formalize the poet she has become. Therefore, in a subsequent collection, *Those Who Ride the Night Winds*, the language and form are very different.

In this collection, Giovanni asserts in the preface that "language has opened . . . becoming more accessible . . . more responsive . . . to what people really think." The poetic style is nontraditional. The lines are fractured by ellipses, and the form resembles a prose passage rather than a stanza of poetry. In an attempt to reunite private and public self as one universal model for African American women, she has dismissed a poetic form that had placed too many restrictions on her as both a witness and participant in this transformation. In "I Am She," domestic chores are sacrificed for a dream, for a creative journey. As a poet, Giovanni seems comfortable with her role, which sometimes can be lonely. Yet the "ride" is worth the price: "When I write I want to write," she explains, "to day trippers . . . urging them to turn/back . . . toward the darkness . . . to ride the night winds . . . to tomorrow." Describing herself as charting the "night winds," she imagines a journey that forces people "to look . . . a little . . . deeper." The tone is encouraging, instructive, and hopeful.

This collection not only marks a significant change in Giovanni's poetic style, but it also provides the foundation for her collection of autobiographical essays and articles entitled *Sacred Cows—and Other Edibles*. This often humorous, cynical, yet challenging poet takes on lofty American institutions such as Miss America pageants, sports, and consumerism. In an essay that echoes the theme of *My House*, she describes the "house" as being in "serious disorder," indicating that "we are still separate and unequal." Unlike in the earlier collection, however, the point of view is one of a unified voice, as exemplified in the "we," which can make a difference. The concluding essay reaffirms this unity and captures the universal theme for all, focusing on "home," not "house," focusing on similarities, not differences, between blacks and whites. "Whether it was a European booking passage on a boat, a slave chained to a ship, a wagon covered with sailcloth, they all headed toward the unknown with all nonessentials stripped away." So she concludes that we are all pioneers, with "a deep desire to survive and an equally strong will to live."

Giovanni has survived inner and outer conflict and emerged with a strong, mature poetic voice. She is willing to ride the night winds to describe her unique, yet universal, experiences as an African American woman.

Bibliography
Fowler, Virginia C. *Nikki Giovanni.* New York: Twayne, 1992. A colleague of Giovanni's at Virginia Polytechnic Institute State University, the author details the evolution of the poet, using her poetry to identify the influences of historical events, personal changes, and maturity on her work. Concluding with an interview of the poet, the work dramatizes the depth of Giovanni's poetry and its literary power. Includes a comprehensive bibliography.
Giovanni, Nikki. *Gemini: An Extended Autobiographical Statement on My First Twenty-Five Years of Being a Black Poet.* Indianapolis: Bobbs-Merrill, 1971. A somewhat self-centered collection of essays linked together by one common theme: the major influences on Giovanni's life and work as she perceives them.
_____. Interview. In *Black Women Writers at Work*, edited by Claudia Tate. New York: Continuum, 1983. Tate's interview of Giovanni reveals the poet's literary philosophy, her unrelenting openness, and her spiritual connections with other black writers.
Giovanni, Nikki, and Margaret Walker. *A Poetic Equation: Conversations Between Nikki Giovanni and Margaret Walker.* Washington, D.C.: Howard University Press, 1974. A dynamic dialogue between two major African American women writers. Reveals an aggressive yet poised Giovanni, who describes her vision of Black Power.
Juhasz, Suzanne. *Naked and Fiery Forms: Modern American Poetry by Women, A New Tradition.* New York: Harper & Row, 1976. Notes the political and social themes of Giovanni's poetry and details the intensely individualistic nature of her work in defining both her public and private roles.
Noble, Jeanne. *Beautiful Also Are the Souls of My Black Sisters: A History of the Black Women in America.* Englewood Cliffs, N.J.: Prentice-Hall, 1978. Captures the importance of the black woman artist during and following the Civil Rights movement of the 1960's. Views Giovanni as a strong voice using explicit language to provoke action and influence the black woman's attitudes.

Cynthia S. Becerra

THE POETRY OF MICHAEL S. HARPER

Author: Michael S. Harper (1938-   )
Type of work: Poetry
First published: Dear John, Dear Coltrane, 1970; *History Is Your Own Heartbeat: Poems,* 1971; *Photographs: Negatives: History as Apple Tree,* 1972; *Song: I Want a Witness,* 1972; *Debridement,* 1973; *Nightmare Begins Responsibility,* 1974; *Images of Kin: New and Selected Poems,* 1977; *Rhode Island: Eight Poems,* 1981; *Healing Song for the Inner Ear: Poems,* 1985

The poetry of Michael S. Harper is eloquent witness to relationships between humans, humankind and cosmology, speech and body, and past and present. It is witness to the historical and personal suffering of people of African American heritage and to the suffering of all humanity. Harper offers healing songs rather than despair and celebrates family, friends, musicians, and heroes in his diverse poetry. He seeks unity rather than diversity, and his themes and interests are wide-ranging, from music, such as jazz and blues, to history, birth, death, and myth.

Michael S. Harper was born at his parents' home in Brooklyn, New York, in 1938. Harper's father, Walter Warren Harper, was a postal worker, and his mother, Katherine Johnson Harper, was a medical stenographer. The family's large record collection first interested Michael in music, which he claims has always been the primary influence on his poetry. He grew up to the sounds of Bessie Smith, Louis Armstrong, Duke Ellington, Billie Holiday, and jazz greats such as Thelonious Monk, Miles Davis, Bud Powell, Sonny Rollins, and Charlie Parker.

When he was thirteen, the family moved, and Harper claims he would not have become a poet had he not moved from Brooklyn to Los Angeles; his world was both collapsing and full of possibilities. Michael, his younger brother, Jonathan Paul, and his sister, Katherine Winifred, moved with their parents to West Los Angeles, where Harper enrolled in Susan Miller Dorsey High School. He was placed in the school's industrial arts program rather than in an academic program until his father spoke to the school counselor about Michael's academic ability.

During high school, Harper's poetic talents lay dormant, and he only occasionally scribbled out what he calls "doggerel" in the back of his English class. He destroyed his early efforts and wrote prose and short drama until he was almost through college. After he was graduated from high school in 1955, Harper attended Los Angeles State College from 1956 to 1961; earning a bachelor's degree in 1961. Throughout his college years, he worked full time as a postal worker, and he claims that that work experience was the real beginning of his life. He was surrounded by educated African Americans who could not get employment in the private sector, and he recalls that he learned a great deal from them. Their sharp wit presented a constant challenge to Harper; they would often stop and discourse on Anton Chekhov or Fyodor Dostoevski, and they told their own stories. It was here that he learned about narrative, silences inherent in speech, and how to pace a good story. He also learned about the country he lived in and about people.

Harper faced the same racial roadblocks that held back his coworkers. While Harper was in a premedical course in college, his zoology professor advised him to give up medicine, saying that blacks could not succeed in medical school. The experiences of racism and rejection that Harper saw in his life and the lives of African American friends and acquaintances were influential in forming the vision of American society that appears in his poetry.

During college, Harper was greatly influenced by his reading of John Keats's letters and Ralph Ellison's *Invisible Man* (1952), and these works prepared him for the University of Iowa Writers Workshop, where he began working toward a master's degree in creative writing in the winter of 1961; he earned the degree in 1963. He claims that while those works were leading him to poetry, he was also influenced by a course called "The Epic of Search," in which the classics were presented as a historical view of the human quest for self-assertion.

At Iowa, Harper began to appreciate his uniqueness—he was the only African American in the poetry and fiction classes there—but he also became aware of racial differences; the university maintained segregated living quarters, and this reinforced Harper's view of society as fragmented. At Iowa, he began writing poetry seriously.

Since his beginnings as a poet, Michael Harper has become the poet laureate of Rhode Island (1988) and a full professor of English at Brown University (1974) as well as visiting professor at many universities, including Harvard and Yale. His honors have included a Guggenheim Fellowship in 1976 and a National Endowment for the Arts grant in 1977; he has read at the Library of Congress and received both a National Institute of Arts and Letters Creative Writing Award and a Massachusetts Council Creative Writing Award. He was nominated for the National Book Award in 1971 and 1977 and was honored with the Black Academy of Arts and Letters Award in 1972.

Harper's poetic vision is mainly of the African American tradition; his vision is rendered in a magical language composed of the oral-musical traditions of jazz, the blues, and spirituals. He employs black literary motifs, black idioms, and black traditions within larger American landscapes, American institutions, and American lexicons. "Most of my ancestors were black; I'm one of their trustees; the context is America . . ." says Harper. The definition of the country is "up for grabs," Harper has said. He feels that much of the country's recorded resonance is mundane and should be heightened by rigor and rhetoric, by some sophisticated truth-telling. Harper agrees with Ralph Ellison's statement that the African American is the most intimate part of American history, and Harper views black contributions to American culture as fundamental. He does not apologize for loving Keats and Robert Frost, however, because he locates himself in their terrain as swiftly as he does in his own family. Therefore, he claims, the way into the family archives of literature must be earned, and this is done by eloquence. Poetry for Michael Harper is not a career and not a choice. It is expiation and bondage. He thinks in sequences of poems with overlapping thematics, and he is intrigued with framing devices, such as those found in *The Arabian Nights' Entertainments* (c. fifteenth century; English translation, 1704). Harper considers himself a narrative poet who plays with syntax for musical overtones, and he hears everything he writes. His poetry is for the ear, he says, but not for a mechanical ear; it is elegant phrasing and perhaps unelegant associations, plus narrative drive, and he enjoys putting things together that do not belong together.

His first book of poetry, *Dear John, Dear Coltrane*, is named for the inspiration that the musician John Coltrane provided for Harper throughout their friendship until Coltrane's death in 1967. Harper refers to Coltrane as his Orpheus, his personal signature for competence, and Coltrane's music has encouraged Harper's belief in his own intuitive power. Thus, Harper named his book for the love he had for a man who never gave up the struggle and whose vision and inner strength encouraged others; the title represented a symbolic love that becomes universal in the poetry. The book pays tribute to many different musicians; the poem "Alone," for example, is dedicated to Miles Davis. The poetry in this book is rhythmic rather than metric, and the poems are meant to be sung or read aloud. Harper mostly writes in free verse and uses rhythms to enhance his images as extended metaphors. *Dear John, Dear Coltrane* is a collection of seventy-two poems with the theme of redemption, and Harper symbolizes the often painful African American experience by portraying the blues musician, who is at his best when he is low and suffering. Harper's poetry never despairs; like the blues, it encourages singing to alleviate pain and sorrow and proclaims the need for people to rise above personal and historical pain and suffering.

Dear John, Dear Coltrane can be divided into three sections. The first category contains poems about Harper's personal relationships, including those with friends and musicians such as Billie Holiday, Charlie Parker, Miles Davis, and James Brown. Harper connects personal experience, family experience, and the experience of African Americans to universal questions of self-assertion and transcendence, but this never leads to failure or despair. His poem "Reuben, Reuben," for example, is about his own loss of a son; in the manner of blues musicians, Harper attempts to transcend his own suffering through creative response to the pain.

The book's second category is made up of geographical poems that evolved out of Harper's travels to Mexico in the summer of 1967 and his search to find himself in relation to humankind's history. To Harper, geography and seminal sites are most important.

The third category is composed of historical or political poems that concern central incidents, such as Lewis and Clark's expedition in "Clark's Way West: Another Version." "American History" uses the more modern incident of the deaths of four black girls in an explosion at an Alabama church as a reminder of "five hundred middle passage blacks."

Harper's eighth book, *Healing Song for the Inner Ear*, is an experiment with elegy organized around certain themes. The text is divided into five sections, with personal history as the central theme. Continuing in the tradition of his other books,

Harper celebrates musicians, folk heroes, poets, friends, and family. There is a feeling of the preciousness of life and an awareness of crimes committed against humanity, as in "The Drowning of the Facts of a Life":

> Tonight we talk of losses in the word
> and go on drowning in acts of faith
> knowing so little of humility,
> less of the body,
> which will die in the mouth of reality.
>
> This foolish talk in a country
> that cannot pronounce napalm
> or find a path to a pool of irises
> or the head of a rose.

Harper includes poems on racial inequities in South Africa, and he questions the myths and lies of politicians, historians, sociologists, and writers. He joyfully sings of the full range of the African American experience while seeking his own personal freedom through his poetic creations. These poems are specifically individual and yet vastly universal. They encompass the earth, reflecting experience as "monuments to history and pain" in such diverse places as Stockholm, Soweto, and Mount Saint Helens. In "The View from Mount Saint Helens," Harper says:

> The flying African would leap from the shores
> of the continent called America,
> though it was really only an island
> in the Caribbean:
> the text demanded the casirenas
> be called cedars,
> what a great poet called
> *the insulted landscape*,
> which is the breast of your forehead
> now, so dense with frenesy
> and greasepaint.

Harper's poetry focuses mainly on exploring the dual consciousness of being an African American poet and an American poet by unifying the past with the present. He seeks unity in diversity and finds universality in the specific. Criticism on Harper's poetry has included that of the conservative critic Edwin Fussell, who wrote that Harper's poetry is very likely the finest poetry being written in a "woe-begone and woe-begotten country." The Pulitzer Prize-winning poet Gwendolyn Brooks finds in Harper's poetry an unafraid strength, his writing vigorous as well as brilliant, and although technically dexterous, magnificently different from most contemporary writing.

Harper balances the past with the present, uncovering stereotypes and myths as he goes, and he uses race as a metaphor. He claims that since he loves people and how they talk and sound, he doubts that he will ever run out of subject matter.

Bibliography
Callahan, John F. "The Testifying Voice in Michael Harper's *Images of Kin.*" *Black American Literature Forum* 13 (Fall, 1979): 89-92. A fairly brief and general examination of Harper's poetic voice, language, images, and idioms. Special attention is paid to his performance poems, such as those that focus on musicians or historical action. Also examines Harper's development of the relationship between himself and his reader.
Callaloo 13, no. 4 (1990). A book-length celebration of Michael Harper. Includes twenty-eight pages of Harper's poetry; a twenty-page interview with Harper; and eight essays on Harper by friends and students.
Fussell, Edwin. "Double-Conscious Poet in the Veil (for Michael S. Harper)." *Parnassus* (Fall/Winter, 1975): 5-28. Mostly about Harper's book *Nightmare Begins Responsibility*, though touching on the other volumes of poetry published by 1975. Fussell discusses what Harper tries to do with his poetry, and the difficulty of Harper's aesthetics for both him and his readers. He also examines Harper's theories on the limitations of language and explores Harper's poetic techniques. The recurrent image of the skeleton throughout Harper's poetry and his concept of "Myth-as-a-lie" are also examined.
Harper, Michael S. "An Interview with Michael S. Harper." Interview by James Randall. *Ploughshares* 7, no. 1 (1981): 11-27. Discussion includes the influence black Africa has on African American writers, Harper's early years, and Harper's teaching experiences.
Stepto, Robert B. "Michael S. Harper, Poet as Kinsman: The Family Sequences." *Massachusetts Review* 17 (Autumn, 1976): 477-502. Stepto is interested in Harper's use of kinship as a recurring metaphor for poetic process and the artist's obligations to traditions. In order to explore these ideas and examine the processes of kinship within the poems, Stepto focuses on Harper's poetic family sequences, such as the twenty-poem series section entitled "Ruth's Blues" from *Song: I Want A Witness.*
_____. "Michael Harper's Extended Tree: John Coltrane and Sterling Brown." *Hollins Critic* 13 (June, 1976): 2-16. Stepto explains that a primary tradition in African American literature is the honoring of kin, especially kin who are also artists. He then takes the reader through an in-depth exploration of Harper's poems on the jazz musician John Coltrane and the poet Sterling Brown, both African American artists whom Harper celebrates.

Rebecca Bliss Herman

THE POETRY OF ROBERT HAYDEN

Author: Robert Hayden (1913-1980)
Type of work: Poetry
First published: Heart-Shape in the Dust, 1940; *The Lion and the Archer,* 1948 (with
  Myron O'Higgins); *Figure of Time: Poems,* 1955; *A Ballad of Remembrance,* 1962;
  Selected Poems, 1966; *Words in the Mourning Time,* 1970; *The Night-Blooming
  Cereus,* 1972; *Angle of Ascent: New and Selected Poems,* 1975; *American Journal,*
  1978, 1982; *Collected Poems,* 1985

On February 24, 1980, the day before Robert Hayden died at the age of sixty-six,
the Center for African American and African Studies at the University of Michigan,
where Hayden had taught since 1969, sponsored a daylong tribute to Hayden. The
occasion served to celebrate Hayden's accomplishment as a poet and his integrity as
a man. The ascendancy of Hayden's critical reputation signified by that occasion has
continued, and Robert Hayden is recognized as one of the significant American
poets of his generation. The quantity of his work is not great; his *Collected Poems,*
published posthumously in 1985, runs to fewer than two hundred pages. Yet it is
work that sustains a high level of artistic merit and that includes a handful of authen-
tically great poems. Hayden's poetry is impressive for the range and variety of form
and theme that it embodies and for the poet's success in fusing a multiplicity of
influences into a body of work as coherent as it is eloquent.

The influences manifest in Hayden's first published book, *Heart-Shape in the Dust*
(1940), are essentially two. The first, and the more fundamental in shaping Hayden's
notions of the nature of poetry, is the example of the Harlem Renaissance, the name
most commonly given to the remarkable flowering of African American art and literature in the 1920's. For an African American looking for his own authentic poetic
voice in the 1930's, the work of the poets of the earlier decade confirmed the possibilities of a poetry beyond the orthodoxies of the established schoolroom anthologies. The second influence was more immediately relevant to Hayden's early sense
of the function, as distinguished from the nature, of poetry. Hayden was as a young
man attracted to the left-wing ideology, loosely Marxist, that more or less intensely
engaged the attention of many young black American artists and intellectuals in the
1930's. Not surprisingly, then, themes of protest play a significant role in this first
collection. The poems themselves would ultimately be dismissed as apprentice work
by their author; the mature Hayden would especially move away from the overt protest poems the primary function of which is to arouse the reader to the correct state
of political awareness. Hayden would never, however, become indifferent to politics
in the broader sense, or to the political dimension of the poet's art. The influence of
the Harlem Renaissance would never be rejected but, combined with other influences Hayden would absorb, would become an integral part of his own developing
identity as a poet.

The development can be traced in two pamphlets, *The Lion and the Archer* (1948) and *Figure of Time* (1955). The poet in full maturity emerges in *A Ballad of Remembrance* (1962), consisting of revised versions of poems from the two pamphlets and a number of new poems. This book represents the poet's own evaluation of his work to 1962, what he thought significant and worth preserving.

The poet of *A Ballad of Remembrance* challenges and may at times even baffle the reader, especially the reader who comes to the book with misguided preconceptions about what to expect from an African American poet. It is not protest poetry that is found here, although Hayden casts a clear-eyed gaze on the tensions and torments—but also on the triumphs—that are part and parcel of the experience of being black and American. It is also not a popular poetry, granting easy access to the casual reader, although it finds much of its inspiration in the genius of African American popular culture. It is not a personal, certainly not a confessional, poetry, although Hayden locates sources of pain and reconciliation in the circumstances of his own life, and although the sense of the author as a feeling moral presence binds together the impressively varied contents of the book.

African American history provides Hayden with the thematic source of some of his finest, most intensely realized poems. "Middle Passage" is inspired by the uprising of slaves, led by one Joseph Cinquez, aboard the slave ship *Armistad* and the incident's aftermath. Rather than taking a straightforward narrative approach to this material, Hayden makes of it a modernist meditation on history, heroism, the inhumanity that is always a human possibility, and the unkillable human wish for freedom. The influence of a key work of literary modernism, T. S. Eliot's *The Waste Land* (1922), makes itself felt in the montage of fragments and multiplicity of voices, ironically juxtaposed, that constitute the first two sections of the poem. In the third section, the focus on the *Armistad* episode becomes clear through the voice of a surviving officer of the slave ship, who, in a telling and typical irony, believes his words will ensure the death of Cinquez and the defeat of his cause. In thus presenting the historical materials of the poem in a nonlinear fashion and through a multiplicity of voices, Hayden observes the impersonality that Eliot and others made central to the modernist aesthetic. At the same time, Hayden adapts the accents of modernism to an affirmation, however removed from sentimentality and soft idealization, of the human. Hayden thus breaks dramatically with the articulation of despair, the "Waste Land motif," associated not only with Eliot but also with many of the major European and European-American works originating from the modernist impulse. Emerging from this, and marking Hayden as the eloquent chronicler of what is most complex in the complex fate dramatized in the poem, is the sense of the Middle Passage as both historical reference and resonant symbol of the American experience, involving both black and white, as an unfinished voyage toward an uncertain shore.

A similar sensitivity to history, its irreducible complexity, and its role in defining the present and in shaping aspirations for the future can be found in other poems in this volume. In "The Ballad of Nat Turner," Hayden imagines the utterances of yet another leader of a slave rebellion. He does not, however, focus on the bloody outcome of the rebellion, but on the moment when Nat awakens to his destiny. Hayden does not write as a polemicist; it is not the rightness of Nat's cause that concerns him, but the awfulness of his awakening. The poem carries a powerful psychological and dramatic charge, intensified by the interplay between the spiritual depth of the human situation the poem depicts and the predictable simplicities of the ballad form Hayden employs. Form and subject interact to different, but equally persuasive, effect in Hayden's sonnet on Frederick Douglass, who is made to incarnate a committed and exemplary awareness of the needfulness of freedom.

In other poems, Hayden draws on aspects of twentieth century African American culture. In "Homage to the Empress of the Blues," a singer reminiscent of the great Bessie Smith wins the allegiance of her audience as she acknowledges, authenticates, and elevates the pain and confusion of their everyday experience and gives it back to them as art. This art belongs to her, in that she is the performer. Yet it is just as much theirs, not simply because she performs for them, but because they are what she performs. "Mourning Poem for the Queen of Sunday" finds irony, but also compassion, in the violent death of a gospel singer. "Tour 5" finds the menace in the eyes of the rawboned Southerner for whom a black man asking directions is the enemy.

Recollections of a more personal sort, though always held at a distance, inform other poems. "The Ballad of Sue Ellen Westerfield" has as its protagonist a composite of Hayden's biological and his foster mothers; the name the character bears is in fact the maiden name of Hayden's foster mother. In "The Whipping," the reminiscence motivated by the sound of a child being beaten is ultimately inspired by Hayden's memories of beatings he suffered at the hands of his foster mother. The poet's insight that the beatings the woman administers are a pathetically inadequate revenge for the beatings life has given her brings the poem to rest in compassion rather than in bitterness. A note of reconciliation is also struck in the fine poem "Those Winter Sundays." Here the poet belatedly recognizes and accepts the love manifested in tending the furnace on cold Sunday mornings and in similarly unrecognized acts of caring performed by an otherwise remote and, at times, frighteningly angry foster father (in the poem, simply "father").

A particular personal experience generates one of Hayden's most powerful treatments of the theme of art, one of the frequent concerns of his mature poetry. Hayden and Mark Van Doren, a white poet, critic, and educator, had read their poems from the same platform at a bond rally in New Orleans in 1946. In accordance with the Jim Crow practices of the period, however, the two men could not sit down to coffee together in any of the city's restaurants. The irony of the situation might easily have given rise to a fairly conventional protest poem. Instead, in "A Ballad of Remembrance," the title poem of the volume, Hayden assaults the reader with a rush of violently juxtaposed images, suggesting a Mardi Gras that has gone over the edge. The poem builds to a chaos in the environment and in the self, a jumble of feelings, attitudes, responses, and hostile presences that the poet transcends by finding the human voice drawn forth by the presence and example of Van Doren, who is identified by name in the poem. That it is the human, rather than the narrowly racial, voice that must be found, and that it can for Hayden be exemplified by a white poet, suggests how far Hayden's thought here is removed from the ideology of Black Nationalism, at least as that ideology would, before the 1960's were over, emerge as a major force within the African American community. It was a force whose impact Hayden would be made to feel.

An especially impressive quality of this book, the mark of the mature poet, is the mastery Hayden demonstrates over a range of formal and tonal strategies. The thematic energy of the poems is consistently echoed in their formal qualities. The baroque elaboration of diction and imagery in "A Ballad of Remembrance," yielding to the almost ingenuous directness of the closing, is one example. The controlled elevation of rhetoric in "Frederick Douglass," the ease and assurance with which the poet has mastered here the influence of Gerard Manley Hopkins, again claiming for African American poetry all that is useful and relevant in the European tradition, lend to the poem its particular kind of eloquence: a grandeur—never grandiosity—of the whole, arising out of language only slightly elevated above the common, intensified by the deliberateness of progression with which the poem moves to its conclusion. In a different register, the blues feeling of "Homage to the Empress of the Blues" and the echoes of gospel music in "Mourning Poem for the Queen of Sunday" give emotional and spiritual definition to their subjects. In "The Whipping" and "Those Winter Sundays," a relative starkness of language, coming as it does from a poet whose virtuosity is elsewhere in the book so dazzlingly on display, makes its own compelling statement.

A Ballad of Remembrance was published in Europe. For his *Selected Poems*, published in 1966, Hayden was able to find an American publisher, a reflection of the degree of recognition he was beginning to enjoy. It was also in 1966 that Hayden was the recipient of the Grand Prix de la Poesie awarded by the First World Festival of Negro Arts held in Dakar, Senegal; Langston Hughes was one of the jurors. It was in that same year, too, that Hayden received recognition of a more troubling sort when the first Black Writers' Conference convened at Fisk University, on whose faculty Hayden had served since 1946. Hayden was distressed to find himself the target of denunciations by black writers who regarded themselves as more militant, more nationalist—more "black," according to the preferred rhetoric of the period—than he. Hayden rejected nationalism as an ideology, separatism as a practice, the notion of a unique black aesthetic, of any set of prescriptions that might limit the freedom of the African American poet to find and follow his own inspiration. He insisted on the integrity of his vision and his art. While Hayden's dedication to his African American heritage is more than adequately manifested in his work, he always regarded that heritage as part of the human heritage, the struggle of African Americans as part of the human struggle toward freedom.

The artistic maturity Hayden achieved in *A Ballad of Remembrance* is confirmed by *Selected Poems* and by the volumes that follow it. "The Diver," which introduces *Selected Poems*, is intriguing for its imagistic vividness and its thematic ambiguities:

Into what depths does the poet descend, and what motivates the ascent that provides the poem with its resolution? In "The Diver," as in earlier poems such as "An Inference of Mexico" and later ones such as "The Night-Blooming Cereus" and "The Peacock Room," Hayden clearly and without apology departs from any overt treatment of narrowly racial themes, a departure that, once again, reflects his rejection of a nationalist agenda for poetry. In these later poems, and perhaps in "The Diver" as well, Hayden's concern is with the mystery and magnetism of the creative power as it reveals itself in the natural world and in the human, especially, in the latter, in the form of art. Yet Hayden by no means abandons his fascination with African American history. "Runagate, Runagate," perhaps less formally complex than "Middle Passage" but comparable to it in its formal strategies, uses the figures of Harriet Tubman and the Underground Railroad in a further meditation on freedom as a fundamental human urge. Phillis Wheatley, Crispus Attucks, Paul Laurence Dunbar, and Paul Robeson are subjects of later Hayden poems, as is John Brown, a white man of special importance in African American history. Hayden's "El-Hajj Malik El-Shabazz" must surely be numbered among the finest poems written about Malcolm X; no small part of its excellence must be attributed to Hayden's characteristic insistence on the full human complexity of the subject. In "Beginnings" and "Elegies for Paradise Valley," Hayden draws, rather more directly than in his earlier work, on his personal and family history.

A theme that is only occasionally present at the surface of Hayden's poetry but that was a fundamental force in shaping his vision was his religious faith. Raised as a Baptist, Hayden in 1943 converted to the Baha'i religion. The tenets of Baha'i certainly bear on the note of hope found even in those poems such as "Middle Passage" that confront most directly the tragic history of race relations in America. Perhaps it is more accurate to say that Hayden's religious faith made it possible for him to see that history as, at least potentially, other than tragic.

Bibliography
Cooke, Michael G. "Intimacy: The Interpretation of the One and All in Robert Hayden and Alice Walker." In *Afro-American Literature in the Twentieth Century: The Achievement of Intimacy.* New Haven, Conn.: Yale University Press, 1984. Argues that Hayden and Walker represent the fullest achievement of intimacy, a sense of power and purpose coming from within. Hayden's stance as a poet is at once passive and militant: passive, in his refusal to force a particular result upon experience; militant, in his insistence that experience has results to which one cannot be indifferent.
Faulkner, Howard. " 'Transformed by Steeps of Flight': The Poetry of Robert Hayden." *College Language Association Journal* 21 (1977-1978): 282-291. Asserts that Hayden's profound theme is transformation. Emphasizing process rather than completed act, he traces the movement up to and down from beauty.
Fetrow, Fred M. *Robert Hayden.* Boston: Twayne, 1984. A biographical and critical study that gives more emphasis than is common to Hayden's early poems. Much

of Hayden's poetry can be most fully understood if read in the light of the poet's biography. Giving voice to the alien and expressing himself through that persona are important strategies for Hayden.

Hansell, William H. "The Spiritual Unity of Robert Hayden's *Angle of Ascent.*" *Black American Literature Forum* 13 (1979): 24-31. Hayden has attempted to portray all human activity as a spiritual journey, however distorted and confused, toward sanctity.

Hatcher, John. *From the Auroral Darkness: The Life and Poetry of Robert Hayden.* Oxford, England: George Ronald, 1977. Notes that Hayden wrote as an African American and as a Baha'i in what he regarded as a crucial period of transition. As a serious artist, his accomplishment, based on a recognition of the timeless requisites of art, was to fuse his feelings and ideas with form and image.

Stepto, Robert. "After Modernism, After Hibernation: Michael Harper, Robert Hayden, and Jay Wright." In *Chant of Saints: A Gathering of Afro-American Literature, Art, and Scholarship*, edited by Michael S. Harper and Robert B. Stepto. Urbana: University of Illinois Press, 1979. States that like Ralph Ellison in *Invisible Man* (1952), Hayden, in "Elegies for Paradise Valley," works toward imparting visibility, and therefore reality, to what had previously been unseen.

Williams, Pontheolla. *Robert Hayden: A Critical Analysis of His Poetry.* Urbana: University of Illinois Press, 1987. A critical study, incorporating a biographical sketch and informed in part by Hayden's personal observations. Hayden fully embraced his black identity, but always as an American poet. He remained true to the primary duty of the artist: to impose form on experience and to derive meaning from art.

Williams, Wilburn, Jr. "Covenant of Timelessness and Time: Symbolism and History in Robert Hayden's *Angle of Ascent.*" In *Chant of Saints: A Gathering of Afro-American Literature, Art, and Scholarship*, edited by Michael S. Harper and Robert B. Stepto. Urbana: University of Illinois Press, 1979. Argues that Hayden, although a symbolist intent on divining the shape of a transcendent order that might redeem a world bent on its own destruction, believed the transcendent realm can be meaningful only as incarnated in human historical experience.

W. P. Kenney

THE POETRY OF GEORGE MOSES HORTON

Author: George Moses Horton (1797-1883)
Type of work: Poetry
First published: The Hope of Liberty, 1829; *The Poetical Works of George M. Horton,*
1845; *Naked Genius,* 1865

In the history of early African American literature, George Moses Horton occupies an indisputably prominent position. Like Phillis Wheatley, he was a slave
poet whose verse earned him renown and respect, and while New Englander Wheatley was the first black writer to have a volume of poems published, Horton was the
first Southern black poet to have a volume of poems published in the United States.
In addition, Horton's was the first black poetic voice of protest against slavery. Horton was also the first black author to earn money from his writings. In fine, "the
Colored Bard of North Carolina," as he used to refer to himself occasionally, is a
seminal figure in the annals of African American literature.

Horton was born a slave in 1797 on the plantation of William Horton in North-
ampton County, North Carolina. Of pure African parentage, a fact in which he took
great pride, he was one of ten children. When Horton was three years old, his master sold his plantation and moved to a farm in Chatham County, a hundred miles
away, taking young Horton and most of his other slaves with him. Horton would
spend the next sixty-five years of his life on the farm, where he taught himself to
read and discovered and developed his gift for writing poetry.

Growing up, Horton devoted what little spare time he had to teaching himself to
read, and in doing so he acquired a deep interest in poetry. He soon recognized that
he had a talent for "versifying" and began to compose poems. Although Horton had
taught himself to read, however, he still could not write and thus had to commit his
poems to memory. In his attempts to improve himself intellectually and culturally,
Horton, unlike Phillis Wheatley, had no one to support him—not his fellow slaves,
who derided his efforts and tagged him "a vain fool" (to use Horton's own words),
and certainly not his master, whom Horton viewed as "a man who had no regard for
liberty, science, or Genius." "No cultivating hand was found," he writes in an autobiographical poem titled "The Obstructions of Genius," "To urge the night improving slave."

What he did have, though, was a nearby college. Fortunately for Horton, his master's farm was located only eight miles or so from the Chapel Hill campus of the
University of North Carolina, at that time a fledgling university, only twenty-five
years old and with a student body of only 100, but nevertheless the state's center of
learning and culture. Convincing his master that it would be profitable for him to
sell some of his goods at the school, Horton obtained permission to travel to the
campus weekly. Hence, on Sundays Horton would walk the eight miles from his
master's farm to the university, where he would sell his master's fruit and farm produce (corn, wheat, and dairy products) and mingle with the students. Before long,

Horton started selling more than produce. What he started peddling were poems, "love pieces," as he termed them. His customers, the students at the Chapel Hill campus, whom he had impressed with his talent for versifying, would eagerly commission him to compose love poems for them, poems which they would send to their ladyloves, passing off those poems as their own. Horton can thus rightly be termed the black Cyrano de Bergerac, for like Edmond Rostand's soldier-poet Cyrano, Horton ghostwrote "love pieces" for Cupid-smitten, less-articulate youths, who took full credit for those poems. "I have composed love pieces in verse for courtiers from all parts of the state," he relates in his autobiographical narrative, "and acrostics on the names of many of the tip-top belles of Virginia, South Carolina, and Georgia." An acrostic poem is one in which the first letter of the first word in each line combines to spell out a word or a name when read downward. It is a particularly difficult kind of poem to write, and it is a tribute to Horton's ingenuity that he was able to compose so many of them (hundreds) and to craft them so well. Moreover, the conditions under which he had to compose these acrostics were grueling and degrading. He reveals that "many of those acrostics I composed at the handle of the plough and retained them in my head (being unable to write) until an opportunity offered, when I dictated whilst one of the gentlemen would serve as my amanuensis." Horton, as one scholar has put it, stands as "one of the most prolific romantic ghostwriters in our history."

By Horton's own account, business was very good. He relates that his poetic talent was acknowledged on campus "as an incontestable fact . . . [and] my fame . . . circulated like a stream throughout the college." For his poems, Horton charged from twenty-five to seventy-five cents, earning from these "love pieces" at least four dollars a week (a far from paltry sum at that time). He also earned the admiration of his customer-students, who often gave him books and clothes.

The students at Chapel Hill were not the only ones who admired Horton. Joseph D. Caldwell, the university's president, was also impressed with him, so much so that the two became close friends. Horton's most ardent admirer at Chapel Hill, however, was Caroline Lee Hentz, a New Englander who arrived at the school in 1826 with her husband, a professor hired to teach modern languages. Mrs. Hentz was to have a profound impact on Horton. A poet herself, she taught him to write, encouraged him to continue to compose, and suggested to him how to improve his poetry. Mrs. Hentz, in fact, was responsible for getting three of Horton's poems published in her hometown newspaper, *The Lancaster Gazette*, in 1828—the first time that any of Horton's poems appeared in print.

It was an auspicious beginning, for July of the next year, 1829, saw the publication of Horton's volume of poems entitled *The Hope of Liberty*. Consisting of twenty-one poems, the volume has the distinction of being the first ever published by a black Southern poet and the first published in America by a black writer. (Although Jupiter Hammond had a few poems published in the United States well before Horton, he never had an entire volume published.) The book is aptly titled, for liberty is precisely what Horton hoped that the money from the sales of the volume would buy him. Sadly, the volume did not sell well enough to raise a sum sufficient to purchase Horton's freedom from his master. (Even if enough money had been raised, Horton's master would not likely have parted with him; Horton had become valuable "family property.")

Horton thus labored on, working in his master's fields, spending as much time as possible at the university, and continually writing poetry. Caroline Hentz left the university in 1830, and her departure left a void in Horton's life. Sometime during this period, Horton got married. There are no records of his wife's name; all that is known is that she was the slave of one of the nearby farmers. The union produced two children but was evidently a loveless one and shortlived. In 1845, Horton published a second volume of poems, *The Poetical Works of George M. Horton.* The volume consisted of forty-five poems and was prefaced by a detailed autobiographical narrative, an account that has proven valuable to Horton biographers and scholars. Horton remained a slave until 1865, when Union troops freed him. His elation at being emancipated is captured in his poem "The Flag of the Free":

> Lift up thy head, exhausted slave,
> Nor to the woods for shelter flee;
> Vain shall the threat'ning tyrant save,
> The flag floats over the free.

One of the Union officers, Captain William Banks, was so impressed with Horton and his poetic talent when he met him that Banks assumed the role of Horton's patron-editor and encouraged him to increase his creative activity. The result was Horton's third and final volume of poems, *Naked Genius.* Published in the fall of 1865, it was also his lengthiest, containing 132 poems (one-third of which had previously appeared in *The Poetical Works of George M. Horton* twenty years earlier).

Emancipated after a long lifetime—sixty-eight years—of slavery, Horton took advantage of his newfound freedom and traveled to Philadelphia, where he spent the last seventeen years of his life. Unfortunately, not much is known about his life in Philadelphia. Horton died in 1883 at the age of eighty-six, but it is not known whether he died in Philadelphia or back in North Carolina.

As a poet, Horton was the perfect fusion of the artist and the pragmatist. He was the poet as businessman and the poet as craftsman, and nowhere can these two sides be seen more clearly than in his love poems. Fittingly enough, Horton's love poetry can be neatly divided into two categories—those poems commissioned by the students at the Chapel Hill campus and those written for Horton's own artistic satisfaction. Many of the commissioned love poems are clever acrostics; unfortunately, not many of these acrostics are extant. The ones that have survived, however, are remarkable for their smooth craftsmanship. Given the grueling conditions under which he composed these poems, as well as the inherently difficult form of the acrostic, Horton's achievement in this area is nothing short of outstanding.

One of these acrostics, untitled, nicely illustrates Horton's mastery of form and content. Like most acrostics, this one spells out a name—in this case, "Julia Shepard."

Joy, like the morning, breaks from one divine—
Unveiling streams which cannot fail to shine.
Long have I strove to magnify her name
Imperial, floating on the breeze of fame.

Attracting beauty must delight afford,
Sought of the world and of the Bards adored;
Her grace of form and heart-alluring powers
Express her more than fair, the queen of flowers.

Pleasure, fond nature's stream, from beauty sprung,
And was the softest strain the Muses sung,
Reverting sorrows into speechless Joys,
Dispelling gloom which human peace destroys.

Another example of Horton's skill is a "double acrostic" written at the request of Chapel Hill student Sion Hart Rogers and addressed to Mary E. V. Powell. Discovered by Horton scholar Richard Walser in 1975, the piece is actually two separate poems, one spelling out Rogers' full name and the other spelling out Powell's name. The two poems, however, are skillfully woven into one complete whole, indicating Rogers' hope that his future and Powell's would similarly be woven together forever. Such a poetic fusion is an ingenious approach on Horton's part.

Not all Horton's commissioned love poems were acrostics, though. Many were conventional love lyrics. Typical of these is the poem entitled, simply, "Love." The poem is an engaging expression of heartfelt love designed to win over the heart of one of the many belles Horton referred to in his autobiographical narrative. Shrewd businessman-poet that he was, Horton frequently recycled many of his non-acrostic poems; if a particular poem proved successful, Horton would sell that same poem to other students.

While Horton composed a multitude of commissioned "love pieces," he also wrote love poems for his own gratification. A noteworthy example of Horton's noncommissioned love poetry is "Early Affection." Moving in its declaration of intense, enduring love and relatively sophisticated in its controlling metaphor (sunrise, sunset), "Early Affection" anticipates some of Paul Laurence Dunbar's love poems, most notable Dunbar's "Love's Apotheosis."

I loved thee from the earliest dawn,
    When first I saw thy beauty's ray;
And will until life's eve comes on,
    And beauty's blossom fades away;
And when all things go well with thee,
With smiles or tears remember me.

I'll love thee when thy morn is past
    And wheedling gallantry is o'er—

> When youth is lost in age's blast,
>   And beauty can ascend no more;
> And when life's journey ends with thee,
> O then look back and think of me.

Horton, however, by no means confined himself to composing only love poems, for despite the financial profit and emotional satisfaction he derived from writing such poems, he never forgot what he was—a slave. Nor did he let the world forget that fact, for in much of Horton's verse one hears for the first time in African American poetry the voice of protest against slavery. In poems such as "Slavery," "The Slave's Complaint," "Liberty and Slavery," and "On the Death of Rebecca," Horton voices his anger and frustration—and at times his despair—at being enslaved and expresses his equally intense desire for freedom. In "Slavery," depicting his condition as wretched and painful, Horton questions the very reason for his existence and laments ever having been born: "Why was the dawning of my birth/ Upon this vile, accursed earth,/ Which is but pain to me?/ Oh! that my soul had winged its flight/ When I first saw the morning light,/ To worlds of liberty!" The poem ends somberly, with a death wish: "Then let me hasten to the grave,/ The only refuge for the slave,/ Who mourns for liberty." Death, Horton goes on to say in the poem, is a kind of blessing—a "sweet and favored friend," as he calls it in another of his antislavery poems—affording peace and relief from the pain of oppression.

In "The Slave's Complaint," Horton again bemoans his condition. He is "a wretch confined," and his life is a "dreary maze," dark and painful. Darkness, in fact, is the poem's controlling image. Like many of Horton's antislavery poems, "The Slave's Complaint" ends with the poet presenting death as a release from "Slavery's night": "And when this transient life shall end,/ Oh, may some kind, eternal friend,/ Bid me from servitude ascend,/ Forever!"

In still another poem entitled "Slavery," Horton begins by recounting the kidnapping of his African "fathers from their native land" and briefly alludes to the arduous Middle Passage. Instead of dwelling on the barbarity of slavery, however, or on the slave's misery, the poem is chiefly concerned with predicting divine vengeance falling upon slavemongers. The poem opens by questioning what kind of God would allow slavery to happen, but it concludes by affirming that God is neither absent nor indifferent but is, on the contrary, just and wrathful—a God who "hurls the vengeance with his rod,/ And thunders, let the slave be free." Given its portrait of a righteously angry God whose maledictions "pervade the dwindling world we see," the poem is certainly the most hopeful of Horton's antislavery pieces.

By far the most effective of Horton's treatments of the slave's condition is found in "Death of an Old Carriage Horse." In it, Horton uses the extended metaphor of a workhorse driven mercilessly until it dies from overwork. With its refrain, "Push along, push along," coming at every fourth line, the poem forcefully conveys the animal-like treatment and existence of the slave, who is, the poem argues, a literal beast of burden. Through this metaphor, Horton accurately captures—for the first time in African American poetry—the racist conception of slaves, and by extension black people as a whole, as subhuman, a motif that pervades African American literature. Horton's poem thus anticipates by more than a century Richard Wright's assertion that to a racist white America "we blacks were not considered human anyway."

In addition to his love lyrics and protest poems, Horton also wrote poems centered on themes such as nature and religion, poetry and death, marriage and women, the Civil War and the historical figures who were a part of it—and even poems about himself. In the final analysis, Horton's poetry is nothing less than remarkable in terms of both quality and quantity. Diverse in subject matter and in several respects ahead of its time, Horton's poetry, like the man himself, commands attention and appreciation.

Bibliography

Cobb, John L. "George Moses Horton's *Hope of Liberty*: Thematic Unity in Early American Black Poetry." *College Language Association Journal* 24 (June, 1981): 441-450. Contends that in Horton's 1829 volume of poems *The Hope of Liberty*, the motif of flight, of escape, gives the collection a fundamental thematic unity and an artistic cohesion.

Farrison, Edward W. "George Moses Horton: Poet for Freedom." *College Language Association Journal* 14 (March, 1971): 227-241. Highly instructive critical article chronicling Horton's life and poetic career. Provides a splendid delineation of the people and forces that shaped Horton's poetry.

Loggins, Vernon L. *The Negro Author: His Development in America to 1900.* 1931. Reprint 1964. Port Washington, N.Y.: Kennikat. Early, classic study of African American literature. Gives a brief overview of Horton's life and an assessment of his literary stature and poetic achievement.

Richmond, Merle A. *Bid the Vassal Soar: Interpretive Essays on the Life and Poetry of Phillis Wheatley and George Moses Horton.* Washington, D.C.: Howard University Press, 1974. Joint study of Horton and Phillis Wheatley, with equal emphasis given to both. Excellent biographical account of Horton, with insightful interpretations of his poetry.

Sherman, Joan R. *Invisible Poets: Afro-Americans of the Nineteenth Century.* Urbana: University of Illinois Press, 1989. Contains a chapter on Horton identifying him as one of many neglected ("invisible") nineteenth century African American poets. Gives a capsulized but enlightening account of Horton's life and an in-depth, perceptive analysis of his poetry.

Walser, Richard. *The Black Poet: Being the Remarkable Story (Partly Told by Himself) of George Moses Horton, a North Carolina Slave.* New York: Philosophical Library, 1966. Groundbreaking study of Horton's life and times. Detailed and vastly informative, drawing heavily—and adeptly—on Horton's brief autobiographical narrative published with *The Poetical Works of George M. Horton* in 1845.

Earle V. Bryant

THE POETRY OF LANGSTON HUGHES

Author: Langston Hughes (1902-1967)
Type of work: Poetry
First published: The Weary Blues, 1926; *Fine Clothes to the Jew,* 1927; *Dear Lovely Death,* 1931; *The Negro Mother,* 1931; *The Dream Keeper and Other Poems,* 1932; *Scottsboro Limited,* 1932; *A New Song,* 1938; *Shakespeare in Harlem,* 1942; *Fields of Wonder,* 1947; *One Way Ticket,* 1949; *Montage of a Dream Deferred,* 1951; *Selected Poems of Langston Hughes,* 1959; *Ask Your Mama: Or, 12 Moods for Jazz,* 1961; *The Panther and the Lash: Or, Poems of Our Times,* 1967

James Mercer Langston Hughes was the most versatile, popular, and influential African American writer of the twentieth century. Hughes published scores of books in his lifetime: two novels, plays, collections of short stories and essays, an autobiography, seven children's books, poetry translations, a number of African American poetry and fiction anthologies—and fourteen volumes of verse. From the 1920's until his death in May, 1967, Hughes was widely recognized as the unofficial poet laureate of the African American urban experience, its most dedicated and passionately eloquent voice; his international reputation has only grown in the years since.

Hughes's career as a poet began, rather abruptly, in the spring of 1916. At the age of thirteen, he was elected class poet of his Lincoln, Illinois, grammar school. Even though he had never written a poem, Hughes dutifully produced sixteen poems in praise of his teachers and class, which he read aloud at graduation, to hearty applause. Soon thereafter, Hughes moved to Cleveland, Ohio, with his mother and stepfather. There he attended the city's Central High School and continued to write poetry, both in the free-verse style of Chicago working-class poet Carl Sandburg and in the dialect style of the African American poet Paul Laurence Dunbar. In the year after his graduation from high school in 1920, Hughes had his first real publications. A number of poems appeared in succeeding issues of *The Brownie's Book,* a junior version of *The Crisis,* the official journal of the National Association for the Advancement of Colored People (NAACP).

Almost immediately, Hughes was graduated to the parent journal. The June, 1921, issue of *The Crisis* published "The Negro Speaks of Rivers," Hughes's first great poem. Written a year earlier, on a train crossing the Mississippi, this short lyric (dedicated to NAACP founder W. E. B. Du Bois) proudly affirms the mystical unity of all persons of African descent, regardless of when or where they happen to live. A poem of praise, rendered in plainspoken free verse, "The Negro Speaks of Rivers" shows the clear influence of Carl Sandburg. Another discernible influence is that of Walt Whitman, whom Hughes regarded as the greatest of American poets. Like Whitman's famous long poem "Song of Myself," Hughes's poem features a first-person speaker, an "I" that refers not only to the poet but also to an entire people he identifies with and, in effect, becomes; when the speaker avers that his "soul has grown deep like the rivers," he assumes the voice of the entire African race throughout history. Finally, in its moving lyricism, "The Negro Speaks of Rivers" harks back to the centuries-old tradition of the African American spiritual.

That Hughes, at the age of nineteen, had already established a unique and powerful poetic voice became fully evident over the next year and a half as Jessie Fauset, literary editor of *The Crisis*, published another dozen Hughes poems. Among them were poems that were to be Hughes's most anthologized, such as "The South," "Beggar Boy," "My People," "Mother to Son," and "Negro." "Mother to Son" is a dramatic monologue that displays one of Hughes's signal strengths as a poet: his ability to adopt a convincing persona. The speaker is the mother alluded to in the title, a (presumably) middle-aged black woman who recounts her arduous life of poverty and toil in metaphorical terms as the endless climbing of a staircase. The goal at the top of the stair is a freer, more dignified life, not just for herself and her son but for her entire people. World-weary but stoical and grimly determined, the mother exhorts her son never to forfeit the struggle by turning back. "Negro" is a free-verse dramatic monologue in much the same vein as "The Negro Speaks of Rivers." The "I" persona that Hughes adopts is, again, universal in scope: that of the black African throughout recorded history. In successive stanzas, the poem's speaker recounts the four basic roles he has been relegated to throughout the ages: slave, worker, singer, victim. "Negro" outlines a saga of suffering and sorrow ("The Belgians cut off my hands in the Congo/ They still lynch me in Mississippi"), yet it eschews self-pity. The last stanza, which repeats the first stanza verbatim and thus frames the middle four, ends the poem as it began, on a note of proud and joyous affirmation: "I am a Negro/ Black as the night is black/ Black like the depths of my Africa."

The emphasis on racial pride in "Negro" is typical of Hughes's early poems, many of which are paeans to the dignity, endurance, and inner strengths of African Americans. Hughes's early verse is not, however, monotonously uniform in style and theme. The poems published by *The Crisis* also include protest poems, elegies, miscellaneous lyrics, and formal experiments that were inspired by, and imitative of, jazz and the blues. Indeed, African American folk music became a major source of inspiration for Hughes after he moved to New York City from the Midwest in the fall of 1921 to attend Columbia University.

The move was a watershed event in Hughes's life, not because of college, which he found uncongenial and quit after his first year, but because it brought him to Harlem, Manhattan's teeming African American district and the locus for the Harlem Renaissance, a burgeoning cultural revival in which Hughes soon immersed himself. Hughes also explored Harlem's vibrant nightlife. Early evidence of its impact on his sensibilities is "The Weary Blues," a 1923 poem about a piano player performing in a Lenox Avenue nightclub. In "a melancholy tone," the man sings the Weary Blues, a song of thoroughgoing dejection and despair, "far into the night." Yet, ultimately, the blues seem to have a salutary effect. Once he has completely drained off his own anguish through the music, the singer is able to at least escape his plight by going to bed, to sleep "like a rock or a man that's dead." The singer's struggle to master his pain captures the cathartic essence of the blues—and something of the deeper nature of Harlem in the 1920's, which was, despite its hectic cabaret life, a place of considerable poverty and hardship.

"The Weary Blues" was a breakthrough for Hughes; it garnered top prize in a literary contest sponsored by the National Urban League in 1925. The award, in turn, won Hughes the support of a prominent literary critic, Carl Van Vechten, who helped Hughes publish his first collection of verse, also entitled *The Weary Blues*, in 1926. Yet the poem stirred controversy among Hughes's peers in the Harlem Renaissance, some of whom objected to the award on the grounds that "The Weary Blues" was not "literary" enough. Not only did it unashamedly draw on folk-music traditions, the poem also featured a blues pianist who sings in dialect such lines as "I's gwine to quit ma frownin'/ And put ma troubles on the shelf." Poetry in the vernacular was deemed politically regressive in some quarters, because it was thought to reinforce white stereotypes regarding African American primitivism. Such criticisms, which were also leveled at *The Weary Blues* as a whole, show exactly how Hughes's aesthetic differed from that of the "Talented Tenth," upper-middle-class black intellectuals who tended to value art that promoted respectability and social advancement through integration. They, therefore, had little use for Hughes's blunt realism.

Hughes's second volume of verse, *Fine Clothes to the Jew* (1927), proved to be even more controversial than *The Weary Blues*. The poems in the new book dealt with aspects of everyday life in proletarian Harlem—fundamentalist religion, low-paying jobs, the cabaret, romance, gambling, fights, prostitution, alcohol—and many of them were written in dialect cast in the form of urban folk blues: the ultimate combination of aesthetic sins, according to Hughes's detractors. Not all critics, however, were disdainful of Hughes's choice of form, diction, and subject matter. Critic Alain Locke and a few others understood that, while apparently artless, Hughes's verse was neither simplistic nor vulgar, that the spare effect he achieved was actually crafted with great care and precision, and that Hughes's portrayal of the joys and calamities of the African American urban masses was executed with honesty and compassion.

The Harlem Renaissance effectively came to an end when the stock market collapsed in October of 1929. The resulting Great Depression, which lasted throughout the 1930's, had a severe impact on the already marginal economy of Harlem. Like much of the rest of the country, Depression-era Harlem was the scene of mass unemployment, bread lines, evictions, and, occasionally, riots. Under such conditions, many of America's leading artists and intellectuals embraced Marxism as an alternative political philosophy. Langston Hughes was no exception. The five books of verse that he published in the 1930's reveal Hughes as an increasingly militant leftist poet. For example, *Scottsboro Limited* (1932) is a book of four poems and a play in support of the "Scottsboro boys," nine young African American defendants in an Alabama rape trial, who were widely thought to be falsely accused. *A New Song* (1938) is Hughes's only book of verse composed entirely of social-protest poems.

After a decade of world travel, activism, and political poetry, Hughes literally and figuratively returned to Harlem. The result was a collection of verse entitled *Shakespeare in Harlem* (1942), which is superficially similar to *The Weary Blues* and *Fine Clothes to the Jew* in its exclusive focus on Harlem as subject and its preponderant use of folk-music forms. Yet Depression-ravaged Harlem in the early 1940's was a vastly different place than it had been in the 1920's. The colorful exuberance of the Harlem Renaissance had long since given way to bitterness and despair, and Hughes's new book reflected the changed mood in the street. Despite some moments of levity, *Shakespeare in Harlem* was an almost unremittingly bleak portrait of an urban ghetto in steep decline, as a sampling of poem titles suggests: "Cabaret Girl Dies on Welfare Island," "Death Chant," "Ballad of the Pawnbroker," "Down and Out," "Midnight Chippie's Lament," "Evil Morning."

One Way Ticket (1949) and *Montage of a Dream Deferred* (1951), are Hughes's verse sketches of Harlem after World War II. Despite the economic boom of the postwar years, Harlem was still grappling with grinding poverty and its attendant social ills and perennially frustrated at the lack of improvement. "Harlem," a short lyric from *Montage of a Dream Deferred*, is justly revered as Hughes's most powerful poem of social protest. In a series of rhetorical questions, the poem's speaker asks what happens when the African American dream of equality of opportunity is endlessly deferred by white society. He conjectures that the dream might "dry up" or "fester" or sag "like a heavy load." Not quite satisfied with these answers, the speaker then asks, "Or does it explode?" The question is a veiled warning that the ghetto may one day erupt in violence. In its brevity, vivid clarity of effect, and moral seriousness, "Harlem" epitomizes Hughes's poetry, which combined consummate artistry with an unflagging social conscience—a relatively rare combination in American literature.

Bibliography
Berry, Faith. *Langston Hughes: Before and Beyond Harlem.* Westport, Conn.: Lawrence Hill, 1983. Sets out to re-create the historical context in which Hughes lived and worked. Quotes an unusual number of poems in their entirety and includes extensive discussions of Hughes's poetry throughout the biography.
Bloom, Harold, ed. *Langston Hughes.* New York: Chelsea House, 1989. A collection of some of the best criticism of Hughes's works, with several articles on his poetry. Supplemented by a useful bibliography and an index.
Emanuel, James A. *Langston Hughes.* Boston: Twayne, 1967. A concise overview of Hughes's extraordinary career. Contains a chronology, an annotated bibliography, and notes.
Miller, R. Baxter. *The Art and Imagination of Langston Hughes.* Lexington: University Press of Kentucky, 1989. Divides Hughes's imagination into the "autobiographical," the "apocalyptic," the "lyrical," the "political," and the "tragicomic." Each chapter focuses on a poem or other work central to an appreciation and understanding of Hughes's imagination.
Mullen, Edward J., ed. *Critical Essays on Langston Hughes.* Boston: G. K. Hall,

1986. Useful for its generous selection of contemporary reviews of the poet's work. An extensive and well-documented introduction surveys and analyzes the critical reception of Hughes's poetry.

Onwuchekwa, Jemie. *Langston Hughes: An Introduction to the Poetry.* New York: Columbia University Press, 1976. Treats Hughes's poetry in thematic terms, with separate chapters on his "black esthetic," the blues, jazz and other musical forms, his social protest verse, his evocation of the ideal ("the dream"), and the poet's place in the "evolution of consciousness in black poetry." Bibliography and index.

Rampersad, Arnold. *The Life of Langston Hughes, 1902-1941: I, Too, Sing America.* Vol. 1. New York: Oxford University Press, 1986. Provides acute interpretations of both Hughes's character and career. Distinguished by its fine style and balance, this volume is the definitive biography of the poet.

Robert Niemi

THE POETRY OF JUNE JORDAN

Author: June Jordan (1936-   )
Type of work: Poetry
First published: Some Changes, 1971; *Poem: On Moral Leadership as a Political Dilemma (Watergate, 1973),* 1973; *New Days: Poems of Exile and Return,* 1974; *Things That I Do in the Dark: Selected Poetry,* 1977; *Passion: New Poems, 1977-80,* 1980; *Living Room: New Poems, 1980-1984,* 1985; *Lyrical Campaigns: Selected Poems,* 1989; *Naming Our Destiny: New and Selected Poems,* 1989

A prolific contemporary poet who merges personal and political concerns, June Jordan has exploited a full range of literary genres in addition to poetry. By turns, her extensive energies have also been devoted to journalism, to teaching, to urban planning, and to political, linguistic, and feminist activism. As Penelope Moffet reported in 1986, it is Jordan's overriding sense that "politics [is] the duty of an artist."

That view can be understood in light of Jordan's background, for her New York City upbringing in a working-class family and her unique experiences as an educationally privileged African American have led her eventually to larger concerns than herself. Of Jamaican ancestry, she was born in Harlem to Granville and Mildred Jordan on July 9, 1936; the family moved to a brownstone in Brooklyn's Bedford-Stuyvesant area when she was five. Both her parents—her father was a postal clerk, her mother a nurse—worked nights at times to help give her advantages.

Frustrated with his own life, her father sometimes beat June physically "to the extent of occasional scar tissue" but also introduced her to literature—notably the Bible and the works of Edgar Allan Poe, William Shakespeare, and Paul Laurence Dunbar—when she was still a young girl. At age seven, Jordan started writing poems herself. Her 1975 essay "Notes of a Barnard Dropout" suggests that her mother, who committed suicide in 1966, had wanted to be an artist but suppressed her own ambitions. Jordan's aggressive lifetime of accomplishments can perhaps be interpreted partly as a compensatory effort to fulfill her mother's thwarted dreams.

In the 1978 essay "Old Stories: New Lives," Jordan reports that during her early days in Bedford-Stuyvesant she surmised that "nobody really liked me or any of the people in my community." For one year in high school, Jordan tolerated a long commute to attend Midwood High School in Brooklyn, where she was the only black among three thousand students; her father then sent her to the exclusive Northfield (Massachusetts) School for Girls. In high school, and subsequently as a student at Barnard College, Jordan found and resisted a white- and male-oriented curriculum that made no attempt to associate itself, as she said, with "my origins: my street, my family, my friends. Nothing showed me how I might try to alter the political and economic realities underlying our Black condition in white America." Jordan's reaction during her twenties was to study African American writers such as Margaret Walker, Robert Hayden, and Langston Hughes; to avoid reading mainstream white authors; and to advocate black English as a respectable medium for writing and communication.

While still at Barnard, Jordan met Michael Meyer, a Columbia University senior who shared her liberal politics; the two married in 1955, and she followed him to the University of Chicago for a year of study there. Their interracial marriage sometimes made them victims of slurs. A son, Christopher David, was born in 1958, the year after Jordan dropped out of Barnard.

Jordan and Meyer divorced in 1966, after a period during which he was in Chicago and she was in New York—a working mother in Queens, writing poetry daily, studying architecture on her own, and doing free-lance journalism to support herself and her son.

In a college teaching career that began in 1967, Jordan has been a member of the English departments of the City College of New York, Connecticut College, Sarah Lawrence College, and Yale University. In 1989, she became a professor at the University of California at Berkeley and concurrently started work as a political columnist for *The Progressive* magazine. Through the years, she has also been poet- and playwright-in-residence, lecturer, and visiting professor with various other colleges and institutions. Since 1969, when she was awarded a Rockefeller Grant, she has received numerous awards, grants, and fellowships, including a National Endowment for the Arts Fellowship (1982) and a National Association of Black Journalists Award (1984).

Though it lacked concrete results, Jordan's work in 1964 with visionary architect Buckminster Fuller on a plan for renovating Harlem gave her a sense of her own potential and helped her get past her "hatred for everything and everyone white." Such essays as Jordan's "Civil Wars" document relevant aspects of her complex career and political development. Jordan's friendships with writer Alice Walker and activist Fannie Lou Hamer both date from her first trip to Mississippi in 1969. Hamer also helped Jordan deal with her racial antipathies.

Jordan's persistent advocacy of black English has triggered much opposition over the years from blacks and many others who see dialectal patterns as detrimental to acquisition by African Americans of the dominant speech and writing patterns of American society. Jordan's juvenile novel *His Own Where—* (1971) was nearly banned by African American parents in Baltimore because it advanced black English, but the same work, which describes an urban renewal project carried out by its protagonist, was central in Jordan's receiving the Prix de Rome in Environmental Design.

Jordan's first collection of poems, *Some Changes*, deals with personal subjects—her parents, her own life as a young woman—and with national events of the 1960's. The book also shows a shift from literary influences to the patterns of black music and speech. Julius Lester, in his introduction to the book, calls the poems "disciplined" and says they are not concerned with "converting the listener . . . to a particular point of view." *New Days*, Jordan's second collection, takes into account her life in Rome as "an exile." One poem in this volume, "Memo to Daniel Pretty Moynihan," uses black English to attack what Jordan takes to be the false notion that African American families are pathologically matriarchal in structure. Jordan's speaker says,

"Don't you liberate me/ from my female black pathology," and concludes, "Clean your own house, babyface." The final poem in *New Days* provided Jordan with the title of her next major collection, *Things That I Do in the Dark.* The theme of that final poem in *New Days* is the idea that a poet's work is a private grasping after public connectedness: "These poems/ they are things that I do/ in the dark/ reaching for you/ whoever you are."

The optimistic tone of the poems that Jordan wrote in the 1980's is colored by an almost paradoxical mix of disciplined aggression and love. In her 1977 essay "Thinking About My Poetry," Jordan notes her own personal transition from "the limitations of a victim mentality" into a sense that she can effectively oppose her enemies, especially "the power of our own fear and our own self-hatred." Jordan's symbiotic concerns with women and Third World peoples are apparent in this essay and in many of her poems.

The collection *Passion: New Poems, 1977-1980* opens with Jordan's praise of Walt Whitman, the father of "New World" poets such as herself; a second motif in Jordan's preface is the difficulty a "dissident American poet" has finding publishers. An essay on Jordan in *African American Writers* (1991), in the context of its full and detailed exposition of her career, suggests rightly that poems in *Passion* are "war cries of women's and Third World peoples' movements."

Jordan's collection *Living Room: New Poems, 1980-1984* appeared in 1985, concurrently with other of her political writings. International concerns and bitter topical satire are bold in such poems as "The Beirut Jokebook":

1. June 8, 1982: This is not an invasion.
2. July 9, 1982: This is a ceasefire.
3. July 15, 1982: This is a ceasefire.
4. July 30, 1982: This ceasefire is strained.
5. August 4, 1982: This is not an invasion.

Jordan's writings in the 1980's, whether prose or verse, often emphasize internationalism and the poet's important role in achieving a worldview and human cohesion. A recurring device is for the personae of her poems to presume to speak for large constituencies: "I am become a Palestinian" or "I am the history of rape/ I am the history of the rejection of who I am." Walt Whitman's "cosmic I" seems to be a precedent in the use of this technique for broadening impact and relevance and giving Jordan's lyric poems a public voice.

The new poems in Jordan's collection *Naming Our Destiny: New and Selected Poems* are clustered under the heading "North Star." Poems in this section, as reviewer Peter Erickson has emphasized, allude to William Butler Yeats's "Leda and the Swan" (in Jordan's version Leda is, as Erickson says, not simply a victim but, rather, strong and aggressive) and the early black American poet Phillis Wheatley, to whom Jordan gives the middle name "Miracle."

The seven poems by Jordan that editor Dudley Randall included in the popular anthology *The Black Poets* (1971) serve to exemplify the elements that have gained

Jordan's poetry a readership. Jordan's "Okay 'Negroes' " opens with a fifteen-line stanza followed by a closing black English couplet, "Come a little closer/ Where you from?" The poem addresses *"American Negroes*/ looking for milk/ crying out loud/ in the nursery of freedomland" and then asks them "where you got that image of a male/ white mammy." This and other parallel questions imply the poem's message: Blacks should grow up, should quit expecting good behavior to bring them nurture from white benefactors.

In "Cameo No. II," a longer poem broken into short stanzaic units, Jordan also uses black English—but here as if in the manner of a grade-school report on George Washington—to discover in Washington an instance of white "privileges of rape and run." Couplets punctuate the dark wit of the poem: "George Washington he think he big/ he trade my father for a pig" and "Americanus Rex/ Secretus Blanco-Bronco-Night-Time-Sex." Thus, with ironic plays on "father," Jordan proceeds to debunk "the father of this country/ stocked/ by declarations at the auction block."

Jordan's "Poem for My Family: Hazel Griffin and Victor Hernandez Cruz" recounts in gruesome detail how a "well-butchered" Kentucky slave named George was killed by Thomas Jefferson's nephews, "Lilburn Lewis and his brother," and thereby "took leave" of that state body part by body part. As elsewhere, Jordan uses a comprehensive "I" voice to speak for blacks: "I am naked/ I am Harlem and Detroit/ currently knives and bullets." To an America (including whites) whom she presumes as her listeners, Jordan's collective persona asserts that "my life is being born/ your property is dying." The poem is at once angry, prosaic, declamatory, and graphic in its imagery.

Jordan's "Poem from the Empire State" is an irregular but sonnet-like poem in which personal experience becomes protest: "Three of us went to the top of the city/ a friend, my son, and I," the poet reports. Their view of "piled-up swill" leads to a concluding rhymed couplet that paradoxically sums up the poem's pessimism: *"No rhyme can be said:/ where reason has fled."* "My Sadness Sits Around Me" is a short, melancholy lyric recording a moment of "boredom without grief." "Nobody Riding the Roads Today," also a brief lyric, has this effective tercet: "Nobody sleeping in my bed/ but I breathe like windows/ broken by emergencies." "What Happens," a cryptic three-sectioned verse contemplation, consists of an extended series of questions whose images of absurdity hint that daily life itself is "the greatest/ show on earth."

June Jordan's writings are available internationally in translation, and some of her poems written in the late 1980's show evidence of experimentations that derive from various international cultural traditions. Domestically, Jordan's accomplishments have established her as an intellectual force in the spheres of twentieth-century American academia, literary life, and political and feminist controversy.

Bibliography
Blassingame, John W., ed. *New Perspectives on Black Studies.* Urbana: University of Illinois Press, 1971. Places Jordan's important essay "Black Studies: Bringing Back

the Person" (1969) in the context of other discussions of programs in black studies.

Erickson, Peter B. "June Jordan." In *Afro-American Writers After 1955: Dramatists and Prose Writers*, edited by Thadious M. Davis and Trudier Harris. Vol. 38 in *Dictionary of Literary Biography.* Detroit: Gale Research, 1985. An illustrated essay by a Wesleyan University professor. Detailed, informative, and insightful. Discusses Jordan's creative works through 1985 in the chronological context of her eventful biography.

Freccero, Carla. "June Jordan." In *African American Writers*, edited by Valerie Smith, Lea Baechler, and A. Walton Litz. New York: Charles Scribner's Sons, 1991. A biographical and critical overview that quotes liberally from Jordan's poems and essays, offers facts and opinions in a clear chronological format, and adds a useful bibliography of primary and secondary works.

Kessler, Jascha. Review of *Some Changes. Poetry* 122 (February, 1973): 301-303. Describes Jordan's poems about the black experience as strong, simple, skillful in adapting the models of earlier poets, and political but not "politicized."

Rollock, Barbara. *Black Authors and Illustrators of Children's Books: A Biographical Dictionary.* 2d ed. New York: Garland, 1992. Summarizes Jordan's biography and lists her six publications for children (1969-1981).

Roy Neil Graves

THE POETRY OF ETHERIDGE KNIGHT

Author: Etheridge Knight (1931-1991)
Type of work: Poetry
First published: Poems from Prison, 1968; *Belly Song and Other Poems*, 1973; *Born of a Woman: New and Selected Poems*, 1980; *The Essential Etheridge Knight*, 1986

There is so much desperation and so much love, so much of death and so much creation in the poetry of Etheridge Knight, as in his life, that reading a collection of his poems can be a delightful and an agonizing experience. People who met him saw that he truly wanted to see them and that he offered his feelings immediately and without reserve, evasion, or disguise. He did so because such an offering and request for reciprocal response was essential to his personality, vision, and struggle to make life and poetry meaningful enough to be worth maintaining. The cost of that maintenance, like its reward, could be very dear (and indeed the poet often lived in or near poverty). Yet the honest and open expression of feelings, always in good will and good faith, was the program of his art, and its purpose was to enact his highest and indispensable value: freedom, for himself and all others. In person and in poetry, Knight tried always to present himself as an expressive model of the free, loving self; but the forces of oppression and constriction appear to have dominated his early life to such an extent that by the time he was an adult and a celebrated poet, the joy of freedom alternated regularly—often day by day—with the desperation of the sprung trap and the cage. Finally, as he said in several poems, his most pervasive problem lay in himself, his addictions that rivaled his enemies, racism and fascism, in their ability to distort and destroy both love and freedom. As he said in a poem about a loved one, "My 'highs' drove her/ down!"

Etheridge Knight was born in 1931 in Corinth, Mississippi, one of seven children in a family with little means or opportunity. Finding himself limited by racism to a world of menial jobs, pool halls, barrooms, and narcotics (his poem dated June, 1981, "Once on a Night in the Delta: A Report from Hell," suggests too little change in fifty years), Knight dropped out of school at fourteen and at sixteen joined the Army. Treatment for a shrapnel wound suffered in Korea increased his addiction to narcotics, and upon his discharge he became a wanderer by necessity as well as inclination, settling at first and then intermittently in Indianapolis, Indiana. There he was sentenced in 1960 to serve a term of ten to twenty-five years in the state penitentiary for having snatched an elderly white woman's purse. Having begun his education, as he remarked, on the streetcorners in the oral tradition of African American blues and toasts, in prison Knight pursued an informal literary education, reading *The Autobiography of Malcolm X* (1965) and the poetry of Langston Hughes and other black poets, including Dudley Randall, Gwendolyn Brooks, Don L. Lee (Haki Madhubuti), and Sonia Sanchez. The latter poets helped him to gain publication of his own poems and earn his parole. He also informed himself eclectically in the canon of Anglo-American poetry and in Greek, Latin, Chinese, and Japanese poetry in translation, especially haiku, a form that he adapted to expression of his blues- and jazz-oriented vision. In the mid-1970's, as he met many of his white contemporaries in poetry, he read their work, especially that of those with whom he became close friends, including Robert Bly, Galway Kinnell, and James Wright. He had not emerged from prison free from his habitual abuse of alcohol and other chemicals, however, and during the remainder of his life he frequently committed himself to Veterans' Administration hospitals for treatment, which he experienced as unavoidable self-incarceration. He was married to Sonia Sanchez, Mary McAnally, and Charlene Blackburn, living with his family or alone in cities in Minnesota, Missouri, Connecticut, Pennsylvania, and Tennessee, and often in Indianapolis, where he died of lung cancer in 1991.

Just as Knight began his writing of poetry in prison, so it appears that in prison his essential purpose as a poet crystallized. Prison, as described in his poems, is a place of unavoidable realism about common human conditions and fate: injustice, deprivation, loneliness, fear and despair, sterility, violence, and death. It is, moreover, preeminently the place of racist and fascist oppression. Thereby, however, it becomes for some a place of truth, brotherhood, heroism, self-discovery and clarification of values, dedication, and finally a place where liberating expression is born and even where love persists and is strengthened. Knight learned from Malcolm X what many slaves had learned, that reading and writing free the soul, and sometimes the body. In his process of becoming an imprisoned writer, "prison" became a central image and metaphor in his poetry, and his essential purpose became liberation, of himself, his readers, humanity. The central image of that purpose is poetry itself—poetry that never attacked or betrayed him and whose creation never let him down but came forth to save him again and again. At its purest, in Knight's vision, poetry takes the form of free singing, and anyone is capable of it. In "On the Projects Playground," a boy declares himself a poet, and Knight completely agrees. In another instance, the "dead world dying" is "reborn" in the words "green grass and yellow balloons" sung in the rain by Alexandria Keller, "poet at four." The sea of life-force rose higher in Knight at such moments, so that in the face of adversity and oppression he could celebrate, as in one of his love poems: "We free singers be, baby!/ We free singers be." The lines suggest the interpretation that people are free when expressive love is unrestricted by racists or fascists or their conventions of behavior, and those who are free singers are wholly alive and (to borrow from an essay by Sonia Sanchez) positively and actively themselves.

Yet "It is hard/ To make a poem in prison." Indeed, it would seem that the condition of imprisonment would make poetry, free singing, impossible. A third central image in Knight's poetry, love, makes poetry possible, however, even as a desire to sing prepares one for love. Love poems, or poems about love relationships, make up a large portion of Knight's poetry. The love may be compassionate, familial, friendly, or sexual. Often in the poems it comes to the male poet-prisoner in the person of a woman—a WASP woman visiting "the least of these" (a black junkie), a poet friend, a lover. In each case, she frees his spirit, for a time, for "our time," love's time, from oppression, desperation, or restrictive conventionality. Walls dissolve, or are seen through. Yet she does not free him from addiction. Readers meet in Knight's poems many of the women who were singers in his life. Few readers would meet even one of these women in life; yet at the time of publication, at least, the women in the poems were as alive and real as were the readers, somewhere in America. If it is one of the charms, perhaps it is also one of the chagrins of reading Knight's love poems that in them he presents persons—women, in a sexist society (in the 1980's Knight was growing in awareness of sexism)—in intimate relation with him, and the reader knows from the poems themselves that the relationships broke, painfully for these women, and knows that the suffering women presented have been viewed only through the eyes of the poet. If Knight looked ahead to the coming of a loving woman, he also looked back at his causing one to leave—for example, he sings in the blues of "Belly Song" about "the yesterdays/ when she opened/ to me like a flower/ But I fell on her like a stone/ I fell on her like a stone." So in the addictive cycle of hope and despair, love too can be a kind of addiction, as can the most selfless junkie's inevitable preoccupation with self in quest for the fix and high. Yesterday's high is yesterday. "Every goodby ain't gone," but neither is it "hello," and neither is it "stay." There are many dark and rainy streets in Knight's poetry; it seems an act of both embracive love and desperate rejection when, in his haiku, "Harlem," he calls the "streetwalking woman" the "sister of my soul."

In prison, Knight began to see a great truth that deepened his images, the ambiguity and ambivalence of all imaginations of life. An eternal high would simply "backflip" to an eternal low. His epigraphs to *Born of a Woman* suggest that he felt himself to be a Job, patiently questioning the injustices of a destructive arbitrary Power, but also that his insistence upon facing the truth was fated and legitimated by his being a junkie. The junkie, if not Job, could see that what appeared to be injustices actually were unjust. In "Genesis," prefatory to *The Essential Etheridge Knight*, he warns that the shape of his poems is the snake's. Like a snake in the grass, these poems might strike a parental Achilles or Eurydicean heel, Or, like a snake under a rock, they might slough off their wrinkled skin to emerge renewed. In a widely quoted statement about his life, Knight said, "I died in Korea from a shrapnel wound and narcotics resurrected me. I died in 1960 from a prison sentence and poetry brought me back to life." Perhaps the essential, patterning rhythm of Knight's poetry, taken as a whole, is the cycle of deaths and renewals—itself ambiguous, since it is a release and a trap. In the poem, the poles of the cycle take various forms: highs and lows, caged or free, loving but leaving, flowing or dammed, empty or full, not enough to too much. A hero appears and is killed, innocence is destroyed, family is torn or reunited, race or class alienation is bridged by a common feeling or word. The poles can exist simultaneously, as when a loving couple hurries home through an oppressive society, or when Knight watches three days of labor pains and then the welcome birth of a black boy in the land of the Ku Klux Klan. In an early poem, Knight insisted that suicidal black poets should choose life; but in the next-to-last poem of *The Essential Etheridge Knight*, his praise song for a young black poet includes an understanding acceptance of his suicide and an affectionate release. The book then closes with the prose poem "Rehabilitation & Treatment in the Prisons of America," the final sentence of which tells the reader, "He was black, so he rushed—*ran*—through that door—and fell nine stories to the street." The person whom readers hear speaking to them through the poems was a desperate victim of American racism, an addict, a lover, an African American singer of the worst and best of common humanity, who in singing was sometimes set free. As he said, his poems love their readers; and to read them well, readers must split their old snake skin with the rock of love.

While Knight was in prison, Martin Luther King, Jr., and Malcolm X rose to prominence among black leaders. The special danger posed by Malcolm X was realized early, and he was assassinated first, but not before his speeches, television appearances, and autobiography gave power to the Black Arts movement and Black Aesthetic. As Knight wrote in one of his poems about Malcolm: "You reached the wild guys/ Like me. You and Bird. (And that/ Lil LeRoi Cat.)" Malcolm X had addressed exclusively black audiences, not caring whether whites listened or what they thought, but fearlessly and articulately "telling it like it is" and demonstrating the liberating power of words spoken with scrupulous honesty, accuracy, and eloquence. LeRoi Jones (Amiri Baraka) and many other black authors, like the men and women of words in the generations of slavery, saw that black writers could and should be doers, liberating black audiences by empowering them with African American images of the true, beautiful, and good, arming them with heroic models from their own history, and calling them to spiritual cohesion in building free and healthful black communities, in which artists would serve the people just as would plumbers and doctors. In that sense, Knight had been a black artist within the oral tradition. As a writing poet, and eventually one with a large white as well as black audience, he continued to consider himself a blues and jazz lyricist, even when experimenting (often very effectively) with Anglo and Japanese lyrical forms; and at readings he would always "say," not read, his poems. Yet his audience was any person who could hear, could feel, what he was saying; he believed that being white did not qualify or disqualify a person to love and be loved, suffer, and seek to sing. In many cities, he offered Free People's Poetry Workshops, at which persons of any color were welcome. Still, it was always clear when he "said" a poem, and is clear to alert readers, that the person speaking in the poem is black, telling it like it is in black experience, and telling it in a black way. In almost every poem there is a prompt, large or small, that the speaking voice is an African American voice. It might be the content, for example praising a black hero and lamenting his destruction (and as the title, "A Poem of Attrition" suggests, even the accidental drowning of a black boy is remembered by Knight as the loss of a potential heroic black man). It might be a touch of standard black diction, grammar, or pronunciation, or a phrase from a song that whites rarely sing or would not hear the same, or the naming of a color with a magical history, like purple (plums and gums). It might be a jazz rhythm or a blues repetition with a telling variation, or the sudden signifying rhythms of an internal rhyme: "me" rhymed with "O.D." in a poem about recovery, for example. The poet might be functioning as a griot for his family or the black community or be keeping alive the tradition of black prophecy ("meddling"). "For Black Poets," he wrote, "belong to Black People." They are the "Flutes of Black Lovers . . . Organs of Black Sorrows . . . Trumpets of Black Warriors."

> Let all Black Poets die as Trumpets,
> And be buried in the dust of marching feet.

Bibliography

Hill, Patricia Liggins. " 'Blues for a Mississippi Black Boy': Etheridge Knight's Craft in the Black Oral Tradition." *Mississippi Quarterly* 36, no. 1 (Winter, 1982-1983): 21-33. Examines Knight's uses of blues and other traditional, African American musical and poetic forms.

_____. " 'The Violent Space': The Function of the New Black Aesthetic in Etheridge Knight's Prison Poetry." *Black American Literature Forum* 14, no. 3 (Fall, 1980): 115-121. Asserts that while in prison, Knight learned to identify with the lives of other African Americans and thereby began writing a poetry that liberates the consciousness of his readers.

Knight, Etheridge. Interview by Steven C. Tracy. *MELUS* 12, no. 2 (Summer, 1985): 7-23. Knight discusses the importance of the oral tradition, poetry by women, the appeal of poetry to the individual spirit of freedom, and the trinity of poet, poem, and people.

Nelson, Howard. "Belly Songs: The Poetry of Etheridge Knight." *The Hollins Critic* 18, no. 5 (December, 1981): 1-11. Argues that the compelling theme in Knight's poetry is human relationships. His major poetic device is the use of sound, especially in the immediacy of the spoken voice.

Pinckney, Darryl. "You're in the Army Now." *Parnassus: Poetry in Review* 9, no. 1 (1981): 306-314. Criticizes Knight's "funky" style.

Tom Koontz

THE POETRY OF YUSEF KOMUNYAKAA

Author: Yusef Komunyakaa (1947-   )

Type of work: Poetry

First published: Dedications and Other Darkhorses, 1977; *Lost in the Bonewheel Factory*, 1979; *Copacetic*, 1984; *I Apologize for the Eyes in My Head*, 1986; *Toys in a Field*, 1986; *Dien Cai Dau*, 1988; *February in Sydney*, 1989; *Magic City*, 1992

Although Yusef Komunyakaa is particularly known for *Dien Cai Dau*, which depicts various aspects of the Vietnam War, he also addresses other dimensions of the African American experience not commonly discussed by other poets. His extensive treatment of the old South, in particular, is unique for its mixture of poignancy and nostalgia. While employing African American art forms such as jazz and the blues, he is also a virtuoso of the dramatic monologue, the soliloquy, and the surrealist juxtaposition of surprising images. Critic Matthew Flamm has described him as "pain's constant witness, often speaking for the historically dispossessed, but with the assumption that he does so only on his own idiosyncratic terms."

Komunyakaa was born and reared in Bogalusa, Louisiana, a Southern town with a Ku Klux Klan presence. During the Vietnam War, he served as a correspondent and editor of *The Southern Cross* (1969-1970), and received the Bronze Star. He returned to the United States to complete his education, receiving a bachelor's degree from the University of Colorado in 1975, a master's degree from Colorado State University in 1979, and a master of fine arts degree from the University of California at Irvine in 1980. Partly because of his academic training, Komunyakaa is extremely well read and very much at home with the writings of American poets past and present. While studying for his degrees, he published two chapbooks, *Dedications and Other Darkhorses* and *Lost in the Bonewheel Factory*, in which he employs the grotesque and the macabre imagination to thematize the moral deformity of the world (symbolized by the skeleton as well as by biblical images and allusions), especially the old South of his youth—a subject that appears to haunt Komunyakaa. He began teaching at Indiana University in Bloomington in 1985, after serving briefly as a poet-in-the-schools in New Orleans. Fascinated with Australia and concerned about its Aborigines, he has spent considerable time there and has written a chapbook, *February in Sydney*, about his experiences.

Komunyakaa's collection *Magic City* serves best as an introduction to his poetry because of its autobiographical nature. According to the book, his maternal great-grandmother was born a slave, and her daughter was married to an illegal immigrant from Trinidad ("Mismatched Shoes"). The volume also reveals that Komunyakaa was born when his mother was fifteen years old ("Family Tree"; "Venus's-flytraps"), and that his father, a worker at a lumber company, was quick to fight back when he was kicked by the foreman ("The Whistle"). Barely literate, his father was sometimes abusive toward Komunyakaa's mother but was nevertheless remorseful whenever she ran away ("My Father's Love Letters"). Judging by the autobiographical poems, the Komunyakaas are a large, extended family in which love, care, and support are generously shared. "Unable to divide love from poverty" ("Banking Potatoes"), the Komunyakaas managed to survive under deprived conditions in spite of various forms of racism. Delineating such a background in his childhood, *Magic City* is a book in which vignettes of pain and joy, work and play, and love and hate interweave into a remembrance that mixes laughter, poignancy, indictment, and nostalgia.

The genealogical pattern found in *Magic City* in fact dates back to the first part of *Copacetic*, which launched Komunyakaa as a contemporary poet to the literary world. For Komunyakaa, the term "copacetic" conjures "jazz-blues feelings" associated with New Orleans. The choice of the word as a title also hints at the poet's awareness of the African American community's remarkable ability to survive. Derived from the Creole word *coupesètique*, "copacetic" is a slang expression for "excellent" or "very satisfactory"; its meaning, however, was "able to be coped with." In general, the volume stresses the idea of "copacetic" as relating to survival or coping, and occasionally the sense of feeling (genuinely or ironically) good about oneself.

The first part of *Copacetic*, "Blackmetal Blues," exemplifies racial matters experienced by a variety of African Americans, mainly in the post-Civil War South. Although the author's family is part of the composite narrative ("Family Tree"), the focus is on how African Americans were invariably affected by their predicament as an ethnic group, whether directly (as in "Reflections," which concerns a lynching) or indirectly (as in "Initials on Aspens," which deals with memories of slavery). The experience of racism is eventually put into a global-historical context (see "An African Exchange Student Awaits the Arrival of an African Princess"), thereby linking racial struggles in America with ones abroad, especially in South Africa ("Blasphemy"). The section concludes with "Lost Wax," a personal meditation on the middle passage of Africans on the slave ships, the gods of Africa, and the "stuff" of which Africans are made. Affirming his ethnicity, the poet states: "I am without mercy/ because I am what/ night poured her lament into/ . . . Woman-mold, man-mold:/ whatever shape we think/ will save us, what's left/ in us preserved by joy./ We won't trade our gods/ for money." Such a mixture of lament and pride is typical of the "copacetic" sentiment of this section.

"Blackmetal Blues" also contains examples of Komunyakaa's most favorite poetic forms—the dramatic monologue and the blues. Some of the poems employ the mask of a persona to explore certain situations associated with African Americans. For example, in "More Girl than Boy," the persona addresses a certain Robert Lee, who has "made it home from Chicago" disillusioned with how "All the man-sweet gigs/ meant absolutely nothing." Remembering how he and Robert Lee played together and embraced each other (before he discovered girls), and how Robert has taught him "a heavy love/ for jazz" and saved him from the streets, the persona welcomes Robert "back to earth" because he "always could make that piano/ talk like somebody's mama." The poet then tells Robert outright that he will always be his friend. The poem thus captures the bond between two young African Americans by dramatizing an episode in the mass migration of blacks to the North. Some poems employing the dramatic monologue are also suggestive of the blues, as, for example, "The Way the Cards Fall," which again deals with the migration of blacks to the North.

In "Mojo" (the second part of *Copacetic*), which consists largely of monologues and soliloquies, Komunyakaa's personal voice begins to play a dominant role. While racial matters reappear (as in "Let's Say"), and musical forms such as jazz (as in "Copacetic Mingus") and the blues (as in "Woman, I Got the Blues") again serve as a motif, the poet ventures into a more modern—and modernist—world. The poems in this section may be challenging to read, but they are essentially written or arranged according to the principles described in "Safe Subjects," which can be regarded as a poetic manifesto.

"Safe Subjects" shows the poet musing upon the possibilities of extending his subject matters and deepening his expressions. There are complex messages in this *ars poetica*, but the imagery suggests that Komunyakaa, acknowledging the darkness and horror afflicting the daily lives of African Americans, would like to probe into the truth hidden behind this sinister mask of reality. In the poem, the juxtaposition of details taken from mundane reality with fragmented images of a horrifying nature also hints at the surrealist style that the poet will be exploiting. At his best, Komunyakaa is able to mix surrealism with the blues technique, creating an interesting expression combining European and African American elements. A good example is "Blues Chant Hoodoo Revival," which, as the last poem of the volume, is also an ironic summation of the "copacetic" theme because of the intensity of the pain that the poet reveals about his African American identity.

I Apologize for the Eyes in My Head, a collection of heterogeneous poems, opens with a powerful declaration of the independence of the self: "I have principles. I won't speak/ on the natural state of the unicorn/ in literature or self-analysis./ I have no birthright to prove,/ no insignia, no secret password, no fleur-de-lis./ My initials aren't on a branding iron." The rest of the volume is informed by this uncompromising self-definition. The book's title is derived from "When in Rome—Apologia," a dramatic monologue depicting a streetwise playboy figure. The poem's persona obviously has been dallying with a woman, but he gets into a potentially troublesome situation when he is confronted by her husband. To defuse the man's anger, the person makes a number of relevant and irrelevant excuses and apologizes—ironically—for the eyes in his head. A few other dramatic monologues are written in a similar vein ("I Apologize"), and humorous satires abound in the book. Other accessible poems include character studies ("Olympia"), soliloquies and masked poems ("Touch-up Man"), and personal reflections and meditations ("Unnatural State of the Unicorn").

Despite its merits, *I Apologize for the Eyes in My Head* can sometimes be puzzling. The reason behind the obscurity is perhaps Komunyakaa's venture beyond "safe subjects," which entails the delineation of what Matthew Flamm calls "difficult truths." For Komunyakaa, truths are necessarily difficult. As an epigraph from

Aimé Césaire suggests, rather than mere concepts, truths involve the totality of one's experience. Moreover, according to an epigraph from Czesław Miłosz, truths are not only personal but also deeply rooted in the interests of the community. This poetics of difficult truths is applied successfully in poems such as "How I See Things" (where Komunyakaa contrasts his experience with a former freedom marcher's rational view of the Civil Rights movement) and "Landscape for the Disappeared" (in which the poet describes a killing field in Louisiana in sensory terms). Komunyakaa's critique of modern technology and Western civilization in the apocalyptic poems "1984" and "Raw Data for an Unfinished Questionnaire" also illustrates that he is ultimately concerned about communal issues, even as he presents truth in terms of the most private experiences.

Dien Cai Dau, by which Komunyakaa's reputation is established, is an important document of the Vietnam War and its aftermath. Some of the poems appeared earlier in Komunyakaa's 1986 chapbook *Toys in the Field*, but, significantly, the title adopted for the book is in Vietnamese. *Dien cai dau*, which means "crazy ones," is a term used by the Vietnamese to refer to American soldiers. The phrase occurs in "Starlight Scope Myopia," a poem with a title that, in turn, puns on the nature of the war. In the poem, the persona recalls how, while spying and preparing to fire on Viet Cong troops who were loading an oxcart with rice and ammunition, he wondered to himself: "Are they talking about women/ or calling the Americans/ *beaucoup dien cai dau*?" The rest of the poem suggests that, for a moment, the soldier enters into an empathy (and sympathy) with those whom he is going to kill. This poem is typical of the way Komunyakaa approaches his subject: Its documentary realism transforms, toward the end, into a critical and humanistic reflection that remains largely unspoken. There is an unmistakable tension between the need to survive and the imperative to commit violence, and the gulf between the moment's violence and the haunting, even remorseful memory long after the act remains unbridgeable. Many other poems dealing with combat situations follow this pattern; the widely praised poem " 'You and I Are Disappearing' " (in which a soldier gazes with prolonged awe at a girl whom he has caused to burn alive) is paradigmatic of this group.

In poems dealing with the facets of warfare, Komunyakaa not only captures the drama of the situations esthetically but also, in the process, hints at the treacherous conditions and moral ambiguity of the war ("Camouflaging the Chimera"). Rather than dwelling upon bloody combats, he underscores the human tragedies afflicting not only the Americans ("Fragging") but also the Vietnamese ("Sappers"). Significantly, the poet often offers a dual perspective on the war itself by dramatizing the encounters and interactions between the opposing forces, so that he presents the war from both sides' point of view. "Night Muse and Mortar Round" shows Americans being easily lured to their deaths regardless of their intentions; "Re-creating the Scene" describes the gang rape of a Vietnamese woman with a baby by Americans. After filing a complaint, the woman simply disappears, leaving behind a baby who "makes a fist & grabs at the air,/ searching for a breast." Poems concentrating on the interactions between American soldiers and Vietnamese women are especially re- markable, not only because they show how such relationships are destined to be circumstantial and abnormal ("The Edge") but also because they epitomize one nation's obscene violation of another at the most intimate level.

The critical stance in *Dien Cai Dau* is further underscored when Komunyakaa begins to introduce the race factor into some poems, thus reminding the reader that the Vietnam War coincided with the era of racial strife, city riots, and the Civil Rights movement in the United States. The distinction between black and white soldiers first emerges as a motif in "Hanoi Hannah," where, ironically, a Viet Cong woman—soon to be killed by the black soldiers—announces the death of Martin Luther King, Jr. In "Report from the Skull's Diorama," when a group of black soldiers "have lost their tongues" after reading propaganda leaflets reiterating that *"VC didn't kill/ Dr. Martin Luther King,"* the lines setting enemies and friends apart are blurred beyond recognition. The death of King is presented as an intensely trau- matic experience in the stageable dramatic monologue in prose "The One-legged Stool," in which a black prisoner of war, after disbelieving and denying King's death to his captors, eventually admits that he has been and will continue to be subject to white racism. The prisoner is so paranoid that he begins to equate the Viet Cong with Southern whites as agents of his oppression. The equation is a little odd but not entirely farfetched, because, according to the implication in "To Have Danced with Death," a black soldier's being wounded in action is no guarantee that he will be accepted by whites as he visits the hospital. The racial distinction between black and white Americans is further problematized, rather inextricably, as black soldiers find racial segregation curiously institutionalized in a Vietnamese bar and yet ironically demolished in a brothel in the same red-light district ("Tu Do Street").

Although Komunyakaa's reflections on the Vietnam War do not hinge on the issue of race alone, his identity as a black man has given the war a special meaning that would otherwise have been lost. Even when he is dealing with the aftermath of the war, he tries to make this clear. In "Face It," the concluding poem of the book, he begins by suggesting his anonymity as he stands before the Vietnam Veterans Me- morial ("My black face fades,/ hiding inside the black granite"). Toward the end, however, he hints at how, before such a memorial, he is meant to be recognized after all: "A white vet's image floats closer to me, then his pale eyes/ look through mine. I'm a window." To some critics, *Dien Cai Dau* is a milestone in poetry by Vietnam veterans; Vicente Gotera, for example, has commented that the volume "points to the possibility and actuality of self-renewal and solace," a transcendent view that helps to "make possible a more accurate national vision of the Vietnam War." Yet it is the racial perspective that Komunyakaa has brought to bear on this transcending vision that makes the book an emergent classic.

Komunyakaa has quoted Ernst Fischer as saying that "beauty holds judgment and pronounces its verdict in lines of tempered steel." Komunyakaa's poetry appears to aspire to a similar condition—to let beauty itself express the truth. Accordingly, he has always disciplined the language in his poems to allow their carefully selected details and images to express themselves. His vision is embedded in his poems' situations rather than declared by their personae. His voice, if often muted because of his "poetics of difficult truths" and his preference for letting the poem dramatize such truths, is distinctive; it has an impact that tends to linger rather than fade. *Dien Cai Dau* proved Komunyakaa's abilities, and *Magic City* also contains sure signs of his maturity as a poet. His subsequent work has suggested that Komunyakaa has in mind further adventures and breakthroughs in both subject matter and artistic expression. Eager to individualize his voice, Komunyakaa thus continues to temper the steel of his poetry.

Bibliography
Cramer, Steven. Review of *Dien Cai Dau*, by Yusef Komunyakaa. *Poetry* 156, no. 2 (May, 1990): 102-105. An elaborate review of Komunyakaa's most celebrated volume.
Ehrhart, W. D. "Soldier-Poets of the Vietnam War." *Virginia Quarterly Review* 63, no. 2 (Spring, 1987): 246-265. Places Komunyakaa in the context of writings inspired by the Vietnam War.
Flamm, Matthew. "Facing Up to the Deadly Ordinary." *The New York Times Book Review* 92 (October 4, 1987): 24. Contains a brief review of *I Apologize for the Eyes in my Head.*
Gotera, Vicente F. " 'Depending on the Light': Yusef Komunyakaa's *Dien Cai Dau.* " In *America Rediscovered: Critical Essays on Literature and Film of the Vietnam War*, edited by Owen W. Gilman, Jr., and Lorrie Smith. New York: Garland, 1990. Discusses *Dien Cai Dau* in the context of the growing body of work devoted to the Vietnam War.
Komunyakaa, Yusef. " 'Lines of Tempered Steel': An Interview with Yusef Komunyakaa." Interview by Vicente Gotera. *Callaloo* 13, no. 2 (Spring, 1990): 215-229. An indispensable interview in which Komunyakaa discusses the sources and models of his poetry, his aesthetic standpoints, and his views on contemporary American poetry.

Balance Chow

THE POETRY OF AUDRE LORDE

Author: Audre Lorde (1934-1992)
Type of work: Poetry
First published: The First Cities, 1968; *Cables to Rage,* 1970; *From a Land Where Other People Live,* 1973; *New York Head Shop and Museum,* 1975; *Between Our Selves,* 1976; *Coal,* 1976; *The Black Unicorn,* 1978; *Chosen Poems: Old and New,* 1982; *Our Dead Behind Us,* 1986

At readings or interviews, Audre Lorde often introduced herself by naming the qualities that defined her: black, feminist, lesbian, poet. After her operation for breast cancer, she frequently added, "post-mastectomy woman." By naming, she brought into the light of day subjects that are often hidden. Lorde insisted on candor, on examining issues that are often viewed as divisive, and moreover, throughout her work she calls for honesty, justice, and bringing together divergent human perspectives that seem to divide, but that Lorde insisted need not.

Her insistence on naming began early. When she was still a child first learning to write, she changed the spelling of her name from Audrey to Audre, a symbolic gesture indicating that she would be her own self. Her direction was thus clearly set while she was still in grade school. She recounts this incident in *Zami: A New Spelling of My Name* (1982), a volume she calls a "biomythography." Naming imparts immense power, and it is therefore no surprise that Lorde seems to have instinctively realized this early in life. She uses naming also when she writes of her recognition of her lesbianism, saying in "Artisan," from *The Black Unicorn,* "I did not recognize/ the shape/ of my own name." In "Between Ourselves," she pleads for tolerance through the use of names: "Do not mistake my flesh for the enemy/ do not write my name in the dust."

When she names herself black, lesbian, feminist, she is clearly and emphatically putting herself with people who have traditionally been excluded or kept on the fringes of society, with the despised and the powerless. It is with these people that she takes her stand.

To be black is the first marginalization that she names. She remembers being spit upon as a child and remembers her strong mother insisting that the perpetrators were rude and ignorant. Her mother, however, did not discuss the obvious factor of racial hatred. In "Story Books on a Kitchen Table," she says her mother "spat me/ into her ill-fitting harness of despair/ into her deceits." Such self-deception may also have contributed to her feelings of marginalization. How could one fight or even oppose something if one could not admit its existence? Moreover, growing up, Lorde did not belong to the majority black society in Harlem. Her parents were immigrants from the West Indies who dreamed of returning home to their island of Carriacou. They spoke the island dialect and used it when they did not want their children to know the gist of their conversation. It is not surprising, then, that in high school Lorde found friends among others who were viewed as outcasts.

In "Coal," however, she names herself black "because I come from the earth's inside/ now take my word for jewel in the open light." This is a celebration of blackness, a celebration that she maintains throughout her work. Her self-assertion continues despite the fact that she knows that strangers who do not want to see her blackness look through her, "cancelling me out/ like an unpleasant appointment." Or they see her as a postage due stamp, undesirable and "stamped in yellow red purple/ any color except Black and choice/ and woman/ alive." Lorde insists that she is all the last three things. She is black, she sees herself as black, and she sees other black people as beautiful as well. Later in that same volume, *Our Dead Behind Us*, she celebrates a snapshot of the last Dahomean Amazons, "three old Black women in draped cloths/ holding hands." From all these people, especially the latter, Lorde draws the strength to resist racism, to proclaim her individuality and beauty.

Unlike most twentieth century homosexual writers, Lorde is open about her lesbianism. She does not disguise the sex of her lovers in her love poems, as, for example, May Swenson, another contemporary poet, did. Lorde says "she" when she means "she," and is similarly frank about her lovemaking. Subterfuge does not seem to be in Lorde's lexicon. In "A Question of Climate," from *Our Dead Behind Us*, she insists that "I learned to be honest/ the way I learned to swim." For Lorde, honesty is a method of lifesaving. She is impelled to honesty about her sexual preferences as well as about other essential aspects of her life. Moreover, she insists that her lesbianism is natural, is something her entire life pointed her toward, although she married at one time and bore two children. In "Outlines," she puts it this way: "When women make love/ beyond the first exploration/ we meet each other knowing/ in a landscape/ the rest of our lives/ attempts to understand." Love poems make up a sizeable portion of Lorde's poetry. There are ten obvious love poems in *Our Dead Behind Us*, and twelve in *The Black Unicorn*. Moreover, her love poems are connected to her other urgent concerns, politics, differences, and art.

Lorde is also a feminist. She calls upon the world to give women equality and justice. In *Coal*, she sees old women in welfare lines, insulted, slow, poor, unvalued. Her poem is an indictment of a society that allows women to be treated this way. She is especially vehement about the treatment of black women in South Africa. In "Sisters in Arms," she writes of a fifteen-year-old girl hanging "gut-sprung on police wheels." Her sympathies coalesce in a number of poems, and she finds that brutality and neglect are the same in New York, El Salvador, or Pretoria.

This knowledge leads Lorde to strong pleas for working together, for sisterhood. Her thesis is that the first step toward cooperation is complete honesty, hence her insistence on her blackness, on her lesbianism, on her feminism. Then she says that matters of color, sexual preference, and politics should not separate communities, especially communities that have been exploited. Nevertheless, there are enormous rifts between the groups whom Lorde addresses. She names the ways people of lighter skin look down on darker blacks. Moreover, she notes that there is enormous pressure from within the black community against lesbians; many blacks view lesbianism as a form of racial suicide, and others, especially black men, see it as an attack on and insult to them. Lorde insists that it is neither. In a speech, she put her case emphatically and clearly: "When I say I am a Black Lesbian, I mean I am a woman whose primary focus of loving, physical as well as emotional, is directed to women. It does not mean I hate men."

Throughout her work, there is a major concern for children, a fact that has been little noted. The beginnings of this concern occur in her early collections and continue in *Coal* in "The Woman Thing," in which she begins to develop a point of view that is vastly expanded and deepened in subsequent work. In this poem, she says, "All this day I have craved/ food for my child's hunger/ Emptyhanded the hunters come shouting/ injustices drip from their mouths/ like stale snow melted in sunlight." Her concern grows more intense and immediate in succeeding volumes. In particular, Lorde focuses on the case of a black ten-year-old named Clifford, who was shot by a white policeman; the policeman was declared not guilty in the subsequent trial. Two poems, "A Woman/ Dirge for Wasted Children" and "Power," concern this incident. The former poem ends "I am bent/ forever/ wiping up blood/ that should be/ you." In the latter poem, which carries a powerful burden of anger, Lorde insists that the policeman after the shooting stood over the body saying "Die you little motherfucker" and that he testified that "I didn't notice the size or nothing else/ only the color."

In *Chosen Poems*, she turns her grief and anger to the case of Emmett Till, a fifteen-year-old black from the North who was visiting relatives in Mississippi when he whistled at a white girl. Some of the local white men saw this as an insult to white womanhood, and Till was taken away, murdered, and mutilated. In "Afterimages," collected in *Chosen Poems*, she focuses on both Emmett Till and a lowerclass white woman who has been caught in a flood and lost everything; Lorde exhibits sympathy for both of them, even though the woman belongs to the oppressor race. The major focus, however, is the tragedy of the murdered child. She compares the newspaper photographs of Till's "black broken flesh" to the face of a raped woman. The parallels between murder and the sexual act are boldly juxtaposed. After the murder and mutilation of the boy, "In the name of white womanhood" his killers "celebrated in a whorehouse/ the double ritual of white manhood/ confirmed." In this way, Lorde equates murder with the white male sexual act, a horrendous and psychologically telling insight.

The first poem in *Our Dead Behind Us* presents images of "Black children massacred at Sebokeng/ six-year-olds imprisoned for threatening the state." In "Diaspora," she juxtaposes Johannesburg and Alabama and presents the nightmare image of a black girl who "flees the cattle prods/ skin hanging from her shredded nails." The images keep coming throughout the volume, including those of the black South African woman who "saw her two-year-old daughter's face/ squashed like a melon/ in the pre-dawn police raids upon Noxolo" and the burned bodies of dead children who had participated in a demonstration "running toward Johannesburg/ some singing some waving/ some stepping to intricate patterns/ their fathers knew tomorrow they will be dead."

Besides her emphasis on children in the later poetry, Lorde has brought the African female gods to American poetry. These gods, their names, and their legends make an excellent match with Lorde's writing. It is from Dan, the ancient kingdom of Dahomey, that the Amazons, the warrior women, came. These women existed in fact, but they exist in myth as well, and their spirits work especially well in the ethos of Lorde's poetry, which is often militant. In "The Women of Dan Dance with Swords in Their Hands to Mark the Time When They Were Warriors," she identifies with these strong, brave women. She would be like them, "warming whatever I touch/ that is living/ consuming/ only/ what is already dead." This is a strong plea for life, for all life, and beneath it, an equally strong call for militant justice. In "125th Street and Abomey," Lorde invokes Seboulisa, the goddess of Abomey. This poem, set in New York City, depicts the narrator walking through the snow. Although "Half earth and time splits us apart/ like struck rock," Lorde calls on the goddess, asking her to "give me the woman strength/ of tongue in this cold season." She also petitions Seboulisa to "see me now/ your severed daughter/ laughing our name into echo/ all the world shall remember." Lorde is calling upon the female African deities to give her strength and laughter to endure difficulties. Such references add a layer of myth that is delightful and interesting and that contributes especially well to Lorde's feminist perspective. By presenting this pantheon in her poetry (*The Black Unicorn* provides a glossary of the names and attributes of African deities), she opens up the myths of Africa to her readers.

Lorde's poetic techniques enhance her message. She writes in free verse, often using the elegy. Although she does not use rhyme, a strong lyrical quality is often the organizing element in her work, the message being carried along by the song. Much of the time, she foregoes standard punctuation. She takes advantage of the patterns of normal speech and lets line breaks fall where commas or periods would naturally occur. When she needs a pause in the middle of the line, she uses a double space. This method does not seem to detract from the substance of her message, but rather seems to give the work an added naturalness and openness. Lorde chooses a vocabulary of ordinary speech most of the time. When she departs from this pattern, as she does when she introduces the African deities or introduces a phrase from the dialect of Carriacou, the reader is alerted to something of importance.

Audre Lorde stood outside most groups in twentieth century America. Her stance gave her a perspective from which to view her country and the world. She used it to bestow new names that impel the reader to take a new look at what is old and ill so that society may be rejuvenated and cured. Her work advocates a cherishing of differences that would, if adopted, enlighten the blackest and the whitest of hearts.

Bibliography
Annas, Pamela. "A Poetry of Survival: Unnaming and Renaming in the Poetry of Audre Lorde, Pat Parker, Sylvia Plath, and Adrienne Rich." *Colby Library Quarterly* 18 (March, 1982): 9-25. An analysis of four women poets exploring the ways they deal with a language that is patriarchal. Annas posits the theory that each

poet goes through a process of recognizing the problem, casting off old names, and then renaming themselves so that they can then rename the world. The material on Lorde relies heavily on her volume *The Black Unicorn.*

Brooks, Jerome. "In the Name of the Father: The Poetry of Audre Lorde." In *Black Women Writers, 1950-1980: A Critical Evaluation*, edited by Mari Evans. Garden City, N.Y.: Anchor Press/Doubleday, 1983. Contends that although the feminist interests in Lorde's poetry have been well documented, her work also expresses a strong attachment for her father and his values. Also notes the lyric quality and tenderness of her love poetry.

Carruthers, Mary. "The Re-Vision of the Muse: Adrienne Rich, Audre Lorde, Judy Grahn, Olga Broumas." *The Hudson Review*, Summer, 1983, 293-322. Carruthers sees these lesbian poets as having used the powers of the muse in familiar, maternal, and sororal ways. Uses Lorde's *The Black Unicorn* to demonstrate these qualities.

DiBernard, Barbara. "*Zami*: A Portrait of an Artist as a Black Lesbian." *Kenyon Review* 13 (Fall, 1991): 195-213. Traces the development of the artist as lesbian and the effects of this orientation on her work.

Lorde, Audre. Interview by Claudia Tate. In *Black Women Writers at Work*, edited by Claudia Tate. New York: Continuum, 1983. The interview covers a number of Lorde's concerns: the difficulty of growing up black in a white society, the antagonism between black men writers and black women writers, Lorde's lesbianism, and her views on the religious aspects of eros. An excellent condensation of Lorde's views.

Martin, Joan. "The Unicorn Is Black: Audre Lorde in Retrospect." In *Black Women Writers, 1950-1980: A Critical Evaluation*, edited by Mari Evans. Garden City, N.Y.: Anchor Press/Doubleday, 1983. Martin finds that Lorde's chief poetic characteristic is honesty and that her poems are intensely personal. Martin also commends Lorde for bringing African female deities into her poetry and hence into the American consciousness.

Ann Struthers

THE POETRY OF CLAUDE McKAY

Author: Claude McKay (1889-1948)
Type of work: Poetry
First published: Songs of Jamaica, 1912; *Constab Ballads,* 1912; *Spring in New Hampshire and Other Poems,* 1920; *Harlem Shadows,* 1922; *Selected Poems of Claude McKay* (introduced by John Dewey), 1953

In the early 1900's, two Jamaicans, almost exact contemporaries, arrived in New York and influenced the course of African American life: in 1916, Marcus Garvey, who organized the Universal Negro Improvement Association; and in 1914, Claude McKay, one of the main inspirers of the Harlem Renaissance, the 1920's cultural development of the arts and literature that, though it lasted for only a decade, permanently influenced the course of black self-expression in the United States. Both men died in relative obscurity after their fame had diminished; Garvey's reputation has since declined, so that he is now known to few except scholars, but McKay's has steadily increased, so that he is considered one of the ornaments of African American literature. He has been posthumously proclaimed Jamaica's national poet, and he has been the subject of an international conference of literary scholars. McKay has retained his stature as both poet and fictionist, even though he was attacked for his presentation of black life in *Home to Harlem* (1928) by the distinguished black intellectual W. E. B. Du Bois, for his left-wing political sympathies and activities by the Howard University philosopher Alain Locke (who is sometimes regarded as the mentor of the Harlem Renaissance), and for his ultimate conversion to Roman Catholicism. Paul Laurence Dunbar, Countée Cullen, and Langston Hughes also helped in the development of modern African American poetry, but only Hughes could legitimately be proposed as a better and more important poet than McKay.

McKay's life (and hence his poetry) was influenced by a number of individuals. His parents, both of whom were Baptists, provided an early and abiding religious disposition and imbued him with a deep sense of racial self-respect. (His father claimed Ashanti origins; his mother was descended from Madagascans.) His brother U'Theo, a schoolteacher, helped to instill in him a deep respect for knowledge and an undiminished appetite for learning. Walter Jekyll, a British expatriate who had become an authority on Jamaican folklife, introduced him to the standard British authors, encouraged him to write poetry in the mode of Robert Burns (and incorporating the use of Jamaican dialect), and became his literary mentor, his collaborator (in the setting to music of some of the poems in *Songs of Jamaica*), and ultimately his patron. McKay was not to develop into a mere mouthpiece for these people, however; he very quickly developed his own philosophy and priorities, which are visible in his themes and poetic subject matter: black self-respect, sympathy for the underclasses, fierce (even propagandistic) advocacy of racial and gender equality, appreciation of natural beauty (whether of Caribbean or European origin), and a dislike of authoritarian and bureaucratic regimentation. Once McKay settled in Harlem, the "black belt" of New York City, he came under the influence of Max and Crystal Eastman, the energetic patrons of *The Liberator,* a socialist publication. These influences were not always compatible, and McKay was, as a result, frequently ambivalent in social and religious matters.

Later in life, McKay described himself as a "troubador wanderer"; this is a most apt sobriquet, for it stresses his primary attachment to poetry and incidentally alludes to his constant search for the ideal life for the black poet in an essentially white culture. This eremetic existence commenced in 1912, a singularly important year in McKay's life, for in that year his first volumes of poetry were published (*Songs of Jamaica* in Kingston and *Constab Ballads* in London); six of his poems, set to Jekyll's music, were issued in London; and he won an international poetry contest sponsored by a London newspaper.

McKay's winning poem was "George William Gordon to the Oppressed Natives," which celebrated the 1865 Morant Bay Rebellion that was supposedly encouraged by the Baptist mulatto politician Gordon. The final stanza of the poem offers a remarkable foreshadowing of what later became McKay's most famous poem, "If We Must Die":

> Gordon's heart here bleeds for you.
> He will lead to victory:
> We will conquer every foe,
> Or together gladly die.

Yet the poem also contains lines that prefigure the exhortation of McKay's great propagandistic poems: "Rise, O people of my kind!/ Struggle, struggle to be free."

Unfortunately, the poem is marred by intrusive approximations of Jamaican dialect in lines that are generally in standard English poetic idiom: "O, you sons of Afric's soil" is followed by "Show dem dat you ha' some brains." It seems improbable that Gordon would have told Jamaicans that they should "Wake . . ./ De gorilla in your blood/ Though you may be coarse and rude." Nevertheless, the poet's enthusiasm, anger, and energy shine through.

In his preface to *Songs of Jamaica,* which is dedicated (rather judiciously) to Sir Sydney Olivier, the governor of the colony, Walter Jekyll describes Jamaican English as "a feminine version of masculine English; pre-eminently a language of love, as all will feel who, setting prejudice aside, will allow the charmingly naive love-songs of this volume to make their due impression upon them." Of the fifty poems in the volume, only a few are undeniably love poems in the traditional manner; more are poems that expound love of nature—especially countryside—and love of family. "To Clarendon Hills and H. A. H." and "My Native Land, My Home" are of the first group, and "Mother Dear" and "To Bennie" illustrate the second. In "To Clarendon Hills and H. A. H." McKay writes to H. A. H. (described in the poem as a "sorrowin' an' sad . . . lad"),

> Love me, frien' o' mine
> Wid that love of thine
> Passin' love of womenkin',
> More dan love of womenkin'.

This may be read in several ways, but it suggests a friendship like that of Saul and Jonathan in the Bible (2 Samuel 1:26), a total male commitment.

Throughout *Songs of Jamaica*, there are intimations that McKay foresaw his imminent wanderings; several poems speak about his intent to return to his native land and to the green hills of the Clarendon district, which held such an attraction for him. "But I'll return again," he says in "My Mountain Home"; "In days to come I shall return/ To end my wand'rin's dere." This attachment to place is deeply felt, frequently repeated, and sadly ironic, for McKay never returned to his native land and his mountain home; though he enjoyed living in the Soviet Union, in France, in Morocco, and in the United States, he was always the troubador wanderer, the poet without national roots—except in Jamaica, to which he felt that he could never return.

Constab Ballads is patently less lyrical than *Songs of Jamaica*, and it is clear that the poems in this second volume by McKay would not have fitted in comfortably with the earlier poems. The poems, the poet writes in a brief preface, were all the consequence of his brief sojourn in the Jamaican Constabulary: "To relieve my feelings, I wrote poems, and into them I poured my heart in its various moods. This volume consists of a selection from these poems." There are twenty-eight poems, many owing inspiration more, perhaps, to Rudyard Kipling than to Robert Burns (whose influence on *Song of Jamaica*, mainly in the incorporation of dialect, had led to McKay's being termed the "Jamaican Burns"). There are poems on drills, marches, fire practices, payday, and comradeship, but none rises above the mundane except "Sukkee River," which seems to have been intended for *Songs of Jamaica*, since it celebrates the poet's love for the countryside, flora, and streams of his native land and for his happiness in swimming, naked and alone, in what he describes as "a fairy dream." Once more McKay comments on the love between him and nature, a love purer than "de love o' men," and vows never to roam again from his Jamaican Eden.

Although there are some true gems of both concept and expression in McKay's initial two volumes of poetry, it is unlikely that any except Jamaicans and scholars will take any real pleasure in reading them. Even in 1912, Jekyll thought it necessary to add extensive footnotes to *Songs of Jamaica* to explain the poems' contractions, allusions, and pronunciation, and both a glossary and footnotes were added to *Constab Ballads.* While for some readers these may be helpful, they undeniably signal difficulties for others and suggest that the dialect poems must be regarded as belonging to a special time and place; that is, that they are not really relevant to the major achievements of Claude McKay as a poet, notwithstanding their unquestionable depth of feeling, value as precursors of subsequent subjects and themes, and place in the development of an indigenous poetic literature in Jamaica.

There is no doubt that McKay's use of dialect in his poems was an advance on the use of dialect by such predecessors as Paul Laurence Dunbar, who used it largely for either comic or role-establishing purposes; McKay used dialect for social verisimilitude, to attempt to capture the Jamaican inflections and idiom, to differentiate the speech of the folk from that of the colonial classes. Upon quitting Jamaica for the United States, however, McKay discontinued his use of dialect, even when, in some of his American "protest" poems that make use of African American diction, dialect would be appropriate and even effective.

Few poets have had such success as McKay had achieved by the time that he was twenty-two. He was little less than a literary phenomenon at a time when A. B. Paterson in Australia and Stephen Leacock in Canada were helping to create the bases for their own colonies' characteristic verse traditions. McKay explored new subjects, new themes, and new forms of speech and language in his poetry.

In 1914, McKay went to New York, where he quickly identified himself with the socialist confraternity—even though he was a black in an essentially white (and largely Jewish) community. Notwithstanding his differences (as a black, a West Indian, and a British subject), he identified with the writers whom he met, and he stressed that the blacks of the United States shared most of the deprivations of the blacks of the Caribbean and Africa. In fact, it has been noted that McKay was the true father of the concept of "negritude"—of pride in blackness—that became a hallmark of advanced literature from Africa and the Caribbean a generation after McKay's Harlem Renaissance days. He was the first and most vocal advocate of racial consciousness, of racial pride for Africans and African Americans alike.

Spring in New Hampshire and Other Poems, McKay's first volume of poetry in Standard English, which was published in London, and *Harlem Shadows,* which appeared two years later in New York, established him as a major poet in the black community and as a potentially important one in English literature. *Harlem Shadows,* with its brilliant evocation of life in the black ghetto of New York City, more than any other book heralded the beginning of the Harlem Renaissance, from which developed the great florescence of African American culture in subsequent years. Immediately after the publication of *Harlem Shadows,* McKay visited the Soviet Union, sojourned in Europe for a decade, and turned his talents to the writing of short stories, novels, and social commentaries; he did not devote his full attention to poetry again until he was in his last years, when he was in physical decline and seemed to lack the poetic inspiration of the earlier period. In fact, the great number of manuscript poems that he left (most never published) are rather saddening: They lack the deftness of construction, the genius for the affecting tone, the brilliance of image that are to be found in both the dialect poems and the two volumes of Standard English poems.

In 1953, McKay's former friend and collaborator Max Eastman was instrumental in arranging for the publication of *Selected Poems of Claude McKay,* which contains an appreciative introduction by the eminent American philosopher and educator Professor John Dewey of Columbia University as well as a brief biographical note by Eastman himself. It is this collection that has maintained the reputation of McKay, and though it is highly selective, it is a fair presentation of the scope of McKay's poetry.

In his post-Jamaican poetry, McKay became attached almost exclusively to the sonnet form, eschewed dialect, and showed no strong inclination to experiment with rhyme, rhythm, and the other components of the sonnet. Further, he displayed the influence of his early reading of the English Romantics (under the tutelage of Walter Jekyll), and in the words of Wayne Cooper, McKay's biographer, "his forthright expression of the black man's anger, alienation, and rebellion against white racism introduced into modern American Negro poetry an articulate militancy of theme and tone which grew increasingly important with time."

Selected Poems of Claude McKay is organized in five sections: "Songs for Jamaica," "Baptism," "Americana," "Different Places," and "Amoroso" (titles invented by the compilers). The first section contains several poems of reminiscence, such as "To One Coming North," "Home Thoughts," "I Shall Return," the beautiful and affecting "Flame Heart," and "The Tropics in New York," with its concluding lines, "And, hungry for the old, familiar ways,/ I turned aside and bowed my head and wept." The second section, which might have been titled "Baptism by Fire," since it contains those protest poems that McKay wrote after his introduction to the racism and segregation that he discovered in New York, includes such well-known poems as "The Lynching," "The Desolate City," and "If We Must Die," a poem that Winston Churchill recited in a speech during World War II (without knowing or acknowledging its author) and that became famous once more when a copy of it was discovered in the possession of one of the inmates during the uprising in the Attica State Prison in New York in 1971. All these poems are fierce in their sentiments and show that the lyrical poet was also the revolutionary poet. Consider, for example, the opening lines of "Tiger": "The white man is a tiger at my throat,/ Drinking my blood as my life ebbs away." Yet McKay's condemnation extends to all who have fallen to hate, disrespect, or discrimination; in "The Wise Men of the East," he says, "From the high place where erstwhile they grew drunk/ With power, oh God, how gutter-low have black men sunk!" It is this condemnation of *all* who have fallen below expectations and generally approved standards of behavior that differentiates McKay's opprobrium from that of other, lesser black poets. He is not ready to condemn whites alone; rather, in the interests of a higher morality than the prevailing one, he calls all to reckoning.

Some of the poems in the Americana sections are famous; "The Harlem Dancer" is perhaps the best of the twenty-one poems, depending for its melancholy effect on the dialectic between laughing male and female youths (the girls prostitutes, the boys "wine-flushed" and "bold-eyed") and a graceful dancing girl, whose beautiful body is "devoured" with "eager, passionate gaze" while she has "Grown lovelier for passing through a storm." The poem presents with great poignancy the contrast between the "superior" Harlemites and the "inferior" dancing girl whose "self was not in that strange place." Of McKay's lyrics, many readers find this the most pleasing because of the extended metaphor of the "proudly-swaying palm" in the storm and the implicit superiority of the apparently inferior.

Those poems collected under the heading "Different Places" are not especially noteworthy except for "St. Isaac's Church, Petrograd," which opens with "Bow down my soul in worship very low/ And in the holy silences be lost." This is the first suggestion that McKay's early religious training had survived his interest in rationalism, socialism, and communism and that he was, fundamentally, a religious person, so that his ultimate conversion to Roman Catholicism was not really so astonishing. (Whether as a Catholic, a Baptist, or a member of some other denomination or sect is not really important, but McKay maintained his fundamental Christian beliefs throughout his sometimes tempestuous first forty years. His becoming a Roman Catholic, an act he termed a "right turn," was in fact a matter of convenience when he was in poor health and almost in despair and was offered succor by Bishop Shiel of Chicago.) "Bow down before the marble Man of Woe," he writes, "Bow down before the singing angel host." McKay had gone to Moscow to participate in the activities of the Communist International, had met Leo Trotsky, and had been feted as an important black delegate; it is clear that this poem, written in 1922, bears a crucial relationship to McKay's subsequent beliefs and life. Only after he had left Moscow (after a six-month stay) did he disclaim his earlier endorsement of communism; this one poem marks the point of change.

McKay's later poems, called the "Cycle Poems" and still in manuscript in the Yale University library, represent an apparent effort to please his Catholic benefactors, but they lack the spontaneity and depth of commitment of the great "St. Isaac's Church, Petrograd," which suggests the closing of the circle of belief.

The sense of being a black man in a white man's world pervades McKay's poetry, as does the sense of being a visionary in the land of the sightless—if not also the sense of being an alien (an islander) in the heart of the metropolis. As John Dewey noted, "I feel it decidedly out of place to refer to him as the voice of the Negro people; he is that, but he is so much more than that." McKay is the voice of the dispossessed, the oppressed, the discriminated against; he is one of the major poetic voices of the Harlem Renaissance; he is one of a select group of poets who have represented the colonized peoples of the world; and he is one of the voices for universal self-respect and brotherhood.

Bibliography

Cooper, Wayne F. *Claude McKay, Rebel Sojourner in the Harlem Renaissance: A Biography.* Baton Rouge: Louisiana State University Press, 1987. Contains a long chapter, "The Jamaican Poetry as Autobiography: Claude McKay in 1912," that offers an excellent introduction to the poet's work.

Gayle, Addison, Jr. *Claude McKay: The Black Poet at War.* Detroit: Broadside Press, 1972. Proposes that McKay was the true warrior-poet of the black people in his era. Offers detailed analyses of four poems: "Flame-Heart," "Harlem Shadows,"

"To the White Fiends," and "If We Must Die."

Giles, James R. *Claude McKay.* Boston: Twayne, 1976. In chapter 2, "The Poetry: Form Versus Content," the author proposes that McKay's poetry pleased everyone because he handled well both rural (the Jamaican) and urban (the American) themes and subjects in his work. He mastered dialect poems early; later, he composed revolutionary poems in traditional forms and language. ~

McKay, Claude. *The Passion of Claude McKay: Selected Poetry and Prose, 1912-1948.* Edited by Wayne F. Cooper. New York: Schocken Books, 1973. Includes several important poems that were omitted from *Selected Poems of Claude McKay* and provides helpful introductory material.

McLeod, A. L., ed. *Claude McKay: Centennial Studies.* New Delhi: Sterling Publishers, 1992. Of the seventeen essays, four are related to McKay's poetry; they consider the relationship of the poetry to politics, to the author's concept of the ideal woman, to the philosophy of passive resistance, and to the writer's biography.

Tillery, Tyrone. *Claude McKay: A Black Poet's Struggle for Identity.* Amherst: University of Massachusetts Press, 1992. Several references to the poems, though no satisfactory analyses; unfortunately, contains errors of fact, and major critical essays are overlooked.

Wagner, Jean. *Black Poets of the United States: From Paul Laurence Dunbar to Langston Hughes.* Translated by Kenneth Douglas. Urbana: University of Illinois Press, 1973. Emphasizes the realism of McKay's Jamaican portraits and favorably compares his dialect verse with Dunbar's American dialect verse, concluding that McKay's was the more authentic.

A. L. McLeod

THE POETRY OF HAKI R. MADHUBUTI

Author: Haki R. Madhubuti (Don L. Lee, 1942-   )
Type of work: Poetry
First published: Think Black, 1967; *Black Pride,* 1968; *Don't Cry, Scream,* 1969; *We Walk the Way of the New World,* 1970; *Directionscore: Selected and New Poems,* 1971; *Book of Life,* 1973; *Earthquakes and Sunrise Missions: Poetry and Essays of Black Renewal, 1973-1983,* 1984; *Killing Memory, Seeking Ancestors,* 1987; *Say That the River Turns: The Impact of Gwendolyn Brooks,* 1987

Haki R. Madhubuti (who changed his name from Don L. Lee in 1973) is a militant African American poet, critic, publisher, editor, and spokesperson—the most vocal and best known of the Chicago school of Black Arts writers who emerged in the late 1960's, and the one of them who has managed to remain in the spotlight as a literary figure.

The focus of Madhubuti's literary career shifted in the mid-1970's from writing small books of poetry to lecturing, literary criticism, editing, and publishing, but his advocacy of a separatist, didactic literature—by blacks, for blacks, and about the black experience—has been consistent. Strong denunciation of "whi-te" values and living patterns—and of "Negroes" who choose to adopt them—is axiomatic, especially in Madhubuti's earlier poems.

Madhubuti's work as editor and publisher began early, in 1967; from the first, it complemented his work as poet, giving him a platform from which to promote his own works and those of others who share his vision.

Madhubuti was born Don L. Lee on February 23, 1942, in Little Rock, Arkansas, to Jimmy L. and Maxine Graves Lee. He attended Dunbar Vocational High School in Chicago. After service in the U.S. Army from 1960 to 1963, he returned to Chicago to attend City College, Roosevelt University, and the University of Illinois, Chicago Circle. While in college, Lee worked as an apprentice curator at a museum of African American history while holding jobs as a clerk and as a junior executive for a Chicago corporation.

Lee's quickly established reputation as a radical poet—and his work after 1967 as editor and publisher at Third World Press in Chicago—brought him early "establishment" recognition that moved him out of the business world and into academia: After teaching at Columbia College in Chicago in 1968, Lee held writer-in-residence posts and lectureships at a number of academic institutions. His career was advanced by a National Endowment for the Arts grant in 1969 and the Kuumba Workshop Black Liberation Award in 1973. He has edited *Black Books Bulletin* and worked as contributing editor of *Black Scholar, Colorlines, GRIOT,* and *The Zora Neale Hurston Forum.* He has also been an executive councilman of the Congress of African People; in 1991, he was made president of the African American Book Centers in Chicago. In 1991, Madhubuti was named Author of the Year for Illinois by the Il-

linois Association of Teachers of English; he also received the American Book Award
in that year. Haki R. Madhubuti has been active in the Black Men's Movement and
has served on the National Commission on Crime and Justice.

By 1991, some seventeen titles and more than three million copies of Madhubuti's
books were in print. He has given more than a thousand readings and workshops at
colleges, universities, and community centers in the United States and many foreign
countries, and his work has been a staple in anthologies of African American poetry
since the late 1960's.

As poet, Madhubuti epitomizes the young blacks of the 1960's who, as editor
Dudley Randall says in his introduction to *The Black Poets* (1983), "turned to poetry
of the folk, of the streets, to jazz musicians, to the language of black people for their
models." Madhubuti and others not only wrote for black readers but also published
mostly in black journals. They brought out books through black presses, and they
sought overall to "blacken" the language, validating black speech and experience
through art—sometimes changing pejorative terms into affirmative ones. Randall
lists coinages by Madhubuti that have gained some currency and helped to modify
stereotypes and to change behavior: "think black," "black pride," "the realpeople,"
"the worldrunners," "blackwriting," "integration of negroes with black people,"
and "talking black and sleeping white" are examples.

The first two of these phrases are in fact titles of Madhubuti's early books. These
and other titles (such as *Don't Cry, Scream*) often carry direct messages to readers.
Two poems from *Think Black*, "Back Again, Home (confessions of an ex-executive)"
and "Re-act for Action (for brother H. Rap Brown)," represent Madhubuti's dominant style and subject matter.

"Back Again, Home," though an open-form poem, has four loose stanzas (each
using hung indention) and is mostly syntactic, with capital letters, dashes, paren-
theses, and some punctuation to guide the reader in construing it. Only the coda-like
fifth stanza—the poet's response to white executives who want to know why he has
resigned his job—breaks the formal pattern of the poem as it drifts to a close:

> "Back Again,
>
> BLACK AGAIN,
>
> Home."

The poem's subtitle underscores the confessional nature of some of Madhubuti's
poetry; like many moderns, he often converts private experiences into poems. His
persona, whether recounting his own life story or not, is always a mouthpiece, and
the message is always unambiguous. In the case of "Back Again, Home," the poet
summarizes his own movement in the late 1960's from the conventional corporate
world to one in which he is "out of a job—broke and hungry" but is "not quiet
now—trying to speak."

"Re-act for Action," also from *Think Black*, is, like many of Madhubuti's poems, a series of imperatives to the reader. The poem, which uses parallel structure and varied repetition, looks irregular and lively on the page, heightened now and then by visually emphatic capitals such as "BAM BAM BAM" or "re-act/ NOW niggers/ & you won't have to/ act/ false-actions/ at/ your/ children's graves." This poem and "The Primitive" both attack "alien concepts/ of whi-teness" that are antagonistic to Madhubuti's program: "nigger toms," "tony curtis & twiggy," "whi-te actors," "faggot actions," "pig-actions," "T. V. & straight hair,/ Reader's Digest & bleaching creams," "reefers & napalm,/ european history & promises." "The Primitive" charges whites with having taken blacks from Africa and "raped our minds" with Christianity, capitalism, and "civilization." "Re-act for Action" calls on blacks to love each other. Some of its lines also suggest violent racial revolt: "re-act to whi-te actions:/ with real acts of blk/action./ BAM BAM BAM."

Madhubuti's basic theme, conflict, and agenda, then, are set in his early poems: Conventional social roles inhibit the "natural" life of blacks, who should "love" the brothers and sisters while hating "whi-te actions."

A preface by the noted African American poet Gwendolyn Brooks, whose patronage was instrumental in the quick success of Madhubuti and other Black Arts writers, spurs on Madhubuti's book *Don't Cry, Scream*, which consists of about forty pages of verse. Calling Madhubuti "A Further Pioneer" who is at "the hub of the new wordway," Brooks notes his rejection of academic poetry (written for whites) in favor of the "healthy, lithe, lusty reaches of free verse" (for blacks). His writing, Brooks says, is "capable of an awful fang." The book's opening poem, entitled "Gwendolyn Brooks," returns the compliment by praising Brooks's sponsorship of younger black poets.

Among the more ambitious poems in *Don't Cry, Scream* is the title piece, inscribed "for John Coltrane," the famed jazz saxophonist much admired by Black Arts writers. The punning "musical" conceit—"soultrane gone on a trip"—allows the poet to discuss a mix of subjects about the growth of black consciousness: "we ain't blue, we are black." More bluntly, the poet says, "i can see my me. it was truth you gave,/ like a daily shit/ it had to come." One section attacks "snagga-tooth niggers" who "play negro" and sleep with blond women, and "negro cow-sissies/ who did tchaikovsky &/ the beatles & live in/ split-level homes & had/ split-level minds & babies." Sound effects visually highlight the text:

SCREAMMMM/we-eeeee/screech/teee   improvise
aheeeeeeeee/screeeeeeee/theeee/ee   with
ahHHHHHHHHH/WEEEEEEEE/scrEEE   feeling
    EEEE
we-eeeeeWE-EEEEEEEEWE-EE-EEEEE.

Other of Madhubuti's titles that hint at their contents include "The Third World Bond," "The Revolutionary Screw," "Malcolm Spoke/who listened?," "History of The Poet as a Whore," and "blackmusic/ a beginning." His "communication in white," a sort of eyepoem, is an onomatopoeic exercise in repetitive letterstrings such as "nig nig nig" and "bom bom bom."

In *We Walk the Way of the New World*, Madhubuti opens with a prose essay and speaks as a black critic. The poet encourages "initiation" rather than "imitation," praising pioneering blacks who have "helped create a New Consciousness"—from W. E. B. Du Bois to the "prophet of Islam" Malcolm X and the poet Amiri Baraka (LeRoi Jones). Poems in the volume include several that Dudley Randall picks as representative: "One Sided Shoot-out" is a topical memorial for Black Panthers killed by the police. The poem "Big Momma" ends with this cadence: "at sixty-eight/ she moves freely, is often right/ and when there is food/ eats joyously with her own/ real teeth." Yet such lyrical understatement is mostly obscured by more prosaic material. The poem "We Walk the Way of the New World" opens "we run the dangercourse" and proceeds with aphoristic advice such as "the breakfast of champions is: blackeyed peas & rice" and "watch yr/every movement."

In *Dynamite Voices*, Madhubuti self-consciously assumes the role of black critic by proceeding to discuss fourteen individual writers. Generally, Madhubuti says, the language of the new black poetry moves "in the direction of actual music" and uses street diction and "its own syntax." An exploration of the various nuances of "muthafucka" expands his point that "black language . . . is not recorded in a dictionary." Among the poets whom he discusses and promotes are Margaret Danner, Sonia Sanchez, Etheridge Knight, Carolyn Rodgers, and Nikki Giovanni. Trying to distinguish what "is poetry" and what is not, Madhubuti as critic often finds "nonpoetry" in their writings. He posits that "a true test for a Black poem is whether one can determine the author's color from a reading of it." Yet he notes that suitably colorized poems are not automatically good ones.

Madhubuti published *Book of Life*, his sixth collection of poetry, in 1973. Though the first part of the volume is similar to his early work, the second is notably different: It is a sixty-page "poem" in ninety numbered segments, each one a saying, in Standard English, about how to conduct one's life as a good Muslim. One is advised, for example, to forgo makeup, respect what is old, eat natural food, and avoid betraying a trust. The notable features of Madhubuti's earlier verse—the imagery and figures, idiomatic tone and flair—are missing. *From Plan to Planet* (1973) offers similar advice in essay form.

In addition to blacks who are out of line with his program, other targets of the poet's satiric barbs or direct frontal assaults have included Catholics, Baptists, Jews, the media, popular whites, cultural heroes of all sorts, and the police. A somewhat mellower tone and calmer style can be seen in Madhubuti's later poems, such as those in *Killing Memory, Seeking Ancestors.*

Critical judgments about Madhubuti's poetry vary. Those who praise him find value in "his distinct voice as a poet of the Black revolution," in his "message of good news" to blacks, and in the lack of an "ironic vision" that keeps his poems "straightforward" and "unpretentious." Jascha Kessler speaks on the other side for those who judge Madhubuti's writings harshly:

I've not seen poetry in Don L. Lee. Anger, bombast, raw hatred, strident, aggrieved, perhaps charismatically crude religious and political canting, propaganda and racist nonsense, yes; and utterly unoriginal in form and style; humorless; cruel laughter bordering on the insane. . . . [I]n Lee all is converted to rant.

Helen Vendler may be right when she says that in Madhubuti's work "the sardonic and savage turn-of-phrase long present in black speech as a survival tactic finds its best poet." Jerry B. McAninch's observation seems concurrently true: "There is no gray in Lee's world, only black and white, and only black is beautiful." Clearly, Madhubuti's ambivalent prophecy that "blackpoems/ will change" finds corroboration in American social and literary history.

Bibliography

Brooks, Gwendolyn. "A Further Pioneer." Introduction to *Don't Cry, SCREAM*, by Don L. Lee. Detroit: Broadside Press, 1969. An influential preface to Madhubuti's third collection of poems by Brooks, a well-known poet herself, who likes Madhubuti's poems' sharp-tongued beauty and their focus on black life. Brooks calls Madhubuti a pioneer and "positive prophet."

Gayle, Addison, Jr. *The Black Aesthetic.* Garden City, N.Y.: Doubleday, 1971. A well-indexed book that discusses Madhubuti in the context of the "new" black poetry of the 1960's. Includes one of Madhubuti's essays on that topic along with a brief biography.

Palmer, R. Roderick. "The Poetry of Three Revolutionists: Don L. Lee, Sonia Sanchez, and Nikki Giovanni." In *Modern Black Poets: A Collection of Critical Essays*, edited by Donald B. Gibson. Englewood Cliffs, N.J.: Prentice-Hall, 1973. Discusses Madhubuti as a "protest poet" who wants readers to "discover blackness." Quotes heavily from his poems to show how they comment on a variety of subjects, including topical events, women's liberation, and education.

Randall, Dudley. "Broadside Press: A Personal Chronicle." In *The Black Seventies*, edited by Floyd B. Barbour. Boston: Porter Sargent, 1970. A poet and editor, Randall clarifies the important relationship between Madhubuti's career and the rise of independent black presses in the 1960's. An essay by Madhubuti also appears in the collection.

Turner, Darwin T. Afterword to *Earthquakes and Sunrise Missions: Poetry and Essays of Black Renewal, 1973-1983*, by Haki R. Madhubuti. Chicago: Third World Press, 1984. An admiring tribute to Madhubuti that summarizes the poet's career, comments on his themes and techniques, and notes the evolution of an "older, quieter voice" in his later works.

Roy Neil Graves

THE POETRY OF THYLIAS MOSS

Author: Thylias Moss (1954-   )
Type of work: Poetry
First published: Hosiery Seams on a Bowlegged Woman, 1983; *Pyramid of Bone,*
1989; *At Redbones,* 1990; *Rainbow Remnants in Rock Bottom Ghetto Sky,* 1991

Thylias Rebecca Brasier Moss, who was born in Cleveland, Ohio, in 1954, has been hailed by the poet Charles Simic as "a major figure in contemporary American poetry." Part of the reason for Moss's steadily growing reputation as a poet and for her steadily growing audience is the unusually wide range of formal styles, voices, and subject matters that make up the poems in her first four books. Although Moss was once considered by critics and by fellow poets such as Marilyn Hacker as primarily an angry and defiant poet whose creativity stemmed from her bitterness over the oppression of African Americans, women, and members of the working class, Moss's poetry is by no means composed strictly of hostile statements about what Hacker called "the black truths behind white lies." Moss's poetry generally, and most specifically in her fourth book, *Rainbow Remnants in Rock Bottom Ghetto Sky,* which was selected by Simic for the National Poetry Series, reveals her wide emotional range. Moss's poetry embraces love, friendship, and visionary and religious experiences, as well as the political themes found in such poems as "Lunch Counter Poem," which reflects Moss's memories of the struggle endured by African Americans to achieve civil rights through the protest movement of the 1950's and 1960's. Moss believes that her poetry has gained in technical control since her first book, *Hosiery Seams on a Bowlegged Woman,* appeared in 1983, when she was not yet thirty and had only recently been graduated from the University of New Hampshire's master's degree program in English. Her work expresses a sense of personal hopefulness and exuberance while remaining sensitive to the difficulties of maintaining this optimism as an African American living in a country with a painful history of racial conflict.

Moss's optimism about life, the sanctity she finds in everyday experiences, and her feeling for community and for a continuity between familial generations stem from her often delightful and nurturing experiences as a child. Moss grew up in what Gerri Bates has described as "a stable, working-class environment in Cleveland." Her mother was a maid, and her father worked for a tire company. Moss's affection for her mother caused her to dedicate her third book, the National Book Critics Circle Award nominee *Pyramid of Bone,* to a woman who, Moss writes, "made it to the dean's list of preferred housekeepers; she is a maid of honor."

Moss's sensitivity to the depth and complexities of the relationship between mother and daughter is especially poignant in the poem that opens *Pyramid of Bone,* "One for All Newborns." While the poem's speaker relishes the joy and hopefulness of a new birth ("Everything about it was wonderful"), this poem also reflects Moss's awareness as a mother of her own children that tensions inevitably surround the mother-daughter relationship, especially as the daughter reaches toward her own maturity. In the poem, the speaker realizes that her personal growth implies her mother's loss of unquestioned authority:

> Then the dark succession of constricting years,
> mother competing with daughter for beauty and losing,
> varicose veins and hot water bottles, joy boiled away
>
> . . .
>
> and the less familiar gait of grown progeny.

The poet is here dealing with a memory of conflict with her mother, but later in the poem, Moss hints that this memory was precipitated by her feelings of sadness and guilt over the recent death of her mother. On a delayed flight home to her own daughter, Moss begins to feel remorse that she did not treat her mother as well as she might have treated her: "I am now at the age where I must begin to pay/ for the way I treated my mother. My daughter is just like me." The last three lines shift the poem's terms away from Moss's relationship to her mother and toward her relationship to "another parent":

> I treated God badly also; he is another parent
> watching his kids through a window, eager to be proud
> of his creation, looking for signs of spring.

The integration of secular and religious relationships in this poem is reminiscent of the unified vision found in the religious lyrics of seventeenth century English metaphysical poets such as John Donne and George Herbert. Like Moss, these poets often described their relationship to deity by using a deeply personal language usually reserved for secular love relationships. Moss's infusion of a theological, or at least a spiritual, dimension to her everyday relationships with friends and family is a consistent feature of many of her poems. The title poem to her third book, *At Redbones*, which is the name for a local gathering place that combined the roles of church and club, again suggests the importance of community and place in Moss's background and in her poetry, as well as the interrelationship she experiences between sacred and secular community.

Although Moss's poetry often conveys a sense of the marvelous and the mysterious aspects of the ordinary experiences of childhood, she also stresses how difficult it was for her to grow up with dark skin in Cleveland, Ohio, in the late 1950's and early 1960's, when the privileged models of youthful beauty in fables, fairy stories, and popular culture (such as Snow White and Heidi) were not often related to her own physical appearance. In "Lessons from a Mirror" and "The Wreckage on the Wall of Eggs," two poems from *Pyramid of Bone*, Moss recalls how easy it was for her to feel invisible in a society that placed an exclusive value on white skin, and, in turn, how easy it was for her to resent other girls in her neighborhood only because their skin was white. In "The Wreckage on the Wall of Eggs," Moss recalls jumping rope in her driveway and noting the "hundreds of girls/ perfect for the part of Heidi." Because she realized that her ancestry "would not lead to Dörfli/ in the Alps," Moss writes, she found it easy to resent the white "girls who couldn't control ancestry." Her mature response to her youthful recognition that her skin color would alienate her from accepted models of beauty is, paradoxically, to experience regret that she "can't hate Heidi well." Moss recalls the story of Humpty Dumpty as a metaphor to describe her own situation as a young girl segregated from other children. Through this conversion of a fairy tale to her own purposes, Moss is able to recognize a connection between her fundamental nature and that of the white children whom she once envied:

> When I look down at the wreckage on the wall of eggs that
> came out of me, I see that what's inside is as white and
> gold as Heidi.

In Moss's poetry, events that might be interpreted by others as violent, dreadful, or tragic are often construed as containing the potential for salvation or the potential for beauty. In this instance, the young girl's fall and her literal breaking apart reveal an "inside" that is equivalent to the valuable "outside" of the girls who could fit the part of Heidi.

In her fourth book of poems, *Rainbow Remnants in Rock Bottom Ghetto Sky*, Moss concentrates her attention on the mysterious rituals of youth that might otherwise be overlooked as insignificant experiences but that are understood by the poet to have been formative expressions of friendship and love. Moss's early relationships shaped her adult perceptions and influenced her mature affection for children. "Poem for My Mothers and Other Makers Of Asafetida" reveals that Moss's embrace of all types of experience in her poetry, whether pleasant or unpleasant, is derived from her mother's and her grandmother's saying that it is "maybe possible to have so much/ death can't take it all." Moss's childhood experiences have influenced not only her subject matter but also her literary style. Her affection for the rhymes, repetitions, and speech rhythms found in children's chants and games is often evident in her poetry. *Rainbow Remnants in Rock Bottom Ghetto Sky* consists of many poems that are filled with the rhythms and music, the sounds, and the ritual games of child's play.

"An Anointing" is an excellent example of Moss's ability to combine her impulse to tell stories about her own past in an incantatory rhythm that is related to a child's speech with her training in traditional forms of English poetry. Besides being a child's chant, "An Anointing" is also a dramatic monologue, or a narrative poem spoken in a voice other than that of the poet. Often, as in the case of the nineteenth century English poet Robert Browning's "Fra Lippo Lippi," which concerns the life of a painter in Renaissance Italy, the poet uses the dramatic monologue to capture the intimacy and nuance of a character from a distant time and place. In "An Anointing," however, Moss uses the dramatic monologue form to recapture the voice and vision of the world of Thylias Moss as a young girl. "An Anointing" is also a love poem, but Moss turns this traditional motif into a celebration of the special affection between two young girls who are best friends, a first-person speaker, referred to in the poem as "Me," and her virtual identical twin, "Molly." The image and anecdotes Moss uses to suggest their closeness reveals one of her mature strengths as a writer. Charles Simic has argued that this strength stems from her "better eyes," by which he means her skill at finding precise yet unusual visual images to convey her emotional life in a colorful and indelible way:

"Boys have to slash their fingers to become brothers. Girls trade/ their Kotex, me and Molly do in the mall's public facility." In this opening stanza, Moss converts the violent and shopworn image of blood brothers into a startling image appropriate for two young women. The sharing of the mystery of menstruation is the perfect way to suggest the depth of the bond between them. The beginning of menstruation suggests both the growth of the young girls into womanhood and also the possibility of their bearing children, a subject that Moss comments upon in other poems, including "One for All Newborns" and "Preferable Truth."

The opening image of the trading of the brand-name good "Kotex" in a shopping mall illustrates another aspect of Moss's originality and freshness. The setting is by itself a statement about where young people spend much of their time and money in a consumer economy in which brand-name goods abound; these brand names become markers that, taken together, convey a sense of personal identity and a collective past.

An anointing usually refers to the application onto the body of an oil at a sacred rite, such as the election of a person to a sacred office. In the context of the poem, however, this act is an induction into the role of womanhood and childbearing. It is also the induction of the speaker into a liberation from social stereotyping. A part of the poem's pleasure is that Molly and her friend form a kind of self-sufficient community of two. They help each other to find the strength and the confidence to "go as who we are" and to "go as what we are": "Me and Molly don't care what people think. We're just glad that/ they do."

While these lines suggest the pithiness, warmth, and infectious energy of a child whose life has been sheltered from the ways the world can hurt those most vulnerable to its dangers, other poems in *Rainbow Remnants in Rock Bottom Ghetto Sky* that are spoken in the mature poet's own voice do not share this tone of innocence. Moss is a public writer who also uses her poetry to call attention to the outrages of the African American experience, from chattel slavery to the Jim Crow laws of the American South to the lynchings and burnings of African Americans by the Ku Klux Klan in the 1950's.

In "The Place That Makes Presidents," Moss meditates about the African American experience from the setting of a Protestant church in Massachusetts. Within the context of this site of "history," "tradition," and "solitude," the "noisy violence" of the lives of contemporary African Americans living in the predominantly black Boston neighborhoods of Roxbury and Mattapan have no place to be heard. The "old theft" of slavery and the "acquisition of the continent" by white settlers through violence are erased within the pious settings of "Pilgrim privilege" and "Yankee superiority." "Quietly a crime becomes heroic," Moss writes.

In "Interpretation of a Poem by Frost," Moss rewrites the American poet Robert Frost's famous poem "Stopping By Woods on a Snowy Evening" from the perspective of "a young black girl" who finds herself trespassing on the property of a white land owner:

> A young black girl stopped by the woods,
> so young she knew only one man: Jim Crow
> but she wasn't allowed to call him Mister.
> The woods were his and she respected his boundaries
> even in the absence of fence.

Moss's ability to turn Frost's poem inside out allows her to express a new way of looking at life, a new way of thinking about an issue from an unexpected perspective. This type of conversion is a general strategy that Moss uses to make poetry out of familiar materials. It is also her strategy for turning scenes of oppression or despair into starting points for poetic insights and for displays of her strength as a poet.

A good example of Moss's ability literally to turn inside out a negative or unpleasant experience in her own life and to remake it into an image of beauty occurs in "The Rapture of Dry Ice Burning Off Skin as the Moment of the Soul's Apotheosis." As in "An Anointing," Moss uses sacred terminology to describe secular events in an unexpectedly heightened way. "Apotheosis" is a term gathered from religious discourse that refers to the moment when an ordinary person is elevated to divine status. The fact that this elevation occurs in her poem through an unpleasant and painful event—dry ice burning off skin—is consistent with Moss's general strategy of transforming unpleasant experiences into events of special, possibly sacred, significance.

"The Rapture of Dry Ice Burning Off Skin as the Moment of the Soul's Apotheosis" expresses the poet's empathetic relationship to the near-extinct buffaloes and to drug addicts whose habits bring them, like the buffaloes, near to the edge of extinction. Within this wide-ranging meditation about such weighty topics, however, a brief anecdote appears that encapsulates Moss's general strategy of conversion of the everyday and mundane experience into the spectacular:

> Every time I use it
> the umbrella is turned inside out,
> metal veins, totally hardened arteries and survival
> without anything flowing within, nothing saying
> life came from the sea, from anywhere but coincidence
> or God's ulcer, revealed. Yet also, inside out
> the umbrella tries to be a bouquet, or at least
> the rugged wrapping for one that must endure much. . . .

In this vignette, the relatively minor discomfort of living in a world that is not always kind—the world of nasty weather—reveals to Moss an ambiguous image that contains within it both chaos and beauty. In one sense, the upturned umbrella reveals a frightening image of decay. The metal ribs of the destroyed umbrella are described as veins and hardened arteries. The destroyed umbrella, however, also causes Moss to think about an image of natural beauty and of human endurance in the face of difficulty. The umbrella reminds her of bouquets, and the rugged wrapping is a thing capable of endurance. Although the image is based in an ordinary ordeal, the process of thinking about it poetically—that is, as a metaphor for something else that is described through images—enlarges and enhances the reader's sense of the world as it is. In "The Rapture of Dry Ice Burning Off Skin as the Moment of the Soul's Apotheosis," the experience of lacking something, the experience of heartbreak, is described as "glorious" and "marvelous" because it is an experience of intense emotion. Moss believes it is necessary to record in her poetry experiences of intense emotion, whether of great joy or of great sadness, because these experiences are a fundamental sign of humanity.

Bibliography

Auburt, Alvin. Review of *At Redbones* and *Rainbow Remnants in Rock Bottom Ghetto Sky*, by Thylias Moss. *American Book Review* 13 (February/March, 1992): 29. Praises Moss's development of an "assertive poetic voice" that is reminiscent of Ishmael Reed's but nevertheless "very much her own."

Bates, Gerri. "Thylias Moss." In *American Poets Since World War II*, edited by R. S. Gwynn. Vol. 120 in *Dictionary of Literary Biography*. Detroit: Gale Research, 1992. A useful overview of Moss's career and poetry.

Clarence, Judy. Review of *Rainbow Remnants in Rock Bottom Ghetto Sky*, by Thylias Moss. *Library Journal* 116 (May 15, 1991): 86. Clarence lauds Moss's "accessible, sensual, feminist poems" for their craft and sense of hopefulness.

Jaskoski, H. Review of *Rainbow Remnants in Rock Bottom Ghetto Sky*, by Thylias Moss. *Choice* 29 (February, 1992): 896. A lukewarm review that argues that Moss "does not (yet) belong with June Jordan, Nikki Giovanni or Audre Lorde" as a talented poet, although "she has set off in the same promising direction."

Waniek, Marilyn Nelson. Review of *At Redbones*, by Thylias Moss. *Kenyon Review* 13 (Fall, 1991): 214. A highly laudatory review that notes that "a fine rage is at play in these pages."

Daniel Charles Morris

THE POETRY OF DUDLEY RANDALL

Author: Dudley Randall (1914-   )
Type of work: Poetry
First published: Poem, Counterpoem, 1966 (with Margaret Danner); *Cities Burning,*
   1968; *Love You,* 1971; *More to Remember: Poems of Four Decades,* 1971; *After the
   Killing,* 1973; *A Litany of Friends: Poems Selected and New,* 1981

Dudley Felker Randall, highly respected by several generations of African American writers, occupies a central position in the development of the "New Black Poetry." As the founder of Broadside Press, Randall contributed an indispensable impetus to the Black Arts movement of the 1960's and 1970's. His poetry, written over
a period of more than six decades, exhibits a wide range of influences, techniques,
and subject matters.

Randall started writing poetry seriously when he was in high school, where he
learned prosody from his teacher and from Henry Wells's *Poetic Imagery Illustrated
from Elizabethan Literature* (1924). At age thirteen, he submitted a sonnet to a poetry contest run by the *Detroit Free Press* and won the first prize. Thanks to his
father, a minister active in the political campaigns of blacks, Randall spent his formative years in an environment associated with intellectual and literary figures such
as W. E. B. Du Bois and James Weldon Johnson. Well read in the writings of black
authors of the time, Randall was thus informed by the Harlem Renaissance, which
had just come to an end when he was graduated from high school during the Great
Depression. His childhood experience is captured in autobiographical poems such as
"Vacant Lot" and "Laughter in the Slums."

After graduation, Randall became a foundry worker at Ford Motor Company. The
poem "George," a tribute to a coworker and lifelong friend, is a product of this
period. Later he worked for the postal service, and in World War II he served in the
South Pacific as a member of the U.S. Army Signal Corps. The wartime experience,
which gave rise to a series of aphoristic sketches entitled "Pacific Epitaphs," proved
an important source of inspiration in his poetry. Returning from the war, Randall
pursued college and graduate studies in earnest, receiving a bachelor's degree in
English from Wayne State University in 1949 and a master's degree in library science
from the University of Michigan at Ann Arbor in 1951. Thereafter, Randall worked
as a librarian at various locations, including the University of Detroit. Meanwhile,
he also completed the coursework toward a master's degree in the humanities at
Wayne State University. His thesis, a translation of Frederic Chopin's music into
words, was left unfinished, though the project itself was not really abandoned (see
"Nocturne," "Impromptus," and "Translation from Chopin"). Randall's extensive
education is evident in his work and sets him apart as a black poet for whom the
African, the American, and the European traditions combine into a triple heritage.

His life having stabilized in an academic setting, the tempo of Randall's literary
activities quickened during the Civil Rights movement era. In 1963, the racially

motivated bombing of a church in Birmingham and the assassination of President John F. Kennedy led Randall to write "Ballad of Birmingham" (1965) and "Dressed All in Pink" (1965, revised 1967). The two poems, later set to music by Jerry Moore, not only spread Randall's reputation but also inspired him to found the Broadside Press in 1965 in order to put poetry, in the form of attractive "broadsides," into the African American household inexpensively. This treatment of poetry as a communal rather than a business enterprise brought Randall into alliance and fellowship with Margaret Danner (founder of Boone House, a black arts center) and Hoyt Fuller (editor of *Black World*), as well as with the Pulitzer Prize-winning writer Gwendolyn Brooks.

In less than a decade, as evident from Randall's *Broadside Memories: Poets I Have Known* (1975) and *Broadside Treasures* (1975; an anthology edited by Brooks at Randall's request), a community of writers had grown around the Broadside Press to fill an honor roll of African American poets now familiar to readers. In addition to the works of Danner, Brooks, and Randall, the press has featured broadsides, posters, books, and audio recordings by Langston Hughes, Jean Toomer, Robert Hayden, Haki Madhubuti, Amiri Baraka, Marvin X, Etheridge Knight, Margaret Walker, Sonia Sanchez, Nikki Giovanni, Stephany, and numerous others. Among this group, not a few younger writers have become published thanks to Randall's generous encouragement and assistance; in return, these writers have also offered him and one another an invaluable sense of community, fellowship, and friendship at a time when a system of mutual support was essential to the survival and development of African American literature. *For Malcolm: Poems on the Life and Death of Malcolm X* (1967), an anthology that Randall coedited with Margaret Burroughs to commemorate the Black Muslim leader assassinated in 1965, could be regarded as a rally in that direction. Realizing that black poets had been suffering from a long history of exclusion by white publishers, Randall ventured further to edit and publish *Black Poetry: A Supplement to Anthologies Which Exclude Black Poets* (1969). This effort to find a forum for black poets and to assert their place in American literature culminated in *The Black Poets* (1971), a comprehensive anthology that Randall edited for publication by Bantam Books. Reprinted many times, the anthology is still one of the best single-volume sources available to general readers and specialists alike. It also stands as a milestone in American literature, in that black poetry as a tradition is now visible and can no longer be ignored by the canon and by academia. Randall has thus played a crucial role in repositioning black poetry from the margin to the center by means of a personal press that not only grew into a community but also outgrew itself into the canon.

Although the Broadside Press and other activities have absorbed most of Randall's energies, he has published six collections of his own poems. His receptiveness to different styles, forms, and expressions makes it difficult to generalize about his poetry, but his earlier work tends to use a literary language characterized by formality, craftsmanship, meditation, and suggestiveness, whereas his later work (after 1971's *More to Remember: Poems of Four Decades*) contains increased colloquialism, shock effects, and experimentation. At home with many techniques but never pursuing them for their own sake, Randall intentionally eschews obscurity, reasoning that lucidity can reach a larger and more varied audience; perhaps for this reason his poetry has been widely anthologized. He has won many honors, including Wayne State University's Tompkins Award (1962 and 1966), a Kuumba Liberation Award (1973), a Literature Award from the Michigan Foundation for the Arts (1976), and other awards from the International Black Writers' Conferences and the Howard University Institute of Afro-American Studies (1977). He was named a distinguished alumnus by both the University of Michigan and Wayne State University. In 1978, the University of Detroit, where he served as a university librarian, poet-in-residence, and lecturer until his retirement in 1975, conferred on him the honorary degree of doctor of literature. These honors were crowned by his appointment as the first poet laureate of Detroit in 1981.

Randall has commented that he considers himself to be a writer of "poetry of the Negro." The importance of this assessment hinges on the issue of his self-identity as a black American poet. Reflecting on his poetry in 1980, Randall identified "Zasha" as his muse ("My Muse"). Comparable to Catullus' Lesbia, William Shakespeare's dark lady, Dante Alighieri's Beatrice, and Edgar Allan Poe's Annabel Lee, Zasha is a beautiful black woman who possesses a combination of tenderness and wrath—a description that in fact applies to Randall's poetry as a whole. Highly conscious of the special place of the black poet in America, Randall satirizes white critics who privilege their values (such as white unicorns) as universal and impose them upon black poets ("Black Poet, White Critic"). Furthermore, he chastises white poets of the Beat generation for being preposterous and admonishes them to act responsibly ("Poet"). His insistence on the black aesthetic notwithstanding, he also distances himself from what he views as the hypocrisy, pretentiousness, and treachery of certain black nationalists ("Nationalists"; "Informer"). It is not surprising to find him portray the ironic shame of a militant black poet who hangs himself after a white suburban woman has commented that his "scariest poems" are not bitter enough ("The Militant Black Poet"). His use of the word "Negro" during the late 1960's and early 1970's, when such terms as "black" and "African American" were gaining currency, seems to set him apart from other black writers; at the same time, however, his deeper concern for the substance of African Americans is clear in his argument that "The spirit informs the name,/ not the name the spirit." As can be seen in "Ancestors," in which he notes with humor his pride in having a swineherd and not a king for an ancestor, it is a humanism rooted in ethnic pride, not facile ethnocentrism, that defines his sense of identity. Free from dogmatic prescriptions from both white and black critics, Randall has made it plain, in his *ars poetica* entitled "A Poet Is not a Jukebox," that he cannot be told to write for the sake of political expediency or propagandist ends.

As a poet, Randall is particularly known for his treatment of cultural and political issues such as African American heritage, racial conflicts, the civil rights struggle, urban realities in America, and life in the modern age. Many of these concerns are already evident in early poems such as 1948's "Roses and Revolutions." During a meditation, the prophetic persona in this poem enters into two apocalyptic visions of the entire continent. The first concerns the reality of urban America in the modern era, a world of darkness where millions of people suffering from pain, alienation, violence, racism, and other social ills regret life and cry for death. In the second vision, he sees an enlightened world in which "the bombs and missiles lie at the bottom of the ocean/ like the bones dinosaurs buried under the shale of eras/ and men strive with each other not for power or the accumulation of paper/ but in joy create for others the house, the poem, the game of athletic beauty." The poem concludes with a radiant explosion that embodies at once the terror of the atomic bomb and the splendor of the French Revolution. Reminiscent of the visions of heaven and hell portrayed by Dante and William Blake, the poem established Randall's reputation as a poet.

Other examples representative of Randall's commitment to the cause of African Americans include "Frederick Douglass and the Slave Breaker" and "Booker T. and W. E. B.," which encapsulate for the general reader the fundamental issues involved in the struggle of African Americans for freedom, identity, and democracy. In connection with the struggle is a group of poems in which the development of ethnic consciousness recurs as a motif. In "A Different Image," he calls for the reanimation of "the mask," the shattering of "the icons of slavery and fear," and the affirmation of the "classic bronze of Benin." In "The Southern Road," which describes the return of a Northern black to the South in search of his roots, Randall poignantly insists on the remembrance of a painful legacy. Comparing the South to a scar left on his father's flesh, he recognizes the South as the source of his grief, but at the same time declares his duty to love and visit it (see also "Legacy: The South"). This historical sense of ethnicity is further exemplified in "Memorial Wreath," in which Randall pays tribute to the black soldiers who served in the Union Army during the Civil War and asserts that "American earth is richer for your bones;/ Our hearts beat prouder for the blood we inherit."

Randall's affirmation of ethnicity often entails the rejection of the exclusive practices of the dominant culture—hence his character Sam's denunciation of "the magic melting pot," out of which he has been thrown a thousand times ("The Melting Pot"). Nevertheless, Randall's poetry is notable for its relevance beyond the African American community. His testimony to the turmoils of the Civil Rights era in "Ballad of Birmingham" and "Dressed All in Pink," for example, exploit the ironic and suggestive naïveté characteristic of the ballad form to give memorable poetic expression to the feelings of an entire nation.

It is significant that Randall's poetry has assumed an increasingly nonsectarian character. He is, of course, mortified by the death of black leaders such as Malcolm X and Martin Luther King, Jr. ("Blood Precious Blood"), and disgusted with traitors to the Civil Rights movement ("Informer"; "F.B.I. Memo"). He is also, however, impatient with the arrogance of activists who attach too much importance to themselves ("Seeds of the Revolution"), with hypocrites who abuse the cause of black nationalism ("Nationalist"; "Words Words Words"), with black males who pretend to be virile by claiming that "white boys are all faggots" ("Tell It Like It Is"), and with those possessed by bloodthirstiness ("Put Your Muzzle Where Your Mouth Is"). In "Abu," he vilifies a "stone black revolutionary" for his terrorist threats to bomb the city hall and assassinate a rich white liberal who "gave only *half*/ a million/ to N.A.A.C.P." As a staunch critic of extremities, Randall is at his best when he confronts his readers' consciences with the consequences of acts of violence, as in "Primitives," in which he laments humanity's failure to exorcise the demonic horror of "hate deified,/ fears and/ guilt conquering,/ turning cities to/ gas, powder and a/ little rubble." Judging by his later poems (for example "Beasts," which identifies bloodthirsty human beings with beasts, and "After the Killing," which mocks the will to kill as the governing principle of humanity), it is apparent that Randall has never slackened his appeal to the nation as a whole to live and let live, to be civilized, and above all to be human. His satire of U.S. war efforts in Vietnam ("Straight Talk from a Patriot"; "Daily News Report") is but an enlargement of this appeal. It is in this ultimate appeal to humanity that Randall has been recognized as a rare humanist.

Randall's humanistic bent is also evident in his treatment of the underclass of American society. In his snapshots of characters ranging from criminals ("The Line-Up") and prisoners ("Jailhouse Blues") to ghetto girls ("Ghetto Girls") and prostitutes ("The Aged Whore"), Randall invariably underscores the predicaments of people who are being dehumanized. Paradigmatically, he would highlight the injury the modern age has done to humanity (see "Old Witherington," a poem about an aging and forgotten man making a spectacle of his drunkenness while brandishing a knife at teasing children); at the same time, however, he also restores his characters' dignity by identifying himself with them (in "Bag Woman," the poet surprises readers with the claim, "Sister . . . But I know that I am you") or by reassuring them of his recognition of their irreducible significance (in "George," the poet encourages an ailing coworker by using the same words the latter had used to encourage him when he was an apprentice). By thus immortalizing personages from among the underprivileged in spite of their otherwise fated commonality, Randall is virtually insisting on the necessity of including the human factor in the definition of modernity itself.

Randall's humanistic temper, in fact, permeates his poetry as a whole. Because of this temper, his satires are typically aimed at those who scandalize mankind (such as the philanthropist in "Interview") and those who abuse the meaning of life (such as the intellectual in "The Trouble with Intellectuals"). Such a temper, which can be found in Randall's poems ranging from the private to the public, is concomitant with the tragic nature of life in the modern world: In a love poem such as "The Profile on the Pillow," the lovers' consummation of love is overshadowed by the prospect of their being consumed in a holocaust, whereas in a war poem such as "Lost in the Mails," a letter full of misspelled words written by the mother of a soldier evokes all at once the double tragedy of the living and the dead.

As a poet, critic, editor, and publisher, Randall serves as an important link both between the Harlem Renaissance and the Civil Rights movement era and between African American and mainstream culture. In developing the African American tradition and nurturing its community of writers while at the same time fostering an independent and open mind of his own, he has enlarged the expressive capabilities, heightened the intellectual interests, and deepened the emotional contents of black literature. Above all, informed by a humanism rooted in his ethnicity and humanity, Randall's own poetry is an important statement of ethics and aesthetics.

Bibliography
Melhem, D. H. "Dudley Randall: The Poet as Humanist." In *Heroism in the New Black Poetry: Introductions and Interviews.* Lexington: University Press of Kentucky, 1990. An article that includes an interview with Randall conducted in 1980 that contains critical insights from the interviewer. The most important study of Randall as a humanist.
Miller, R. Baxter. " 'Endowing the World and Time': The Life and Work of Dudley Randall." In *Black American Poets Between Worlds, 1940-1960.* Knoxville: University of Tennessee Press, 1986. Comprehensive overview of Randall's career, with evaluation of his poetry.
Nicholas, A. X. "A Conversation with Dudley Randall." *Black World* 21 (December, 1971): 16-34. Contains detailed autobiographical information as well as Randall's views on black literature. Randall quotes and approves of Terence's motto, "Nothing human is alien to me."
Randall, Dudley. "The Black Aesthetic in the Thirties, Forties, and Fifties." In *The Black Aesthetic*, edited by Addison Gayle, Jr. Garden City, N.Y.: Doubleday, 1971. Discusses Randall's views on the "Black Aesthetic."
Redding, Saunders. "The Black Arts Movement in Negro Poetry." *The American Scholar* 42 (Spring, 1973): 330-335. Argues that Randall was at odds with the younger poets of the Black Arts movement and belongs to a different tradition.

Balance Chow

THE POETRY OF CAROLYN M. RODGERS

Author: Carolyn M. Rodgers (1940's-   )
Type of work: Poetry
First published: Paper Soul, 1968; *Two Love Raps,* 1969; *Songs of a Black Bird,* 1969; *Now Ain't That Love,* 1969; *For H. W. Fuller,* 1970; *Long Rap/Commonly Known as a Poetic Essay,* 1971; *How I Got Ovah: New and Selected Poems,* 1975; *The Heart as Ever Green,* 1978; *Translation,* 1980; *Eden and Other Poems,* 1983

Carolyn M. Rodgers was born in Chicago in the 1940's (sources do not give her birth date), the youngest child of Clarence and Bazella Rodgers, natives of Little Rock, Arkansas. Rodgers was reared near Forty-Seventh Street in Chicago, an area that was home to many popular blues singers. As a child she was active in the African Methodist Episcopal Church. Her poem "Portrait" speaks personally: "mama . . . / saved pennies/ fuh four babies/ college educashuns." In "I Have Been Hungry," she confides, "my father never wanted three girls/ and only one son." An avid reader, young Carolyn took dramatic elocution lessons, memorizing and reciting works by such black poets as Paul Laurence Dunbar and Langston Hughes. At nine, Rodgers started keeping a journal, and in her teens she began writing poems. After high school, Rodgers sang and played the guitar in coffeehouses and even contemplated a singing career. "But," she says, "the night life scared me away from singing professionally."

After she was graduated from Hyde Park High School, Rodgers attended the University of Illinois at Urbana, where her first published poems appeared in a literary magazine, and then finished all but one course in the bachelor's degree program at Roosevelt University. (In the 1980's, she completed her bachelor's degree and also earned a master's degree in English at the University of Chicago.) During her Roosevelt University years, Rodgers met Gwendolyn Brooks, who proved to be a supportive critic; within a year or so after sending out poems for publication, Rodgers had work accepted and published in *Negro Digest.*

Rodgers found employment with the Young Men's Christian Association (YMCA) in the mid-1960's, working with high school dropouts who, she says, helped provide her with subject matter for her poems, stories, and plays. As a young free-lance writer, she traveled, gave readings, and met many established black writers.

Rodgers' reputation as a poet dates from her publication of several small books of poems in 1968, 1969, and 1970—first at Third World Press in Chicago and then at Broadside Press in Detroit. Though her reputation rests more on her bold writings during these years than on any of her later publications, she has continued to write, progressively moving away from her early militant stance and toward more relaxed, even humorous, poems that focus on religion, traditional morality, and the poet's private life—though Rodgers does not forsake the black experience as subject.

In 1968, while still in her twenties, Rodgers was a recipient of the first Conrad Kent Rivers Writing Award. She has also earned a National Endowment for the Arts grant, a Society of Midland Authors award, and a Carnegie Award. Her book *How I Got Ovah: New and Selected Poems* was nominated for a National Book Award in 1976. Even with such recognition, her career has not always been easy; there were times before 1984, she says, when "I continued writing and publishing and practically starving to death."

Despite Rodgers' evolution toward poems that are calmer in tone, her early subject matter, stance, and association with other African American activists in the late 1960's allied her initially with the Black Arts group in Chicago, a school of militant liberationist poets, of whom Don L. Lee (who later took the name Haki Madhubuti) is best known. Critics also identify Rodgers as an "OBAC poet" because of her active membership after 1967 in the Writers Workshop of the Organization of Black American Culture. A participant in the Gwendolyn Brooks poetry workshop in the late 1960's, Rodgers acknowledged her affection and indebtedness in "To Gwen with Love" in 1971.

Rodgers' career has included lectureships or writer-in-residence appointments at Columbia College and City College, Chicago, the University of Washington, Albany College, Georgia, Malcolm X College, Chicago, and Indiana University at Bloomington. Her many publications include poems and articles in such magazines as *The Nation, Ebony, The Black Scholar,* and *Black Arts Anthology.* Since the early 1970's, her work has been regularly anthologized in collections of modern black poets, and Rodgers has made frequent appearances as lecturer or as reader of her poems.

Displaying open form—a free-verse medium that is not rhymed or metrical—Rodgers' best-known poems employ street language, eccentric lower-case letters, texts erratically placed on the page or spaced within the line, oddly placed capitals, capital-letter strings, italics, dialectal spellings (such as "sistuhs"), clippings ("sd" for "said," "u" for "you"), nonsyntactic phrases, elliptical dots, unpunctuated lines that suggest associative (or dissociated) thought or speech, and lines linked by initial parallel structure, as in "Poems for Malcolm":

> I want uh love poem
> I want uh trust poem
> I want uh unity poem
> I want uh Liberation poem.

Rodgers' verse after 1970 uses fewer typographic effects and is quieter on the page, but it remains loosely and informally structured.

In subject matter and theme, Rodgers shared in the beginning the didactic program of the Black Arts and OBAC poets, who wanted African American writers to stop trying to please whites and instead to assert a black identity to which ordinary black readers could respond, thus moving the race toward radical independence from mainstream aesthetic (and political) traditions. Such ideas grew in the context of the freedom-minded 1960's and the Black Power movement in politics. Malcolm X, the Black Panther Party, and Martin Luther King, Jr., recur as heroes in poems by the Black Arts writers; the villains are not only "honkies" but also "Negroes" who try to "act white" and thus betray their race. Though Don L. Lee, an early compatriot, found the book weaker than *Paper Soul*, Rodgers' *Songs of a Black Bird* represents her early writings fairly. Race is the book's theme; being young, black, and involved as a poet in "The Movement" is its subject; and its dedication, "to/ Love/ Truth/ Organization/ Discipline/ Liberation," summarizes its strident, rigidly exclusive idealism. Its twenty-five poems, ranging between nine lines and three pages in length, show some tension between Rodgers' committed advocacy of revolution (and the "brothas") on the one hand and her defense of the "sistuhs" (and disillusionment with black males) on the other. The book's preface by fellow OBAC writer David Llorens praises Rodgers' "new energy" while conceding that sometimes her verse "comes down hard on brothers." Rodgers' short poem "Untitled No. Hurt," a case in point, is an apostrophe to "all my men"—who were supposed to embody "strength and beauty" but "could not love me,/ because you hate your/ Black/ momma."

The longest poem in *Songs of a Black Bird* is "JESUS WAS CRUCIFIED, or, It Must Be Deep (an epic pome)," which Don L. Lee found too burdened with narrative to be "poetic." This confessional monologue reveals a generational and cultural gap between a radicalized black girl with "educashun" and her working-class mother, who thinks her activist daughter is literally going to hell. The young speaker's dialectal recounting of a late-night phone conversation moves through a conflict stage (heightened by an all-caps text) to a calmer resolution: "she sd i mon pray fuh u tuh be saved. i sd thank yuh." The speaker in "It Is Deep," with a similar mix of frustration and love, describes her mother's worries "that I am under the influence of/ **communists**/ when I talk about Black as anything/ other than . . . ugly. . . ." Nevertheless, this "religious-negro" mother is "a sturdy Black bridge that I/ crossed over, on."

Poems that show standard Black Arts positions include "Greek Crazeology," a diatribe against black fraternities and sororities for "whitening the minds of their members," treating pledges as "slaves," and wasting "TIME & MONEY" that should go "for the r(evolution)." "Unfunny Situation" ridicules readers' calls for witty poetry: "will we laugh our heads off when our brother's bodies/ are blown to bits in vietnam . . . ?" One short poem puts "hunkies" at the end of a list of "animals" that "We have always imitated." "The Last M. F." has the speaker defend using "the word/ muthafucka" by explaining that the epithet applies only to "pigs and hunks and negroes who try to divide and/ destroy our moves toward liberation." "Let uh revolution come," says the poem "U Name this One." More subtle and poignant is "What Color Is Lonely?," in which the poet, writing "poems about Black Unity," sits "for hours that/ trickle befo me like unfreezin water."

Two poems in *Songs of a Black Bird* stand out for their drama and their pictographic views of third-person subjects. "5 Winos" sketches down-and-out black men whose drunken music becomes a "most carefully/ constructed a-melodic coltrane psalm." (The name of jazz saxophonist John Coltrane punctuates poems by the Black Arts poets.) Rodgers' poem "For H. W. Fuller" memorializes a quiet black man "standing in the shadows of a/ white marble building/ chipping at the stones. . . ." Unnoticed, the man eventually effects the building's downfall. Here Rodgers finds a figurative paradigm for all the patient blacks who ever worked quietly for freedom, laying careful groundwork for toppling the power structure.

In *Dynamite Voices* (1971), an anthology of black poetry, editor Don L. Lee featured Carolyn Rodgers but noted her "ineffective, unconscious writing" and use of "too many words." (Given Lee's own verbose early style, the comment has its ironies.) Lee preached against "writing Black and publishing white," favoring instead a separatist publishing network for African American writers. In this light, Rodgers' decision to bring out her 1975 collection *How I Got Ovah* with Anchor Press/ Doubleday in Garden City, New York—with an establishment rather than a black press— appears modestly defiant, a self-assertive act altogether consistent with the independent spirit that her poems show. Rodgers' selection of previously published poems for *How I Got Ovah* seems to pay Lee's dogmatic evaluations little heed; her author's note implies that she has partly changed her "style" and "mind," distancing herself somewhat from the movement that Lee dominated: "I want my work to interest as many people as possible," she says simply. Revised details in several previously published poems confirm her independent drift. The poem "Love—The Beginning and the End," for example, as it originally appeared in *Songs of a Black Bird* ended with the intersecting acrostic of the words "WOMAN and BLACKMAN" (sharing an "M" where they crossed), capped by the line "the last aspect is Love is Revolution." By contrast, the same poem closes *How I Got Ovah* in a toned-down version that concludes this way:

W
O
M A N
A
N

the last aspect is Love.

Other poems entitled "The Revolution is Resting" and "I Have Changed So Much in This World" likewise suggest moderations in Rodgers' career as she progressed into the less-turbulent decades after 1970.

Nevertheless, Rodgers' work in *How I Got Ovah* crystallizes rather than reforms her earlier work. The truth, as she surely knew, is that the strong young voice that brought her to early prominence was also her assurance of a place in the history of modern African American poetry.

In a comment printed in 1985, Rodgers asserts: "I seek to tell the truth. To explore the human condition, the world's condition. To illuminate the ordinary, the forgotten, the overlooked, to show that the specific me is often the general you and us. To exemplify God working in man. . . ." Rodgers wants to write both "simply" and "profoundly," and feels she may be God's instrument for doing so. Her 1969 poem "Breakthrough" seems, in the subsequent context of *How I Got Ovah*, to encapsulate well the "many changes," the "several of me," the "consistent incongruity" of life, as she oxymoronically puts it, that her poems seek to define. In "To the White Critics," Rodgers asserts simply, "my baby's tears are . . ./ a volume of poems." In "I Have Been Hungry," the speaker asks, "and you white girl/ shall i call you sister now?" In "Some Me of Beauty," Rodgers concedes, "the fact is/ that i don't hate any body any more/ i went through my mean period."

Though the revolutionary passion of the late 1960's that undergirded the first voice of Carolyn Rodgers has long ago cooled, poems such as "What Color Is Lonely?," "For H. W. Fuller," and "Breakthrough" remain to speak of that lost time. One key role of hers, in fact, appears in retrospect to be that of chronicler to the Chicago movement and the OBAC phenomenon. Thus the chantlike rhythms of the 1970 poem "Yuh Lookin GOOD" catch indelibly an image of the "Meetings meetings meetings . . ./ about us makin it,/ as a people/ as a nation."

Bibliography

Colby, Vineta, ed. *World Authors, 1980-1985.* New York: H. W. Wilson, 1991. Features Rodgers' own autobiographical report on her life and career and includes chronologically arranged criticism that quotes liberally from her poems.

Evans, Mari, ed. *Black Women Writers, 1950-1980: A Critical Evaluation.* Garden City, N.Y.: Anchor Press/Doubleday, 1983. Includes discussions of Rodgers' work by various critics, along with editor Evans' interview with Rodgers.

Gayle, Addison, Jr., comp. *The Black Aesthetic.* Garden City, N.Y.: Doubleday, 1971. A well-indexed book that discusses Rodgers in various contexts relevant to the literary movements of the 1960's. Calls her essay "Black Poetry—Where It's At" (published in *Negro Digest* in 1969) "the best essay on the work of the new black poets."

Lee, Don L. *Dynamite Voices Volume 1: Black Poets of the 1960's.* Detroit: Broadside Press, 1971. Poet/critic Lee (Haki Madhubuti) evaluates Rodgers' "strengths" and "weaknesses"—which, he says, include occasional "misuse of language." Lee quotes liberally from Rodgers' poems to illustrate his points.

Turner, Roland, ed. *The Writers Directory, 1988-1990.* 8th ed. Chicago: St. James Press, 1988. Contains a factual outline of Rodgers' literary achievements through the mid-1980's.

Roy Neil Graves

THE POETRY OF SONIA SANCHEZ

Author: Sonia Sanchez (1934-   )
Type of work: Poetry
First published: Homecoming, 1969; *We a BaddDDD People,* 1970; *It's a New Day: Poems for Young Brothas and Sistuhs,* 1971; *Love Poems,* 1973; *A Blues Book for Blue Black Magical Women,* 1974; *I've Been a Woman: New and Selected Poems,* 1979; *Homegirls and Handgrenades,* 1984; *Under a Soprano Sky,* 1987

Sonia Sanchez's widely acclaimed poetry eloquently reflects her personal trials—childhood loneliness that caused a speech impediment, unhappy marital relations, life-threatening illness—as well as the joy she has found in husband, friends, and—most enduringly—her three children. Her poetry also compassionately expresses deeply felt social and political concerns. Her major theme is not merely survival but the will to renewal; the personal and political are often combined in Sanchez's poems, one dimension of experience illuminating the other.

This poetry is also often public poetry, in the sense that Sanchez crafts orations intended to address and awaken public awareness of issues that range from international politics to family relationships and personal consciousness of the self, particularly the female self. While not usually bookish in its allusions, her poetry can also deftly build on history and mythology as useful reflections of the personal drama that is the life of every human being. Sanchez also draws quite effectively on the legacy of African American song, both secular and spiritual, and dynamically extends the African American literary tradition. As did Frances Harper and Paul Laurence Dunbar, Sonia Sanchez addresses the African American community and creates "songs for the people"; like Langston Hughes, Gwendolyn Brooks, and Margaret Walker, she has mastered twentieth century modernism while remaining sensitive to the intricacies and expressive nuances of African American vernacular.

Sanchez's poetry not only has received recognition such as the 1984 Lucretia Mott Award, the Before Columbus Foundation's American Book Award, and a fellowship from the National Endowment for the Arts, but also has acquired an enormous popular readership in the African American community. Born September 9, 1934, in Birmingham, Alabama, Sonia was only a child when her mother, Lena Jones Driver, died. For the next several years, she and her sister were cared for by various relatives, and the emotional dislocation caused her to develop a stutter that she compensated for by writing poems. Her father, Wilson L. Driver, moved the girls to New York's Harlem community in 1943. The poet attended public schools there and, in 1955, graduated with a degree in political science from Hunter College of the City University of New York. She spent the next year studying poetry with Louise Bogan at New York University.

After college, Sanchez was active in the drive for desegregation as a member of the Congress for Racial Equality (CORE), but she was also skeptical of mainstream American culture and its materialistic focus. In Sanchez's view, integration did not include abandoning what was vital in African American culture. *Homecoming*, her first book, includes a "Memorial" for the popular female singing group The Supremes: "cuz they dead," having changed their rhythm and blues performance style and "bleached out/ their blk/ness" in order to appeal to a white, mainstream audience. Consistent with this outlook, Sanchez was closely involved with efforts to establish black studies in the college curriculum during the 1960's, working with others such as playwrights Ed Bullins and Marvin X. She began her own teaching career at the Downtown Community School and at San Francisco State College. She was also to teach at the University of Pittsburgh, Rutgers University, City College of the City University of New York, and the University of Massachusetts. In 1977, Sanchez was appointed a professor of English and women's studies at Temple University in Philadelphia.

Sanchez's commitment to social change is evident throughout her poetic work (which includes plays and poetic prose that could also be called vignettes or short stories), but her concerns expand over time from the specific issues of the American Civil Rights movement to global interest in the relief of racial and political oppression. The poet's frequent travels to Europe, Cuba, Central America, and China also brought her into personal contact with similarly committed writers whose works address the same concerns. Sanchez is fluent in Spanish, and her work reveals the influence of poets such as the Chilean Pablo Neruda and Cuba's Nicolás Guillén.

Sanchez's published work is a chronicle of her own progress from Westernized values to what she has called a "blacker" point of view. "Each of us," she wrote in *We Be Word Sorcerers* (1973), "was born a Negro with no knowledge of himself or history. Each one of us was the finished product of an American dream, nightmarish in concept and execution. Each one of us has survived to begin our journey toward Blackness." This cultural/ nationalist stance is evident in early poems such as "Listen to Big Black at S.F. State," from the collection *We A BaddDDD People*. The poem exemplifies Sanchez's characteristic and effective strategy: Protest against racism leads to a call for self-realization, both personal and communal. In lines that sometimes demonstrate her use of onomatopoeic imitation of the sound of conga drums, Sanchez lauds the jazz drummer Big Black's celebration of African culture and calls for "no mo meetings/ where u talk bout/ whitey. the cracker/ who done u wrong." Such angry recrimination should, the poet feels, be replaced with racial self-affirmation and the moral regeneration of the African American community, which will be made evident by "just a sound of drums./ the sonnnnnNNg of chiefs/ pouren outa our blk/ sections." This poem also vividly exhibits Sanchez's reshaping of lines and standard spelling to approximate the rhythms and sounds of urban African American speech. In an analogy to the way the African "talking drum" mimics the sound of West African tonal languages, Sanchez attempts to make printed words visually echo her sung and spoken language.

Sanchez's brilliant recitation of her own work spurred its popularity. *A Sun Lady for All Seasons*, an album issued by Folkways Records in 1971, reveals that Sanchez's oral presentation of these early poems blends chanting and sung passages that are akin to the modulations of both blues and spirituals. She also, in an avant-garde manner, sometimes included jazz "scat" singing of nonlexical syllables with dramatic shrieks of agony and keening cries.

Not all Sanchez's work is written in open or speech-inflected forms. *Love Poems* and *I've Been a Woman: New and Selected Poems* present many examples of Sanchez's handling of the Japanese haiku (a strict three-line, seventeen-syllable form notable for its compression). This ancient form was also a favorite of Richard Wright's, and like him, Sanchez does not limit herself to the original nature imagery and philosophical content of the form's medieval conventions. Her haiku poems range in subject matter from tender love lyrics to bitter social comment, as well as the philosophical meditation so well suited to the form.

Among Sanchez's frequent themes in both poems and prose pieces is the denunciation of self-destructive behavior in the African American community. "After Saturday Nite Comes Sunday," in *Homegirls and Handgrenades*, shows the pain and poverty a man's narcotics addiction causes his wife and children. Despite the power of her love for him, the man cannot be saved; yet the poet makes clear that such tragedies are merely the symptoms of a deeper problem—the lack of self-esteem caused by a system of racial oppression. This theme is often also presented in political terms with a sense of deep compassion for all those who suffer. The poem "MIAs" speaks of blacks detained without bail by the South African police, the "disappeared" villagers of El Salvador's repressive government, and the string of abductions and murders of black children from the streets of Atlanta, Georgia. The poet declaims a sense of solidarity with all these victims and ends on a note of determined resistance to terrorism:

> let there be everywhere our actions.
> breathing hope and victory
> into their unspoken questions
> summoning the dead to life again
> to the hereafter of freedom.

Sanchez's ecumenical social consciousness is displayed in *Under a Soprano Sky* with effective and moving poems memorializing victims of oppression as well as a survivor of the Hiroshima nuclear bombing and a brother who died of AIDS (Acquired Immune Deficiency Syndrome). A series of intense poems focuses on those who died in the police assault on a dissident Philadelphia group called MOVE. When police actually bombed the group's headquarters on May 13, 1985, more than forty surrounding homes were destroyed. The poet, in utter disbelief, asks "how does one scream in thunder?" and prays with a determined hope "for honor and peace./ one day." In a world that can produce such tragedy, Sanchez searches for hope in a sense of family and community. The beautiful "Dear Mama" is a prose piece that recalls the poet's childhood and the strength that can be found in adversity; it is nominally addressed to the parent who died when the poet was an infant:

My life flows from you Mama. My style comes from a long line of Louises who picked me up in the nite to keep me from wetting the bed. A long line of Sarahs who fed me and my sister and fourteen other children from watery soups and beans and a lot of imagination.

Finally, Sanchez celebrates the collective nurturing and sees that her true heritage is "A long line of Black people holding each other up against silence." A significant stylistic development in Sanchez's work supports this war against the isolation figured in the word "silence." The body of Sanchez's work shows the increasing use of a surrealistic imagery similar to that of Negritude poets such as Aimé Césaire and Léon Damas. These images often combine bodily references and natural forces, creating the impression of an animated world of wonder that recalls ancient African religions and mythologies. An excellent example of this technique is found in "Under a Soprano Sky":

> the woods, tall as waves, sang in mixed
> tongues that loosened the scalp
> and my bones wrapped in white dust
> returned to echo in my thighs.

Such imagery makes the human body a responsive part of nature and blends physical and emotional levels of consciousness. Some have suggested that this type of imagery also represents a feminine sensibility.

For a period in the early 1970's, Sonia Sanchez was a member of the Nation of Islam and, under the Islamic name Laila Mannan, wrote a series of important articles for the *Muhammad Speaks* newspaper. The patriarchal regimen of the Nation of Islam under Elijah Muhammad's leadership apparently created a certain amount of tension for the poet, and many of her *Muhammad Speaks* articles explored the basis for equality of the sexes as she found it through extensive research into African history. This period also saw the publication of her most ambitious poetic work, a long poemsequence entitled *A Blues Book for Blue Black Magical Women*, which combined her historical research with Black Muslim motifs and an exploration of what it means to be female. Sanchez's long poem is a major work structured as the performance of a ritual modeled on ancient Greek and Egyptian mysteries. Like most initiation rituals, this one involves a symbolic death and rebirth, and the poem dramatically details a spiritual "possession" that leads the performer (or speaker) and her audience to a level of greater self-awareness. The poem also provides Sanchez with an opportunity to demonstrate her virtuosity in handling several different rhetorical modes.

The book opens with an introduction entitled "Queens of the Universe." This rhythmical prose section restates many of Sanchez's familiar exhortations to African American women to improve their lives, heighten their consciousness, and nurture their families. She urges women to embark on a mystical journey to achieve self-knowledge: "we must looook/ at our past. not be angered at it. nor upset." Such an attempt will result in a valuable inventory of both strengths and weaknesses (much as Sanchez records in her later "Dear Mama"), providing the necessary knowledge for building a better future. The next section, titled "The Past," presents five interconnected poems that reexamine the autobiographical material from childhood into an imagined old age. Part 3, "The Present," is a transition from the trance-like voices of the previous section and allows the poet to reveal the insights gained from her "possession" by those spiritual voices.

Among the allegorical figures utilized by the poet are the archetypal Earth Mother and Maat (or Mayet), the twin goddesses of Right and Truth symbolized in ancient Egyptian mythology as upright feathers. Sanchez redefines Maat as "love of Black self and/ righteousness." Many passages of the poem also present the poet's affirmation of the principles of Islam, including the teachings of Elijah Muhammad; the second half of the book, made up of sections entitled "The Future" and "Rebirth," is particularly rich in allusions drawn from both the Koran and the Bible.

At the end of *A Blues Book for Blue Black Magical Women*, the poet celebrates not only a personal rebirth but also hears "the trumpets of a new age." By facing her own life squarely, the poet has performed a sort of purification ritual and is able to affirm that "i carry truth and righteousness/ on my body like emeralds," which is the reward for the labor and pain of "giving birth to ourselves." Like the Egyptian Book of the Dead and the Bible's Book of Revelation, both of which are frequently alluded to in the second half of the work, Sanchez's volume might properly be called apocalyptic literature in the literal sense of the Greek word *apokalypsis*, meaning an "unveiling" of true meaning. As in any initiation ritual, the candidate has undergone a process designed to unveil the real nature of the self and its true potentialities. Such a process can only be successful if the protagonist of the ritual is willing to relive the pain of false or mistaken identities and to suffer the symbolic shock that accompanies a psychological rebirth. Clearly, also, shedding falsehood and error results in the elevation of truth and righteousness.

The intense drama that is celebrated in *A Blues Book for Blue Black Magical Women* is also played out in the shorter poems that bear witness to the human ability to survive cruelty and self-delusion, whether on a personal level or as it has been demonstrated historically on oppressed populations. Sonia Sanchez's political and ideological commitment, as reflected in her poetry, is to the freedom of the individual for spiritual and moral self-realization. The message Sanchez presents in her most public orations and the poems that are most personal is, in this sense, the same message. The healthy family and society depend upon the freedom of the individual's self-affirmation, just as the oppression of that freedom results in dysfunctional families and the ultimate corruption of society. For Sonia Sanchez, regard for African tradition, the celebration of freedom, and watchful criticism of its suppression are accomplished best through song.

Bibliography
Bell, Bernard W. *The Folk Roots of Contemporary Afro-American Poetry.* Detroit:

Broadside Press, 1974. Discusses Sanchez and her early contemporaries as the extension of African American folk traditions. Provides a helpful historical context for interpreting her work.

Evans, Mari, ed. *Black Women Writers, 1950-1980: A Critical Evaluation.* Garden City, N.Y.: Anchor Press/Doubleday, 1983. Contains an interview with Sanchez entitled "Ruminations/Reflections" and an overview of her poetry.

Joyce, Joyce. "The Development of Sonia Sanchez: A Continuing Journey." *Indian Journal of American Studies* 13 (1983): 37-71. A lengthy, thorough discussion of Sanchez's evolution as a poet.

Palmer, R. Roderick. "The Poetry of Three Revolutionists: Don L. Lee, Sonia Sanchez, and Nikki Giovanni." *College Language Association Journal* 15 (1971): 25-36. An early but still accurate assessment of Sanchez's work. Views her in the context of other leading poets of the Black Arts movement.

Sanchez, Sonia. "Exploding Myths: An Interview with Sonia Sanchez." Interview by Herbert Liebowitz. *Parnassus* 12/13 (1985): 357-368. An illuminating exploration of Sanchez's views on her life and works.

Lorenzo Thomas

THE POETRY OF MELVIN B. TOLSON

Author: Melvin B. Tolson (1898-1966)

Type of work: Poetry

First published: Rendezvous with America, 1944; *Libretto for the Republic of Liberia*, 1953; *Harlem Gallery: Book 1, The Curator*, 1965; *A Gallery of Harlem Portraits* (edited by Robert M. Farnsworth), 1979

Melvin Beaunorus Tolson never contrived to be a secret passion for the students and writers who idealized him. His ambitions were singularly public. Indeed, he cast himself in the mold of his own idols, the slightly older icons of the Harlem Renaissance. Publishing just past the Harlem heyday, he became a poet lauded but seldom anthologized by a largely segregated literary establishment that Karl Shapiro called a "closed corporation."

Harlem was the subject of Tolson's most prolific poetic output. Harlem was the site of his poetic mythos, his religion, his Metropolis and Mecca. In this literary geography, he made a compassionate body of work now curiously underread, shining between literary booms. As a writer, he blossomed independently: a postrenaissance Harlem bard and a premovement advocate for civil rights.

Tolson's reputation reveals itself from back to front; it was not a career of celebrated cub to proud lion. His star shone brightest with the publication of his last book, *Harlem Gallery: Book 1, The Curator. Harlem Gallery* appeared just a year before the poet's death. The late book is a polished tour de force of modernist technique superimposed on racial insight and whimsey. The book evolved from the more recently published early sketches and was planned as the first in a five-part epic history of the African American in America.

Those sketches, published as *A Gallery of Harlem Portraits*, effectively illuminate Tolson's process as an artist. While he found his subjects early, he developed his approach with care, across a career that embraced a far wider cut of society than the literary world alone.

Tolson's public persona reflected that embracing vision. Testimonies from his students at Wiley College, Tuskegee Institute, and Langston University are filled with adulation for his informal, caring style and immersion in his students' intellectual growth. A skillful, demonstrative actor, he declaimed in the classroom, sometimes from atop his desk. The most frequent issue upon which he held forth was the power of a wide, active vocabulary—clarity, for Tolson, was paramount.

The search for clarity demanded more than one mode of presentation. Interest in oratory committed him to coaching debate at Wiley, and he composed a number of full-length plays on racial situations. Further, he adapted novels to the stage, including George Schuyler's *Black No More* (1931) and Walter White's *The Fire in the Flint* (1924). More than five thousand people were in attendance at a performance of the adaptation of White's book in 1952 in Oklahoma City as part of a convention for the National Association for the Advancement of Colored People.

At Langston, he directed the Dust Bowl Theatre. A restless creator and active participant both at the college and in the community, he found his most productive writing time in the middle of the night, after napping in the early evening hours. While he worked on novels and short stories early in his writing career, it was poetry that gave him truest voice.

Born in Moberly, Missouri, Melvin Beaunorus Tolson was the eldest of four children. Melvin's parents encouraged his interests in music, painting, and reading. In high school, he distinguished himself in public speaking with dramatic recitations of the work of Paul Laurence Dunbar and with performances both in theater and on the football team.

In 1920, he entered Lincoln University, near Philadelphia, where he met Ruth Southall, a Virginian visiting Pennsylvania relatives. They married after his graduation and settled in Marshall, Texas, where they reared three sons and one daughter.

Tolson met Harlem, his steady muse, as the community met economic bleakness. Beginning work on a master's degree at Columbia University in 1930, he found a community he loved, but one that was inexorably being ravaged by the Depression. The president of the Harlem Savings Bank in *A Gallery of Harlem Portraits* is a hypocritical figure who boasts of his sacrifice while abandoning those whose sacrifice made him rich. The banker figure reflects that moment's reality. While Connie's and The Cotton Club still swelled with the rich forgetting the troubles of Wall Street, median income in the community was falling fast.

Tolson's thesis, "The Harlem Group of Negro Writers," attempted to interpret the artistic and literary development of the artists in whose company he set out to establish himself. The boom of 1920's creativity was undiminished, and he celebrated his contemporaries the world of literature had embraced: Wallace Thurman, Zora Neale Hurston, Claude McKay, Sterling Brown, Langston Hughes, Countée Cullen. Curiously, Tolson grew closer to Harlem through the economic pinch. He considered himself a Marxist; his poetic testimonies of economic pain are unflinching. He was a regular follower of the leftist periodical *The New Masses*, and as an instructor at Wiley College he developed a close friendship with the economist Oliver Cromwell Cox, who recorded his indebtedness to Tolson in *Class, Caste, and Race: A Study in Social Dynamics* (1970).

The enthusiasm of *The Modern Quarterly*'s editor, V. F. Calverton, ensured Tolson's introduction to Harlem literary society, and Tolson repaid the kindness by bringing Calverton to lecture at Wiley. It was during and following the work on his thesis that Tolson composed *A Gallery of Harlem Portraits*. Calverton encouraged him in 1939 to send the manuscript to editors Bennett Cerf and Maxwell Perkins. Tolson took their rejection hard; for a period he stopped writing and stored the manuscript in a trunk.

The manuscript can be seen as a watershed for the published work that was to come. Formally, the book is modeled on Edgar Lee Masters' *Spoon River Anthology* (1915): a collection of free-verse monologues wherein the speakers reveal their inner lives. These monologues reveal the crosscultural energy of Harlem life with a fascination for the ethnic mix there. It is fair to speculate that Tolson's own African-Irish-French-Indian lineage finds reflection in the book's testimonies. Even more stunning is the range of topics covered by these voices. Class and cultural concerns fuse in these vignettes, small powerful dramas using a playwright's declamatory gift. Masters' subjects offered a model of narrative, and these poems add the element of music. The characters sing italicized stanzas almost as frequently as they speak, and the blues is their language.

In addition to the color of everyday life, the poems embrace the heroism of working people, and the book closes with "The Underdog," a furious proletarian jeremiad. This poem thematically expresses Tolson's work organizing sharecroppers in Texas—a theme he returned to in *Rendezvous with America* in "Ballad of the Rattlesnake." At 340 pages, the manuscript was enormous.

The year 1944 brought Tolson's first published book, *Rendezvous with America*, including his most popular poem, "Dark Symphony." "Dark Symphony" combines the aesthetic theme of "The New Negro," Tolson's thesis subject, with the celebration of the common man. The poem, later set to music by Earl Robinson, continues Tolson's formal interest in the structure of music. In six "movements," "Dark Symphony" works a sequence of contrasts in African and white American history. Beginning with the revolutionary war, the poem records mythic and actual slave history from points further past. It follows slaveships to the new continent and picks up a faster, more rhythmic energy as it enters a paean to the accomplishments of the proud "New Negro."

A Gallery of Harlem Portraits presented the culture of the African American struggling upward, in fits and starts, toward cultural expression and dignity. In *Rendezvous with America*, the less individualized and more mythic form emerges triumphant. The last sections of the poem document a political manifesto. Part 5 documents the shortcomings in race relations of white Americans; in part 6, the New Negro comes forward as an equal in human and national recognition:

> Out of dead-ends of Poverty,
> Through wildernesses of Superstition,
> Across barricades of Jim Crowism . . .
> We advance!

The book brought Tolson favorable recognition, and the critical emphasis was on the writer's breadth of intellect. It also brought a highly unusual appointment some three years later. One of his students at Wiley introduced Tolson to the daughter of a consul at the Liberian embassy. This was the only connection Tolson had to that country when, in 1947, he was appointed poet laureate of Liberia and commissioned to work on a poem to celebrate the centennial of the founding of the republic. *Libretto for the Republic of Liberia* was completed within a year. The libretto was an extended ode that posed the question "Liberia?" to be answered in eight sections, each one named for a note of an ascending diatonic scale. The poetic model borrowed from Tolson's reading of the modernists; he cited Hart Crane's "The Bridge" as the contemporary ode he most respected.

Libretto for the Republic of Liberia received widely varying reviews upon publication. The harshest critics associated the book with the strongest excesses of modernism. The manuscript was attacked as too scholarly, as unmusical, as too deliberately academic and referential. The favorable criticism praised Tolson's seriousness as much as his craft. When lauded, the poem was praised as a complex work worth many rereadings for the torrent of language and magnificence of subject.

The sound and the fury of critical debate focused on style more than substance. The book is a very serious ode and works methodically at once to elevate and to understand its subject. Tolson's Liberia, the "quicksilver sparrow that slips/ The eagle's claw," is a trickster, a Promethean plotter that slips the coils of a long European colonial parade. Included are not only political and tribal histories but also tributes to African contributions across scientific and literary knowledge. In addition to the European connection, Tolson directly addresses America's colonial association: the American Colonization Society's plan to send freed slaves to Africa.

Here is Tolson at his slyest. The "Mi" section of the ode runs historical hypocrisy against itself. While the Colonization Society's goal was to promote a "civilized" Africa, its proposition fit readily the aspirations of antebellum holdovers who would happily have drained the slaveholding states of free African Americans. The irony Tolson focuses is that the would-be colonists and white sponsors did not envision the need for these freed slaves in winning a war. For Liberia had in recent memory provided the Allies with rubber and the airfields from which Erwin Rommell's Afrika Korps was savaged:

> *The rubber from Liberia shall arm*
>
> *Free peoples and her airport hinterlands*
> *Let loose the winging grapes of wrath upon*
> *The Desert Fox's cocained nietzcheans*
> *A goosestep from the Gateway of the East!*

Ranging between prophecy and proverb, the poem ends with an internationalist and Blakean political vision: an Africa of more than thirty free and independent nations.

For a time, Tolson felt that he had exhausted his work as a poet. Thirteen more years were to pass before the publication of *Harlem Gallery*. He had learned lessons of craft while extending the poetry of common people's struggle in his published books. Now he returned to the expansive Harlem of his epic, synthetic early work. In addition, the intervening years brought new demands: four terms as mayor of Langston, Oklahoma, and numerous honors, including a permanent fellowship in poetry and drama at Bread Loaf and the Order of the Star of Africa, conferred by the ambassador of Liberia. The kudos illustrated Tolson's peculiar position in the literary community: acclaimed but rarely anthologized, honored but infrequently published.

Harlem Gallery transforms the work of the early thesis and manuscript into a complex work of art. It is at once a playful illumination of colorful Harlemites and a serious discourse on the situation of art in African American culture. The character of the curator is an octaroon who is drawn to the darker culture; around him revolve the varied and curious gallery patrons. These figures, eccentric and humorous, are the wry foils for social and aesthetic analysis throughout. Tolson's death in 1965 interrupted the composition of the successive books that this was to introduce; still, it stands as a major work in its own right.

More than any of Tolson's previous work, the comic dialogue mediated by the appreciative curator combines dramatic and poetic elements. The work is self-described as referential and intertwined, as are the lives of the book's characters:

> Sometimes a work of art is bitter crystalline alkaloid
> to be doled out
> at intervals, between the laugh and flout
> of an Admirable Doctor; but, if taken too much
> at a time, it delivers the cocainizing punch
> of a Jack Dempsey nonesuch.

As the curator summarizes, the book is thick, splendid, and powerful. The give-and-take of gallery characters builds a narrative among three-dimensional personalities: Bantu expatriate Doctor Nkomo, half-blind artist John Laugert, Boa Boa Enterprises president Guy Delaport III, his striptease mistress Bamboo Kraal, beatnik poet Hideho Heights, and a wide assortment of Harlem society from the 1920's on.

Tolson's colleague Joy Flasch called him a "universalist," a term that applies to style as well as content. *Harlem Gallery* brought Tolson more international attention and fame than any of the previous work. In it, he asserts the humanity encapsulated in his beloved Harlem's music and figures. Formally, too, it is a universalist's book, combining jokes with philosophical dialogue and blues with history.

Tolson's work best succeeded in giving dramatic life and identity to high idealism. This idealism took Tolson through a variety of incarnations: as a rural civil rights organizer in the face of racist attack, as a debating coach and lecturer, as an actor and dramatist, and as a poet. The poetry, as a published legacy, is a difficult one. It bridges styles and schools, functioning as a record of an intellectual fabric rather than as the product of any given school. The evaluation remains incomplete, and Tolson's unique contribution continues to unfold.

Bibliography

Bérubé, Michael. "Avant-Gardes and De-Author-izations: *Harlem Gallery* and the Cultural Contradictions of Modernism." *Callaloo* 12 (Winter, 1989): 192. Bérubé studies Tolson's *Harlem Gallery* as a measure of the conflict between the sources of modernist poetry of the oral and the written traditions. The figures of the beatnik poet Hideho Heights and the Curator serve as respective totems for these forces.

_____. *Marginal Forces/Cultural Centers: Tolson, Pynchon, and the Poli-*

tics of the Canon. Ithaca, N.Y.: Cornell University Press, 1992. An analysis of the literary and cultural politics surrounding canonization. The author pairs Tolson, the "marginal figure who wanted nothing more than to be central," with Thomas Pynchon, the "newly central figure who wanted nothing better than marginality." The chapter on "Tolson's Neglect" clarifies the politics of race in the modernist movement.

Farnsworth, Robert M. *Melvin B. Tolson, 1898-1966: Plain Talk and Poetic Prophecy.* Columbia: University of Missouri Press, 1984. A thorough literary biography that reviews Tolson's many facets. Comprehensive; discusses Tolson's range as poet, essayist, and journalist.

Flasch, Joy. *Melvin B. Tolson.* New York: Twayne, 1972. A sensitive early survey of the work and the educator, written by one of Tolson's faculty colleagues. Flasch evaluates the poet as a major modernist figure and covers all of his poetry then in print.

Russell, Mariann. *Melvin B. Tolson's Harlem Gallery: A Literary Analysis.* Columbia: University of Missouri Press, 1980. A critique that emphasizes Tolson's conception of the social role of the poet. The book contains a sound analysis of Tolson's reinterpretations of mass culture and history. Contains extensive notes and bibliography.

Tolson, Melvin B. "Melvin B. Tolson, an Interview." Interview by M. W. King. In *Anger, and Beyond: The Negro Writer in the United States,* edited by Herbert Hill. New York: Harper & Row, 1966. Subtitled "A Poet's Odyssey," the interview allows Tolson to express his sense of his place in the range of world writers. The springboard for the discussion is Tolson's "The Poet" from the book *Rendezvous with America.*

Tolson, Melvin B., Jr. "The Poetry of Melvin B. Tolson (1898-1966)." *World Literature Today* 64 (Summer, 1990): 395-400. The writer's son evaluates his father's legacy in a lecture prepared for a Black History Month presentation. This survey emphasizes both Tolson's poetics and the publication history of his major works.

David Shevin

THE POETRY OF DEREK WALCOTT

Author: Derek Walcott (1930-   )

Type of work: Poetry

First published: Twenty-five Poems, 1948; *Epitaph for the Young: XII Cantos,* 1949; *Poems,* 1951; *In a Green Night: Poems 1948-1960,* 1962; *Selected Poems,* 1964; *The Castaway and Other Poems,* 1965; *The Gulf and Other Poems,* 1969; *The Gulf,* 1970; *Another Life,* 1973; *Sea Grapes,* 1976; *The Star-Apple Kingdom,* 1979; *The Fortunate Traveller,* 1981; *Midsummer,* 1984; *Collected Poems, 1948-1984,* 1986; *The Arkansas Testament,* 1987; *Omeros,* 1990

Winner of the Nobel Prize for Literature in 1992, Derek Walcott is a major figure of contemporary literature. Scion of both the Anglo-European and the Afro-Caribbean heritage, he has conducted a lifelong struggle to integrate the divided self engendered by the duality of his legacy. Dedicated to art as a means of coming to terms with the colonial and postcolonial conditions of the Caribbean, Walcott has braved controversies and labored furiously to define himself as a citizen of the New World while maintaining vital links with the Old. Writing as both a West Indian and an American, he also offers imaginative insights into racial matters in the United States and the relationship between the United States and the Third World.

Derek Walcott's career can be understood in the context of the colonial condition and marginalized predicament that he epitomizes but endeavors to redress. Descended from mulatto parents with a Methodist background, he was born in 1930 in St. Lucia, a small Caribbean island (under British rule until 1979) with a largely poor, black, and Catholic patois community. His situation as a "divided child" was complicated by the loss, at the age of one, of his father, a civil servant (also an amateur painter and poet). Thanks to his mother (a schoolteacher active in the local theater) and to the books and paintings that his father left behind, Walcott had an excellent education, and he began to write at a young age. He also learned to paint under the tutelage of "Gregorias" (Dustin St. Omer), his mentor, to whom he was to pay tribute in the poem "Homage to Gregorias" in *Another Life.* Psychologically isolated, early on he developed a sense of being "chosen" to speak for his generation and his community and to immortalize their unique but neglected legacy.

Walcott published his first poem at fourteen and created a controversy in the local newspaper. At eighteen, he published his first book, *Twenty-five Poems,* with two hundred dollars that his mother had raised for him. During this formative period, the major literary influence on his writing was the European classics, especially the English literary canon. Representative of this period is *Epitaph for the Young: XII Cantos,* which was modeled upon James Joyce's *A Portrait of the Artist as a Young Man* (1916). Thereafter, he published one more volume privately (*Poems* in 1951); along the way, his interest in the theater also developed. While receiving his college education (1950-1954), he started writing and producing dramatic plays on Caribbean subjects. This new development culminated in the success of *Drums and Col-*

ours (produced in 1958), which won him a Rockefeller Fellowship to study theater in the United States. Upon his return in 1959, he founded the Trinidad Theater Workshop, and from then on he has been playing an eminent role in the West Indian theater.

Walcott's apprenticeship in poetry came to fruition with *In a Green Night: Poems 1948-1960*. The book's title is derived from Andrew Marvell's "Bermudas," and many poems evoke the beauty of the islands, with echoes of François Villon, Dante Alighieri, Catullus, and others. The most significant pieces, however, are those dealing with various aspects of colonialism and Walcott's sense of cultural confusion. Examples include "Ruins of a Great House" and "Two Poems on the Passing of an Empire." The often-anthologized poem "A Far Cry from Africa" is the most memorable in this group. Occasioned by the Mau-Mau Uprising and its bloody suppression, the poem dramatizes Walcott's agony over the political and cultural tensions between the declining British Empire and the insurgent Africa. This poem exemplifies the divided voice that is the hallmark of much of Walcott's poetry.

During the 1960's and the 1970's, at the height of the Black Power movement and the Third World's campaign toward independence and self-determination, Walcott's divided voice was heard but not readily appreciated by his fellow Caribbean natives with zealous nationalist sentiments. This was compounded by the fact that his earlier poems tended to be written in a high-style language that is formal, ornate, and replete with classical allusions, poetic devices, and complex rhyming schemes that are associated with the polite learning of colonial education. Although such a cultural tension was to remain unresolved, the drive toward synthesis brought about a significant response to his critics with the publication of *The Castaway and Other Poems*. The book, which recalls William Cooper's poem of the same title, contains important poems such as "Laventille" and "Codicil," but its unity has to be found from poems such as "The Castaway," "Crusoe's Island," and "Crusoe's Journal." Robinson Crusoe, the "castaway" of the book, had been occupying Walcott's attention for some time. Although Crusoe suffers from an interminable isolation that bespeaks Walcott's situation, this shipwrecked hero personifies Walcott's view that it is important for colonized peoples to regard their predicament not in terms of loss and nothingness but rather as a beginning; instead of lamenting their past and their suffering, it would be more fruitful to start creating a new world. The Crusoe figure is a significant emblem of Walcott's synthesizing impulse in that, as a composite of Adam (the archetypal man of the Old World) and Columbus (the archetypal discoverer of the New World), Crusoe is one who can create his own world by adapting to an environment akin to the geographical and cultural isolation of the West Indies. Walcott's concept of a new beginning made possible by the shipwreck is associated with the condition of amnesia—the erasure of the burdens of the past—and with the notion of the *tabula rasa*, the unfolding of history on the blank page of the present. These and other related ideas were later articulated, with great passion and eloquence, in his crucial but at the time controversial essays "What the Twilight Says: An Overture" (1970) and "The Muse of History" (1974). Informed by the composite myth of Crusoe, Walcott's poetry subsequent to *The Castaway* begins to quicken its pace in the direction of reconciling and synthesizing the dualistic opposites in his psyche.

As Walcott's ties with the United States became closer during the late 1960's, the frequent plane flights over the Gulf of Mexico inspired him to use the image of the gulf as the title for his next book, *The Gulf and Other Poems*, which was combined with *The Castaway* and republished as *The Gulf* in 1970. The title can be traced to an epigram in "Crusoe's Journal" in *The Castaway*, where Crusoe states that there is "a great gulf fixed" between him and the (old) world he has come from. The "gulf" is both geographical and symbolic. Accordingly, many important poems in *The Gulf* deal with connections and disjunctions, especially those between the two Americas and between the New World and the Old (for example, "Elegy" and "Negatives"). Significantly, a new element in the book is Walcott's use of the myth of Odysseus to explore the themes of home, homecoming, exile, memory, and art.

With the publication of *The Gulf*, Crusoe recedes into the background and becomes absorbed into the Odysseus figure. As a matter of fact, references to Odysseus started appearing even in the earliest of Walcott's poetry, but their conscious use for thematization rather than embellishment is more recent. As such, the focus on Odysseus can be regarded as a pivotal point in Walcott's poetic career. In contrast to Crusoe, Odysseus is a more suitable emblem for Walcott's project of synthesis, because an important part of Odysseus' character—as portrayed in Homer's *Odyssey* (c. 800 B.C.)—is his stubborn resistance against forgetfulness and erasure; memory, instead of being a source of nostalgia to be indulged in, provides Odysseus with the creative impetus needed for the new beginnings and reconnections that are essential to his homecoming. Subsuming aspects of Adam, Columbus, and Crusoe, the Odysseus myth can be seen in Walcott's *Another Life*. This intellectual autobiography in verse represents a return to the poet's childhood, home, and spiritual source by way of memory; but although it stands on its own, as a statement of rediscovery and affirmation of the past, it is also an integral part of a bigger pattern that includes the subsequent volumes, for which the autobiography would serve as a prelude. Walcott's Odyssean myth, eventually, would metamorphose into *Omeros*, an epic-size narrative that recasts the *Odyssey* in Caribbean settings and redefines the meaning of Western civilization in the terms of the New World (St. Lucia, for example, is embodied by a black Helen).

Sea Grapes, the title of which refers to a coastal plant found in tropical America, can be regarded as Walcott's first organically structured collection, with the myth of Odysseus' return ("Sea Grapes") serving as a unifying factor. The title poem also hints at the poet's desire to venture beyond the bookish solace provided by the Anglo-European tradition. Related themes such as Adam and the New World ("The Cloud"; "New World"; "Adam's Song"), exile ("Preparing for Exile"; "At Last"), and naming ("Names") also figure large. Significantly, at the center of the volume Walcott pays tribute to his home island, St. Lucia, in a sequence of poems that employ patois as well as English ("Sainte Lucie"). The desire to immortalize his home island, the sea, and the Caribbean has always been strong in the poet's life, but here such a desire is expressed with an indulgent tenderness that suggests that Walcott—an Odyssean wanderer—has found memory to be the medicine for his cultural schizophrenia.

The next volume's title, *The Star-Apple Kingdom*, is again derived from an indigenous fruit of the Caribbean (the fruit's "star design" can be seen when it is cut open). The volume opens with "The Schooner *Flight*," a narrative poem about a Trinidadian sailor, Shabine, who goes into exile. This Odysseus-like mulatto, whose most memorable line is "either I'm nobody or I'm a nation," bears many resemblances to Walcott and hence serves as his mask. Concluding the volume is the title piece, "The Star-Apple Kingdom," a meditation on the colonial and postcolonial history of the West Indies and on the relationship between the Third World and the British Empire as well as the United States. In the middle of the book is "The Sea Is History," in which Walcott once again reiterates the notion of a new beginning; here, though, the beginning is not "new" because of forgetfulness, but because of the cathartic and transcendental function of nature represented by the sea.

Both *Sea Grapes* and *The Star-Apple Kingdom* suggest that the poet has located the Caribbean as the center of his consciousness. With the publication of *The Fortunate Traveller*, which is directly related to Walcott's frequent travels between the two Americas, it is increasingly evident that he no longer operates on the basis of being "divided" as a person and "split" as an artist, but rather on his new synthesis, the Caribbean consciousness that is at the very core of his existence. St. Lucia, the center of his universe, is where he begins and must return. Alluding to *The Unfortunate Traveller* (a picaresque tale by Thomas Nashe dated 1594) with a degree of irony, the book rehearses the bittersweet pleasures of exile and travel and attempts to resolve the dilemma by exploring the differences between the North and the South in terms of geography, politics, economics, culture, and so forth. Divided into three sequences (*North I*, *South II*, and *North III*), the book follows a circular pattern typical of a journey with return, though it is also important to note that the persona here is an Odysseus figure with the qualities of a picaro as well. Walcott's Aegean-evoking Caribbean home is placed at the center, at which the myth of Odysseus reappears (in the lyrical "Map of the New World" and the carnivalesque "The Spoiler's Return"). The most important poem in *North I* is "North and South," in which Walcott meditates on his psychological break with the British Empire, on the predicament of the African diaspora, and on the problem of racism. In *North II*, the most important poem is the title piece, "The Fortunate Traveller," in which the poet—by way of self-mockery—dramatizes the disparity between the industrialized nations and the Third World, expresses his disgust with colonialism, and comes to the bitter conclusion that "The heart of darkness is not Africa./ The heart of darkness is the core of fire/ in the white center of the holocaust." As "England recedes" ("The Fortunate Traveller") and as the poet is "falling in love with America" ("Upstate," from "North I"), the dualistic existence that has dogged Walcott for many years is being supplanted by an Afro-Caribbean-American identity—an identity yet burdened with a new baggage, for example, the military role of the United States in the Third World that is alluded to in some poems.

Midsummer is a collection of untitled meditations on a wide range of subjects such as self, memory, art, poetry, language, the imagination, colonialism, Africa, and racial conflicts, with a particular focus on the unifying diversity of the poet's personal experience as an Afro-Caribbean-American. In one of the volume's best poems (known simply as "XXIII"), Walcott ponders bitterly on the relationship between the Shakespearean theater and the practice of racism. Walcott is no longer able to see the English language and the English literary canon as something separable from the imperialism of the British Empire. Such a poem would very likely have startled the Walcott of yore. He has come a long way in his spiritual odyssey, and it is only appropriate that such a triumph should find its commemoration in a retrospective volume, *Collected Poems, 1948-1984.*

Walcott's next book, *The Arkansas Testament*, is divided into two sections: *Here*, which deals mainly with his reconnections with the people and places of his childhood in St. Lucia (see "The Lighthouse"), and *Elsewhere*, which is concerned with the rest of the world. St. Lucia and the West Indies and the Third World in general continue to occupy a central position in the poet's universe and loom large even in the *Elsewhere* section of the book. In "Elsewhere (for Stephen Spender)," for example, the poet notes that "we are free for a while, but/ elsewhere, in one-third, or one-seventh/ of this planet, a summary rifle butt/ breaks a skull into the idea of a heaven/ where nothing is free, where blue air/ is paper-frail, and whatever we write/ will be stamped twice, a blue letter,/ its throat slit by the paper knife of the state." Even the United States has become a new source of ambivalence in Walcott's consciousness as he tours around the country. For example, the poet remarks, apropos of the irrelevance of America's entertainment industry, that "Nothing hurts as much as the word 'California'" because "There's sometimes more pain in a pop song than all of Cambodia" ("Summer Elegies II"). Such observations are important hints about the nature of the volume, the title of which is taken from a sequence of twenty-four poems occasioned by Walcott's visit to Fayetteville, Arkansas, an experience that triggered a revelation for the poet. Checking into a "$17.50 motel" and waking up early to get his coffee and breakfast, Walcott muses on the dark side of the history of the United States: as the Puritan ideology, the Indian Wars, the slavery of Africans, the Civil War, the Ku Klux Klan, the prolonged racism in not only the South but also the North, and so forth. One of the most horrible realizations is that there was a "recently repealed law/ that any black out after curfew/ could be shot dead in Arkansas." These poems constitute a "testament" in the sense that Walcott, then considering whether to become an American citizen or to remain St. Lucian, was wrestling with the meanings and implications of what it is to be an American for a person of color. Wryly ironic and self-mocking, *The Arkansas Testament* problematizes Walcott's new Afro-Caribbean-American identity and thus arrives at yet another level of complexity.

Developed over half a century, Walcott's poetry amounts to a formidable corpus;

essentially, though, it emanates from his Caribbean existence, which is the center of his consciousness and the source of his inspiration. Owing to—and in spite of—the many opposites, conflicts, tensions, and confusions inscribed in his mixed heritage, he demands readers to see his poetry in terms of complex negotiations, or navigations, toward resolutions. Such maneuvers make him more than an island poet, and indeed more than an African American poet. To characterize Walcott, it may be appropriate to borrow a line from one of his characters: "I had no nation now but the imagination." In the final analysis, however, Walcott's imagination does not create its own universe out of nothing, but rather out of an inexhaustible energy toward synthesis. It is this propensity toward synthesis, in the interest of a new world, that allows him to transmute the myth of Crusoe into the myth of Odysseus, and himself into the Homer of *Omeros.*

Bibliography
Baugh, Edward. *Derek Walcott: Memory as Vision: "Another Life."* London: Longman, 1978. Focuses on Walcott's autobiographical poem.
Brown, Stewart, ed. *The Art of Derek Walcott.* Chester Springs, Pa.: Dufour Editions, 1991. Indispensable anthology of essays discussing all the poetry collections and major plays by Walcott; extensive bibliography.
Goldstraw, Irma. *Derek Walcott: An Annotated Bibliography of His Works.* New York: Garland, 1984. Includes secondary sources and uncollected materials.
Hamner, Robert. *Derek Walcott.* Boston: Twayne, 1981. A comprehensive introductory study by an authority on Walcott.
Terada, Rei. *Derek Walcott's Poetry: American Mimicry.* Boston: Northeastern University Press, 1992. Discusses Walcott's poetry from a postmodern/postcolonial perspective. Select bibliography.

Balance Chow

THE POETRY OF ALICE WALKER

Author: Alice Walker (1944-   )
Type of work: Poetry
First published: Once, 1968; *Revolutionary Petunias and Other Poems,* 1973; *Good Night, Willie Lee, I'll See You in the Morning: Poems,* 1979; *Horses Make a Landscape Look More Beautiful,* 1984; *Her Blue Body Everything We Know: Earthling Poems, 1965-1990 Complete,* 1991

Although it is less well known than her fiction, Alice Walker's poetry is integral to her development as a writer. The restorative power of poetry, Walker claims, has continually saved her from hopelessness and suicide. In her poetry, Walker records intensely felt emotions, purging the psyche of stultifying mental states that hamper growth. Written out of firsthand experience, Walker's poetry reveals a sensitive African American intellectual coming to terms with disparate strands of her own existence. Along with her other literary achievements, essays, and long and short fiction, Walker's poetry is a significant contribution to American letters, expressing the African American female consciousness.

The work with which Walker's name is most often associated is the epistolary novel *The Color Purple* (1982), for which she won the 1983 Pulitzer Prize. Steven Spielberg, the well-known director of such films as *Star Wars* (1976) and *E.T. the Extra-Terrestrial* (1982), directed the movie version of the book that catapulted Walker to international celebrity status. Having been writing for fifteen years before the publication of *The Color Purple,* Alice Walker had been known mainly among literary audiences as one of a number of African American writers who became visible in the late 1960's and early 1970's. With *The Color Purple,* Walker's niche as a writer was secured. A skillfully written story about the travails of Celie, a black woman living in the South under oppression imposed by whites and by black males, the novel is a poignant commentary on the spiritual liberation of Celie. For the most part, Walker's writing, controversial in its portrayal of character, has evoked strong reaction.

Given the circumstances of Alice Walker's early life, it seemed unlikely that the young girl would overcome poverty and deprivation to become an educated woman, much less a noted writer. Born February 9, 1944, Alice was the eighth and last child of Willie Lee and Minnie Tallulah Grant Walker, sharecroppers earning about $300 a year working in the cotton fields of Eatonton, Georgia. An eye injury Walker suffered when she was eight helped steer her to a literary life. Self-conscious of the resulting scar tissue and impaired vision, Walker, although prom queen as well as class valedictorian, became reflective, turning her attention to reading, observing people, and writing poems, unwittingly developing a writer's sensibility.

Paradoxically, it was also the eye injury that enabled Walker to go to college by entitling her to a scholarship to Spelman College, an elite black women's school in Atlanta. Walker became active in civil rights activities while in Atlanta. Yet she felt stifled by the conservatism at Spelman, so she transferred to Sarah Lawrence College, an exclusive women's school in Bronxville, New York. While at Sarah Lawrence, Walker gained the education and exposure she needed to master her craft. Her literary talents were soon noticed, and Walker won fellowships to various writing conferences. By 1967, Walker was on her way to a professional writing career, finding several outlets for her work. While a contributing editor to *Ms.* magazine, Walker published short pieces with feminist overtones. The poet Muriel Rukeyser, one of Walker's teachers at Sarah Lawrence, took a special interest in her writing and sent it to an editor at Harcourt, Brace, Jovanovich, resulting in 1968 in her first publication, *Once*, a volume of poems. Throughout her career, Alice Walker has continued to write in different genres, moving outward to create fiction and then inward to create essays and poetry.

The range of topics in Alice Walker's poetry can be described as anything with which the poet has come in contact. Thus, themes in her work include her rich African American heritage, failures and successes in relationships, the ramifications of living in a family and in a community, and social and political issues. Walker often denounces racial injustice and prejudice, sometimes showing anger and resentment toward the oppressors without becoming militant. Convictions are strong, but they remain part of a process, as if Walker is continually listening to her own voice, then adjusting volume and tone so that she might best achieve a mature perspective. Even in poems written about specific instances of prejudice, although Walker shows indignation, her ultimate conclusion is that change must take place within the individual, that only those with myopic vision believe that wholesale racial reform can be imposed from without.

Always confessional, Walker's poetry closely resembles the art form she envies most, music; like the musician, she strives to achieve unity with her creation. For Walker, this effort translates into capturing the poet's authentic feelings, including all nuances of emotion, in her poems. The effect is both a strength and a weakness, as the resulting poems are often vigorous yet sometimes overly sentimental. The reader suspects that what Walker says of journal writing also can be said of her poetry: "In my journal/ I thought I could/ capture/ everything. . . ." To project personal reality, Walker exercises stylistic freedom, creating free verse that is often prosaic rather than rhythmic. In her effort to write realistically, Walker avoids symbolic language, preferring language that is colloquial and direct, candid, expressive, and generally forceful. With a predilection for terseness, Walker forges lines that are straightforward, free of flourishes and decoration.

Alice Walker's stories and novels are populated by characters who might be tangentially related to the author, but the persona of her poetry is the voice of the speaker. In her poetry, Walker works through personal conflict, feelings, moods, and concerns, thus freely exposing the self. All Walker's poetry can be viewed as a self-study. In fact, in her fifth volume of poetry, a compilation of Walker's first four books of poetry, some uncollected poems, and some never-before-published pieces, *Her Blue Body Everything We Know: Earthling Poems, 1965-1990 Complete*, the reader is encouraged to read the poems as a narrative of Walker's past. She has even added contextual prefaces that explain the biographical circumstances of each book of poems.

In the preface to *Once*, Walker explains that she wrote most of these poems while sitting under a tree in Kenya; the others she wrote at Sarah Lawrence. The voice in this book is that of a young idealist whose desire to understand herself takes her to Africa, to the inner workings of romantic relationships and to experiences with racial prejudice in the South. Walker communicates the grandeur of the African landscape through description and the unobtrusive posture she takes. She observes, then recedes into the background. Commentary is minimal; imagery tells all. There is indirect commentary, however, as in these lines, "Holding three fingers/ The African Child/ Looked up at me/ The sky was very/ Blue." An obvious problem for Walker is her relationship to her African heritage. With her usual wry humor, Walker writes of African custom and ritual; she mimics her own pretentiousness in reenacting the life of the African nobility as she says, "I try to be a native/ queen," then she observes a giraffe that "turns up/ his nose" at the sham. Aware that she will never reconcile her two geographical selves, Walker describes a Harvard-educated friend in Africa whose education, like her own, pales in comparison to the vastness of the continent. Walker is aware of the incongruity, just as she is aware of many incongruities in Africa; to convey inconsistency, Walker uses juxtaposition, as in the poem that shows a "Noble Savage" with infected pierced ears.

Often Walker uses the element of surprise, which works well in poems about love and home as well as in those about Africa. In her title poem "Once," one vignette presents a young white civil rights worker who disowns her racist mother; in another poem, Walker brazenly announces, "I/ never liked/ white folks/ really." Such forthrightness is characteristic of Walker's poetic voice, which unrestrainedly addresses such issues as abortion, interracial dating, and suicide.

An increasingly mature vision marks Walker's second book of poems, *Revolutionary Petunias and Other Poems*, for which she received a National Book Award. In the introductory background essay to these poems in *Her Blue Body Everything We Know*, Walker explains that the context of these poems is her return to the South from New York, where she had been working for the city welfare department. In *Revolutionary Petunias*, Walker embraces her native African American culture, acknowledging that it possesses wisdom as well as life-sustaining rhythms, and indicates in a poem describing her grandmother's funeral a desire to transmit her own cultural richness to her daughter. With originality and grace, Walker writes affectionately of family, describing men so in tune to the life cycle that they naturally know how to "Gently swing/ A casket," and the women, or "Headragged Generals," who, though uneducated, "knew what we/ *Must* know."

Walker carefully culls her memories, suggesting that she is poised between two worlds, like the sister in "For My Sister Molly Who in the Fifties," whose relationship to her family once she has left it for wider vistas becomes precarious. Bringing knowledge and manners to those who have never left home, as Molly does, brings both admiration and disdain. Certainly, Walker knows how being enlightened is enhancing and threatening. Walker is also wise enough to see herself in the old women in the poem who sing with cracked voices about Jesus. Another sign of understanding is evident in Walker's multiple references to spiritual forces outside herself that she cannot control, references that indicate that Walker is becoming increasingly comfortable with the inexplicable and with uncertainty. Taking the position of the poet Rainer Maria Rilke, Walker perceives the theme of search as a mandate, announcing, "I must love the questions."

This second book of poems is also stylistically more mature than the earlier work. Gone are excessive pathos and the overabundant use of dashes of the first book. Images are sharper and wittier; some lines with their clever playfulness are reminiscent of Emily Dickinson, as in one monologue in which the persona states "Coincidence makes me laugh/ out loud."

Several poems addressed to lovers, including the poem dedicated to her husband Mel, show passion and romance as revolutionary forces. Bridging racial and cultural barriers to marry the young Jewish lawyer, whom she had met while they were both working in a voter registration campaign in New York, Walker creates lyrics in protest of the status quo in which love is "unfashionable" and some relationships "forbidden." That resistance is both natural and necessary is underscored by the emblem of revolutionary petunias, bold blossoms commonly found in Southern gardens, that are impervious to any "Elemental Crush."

Two landmark events, the breakup of her marriage and the death of her father, guided the poetic voice in Alice Walker's third volume of poetry, *Good Night, Willie Lee, I'll See You in the Morning: Poems*, through the grief process. The sections in the book, beginning with "Confession" and ending with "Forgiveness," expressly re-create the pain necessarily suffered in the process of coping with loss. To describe the dissolution of a love relationship, Walker uses pointed questions, monologue, and dialogue, honestly conveying anger, fear, and pain. In the section entitled "Early Losses: A Requiem," Walker delves into a lifetime of bereavement. Included are a poem examining an early loss of love, an expression of guilt following a father's death, and lyrics about the death of Malcolm X. As Walker explores the deaths of loved ones, she seeks to understand their impact on her present and future existence. Regret, a sentiment associated with life and death processes, is obviously experienced and openly expressed in these poems. The lesson that the speaker hears in the title poem is one of acceptance and understated hope, for as Alice Walker's mother speaks the parting words to her husband, "Good night, Willie Lee, I'll see you/ in the morning," the healing process of forgiveness has already begun.

Dedicating her fourth volume of poetry, *Horses Make a Landscape Look More Beautiful*, to her Cherokee great-grandmother and her white great-great-grandfather, Walker resurrects these family members, believing that their existence is closely tied to her own and that they may shed light on her own identity. In the book's dedication, she addresses them saying "the meaning of your lives/ is still/ unfolding." Walker focuses especially on her Native American ancestry, sensing that her own reverence for plants, trees, the sun, and the earth can be traced to the reverence Native Americans held for a harmonious relationship with nature. (The book's title is taken from a speech by a Native American.) In the poem "These Days," Walker enumerates many friends for whom she hopes "*the earth can be saved.*" A consistent theme is the lamentation of destruction, whether it is the deterioration of the planet or the degradation of women. While message and intent are unmistakable, Walker's tone does show some musicality and mellowing as her universe expands backward into personal history and forward to the future of the globe.

Walker's highly personal poetry, to some extent her own shrine that draws the reader into an intimate relationship, is at once art, process, and struggle. Affirmation, sometimes triumphantly proclaimed, is temporary, yielding to pessimism in a continuous cycle. Walker's poetry mirrors the ongoing dialectic of hope and despair. Even the poetic process, which Walker describes as "Having to almost die/ before some weird light/ comes creeping through," involves an act of faith in the redeeming power of words.

Bibliography

Banks, Erma Davis, and Keith Byerman. *Alice Walker: An Annotated Bibliography, 1968-1986.* New York: Garland, 1989. A thorough catalog of writings by and about Walker, this bibliography includes numerous book and poetry reviews. An introductory essay provides an overview of Walker's life and her literary contributions.

Christian, Barbara. "Alice Walker: The Black Woman Artist as Wayward." In *Black Women Writers, 1950-1980: A Critical Evaluation*, edited by Mari Evans. Garden City, N.Y.: Anchor Press/Doubleday, 1983. Examines thematic patterns in Walker's work. Points out issues inherent in the role of the black female artist, such as the need for conflict leading to change.

Davis, Thadious M. "Alice Walker's Celebration of Self in Southern Generations." In *Women Writers of the Contemporary South*, edited by Peggy Whitman Prenshaw. Oxford: University Press of Mississippi, 1984. Focuses on themes and patterns apparent in Walker's work from her poetry through *The Color Purple.* Shows Walker's need to reconcile her intellectualism with her rural roots.

Turner, Darwin. "A Spectrum of Blackness." *Parnassus: Poetry in Review* 5 (Spring/ Summer, 1976): 202-219. An analysis of Walker's direct poetic expression. Commends Walker for seeking individualism and for her frankness in conveying the world as fragmented.

Williamson, Alan. "In a Middle Style." *Poetry* 136 (March, 1980): 348-354. Commentary on the poetry collection *Good Night, Willie Lee, I'll See You in the Morning.* Demonstrates Walker's weakness in at times using a moralistic tone and yet acknowledges the strength of her crystal-clear imagery.

Mary Brantley

THE POETRY OF PHILLIS WHEATLEY

Author: Phillis Wheatley (1753?-1784)
Type of work: Poetry
First published: Poems on Various Subjects, Religious and Moral, 1773

When Phillis Wheatley wrote *Poems on Various Subjects, Religious and Moral,* the first book published by an African American, she began two traditions simultaneously: the African American literary tradition and the African American women's literary tradition. This was a monumental accomplishment for a slave. Phillis belonged to the John Wheatley family in Boston. A letter from her owner to her publisher, also included in the book, provides the first account of her early years. It states that she was brought from Africa to America in 1761, being at that time seven or eight years old. Without formal schooling but with tutoring by the family, especially Mary Wheatley, the family's daughter, Phillis learned the English language in sixteen months to the extent that she could read the most difficult parts of the Bible.

Wheatley started writing poetry at the age of twelve and quickly gained recognition as an occasional poet. Since the occasion was usually death, and the preponderance of her poems were elegies, she soon became Boston's muse of comfort. Her elegy "On the Death of the Rev. Mr. George Whitefield, 1770," gained her instant recognition in England as well as America. Sending this elegy along with a cover letter to Selina Hastings, the countess of Huntingdon, an early promoter of English Methodism who had in 1748 appointed Whitefield her chaplain, Wheatley acquired the countess' patronage. Published first as a broadside, this widely printed elegy was also included by the Reverend Ebenezer Pemberton of Boston as an addendum to his funeral sermon for Whitefield, which was published in 1771 in London.

The publicity generated by this elegy spurred Mrs. Susanna Wheatley's efforts in 1772 to publish Phillis' small collection of poetry. Although proposals for the book were advertised four times, subscribers did not respond in sufficient numbers for the book to be printed. Thoroughly exasperated, Susanna Wheatley began to seek a London publisher for the poems. One was found, Archibald Bell, a printer of religious works. After being acquainted with the troubled history of the project, he insisted on a written verification of Phillis' authorship. The Wheatleys complied by having an attestation signed by the Massachusetts governor and lieutenant governor along with sixteen other notable Bostonians, including John Hancock. Next, the Wheatleys in the spring of 1773 sent Phillis to London to superintend the publishing of the book. Accompanied by their son Nathaniel, who was going to London to expand the family's business, Phillis sailed from Boston on May 8 and arrived in London on June 17. Phillis had also been sent on the trip because doctors thought the sea air might mitigate her chronic respiratory ailments. From her arrival to her departure on July 26, 1773, because of the serious illness of Susanna Wheatley, Phillis was lionized in London. She visited and was visited and escorted by English philanthropists, statesmen, members of Parliament, abolitionists, titled men and women, politicians, merchants, a female writer, a botanist and explorer, and a fellow American, Benjamin Franklin. Clearly this was the social and professional apex of her life.

The slim volume, consisting of 127 pages, does not contain her complete canon. In addition to her twenty-two extant letters, her canon consists basically of four groups of poems: thirty-eight written by 1773 and published in her book, eight written by 1773 but not published in the book, twenty-eight or possibly twenty-nine written after 1773 but not extant, and ten written after 1773 and extant. Thirty-three poems and thirteen letters were collected for a proposed 1779 volume, but again Bostonians did not respond to advertisements for subscribers. Not only was this book not printed, but also the manuscript was eventually lost after Phillis' death; the manuscript was probably abandoned by her improvident husband, John Peters, whom she had married on April 1, 1778.

Wheatley's New England education, acquired through informal tutorial sessions, influenced her poetry. According to Margaretta Matilda Odell, who wrote a brief account of Phillis' life, that education consisted of astronomy, ancient and modern geography, ancient history, the Old and New Testaments, and Greek and Roman mythology. Odell also observed that Alexander Pope's translation of Homer was one of Phillis' favorite books. As a consequence of this education, Phillis' poetry emphasizes the classics and the Bible.

Phillis' exposure to the classics influenced her to write in the neoclassical style of the time. Examples of that style abound in *Poems on Various Subjects*. Like other neoclassical poets, she wrote public poetry celebrating events of historical importance. In "To the King's Most Excellent Majesty," Wheatley expresses the nation's gratitude to King George III for the repeal of the Stamp Act. In "To the Right Honourable William, Earl of Dartmouth, His Majesty's Principal Secretary of State for North-America," Wheatley praises an administrative appointment to the colonies. It should be noted that in writing these and similar poems, Wheatley was the first American female poet to speak of politics.

Another example of the neoclassical influence is the personification in Wheatley's poetry of such abstractions as virtue, recollection, imagination, and humanity. Yet another is her use of invocation to the muse. The opening lines of "Goliath of Gath" resound with an invocation, as do those of "Niobe in Distress for Her Children Slain by Apollo." Wheatley did not restrict the invocation to these two epic-like poems; she used it in at least nine other poems in her book. Additional evidence of Wheatley's neoclassicism can be seen in her Latinate vocabulary, circumlocution, formal tone, and closed heroic couplets.

Finally, allusions to Greek and Roman mythology abound in her poetry; classical mythology inspired her imagination and fancy, so that in rendering Ovid's story of Niobe, for example, she added interpolations and her own interpretations.

In addition to classical and neoclassical influences, her poetry also evinces emphasis on religion and the Bible. She occasionally assumes the persona of a preacher. In "To the University of Cambridge, in New-England," she admonishes the young men at Harvard to shun sin: "An *Ethiop* tells you 'tis your greatest foe." She further evangelizes in "On Being Brought from Africa to America": "Remember, *Christians*, *Negros*, black as *Cain*,/ May be refin'd, and join th' angelic train."

Her elegies represent a marriage of the classical and Biblical influences on her poetry. They constitute a major genre in her canon; of her eighty-five poems, extant and nonextant, twenty-five are elegies, of which four are nonextant. Her early ones were written primarily upon request. *Poems on Various Subjects* contains fourteen elegies, including six on the deaths of children. Wheatley individualizes her treatment of this genre by elegizing the deaths of babies and children and by describing the grief of both parents. Although elegies for children were not unusual at that time, those for adults were more prevalent. Wheatley, however, consistently affirms the importance of children both on Earth and in an afterlife.

Although her elegies represent one of the classical genres, and although they utilize neoclassical conventions,.they contain few allusions to Greek and Roman mythology. Probably Wheatley thought that paganism was not consonant with their Christian theme. Since elegies span her poetry, a comparison of her last five with her earlier ones can reveal her improvement and maturity as a poet. The later ones are less formulaic and predictable; also, they seem more sincere in the conferment of honor and in the expression of grief—in most instances her personal grief. Certainly, after the death of two of her own babies she could empathize more with other parents on the loss of theirs.

In her last poems, another change appears—Wheatley's increased nationalism. During and immediately after the revolutionary war, "the Afric muse" wrote poems celebrating America and liberty. Her inclination to speak of politics and to celebrate liberty combine to produce the nationalistic tone in "To His Excellency General Washington" (1775), "On the Capture of General Lee" (1776), and "Liberty and Peace" (1784). In all three of these poems, she warns England to curb its thirst for power and wild ambition. In "Liberty and Peace," Wheatley quotes her own lines from "To His Excellency General Washington": "The goddess comes, she moves divinely fair,/ Olive and laurel binds her golden hair." Wheatley proudly reminds the reader of her accurate prophecy that the United States or its personification, Columbia, would eventually offer peace (olive) and honor (laurel). Paradoxically, she developed her strongest nationalistic and anti-British sentiments despite the increased knowledge and appreciation of Great Britain she acquired during her trip to London.

Two arguments against Wheatley's poetry have been discussed through the years by critics. One is that she was an imitator of imitators; the other is that she lacked interest in fellow slaves, Africa, and Africans. Much of her poetry is derivative, as was that of many poets and poetasters of mid-eighteenth century America. Like them, she used Pope and John Milton as models. Her own imagination and fancy, however, prevented her from following her models slavishly.

Early twentieth century critics discerned Wheatley's alleged lack of interest in Africa and blacks in part in her stance and tone in poems such as "On being brought from Africa to America," which states, " 'Twas mercy brought me from my Pagan land." Several factors influenced her thoughts on the subject. She grew up among Bostonians who regarded Africa as a primitive and heathen place, and she was likely constrained as a slave writing for a predominantly white reading public. Yet she was herself a constant statement against slavery; abolitionists used her as an embodiment of their argument of what the slave could become if freed and educated. Although occasionally her poetry reveals her as more interested in slaves' souls than in their bodies, she was, even in her early years, opposed to slavery. A growing chorus of critics, having benefited from recently discovered poems and letters, argue convincingly that Wheatley was not devoid of racial feelings. The strongest indictment of slavery in her book is in her poem to the Earl of Dartmouth:

> I, young in life, by seeming cruel fate
> Was snatched from *Afric's* fancy'd happy seat;
> What pangs excruciating must molest,
> What sorrows labour in my parent's breast?
> Steel'd was that soul and by no misery mov'd
> That from a father seiz'd his babe belov'd:
> Such, such my case. And can I then but pray
> Others may never feel tyrannic sway?

Two pivotal events in Wheatley's life further galvanized her opposition to slavery. During the five weeks in 1773 when the poet was in London, she was legally a free woman under English law. Moreover, sometime during the fall or winter of 1773, Phillis was manumitted by the Wheatleys; she then began to write in a stronger, more confident voice. In seven of her extant letters, six written during and after the summer of 1773, she acknowledges her concern for Africans and blacks. Her strongest antislavery sentiments in a letter appear in one written to the Reverend Samuel Occom on February 11, 1774. In controlled but passionate words, she equates contemporary white racists, including Christian ministers who owned slaves, with the ancient Egyptians. By far her strongest overt statement against slavery in poetry is found in "On the Death of General Wooster" (1778). She speaks in the persona of the dying general, who in his final prayer importunes God to lead America through the revolutionary war successfully and keep it "virtuous, brave, and free"; but he deplores America's withholding freedom from its slaves:

> But how, presumptuous shall we hope to find
> Divine acceptance with th' Almighty mind—
> While yet (O deed ungenerous!) they disgrace
> And hold in bondage Afric's blameless race?

While Wheatley was developing stronger antislavery feelings, she was also learning more about Africa. She writes in one of her letters that she is studying maps of Africa and a gazeteer. No more does she allude to Africa as a "pagan land" or the "land of errors, and Egyptian gloom." Instead, she finds much about it to praise. In her "Reply to the Answer in our last by the Gentleman in the Navy," she recalls a description of the luxuriant beauty of the Senegal/Gambia area, the land of her birth:

> Charm'd with thy painting, how my bosom burns!
> And pleasing Gambia on my soul returns,
> With native grace in spring's luxuriant reign,
> Smiles the gay mead, and Eden blooms again.

One regrets not only that Wheatley's poetic productivity was not greater after 1773 but also that much of what she did write during that period has disappeared. There were, of course, understandable reasons for her limited productivity: the demise of the entire Wheatley nuclear family, the revolutionary war, a disappointing marriage, three sickly children born in six years, and deteriorating health ending in Wheatley's untimely death on December 5, 1784.

In "An Elegy on Leaving _____ ," published five months before her death, she recalls when first she felt the poetic flame inspired by Cynthio (or Apollo). Prospero-like, she breaks her staff and bids farewell to her magic:

> But, ah! those pleasing hours are ever flown;
>   Ye scenes of transport from my thoughts retire;
> Those rural joys no more the day shall crown,
>   No more my hand shall wake the warbling lyre.

Thus was she precluded from fulfilling her desire stated in "To Maecenas"—to "mount and ride upon the wind." Yet she was able to write poetry that nurtured and fed not only her own spirit and being but also the spirits and beings of her admirers.

Bibliography
Hayden, Lucy K. "Classical Tidings from the African Muse: Phillis Wheatley's Use of Greek and Roman Mythology." *College Language Association Journal* 35 (June, 1992): 432-447. That Wheatley, influenced by Alexander Pope and neoclassicism, used classical mythology throughout her poetry is the main focus of this essay. Wheatley's poem "Niobe in Distress for Her Children Slain by Apollo from Ovid's *Metamorphoses*, Book VI, and from a View of the Painting of Mr. Richard Wilson" provides the centerpiece of the discussion.
Richmond, Merle. *Phillis Wheatley.* New York: Chelsea House, 1988. This 111-page biography provides an overview of Wheatley's life and is written primarily for the younger reader. Illustrated.
Robinson, William, ed. *Critical Essays on Phillis Wheatley.* Boston: G. K. Hall, 1982. Robinson's introductory essays on Wheatley and his chronology of important dates in her life precede the essays, which provide reliable scholarship on Wheatley's canon.
Robinson, William H. *Phillis Wheatley: A Bio-Bibliography.* Boston: G. K. Hall, 1981. A brief but scholarly introduction is followed by a chronological list of Wheat-

ley's poems and letters and an annotated bibliography of writings about her from 1761 to 1979.

———————. *Phillis Wheatley and Her Writings.* New York: Garland, 1984. Robinson's sixty-six-page critical biography "On Phillis Wheatley and Her Boston" and his thirty-nine-page essay "On Phillis Wheatley's Poetry" introduce a comprehensive collection of Wheatley's work. Includes all of her extant poems and letters, a selection of her letters and various poems in facsimile, and a facsimile of her entire volume *Poems on Various Subjects, Religious and Moral.* In the appendices are the 1834 memoir of Wheatley, the biblical and Latin originals that she paraphrased and translated, and two letters by George Washington, one discussing Wheatley and the other written to her. The fountainhead for much of the subsequent scholarship on Wheatley.

Wheatley, Phillis. *The Poems of Phillis Wheatley.* Edited by Julian D. Mason, Jr. Chapel Hill: University of North Carolina Press, 1966. Contains Wheatley's complete canon: all her poems, as well as their variants, and all her letters. Mason's scholarly footnotes and essays are valuable additions.

Lucy K. Hayden

THE POETRY OF SHERLEY ANNE WILLIAMS

Author: Sherley Anne Williams (1944-   )
Type of work: Poetry
First published: The Peacock Poems, 1975; *Some One Sweet Angel Chile*, 1982

Sherley Anne Williams, whose reputation as a writer has been fortified by her novel *Dessa Rose* (1986), is an accomplished poet. Developing a poetics of blues drawn from the African American cultural tradition, Williams has turned her experience of life's hardships and her struggles into an aesthetic triumph in *The Peacock Poems*, which was nominated for the National Book Award in Poetry for 1976, and *Some One Sweet Angel Chile*. Sophisticated in structural design and original in thematic exploration, Williams' poetry has added new dimensions and fresh perspectives to contemporary American literature by giving a voice to black women of the economic underclass.

Williams' writing is inseparable from her will to rise above the deprivations of her childhood—she grew up in a housing project in Fresno, California, her father died when she was eight years old, and her mother died eight years later. Despite her disadvantaged background, Williams managed to go to college, earning a B.A. from Fresno State College in 1966 and an M.A. from Brown University in 1972. She published *Give Birth to Brightness: A Thematic Study in Neo-Black Literature* in 1972 and became a professor of Afro-American literature at the University of California at San Diego in 1982.

In her creative writing, Williams is informed by a literary aesthetic developed from critical analyses of African American culture and history. As is evident from her critical writings, this aesthetic draws heavily from the traditions of the blues, slave narratives, and black speech.

The Peacock Poems exemplifies Williams' ingenuity in expression. It employs a nonlinear design suggestive of the fragmented life led by a woman who has to cope with the demands and constraints of reality in order to survive. The book's structure is closely tied to the subject matter and the main theme of the poems, of which there are two types. The first type is situational poems dealing with significant aspects of Williams' life experiences. Interweaving such experiences are poems in "classical blues" format that heighten the effects of the situations by acting as their lyrical commentaries. The situational poems and the literary blues reinforce and complement each other, so that the autobiographical sketches of the poet as a young, black, single mother in the first type of poems are thematized, in the second group, into a general history applicable to any woman with a background comparable to Williams'. This movement from the individual to the communal is implied in the three divisions of the book. Their subtitles—"every woman is a victim of the feel blues, too," "I neva thought I'd sing this song," and "the lines converge here"—indicate that the poet's task in the collection is to adopt the blues format as a vehicle for her personal experience, so that the blues that she sings can become a communal expression.

Williams' thematization of her personal experience begins with "Any Woman's Blues," which is paradigmatic of the literary blues in the collection. Having established the connection between the poet and the blues tradition, the poem employs a bed as a "mascon" (an object, image, or metaphor, often used in blues, characterized by the "massive concentration" on its potential suggestions) to highlight how the bed has become "one-sided" from the woman's "sleepin alone so mucha the time" and how it has been empty because "this man is messin with my mind." As a prologue to the drama of black womanhood, the commentary in "Any Woman's Blues" is borne out by the black woman's predicament in the next few poems, in which readers witness a man confusing and alienating her in a sex-driven relationship ("This Is a Sad-Ass Poem for a Black Woman to Be Writing"), her sister chastising her for giving birth at an inappropriate moment ("Say Hello to John"), and the young mother plucking up enough courage to leave the man ("If he let us go now"), thus starting an odyssey between the coasts with a baby ("Time"). Although these experiences culminate in a crisis of anonymity ("A Walk into the Soft Soft"), they also strengthen the bond between a mother and child who spend their time together ("Time") and above all contribute to the woman's determination to make her life whole by integrating her memories of childhood in the San Joaquin Valley in California and her present predicament as a mother and student on campus in Providence, Rhode Island ("2½ Poems"). Psychologically, the woman begins to mature in "Time," a long poem charting the child's growth and the woman's development of rage. Her rage develops further into a feminist outrage in "Drivin Wheel," in which the poet uses black English and slang to criticize black men for their "jiveness" and their subjugation of black women as a means of proving their manhood. The bitter and sometimes stormy tone provides a radical and militant variation to the blues.

The next two sections of *The Peacock Poems* can be seen in terms of the "new respons" and "another ending" that she calls for. Mixing anger and militancy with reflection and meditation, the poems of "I neva thought I'd sing this song" revolve around Williams' childhood experience and her relationships with her parents, other relatives, and lovers. While documenting the hurt of life (compared to the trimming and folding of a peacock's feathers), they also focus on the struggle of a black woman who, with support from other black women, fashions a new self in order to sing a new song ("The Peacock Song"). The peacock, which recurs as a leitmotif throughout this section, both in the titles and in the texts of various poems, is Williams' emblem for the "strife" toward a new identity: "But if I'm a peacock/ my feathers' s'posed to cover/ all hurts and if you want to/ stay one then you got to keep/ that tail from draggin so mines/ is always held up sky high." She has always wondered "How a peacock/ gon speak" because "I got no tongue," but by dignifying her individuality as a black woman, the poet has nevertheless achieved the extremely difficult task of singing the song that she never thought to sing.

The blues commentary introduced in the first section is transformed, in "The Collateral Adjective," into a critique of the subject matter—blackness and womanhood—of blues, alluded to as "the adjective the noun." In this difficult poem, Williams announces her ambivalence toward the blues, observing that "Without a drum/ that sings soprano/ the tongue's only a/ wagging member in/ the void of the mouth/ speechless in the face of what it has said." What this implies is that without a battle drum, she would not have been able to sing the song that she never thought to sing, that is, "The Peacock Song." In the chorus, the women ("we") recognize the importance of blues, but they also express their reservations about it because "we've been carried away/ in what's become/ a mindless tune." To this, the poet ("I") responds that "I'm/ talking about more/ than just love" when she seeks to sing her song. In the refrain, the poet resolves the conflict between the two understandings of blues, as life lyric and as love song, by identifying herself with blues, qualifying such an identity with the remark that "I never heard/ the drum sound more than/ just that same old blue/ note." The implication is that to Williams, blues not only includes the frustrations of love but also subsumes the struggle in life's battle. The significance of the drum, which appears in all three parts of "The Collateral Adjective," is clarified as Williams begs to differ from the old folks' admonition that the purpose of battle is peace by remonstrating that "peace isn't always worth the battle." Through this series of dialogues between self and community, Williams has invigorated African American sensibility by implying that women's well-being ought to be on the agenda of the community's struggle.

In "Quartet," the first poem of "the lines converge here," Williams makes it clear that the previous section has been designed as a "word ritual" woven "in anger and love" to educate her son, "giving him/ sounds to link what's gone with what/ we renew in our coming." In this section, the dialogue started earlier is extended to a broader community of men and women, of generations past, present, and future— hence the convergence of lines. Identifying herself as the "town-bred descendant of slaves" in "North County," she pays tribute to women who have assisted in her coming of age as well as to men who have in one way or another contributed to the formulation of her "Peacock Song." Of particular interest is "I Sing This Song for Our Mothers," in which she contrasts the heroism of Odessa, a pregnant fugitive slave (later to become the heroine of *Dessa Rose*), with the senseless drunkenness of Mayri, a "no-good daughter" messing around with "low down scum" at parties. Mayri in turn is juxtaposed to "Ruise," Williams' sister "who took the womanme in/ saw so clearly what it was/ that would save me for my/ self and so let me be a/ child again." Epitomizing Williams' entire life, what she is and what she could have been, this is a poem that she would like her son to remember, just as Odessa's son remembers Odessa herself in the poem.

Considered as a whole, the major merits of *The Peacock Poems* are not only the complexity of its design and the sophistication of its thematic exploration, but also its faithfulness to the sordid reality in which Williams has created her peacock's identity and her "voiceless" voice. Her stance as a woman singing the blues of life's hurt at the height of the Civil Rights movement also deepened that struggle with the message that to be worthwhile it had to be as much a women's as a men's movement.

In her second volume of poetry, *Some One Sweet Angel Chile*, Williams continued to exhibit the same merits, and her style mellowed. The book contains three distinct sections, each made up of a series of interwoven poems written from the perspectives of the personae involved.

The first section, "Letters from a New England Negro," is a story in verse. Patient Herald (Hannah), the "herald of Emancipation's/ new day," sends a series of letters to Mrs. Josiah Harris (Miss Nettie) and Mr. Edward Harris, both in Newport, Rhode Island, as well as to Miss Ann Spencer of New Strowbridge, Connecticut. In her letters, she describes her experience as a black teacher in the South during 1867 and 1868. From the last letter, addressed to "Dearest One" (God), readers learn that Hannah had been a servant to the Harrises, a religious but liberal family to whom she is indebted for her education, which she has applied toward the uplifting of her race. The quasi-historical letters capture precious moments of humor, pride, humiliation, anger, perseverance, dedication, and courage when taken individually. As a whole, they are most striking for their treatment of an amicable and genial relationship between a white family and a black woman who possesses the best qualities of Frederick Douglass, Booker T. Washington, and W. E. B. Du Bois. The story also prefigures the black-white friendship in *Dessa Rose*.

"Regular Reefer," the second section, is a composite portrayal of the celebrated blues singer Bessie Smith. The volume's title comes from "some sweet angel chile," a line in Smith's "The Reckless Blues." Structured like a montage, the series features a variety of poems including verse-pictures, simulated reminiscences, biographical portraits, approximations of Bessie's speech and song, eulogies, and personal lyrics expressing the poet's desire to be Bessie. The poems slide from one to the next, often making it difficult to determine not only where a poem begins and ends but also which voice—the poet's or Bessie's—is speaking. Bessie is a particularly appropriate mask for Williams, because she allows Williams to explore whether "if mask and woman/ are one, if pain is/ the sum of all your/ knowing, victim the/ only game you learned." In the end, the identities of both the poet and the poet's subject merge into one. Echoing *The Peacock Poems*, but with greater coherence, "Regular Reefer" demonstrates how Williams has shaped her imagination by harnessing the power of the blues, both as a literary source and as a sociohistorical phenomenon.

The final section of *Some One Sweet Angel Chile*, titled "The Songs of the Grown" and written for Williams' son John Malcolm, can be subdivided into "Witness" and "The Iconography of Childhood," each part once again a series of interwoven poems.

The poems in "Witness," which serves as a testimony to the Black Power movement during the civil rights era, are linked together by flashing montages of drumbeats (represented by the bass clef) as well as whistles and rally cries inserted at various places. Because of the setting, which is mainly Washington, D.C., during 1967 and 1968, when Williams was studying at Howard University, the poet is able to capture a unique aspect of the movement. The fraternity students and ghetto boys from across the campus (the two groups were known to be "Niggas fightin otha niggas") somehow set aside their differences and, united under the banner of Black Power, "together/ burned the effigy of a General/ Named Hershey And one of Howard." Howard University was named for a white man. Williams' treatment of the Black Power movement, however, goes beyond these dramatic spectacles. As is clear from her tribute to Malcolm X ("Big Red and His Brothers") and the portrayal of the black women of her times ("a young woman's blues"; "Straight Talk from Plain Women"), she is more interested in the spirit-transforming and consciousness-raising potentials of the movement. It is significant that in "generations," the poem concluding the "Witness" series and prefiguring "The Iconography of Childhood" series, Williams writes of her parents in a celebratory tone. It seems that the poet, after years of hardship, has come of age and gained confidence in her total being during this "season/ of singing in the/ towns and the cities/ from coast to coast of/ searching in the/ wilderness for what/ we thought was loss."

"The Iconography of Childhood," which recaptures memories once thought to be lost, reads like the autobiography of a person no longer confused and troubled by the hurtful life introduced in *The Peacock Poems*. Lifting her reticence, Williams writes, often with unexpected tenderness, about the housing project, the fields, the orchards, the towns, the freeways, the segregated buses, the county hospitals, and the welfare offices, as well as the tales, songs, and excursions, that constituted her childhood. Readers are given glimpses of the personalities of Williams' parents, sisters, and other relatives. The focus is not so much on the hardships of life as on the realistic, humanistic, and even heroic disposition with which Williams' family, particularly her mother, coped with those hardships. Williams' purpose, it is implied, is not to indulge in the memories themselves but rather to create "symbols of memory" in order to unfold "the meat of vision" ("California Light"). It is perhaps thanks to this memory-generated vision that Williams eventually finds a voice that is entirely her own. The autobiographical situations in *The Peacock Poems* called for blues commentaries; here blues are conspicuously absent. As suggested in "The Janus Love," a poem in which the persona conquers her fear of a new relationship with a man and celebrates her sexuality, masks—including the blues mask—are no longer adequate for her: "masks are part self/ not myself's total." She has triumphed, the entire volume seems to suggest, over the hurt of life itself.

In *The Peacock Poems* and *Some One Sweet Angel Chile*, Williams has accomplished many things for which her poetry will be remembered, from the dexterity of expression to the application and transformation of her cultural tradition, from the fashioning of the self to the visionary outlook of life, and from capturing historical truth in fiction to digging into contemporary reality. Giving birth to a voice to which deprived members of society can relate, she has not only broadened the possibilities of African American poetry but also redefined the meaning of poetry itself.

Bibliography

Gable, Mona. "Understanding the Impossible." *Los Angeles Times Magazine*, December 7, 1986, 22-28. An interview containing extensive biographical information.

Jones, Gayl. "Multiple-Voiced Blues: Sherley Anne Williams' 'Some One Sweet Angel Chile.'" In *Liberating Voices: Oral Tradition in African American Literature*. Cambridge, Mass.: Harvard University Press, 1991. Discusses Williams' use of multiple voices in her poetry, which is inspired by the blues tradition.

Koolish, Lynda. "The Bones of This Body Say, Dance: Self-Empowerment in Contemporary Poetry by Women of Color." In *A Gift of Tongues: Critical Challenges in Contemporary American Poetry*, edited by Marie Harris and Kathleen Aguero. Athens: University of Georgia Press, 1987. Contains a section on Williams' poetry discussing how she borrows from the slave narrative tradition for formal and thematic inspiration.

Tate, Claudia. "Sherley Anne Williams." In *Black Women Writers at Work*. New York: Continuum, 1983. An interview in which Williams discusses her identity as a black woman writer, her writing process, and her views on the teaching of American literature.

Williams, Sherley Anne. "The Blues Roots of Contemporary Afro-American Poetry." *Massachusetts Review* 18 (Autumn, 1977): 542-554. Discusses the history and techniques of blues. Important for understanding Williams' poetics.

Balance Chow

THE POETRY OF JAY WRIGHT

Author: Jay Wright (1934 or 1935-   )
Type of work: Poetry
First published: The Homecoming Singer, 1971; *Soothsayers and Omens,* 1976; *Dimensions of History,* 1976; *The Double Invention of Komo,* 1980; *Explications/Interpretations,* 1984; *Selected Poems* (edited by Robert B. Stepto), 1987; *Elaine's Book,* 1988; *Boleros,* 1991

Jay Wright's poetic ventures into the manifold layers of African American spiritual and intellectual history defy critical attempts at containing African American literature within paradigms of cultural nationalism and Afrocentricity. On the one hand, Wright has been celebrated as one of the most original and powerful voices in contemporary American poetry and has received prestigious awards throughout his career, including a Guggenheim Fellowship (1974), an American Academy Literature Award (1981), and a MacArthur Fellowship (1986). On the other, his refusal to follow Amiri Baraka and others in renouncing Western European and Euro-American poetic traditions and to make his poetry more accessible to popular audiences has led to charges of willful obscurantism and political aloofness. Unlike most African American poets of his generation, Wright insists that grounding in other cultures is a vital part of African American creativity.

Few poets are as conversant with as many different poetic and cultural traditions as Jay Wright is. Inspired by what he calls in *Elaine's Book* a "passion for what is hidden," Wright delves into the histories and mythologies of Western Europe, Africa, North and South America, the Caribbean, and Asia in an impressive effort to restore to African American literature all of its cultural, historical, social, artistic, intellectual, and emotional resources. During the course of a spiritual quest that is at once personal and collective, Wright calls attention to myriad invisible threads that subtly weave together cultural traditions often believed to have evolved separately. Though firmly grounded in African American historical experience and expressive culture, Wright's work exemplifies what Guayanese novelist Wilson Harris, whom Wright has frequently acknowledged as one of his guides, calls a poetics of the cross-cultural imagination.

Wright's multiculturalism has strong autobiographical resonances. Of Irish, African, and Native American descent, Wright grew up in the ethnically diverse settings of Albuquerque, New Mexico, and San Pedro, California, making frequent trips to Mexico as part of his work as a minor-league baseball player in the early 1950's. His early poems, collected in *The Homecoming Singer,* best exemplify the way in which autobiographical experience can serve as a catalyst for constructing an African American cultural and literary tradition. "A Non-Birthday Poem for My Father," "Origins," and "The Hunting-Trip Cook" are homages to Mercer Murphy Wright, Wright's biological father, and to his foster father, Frankie Faucett, that serve as occasions for examining the responsibilities with which the dead charge the living.

Such ancestral charges are what connect presences from Wright's personal past to "the intense communal daring" of Crispus Attucks and W. E. B. Du Bois.

The Homecoming Singer also sketches geographies to which Wright will return throughout his work. The Southwest and California emerge as important places of origin and communion, as does Mexico. "Morning, Leaving Calle Gigantes," "Chapultepec Castle," "Jalapeña Gypsies," and "Bosques de Chapultepec" are chronicles of the time Wright spent in Guadalajara and Jalapa, Mexico, between 1968, the year in which he married Lois Silber, and 1971. In "An Invitation to Madison County," the black American South offers additional possibilities for community to the displaced poet, whose pilgrimage in this instance retraces that of many African American writers before him. "A Month in the Country," in turn, offers a first glimpse of the landscape of New Hampshire, which became Wright's residence in 1973. In later poems, these and other places come together in full-fledged imaginary geographies.

The Homecoming Singer is more than a record of Wright's early artistic development, however; it also contains the seeds of his later writing. "Wednesday Night Prayer Meeting" and "The Baptism," for example, deplore the spiritual paucity of institutionalized African American religions. The lack of "myths to scale your life upon" produces "the senseless, weightless,/ time-denying feeling of not being there" in "Reflections Before the Charity Hospital." Yet rather than escalating in the violent despair of "A Poem for Willie Best" by Amiri Baraka (LeRoi Jones), on which Wright brilliantly improvises in "The Player at the Crossroads" and "Variations on a Theme by LeRoi Jones," this dispossession heightens the poet's awareness that the "tongues of the exiled dead" continue to speak to the living. This awareness gradually matures into the death-defying search for new spiritual and poetic categories that directs Wright toward traditional African societies, rituals, and mythologies in "A Nuer Sacrifice" and "Death As History." "Sketch for an Aesthetic Project" and "Beginning Again," which close *The Homecoming Singer*, are tentative efforts at weaving memories and discontent into a poetic design beyond individual experience.

The Homecoming Singer is a prelude to *Soothsayers and Omens*, the first volume of a poetic cycle that includes *Explications/Interpretations*, *Dimensions of History*, and *The Double Invention of Komo*. Placed in this order, these formidable book-length poems delineate a meticulously conceived dramatic movement. The formal procedures in these and later volumes are extravagant; the linguistic and semantic texture is often of an almost forbidding density. An amalgam of Italian, German, and Spanish interspersed with Dogon and Bambara ideograms, Wright's language is only inadequately described as "English." Employing African American musical forms such as the blues and jazz as well as a host of Caribbean and Latin American song and dance forms, Wright's poems also attempt to make English verse a hospitable environment for grammars and metrics of other languages.

Significantly titled "The Charge," the poem that opens *Soothsayers and Omens* focuses on a gathering of fathers and sons "in the miracle/ of [their] own memories." With the rise of a female principle in "The Appearance of a Lost Goddess," the poet identifies himself as an initiate charged with the responsibility to reconstruct eclipsed and severed ties between generations and cultures. This reconstruction begins to take shape in the six short poems entitled "Sources" that commence Wright's systematic investigation of African cosmologies. The "Sources" poems rely heavily on West African and pre-Columbian mythologies, both of which become part of cross-cultural memory. The two longer poems that follow and change the pace of the first part, "Benjamin Banneker Helps to Build a City" and "Benjamin Banneker Sends His 'Almanac' to Thomas Jefferson," weave elements of Dogon theology around excerpts from the letters of the African American astronomer, an "uneasy" stranger in his own land who laments slavery's injustices.

Dogon ritual plays an even more significant role in part 4, the title of which, "Second Conversations with Ogotemmêli," refers specifically to Marcel Griaule's studies of Dogon religion and, more broadly, to Wright's extensive research in cultural anthropology. These poems of apprenticeship invoke different elements and stages of the creation of the universe, represented by the water spirit Nommo, creator of the First Word, his twin Amma, Lébé, guardian of the dead, and the Pale Fox, agent of chaos. Wright's "Conversations" are substantially different from Griaule's field notes. For Wright, Ogotemmêli is not an informant but a spiritual guide, a "nani" whose silences presage the language of redemption with which to mend the cracked universe. As "Homecoming," a poem laced with quotations from Dante Alighieri's *La divina commedia* (c. 1320; *The Divine Comedy*) demonstrates, the terms and trajectory of Wright's passage to Africa are also indebted to Dante's search, even if the spiritual map Wright's initiate designs is rather different.

If *Soothsayers and Omens* is the first step in the articulation of a spiritual order, *Explications/Interpretations* marks the next logical stage in Wright's African-Hellenic-Judaic discourse. Recalling his stay in Scotland from 1971 to 1973, this volume introduces a new cast of characters on the stage of the central dramatic poem, "MacIntyre, the Captain, and the Saints." The "dialogues" in this poem bring into view personal and intellectual ties with Scotland. MacIntyre, the Irish/Scottish clan to which the names Murphy and Wright can be traced, is Wright's autobiographical persona who, instead of conversing with Ogotemmêli, now turns for inspiration to astronomer David Hume, poet Hugh MacDiarmid, and anthropologist Robert Rattray. This poem acknowledges its debt to Ezra Pound's *Cantos* (1925, 1969) by introducing the use of ideographs, which Wright takes further in *Dimensions of History* and *The Double Invention of Komo*.

Explications/Interpretations is also energized by the rhythms of African American music. The poem is divided into three parts, "Polarity's Trio," "Harmony's Trio," and "Love's Dozen," titles that indicate Wright's concern with music and number. That the rhythms of writing and speaking are formal articulations of the poet's being is crucial to understanding the dynamics of *Explications/Interpretations*, and indeed of all Wright's poems. The division of the poems into groups of three, six, and twelve (plus one) already creates a sense of rhythm, which is then rendered explicit in "The Twenty-Two Tremblings of the Postulant." Subtitled "Improvisations Surrounding the Body," this poem exemplifies Wright's kind of blues poetry: The compositional principle derives not from the call-and-response structure of the blues stanza but from the arrangement of the twenty-two short poems across sequences of chords. Each poem corresponds not only to a part of the human body but also to a musical bar associated with a specific chord, either I, IV, or V. That the final two bars are "tacit" brings the total number of bars to twenty-four, the musical equivalent of a (doubled) blues line. These distinctive rhythms of African American culture are the sounds of flesh and bone that constitute the poems' (and the poet's) ontology, their "grammar of being."

Explications/Interpretations' emphasis on the body as a site of knowledge and action is indicative of Wright's rejection of dichotomies: For him, spirituality is no more separate from materiality than male is from female. Each is a "twin" of the other; the desired relationship between them is balance. This is most clearly articulated in "The Continuing City: Spirit and Body" and "The Body," two poems that lay out aesthetic and philosophical principles indebted to Ghanian politician and philosopher J. B. Danquah. Wright gives further insight into these complex designs in an essay that may well be called his poetic manifesto: "Desire's Design, Vision's Resonance: Black Poetry's Ritual and Historical Voice" (1987).

Wright's project of claiming the knowledge of European and African theologies as part of the creative life of the Americas comes into full view in *Dimensions of History*. Though dedicated to the late Francis Fergusson, this book owes its most significant debt to Wilson Harris' notion of "vision as historical dimension." In *Dimensions of History*, the tripartite structure of *Explications/Interpretations* is more explicitly associated with the stages of an initiation ritual: separation, transition, (re)incorporation. Part 1, "The Second Eye of the World. The Dimension of Rites and Acts," performs this link by being itself divided into three poems. It also includes a Dogon ideogram that represents the separation of the twins, male and female, at the moment of circumcision. According to Wright, the historical dimension of that separation within an African American context is (enforced) exile. This predicament becomes the ground for the special kinship the poet shares with his other selves, the dead whose claims he seeks to understand in a godless land. Du Bois and Crispus Attucks are now joined by Frederick Douglass, Saint Augustine, the Haitian insurrectionist Toussaint Louverture, and many others who meet in a text that abounds with allusions and references to Aztec, Mayan, Incaic, Egyptian, Arabic, Christian, Yoruba, Akan, and, of course, Dogon and Bambara mythologies. Ogotemmêli's return as the blind sage at the beginning of the second poem prophesies healing: "Anochecí enfermo amanecí bueno" (I went to bed sick, I woke up well).

"Modulations. The Aesthetic Dimension" introduces various Caribbean and Latin American musical forms and instruments such as the Cuban *son* and the *bandola*, a fifteen-string Colombian guitar. These shorter poems, distributed across "Rhythms, Charts, and Changes," "The Body Adorned and Bare," and "Retablos" (votive paintings), prepare the ground for Wright's "Log Book of Judgments," a series of ethical and aesthetic principles distilled from the persona's historical and ritualistic experiences. They culminate in these lines from "Metà-A and the A of Absolutes":

> I am good when I hear the changes in my body
> echo all my changes down the years,
> when what I know indeed is what I would
>   know in deed.

Dimensions closes with "Landscapes. The Physical Dimension," the literary architecture of which returns to the history of the conquest of the Americas and to Náhua (Aztec) mythology and poetry. The most notable formal aspects of this final part are the encyclopedic monoliths that list the vital statistics of five American nations: Venezuela, Colombia, Panama, Mexico, and the United States. The spaces between these building blocks are filled with Wright's own enchanted mortar, an appropriate translation of the Náhuatl-infused Spanish idiom "cal y canto" (literally, mortar and song) Wright uses to join compositional principles with cross-cultural concerns. Wright's syncretic idiom represents the rhizomic weaves Wright's poem uncovers and refashions into what he calls "emblems of the ecstatic connection."

Dedicated to Griaule, *The Double Invention of Komo* qualifies as the most African of Wright's poems. Unlike *Elaine's Book*, Wright's feminist poem, or even *Boleros*, *The Double Invention of Komo* approaches (self)-knowledge from a decidedly masculine perspective. Wright's most sustained and ambitious effort in the genre of dramatic poetry, *The Double Invention of Komo* is a poetic performance of the initiation ceremonies of the all-male Komo society among the Bambara. These highly formalized procedures, detailed in Germaine Dieterlen and Youssouf Tata Cissé's *Les fondements de la société d'initiation du Komo* (1972), maintain the Bambara's traditional intellectual, religious, and social values. *Double Invention*'s conceptual and literary structures are based on the logic of this ritual. Of special importance are the 266 Great Signs that organize Bambara cosmology. Each ideogram inscribes a different "name" of the god in connection with the material objects and substances associated with Komo's altars, as in "*Sele*—tomb—copper." This sacred "grammar" of names Wright translates into a secular "alphabet" of creation and creativity.

The main task of *The Double Invention of Komo* is to fashion a language that would overcome exile and dispossession. To that end, writing simultaneously dismembers and reassembles meaning and community. Like the ritual scars on the body of the initiate, poetic writing confers kinship through knowledge of traditional values from different cultures. The poet's pen becomes something akin to a ritual knife cutting the initiate into kinship, marking him as a member of a special community. As the persona is promoted from an initiate to a "delegate," the statements made in *Dimensions* undergo reformulation:

> What is true is the incision.
> What is true is the desire for the incision,
> and the signs' flaming in the wound.

The Middle Passage, which the poet's journeys retrace and reverse, becomes a rite of passage that both remembers and heals the violent ruptures and dispersals of Africa's traditional cultures. Wright's key metaphor, the limbo, refers once again to

Harris, who conceives of this dance, created on the crowded slave ships, as a form of silent collective resistance. This "black limbo," first thematized in "The Albuquerque Graveyard" in *Homecoming Singer*, offers both mythic and historical grounds for Wright's continuing poetic explorations of music and dance as possible "gateways" toward cross-cultural kinship.

Bibliography
Benston, Kimberly W. "'I Yam What I Am': The Topos of (Un)naming in Afro-American Literature." In *Black Literature and Literary Theory*, edited by Henry Louis Gates, Jr. New York: Methuen, 1984. Situates the ways in which Wright names his poetic "self" in *Dimensions of History* and *Soothsayers and Omens* within the larger context of African American writing.

Callaloo 6 (Fall, 1983). This special issue includes an excellent interview in which Wright outlines the theories behind his poetry. Also contains a general introduction to Wright's poetry by Robert B. Stepto, an assessment of his early poetry by Gerald Barrax, and detailed commentary on the Benjamin Banneker poems by Vera M. Kutzinski.

Clifford, James. *The Predicament of Culture: Twentieth-Century Ethnography, Literature, and Art.* Cambridge, Mass.: Harvard University Press, 1988. This critical look at the rise of modern anthropology and its entwinement with literature is useful background reading for some of Wright's main sources, notably Marcel Griaule and his team. Equally relevant are Clifford's comments on the West's representations of other cultures and the negotiation of cultural differences.

Harris, Wilson. *The Womb of Space: The Cross-Cultural Imagination.* Westport, Conn.: Greenwood Press, 1983. While this study includes a brief discussion of *The Double Invention of Komo*, it is valuable primarily for its conceptualization of the literary dynamics of "the cross-cultural imagination." Though Wright's debt is to Harris' earlier writings, this book summarizes the main concepts and ideas that have guided Harris' thinking since the beginning of his career.

Kutzinski, Vera M. *Against the American Grain: Myth and History in William Carlos Williams, Jay Wright, and Nicolás Guillén.* Baltimore: Johns Hopkins University Press, 1987. The second part of this book, "The Black Limbo: Jay Wright's Mythology of Writing," provides the fullest available commentary on Wright's poetry. Focusing on *Dimensions of History* and its historical and theoretical sources, the discussion places Wright's cross-cultural poetics within the context of the diverse cultural and literary histories of the Americas. Detailed notes, index.

Okpewho, Isidore. "From a Goat Path in Africa: An Approach to the Poetry of Jay Wright." *Callaloo* 14, no. 3 (1991): 692-726. Locates Wright's exploration of cultural history within an African context. Focuses on *The Double Invention of Komo*.

Vera M. Kutzinski

THE POETRY OF AL YOUNG

Author: Al Young (1939-   )
Type of work: Poetry
First published: Dancing, 1969; *The Song Turning Back into Itself*, 1971; *Geography of the Near Past*, 1976; *The Blues Don't Change: New and Selected Poems*, 1982

Al Young's distinctive and finely wrought poetry documents the personal odyssey of a clear-sighted and sensitive man in a period of social and political turmoil. Young's poetry is seldom overtly political manifesto or social commentary. He is a practitioner of a time-honored tradition of lyric poetry that comments on the larger issues of society by a close introspection of everyday life and private emotions.

Young's writing has earned him numerous awards, including a Wallace E. Stegner Creative Writing Fellowship, the Pushcart Prize, a Guggenheim Fellowship, the Before Columbus Foundation American Book Award, a National Endowment for the Arts Fellowship, and a Fulbright Fellowship that enabled him to travel and work in Eastern Europe. He has taught at several institutions, including Rice University, Stanford University, and the University of California at Santa Cruz and at Berkeley. In addition to poetry, Young is also the author of several highly acclaimed novels, a trilogy of innovative "musical memoirs," and screenplays for such Hollywood films as *Sparkle* (1976) and *Uptown Saturday Night* (1974). It is poetry, however, that first brought him to attention as an important voice in contemporary American letters.

The son of Albert and Mary Campbell Young, poet Albert James Young was born in Ocean Springs, Mississippi, on May 31, 1939. His father, a professional jazz musician during the 1930's, became an autoworker when he moved the family to Detroit, Michigan, in 1946. During his youth, Young spent summers in rural Mississippi but attended public schools in Detroit, graduating from Central High School. Young attended the University of Michigan at Ann Arbor and the University of California at Berkeley while also pursuing his own professional career as a jazz flutist, singer, and guitarist in the folk music style popular on college campuses in the early 1960's. He received a B.A. from the University of California in 1969 and published his first collection of poems that same year.

"The coming of age of America's black artists continues to be a subject that's rarely touched upon," Young has written. In his own case, he was from his early years a voracious reader and avid listener to all types of music, and his early poetry shows the influence of these wide-ranging interests. Jazz music made a lasting impact. In the late 1950's, he attended concerts at Detroit's New Music Society that featured local musicians such as Yusef Lateef, Charles McPherson, Donald Byrd, Kenny Burrell, Pepper Adams, and others who would later achieve international reputations. Young was impressed both by the respect these musicians enjoyed in the community and the seriousness with which they approached their art. Jazz at that period was not viewed merely as entertainment. In *Bodies and Soul: Musical Memoirs* (1981), Young recalled that any jazz worthy of the name was expected to be *about* something. The main idea was still to venture out there and play what you had to say meaningfully, with as much feeling and personal inventiveness as you needed to get your story across to those with whom you were communing. It was a two-way avenue of expression along which player and hearer drove and refueled one another and yet, at heart, were one.

As he made the transition in the late 1960's from playing music professionally to writing poetry, Young adapted the ideal of jazz performance to literary composition. The interest in jazz from his teenage years was blended with experiences of Negro spirituals and tales learned from his grandmother Lillian Campbell in the small hamlet of Pachuta, Mississippi. He later wrote of her, "She is as Southern as meat brown pecans,/ or fried green tomato, or moon pies." It is this African American heritage, both rural and urban, that Young's poems record and examine. Like poet Michael S. Harper, Young focuses on the personal testimony that is inherent in jazz playing and in the African American religious tradition as the most authentic element of his aesthetic approach. Young's work, as he states in "Poetry," is based on his own personal experience but reflects the universal "longing to have known everything/ & to have been everywhere/ before the world dissolves."

A poem such as "Myself When I Am Real," written in 1967, demonstrates Young's handling of his diverse sources. The title is taken from a recording by jazz bassist and composer Charles Mingus. The poet intends the work partly as a tribute to the musician and partly as an impressionistic report of the mood inspired by Mingus' music. Music is never actually mentioned in the poem, which begins with a paraphrase of a traditional blues verse: "The sun is shining in my backdoor/ right now." The poet then expresses, in lines reminiscent of the metaphors of the Persian poet Jalal al-Din Rumi, a mystic of the Islamic Sufi tradition and founder of an order of dervishes whose dance meditations are performed to the text of his poems, a feeling of losing his individual personality and "melting" in the penetrating sunlight that seems to represent a spiritual reality:

> Love of life is love of God
> sustaining all life,
> > sustaining me
> when wrong or un-self-righteous
> in drunkenness & in peace

This sudden awareness leads to a reintegration of the individual self with both God and nature:

> > He who loves me
> is me. I shall return to Him always,
> my heart is rain, my brain earth,
> but there is only one sun & forever
> it shines forth one endless poem
> of which my ranting, my whole life
> is but breath.

The symmetry of this poem is accomplished in the final lines, which return to the opening blues motif and create a meaningful variation: "I long to fade back/ into this door of sun forever." These lines show a skillful and sophisticated poet at work, one able to simultaneously project the cosmic humanism of Walt Whitman, the life-affirming sensibility of Negro spirituals and the blues, and a convincing adaptation of classical Islamic poetic conventions.

The unexpectedly logical metaphor of "melting" in sunlight is taken literally in a spiritual sense and followed by the even more unexpected metaphor of "fading" into the bright sunlight that becomes surrealistically synonymous with a door that serves as an entrance to the infinity of the universe. Although Young's later poems do not reveal their literary influences as immediately as does "Myself When I Am Real," all of his work is grounded in a thorough knowledge and recall of a wide spectrum of classical and contemporary literature, philosophy, and folklore. Young's use of such sources, however, is not academic or pedantic. "As a kid," he has written, "I got the idea that still persists with me, that when we look at any painting or piece of writing or listen to any piece of music, what we are actually doing is searching for the human spirit."

Each of Young's collections of poems demonstrates his firm commitment to such a humanistic aesthetic. *Dancing* contains twenty-seven poems, most of which deal explicitly with the theme or metaphor of the dance. The opening poem of the sequence, "A Dance for Militant Dilettantes," positions Young in opposition to the so-called "revolutionary black poets" who achieved popularity during the 1960's. Using satire, Young presents a poem intended to offer "advice to young poets":

> You got to learn to put in about
> stone black fists
> coming up against white jaws
> & red blood splashing
> down those fabled wine & urine-
> soaked hallways

Such a poetry of unsavory detail, a parody of Amiri Baraka's well-known poem "Black Art," will bring its author popularity because readers of black poetry "don't want no bourgeois woogie/ they want them a militant nigger/ in a fiji haircut."

Although Young clearly is opposed to irresponsible rabble-rousing presented in the guise of poetry, he does not himself avoid confronting and protesting what racism has done to African American people. In "A Dance for Ma Rainey," he declares that he will create a song in honor of the great blues singer that will embody the "redblooded american agony . . . that bred/ & battered us all." He intends the poem to reverse the detrimental affects of racism by depicting

> our beautiful brave black people
> who no longer need to jazz
> or sing to themselves in murderous vibrations

> or play the veins of their strong tender arms
> with needles
> to prove that we're still here

Young's collaged images of music and social dislocation, of the needles that play phonograph records and the needles used by drug addicts, force the reader to consider whether the sorrow and desperation that is often the subject matter of the blues singer is really equivalent to the antisocial and self-destructive behavior caused by racism's attempt to deny that African Americans are beautiful, brave, or entitled to the same respect and opportunities enjoyed by others.

Similarly, in "Dancing in the Street," the poet announces his desire to "bring back a more golden picture of us . . . healthy black masters/ of our own destiny." Other poems carefully present the tragic alternatives to such a positive self-image. In "2 Tales from *Love in Los Angeles*," Young contrasts portraits of a penurious old man barely surviving in his rented room and a reckless young black man distracted by the so-called prizes of American society. The young man's expensive imported sports car, white female companion, and chemical hairstyle are emblems of prodigality that clearly rate the old man's (and the poet's) disapproval. Young makes his point without strident rhetoric.

Young's poetic themes often reflect quiet introspection, love for women, concern for friends, and impressions recorded while traveling in cities in many different countries. "Paris" embraces several of these themes. The poet notes his foreignness even though he is excited by the fabled glamour of the city. His ruminations soon turn to politics and personal memories. Soberly, he notes:

> this is France
> another colonial power environment
> far from Richard Wright's
> or my own wrong Mississippi

Paris, the poet and reader understand, is also the adopted home of Richard Wright, the older African American novelist who moved there to escape American racial inequities only to discover that European imperialism produced similar problems. Young's own childhood memories of Mississippi are the subject of many poems and elicit both nostalgia and bitterness. He recalls, in "A Little More Travelling Music," the poverty of his youthful surroundings and the way that people found a way to help one another. He speaks of his mother, who "had a knack for snapping juicy fruit gum/ & for keeping track of the generations of chilrens/ she had raised, reared & no doubt forwarded." Depicting himself as one of those Southern children sent north to get a better education and avoid the hard life of farm labor, the speaker of the poem studies hard in Detroit, goes to college, and becomes conversant with the world of books and ideas. He is never able, however, to "forget all that motherly music."

The Song Turning Back into Itself includes further reminiscences of Mississippi and the poet's struggle to realize his own identity. The play on words in the book's

title prefigures the ambiguities of race and class that are the subject of several poems. "The Problem of Identity," a prose poem, presents early male role models
including the persona's father, the heavyweight boxing champion Joe Louis (a native
of Alabama who also migrated to Detroit), and a family friend named Otis who had
a talent for drawing but "went up to Chicago, sadness, madness, wed, bled, dope,
hopelessness, catapulted into the 20th century." Many of the poems that follow recount a personal struggle to avoid the fate that befalls Otis. "Sunday Illumination"
celebrates the joy of small pleasures such as hiking in the Berkeley, California, hills.
The physical exertion and the beauty of both the natural landscape and the suburban
skyline in the distance bring the poet a restorative vision that he feels is similar to
the Buddhist concept of *satori*, or enlightenment. Appropriately, the poem is written
in the verse paragraph form used by William Blake and Walt Whitman, both of
whom recorded similar messages about the human being's relationship to both the
natural and the constructed environment.

Young, however, is not a poet much attracted to landscapes; his primary concern
is with other people. In "I Arrive in Madrid," he notes that "The wretched of the
earth/ are my brothers." He is immediately aware that this perception is not much
more than a facile political slogan that rings as hollow as the travel agent's or the
government's "publicity" that gives Madrid, and other cities, false faces that actually mask their human realities.

Seeking the insight to penetrate such misleading superficiality remains the poet's
goal in *Geography of the Near Past*, which is notable for a series of satirical poems
titled "Boogie with O. O. Gabugah," purporting to be the works of a stereotypical
"street poet." Young's parody of militant "rappers" is pointedly funny and can be
read as a restatement of the early "A Dance for Militant Dilettantes." Other poems
in this collection present a darker mood. Works such as "Herrick Hospital, Fifth
Floor," "Visiting Day," "Roland Navarro (1939-1961)," "Ho," and "Some Recent
Fiction" attempt to count the losses and map some understanding of how racism,
drugs, cynicism, and violence are destroying America's youth. These poems, however, are balanced by lyrics about the birth of the poet's son and buoyant memoirs
such as "New Orleans Intermission." Here, an encounter on the St. Charles Street
trolley causes Young to question the very necessity of poetry:

> an old American, classically black,
> spots me as a tourist & softly explains
> how he dont have to take snapshots
> no more since he can more or less
> picture in his mind what's keepable

Young's poems, of course, are more than mere snapshots and are also his way of
highlighting "what's keepable" from his travels and personal interactions.

Young's employment of subtle visual imagery, in a manner that suggests the Spanish poet Federico García Lorca, is evident in lines such as "Old emotions like pow-
dery tenements/ undulate in the July heat" from the poem "City Home/Detroit." In

such works, as in those that almost imperceptibly radiate the wisdom in vernacular African American speech, Young focuses his own and the reader's attention and goes about the crucial business of "refining your eyesight, opening your ears/ for a liberating music."

The twenty-six new poems included in *The Blues Don't Change: New and Selected Poems* offer treatment of familiar themes such as the creative impulse represented by jazz, meditations on nature, and the nature of friendship. Tight in structure (often only nine or twelve lines), written in a simple but elegant vernacular diction, these are the work of a mature poet who has mastered all elements of his craft. All of Young's poetry—brilliant in perception, subtle in its understated eloquence, always reaching toward spiritual insight—represents the tradition of "testifying" that can be found both in the aesthetic of jazz performance and in the Southern church that is the matrix of much African American art and folklore.

"Sadness is the theme of existence," Young writes in the poem "Detroit 1958," "joy its variations." What must not be missed, however, is that his poems do not dwell on painful moments; like a true jazz improviser, Young is more concerned with spinning out ever more marvelous and inventive variations. "Let us laugh/ each at the other/ & be friends," he sings. Assembled from the diverse impressions, observations, and reminiscences of his world, Young's variations—and the message of his poetry—simply remind readers that their business is to create more joy.

Bibliography

Broughton, Irv, ed. *The Writer's Mind: Interviews with American Authors.* Vol. 3. Fayetteville: University of Arkansas Press, 1990. Contains an overview of Young's literary career.

Johnson, Charles. "The Men." In *Being and Race: Black Writing Since 1970.* Bloomington: Indiana University Press, 1988. Commentary on Young by a celebrated novelist, who notes that Young "is distinguished by the emphasis in his large body of work on a gentle vision of black American life that is, at bottom, harmonious and spiritual."

O'Brien, John, ed. *Interviews with Black Writers.* New York: Liveright, 1973. Includes a concise but important interview focusing on Young's early poems and the novel *Snakes.*

Schultz, Elizabeth. "Search for 'Soul Space': A Study of Al Young's *Who Is Angelina?* (1975) and the Dimensions of Freedom." In *The Afro-American Novel Since 1960,* edited by Peter Bruck and Wolfgang Karrer. Amsterdam: Grüner, 1982. Excellent analysis of Young's novel, offering comment on his poetic technique and attitudes on racial issues.

Young, Al. "Interview with Al Young." Interview by Nathaniel Mackey. *MELUS* 5 (Winter, 1978): 32-51. Detailed and useful interview covering Young's work as poet, novelist, and Hollywood screenwriter.

Lorenzo Thomas

POSSESSING THE SECRET OF JOY

Author: Alice Walker (1944-   )
Type of work: Novel
Type of plot: Social realism
Time of plot: The 1920's to the 1980's
Locale: The United States, Europe, and Olinka (Africa)
First published: 1992

Principal characters:

TASHI EVELYN JOHNSON, the protagonist, reared until she is a
  young woman as a member of the Olinka tribe
ADAM, Tashi's husband, on the surface a good husband and
  provider
OLIVIA, Adam's sister and Tashi's best friend since they were
  prepubescent girls in Africa
MZEE, (CARL JUNG), a friend to Tashi and Adam, a therapist, for
  a while, to Tashi
BENTU MORAGA (BENNY), Tashi and Adam's son, who is slightly
  retarded
LISETTE, Mzee's niece and Adam's lover, a white woman who is
  the mother of Adam's son Pierre
PIERRE, Lisette and Adam's son
M'LISSA, the Olinkan who circumcises young Olinkan girls

The Novel

In *Possessing the Secret of Joy*, Alice Walker displays her evolving inventiveness in
telling a story. The novel is a series of interior monologues interspersed with a few
letters that describe the story's major events and the major character's interpretations of and reactions to those events.

Tashi Evelyn Johnson, as the novel's central focus, has the first interior monologue, which begins "I did not realize for a long time that I was dead." Subsequent
monologues by Tashi and others reveal what leads Tashi to this assessment of her
life. Tashi's opening line gives in miniature Tashi's state of mind. Walker's attention
to the states of mind of characters provides the novel's structure.

Shortly into the novel, as Tashi tells about her life, the final major events are
revealed. Tashi is in prison awaiting her execution for murdering M'Lissa, a *tsunga*,
the Olinkan woman who has become celebrated in her own country and in the rest of
the Western world for her life's work as a circumciser of females. The novel's task is
to show what led Tashi to kill and why M'Lissa is so celebrated.

As Tashi tells about key moments in her life, she emphasizes the fact that many
people believe her to be psychotic. She then begins the process of talking about the

vast amount of formal therapy she has received and how none of it has been effective in helping her. If she is insane, then her emotional and mental illness must be connected to why she is in prison awaiting execution for murdering M'Lissa. If so, what did M'Lissa do that could create so much damage in Tashi's life?

Tashi, Olivia, Adam, Lisette, Benny, Pierre, and a few other characters collectively reconstruct the history that accounts for the novel's present-time events and that explains the final forms that Tashi and other characters have taken.

Weaving in and out of time from the 1920's, when Tashi is a child in Africa, to the late 1980's, when Tashi is awaiting death, the novel scrutinizes an Olinkan ritual and its trail of destruction. Tashi and the females of her tribe are circumcised when they are between the ages of five and eleven. The circumcision is revealed to be one of the most barbaric forms of female mutilation known. Many of the girls die from infections soon after the ritual is performed. Tashi's favorite sister, Dura, dies in this way. More important to the novel's progression are the effects the ritual has on those girls who do not die. Most of them have numerous urinary tract infections throughout their lives. Many of them cannot have sexual intercourse without great pain. Many of the women experience so much pain that their husbands either refuse to have sex with them and seek partners elsewhere or insist that their wives have anal intercourse. If a woman becomes pregnant, which does happen in spite of the fact that sexual penetration is difficult, she almost always has a painful delivery.

In detailing what the Olinkan ritual does to women, Tashi tries to understand why the practice was never stopped. In remembering her own circumcision, she recalls that no one protested against the ritual. She then becomes obsessed with the woman who performed the ritual on her and who killed her sister Dura.

The difficulty of trying to live a normal life after the ritual has been performed is the focus of the novel. Tashi's monologues reveal that the aftermath of the ritual has literally driven her insane. Her insanity is exacerbated by the fact that once she moves to the United States there are no therapists who can understand the ritual's long-lasting human damage and help her. As a middle-aged woman, she finally comes to understand that only she can cure herself, by taking action against the woman who has literally or figuratively killed so many Olinkan girls and women.

The Characters

Tashi, who was only a sketch of a character in *The Color Purple* (1982) and *The Temple of My Familiar* (1989), is one of the more memorable characters to people Walker's fiction. Because Walker chooses to present her characters' traits from a subjective perspective, by using the device of the interior monologue, Tashi is able to say that which she has been unable to express to others, including her husband, Adam, and her sister-in-law, Olivia.

Moreover, through interior monologues, Walker shows how Tashi deals with a lifetime of pain and suffering that has its genesis in the female circumcision ritual of the Olinka. Tashi's character is portrayed as "damaged goods," and she tells the extent of the damage and how it has altered almost every aspect of her life.

A major problem for Tashi is that she thinks of herself as insane because no one is able to understand the horror of her childhood and how physical and emotional scarring have made her a shell of a woman. Tashi feels inadequate and unloved—even though she intellectually knows that Adam loves her—and less than whole.

As she revisits through memory what the *tsunga* did to her, her sister Dura, and other young girls, Tashi becomes obsessed with analyzing what the circumcision ritual means and why it continues. Her reflection becomes an examination of the impact of the ritual on herself and on her culture, and it is through examination, facing the horror directly, that she resolves to do something about it. When she decides to act, to return to Africa and kill M'Lissa, she gains the first semblance of an authentic self that can live and be a part of the world again. In Africa, when she confronts M'Lissa directly and asks her why she mutilated girls, Tashi comes to understand the power of the ritual in her culture and why it must be stopped. She believes that her own death is a small price to pay to save some young girls' lives.

Walker's headings for Tashi's monologues are inventive and relate to Tashi's movement toward wholeness. Early in the novel, many headings are labeled with a single name, such as Tashi or Evelyn. As the novel progresses, headings are often two names, such as Tashi-Evelyn or Evelyn-Tashi, suggesting the duality of American and African experiences that have had a major impact on who Tashi is. Toward the novel's end, as a way to indicate Tashi's movement toward a fuller sense of self, the headings for Tashi's interior monologues are Tashi-Evelyn-Mrs. Johnson, and later Tashi-Evelyn-Johnson-Soul.

Other characters are developed in a similar way. They tell their own stories. All of them in one way or another have been influenced by the Olinkan ritual. Adam, who has devoted his life to Christian missionary work, discovers that having a healthy sexual relationship with Tashi is more than he can handle, for the act of sexual intercourse is always painful for Tashi. He has a longtime affair with Lisette, even though he knows it is not Christian to do so. Tashi's emotional problems also wear Adam out, and he looks forward to the twice-yearly visits to Europe to be with Lisette.

Olivia, Tashi's childhood friend, reveals through her monologues her own struggle to understand Tashi. Even as she acknowledges that her attempts to assist Tashi have failed, she is always there for Tashi. She is the one who takes the lead in trying to acquire adequate defense representation for Tashi at her trial. At the novel's end, she is the one to continue Tashi's efforts to destroy the ritual.

Pierre, Adam's son by Lisette, is one of the few characters who actually understands something of what it means to be Tashi. As a male, he perhaps does not understand all that female circumcision entails in a woman's life, but he does understand what it means to be split between two cultures. As the product of a white European woman and an African American man, Pierre identifies with both parents but does not feel complete acceptance by either. He reveals to Tashi that his sense of duality extends to his sexual orientation. He is bisexual and comfortable with that.

Benny, presented in a way not too different from how William Faulkner developed the character of Benjy in *The Sound and the Fury* (1929), is a slow thinker, but he is remarkably wise. Walker's rendering of his lists and how he uses them to make sense of what is happening to his mother and the spectacle of her trial is a masterful achievement. Like the Faulkner character, Benny intuitively knows what is right and wrong, and he knows that something very wrong has been inflicted on his mother.

Themes and Meanings

Possessing the Secret of Joy advances two major ideas simultaneously: African girls and women are victimized by traditions that do not value the life of girls and women, and Africa should not always be viewed as a panacea of cultural "goodness." Walker, through Tashi's story, looks at African traditions and rituals and says that not everything in one's cultural past should be honored or kept alive.

The novel carefully details how pervasive and destructive the ritual of female circumcision is in several African ethnic groups. In showing one woman's experience with the effects of the ritual and how Tashi resolves to symbolically end it when she murders M'Lissa, Walker suggests that no cultural tradition is so monolithic that it cannot be defeated.

To indicate how terrible the ritual is, Walker devotes significant amounts of narrative space to graphic renderings of how the ritual is performed, the instruments used, the physical consequences on the subjects of the ritual, and the gynecological problems subjects bear for the remainder of their lives. Walker, in providing such graphic details, insists that readers know and understand the severity of the ritual and its toll on human lives. The novel begins with Tashi saying that she is dead.

As if the rendering of the physical aspects of the ritual is not enough, the novel also charts the heavy psychological toll it has on women. The novel becomes a record of the process through which Tashi tries to recover a lost and defeated self, a self defeated by people of her own culture, not some outside oppressor. In the revelation of the psychological costs of the ritual, Walker welds content to form. The story can be told only from the perspective of a woman who endured the ritual's physical and mental destruction. Moreover, only a victim can make the choices and create the strength to take actions to let the world know what silently happens to African girls and women. Tashi's act of murdering M'Lissa focuses worldwide attention on a problem that no one had noticed or protested against. Beginning in the silence of her own mind, with its pain and suffering, Tashi refuses to forget what happened to her as a child. Her pain and her memories help her to accomplish two things: She kills M'Lissa and she recovers, even if only until her execution, a sense of wholeness.

Whether or not Tashi's killing of M'Lissa symbolically puts a stop to the ritual or actually destroys it is left to those who remain after Tashi is executed. Adam, Olivia, and Pierre, who lived through Tashi's pain and who are witnesses to the meaning of her death, stand ready to continue Tashi's private, then public, outcry against female circumcision. Equally significant, Tashi's African sisters have Tashi as a model to follow in speaking out against an outdated and dangerous tradition.

Critical Context

Possessing the Secret of Joy joins Walker's previous fiction in attempting to make the world better for black people. In Walker's fiction, black communities, cultural attitudes, and values must be revised before such communities adequately serve all of their members, particularly black women. Walker's first cycle of fiction, which includes *The Third Life of Grange Copeland* (1970) and *In Love and Trouble: Stories of Black Women* (1973), presents the dilemmas of several black women who silently obey cultural traditions that are not always in their best interests. In these two works, African American women do all they can for the group. The group often is not appreciative of the women's efforts and requires black women to act according to outdated cultural scripts that impede the women's choices for growth and development as individuals.

Meridian (1976) and *You Can't Keep a Good Woman Down* (1981) represent an intermediate stage in Walker's fiction. Black women discover alternative ways of serving their communities and serving themselves. This discovery often means that black women reject some of the sexist assumptions that are part of some black communities.

Possessing the Secret of Joy belongs most clearly to a third cycle of fiction, which includes *The Color Purple* and *The Temple of My Familiar.* Black women are presented as taking charge of their lives, no matter what state they may be in. From the physically and psychologically abused Celie of *The Color Purple* to Tashi, these women are determined to make changes in their lives and in their communities. They are bent on revising their communities so that what happened to them will not happen to others. They create new options for both men and women and healthy environments for black children.

This novel, along with Walker's other fiction, is a major part of the growing tradition of black women's literature that creates new visions for readers and new possibilities for black communities. Works by Gloria Naylor, Toni Morrison, Gayl Jones, Terry McMillan, and others have created a new literary landscape, complete with new characters, new issues, new language, and new themes that mark a major new achievement in African American literature.

Bibliography

Banks, Erma, and Keith Byerman. *Alice Walker: An Annotated Bibliography.* New York: Garland Press, 1989. Collects the major and minor material written on Alice Walker from 1968 to 1986.

Bloom, Harold, ed. *Alice Walker.* New York: Chelsea House, 1989. Major critics from a variety of critical and theoretical perspectives discuss Walker's fiction, nonfiction, and poetry.

Gates, Henry Louis, Jr., ed. *Reading Black, Reading Feminist: A Critical Anthology.* New York: Meridian, 1990. Gathers major criticism from a black feminist perspective. Discusses major black women writers, including Walker.

Wall, Cheryl A., ed. *Changing Our Own Words: Essays on Criticism, Theory, and*

Writing by Black Women. New Brunswick, N.J.: Rutgers University Press, 1989. Major black feminist critics analyze the black women's literary tradition.

Willis, Susan. *Specifying: Black Women Writing the American Experience.* Madison: University of Wisconsin Press, 1987. Considers the many alternative creative visions that black women writers contribute to American literature. Places black women in four traditions: American literature, African American literature, black women's literature, and women's literature.

Charles P. Toombs

PRAISESONG FOR THE WIDOW

Author: Paule Marshall (1929-   )
Type of work: Novel
Type of plot: Social realism
Time of plot: The late 1970's, with flashbacks to the 1940's, 1950's, and 1960's
Locale: Grenada and Carriacou; Brooklyn and North White Plains, New York; South
  Carolina Sea Islands; Tatem, South Carolina
First published: 1983

> *Principal characters:*
> AVATARA "AVEY" JOHNSON, a middle-aged, middle-class African
>   American widow
> LEBERT JOSEPH, the old rum-shop proprietor who serves as Avey
>   Johnson's spiritual mentor

The Novel

  Praisesong for the Widow traces Avey Johnson's journey toward self-knowledge, a process involving not only her own personal identity but also her identification with her family, her past, and her African heritage.

  The novel begins in the late 1970's, during Avey Johnson's third Caribbean cruise. Suddenly she begins to experience an uneasy, unspecified feeling, not quite illness but a "mysterious welling up in her stomach," "a clogged and swollen feeling." Two additional occurrences alarm her: First, she does not even recognize herself in the dining-room mirrors one evening, and then she begins to dream again (something she had not done since 1963). In her dream, Aunt Cuney, whom she had not thought about for years, drags a resistant Avey, in high heels and mink stole, toward the Ibo Landing in Tatem. This dream (so real that Avey's wrists are sore the next morning) and her vague sick feelings convince Avey that she must leave the ship, and she disembarks at Grenada to await the first flight back to New York.

  In a second dream at the hotel, Avey's dead husband appears to her, accusing her of wasting their money by forfeiting fifteen hundred dollars in leaving the cruise early. Money had become "the whole of his transubstantiated body and blood." That and his tone of voice remind Avey of a night in 1945 when their lives changed forever. Jay Johnson, Avey's husband, had always been fun and affectionate. He worked hard as a department-store warehouse clerk while Avey advanced at the state motor vehicles department between her pregnancies. Avey's third unexpected pregnancy drove a wedge between husband and wife, however; her unsuccessful self-abortion attempts and Jay's refusal to accept responsibility for the pregnancy led to a crisis. Barely able to walk or manage the five flights of stairs, lacking warm clothing and adequate heat while caring for the other two children, Avey resented Jay's freedom, and her jealousy increased as she imagined her husband alongside the department store's flirtatious white salesgirls. When Jay returned home late one evening and Avey confronted him with her suspicions, she heard the question that she would always remember: "Do you know who you sound like, who you even look like . . . ?" He meant the rowdy woman who could be heard in their apartment from the street below fetching her drunken husband home from the neighborhood bars every Friday night. For Jay, at that moment, the corruption of the street changed everything. On that night, Avey perceived Jay "take a slight step backwards," "straining to make his escape," and only through an act of sheer will returning to his wife and family. The man who enters the apartment that night is not the same man, though; he works two jobs from then on, takes correspondence and night-school courses, and eventually builds an accounting business so he can move his family from Halsey Street to North White Plains, from the ghetto to the suburbs, from a black life to an almost white one. Her dream and further contemplation cause Avey Johnson to realize that she did not mourn her husband's death because the man she loved had died in 1945. It is only in Grenada that Avey comes to terms with her loss.

When Avey Johnson ducks into Lebert Joseph's rum shop, the course of her life is forever altered. She feels an inexplicable need to confess everything, including her odd dreams, to the old man who can read such dreams. When he convinces her to accompany him on the Carriacou Excursion (an annual pilgrimage by the island's former inhabitants), she hesitates. When he asks her, "And what you is?"—from what nation do you come?—and she cannot answer, he diagnoses her illness immediately: She is one of those people "who can't call their nation." Through songs, prayers, and dances, Avey Johnson is purged both physically and spiritually of excess—of too much food on the ship and in her own pantry, too much furniture, too many suitcases and clothes, too much of everything. Her participation in the inclusive "Carriacou Tramp" allows her to identify with the African diaspora, which will lead her to sell the house in North White Plains, return to her roots in South Carolina, and pass on to her grandsons and to her daughter's students the stories, history, and culture she has inherited.

The Characters

Avatara "Avey" Johnson is not a stereotypical African American protagonist. She is middle-aged, middle-class, and widowed. Her material comfort is by no means synonymous with satisfaction, however; Avey is a sixty-year-old woman who does not know who she is.

As her name implies, Avatara (from the root "avatar") is the incarnation of what has come before her, though she is unaware of that fact. Yet Avey is not merely a flat, symbolic representation of African American culture. She is a developing character struggling with her personal and racial past.

Avey's character is developed through a series of flashbacks, dreams, memories, and even vague, slightly nauseous feelings that she cannot completely identify. The novel traces Avey's growing awareness of how her childhood in Harlem, her annual trips to South Carolina, and her long marriage to Jerome "Jay" Johnson all readied her for her self-discovery on Carriacou as part of the larger community of African peoples.

Presented only through Avey's recollections and dreams, Jerome Johnson is a strong, middle-class black man who achieves the American Dream but, in the process, loses his soul. After years of working on a loading dock, selling vacuum cleaners door-to-door, studying correspondence courses, and eventually earning a college degree, Jerome Johnson becomes a successful accountant, a member of the Elks Lodge, and a respected Mason, but he has sacrificed his passion, his past, and his own people to do so. He is characterized as a man who gradually accepts his relationship to his wife as an obligation rather than as a delight and his family responsibilities as a sheer matter of will. Social and material success wholly determines his actions. It is for this reason that Avey cannot cry when he dies. The man she had loved and married, Jay Johnson, had passed away years before Jerome Johnson's death. His stasis becomes apparent to Avey only in her revelatory dream in the Grenada hotel room years later, when she sees him in his casket, adorned in his Mason's apron, hardly even recognizable to her. This vision of her husband and her life with him in the suburb of North White Plains, New York, pushes her onto Grenada's beach and toward her true self.

Lebert Joseph, the old rum-shop proprietor whom Avey meets on the beach, serves as Avey's spiritual mentor. A very old man, feeble and crippled, he plays a key role in Avey's search for identity. Avey is a woman without a nation, a past, or a family; Lebert Joseph is the archetypal patriarch and historian, "like some Old Testament prophet chronicling the lineage of his tribe." He is the all-knowing seer who can peer into Avey's heart and guide her to Carriacou and to her own racial and cultural roots as a member of the African diaspora. He is an almost mystical figure, seemingly able to transform himself into a feminine shape as he lithely and spiritedly demonstrates for Avey the Juba dance practiced on Carriacou. Avey notes that "even his foreshortened left leg had appeared to straighten itself out and grow longer as he danced." When he is leading the "Beg Pardon" ceremony, the diminutive old man appears overpowering as a consequence of his spiritual connections to his past and that of the African people.

Themes and Meanings

In *Praisesong for the Widow*, Paule Marshall examines the high cost at which African Americans purchase success in American society: the relinquishment of their history, their culture, and their individual identities. Avey Johnson represents the contemporary African American woman who has gained the American Dream and lost her soul. The novel traces her quest to recover her lost identity, which is only possible through the sacrifice of her middle-class trappings and the recovery of the rituals of her family and the other people of the African diaspora.

Cuney appears first in Avey's dream because she represents the most important piece of her past that Avey Johnson needs to recover: the stories of the Ibo Landing, the summers in Tatem, and the old folks circling in the Ring Shout. Avey remembers her walks with her aunt as a ritual, both she and Cuney donning ceremonially their two belts: one for practicality's sake and one for strength. As the old woman and little girl walked across the island, Avey learned the history of the place and its people, especially the slave Ibos who refused to set foot on the land because, as Cuney observed, "those pure-born Africans was people my gran' said could see in more ways than one. The kind can tell you 'bout things happened long before they was born and things to come long after they's dead." Cuney's grandmother reported that, seeing the awaiting slave owners, the Ibos simply walked across the water back to Africa. "Her body she always usta say might be in Tatem," Cuney said of her grandmother, "but her mind, her mind was long gone with the Ibos." Her African connection was never severed. On these walks, also, Avey watched the old Ring Shouters dancing. The stories and the dance were all part of Cuney's plan for Avey to engage in "a mission she couldn't even name yet had felt duty-bound to fulfill." The trappings of material success, however, bury Avey Johnson's sense of duty, her commitment to Cuney's legacy. Tatem's rituals become lost.

Sacrificing the rituals Jay and Avey Johnson shared on Halsey Street in Brooklyn early in their marriage to middle-class assimilation also contributes to Avey's loss of self. At one time, each album of Count Basie, Coleman Hawkins, and Ma Rainey (Jay's inheritance from his father) "became a sacred object, and each record inside an icon." Avey remembers that "the Jay who emerged from the music of an evening, the self that would never be seen down at the store, was open, witty, playful, even outrageous at times." He was a passionate man with a large mustache who danced barefoot with his wife on the wooden floor he had refinished himself. As he recited Langston Hughes's poetry, they ate coffee cake together every Sunday morning. Her fitful dream in the Grenada hotel room convinces Avey that when "the little private rituals and pleasures" she and Jay shared gave way to correspondence courses and door-to-door vacuum-cleaner sales after that Tuesday night, something terribly important had been lost: "something in those small rites, an ethos they held in common, had reached back beyond her life and beyond Jay's to join them to the vast unknown lineage that had made their being possible." Jay Johnson's search for middle-class status denied those rites.

The Carriacou rituals finally provide Avey Johnson with a clear sense of identity. The other pilgrims make her recall the wharf filled with Harlem picnickers, when she felt "a part of, indeed the center of, a huge wide confraternity," and now she begins to feel something akin to that again. Her transformation, however, is not immediate. A condition of her participation in the ceremony is clearly purification through purgation. The passage to the island proves both humiliating and healing to her; her physical illness returns, but this time in the form of uncontrollable vomiting and a "bloated mass . . . being propelled down also." Afterward, that bloated, welling feeling is gone, soothed by the kindness of the women elders and by the healing hands of Lebert Joseph's daughter. Rosalie and her maid perform a further symbolic cleansing, a laying on of hands, that prepares the way for Avey Johnson's acceptance into the community. Through a ritualistic bathing, "the emptiness at her center" evokes "a sense of a chord being struck." Following prayers and songs, nation after nation is called upon to dance, but not until the inclusive Carriacou

Tramp can Avey join in. She knows this dance; it is the Ring Shout the church people in Tatem performed many years before. Avey had finally made it across the road to the Ring Shout. "And for the first time since she was a girl, she felt the threads, that myriad of shiny, silken, brightly colored threads . . . which were thin to the point of invisibility yet as strong as the ropes at Coney Island. . . . she felt the threads streaming out from the old people around her in Lebert Joseph's yard." When the dance is over and again Avey Johnson is asked who she is, she recalls what Cuney had instructed her to respond always when she was a girl: "Avey, short for Avatara." She knows who she is and where she belongs.

Critical Context

Paule Marshall first gained attention in 1959 with the publication of her first novel, *Brown Girl, Brownstone*, a coming-of-age account in the tradition of Zora Neale Hurston's *Their Eyes Were Watching God* (1937) and Toni Morrison's *The Bluest Eye* (1970). It was followed by a short-story collection, *Soul, Clap Hands and Sing* (1961). Her second novel, *The Chosen Place, The Timeless People*, published in 1969, takes place in the Caribbean and, as critic Barbara Christian has noted, "Her emphasis moves from the way the world affects an individual psyche to how many psyches create a world." *Praisesong for the Widow* is Marshall's third novel. It has drawn steady critical attention since its publication and has been admired especially for its portrayal of that rare character in African American fiction, the middle-aged and middle-class woman. Critics also point to Marshall's effective use of myth, the heroic quest, and ritual in the novel. Though Marshall's works have never had the wide audience that Alice Walker's or Toni Morrison's fiction has had, they are important, powerful, and influential. Marshall's *Daughters* (1991) has also gained wide praise.

Bibliography

Busia, Abena P. "What Is Your Nation? Reconnecting Africa and Her Diaspora Through Paule Marshall's *Praisesong for the Widow*." In *Changing Our Own Words: Essays on Criticism, Theory, and Writing by Black Women*, edited by Cheryl A. Wall. New Brunswick, N.J.: Rutgers University Press, 1989. Maintains that the journey Marshall presents is not just that of Avey Johnson but also a journey on which the reader must embark to recognize the cultural signs and symbols that would lead to a reunification of the African diaspora. Avey's quest is that of "all New World diaspora children."

Kubitschek, Missy Dehn. "Paule Marshall's Women on Quest." *Black American Literature Forum* 21 (Spring/Summer, 1987): 43-60. Demonstrates how Marshall's first three novels make use of Joseph Campbell's universalist mythos, Robert Stepto's racially based journey patterns, and Carol Christ's gender-specific heroic patterns.

Sandiford, Keith A. "Paule Marshall's *Praisesong for the Widow*: The Reluctant Heiress, Or Whose Life Is It Anyway?" *Black American Literature Forum* 20 (Winter, 1986): 371-392. Sees the novel as presenting a character who must confront the antagonism between history and myth, between the diachronic view of history and the synchronic view of myth and ritual.

Scarboro, Ann Armstrong. "The Healing Process: A Paradigm for Self-Renewal in Paule Marshall's *Praisesong for the Widow* and Camara Laye's *Le Regard du roi.*" *Modern Language Studies* 19, no. 1 (Winter, 1989): 28-36. Finds six elements in the model for self-renewal in both Marshall's and Laye's works: "The decision to depart, psychological disorientation, interaction with a mentor, episodes of purification, psychological reintegration and arrival home."

Waxman, Barbara Frey. "The Widow's Journey to Self and Roots: Aging and Society in Paule Marshall's *Praisesong for the Widow.*" *Frontiers* 9, no. 3 (1987): 94-99. Maintains that Marshall's novel, along with others written by contemporary women, traces the "young-old" widow who undergoes a transformation of soul and spirit through the rediscovery of her racial and cultural heritage.

Laura Weiss Zlogar

PURLIE VICTORIOUS

Author: Ossie Davis (1917-   )
Type of work: Play
Type of plot: Comedy
Time of plot: The 1950's
Locale: A Georgia cotton plantation
First produced: September 28, 1961, at the Cort Theatre, New York City
First published: 1961

> *Principal characters:*
> PURLIE VICTORIOUS JUDSON, the protagonist, an African American
> in his mid- or late thirties
> LUTIEBELLE GUSSIE MAE JENKINS, a young African American
> woman
> MISSY JUDSON (AUNT MISSY), Purlie's sister-in-law and the
> matriarch of the Judson clan
> GITLOW JUDSON, Purlie's brother but in many ways his antithesis
> OL' CAP'N COTCHIPEE, the white plantation owner and Purlie's
> antagonist
> CHARLIE COTCHIPEE, the Ol' Cap'n's son, a representative of the
> new South
> IDELLA LANDY, a tiny old African American woman who was
> Charlie's nurse and is still his confidante

The Play

Purlie Victorious relates Purlie's dream of becoming a preacher to the African American community in southern Georgia, where he and his family live and where little has changed over the generations. It is the 1950's, and change has begun. Reference is made to the Montgomery, Alabama, bus boycotts, Martin Luther King, Jr., and the National Association for the Advancement of Colored People. Purlie is influenced by all of these, but his motives come primarily from within himself and his own experiences as an African American in the traditional South.

Twenty years earlier, Purlie had been beaten by the white owner of the plantation, Ol' Cap'n Cotchipee, and he has neither forgotten nor forgiven. Self-educated, a rebel and a dreamer, Purlie has gone through several metamorphoses and has finally settled on the role of a preacher. He preaches not of a heaven obtainable only after death but of a new heaven on earth, a heaven of freedom, a word he often invokes. He needs a church, and he chooses Big Bethel, an old barn that in the past had held a black congregation. To acquire Big Bethel, Purlie must obtain a $500 inheritance left to a deceased member of the Judson family, an inheritance controlled by the Ol' Cap'n. Purlie plots to have a young black woman, Lutiebelle Jenkins, impersonate the dead heir.

Unfortunately for Purlie but fortunately for the play, things do not go according to plan. In this satire on the people, institutions, and racism of the Old South, Davis has created broad stereotypes. Purlie's choice to have Lutiebelle impersonate the dead Cousin Bee is from the beginning an unlikely prospect. Lutiebelle looks nothing like Cousin Bee. Cousin Bee had been a college student, while Lutiebelle's background is that of a servant. Purlie likely chose Lutiebelle because, perhaps unconsciously, he was attracted to her looks and personality. Lutiebelle's personal desires are primarily domestic, but she is willing to do her best for Purlie, and he coaches her for the crucial meeting with Ol' Cap'n Cotchipee.

Another difficulty for Purlie comes from his brother, Gitlow. Unlike Purlie, Gitlow has seemingly made his peace with the existing social system, accommodating himself to the Ol' Cap'n's racist regime. Selected by the Ol' Cap'n to be the "Deputy-for-the-Colored," Gitlow picks cotton, spends time in the fields, and even sings spirituals for Cotchipee, spirituals with obvious themes of resignation and acceptance. Gitlow fears that the plan to impersonate Cousin Bee will not succeed and that its failure can only cause more difficulties for the African Americans on the plantation.

Gitlow is an obstacle to Purlie's aims, but Ol' Cap'n Cotchipee also has problems, with his son, Charlie. Charlie is among the first Southern whites to support the recent court decisions voiding segregation. When he expresses these opinions to his father, the Ol' Cap'n rejects them, rhetorically asking, "Do you think ary [sic] single darky on my place would ever think of changing a single thing about the South, and to hell with the Supreme Court . . . ?" For his beliefs, Charlie is beaten by local rednecks and becomes an object of ridicule to his father.

Pushed by Purlie to present Lutiebelle—the false Cousin Bee—to the Ol' Cap'n, Gitlow resists. Cotchipee unexpectedly enters the plantation store, where Purlie is rehearsing Lutiebelle, and the impersonation begins. Lutiebelle does her best, and Cotchipee seems convinced, but more by her attractive looks than by the effectiveness of her act. Purlie also presents Cotchipee with a supposed sheepskin scroll naming him the "Great White Father of the Year!" and "the best friend the Negro ever had." Coming from Gitlow, the citation would have been a manifestation of the Uncle Tom syndrome of accommodation. From Purlie it drips satire, as he gratefully notes that the African Americans on the plantation are allowed to pick Cotchipee's cotton and receive hominy grits on credit at the plantation store, and that the Ol' Cap'n "never resorts to bull whip except as a blessing and benediction." Cotchipee appears genuinely touched by the tribute and orders Charlie to get the $500. The Ol' Cap'n asks for a receipt, and Lutiebelle signs her own name, not that of Cousin Bee. Cotchipee has already alerted the sheriff, who attempts to arrest Purlie. Cotchipee wants more than Purlie's arrest: He wants to again beat Purlie with his bullwhip. Purlie resists, a fight breaks out, Charlie tries to break it up and is knocked unconscious, and Purlie escapes.

In the aftermath of the failed plot, Missy tries to convince Purlie, her brother-in-law, that he should give up his dream of regaining Big Bethel and marry Lutiebelle instead. Purlie objects, arguing that "the crying need of this Negro day and age is not grits, but greatness; not cornbread but courage; not fat-back but fight-back." Gitlow appears, claiming that he has obtained the $500 from the Ol' Cap'n. Cotchipee, however, has merely promised to give the money to Gitlow as a reward for leaving Lutiebelle at the plantation house to help with the Sunday dinner. Purlie suspects that the Ol' Cap'n intends to seduce Lutiebelle. Gitlow defends himself by asking Purlie whether he wants Big Bethel or not, the price implicitly being Lutiebelle. Lutiebelle then walks in, disheveled and without the money. Cotchipee had pinched and kissed her, and she ran away in disgust. Purlie vows revenge, and the others attempt to restrain him, Gitlow noting that the Ol' Cap'n had only kissed Purlie's woman. Purlie's response echoes the long lament of African Americans regarding violence from the white community: "Yeah! And what you suppose he'd a done to me if I'd a kissed his?"

Purlie charges off to confront the Ol' Cap'n and returns with the money and the Ol' Cap'n's bullwhip. Lutiebelle and Missy assume that Purlie had a fight with the Ol' Cap'n. Purlie, swept up in their adoration, enthusiastically relates how he brought the Ol' Cap'n down: "I beat him—I whipped him—and I flogged him—and I cut him—I destroyed him!" At that climax, Idella enters and explains that in reality Purlie broke into the commissary and did not beat Cotchipee. Lutiebelle, Missy, and Gitlow turn against Purlie, who defends himself by claiming "I ain't never in all my life told a lie I didn't mean to make come true some day."

The Ol' Cap'n and the sheriff appear, but instead of arresting Purlie, Charlie Cotchipee is charged with theft. Charlie admits to having taken the money in order to save his father from Purlie's anger. The Ol' Cap'n then orders Gitlow to seize Purlie, but Gitlow breaks into song instead, singing "Gone are the days." The Ol' Cap'n informs the group that he, through Charlie, has bought Big Bethel. In yet another twist, Charlie confesses that he has put the deed not in the Ol' Cap'n's name but in Purlie's. After giving the deed to Purlie, Charlie asks if he, a white man, can become a member of Big Bethel. He is unanimously accepted. This deals a fatal blow to the Ol' Cap'n, who dies while still standing up.

The epilogue sees Purlie as the minister of Big Bethel, presiding at the funeral services for the Ol' Cap'n, who is appropriately buried upright with his casket draped with the Confederate flag and his bullwhip. The play closes with Purlie giving a panegyric to African American pride: "Accept in full the sweetness of your blackness—not wishing to be red, nor white, nor yellow: nor any other race, or face, but this . . . be brave, keep freedom in the family, do what you can for the white folks, and write me in care of the post office."

Themes and Meanings

In the published edition of *Purlie Victorious*, Davis gave his justification for the play:

Our churches will say that segregation is immoral because it makes perfectly wonderful people, white and black, do immoral things. Our courts will say segregation is illegal because it makes perfectly wonderful people, white and black, do illegal things. And, finally, our theatre will say segregation is ridiculous because it makes perfectly wonderful people, white and black, do ridiculous things.

In *Purlie Victorious*, whites and blacks do many ridiculous things. The play is a comedy, a farce, and a satire, and its characters are stereotypes. Purlie is the traditional African American preacher, ever influential in the black community, with a great gift of language. Gitlow "gits low" in his acceptance of the system. Among the whites, Ol' Cap'n Cotchipee symbolizes the historical reality of racial intolerance in the white-dominated South. The Ol' Cap'n's bullwhip is the force that underlies the entire system of segregation. The author argues that these stereotypes were rooted in history.

Although *Purlie Victorious* is comedy, satire, and farce, Davis' choice of humor was, he argues, a realistic portrayal of the African American experience. "We told jokes . . . but we weren't telling jokes for the sake of getting off fast quips and gags. That stream of humor had to carry our sense of self, our sense of history, our hope of the future." Underneath the comedy and parody is a profoundly serious critique of American society with its racist practices, its class differences, and its violence. When Idella, Charlie Cotchipee's African American nurse and confidante, urges him to be less vocal about his support for the ending of segregation, she is speaking from the African American experience. Charlie, a white man, might get beaten by rednecks for uttering his opinions, but an African American could well be killed for saying the same things.

When the play was first produced in 1961, civil rights had become a central issue in American society. Legal segregation had not vanished, but federal courts were regularly voiding laws enforcing racial discrimination. There were many Ol' Cap'ns still extant, but it seemed that their day was waning. The burial of the Ol' Cap'n at the end of *Purlie Victorious* is thus the author's metaphor for the burying of segregation, and Charlie's request to join Big Bethel signifies the author's commitment to an integrated society based on freedom and equality. Davis has written a serious play in satirical form, a subversive but hopeful commentary on African Americans in American society.

Critical Context

Starring the author in the title role, *Purlie Victorious* ran for 261 performances when first produced. Critics were divided about the play. The reviewer for *The New York Times*, Howard Taubman, praised it as an affirmation of progress and change, a "farce with a slashing viewpoint" that "provokes as it disarms." *Ebony*, published primarily for African Americans, noted with approval Eleanor Roosevelt's comment that "mixed with the humor there is intelligent, incisive commentary on segregation, discrimination and the slow pace of integration."

Others were less enthusiastic. In the *Saturday Review of Literature*, Henry Hewes admired the satire but found the characters uninvolving and the plot predictable. Edith Oliver, writing in *The New Yorker*, found the play similar to many left-wing dramas of the 1930's for its simplistic heroes and villains. Accusing Davis of "playing it safe," Oliver argued that to make the Ol' Cap'n the symbol for the realities of racism and segregation was to imply that the problems were easily solved. Robert Brustein, drama critic of *The New Republic*, was appalled at the message of *Purlie Victorious*, claiming that the play "set back inter-racial harmony, by my calculations, about fourteen years." He was disturbed by the "hate and violence under the shut-my-mouf benevolence of these cardboard characters."

The satirical and humorous approach was a contentious issue for critics. Can such techniques be applied to serious issues? The play was translated into film in 1963 under the title *Gone Are the Days*. Davis remained active in the movement for African American rights. He has received many awards for his writing and acting and for his commitment to African American causes.

Bibliography
Abramson, Doris E. *Negro Playwrights in the American Theatre.* New York: Columbia University Press, 1969. This work concentrates on African American playwrights from the 1920's through the 1950's, but the author includes perceptive comments on Davis and other writers of the 1960's.
Brustein, Robert. "Down Among the Dead Men." *The New Republic* 145 (November 6, 1961): 22. In this critical review of *Purlie Victorious*, Brustein interprets the play as giving encouragement to racial antagonisms and potential violence, but now from African Americans.
Hatch, Robert. "Theatre." *The Nation* 193 (October 14, 1961): 254-255. In this liberal journal and traditional defender of African American rights, Hatch praises Davis' work as a considerable achievement but fears that the author's tone was uncertain concerning whether the characters knew they were being humorous.
Hewes, Henry. "Laughing Matters." *Saturday Review of Literature* 44 (October 14, 1961): 78. This review in an influential national publication is generally favorable. The reviewer would like to have seen even more satire and categorizes the work as a "cheerful comedy."
Hill, Herbert, ed. *Anger and Beyond: The Negro Writer in the United States.* New York: Harper & Row, 1966. Included in this collected work are articles by and about such writers as Arna Bontemps, LeRoi Jones, Harvy Swados, and Richard Wright. Includes a valuable discussion by Ossie Davis of his aims and ambitions in writing *Purlie Victorious*.
Oliver, Edith. *The New Yorker* 37 (October 7, 1961): 130. A generally critical review. Oliver claims that the plot is unconvincing and that perhaps satire and stereotyping were insufficient techniques to explore serious and complicated social problems.

Eugene Larson

QUICKSAND

Author: Nella Larsen (1891-1964)
Type of work: Novel
Type of plot: Psychological realism
Time of plot: The 1920's
Locale: The American South; Chicago, Illinois; New York City; and Copenhagen, Denmark
First published: 1928

> *Principal characters:*
> HELGA CRANE, a young woman searching for personal fulfillment
> DR. ROBERT ANDERSON, the principal of the school where Helga teaches
> ANNE GREY, a widow deeply involved in racial causes
> AXEL OLSEN, a conceited Danish artist
> THE REVEREND MR. PLEASANT GREEN, an overweight, lustful preacher who marries Helga

The Novel

Nella Larsen's *Quicksand* is the story of a mulatto woman who cannot find happiness and fulfillment in any of the worlds in which she lives. Her dual origins permit her to pass from one culture to another, but her outsider perspective gives her the ability to discern serious flaws in both societies, thus causing her to feel nowhere at home.

Although Nella Larsen employs a third-person omniscient point of view, Helga Crane's character is the central consciousness within the story. Perceptions of various events and interpretations of experiences are those formulating within the mind of Helga. From the start of the novel, the reader is drawn immediately into her thoughts and feelings.

Helga is a young schoolteacher in the black Southern community of Naxos. At first, she is happy there; however, after two years of living in an oppressive atmosphere in which black students and teachers are molded into the forms of the white middle class, Helga decides to leave. She meets with the new principal, Dr. Robert Anderson, who seems cool and controlled to her. He pleads with Helga to stay and almost convinces her, until he calls her a fine lady. This remark angers Helga, because it indicates he is presumptuous about her and sees her as less than a full-bodied woman. Thus, she bids farewell to Naxos.

Helga travels to Chicago, where she was born. There, she looks up her Uncle Peter, whom she remembers fondly. She discovers that he is now married and that his wife wants nothing to do with a family member of mixed blood. Desperate, Helga seeks employment, and she finds a position with a wealthy widow, Mrs. Hayes-Rore, who needs someone to help her write and edit speeches on racial matters that she delivers at conferences. Mrs. Hayes-Rore takes Helga with her to New York City and convinces her to live in Harlem with her friend Anne Grey.

In Harlem, Helga is fascinated with the excitement of the crowds, the nightlife, parties, conversations—all the activities of the animated black men and women of the bustling city. She enjoys living in Anne's luxurious home and accompanies her to gatherings at which guests seriously discuss issues of racial uplift. Helga, however, begins to notice Anne's weakness for white society's upper-class values and manners, despite the fact that Anne takes every opportunity to express distaste for all whites. She especially criticizes those white persons who come to Harlem to indulge themselves in "Negro life" and to seek out sexual liaisons.

At a social function in Harlem, Helga encounters Robert Anderson, who is now living in New York. Although she continues to run into him at other affairs, he seems distant toward her. Helga realizes, however, that she is emotionally stirred by his presence.

Soon, Helga begins to see Harlem in a different light. The partying and dancing now seem wild and disgusting to her; she tells herself that she is not a "jungle creature." Furthermore, she considers the Harlem men and women narrow and hypocritical in their views.

One day Helga receives a letter from Uncle Peter containing five thousand dollars, the amount of money he has designated for her in his will. He believes that she needs the money now, and he gives it to her with the understanding that she should never come to his door again. The money allows Helga to escape her now unsatisfactory life with Anne in Harlem and to go to Denmark. Helga remembers how her mother's family expressed kindness to her during a visit to Copenhagen when she was a child.

In Denmark, Helga becomes the star attraction of white society. Her Aunt Katrina and Uncle Poul Dahl treat her royally and introduce her to many important men and women, especially in the world of art. In the two years Helga stays in Copenhagen, she is regarded as a dark, sensuous beauty who appears clothed in extraordinary fashions and jewelry at the numerous teas and dinners to which her relatives take her. By showing her off, they wish to promote their own entrance into high society. At one of the gatherings, Helga meets the famous portrait painter Axel Olsen, who later expresses his desire to draw her likeness on canvas. The pompous Axel eventually reveals himself to Helga as a self-centered man who views her as an exotic ornament. Subsequently, she refuses his approaches to her, including a proposal of marriage.

Unhappy with being treated in a stereotypical way by the Danes, Helga leaves Copenhagen. She also realizes that she is homesick, "not for America, but for Negroes." Back in Harlem, she runs into James Vayle, a stuffy schoolteacher from Naxos whom she almost married. He still wants her, but Helga expresses her lack of interest in him. At a party, Robert Anderson, now married to Anne Grey, furtively kisses Helga. Some time later, he signals that he wants to see her; Helga, thinking that he wants to start an affair, agrees to go to him. At their meeting, however,

Robert merely apologizes for his behavior.

This last disappointment sends Helga into a state of hopelessness that results in her literal descent into the gutter on a rain-driven Harlem street. She finds refuge in a storefront church, where a frenzied revival is taking place under the direction of the Reverend Green, who inspires her to be saved. Green escorts her home, spends the night with the now grateful Helga, and later persuades her to marry him.

Green takes Helga to live with him in the poor rural Alabama community where he is idolized by his black parishioners. In the beginning, Helga enjoys the simple, structured existence of a minister's wife; however, as the years go by and she gets bogged down in the arduous and thankless tasks of housework, childrearing, and service to her husband, she once more becomes dissatisfied with her way of living. Her fourth childbirth causes her to become gravely ill, and the doctor informs her that another pregnancy will kill her. Helga is now a bitter and disillusioned woman who sees herself as a victim of a racist, oppressive system—a system in which the institutions of church and marriage are especially blameworthy. At the end of the novel, Helga is pregnant with her fifth child.

The Characters

Helga Crane is beset by many demons throughout her life. Her mixed racial heritage makes her especially sensitive to the agonizing experience of living in a racist society and interferes with her quest for identity and self-fulfillment. The rejections that she suffers in childhood set her on a search for love, understanding, and emotional security; these are difficult goals for her to achieve in the American society of the 1920's, a time of rapidly changing, and thus conflicting, sexual mores and racial attitudes. Helga seeks to enjoy a healthy sexual life as a woman, but she is blocked from doing so by the narrow and unenlightened attitudes of the men that she encounters. Moreover, she is plagued by her own confusion about which roles are proper to choose. Several times, Helga goes from supporting the traditional norms of society to flinging herself into the freedom and excitement of a nonconformist life.

In choosing a mulatta as her protagonist, Nella Larsen allows the reader to observe the experiences of both the white and black worlds. Helga is able to move from one society to another, even though she cannot feel at home in either one. Her position as an outsider causes her much difficulty, but it also endows her with a more insightful perspective than she would have if she belonged only to one culture. Yet her insight is her undoing, because the truth she discovers about each culture is the cause of her unsatisfied life and discontented spirit. She understands this perfectly well at the end of the novel, when she looks back on her experiences and realizes that "happiness and serenity always faded just as they had shaped themselves."

The other women characters in *Quicksand* do not play very significant roles. They are one-dimensional representations of attitudes on race; Anne Grey is the only one who is presented with some degree of development. She is a proponent of racial uplift for African Americans, and Helga admires her before coming to understand

Anne's contradictory and negative behavior: "She hated white people with a deep and burning hatred. . . . But she aped their clothes, their manners, and their gracious ways of living." Anne's hypocritical actions symbolize for Helga the general practices of the black dwellers of Harlem, and this realization helps to drive her to the white society of Denmark.

The men in Helga's life are more fully drawn. Robert Anderson is presented as a detached and pretentious man whose middle-class inhibitions ruin any possibility of a deep relationship with Helga at a time when she is willing to respond with her honest feelings for him. The Danish artist, Axel Olsen, is characterized as a pompous egoist. His extreme self-love prevents his becoming aware of the true nature of any person. He sees Helga as a stereotypical African endowed with sensuous beauty and exotic charm. His only interest in her is that she become an adornment for his public enhancement.

The Reverend Mr. Pleasant Green is probably the most unfavorably depicted character in the novel. His corpulent, stale-smelling body, his dirty fingernails, and his extreme sexual appetite are excused by Helga until she realizes that he has trapped her in a grim domestic prison of backbreaking work, daily boredom, constant fatigue, and ill health. Through all this, he spouts religious platitudes, and his only interest in her is for the gratification of his sexual desires.

Themes and Meanings

Quicksand is more than a novel about a person's search for identity. It offers a critical commentary on diverse cultural and racial societies—their oppressive institutions, outmoded traditions, false values, and distorted ways of perceiving reality. Because the protagonist is a woman of mixed racial heritage, Nella Larsen can easily shift her character from one different community to the next. Furthermore, because Helga's less-than-full commitment to either black or white society provides her with special insight, Larsen can illustrate and criticize the distinguishing elements that make up the different racial cultures.

Larsen communicates many important ideas to the reader through Helga's central consciousness in the novel. The Naxos school is a black middle-class training ground where new ideas are not tolerated and individual freedom is discouraged. The name "Naxos" is probably used by Larsen as an anagram for "Saxon," to denote the school's obedience to the dominant Anglo-Saxon society. This kind of life is in contrast to the free and joyous existence of the black residents of Harlem, where Helga temporarily finds escape. In Harlem, however, she soon realizes that there, too, black men and women are imitating white patterns of life, even as they denounce the actions of white persons. Furthermore, she finds the sensual excesses practiced in Harlem to be repulsive to the values of her moral upbringing.

Again seeking refuge, Helga lives in the white society of Denmark, but once more she encounters hypocrisy and false attitudes. The Danes pride themselves on their nonracist ideas, but they are oblivious to the fact that they see Helga as a stereotypical black woman rather than as an individual person. Finally, living in a rural community in Alabama, Helga thinks that she has at last found her identity and a sense of belonging with these simple black folk; soon, though, she finds herself constrained and trapped again. This time, the oppressive forces are the institutions of marriage, church, and family.

Helga is also tossed around in her emotional life. The men she knows are for the most part self-centered, shallow-thinking, and, in the case of Robert Anderson, too restrained to give fulfillment to Helga's life. Some of the blame for their actions can be placed on the times in which they live. During the sexual revolution of the 1920's, the demand for openness in sexual relationships caused much confusion and conflict between men and women. Helga herself has sexual feelings that confuse her and sometimes lead her astray, as in the incident with Anderson that sends her into the arms of the Reverend Green. She opts for marriage at the end because she gives into her ingrained sense of propriety, which allows her to think that marriage might be the solution to her problems. Instead, Helga finds herself pushed deeper down into the quicksand that finally suffocates and destroys her. She has been unable to find fulfillment of her sexual nature, happiness in her role as a woman, or a satisfactory identification with any part of her racial heritage.

What Nella Larsen displays in her novel is a realistic and damning study of white and black societies. She focuses on their oppressive institutions and on all their negative practices in relation to race, class, and gender. In writing her story, Larsen reverses the pattern of the nineteenth century slave narratives that chronicle a captive's journey to the North, where freedom and identity can be secured. Helga's journey is to the North and back to the South, and in neither place is there any escape for her.

Critical Context

When Larsen's novel about the life of Helga Crane appeared in 1928, the Harlem Renaissance was at its height. Works by African American writers were in great demand, especially those stories that depicted the fantasies of white men and women about the sexual freedom and happy excitement they associated with the black experience. Despite the white public's expectations, however, many African American literary artists, including Larsen, wrote novels and poems that presented fuller and more accurate portraits of black men and women. When *Quicksand* was published, it received praise from critics of both races. W. E. B. Du Bois, the great black intellectual writer and editor, reviewed the book and called it the "best piece of fiction that Negro America has produced since the heyday of [Charles] Chesnutt." In 1929, Larsen published her second novel, *Passing*, which was also well-received; her career foundered in the ensuing years, however, and she stopped writing.

Like the work of many other writers of the Harlem Renaissance, Larsen's work was largely forgotten until she was rediscovered by feminist critics in the 1970's. Since then, her novels have been republished numerous times and have received serious scholarly analysis. Larsen's work was seen in the 1920's as a variation of the "tragic mulatto" theme in literature; however, most critics now value Helga Crane as a probing study of a woman's conflicts along the intersecting lines of race, class, and gender. As a result, years after her death, Larsen has gained more widespread respect and appreciation than she ever attained during her brief literary career.

Bibliography

Ammons, Elizabeth. *Conflicting Stories: American Women Writers at the Turn into the Twentieth Century.* New York: Oxford University Press, 1991. Claims the ideas in *Quicksand* "declare their author's rebellion as an artist." Notes that, in Helga, Larsen creates a character who refuses to act out the white fantasies she would be expected to perform. Also compares Larsen with her contemporary Zora Neale Hurston.

Carby, Hazel V. *Reconstructing Womanhood: The Emergence of the Afro-American Woman Novelist.* New York: Oxford University Press, 1987. Treats Larsen's use of the mulatto figure as a "narrative device of mediation." Explores the interconnections of sexual, racial, and class identity and makes the claim that Larsen offers no resolutions to the contraditions she raises in the novel.

Christian, Barbara. *Black Women Novelists: The Development of a Tradition, 1892-1976.* Westport, Conn.: Greenwood Press, 1980. Presents an analysis of Helga as a mulatto and discusses Larsen's attempted innovations in the depictions of women characters.

Huggins, Nathan Irvin. *Harlem Renaissance.* New York: Oxford University Press, 1971. Sees Helga as struggling against her sensuality, but surrendering to it in the frustrating experiences she undergoes. Her final surrender to sensuality, in the marriage to Reverend Green, results in her death.

McDowell, Deborah E. Introduction to *"Quicksand" and "Passing,"* by Nella Larsen. New Brunswick, N.J.: Rutgers University Press, 1986. Extensive analysis of *Quicksand.* Deals with Larsen's exploration of female sexual fulfillment and studies the novel's narrative strategy, which reflects the tension between sexual expression and repression.

Angelo Costanzo

A RAISIN IN THE SUN

Author: Lorraine Hansberry (1930-1965)
Type of work: Play
Type of plot: Problem play
Time of plot: Between the 1940's and the 1950's
Locale: South Side of Chicago
First produced: March 11, 1959, at the Ethel Barrymore Theater, New York City
First published: 1959

> *Principal characters:*
> MAMA (LENA YOUNGER), the matriarch of the Younger family, a
> woman in her early sixties
> WALTER LEE YOUNGER, the son of Lena Younger and the major
> protagonist of the play
> BENEATHA YOUNGER (BENNIE), Lena's twenty-year-old daughter, a
> university student who dreams of becoming a doctor
> RUTH YOUNGER, Walter Lee's wife, a woman in her early thirties

The Play

According to Lorraine Hansberry's stage directions at the beginning of the play, the action occurs sometime between the end of World War II and the 1950's. The play is set in an urban ghetto and deals with the problems encountered by a poor black family as it tries to cope with the realities of life on Chicago's South Side. It reveals the devastating effects of poverty and oppression on the African American family. Even before the play begins, Hansberry's stage directions, both in tone and substance, suggest the extent of that devastation. The furnishings in the Younger family's apartment, she says, are "tired," and the "once loved couch upholstery" has to "fight to show itself from under acres of dollies and couch covers." The very environment in which the Youngers live mirrors the struggle for survival that is waged daily in this household.

As the play progresses, the frustration born of this poverty and oppression mounts. The anger and hostility that it spawns begin to erode the foundations of the family structure. This erosion begins early in the play, exhibiting itself in the strained relations between Walter Lee and his wife Ruth as they argue over the disposition of money coming from insurance on Walter's father. Walter Lee wants to use the money to purchase a liquor store. He is convinced that such a business venture will be his ticket out of the ghetto. His marriage threatens to collapse under the constant bickering. Ruth, having just discovered that she is pregnant, contemplates abortion to avoid bringing a new life into this hostile, poverty-ridden environment.

As the family anticipates the arrival of the insurance check, the tension grows and Walter becomes more agitated. He is resentful of his sister, whose medical-school expenses, he thinks, will consume money that he might otherwise use to finance his liquor store. When the check finally arrives and he finds that Mama Younger has used part of the money to make a down payment on a new house and plans to use the rest for Beneatha's medical-school expenses, Walter explodes, spending his days driving around town and his nights brooding in the local bar.

When Mama begins to understand the depth of damage to Walter Lee's feelings and manhood, she turns over the rest of the money to him to do with as he pleases. She makes one request, however: that he put aside the money for Beneatha's education. Still pursuing his dream, however, Walter gives Willie, one of his friends, the money to purchase the liquor store for him. Willie absconds with the money, dashing Walter Lee's hopes and dreams as well as those of the entire Younger family.

In an effort to recover his losses, Walter Lee decides to accept the money that has been offered earlier by their prospective white neighbors as a bribe to keep the Younger family out of an all-white neighborhood. In the last scene of the play, however, under the watchful eye of his son, Walter finds the courage to reject the offer. The family takes its leave of its ghetto apartment and heads for its new home and anticipated better life.

Themes and Meanings

In 1957, when Lorraine Hansberry began work on *A Raisin in the Sun*, she titled it *Crystal Stair*, taken from a line in a Langston Hughes poem, "Mother to Son." The final title, like the original one, also comes from a Hughes poem, "Harlem," which asks the question, "What happens to a dream deferred/ Does it dry up like a raisin in the Sun?" Either title is appropriate, for certainly this is a play about a mother-son relationship, but it is no less a play about dreams, dreams too long deferred. These unfulfilled dreams are at the center of the play and are the source of the varied problems in the play. The manner in which Hansberry presents these problems and the skill with which she weaves them into the basic theme of the work attest the artistry of the playwright.

A Raisin in the Sun is rife with conflicts: generational conflicts, gender conflicts, ideological conflicts, and perhaps most important, conflicts of dreams, which are at the center of the play. By placing three generations in the same cramped quarters, Hansberry focuses dramatically on some of the essential differences between age and youth. Mama Younger's concern is always for the welfare of her children. She wants to provide for Beneatha's education and find a comfortable home for the family. She and her husband, Big Walter, had struggled to make life better for the children. Although he had literally worked himself to death, he had taken out the $10,000 life insurance policy as security for them.

Beneatha and Walter Lee, on the other hand, are more selfish in their concerns. Beneatha squanders money on frivolous pursuits and devotes her attention to her personal relationships, while Walter is oblivious to the needs of everyone else, with the possible exception of his son, in his obsession with the dream of becoming a businessman. Travis, in typical childlike fashion, manipulates all the adults in the play in order to achieve his own ends.

Ideological conflicts also abound, feeding into the major theme of the novel. Beneatha, having been newly exposed to some radical ideas in the university setting, has abandoned the God-centered Christian faith of her mother and has embraced atheism, or at least secular humanism. The major clash between these two ideologies comes in a dramatic scene in which Mama forces Beneatha to acknowledge, at least verbally, the existence of God by forcing her to repeat the phrase "In my mother's house, there is always God." In sharp contrast to Mama Younger's philosophy of success through faith and hard work is Walter Lee's philosophy of the "takers and the tooken." He adopts this philosophy after being deceived by his friend, Willie. Mama Younger denounces this philosophy when, in a powerful speech reminding Walter Lee of his heritage, she says, "Son, I come from five generations of slaves and sharecroppers—but aint nobody in my family never let nobody pay 'em no money that was a way of telling us we wasn't fit to walk the earth. We aint never been that poor."

In George Murchison, a rich young African American college student, and Asagai, a poor Nigerian college student—both suitors of Beneatha—Hansberry focuses on the conflicts between wealth and position versus heritage and tradition. Murchison offers Beneatha a life of opulence and comfort, while Asagai offers her a life steeped in ancestral tradition but devoid of creature comforts. Hansberry does not attempt to resolve this conflict, choosing rather to leave Beneatha undecided at the end of the play, suggesting the difficulty of such a choice. The Beneatha-Asagai relationship also introduces into the drama the theme of pan-Africanism, a theme unique to African American drama of this period. Through the romantic involvement of these two, Hansberry manages to link the African struggle for independence with the African American struggle for self-identity and self-determination.

Furthermore, in her portrayal of Beneatha as a fiercely independent, self-assured woman, determined to succeed in the medical profession, Hansberry introduces the theme of feminism, a novel one at this time not only in African American literature but also in American literature in general. Even Walter Lee expresses the typical male-chauvinist point of view as he taunts Beneatha about her ambitions: "If you are going to medical school, why not be a nurse like everyone else."

The feminist theme is enhanced by the portrayal of the two other women in the play. Each in her own way reflects some aspect of feminism. Lena Younger (Mama) is the epitome of the self-reliant woman, having worked side by side with her husband to provide for the family and continuing to be its stabilizing force. Ruth, on the other hand, seems to hold fairly traditional ideas about motherhood, but she finds herself, without the counsel of her husband, considering abortion as an alternative to bringing another child into the world. Although the abortion theme is merely touched on in this play, the way is opened for other writers to treat it more thoroughly in future plays.

In *A Raisin in the Sun*, Hansberry raises many issues of race, gender, family values, religion, and ethics. The play poses many more problems than it resolves or even attempts to resolve; therein lies the complexity and the realism of the drama.

Critical Context

The single most important achievement in African American theater in the 1950's was the production of Hansberry's *A Raisin in the Sun*. It was first produced Off-Broadway, in New Haven, Connecticut, and Philadelphia, Pennsylvania, because it was rejected by Broadway producers as being "too unlike the typical Broadway play" and because of the perceived lack of interest in African American family life. When it did open on Broadway, however, it received exceptional reviews and ran through 530 performances. Since its Broadway production, it has attracted the widest viewing audience of any play by an African American.

The play has been performed by both professional and amateur groups all over the United States, in large cities and small towns, on college campuses and in community centers. It has also been reproduced on film and on videocassette. It has been widely anthologized in high school and university textbooks and has been published singly in hardcover and inexpensive paperback volumes. Because of this wide accessibility, it is fair to speculate that most Americans, even if they have not read or seen the play, at least know about it.

Although *A Raisin in the Sun* is held in high esteem by most critics, some have criticized it for what has been called its "soap opera" quality, primarily its perpetuation of stereotypes: the black matriarch (Mama Younger), the frustrated African American male (Walter Lee), the free-thinking college student (Beneatha), the black bourgeois (George Murchison), the "poetic revolutionary" (Asagai), and the white bigot (Mr. Linder). Others have damned its sentimentality, particularly the idealization of the black matriarchical character, Mama Younger.

Most critics would argue, however, that *A Raisin in the Sun* attests the artistry of Hansberry in being able to explore, in the lives of the Younger family, myth structures and styles formerly ignored by dramatists, especially African American dramatists. They would also concur that the skill with which she interweaves the various themes of the work into a homogeneous whole is testimony to her skill in dramaturgy. Finally, critics agree that the universality of the themes and the variety of social issues raised in the play give *A Raisin in the Sun* lasting appeal.

Bibliography

Abramson, Doris. *Negro Playwrights in the American Theater: 1925-1959*. New York: Columbia University Press, 1969. The definitive work in African American drama. Treats the origin and development of the black drama—its structure, themes, innovations, and impact—from its nineteenth century beginnings through Hansberry.

Bennett, Lerone, Jr., and Margaret G. Burroughs. "A Lorraine Hansberry Rap." *Freedomways* 19, no. 4 (1979): 226-233. A discussion between Bennett, a historian and editor of *Ebony* magazine, and Burroughs, an artist and teacher. The article focuses on Hansberry's career, with much of the discussion devoted to an assessment of the themes and characters in *A Raisin in the Sun* and the reasons for its popularity with both black and white audiences.

Cruse, Harold. *The Crisis of the Negro Intellectual.* New York: William Morrow, 1967. In the chapter on Hansberry, Cruse criticizes *A Raisin in the Sun* for what he sees as its soap opera qualities and for its failure to deal realistically with the problems of the black underclass.

Hairston, Loyle. "Portrait of an Angry Young Writer." *Crisis* 86 (April, 1969): 123-124. Examines the ways in which Hansberry's activist philosophy and rebellious attitude influence her work, especially in terms of themes and character development.

Isaacs, Harold R. *The New World of Negro Americans.* New York: John Day, 1963. In the section on Hansberry, the author discusses the origin and development of Hansberry's ideas on pan-Africanism and the degree to which these ideas are reflected in *A Raisin in the Sun.*

Riley, Clayton. "Lorraine Hansberry: A Melody in a Different Key." *Freedomways* 19, no. 4 (1979): 205-212. Focuses on the universality of themes in Hansberry's plays. It emphasizes the fact that because black experience strikes "a different key" in the American experience, this universality is frequently overlooked.

Ward, Douglas Turner. "Lorraine Hansberry and the Passion of Walter Lee." *Freedomways* 19, no. 4 (1979): 223-225. An in-depth study of the character of the protagonist of *A Raisin in the Sun*, Walter Lee Younger. Asserts that the character is much more complex than generally thought to be and that Hansberry's skillful portrayal of him reveals these complexities.

Wilkerson, Margaret B. "Lorraine Hansberry: The Complete Feminist." *Freedomways* 19, no. 4 (1979): 235-245. Looks at Hansberry's plays as they reflect the feminist point of view, noting that as a descendant of early feminists such as Sojourner Truth and Ida B. Wells, Hansberry centers her feminism in human dignity and thus includes both men and women in her concept of feminism.

Gladys J. Washington

A RAT'S MASS

Author: Adrienne Kennedy (1931-   )
Type of work: Play
Type of plot: Surrealistic
Time of plot: Unspecified
Locale: The rat's house
First produced: 1966, at the New American Theatre, Rome, Italy
First published: 1968

> *Principal characters:*
> BROTHER RAT, also known as BLAKE, a character with a human
>   body but a rat's head and tail
> SISTER RAT, also known as KAY, Brother Rat's sister, who has a
>   human head but a rat's belly and tail
> ROSEMARY, a white girl who claims to be the heir to both the
>   Roman Catholic Church and the Roman Empire
> JESUS,
> JOSEPH,
> MARY,
> TWO WISE MEN, and
> A SHEPHERD, symbolic religious figures who form a procession

The Play

A Rat's Mass is a one-act play that poetically combines a wealth of linguistic and theatrical images. The brevity of the piece intensifies its already jarring style of presentation, which features characters who are part human and part animal, superficially nonsensical dialogue, and highly charged spectacle and sound effects. The style of this play is surrealistic, expressionistic, and absurdist; the plot of the play should not, therefore, be regarded as a credible or realistic story, nor should readers attempt to make literal sense of the dialogue or visual effects.

Because the play makes most sense on a symbolic level, readers should first try to imagine how the playwright intends the fully staged work to be seen and heard by an audience. The appearance of the stage itself, the use of movement on the stage, and the use of nonlinguistic sound are key to an understanding of *A Rat's Mass*.

The visual dimension of a production of this play would perhaps be the most immediate aspect of *A Rat's Mass* that a theater audience would be able to relate to meaningfully. The dreamlike set, deliberately stark, quickly seems to acquire significance: Although the scene is described as the rat's house, the setting consists of a red carpet runner and candles and thus suggests a church with a long, narrow aisle and votive candles. The lighting, which is to imitate the light at the end of a summer's day, is waning, implying a finality or an ending.

Movement through this stage space also acquires added importance. From the beginning of the play, the characters' positions on stage are clearly and specifically noted; Brother Rat is placed directly facing the audience, while Sister Rat stands at the far end of the long red aisle defined by the carpet runner. The procession of religious figures, Jesus, Joseph, Mary, two wise men, and a shepherd, are placed to the far left of the "rat's house" area on stage. As the play progresses, characters move about the stage with carefully choreographed directions. For example, the procession of religious figures marches across the stage, then goes to center stage, then comes all the way down to the edge of the stage, close to the audience, then goes back to the center of the stage, and exits, only to return and exit once more. Similarly, Brother Rat and Sister Rat, throughout the play, are given specific actions to perform (kneeling and rising, marching, and saluting) that accompany their dialogue. Because the play seems to lack traditional action—there is no standard use of plot or story, and whatever it is that "happens" during the course of the play remains obscure—these smaller actions (movements, gestures) stand out as significant.

Just as there appears to be no real plot, what the characters have to say may strike the reader as bizarre or even as utterly meaningless. Yet the playwright seems to emphasize sound apart from spoken language. Early in the play, the sound of rats may be heard as the processional characters march across the stage, and later, when the procession exits, a gnawing sound is heard. Toward the end of the play, gnawing sounds are accompanied by battlefield sounds, and just before the curtain falls, the procession returns with guns and the sound of shots rings out. At the same time, the playwright indicates moments throughout the play when there is no sound at all, when the absence of sound—silence—is reserved for effect.

If readers can keep these aspects of the script in mind, *A Rat's Mass* becomes easier to follow and perhaps to understand. The opening of the play, with its long interchange between Brother Rat and Sister Rat, sets up a tone of ambiguity that the dialogue maintains. Just as Brother Rat and Sister Rat look as if they are part rat and part human (he has a human body but a rat's head, she a human head but a rat's stomach), their speeches referring to their lives are similarly mixed: Like rats, they have lived in a holy chapel, eaten sunflower petals, and are afraid of cats, but in a very human way, they speak of Sister Rat being sent to the state psychiatric hospital, remember Rosemary taking them on a picnic, and fear being caught by the Nazis. Quite intentionally, the playwright mixes ideas and linguistic images so that they do not make sense in a logical or predictable way. As Brother Rat and Sister Rat speak of their lives, of their childhood in a neighborhood that was ethnically and religiously mixed, of their baby or babies, of Sister Rat's mental illness and her time in the state hospital, of Brother Rat's infatuation with Rosemary, the contradictions and confusions in what they say are of less importance than the suffering and feelings of oppression that they convey. Their emotional cries proceed in an orderly, almost ritualistic pattern, like the mass that they say that they are performing.

Amid the rats' expression of their sad lives, the procession of religious figures intrudes only at particular moments. When they march across the stage, they are sometimes oblivious to the rats' sadness; at other times, they seem all too aware that they have entered the rats' lives. Their final entrance, just before the curtain, turns them from the benevolent Christian icons they represent (the holy family and characters from traditional Christmas nativity pageants) into a line of gun-carrying soldiers.

Although the processional figures speak (in unison) to Brother Rat and Sister Rat a few times during the play, the only character who genuinely converses with Brother Rat and Sister Rat is Rosemary. Dressed in a communion dress and sporting worms in her hair, Rosemary is an Italian Catholic girl who has befriended the two rats. She has read to them from her catechism book and claims to be the descendant of Julius Caesar, the Virgin Mary, and the pope; the rats remember Rosemary with enormous affection and revere her quite religiously, and it is even suggested that Brother Rat had sex with Rosemary during the previous spring. Yet Rosemary seems distant, recommending repeatedly that the only thing left for the rats to do is to kill themselves.

Given the distance of the religious figures and the ambivalence of Rosemary, Brother Rat and Sister Rat become increasingly frantic as their rat's mass progresses. They speak of their impending capture by the Nazis, who they fear are pursuing them, and refer to events in their own past, such as Sister Rat's hospitalization and Brother Rat's reluctance to visit her. They seem to adore Rosemary, repeating what she has told them and holding her in great esteem, as if they have internalized all the teachings that she has imparted to them. The conclusion of the play, with the religious figures turning into a firing squad and shooting the rats while Rosemary looks on, is a chilling final tableau.

Themes and Meanings

The playwright uses techniques that may be described as surrealistic and also as expressionistic and absurdist. The surreal world created by *A Rat's Mass* appears to emanate, much like a dream, from the subconscious. Thus, the visual images and dialogue do not seem to make sense in a rational way, and the play as a whole manages to embody contradictions that, by the time the play has concluded, have ceased to appear contradictory.

At the same time, the playwright employs expressionistic devices—that is, she depicts the main characters' internal, rather than external, notions of reality. The rigidity of the religious procession, for example, may physically embody how Brother Rat and Sister Rat feel about the Church, and Rosemary's appearance (the communion dress and wormy hair) indicates how the two rats perceive her: childlike, religiously pure, and yet rotting, as if dead.

The play also relies on some of the conventions of what has become known as the Theater of the Absurd. Thus, the plot seeks to explore how certain situations feel rather than to tell a story (hence the absence of a traditional plot), and the importance of language is diminished, while spectacle and nonlinguistic sound take on a larger, highly symbolic meaning. The play appears to be fragmented and illogical, progressing with irrational, seemingly circular dialogue and bizarre visual effects.

The often repetitive and nonsensical speeches by Brother Rat and Sister Rat make the audience look to the sights and sounds of the play for meaning.

Yet the symbolism of the play remains, perhaps quite deliberately, elusive. Rosemary's insistence that people of color are not Catholic does, however, offer an important clue to what the play may signify: the rats, depicted as half human and half animal, may represent African Americans, who have been made to feel less than human by Western culture in general and by the Church or organized Western religion in particular. The connection between Western culture and Western religion is drawn emphatically by Rosemary, who claims to be descended from the Virgin Mary, Julius Caesar, and the pope, and who has taught the rats Latin (the language of the Roman Catholic Church and of the Roman empire) and Italian history. The emergence of the religious figures with guns at the close of *A Rat's Mass* fulfills the rats' worst fears of being captured by the Nazis: The benevolent religious figures in effect become the representatives of oppression, just as European culture evolved into a collection of imperialistic states that overran and colonized much of the world.

A Rat's Mass, with its references to rats and the Nazis, evokes a terrifying image of extermination. The play seems to imply that Western civilization is bent on destroying what it cannot claim as its own. At the same time, Brother Rat and Sister Rat, having internalized the anti-rat teachings imparted by Rosemary, have tried their hardest to conform to what they perceive as the demands of the culture.

The title, with its Catholic ceremonial connotations, not only sets the ritualistic and religious tone for the play as a whole, but also contains a pun (the colloquial figure of speech is "a rat's ass") that betrays the play's basic irreverence for the society (and its institutions) that are critiqued and even satirized. The incongruity of the characters (the part-rat, part-human costuming of Brother Rat and Sister Rat and the worms in Rosemary's hair, for example) and some of the dialogue (Rosemary's insistence that she is descended from the Virgin Mary and the pope), true to the tradition of the Theater of the Absurd, seem humorous.

Yet, ultimately, the play poses more questions than it answers. In this highly ritualized setting, where is God? If organized Western religion is bankrupt of meaning for Brother Rat and Sister Rat, does this mean that all religious experience remains irrelevant? Are the rats doomed to die in this nightmarish world, or is there an escape? Can the rats' beliefs in what Rosemary has taught them (which inevitably leads to their deaths) be turned into a belief in themselves?

Critical Context

Critics who have studied *A Rat's Mass* tend to see in it issues concerning race. The division of minorities into ghetto communities has been noted. Some writers have noted Kennedy's use of animal imagery, relating it to her use of similar imagery in other plays. The idea that the rats in the play are regarded as vermin is of special importance. Other writers have discussed the premiere of this play, which, unlike most of Kennedy's other plays, was held not in America but in Europe—in fact, in Rome. In light of the play's use of the Roman Catholic church and the Roman Empire to represent European civilization, the locale of the premiere seems particularly significant.

Adrienne Kennedy's work has, from the beginning of her career, attracted much interest. Her plays demonstrate her unique and innovative abilities as a theater artist, and perhaps no Kennedy play more succinctly illustrates her desires to experiment with dramatic form and content than *A Rat's Mass*. On the whole, however, critics of Kennedy's work have tended to overlook *A Rat's Mass*, possibly because it is far shorter than most of her other theater pieces. Those commentators who do mention the play find it consistent with her overall vision and technique; perhaps its intensity and its intentional obscurity make it more difficult to write about. In any case, few have attempted to make sense of this challenging work.

Bibliography
Blau, Herbert. "The American Dream in American Gothic: The Plays of Sam Shepard and Adrienne Kennedy." *Modern Drama* 27, no. 4. (December, 1984): 520-539. A crucial piece by distinguished insightful critic of the theater. Compares playwrights Shephard and Kennedy, noting why they ought to be considered two of the most important dramatists working on the American stage. Most critics writing on Kennedy since Blau published this article refer back to it.
Bryant-Jackson, Paul K., and Lois More Overbeck, eds. *Intersecting Boundaries: The Theatre of Adrienne Kennedy*. Minneapolis: University of Minnesota Press, 1992. An interesting collection of articles. Includes critiques by literary and theater scholars, pieces dealing with the production of Kennedy's plays, and several extensive interviews with Kennedy. Overbeck's "The Life of the Work: A Preliminary Sketch" offers important information on the original production and first publication of *A Rat's Mass*, as well as on the production and publication of Kennedy's other plays.
Kennedy, Adrienne. "A MELUS Interview with Adrienne Kennedy." *MELUS: The Journal of the Society for the Study of the Multi-Ethnic Literature of the United States* 12 (Fall, 1985): 99-108. The playwright talks about issues of race and culture, on a personal and professional level, and discusses how politics and gender have an impact on writing for the modern theater. Kennedy offers a frank discussion of how her private and public lives have fused in the creation of her art.
_____. "An Interview with Adrienne Kennedy." *Studies in American Drama, 1945-Present* 4 (1989): 143-157. In this intimate and often revealing interview, Kennedy discusses her career. The experiences she shares with the interviewer illuminate how her personal life has had an impact on her dramatic works.
Shinn, Thelma. "Living the Answer: The Emergence of African American Feminist Drama." *Studies in the Humanities* 17 (December, 1990): 149-159. A view of how Kennedy's works fit into the broader field of plays by African American women dramatists. The writer suggests how such dramaturgy has evolved from the works of Lorraine Hansberry onward and notes that African American feminist writers tend toward nonrealistic conventions. Shinn also compares the rattraps of *A Rat's*

Mass to the ghetto setting of Hansberry's *A Raisin in the Sun* (1959).

Sollors, Werner. "Owls and Rats in the American Funnyhouse." *American Literature: A Journal of Literary History, Criticism, and Bibliography* 63 (September, 1991): 507-532. A fascinating study of several of Kennedy's plays, including *A Rat's Mass*. The author discusses imagery found in Kennedy's work and attempts to synthesize the playwright's view of America. Helpful in interpreting some of Kennedy's obscure and nightmarish motifs.

Kenneth Krauss

RECKLESS EYEBALLING

Author: Ishmael Reed (1938-   )
Type of work: Novel
Type of plot: Satire
Time of plot: The 1980's
Locale: New York City and the fictional Caribbean island of New Oyo
First published: 1986

Principal characters:

IAN BALL, a black playwright in his late twenties or early thirties
TREMONISHA SMARTS, a playwright and a black feminist
BECKY FRENCH, a director and white feminist
JAKE BRASHFORD, a black playwright
LAWRENCE O'REEDY, a white detective
RANDY SHANK, a black playwright

The Novel

Reckless Eyeballing is a work written in the third person that closely follows the life of black playwright Ian Ball over a period of weeks in Manhattan as he tries to get his second major play produced. Having left the Caribbean island of New Oyo to become a famous writer, Ian is caught between the conflicting political demands of a small group of theater people. Ian emotionally and philosophically vacillates between feuding factions that argue over his position as playwright and the political correctness of his play. He is torn between loyalty to a simpler Southern way of life and the hectic, conflicting social interactions in a major Northern city. Ian is also philosophically trapped between an older generation of black, male, radical, antifeminist playwrights and an emerging group of white and black radical feminist playwrights and directors. A series of short vignettes shows the increasing demands put on Ian by his producer, Becky French, and his director, Tremonisha Smarts. His chief supporter, a white director named Jim Minsk, is brutally sacrificed in a racist and sexist ceremony held at a fraudulent "college" in the South. At the same time, a bizarre series of attacks on leading feminists in the arts is perpetrated by the Flower Phantom, a masked intruder who cuts off his victims' hair and leaves a chrysanthemum at the scene of his crimes, claiming the women deserve the same punishment that French female collaborators with the Nazis received after World War II. White detective Lawrence O'Reedy is assigned to the case. Nearing the end of his tenure as a New York police officer, O'Reedy is suffering from hallucinations in which the black and Hispanic victims of his quick gun come back to haunt him. The Flower Phantom continuously strikes throughout the novel, as O'Reedy's investigation becomes more and more muddled. Ian's mixed reaction to the Flower Phantom reflects his troubled state of mind. He refers to himself as a Dr. Jekyll and Mr. Hyde; he rationally feels the attacker is crazy but emotionally supports his actions.

Becky French demands that Ian's play, slated to be shown at the prestigious Mount-batten Theater, be produced instead at a smaller venue. In place of Ian's play, Becky plans to produce *Eva's Honeymoon*, a play that takes place at the end of World War II in Adolf Hitler's bunker. In this play, Eva Braun rebels against Hitler, claiming that she as well as other German women have been victimized. Eva shoots and kills Hitler and then runs away with Hitler's chauffeur. During a meeting at Becky's office, Ian finds out his play will receive little support. Becky vehemently objects to Ian's depiction of female characters, claiming that Ian's male gaze has perverted their position in the drama; Ian proclaims the authenticity of his vision. Becky has him thrown out of her office, and over a series of days Ian succumbs to the seemingly inevitable alterations of his work, hoping that he can still get his play produced. His new director is Tremonisha Smarts, a leading black feminist playwright recently victimized by the Flower Phantom.

In the process of rewriting the play, Ian feels that Tremonisha brings knowledge and dramatic savvy to the piece. Yet he continues to balk at a major alteration of the drama concerning a black male named Ham Hill. *Reckless Eyeballing* is a play about Ham, who was lynched for "recklessly eyeballing" a white woman named Cora Mae. Ham's body is disinterred, and the skeleton is put on trial by Cora Mae to legally prove that Ham was guilty of sexual misconduct. Originally, Ian had Ham proven not guilty, but Becky insists that Ham be indicted and condemned again for a sexual crime. Tremonisha refuses to change the original idea. She and Becky argue vehemently over Becky's radical stance, and Tremonisha accuses Becky of being a white feminist who does not sympathize with black feminists.

Jake Brashford, an aging black playwright famous for his play *The Man Who Was an Enigma*, has sponsored Ian for artistic grants in the past. Jake is a staunch black radical who represents a protest philosophy that Ian increasingly finds out of date. Jake vehemently objects to Ian's working in consort with feminists and rails against any compromising tendencies Ian voices. Randy Shank, another older black play-wright famous for the play *The Rise and Fall of Mighty Joe Young*, is known for his radical message of black male sexual supremacy. After failure in Europe and black-listing at home, Randy is reduced to working as a doorman at Tremonisha's apart-ment complex. Randy distrusts all feminists, black or white, and is extremely anti-Semitic. Ian also deals with Shoboater, a black critic originally from New Oyo. Shoboater mocks Ian's lack of continental taste in food and liquor and warns Ian against collaboration with any feminists.

Ian's play is successfully staged after Tremonisha leaves for California and Ian agrees to all Becky's changes. Jake appears at the production and, in a drunken rage, accuses Ian of compromising with feminists. Shoboater writes a critical review of the play, but it is put on a back page of his paper. Randy Shank is shot by O'Reedy. Ian returns to New Oyo, where his mother's chauffeured car brings him to her pala-tial house. On the way, Ian reads a letter from Tremonisha Smarts in which she renounces her radical black feminism and condemns the theater world of Manhat-tan. She plans to let herself gain weight, have children, and continue to write. Ian's mother has a house guest named Johnnie Krenshaw, a "goddess" of the feminist movement, who wrote a famous play *No Good Man.* Johnnie is also undergoing a change in attitude, rejecting feminism and writing plays that she could read in church. Martha Ball leaves Johnnie and Ian to talk and goes upstairs to unpack her son's clothes. She finds a crumpled leather coat, a beret, a black mask, and human hair of many textures and colors, suggesting that Ian was the Flower Phantom all along.

The Characters

Ian Ball is the principal character in the book. As a young playwright from the fictional Caribbean island of New Oyo, Ball is undergoing an identity crisis in the high-pressure theatrical world of New York. All the other characters can be seen in relation to Ian, who is at the center of a battle between male and female viewpoints.

The crux of the novel involves Ian's attempts to get his second play, *Reckless Eyeballing,* published. Becky French, director and white feminist, and Tremonisha Smarts, playwright and black feminist, oppose the production. Jake Brashford and Randy Shank, both black playwrights, urge Ian not to change his mind and give in to feminist pressure to rework his play.

Detective O'Reedy seems a caricature of a sexist, racist white policeman. His frequent use of violence on black and Hispanic subjects suggests mental instability. His search for the Flower Phantom, who defiles women by shaving off their hair, seems anything but authentic.

In fact, the characters in the novel are difficult to picture as real human beings, because they exist principally as mouthpieces for ideas. Consequently, it is hard to develop sympathy for them as characters with real problems. Throughout the novel, few of the characters change or question themselves; they have the feel of types rather than individuals.

Ian appears to be an exception; he gives in to the demands of his feminist producers and changes the focus of his play. The reader is cautioned, however, concerning Ball's own motivations. Ian describes himself as a Jekyll-and-Hyde sort, giving rise to questions about his own characterization.

In fact, the author is pulling a sleight-of-hand trick with his characters. Drawing strict ideological lines is part of his satiric intent. The feminist debates that occur throughout the novel depict the women characters Tremonisha and Becky as unrelentingly hostile to male viewpoints. The black men Jake and Randy are equally inflexible. By making the characters behave in this way, certain viewpoints are ridiculed, showing the dangers of extreme behavior and political correctness. The one sympathetic character in the novel besides Ian's mother is Jim Minsk. Minsk is a Jewish director who supports Ian but who is killed early on in a public execution that satirizes Ku Klux Klan activities.

Tremonisha Smarts revokes her hard-line feminist perspective at the end of the novel, but this sudden about-face rings false. There is no preparation given in the text for this radical change of attitude, and the episode is only one of many character surprises that occur in the text without warning.

The narrator of the novel is unreliable. Information is withheld at the will of the nameless but omniscient narrator. The prime example of this manipulation concerns the identity of the Flower Phantom, which is hidden until the last page of the novel. The reader is given much information about Ian without any clues as to his true identity. Therefore, the revelation of his true nature as the Flower Phantom seems somewhat contrived and out of character.

Themes and Meanings

Reckless Eyeballing is written in broad, extravagant gestures that often have the characters lecturing one another at the tops of their voices. Each character represents a particular viewpoint; there is little agreement and no sympathy among them, and the novel thus has a chilling, satiric quality. The wanton attacks of the Flower Phantom and Jim Minsk's brutal death at the hands of anti-Semitic extremists contribute to this sense of frozen hatreds incapable of thaw. Ian Ball is caught in the middle of philosophical fights between black males and black feminists and between white and black feminists. The powerful prejudices of each group are magnified by the intense competition in the Manhattan theater world. As a social satire, the novel portrays the contradictory aspects of political correctness that lie behind the main characters' behaviors and decisions. The extreme stances of Jake Brashford and Randy Shank are diametrically opposed to the equally fanatic postures of Tremonisha Smarts and Becky French. Ian's overweening ambition to be a famous playwright puts him in a difficult position. He pays lip service to Randy Shank while seeing him as a buffoon, and he silently ridicules Jake Brashford, who has provided him with grants and support. At the same time, he wants to co-opt their black protest reputations without declaring himself a member of their group. In addition, Ian's first play, *Suzanna*, about a black female plantation hand who uses sexual manipulation to survive, has gotten him in trouble with both black and white feminists. Ian desperately wants his play *Reckless Eyeballing* produced, and this leads him to make concessions that run contrary to his natural inclinations. He consents to the drastic alteration demanded by Becky French that Ham Hill be in effect condemned twice for the indiscretion of looking at a white woman.

The state of Ian's mind is suggested in the opening sequence of the novel, in which Ian dreams that Becky French and Tremonisha Smarts are Puritan judges condemning him to the gallows. Ian's relationships to women in the novel are casual, incomplete, and sexually manipulative. He is closest to his mother, on whom he relies for support and money. Other women are simply bed partners cast off at the first opportunity. Furthermore, Ian is less than honest in his everyday social interactions. With Jim Minsk, he vehemently rejects any control over his work by feminist directors and criticizes them brutally. Yet, when Jim is killed, Ian quickly acquiesces to Becky French's alterations. Likewise, Ian's male-dominant sexual fantasies concerning the major female characters are delivered through interior monologues that run counter to his voiced agreements with radical feminist ideas. The Jekyll-and-Hyde quality of his behavior extends to the very end of the novel, when the reader discovers on the last page that Ian is actually the Flower Phantom. Detective O'Reedy continues the stereotypic characterization, resembling overblown cinematic detectives. In fact, frequent references to films and film stars in the text reinforce the cartoon quality of the action. Reed also refers to real African American artists such as Chester Himes, Josephine Baker, and Langston Hughes. The dramatic action of the play *Reckless Eyeballing* brings to mind the tragedy of Emmett Till, who was murdered in Mississippi for similar indiscretions with a white woman. Tremonisha is the name of a character from a Scott Joplin opera who is assimilated into white culture. This mixture of fact and fiction complicates the narrative, bringing into question the very notion of what makes a novel. The self-reflexive texts of this and other Reed novels work as vehicles of expression in which Reed stresses the importance of African American and Afrocentric traditions.

The heavily drawn confrontations of the novel, coupled with characters with little psychological nuance, mirror the burlesque qualities of the plays within the text. The plays *Reckless Eyeballing* and *Eva's Honeymoon* appear to be absurd social satires. In the same way, the bold, exaggerated characterization and action of the novel satirize extreme viewpoints. For all the discussion about changing sexual identity in the novel, nobody really changes. The last-minute renunciations of arch feminism by Tremonisha and Johnnie Krenshaw come without any foreshadowing in the novel and therefore ring false. They simply serve Ian's predominant viewpoint and reinforce the textual theme satirizing empty rhetoric. The brutal slaying of Jim Minsk at an outdoor ceremony by extremist perverts masking as academics suggests parody. The final revelation that Ian Ball is actually the Flower Phantom completes the implication that the novel is a satiric portrait of human fallibility. The central conceit of the theater, with its conventions of masquerade, completes the metaphor. The novel suggests that human nature is prone to masks of duplicity and that political and sexual correctness is simply another facet of the bitter human tradition of deceit used for personal gain.

Critical Context

Reckless Eyeballing fits into a personal literary tradition established by Reed through the publication of other satiric novels such as *The Free-Lance Pallbearers* (1967), *Yellow Back Radio Broke-Down* (1969), *Mumbo Jumbo* (1972), and *The Last Days of Louisiana Red* (1974). These novels suggest that Reed is not afraid to tackle dangerous social subjects or critique prevalent or accepted stereotypes. In his novels, Reed builds a landscape that blends fantasy with reality, ignoring conventional characterizations and distorting linear time frames. He blends popular culture figures and genre conventions into his fiction, so that his novels evoke archetypal images without conforming to any specific formula. His satire ranges from subtle parody to outright buffoonery while lampooning varied concepts of race, class, and gender. His exaggerated characters have often proven difficult for critics to handle. In particular, feminist critics have questioned his portrayal of women. Yet Reed's reworking of African American cultural identity, stressing Afrocentric origins, black vernacular creativity, and black survival abilities, puts him at the forefront of African American postmodernism. Nominated for two National Book Awards, Reed is a prolific and important African American writer who has published novels, poems, plays, and essays. His critical stature continues to grow as he explores the varied world of African American and American cultures with a unique voice.

Bibliography

Byerman, Keith E. "Voodoo Aesthetics: History and Parody in the Novels of Ishmael Reed." In *Fingering the Jagged Grain: Tradition and Form in Recent Black Fiction.* Athens: University of Georgia Press, 1985. Focuses on Reed's use of parody and reworking of history. Suggests that Reed uses a unique combination of metaphysical form and social critique in his work.

Fox, Robert Elliot. "Ishmael Reed: Gathering the Limbs of Osiris." In *Conscientious Sorcerers: The Black Postmodernist Fiction of Leroi Jones/Amiri Baraka, Ishmael Reed, and Samuel R. Delany.* New York: Greenwood Press, 1987. Fox studies in depth seven of Reed's novels and finds that each work builds on the previous one, expanding Reed's aesthetic. Sees *Reckless Eyeballing* as having elements of farce that add to the trickster tradition of African American narrative.

Harris, Norman. *"The Last Days of Louisiana Red:* The Hoodoo Solution." In *Connecting Times: The Sixties in Afro-American Fiction.* Jackson: University Press of Mississippi, 1988. Analyzes *The Last Days of Louisiana Red* in relation to Reed's insistence that racial histories be reviewed and rewritten. Comments on Reed's methods are helpful for understanding Reed's later works such as *Reckless Eyeballing.*

Martin, Reginald. *Ishmael Reed and the New Black Aesthetic Critics.* New York: St. Martin's Press, 1988. Martin closely analyzes Reed's evolving notion of Neo-HooDoo aesthetics and how it relates to new black aesthetic critics such as Clarence Major, Houston Baker, Jr., Addison Gayle, Jr., and Amiri Baraka. Comes to the conclusion that Reed refuses to acknowledge any mode of criticism, whether white or black. Discusses *Reckless Eyeballing* as a satiric allegory that demonstrates Reed's constant ability to change.

Settle, Elizabeth A., and Thomas A. Settle. *Ishmael Reed: A Primary and Secondary Bibliography.* Boston: G. K. Hall, 1982. Covers all aspects of Reed's publishing career, including sound recordings and videotapes, through 1981. A valuable resource guide for articles and essays by Reed as well as reviews of his work.

Whitlow, Roger. "Ishmael Reed." In *Black American Literature: A Critical History.* Chicago: Nelson-Hall, 1973. Covers the early career of Reed, including his poetry, and makes a strong argument for his inclusion in the absurdist literary tradition.

Stephen F. Soitos

REFLEX AND BONE STRUCTURE

Author: Clarence Major (1936-   )
Type of work: Novel
Type of plot: Metaphysical detective
Time of plot: The late 1960's or early 1970's
Locale: New York City
First published: 1975

>
> *Principal characters:*
> THE NARRATOR, a primary character although nameless and never
>   described
> CORA HULL, a black actress
> CANADA JACKSON, a serious suitor of Cora
> DALE, an Off-Broadway actor

The Novel

The interrelationships of four characters are examined in this novel of discursive experimentation. The main protagonists of the novel are the narrator, Cora Hull, Canada Jackson, and Dale. Cora Hull is present during most of the action, which takes place primarily in New York City, with occasional trips to places such as the Poconos and New England. Since none of the trips is described in any detail, the reader cannot be sure if they really take place. The characters can travel as easily to the South Pole as to the neighborhood theater. The novel is written in the first person and in the present tense, which gives the narrator complete control over what takes place. In fact, the narrator tells the reader that he is unreliable and consciously manipulating the text. He stresses the fact that he is simply an act of his own imagination. Because of the episodic, often contradictory form of the novel, the reader's suspension of disbelief is challenged. There is little certainty about anything in this novel, which is one of the implied intents of the narrator, who often claims that forgetfulness or simple arbitrariness purposely alters the text.

There are, however, certain motifs that recur throughout the text that provide stable points of reference. The primary frame of reference is the narrator, who tells the reader that he is writing a novel while he is writing it. The narrator comments continuously on the problems he has in constructing the text as a result of his own misinterpretations, his forgetfulness, his difficulty in describing how things appear or are, and his constant flights of fancy. All the other characters are at the mercy of the narrator's whims. Thus, they are at times sent away or drop out of the action depending on the narrator's moods. Often, the narrator will contradict himself or even blend himself into the other characters. While the activity of all four characters takes place in a skewed, apparently haphazard time frame, the story obviously centers around Cora Hull. Cora is presented in a variety of ways. At one time, she is studying feminist theory. Often she is appearing in a play, but the reader learns little about the drama. Usually, she is presented in relation to one of the three other characters in an indeterminate time frame. Cora is the center of the novel, and all the other characters are redefined through her, but she too is endlessly mutable. Commonly, she is the locus of their sexual attention as well as a physical presence to which the narrator returns again and again.

Although Canada, Dale, and the narrator are fixated on Cora, none of them maintains any long-term relationships. They revolve around one another without really understanding one another. Their closeness is suggested by the interwoven repetition of their personal and sexual encounters, which are presented in matter-of-fact terms. The narrator claims they all have problems focusing on anything. At various times, they either live in the same apartment or in close proximity to one another. Much of the novel takes place inside apartments, in rooms ill-defined and vague. The narrator complains about this, claiming they stay inside with closed-in thoughts too much.

From the various locales mentioned, the reader can tell that the characters live in Manhattan. Cora is an actress often at rehearsals or trying out for plays. Dale and Canada have no known occupations, although they are associated with the theater as actors. The narrator at one point calls himself a theater director. They drift in and out of the timeless plot, sometimes threatening, sometimes friendly, but never really defined. Another recurring motif is a young Puerto Rican boy who wears a green shirt. The boy is seen everywhere and somehow has access to the apartments of the characters. He is mysteriously attracted to Cora and appears at regular intervals throughout the novel without altering the direction of action or having anything to do with the rest of the characters.

There are other repeated motifs that give the novel the eerie sense of suspense associated with detective fiction. A bomb has exploded on the street, and the police are investigating the apparent assassination of two people. Somebody with a suitcase has been murdered. There are indications that the murder has been committed by an unnamed revolutionary group. Hints are given that Canada is a member of a black revolutionary group responsible for the bombing; all the characters are fingerprinted as suspects. The nameless police return again and again to the scene of the crime with no apparent success in their investigation. The boy with the green shirt says he knows who owned the suitcase that exploded. The narrator says that the boy lies. The narrator also says that the crime occurred just outside his apartment. At times, the narrator states that it was Cora who was killed, but a few pages later, Cora is back. In the end, the narrator claims that it was he who murdered Dale and Cora, suggesting that the murder is a figment of his literary imagination.

Likewise, at various times in the course of the narrative, well-known literary and cinematic icons such as Agatha Christie and John Wayne appear. The narrator makes numerous references to old movies and actors from early crime films; the cinematic references reflect the narrator's interest in film and mirror the cinematic quality of the text, which occurs in small "takes." There are also a number of sections that consist simply of lists, more often than not lists of black musicians or other well-known African American artists. These lists seem to function as a type of naïve empiricism, proving by their very existence that a world outside the text does exist as well as affirming the positive quality of African American cultural expression.

The novel is composed of small vignettes broken into two sections, entitled "A Bad Connection" and "Body Heat." Approximately equal in length, these two sections offer no clue as to the meaning of their titles or their function in the overall narrative. There is no discernible change in storytelling method or characters from one section to the next. In fact, the novel ends much as it began, with the narrator slipping in and out of surreal dream sequences in which the characters blend with one another and into absurd scenarios.

As these characters intermingle, connect, and disconnect, however, there is a curious static quality about the text. The reader is never sure if anything happens. In fact, the reader becomes the detective of the novel, trying desperately to put all the disparate pieces together. A perverse, unnameable menace seems to keep anything from occurring in ways that can be understood. This menace may simply be the avowed manipulation of the narrator—or it may be the intent of the narrator to suggest that the true nature of existence consists of these seemingly random encounters with people and places to which there is no rhyme or reason.

The Characters

There are no characters as such in this experimental novel. The reader is given very little reliable information about the four people mentioned in the text, Cora Hull, Canada Jackson, Dale, and the narrator.

Cora Hull is at the center of the novel; the other characters, including the narrator, are usually described in relation to her. Cora may have been killed at the beginning of the novel. Therefore, the rest of the novel may be looked at as an attempt to explain and define Cora's life. The short, episodic quality of the text includes many intriguing and sometimes contradictory descriptions of Cora.

Cora is presented in many moods and in many ways. Her life, however, does not seem to have a center or a definitive purpose. At one moment, she is a beginning actress who tries out for Off-Broadway shows. Later, she is described as being a famous actress. She is also described, variously, as a member of a black revolutionary group, a member of a white revolutionary group, and a feminist. Cora is a complicated character described in fleeting images that do not give a complete picture of her.

All three of the other characters, including the narrator, are described in relation to Cora. Canada, Dale, and the narrator are suitors of Cora, but none has any lasting relationships. These characters are also described in images that give impressions but form no clear picture. All the characters are in a constant state of flux, never staying in one place long enough to be fully described or analyzed.

The most interesting aspect of this experimental approach to characterization is the relation of the narrator to the text and to the other characters. The narrator informs the reader early on in the book that the other characters are under his control. The narrator confesses to being unreliable, forgetful, and absentminded. The use of fantasy and surreal episodes springing from the narrator's imagination makes the characterization even harder to analyze. Also, the narrator confesses to being in love with Cora. As he is presented as one of three suitors to Cora's affections, the way he describes Cora may be attributed to his jealousy or to his feelings of inferiority.

This nontraditional use of character description and motivation makes for an intriguing fictional presentation. The whole question of narrative control through the process of naming and describing is examined. Furthermore, the main character becomes the narrator; since he is writing the novel, his freedom of perception affects the way the novel is understood.

Major's use of characterization in *Reflex and Bone Structure* forces the reader to reexamine received notions of fictional presentation. The abstract flow of words functions nonrepresentationally on the page, in much the same way that abstract painting forces the viewer to see the paint before the image. In this sense, the book's characters are more poetic constructs than realistic presentations.

Themes and Meanings

The title of *Reflex and Bone Structure* suggests a way to interpret the characters and plot. Cora Hull has X rays of her brain, heart, womb, and bone structure framed and hanging in her living room. For all the intimacy that this might suggest, the reader really learns little about Cora. The stark, negative images of X rays suggest only the essential outlines of things. The novel itself, like the image of an X ray, is reduced to its bare bones in this text. Aristotle's dramatic verities of time, place, and action are subverted, and there is virtually no characterization and very little plot development. The novel revolves around four shadowy characters interacting in ambiguous and contradictory ways. The episodes of the novel seem to ignite spontaneously from the mind of the narrator. The plot reads like the reflex reactions of the narrator, who puzzles out his existence among characters who may or may not be real. Since everything is consciously filtered through the narrator's viewpoint, and since he says that he is lying, the reader's response is also much like a reflex reaction; that is, the reader is constantly bewildered and under attack as much as are the narrator and the other characters.

Because there is a crime, detectives, and an investigation, certain rudiments of the detective novel genre are satisfied. Yet the investigation stalls, and the unsolved crime stands as a metaphor for the rest of the novel, in which nothing gets resolved. The reader is forced to assume the detective role, amassing clues that go nowhere. The reader's role as detective also ends in failure, since the key to the crime and the book lies with the narrator, who refuses to relinquish his hold.

As a metaphysical detective novel, the book meets the criteria of other postmodernist detective novels. One of the assumptions of classical detective fiction is that the detective can solve the crime. In metaphysical detective novels, the formula of detective fiction is subverted. The details are twisted, the plot is awkward, the characters are strange—nothing can be solved. The detective in these novels is often ineffectual, and the reader is forced to assume the role of detective in trying to bring order to the text. Often, however, order cannot be imposed, suggesting that the novel might be about the process of understanding itself as well as about the nature of language. In the end, nothing makes sense but the poetry of the words. This contradiction of readers' expectations is a decided ploy on the part of the narrator. *Reflex and Bone Structure* is a conscious attempt to take away plot, characterization, and motivation, leaving little connective narrative tissue. This type of confrontational and self-reflexive text is often called metafiction. It is a trademark of metafiction to emphasize the artifice of fiction, thereby questioning the very notion of what a novel is.

Indeed, the author, Clarence Major, is quite aware of the conundrums preferred by this type of fiction and gives the reader some warning of what is coming. On the book's inscription page, there is an enjoinder that reads, "This book is an extension of, not a duplication of reality. The characters and events are happening for the first time." The author's preamble suggests the spontaneous quality of *Reflex and Bone Structure*. The very short, elliptical, and confusing vignettes bewilder the narrator as much as the reader. The narrator is a character in his own narrative, but he does not possess the omniscient quality of most narrators. The present-tense format also adds to the sense that the story is unfolding immediately in front of the reader.

If there is a death in this text, it is the death of the novel as commonly experienced. The characters in *Reflex and Bone Structure* sometimes blend into one another. Insects and frogs mysteriously appear in large numbers, inhabiting rooms or dropping from Cora Hull's dress. The characters are often described as being in a room; suddenly, in the same paragraph, they are transported to some remote beach. This fluid and strangely melting quality of the text gives it a surreal quality. The absurd and unreal scenes reel out in a seemingly random fashion, as if the narrator were asleep or hallucinating. None of the characters acts consistently and with purpose. For all this movement and spontaneity, *Reflex and Bone Structure* projects claustrophobia and paranoia. Nothing is ever done or accomplished in the novel, and none of the mysteries of its text is elucidated. None of the characters changes or develops, because the reader does not really know who they are. The narrator continuously bemoans his increasing age but never reveals what that age is. The novel is reduced to an obsession for indeterminacy. This sense of incompleteness is what people normally fight against by writing books, creating plays, believing in something. This indeed may be the warning of the narrator in writing such a novel—that one must know oneself first so that one in turn may know the world.

Reflex and Bone Structure confronts the accepted notions of the novel. It demands to be met on its own terms, suggesting that the key to all reality is elusive and that fiction has a life of its own. With the novel's pastiche construction, it is much like an abstract canvas creating a new perspective on fiction. The reader is forced to interact with the text and, in so doing, question the nature of fiction and of reality.

Critical Context

Reflex and Bone Structure is a good example of Clarence Major's continuing experiments in trying to erase the boundaries between prose and poetry. The novel fits into a body of work by the author devoted to innovative narrative techniques. In novels such as *All-Night Visitors* (1969), *No* (1973), and *Emergency Exit* (1979), the author uses a combination of prose experiments to present an alternative viewpoint of the African American experience. Major infuses language with new power through radical alterations of conventional plots and characterization. He stresses the beauties of sensual experience and the special gifts of black Americans.

Major is an African American poet and the author of the *Dictionary of Afro-American Slang* (1970); he is often cited as one of the founding theoreticians of the 1960's new black aesthetic movement. As editor of the poetry anthology *The New Black Poetry* (1969), Major stresses the importance of African American poetic identity in collectively attempting to revolutionize social and political relationships through creation of a brotherhood of black consciousness. This African American cultural emphasis and heightened sense of the positive black identity is shared by other black writers such as Amiri Baraka (LeRoi Jones), Addison Gayle, and Ishmael Reed.

Bibliography
Bell, Bernard W. "Modernism and Postmodernism." In *The Afro-American Novel and Its Tradition.* Amherst: University of Massachusetts Press, 1987. Places Major in the African American postmodern tradition of experimenting with language and form. Sees Major as parodying the detective novel and testing the boundaries of its form.
Black American Literature Forum 13, no. 2 (1979). This special issue is devoted to Clarence Major and contains a number of interesting articles. Among these are "Towards a Primary Bibliography of Clarence Major," by Joe Weixlmann and Clarence Major, and "Major's *Reflex and Bone Structure* and the Anti-Detective Tradition," by Larry McCaffrey and Linda Gregory.
Klinkowitz, Jerome. *The Life of Fiction.* Urbana: University of Illinois Press, 1977. Includes a discussion of the disruptive qualities of Major's work in relation to the postmodern text. Sees Major as an instrumental African American writer who blends social and racial critique into experimental texts.
——————. *The Self-Apparent Word: Fiction as Language/Language as Fiction.* Carbondale: Southern Illinois University Press, 1984. Places Major in a postmodern tradition of writers including William S. Burroughs and John Barth. Considers *Reflex and Bone Structure* a text that draws vitality from the "self-apparency" of its construction.
Major, Clarence. *The Dark and Feeling: Black American Writers and Their Work.* New York: Third Press, 1974. A collection of varied essays, including Major's seminal essay "Black Criteria." Also a number of interviews, including a self-interview.

Stephen F. Soitos

ROLL OF THUNDER, HEAR MY CRY

Author: Mildred D. Taylor (1943-   )
Type of work: Novel
Type of plot: Historical realism
Time of plot: October, 1933, to August, 1934
Locale: Rural Mississippi
First published: 1976

Principal characters:

CASSIE LOGAN, the narrator, a nine-year-old black girl
STACEY, Cassie's twelve-year-old brother
CHRISTOPHER-JOHN, another brother, age seven
CLAYTON CHESTER ("LITTLE MAN"), the youngest Logan, age six
DAVID LOGAN (PAPA), the Logan family's father, a farmer and laborer
MARY LOGAN (MAMA), the Logan family's mother, a schoolteacher
BIG MA, Cassie's grandmother
UNCLE HAMMER, Papa's hot-tempered older brother
MR. MORRISON, a huge "human tree"

The Novel

Roll of Thunder, Hear My Cry is a psychologically realistic, historically accurate picture of black family life in rural Mississippi. It is also an excellent initiation novel about a young girl growing up to learn about the values and dangers of her Depression-era world.

The Logan family lives in Spokane County, Mississippi, on four hundred acres of land that Cassie Logan's grandfather, a former slave, purchased years before. Harlan Granger, whose family originally owned the Logan property and who owns all the farms around it (now sharecropped by poorer black families), wants the Logan parcel back, and it is a struggle for the Logan family to hold on to their land. The novel is set in rural Mississippi in the early 1930's, and conditions for blacks could hardly be worse. Just how bad they are, Cassie Logan soon learns.

Cassie, who narrates the novel, is a smart, curious girl who loves her parents, especially her father, who is off working in Louisiana. When Papa Logan returns home in chapter 2, he is accompanied by Mr. Morrison, who has been fired from his railroad job for fighting with whites and whom Papa is bringing home to help protect the family against a recent wave of vigilante terrorism; distant neighbors have just been visited by the dreaded night riders, and one man has already died of burns.

Several plot lines grow out of this opening situation. Papa tells the children to stay away from the Wallaces' crossroads store, knowing the Wallaces are involved in the recent terror, and he organizes a boycott. Mama is soon fired, allegedly for teaching black history but actually for being involved in the boycott. When Papa and Morrison go into Vicksburg for supplies, Papa is shot, and his leg is broken. Morrison saves Papa, but another income has been lost. As the momentum of the novel builds, these two stories coalesce: The fight to save the land from Harlan Granger and the fight against the racism and brutality of the Wallaces are intertwined, because the Wallace store is on Granger land.

After a series of adventures for both children and adults, the exciting climax comes when the night riders try to lynch T. J. Avery, a friend of the children who has been involved in a robbery. Stacey acts quickly, sending the other children to warn the Logans that the crowd will come to their house next. The resourceful David Logan sets fire to his own cotton field, which borders Harlan Granger's land, and the mob rushes to put it out. Black and white, men and women, the community fights the fire through the night.

Yet the crisis is not over. The land has been saved, the Logans have survived as a family and are probably even stronger, and two of the children—Cassie and Stacey—have learned more about the world of cruelty and injustice and how to maneuver in it safely. The novel does not end on any note of false optimism, however: the Logans are still poor, and racism and violence are still everywhere about them. "I cried for T. J.," Cassie says at the end of the novel, "For T. J. and the land." Her growth over the course of the novel indicates that the strong, independent Cassie will be able to operate in this racist society after the novel closes, but her tears at the end are also a sign of sadness for her loss of innocence.

In the course of the novel, Cassie comes to learn a great deal about the sacrifices her family is making to keep their land, about their struggle for equality, and about their pride in themselves and their heritage. As much as from anyone else, Cassie learns these lessons from her family; the Logans overwhelm readers with their warmth and mutual support. Big Ma tells Cassie about the importance of the Logan land and, by the lesson of her hard work in the Logan household, how much she is willing to do to hold on to it. Cassie's mother is, like her daughter, a real rebel, but she is fired for holding on to her principles.

The Characters

Characterization is one of the real strengths of *Roll of Thunder, Hear My Cry*. The book's characters are believable and, for the most part, sympathetic, and younger readers can easily identify with them.

The narrator and central character of the novel is nine-year-old Cassie Logan, a bright (some might say precocious) rebel who gains a fuller identity in the course of the novel through her family's struggles with racism and injustice during the Depression. She is, of course, no blank slate when the novel opens (she knows, for example, that "punishment was always less severe when I poured out the whole truth to Mama on my own before she had heard anything from anyone else"), but she still cannot understand why Mr. Barnett will not wait on them at his store in Strawberry. Through the actions of the novel, Cassie learns that—as Mama puts it—"in the world outside this house, things are not always as we would have them to be." Cassie's treatment of Lillian Jean Simms toward the novel's end is an indication that she will survive in this society, and her first-person narration allows readers to witness her growth and development through the novel.

One of the unusual qualities of *Roll of Thunder, Hear My Cry* as an initiation novel is that it has not one but two protagonists. While Cassie is learning about the world and moving from innocence and naïveté, she is also telling about her older brother Stacey's taking more responsibility and growing into maturity himself. At the opening of the novel, with his father away working on the railroad, Stacey is anxious to become the man of the family, and he resents the arrival of Mr. Morrison. He is already a young man with several clear Logan traits: It is his loyalty to his brother Little Man (humiliated when the white school bus muddies him) that leads to his plan of revenge, and he refuses to betray his friend T. J. when he gets caught with T. J.'s "cheat notes." Yet Stacey is still learning. When he gives away his new coat to T. J. because the other boy ridicules him for wearing it, Uncle Hammer warns him: "You care what a lot of useless people say 'bout you you'll never get anywhere, 'cause there's a lotta folks don't want you to make it." In the attack on the wagon, Stacey is unable to hold the horse; his father's leg is broken, and Stacey feels responsible. In his actions at the end of the novel, however, Stacey demonstrates that he has become his own man. When T. J. shows up hurt at the end of the novel, Stacey responds with loyalty, and his actions help to save the Logan family. In the sequel to *Roll of Thunder, Hear My Cry*, Stacey emerges as the central character.

The Logan parents have a similar complexity and depth. Although she has been teaching for fourteen years, Mrs. Logan is still considered something of a disruptive maverick by her fellow teachers. Children may have to learn the realities of race relations, she tells a colleague early on, "but that doesn't mean they have to accept them." She is eventually fired for adhering to this principle. She is also sensitive and loving: When Papa surprises her by arriving with Mr. Morrison, for example, she graciously accepts him. David Logan, on the other hand, is a compassionate man who "always took time to think through any move he made," but his quick thinking at the end of the novel saves the Logan family.

Even minor characters play important roles in the novel. Uncle Hammer is a "tall, handsome man" who is more hot-tempered than his younger brother and who provides an interesting contrast to Papa for the children. Jeremy Simms is a poor, sad boy who wants to do the impossible—befriend the Logan children—but whose actions underline the important theme of friendship in the novel. Only the adult whites, liberal (like the lawyer Mr. Jamison) or racist (like the Wallaces and the Simmses), seem two-dimensional and stereotypical—quite a triumph in a novel aimed primarily at young readers.

Themes and Meanings

There are a number of complex ideas at work in *Roll of Thunder, Hear My Cry.* The overriding theme is the initiation of the two eldest Logan children into the real world of Depression-era Mississippi, and they learn a number of lessons along their road to self-discovery. Two general subthemes are visible within the framework of initiation, two areas of adult life that Cassie and Stacey must learn about in order to survive. One is the negative pole: injustice and discrimination and the cruelty that follows from them. The other is almost the antidote to the first: the pride and self-respect that come from the Logan land and heritage.

Roll of Thunder, Hear My Cry is historically accurate and psychologically realistic—and brutal. The uneasy relations between the races established in rural Mississippi since Reconstruction are coming apart under the multiple pressures of the Depression (which began in the South before the 1930's), and the "night men" are riding again. While Mr. Jamison may be correct in saying that not all Southerners are bigots, characters such as the Wallaces and the Simmses predominate in this world of poor whites and blacks, and the novel is filled with incidents of discrimination and brutality. It is an ugly, violent world in which the Logan children are growing, but their parents try to give them the skills and support to make their journey a little less hazardous.

The theme of discrimination is thus from the beginning set against its opposites: self-respect, black pride, and the struggle to overcome prejudice and injustice. The physical embodiment of this positive pole is the Logan land, which gives the Logans freedom and a sense of their own worth and helps them hold themselves up in a world of white power and discrimination. Cassie's tears for "the land" at the end of the novel symbolize her recognition of the enormous price of this struggle.

The Logans are historically realistic and overwhelmingly positive in their love and their pride. These values are grounded in the land, Mildred D. Taylor is telling her readers: Give all the other families here—white and black—land of their own, and they would not witness bloodshed and humiliation. *Roll of Thunder, Hear My Cry* is a novel woven out of black history, a story not only of economic survival but also of the survival of the human spirit in the face of incredible obstacles.

The language of the novel is as local and natural as the land. Big Ma is "the color of a pecan shell," and Mama always "smelled of sunshine and soap." When Papa explains to Christopher-John why Mama's firing is so hard on her, he says that "she's born to teaching like the sun is born to shine." The first-person narration by Cassie is easy and consistent (if often adult in its vocabulary) and, like the conversations Cassie quotes, captures the black dialect of rural Depression Mississippi.

Another distinctive characteristic of this novel is the richness of its detail. Domestic life on this Southern Depression-era farm is rendered sensuously: Readers witness Big Ma ironing (with a second iron always heating in the fireplace); see Cassie churning, picking cotton, and lying under her patchwork quilt; feel the red Mississippi mud oozing through the children's toes on their way to school; and get hungry at the descriptions of food at the family get-togethers.

Finally, the novel is noteworthy for its unforced symbolism. Objects and incidents in the novel are important for their narrative value, and at the same time they often represent something larger. The Logan land, for instance, is a motivating force in the story, but it also symbolizes the Logan history in slavery and freedom. Weather, likewise, has a double meaning: The title's "roll of thunder" (taken from a verse that Mr. Morrison sings at the opening of chapter 11) is not only a presage of rain but also the heavenly response to a cry of anguish. Finally, even manmade objects can have this symbolic import: Uncle Hammer's silver Packard is an assertion of his own worth against the power of whites, while the gun that T. J. Avery hungers for is a sign of his need for that power but a clue to his ultimate weakness. The style and language of *Roll of Thunder, Hear My Cry*, in short, work against the didactic qualities of this fine novel and help to underscore subtly its significant themes.

Critical Context

Roll of Thunder, Hear My Cry won the 1977 Newbery Medal for "the most distinguished contribution to American literature for children." Taylor dedicates the novel to the memory of her father, "a master storyteller" who gave her countless oral histories

> of great-grandparents and of slavery and of the days following slavery; of those who lived still not free, yet who would not let their spirits be enslaved. From my father the storyteller I learned to respect the past, to respect my own heritage and myself.

Like Alex Haley in *Roots*, which was also published in 1976, Taylor was tracing her own black history and retelling a story, as she describes it in her Newbery Award acceptance speech, "about human pride and survival in a cruelly racist society."

Roll of Thunder, Hear My Cry is the central work in the cycle of novels about the Logan family, works aimed at both elementary and adolescent readers. The first was *Song of the Trees* (1975), a story for elementary readers concerning the Logan forest; *Let the Circle Be Unbroken* (1981) is the sequel to *Roll of Thunder, Hear My Cry* and focuses on Stacey Logan and the trial of T. J. Avery. *The Friendship* (1987) continues the Logan history in a story for younger readers centering on a confrontation with an elderly black man at the Wallace store. Finally, in *The Road to Memphis* (1990), Cassie helps a black youth to flee the state after a fight with white youths. *Roll of Thunder, Hear My Cry*, however, remains the best work in the series, as the numerous awards to it attest. Besides the Newbery Medal, the novel was awarded the American Library Association Notable Book Citation and was a National Book Award finalist.

Like a number of writers in the last decades of the twentieth century—William Armstrong in *Sounder* (1969), Paula Fox in *The Slave Dancer* (1973), or Virginia Hamilton in *Sweet Whispers, Brother Rush* (1982), for example—Mildred D. Taylor is giving back to her readers authentic and positive portraits of earlier black life.

Bibliography

Fogelman, Phyllis J. "Mildred D. Taylor." *The Horn Book Magazine* 53 (August, 1977): 410-414. A brief description of Taylor's early life and the influences on her first two books.

Harper, Mary Turner. "Merger and Metamorphosis in the Fiction of Mildred D. Taylor." *Children's Literature Association Quarterly* 13, no. 1 (Summer, 1988): 75-80. Harper analyzes the communal oral and musical tradition in Taylor's novels and states that the tradition "infuses Mildred Taylor's work, resulting in an imaginative blending of history, cultural traditions and practices so as to create a sequential *Bildungsroman* in four works."

Peterson, Linda Kauffman, and Marilyn Leathers Solt. *Newbery and Caldecott Medal and Honor Books: An Annotated Bibliography.* Boston: G. K. Hall, 1982. The authors identify most of the novel's strengths: "Although the family's problems are not solved by the book's end, spunky Cassie and her brothers have experienced some triumphs in the racist society in which they live. These bring both humor and satisfaction to a story that has many grim and frightening moments."

Rees, David. "The Color of Skin: Mildred Taylor." In *The Marble in the Water: Essays on Contemporary Writers of Fiction for Children and Young Adults.* Boston: The Horn Book, 1980. A comparative study that asserts that Taylor "comes closer than anyone else to giving us a really good novel about racial prejudice."

Taylor, Mildred D. "Newbery Award Acceptance: Address." *The Horn Book Magazine* 53 (August, 1977): 401-409. Taylor describes the origins of her prize-winning novel, which she says is "about human pride and survival in a cruelly racist society."

David Peck

ROOTS
The Saga of an American Family

Author: Alex Haley (1921-1992)
Type of work: Novel
Type of plot: Historical realism
Time of plot: 1750 to 1967
Locale: The Gambia, West Africa; and the Southern United States
First published: 1976

> *Principal characters:*
> KUNTA KINTE, "the African," progenitor of the American line of
>   Alex Haley's family
> KIZZY, the daughter of Kunta and Bell
> CHICKEN GEORGE, Kizzy's clever and resourceful son
> TOM MURRAY, the son of Chicken George
> CYNTHIA MURRAY PALMER, the daughter of Tom Murray and
>   grandmother of Alex Haley
> GEORGIA ANDERSON, the sole survivor of the "graying ladies" who
>   perpetuated the family narrative on Cynthia Palmer's porch
> ALEX HALEY, the great-great-great-great-grandson of Kunta Kinte

The Novel

Roots is, in Alex Haley's words, a "novelized amalgam" of documented historical and fictionalized events. Haley's artistic intent, that his family's narrative should serve as a symbolic saga for all Americans of African descent, pervades the novel on all levels. With the exception of the last three chapters, the novel is told from an omniscient, third-person perspective.

In the spring of 1750 in Juffure, The Gambia, a son is born to Omoro Kinte and his second wife, Binta. The child is named Kunta. As a member of the old and highly esteemed Kinte family, Kunta is schooled in the customs and traditions befitting a future Mandinka warrior. Throughout his childhood, Kunta is taught to avoid and fear the "toubob," white men who capture African people for evil purposes.

Despite these tribal caveats, Kunta is captured by white slave traders in 1767 while searching for a tree section to make a drum. Along with 140 Africans of various tribes, Kunta is shipped as cargo on the *Lord Ligonier*. Pestilence, filth, depravity, and cruelty fill this episode, serving as a controlling metaphor for the inhumanity of the institution of slavery. The captives unsuccessfully stage a revolt, resulting in the deaths of many. Kunta admires the courage of these dead, for they died as warriors. He, as a survivor, dreads what is to come, for he instinctively knows that his eventual fate will be worse than the ocean voyage.

In Annapolis, Maryland, Kunta is sold to John Waller and given the name "Toby." Appalled by the toubob and their pagan ways, Kunta attempts to escape four times. After his last attempt, he is apprehended by two slave catchers. Given the choice of castration or foot amputation, Kunta chooses the latter. John Waller's brother William, a physician, is outraged at the mutilation and buys Kunta.

Kunta, through the ministrations of William Waller's cook, Bell, recovers from this last ordeal. After a lengthy courtship, he "jumps de broom" (the slave equivalent of the marriage ceremony) with Bell. A daughter is born to the couple. Kunta gives her the Mandinka name of "Kizzy," meaning "you stay put." Now crippled and unable to run away, Kunta is entrusted with driving Dr. Waller on his calls, which enables him to hear news of the outside world. Of particular interest to Kunta are the accounts of Toussaint Louverture's revolt in Haiti, which he sees as paralleling his own struggle for freedom, especially when Napoleon Bonaparte captures Toussaint.

Kunta persists in keeping alive his dream of freedom and his pride in his African heritage, both of which he passes on to Kizzy. A clever child, Kizzy is entranced by her father's African tales and learns many Mandinka words. At the age of sixteen, she is sold to the dissolute Tom Lea as punishment for aiding another slave to escape.

Lea rapes Kizzy repeatedly for several months, eventually fathering a son, George. Kizzy, a devoted mother, regards her son as the descendant of "the African," not as the son of Tom Lea. She instills in her son both her pride in their African heritage and Kunta Kinte's dream of freedom.

As George grows to manhood, he exhibits traits of both parents. Like Tom Lea, he loves cockfighting and carousing. The rakish George becomes such an accomplished trainer of gamecocks that he earns the sobriquet of "Chicken George." From Kizzy he has inherited the desire to be free, and he is determined to buy himself and his family. When Lea loses Chicken George in a bet with an Englishman, he promises Chicken George his manumission papers upon his return.

Years later, Chicken George returns and is grudgingly freed by Lea. Kizzy has died during his absence, but Chicken George seeks to reunite his family, whom Lea had sold to the Murrays. When he finds the family, Chicken George gathers them around and relates the family narrative.

After the Civil War, the family moves to Henning, Tennessee. Upon Chicken George's death, Tom Murray, his son, asserts his position as patriarch and emphasizes the importance of the family and the oral tradition to his children. Both of these ideas are perpetuated by Tom's daughter, Cynthia, and other female members of the Murray family. Cynthia's daughter Bertha, who evinces little interest in the family narrative, goes away to college, where she meets and marries Simon Alexander Haley.

While Haley is a graduate student at Cornell, their first son is born, Alexander Haley. At this point, the novel abruptly shifts to Haley's first-person narrative, which recounts the death of his mother and the summers he and his brothers spent at Grandma Cynthia's house listening to the "graying ladies" tell the story of "the African Kin-tay" who called a guitar a "ko" and the river "Kamby Bolongo." In the final two chapters, Haley details the research and writing of *Roots*, addressing the fact/fiction elements of the novel.

The Characters

Kunta Kinte dominates the novel, within the narrative of his life story and within the context of the influence his story exerts over his descendants. Kunta is the only fully developed character in the novel. All others are on the periphery of the family narrative or are secondary characters, such as Chicken George, Kizzy, and Tom Murray. Characters such as Bell (Kunta's wife) and the fiddler (his friend) are one-dimensional. Their sole purpose is to provide points of view that differ from Kunta's.

For example, Bell represents the docility of the born slave. A strong, mature woman who loves her husband, she nevertheless is constantly disturbed by Kunta's African-isms. She takes umbrage when Kunta remarks that she looks like a Mandinka woman. "What fool stuff you talkin' 'bout? . . . Don' know how come white folks keep on emptyin' out boatloads a you Africa niggers!" Like most slaves, Bell has severed any ties or reminders of her African heritage. Furthermore, she regards Kunta's adherence to Mandinka practices as dangerous, always fearing what the massa's re-action might be, and with good reason. Bell's two daughters from a previous mar-riage were sold. Ever obedient, ever wary, Bell fears the breakup of her new family.

The fiddler represents the talented, enterprising, yet naïve slave who offers a de-cided contrast to Kunta, who hates and distrusts all toubob. The fiddler's story rein-forces Kunta's negativity. Essentially cheated out of his right to buy himself, the fiddler dies a broken and embittered old man. The knowledge of white treachery crushes his exuberance, whereas Kunta continues to resist and live.

Because he is the predominant character in the novel, his tale underscores the theme of freedom and the search for dignity. It is through Kunta's eyes that the reader is drawn into the horrors of the slave ship, witnesses the strangeness of the New World, and encounters the dilemma facing a devout Muslim in a Christian slave culture. Particularly repugnant to Kunta is the American—black and white—penchant for eating pork, considered to be a filthy and profane practice for a Muslim.

By making Kunta the driver for Dr. Waller, Haley is able to expose popular mis-conceptions about historical personages. For example, on his travels to other planta-tions, Kunta learns Thomas Jefferson's real views on the slavery issue: "I heared Massa Jefferson say slavery jes' bad for white folks as for us'ns, an' he 'gree wid Massa Hamilton it's jes' too much nachel diff'rence. . . . Dey say Massa Jefferson want to see us sot free, but not stickin' roun' dis country takin' po' white folks' jobs—he favor shippin' us back to Africa, gradual, widout big fuss an' mess."

The abrupt intrusion of Haley as the first-person narrator at the end of the novel serves a dual purpose. First, it allows Haley to outline explicitly the overarching agenda that permeates *Roots*. Second, the almost journalistic style employed vali-dates the novel's historical authenticity and importance.

Themes and Meanings

The oral tradition remains an important part of African American culture; thus the retelling of Haley's family history becomes the central theme of *Roots*. Great emphasis is placed on each generation's handing down of the tale of "the African." .

Throughout each retelling, the key words "ko," "Kin-tay," and "Kamby Bolongo" are transmitted to a new generation. These words will become the keys with which Haley will unlock and recover his family's heritage.

Other African-based traditions are expanded upon throughout the novel as well, especially the naming ritual. The Mandinka people believe that a child develops seven traits of the person for whom he or she is named. Kunta was named for his grandfather, a holy man known for his courage and honor. Thus Kunta's name reflects the characteristics he will evince as a slave: courage, piety, and dignity.

Kunta carries out the Mandinka custom when naming his own child, in an effort to thwart the toubob. By naming the child "Kizzy," Kunta believes that he has metaphysically ensured that the child will never be sold. In addition, the naming ritual endows the child with a sense of self and dignity. She will always know who she is. Ironically, Kizzy's sense of self, instilled in her by her father, leads her to aid another slave to escape. She is not permitted to "stay put"; instead, she is sold away.

Another theme present in *Roots* is the never-ending quest for freedom. The first four generations refuse to allow the dream of freedom to die. In the story of Chicken George, who successfully bargains with his white father for his freedom, this theme is actualized. Chicken George's gamecocks provide an analogy for the plight of the slaves. Originally from the jungle, the gamecockerel is not like domesticated birds, which are only fit for consumption. Moreover, the gamecock is as fierce and cunning as the ancient jungle cockerels. Like the gamecocks he trains and identifies with, Chicken George has lost none of the qualities passed down from his African ancestors. Also like the gamecock, he shares none of the docility of his domesticated counterparts, the plantation slaves, and like the gamecock, he is owned by the massa.

Another analogy employed in the novel is that of the Rosetta Stone to the oral history that provided the impetus to Haley's quest. The French scholar Jeań François Champollion deciphered the unknown script of the Rosetta Stone by matching it with the known Greek text chiseled in it. Haley's fascination with the Rosetta Stone and its history induced him to postulate that by discovering the origin of the phonetic snatches orally transmitted by his family, he, like Champollion, could crack the linguistic code and recover his early familial history.

Subsequently, the themes of the perpetuation of oral history, the quest for freedom, and Haley's search for his family's origins become inextricably intertwined. Through the use of multinarrative structure, symbolism, and analogy, the novel's themes address the shared heritage of all African Americans.

Critical Context

Roots was Haley's second book; he served as collaborator on *The Autobiography of Malcolm X* (1965). *Roots* appeared in condensed form in *Reader's Digest* in 1975. The first work by an African American based on genealogical research, *Roots* was lauded, even before its publication as a full-length novel, as certain to become an American classic. The novel was both a financial and a critical success, receiving a special Pulitzer Prize and the National Book Award in 1977 and spawning the most popular television miniseries up to that time.

More important, the publication of *Roots* signaled a resurgence of the reading public's interest in the African American oral tradition. Although the bulk of the book is a novelized account of the saga of Haley's maternal family, the detailed explanation of his research methods and encounters at the end chronicles not only the American perpetuation of the oral tradition by an African American family but also the larger role the griots (African oral historians) played in this amalgam of fact and fiction. The griots are able to retell centuries of village and clan histories. They are living libraries of African history and lore. The griot's history accurately corroborates the story of Kunta Kinte painstakingly handed down through seven generations in the United States.

Another important component of the novel is the vivid description of the early life of Kunta Kinte, based on extensive library and archival research. The novel almost singlehandedly dispelled the American notion of African life as depicted in Tarzan films and inferred by perusal of *National Geographic*. Haley himself admitted to having held these same popular erroneous conceptions of Africa.

It is the author's desire that *Roots* as the "story of our people can help to alleviate the legacies of the fact that preponderantly the histories have been written by the winners." In essence, by recapturing his family's history through blending historical fact and fiction, Haley has, on a greater scale, retold the legacy of all Americans of African origin and recovered their cultural heritage, one that had been stripped away under slavery.

Bibliography
Blayney, Michael Steward. "*Roots* and the Noble Savage." *North Dakota Quarterly* 54 (Winter, 1986): 1-17. Provides a correlation between the popularity of the novel and the American fascination with the romantic ideal of the noble savage. Sees Kunta Kinte as a character in that tradition. In addition, shows how Haley inverts the notion of the American Eden: Africa, not America, represents the Edenic paradise in the novel.
Courlander, Harold. "Kunta Kinte's Struggle to Be African." *Phylon* 47 (December, 1986): 294-302. Discusses Haley's characterization of Kunta Kinte as a primitive being. Perceives some of the questions first raised about *Roots* as a result of its ambiguous generic underpinnings. Asserts that *Roots* should be viewed as a work of fiction, not as pure history.
Gerber, David. "Haley's *Roots* and Our Own: An Inquiry into the Nature of Popular Phenomenon." *Journal of Ethnic Studies* 5 (Fall, 1977): 87-111. A review essay that analyzes the popular cultural phenomenon generated by the novel and the subsequent airing of the television miniseries. Analyzes Haley's treatment of historical material in general and his treatment of slavery in particular.
Marsh, Carol P. "The Plastic Arts Motif in *Roots.*" *College Language Association Journal* 26 (March, 1983): 325-333. Discusses how the characters master the plastic arts of carving, weaving, and forging, all of which enable the Kinte clan to

become successful within the context of the Protestant work ethic.

Miller, R. Baxter. "Kneeling at the Fireplace: Black Vulcan—*Roots* and the Double Artificer." *MELUS* 9 (Spring, 1982): 73-84. Analyzes Haley's attempt to celebrate the artisan within the novel. The use of the figures of painters, blacksmiths, and fireworkers subtly alludes to the Hephaestus/Vulcan story of ancient mythology.

Othow, Helen Chavis. "*Roots* and the Heroic Search for Identity." *College Language Association Journal* 26 (March, 1983): 311-324. Offers a discussion of the organic unity of the novel. Cites as problematic the shifting of protagonists, abrupt endings of generational episodes, and authorial intrusion. The work is viewed as an epic in a tradition found in Greek classical literature.

Pinsker, Sanford. "Magic Realism, Historical Truth, and the Quest for a Liberating Identity: Reflections on Alex Haley's *Roots* and Toni Morrison's *Song of Solomon*." In *Black American Prose Theory*, edited by Joe Weixlmann and Chester J. Fontenot. Vol. 1 in *Studies in Black American Literature*. Greenwood, Fla.: Penkevill, 1984. Examines the role of the storyteller in conjunction with African American identity in *Roots* and in Toni Morrison's *Song of Solomon* (1977).

Anita M. Vickers

RUNNER MACK

Author: Barry Beckham (1944-   )
Type of work: Novel
Type of plot: Social criticism
Time of plot: The early 1970's
Locale: An unnamed Northern city, Mississippi, Alaska, and the Pacific Northwest
First published: 1972

> *Principal characters:*
> HENRY ADAMS, the protagonist, a twenty-year-old black man from
>   Mississippi
> BEATRICE MARK ADAMS, Henry's young wife
> RUNNINGTON (RUNNER) MACK, Henry's well-read mentor

The Novel

A nightmare vision of the African American experience, *Runner Mack* fittingly opens with Henry Adams dreaming of a painful encounter with a dentist. Awakening to discover a leaking ceiling to be the source of his nightmare, Henry soon finds himself in a violent encounter with Alvarez, the building superintendent. Alvarez's refusal to speak English, his having stolen Henry's pajamas, and his using a guard dog to protect him from the tenant quickly establish the motifs of the inability to communicate, exploitation, oppression, and Henry's general sense of alienation.

On the way to a job interview in a crowded, noisy, impersonal metropolis resembling New York City, Henry is struck by a truck but continues on, with minor injuries, because of his determination to make a successful life for himself and his wife, Beatrice, in the North. Despite the clearly racist attitudes of the executives at Home Manufacturing, the desperate Henry, who has washed dishes, delivered fish, and sold encyclopedias since arriving in the city, accepts a position. He is disturbed by not knowing exactly what products the company makes and how the tasks he performs in the section known as "identification and recovery" fit into the greater scheme. Home Manufacturing controls its employees through indifference and intimidation.

Henry's supervisor, the ironically named Mister Boye, crudely attempts to make Henry feel at ease by showing him pornographic photographs he has taken of black women. The depressing impersonality at Home Manufacturing reminds Henry of the warnings about life in the North offered by Beatrice's father, Mister Mark. Henry sees the jobs he has held as temporary measures while he waits to realize his dream of playing major league baseball, the dream he has pursued north that makes him willing to undergo a degree of humiliation. Back home in Mississippi, he had been promised a tryout with the Stars, and Henry knows he will eventually get an opportunity to prove himself, a chance Mister Mark predicted would never come. The dangers of living in the North are underscored when unknown intruders break into the Adams' apartment in the middle of the night and assault them.

When Henry finally has his tryout with the Stars, Stumpy, the midget manager of the team, sabotages Henry's performance. Still, Henry cannot bring himself to leave the North, feeling he has nowhere to go. His dilemma is solved for him when he is drafted to fight his country's unnamed enemy in a war in Alaska. Beatrice, revealing she is pregnant, accuses him of abandoning her.

In Alaska, Henry is befriended by fellow soldier Runnington Mack, also known as "Runner" and "the Run." The well-read Mack understands the world much better than the naïve Henry and becomes his teacher and guide through life's complexities. Even Mack, however, cannot explain this war, in which troops are ordered to slaughter caribou so that the enemy will not be able to eat them.

Mack decides that they should run away from the war and, with the help of a network of followers he claims to have developed, make their way to Washington and bomb the White House. After Henry is slightly wounded, he and Mack escape the Army and into a world of paranoia. When Mack's revolution breaks down, he hangs himself. The novel ends with Henry being struck, ironically, by another Mack truck.

The Characters

Henry Adams is presented as an innocent who must be battered about by life before he can begin understanding his racist, militaristic, insensitive society. He is a victim of this society, wanting success desperately but being denied even meager rewards. He trusts in the American Dream, believes that his country is the land of opportunity, and thinks that, since baseball is America's pastime, he must be treated fairly in his effort to break into the sport. His naïve belief that "through faith and perseverance and trust" he can create a meaningful life is dispelled by each of his experiences, making him just "a lost Southern nomad, bewildered in the big city." Beckham presents him more as a type than as a fully realized character, representative of the effects of the contradictions in American life on a typical African American.

Henry's goal, beyond providing for Beatrice and playing baseball, is to understand these contradictions: "That's all I want: just for things to mean something, to make sense." He is handicapped by not knowing how to do anything other than play baseball. "He felt he knew how dreadful a fish stuck in the sand felt," the author writes at one point. Henry attempts to overcome his insecurity through clichés: "Well, keep the faith, he told himself. Things will look up if you don't give up. Keep on pushing." Such banalities are poor armor in a hostile environment.

A contradictory side of Henry himself becomes apparent during the war. He enters the Army with a simplistic patriotism, and once in combat, he discovers that he does not want to kill anyone or anything. Yet he finds himself enthusiastically clubbing seals to death. He is an unformed man too easily swayed by the emotions of the moment. Under Mack's tutelage, Henry becomes politically committed without truly understanding his friend's revolutionary rhetoric. He becomes engaged emotionally rather than intellectually and pays for his naïveté. Beckham depicts him as a good-hearted but shallow man, the type easily led—or misled—by a stronger influence. Henry feels transformed by Mack but is left without a definite new identity to replace the old one he has discarded.

Beckham employs Beatrice as a means of displaying other weaknesses of Henry. He sincerely loves her but still lusts after other women, fondling one on the subway. He sees Beatrice's role solely as that of the dutiful wife, refusing to allow her to work. Knowing little about her, Henry discovers, just before leaving for the Army, his wife's unfulfilled ambition to write poetry. More romantic and idealistic than her husband, Beatrice wishes she could "write a poem about a clearing and we could run into it. . . . We could get to know each other. We could be free. . . . We have to get out of here because there's no sun or trees, no peace or love." Her vision encompasses escape for them both; his ambitions are more selfish. Unable to understand this poetic longing, Henry becomes angry but begins to recognize Beatrice's complexity.

Just as he decides that he must protect this spirit he senses in all African American women, Henry is drafted and leaves his pregnant wife. He naïvely feels a greater sense of responsibility toward a country that neglects and exploits him than toward the person who cares the most for him. Returning to the city after Mack's revolution fails, Henry discovers that Beatrice has become deaf, posing yet another barrier to their communication. Beckham uses this marriage to criticize African American men's often unconscious neglect of their women.

Runner Mack is also more symbol than fully developed character. A larger-than-life figure, he flies a combat helicopter without ever having done so. Henry is drawn to him because Mack knows so much, has experienced so much of life, and seems so certain of himself: "The man was vibrant, forceful, hard to ignore. . . . Henry even forgot they were in a war and that his wife was pregnant miles away." Mack suggests escape from reality more than confrontation with it. On one hand, he forces Henry to think for the first time; on another, his solutions to life's intertwined problems seem simplistic. Blowing up the White House will merely create more chaos. Freedom for them both is as elusive as the symbolic polar bear that Mack chases in Alaska.

Mack is not a completely ironic character, however, for Beckham uses him to demonstrate the importance of learning: "Mack had read all, everything, and . . . this was the absolute strength of Mack, that he had consumed the written word voraciously, like a tiger, and the ideas, the concepts were boiling within him." Unfortunately, Mack is unable to use his learning to benefit either himself or others, as Beckham implies that education is only part of the solution to the predicament facing African Americans.

Themes and Meanings

Racism and forms of oppression are at the center of everything in *Runner Mack*. When Henry arrives at Home Manufacturing, Peters, the personnel officer, gets details wrong in discussing the local professional football team, but Henry has learned that a black man dare not correct a white man. Another executive says, "They all believe in God," one of several instances of racial stereotyping uttered by Henry's bosses. The executives examine his teeth and, in a restroom, stare at his penis, making Henry feel as if he is a slave.

Henry recalls a central event of his Mississippi childhood: A neighboring white family wants to buy his younger brother's dog, and when his father refuses, the whites kill it. John Adams sees this incident as yet another example of why blacks must give in to whites if they are to survive, an attitude the adult Henry understands but rejects.

Racism is only part of the pervasive sense of oppression that retards the development of any individuality in *Runner Mack*. When Henry goes to the restroom during his Home Manufacturing interview, the executives chase after him, shouting, "Don't try to run away, you can't escape!" Privacy is impossible in a world controlled by a paranoid corporate mentality.

This oppression is best illustrated by the invasion of Henry and Beatrice's apartment. Such inexplicable violence can occur to anyone at anytime or anywhere. Worrying about Beatrice later, Henry thinks that her sudden disappearance would "seem almost naturally unnatural." In Henry's world, psychological unease and racial/social pressure are inescapable. One of the most ironic moments in this heavily ironic novel comes when Henry defends his being drafted to Beatrice: "I have to fight for my country—it's our country. . . . How do you expect me to play ball for a team if they know I didn't want to keep this country safe?" The country has hardly been a safe place for him and his family.

Three major agents of oppression in *Runner Mack* are big business, the military, and professional sports. When Henry arrives at Home Manufacturing, he is told, "You can go straight to the top." Boye, however, has been there for forty years and has not been promoted in thirty years. Henry would be foolish to think that things will be different for him at a place where only "a few black faces" are visible.

Even Boye cannot explain what the company does, falling back on mindless slogans: "It may seem senseless, but every piece of work, every operation performed by Home's dedicated and faithful workers is an inestimably important contribution to the progress of this company. This is a great company, and we are great because our people are great." Meanwhile, workers constantly drop from heat and exhaustion. When two employees are to be honored for their promptness and production, they cannot accept their awards because they are in the infirmary.

Such Kafkaesque impersonality also appears in the military. In the war in Alaska, the enemy and the issues are never identified. The soldiers spend much of their time killing defenseless animals, because at least beasts can be seen. The presence of the invisible enemy is obvious only when the American soldiers are killed. Beckham is satirizing the Vietnam War, during which the Viet Cong were often concealed by nature, causing American troops to resort to "deforestation." The military does almost nothing to prepare soldiers for combat, numbly sending them to their slaughter.

Henry's primary refuge during all these travails is baseball. John Adams, knowing little about the sport, encourages his son, since sports seem to offer African Americans one of their few opportunities for economic success. Henry sees the unfamiliar in baseball terms because of the comforting nature of a sport bound by logical rules in which those with talent, like him, will flourish. A hallway at Home Manufacturing looks like "one long, unending dugout." The way the executives hold their pipes reminds him "of a pitcher preparing for a slider." Henry can deal more easily with baseball than with real life. His confusing treatment at Home Manufacturing is "worse than trying to steal home, it was a larger dilemma than being run down between second and first, and far worse than guarding the bag when a cleat-spitting runner was heading toward you."

Henry loves baseball because it is the one thing he can do well, and he is only truly in control of his life when playing the game. Beckham suggests that talent and ambition are not enough in a racist society. Stumpy rigs the Stars tryout to humiliate Henry through such ploys as setting the pitching machine to throw pitches to Henry at 150 miles an hour. Despite such treatment, Henry persists in his potentially destructive belief in baseball's representing fair play. Mack tries to explain why baseball will not give him a fair chance: "It's our history. Can't you see?"

Critical Context

The protagonist and his father are named for the nineteenth century American historian and his great-great-grandfather, the second American president, men with the power and influence Beckham's Henry and John Adams lack. The former's most famous work, *The Education of Henry Adams* (1907), deals with theories of history and examines chaos, just as Beckham looks at the chaos inherent in the history of African Americans. The views of both Adams and Beckham are tinged by cynicism and skepticism.

The major influence on *Runner Mack*, however, is Ralph Ellison's *Invisible Man* (1952), the protagonist of which comes north to encounter the impersonality, violence, and racism of life in a crowded metropolis, where he works for an oppressive corporation. *Runner Mack* is a nightmare vision of the African American experience clearly influenced by Ellison and Richard Wright. Henry resembles the naïve Bigger Thomas, who gets caught up in events he cannot control in Wright's *Native Son* (1940), a novel to which Mack refers.

One of the few African American novels to deal directly or indirectly with the Vietnam conflict, *Runner Mack* was the first African American sports novel, an interesting phenomenon given the historical importance of athletics in black culture. Beckham's main concern is to use baseball to argue that sports may be, for blacks, a false avenue of escape from the daily ordeal of life in an inescapably racist society. The novel also stands out for its skepticism about the value of revolutionary rhetoric and violence at a time when such attitudes were influential among African Americans.

Bibliography

Klotman, Phyllis Rauch. *Another Man Gone: The Black Runner in Contemporary Afro-American Literature.* Port Washington, N.Y.: Kennikat Press, 1977. Places *Runner Mack* in the context of the African American literary tradition, growing out of the slave narrative, of the symbolic run toward freedom. Analyzes the novel as a satirical quest.

Pinsker, Sanford. "About *Runner Mack*: An Interview with Barry Beckham." *Black Images* 3 (Autumn, 1974): 35-41. Beckham discusses the comic elements in his novel in detail. He explains the influence of *Invisible Man* and *The Education of Henry Adams* and the reasons he chose to use baseball as a subject and Alaska as a setting. He comments on the ambiguous ending.

Umphlett, Wiley Lee. "The Black Man as Fictional Athlete: *Runner Mack*, the Sporting Myth, and the Failure of the American Dream." *Modern Fiction Studies* 33 (Spring, 1987): 73-83. Examines *Runner Mack* as the first example of African American sports fiction and places it in the larger context of American sports literature. Shows how Beckham combines sociopolitical elements with American sporting myths.

Watkins, Mel. Introduction to *Runner Mack*, by Barry Beckham. Washington, D.C.: Howard University Press, 1983. Shows how the novel is an allegory of the historical injustices against African Americans. Compares *Runner Mack* to *Invisible Man* and to works by Franz Kafka. Argues effectively that Beckham uses baseball as a metaphor for the false hopes offered by American society to African Americans.

Weixlmann, Joe, "The Dream Turned 'Daymare': Barry Beckham's *Runner Mack*." *MELUS* 8 (Winter, 1981): 93-103. Deplores the lack of critical attention to *Runner Mack* and compares the novel favorably with *Invisible Man*. Ably analyzes the novel's structure and pays considerable attention to the apparently pessimistic ending. Depicts Runner Mack as a flawed hero.

Michael Adams

SALLY HEMINGS

Author: Barbara Chase-Riboud (1939-   )
Type of work: Novel
Type of plot: Historical realism
Time of plot: 1787-1835
Locale: Albemarle County, Virginia, and Paris, France
First published: 1979

Principal characters:
   SALLY HEMINGS, the protagonist, based on a real slave owned by
      Thomas Jefferson
   THOMAS JEFFERSON, a character based on the actual politician
   NATHAN LANGDON, a fictional character, a white Southern lawyer
      educated in the North
   JAMES HEMINGS, a character based on the historical son of John
      Wayles and Elizabeth Hemings; Sally's older brother
   ELIZABETH HEMINGS, a historical character, the slave mother of
      twelve children, including James, Sally, and three others by
      John Wayles
   MARTHA JEFFERSON RANDOLPH (PATSY), a character based on the
      historical daughter of Thomas Jefferson and Martha Wayles

The Novel

Dedicated to "the enigma of the historical Sally Hemings," *Sally Hemings* is a work of fiction about historical personages and events. In the historical record, Sally Hemings and her children appear as items of personal property in Thomas Jefferson's inventories, and "Dusky Sally" appears as the object of salacious accusations in the writing of Jefferson's political enemies. Chase-Riboud draws on history professor Fawn McKay Brodie's 1974 biography, *Thomas Jefferson: An Intimate History*, as well as on her own examination of source documents to interpret a historical record in which white males have traditionally assumed the right to define the experience of women and black people, and in which the voice of Sally Hemings herself is silent.

Chase-Riboud imaginatively re-creates Hemings' life. Hemings grows up happy and well cared for in a large and closely knit family; slavery rests easily on her. Like her playmate and niece, Martha Jefferson, she adores the domineering and kindly master of Monticello, Martha's father and Sally's owner. She blossoms into womanhood in ladies-maid status in France, where her life options are not defined by her race. She learns to converse in two languages and acquires fashionable clothing and manners. When her brother James tells her they must stay in France as free people, she asks, "What do 'free' people do?" Hemings' return to Monticello, though she was legally free in France, is a historical fact, one the novel must explain. Chase-Riboud's fictional Hemings knows "as sure as death that I belonged to Thomas Jefferson" and welcomes as ardently as Jefferson does the beginning of their sexual relationship. She chooses to trust her lover's assurance of their eventual return to France. As his responsibilities to the new republic increasingly absorb him, Hemings realizes that she and her children are trapped in her choice of love over freedom. Even if Jefferson had been willing to free them, free black people at that time could not legally reside in Virginia. Of her seven children, two die in infancy, three run away to the North, and two stay with her throughout her life. Jefferson promises her that there will be no white mistress at Monticello but nevertheless allows his daughter Martha to assume that role. As she grows older, Hemings increasingly suffers from the indignities and powerlessness of her situation, but her love for Jefferson survives. After his death and the sale of Monticello, she continues to live in a cabin close by with her adult sons Madison and Eston. She frequently visits the cemetery where the members of her intricately linked black and white family are buried.

Chase-Riboud's chronological account of Hemings' life is placed within a framing story of the fifty-six-year-old freedwoman's relationship with a young white lawyer, a relationship that brings Hemings to a reassessment of the meaning of her life. The novel begins in 1830, when Nathan Langdon, a census taker, interviews Sally Hemings in her cottage near Monticello. A mutual attraction flourishes between the fascinated youth, who is an enthusiastic admirer of Thomas Jefferson, and the still-beautiful woman, starved for cultivated male conversation. Langdon's interest leads Hemings to recapitulate the story of her life, a story that is the only thing of value she has. Wishing to protect Jefferson from the crime of miscegenation in the eyes of future generations, Langdon decides to list Hemings and her sons in the census as white. Furious, Hemings lashes out at another white man's "playing God" with her body and her life; she "had been raped of the only thing a slave possessed: her mind, her thoughts, her feelings, her history." She refuses to see the bewildered lawyer again. Subsequently, Hemings (in disguise) and Langdon both attend the trial of Nat Turner, an experience in which both see their lives nullified, Hemings because she has "loved the enemy" and Langdon because he has never before questioned the idea that the system of slavery was based on the natural submission of an inferior race.

Chase-Riboud then moves into the chronological sequence of Hemings' life story, interrupting it twice with sections set in the 1830's. In one, Langdon pursues his rebuffed fascination with Hemings by interviewing men who had met her: John Quincy Adams, Aaron Burr, and John Turnbull. In another, Hemings attends the auction at which all the human and nonhuman assets of the Monticello estate are sold.

At the end of the novel, both Langdon, who has discovered that his life consists only of "infinite shades of gray," and Hemings, who has concluded that "love had been more real to her than slavehood" and that she had "survived both," recede into "the infinite chiaroscuro of silence, where all biographies become one."

The Characters

For a historical novelist, the freedom a fiction writer has to create plausible and coherent characters is disciplined by the need for historical characters to conform to the historical record. Chase-Riboud follows Brodie's biography in interpreting the relationship between Hemings and Jefferson as a story of mutual love that began in Paris in 1788 when she was fifteen and he forty-five and that lasted thirty-eight years, until Jefferson's death.

Sally Hemings is characterized as an intelligent and beautiful woman whom slavery has taught "never to hope, never to anticipate, and never to resist." Hemings accepts her role of slave "wife," which gives her paradoxically combined feelings of passivity and power. Slavery only reinforces her culture's training in submission as the proper role of women. Dependent on a loving, powerful man, she abandons herself to "that particular joy of not being responsible for oneself." At the same time, she takes pride in her power—power to invoke Jefferson's intensely passionate love, power to exert occasional influence over his political decisions, and power to exercise real if unacknowledged authority as mistress of Monticello. At times, the cruel realities of slavery force her into agonized reappraisal of her situation—when she reviews her mother's life, when Jefferson refuses to acknowledge her sons as his, when the murder of slave friends by their masters goes unpunished, and when she attends Nat Turner's trial. Although she continues to affirm that her love for Jefferson has been the meaning of her life, in repudiating Nathan Langdon she asserts her right to control and interpret that life for herself.

Chase-Riboud depicts Jefferson's feeling for Hemings as genuine though possessive love, including and transcending sexual passion. His love originates in the desire to retain the image of his dead wife in the person of her half-sister Sally, but "he liked owning her." Jefferson is characterized as a man at war with himself on the question of slavery. Convinced that slavery is morally wrong and dedicated to abolishing the slave trade, he nevertheless continues throughout his life to own slaves. His draft of the Declaration of Independence includes language that would have abolished slavery in the new nation, but he does not fight to prevent its excision. Convinced that free blacks and whites cannot live together in the same country, he nevertheless takes a slave "wife" and fathers seven children whom he refuses to acknowledge.

Minor characters enrich the historical texture of the novel's plot and setting. They also function to provide different perspectives on the Hemings-Jefferson relationship. James Hemings forces his sister to choose between freedom and love. Elizabeth Hemings' realistic self-assertion against her slave status contrasts with her daughter's more romantic submission to the power of love. Nathan Langdon, who thinks that Sally Hemings' submissiveness makes her both "the perfect slave" and "the perfect woman," provides a catalyst for the freedwoman's reassessment of her life. Langdon's interviews of men who had met Hemings create an opportunity for Chase-Riboud to imagine how several historical contemporaries would have viewed the Hemings-Jefferson relationship. John Quincy Adams attributes it to mutual deception, Jefferson having deceived both himself and Hemings into believing that a master could truly love a slave. Hating Jefferson, Aaron Burr describes Hemings as "the only woman in the South capable of being self-righteous about concubinage," and painter John Turnbull destroys his sketches of her, because "The history of private passions has no place in public history." Other historical characters appear in brief sketches, including John and Abigail Adams, Dolly Madison, and the feminist abolitionist Frances Wright.

Chase-Riboud occasionally places actual historical documents in contexts where their interpretation contributes to characterization. For example, Jefferson's 1815 letter to Francis Gray minutely detailing the genetic and legal process through which a "pure negro" can become "a free white man, and a citizen of the United States" illuminates the ambivalent feelings of her fictional Jefferson when his slave children leave Monticello, go north, and pass for white. Occasionally Sally Hemings appears overtly in actual historical documents, such as James Callender's 1802 newspaper accusation and the "Black and White Ballad" of 1803.

Themes and Meanings

Thomas Jefferson's declaration that "all men are created equal, that they are endowed by their Creator with certain unalienable Rights, that among these are Life, Liberty, and the pursuit of Happiness" enunciates the most basic political values by which Americans define themselves. Although Jefferson's ownership of slaves seems a troublesome contradiction of those values, it can be rationalized in the context of his times. Jefferson wrote in his *Notes on the State of Virginia* (1790) that "The whole commerce between master and slave is a perpetual exercise of the most boisterous passions, the most unremitting despotism on the one part, and degrading submissions on the other." To assert that he maintained for thirty-eight years a sexual relationship with a woman whose body and children were his property, in violation of law and his own stated moral principles, calls for a serious reassessment of a national hero and also for a deeper awareness of moral ambiguity in the American self-image. That reevaluation is clearly one of Chase-Riboud's main purposes in this novel, along with the attempt to recover the story of a black woman whose experience has been erased from historical consciousness.

Chase-Riboud also forces a reexamination of the meaning of the term "the American family." Sally Hemings and Martha Jefferson Randolph watch by Elizabeth Hemings' deathbed in a "strange and southern circle of complicity," bound by "intricate and convoluted ties" of "blood, love, servitude, hate, womanhood, time." When the Jefferson family and their slaves gather on Christmas Day in 1795 in the central hallway at Monticello for the gift-giving celebration, Chase-Riboud notes that Elizabeth Hemings was "either mother, stepmother, grandmother, aunt, or great-aunt to practically everyone present." In constantly stressing the interrelationships among the Jefferson, Wayles, and Hemings families, Chase-Riboud exposes how recognizing the effect of exploitative miscegnation on national life and character can significantly alter historical perspective.

While refuting what she considers to be overly idealistic interpretations of American history and values, Chase-Riboud also challenges the interpretation of slavery as unmitigated degradation. Elizabeth Hemings passes on to her children a sense of dignity and self-control, saying "I made up my mind I might be called a slave, but I wasn't going to live no slavish life." Although Sally is a victim of her circumstances, she also makes choices appropriate to her own values. In imagining the relationship between Hemings and Jefferson, Chase-Riboud explores a paradoxical interdependence of slavery and power. She demonstrates that the role of "master" depends for its definition on the role of "slave," a theme to which she returns in her subsequent historical novels *Valide: A Novel of the Harem* (1986), set in the harem of the Ottoman Empire, and *Echo of Lions* (1989), about the Amistad rebellion.

Critical Context

Sally Hemings was Chase-Riboud's first novel, though she had previously established an international reputation as a sculptor and published a book of poems, *From Memphis and Peking* (1974). *Sally Hemings* was widely and favorably reviewed when it appeared in 1979. It was a Literary Guild selection and won that year's Janet Heidinger Kafka Prize for Excellence in Fiction by an American Woman.

Sally Hemings has appeared in a French edition and stimulated some critical commentary in French; Chase-Riboud has lived in France for much of her life. The surprisingly little critical attention to the novel in English has focused more on debating the historical accuracy of its premise than on literary analysis.

In her acknowledgements, Chase-Riboud links *Sally Hemings* to the "roots of Afro-American writing" in William Wells Brown's *Clotel: The President's Daughter, a Narrative of Slave Life in the United States* (1853), generally identified as the first novel by an African American writer, though she read Brown's book only after completing her own. Brown's novel is also based on the premise that Thomas Jefferson had children by a slave mistress, a premise that historian Fawn Brodie says black historians have long accepted as accurate. In imaginatively re-creating the life of Sally Hemings, Chase-Riboud gives a voice to an African American woman whom history has silenced.

Bibliography

Brodie, Fawn M. *Thomas Jefferson: An Intimate History.* New York: W. W. Norton, 1974. The controversial biography upon which Chase-Riboud's novel is based. Brodie combines historical and psychological analysis to interpret the extensive historical record of Jefferson's life.

Dabney, Virginius. *The Jefferson Scandals: A Rebuttal.* New York: Dodd, Mead, 1981. Dabney rejects Brodie's and Chase-Riboud's premise that Sally Hemings was Thomas Jefferson's mistress, analyzing their sources and disputing their conclusions. Chapter 5, "Fiction Masquerading as Fact," focuses specifically on *Sally Hemings*, pointing out minor historical inaccuracies as well as rejecting its basic premise.

Heidish, Marcy. Review of *Sally Hemings*, by Barbara Chase-Riboud. *The Washington Post*, June 15, 1979. A dissenting review that faults *Sally Hemings* for its shifts in voice and chronology, which Heidish sees as disruptive to the narrative.

McHenry, Susan. "Sally Hemings: A Key to Our National Identity." *Ms.* 9 (October, 1980): 35-40. Both a review of *Sally Hemings* and a profile of Chase-Riboud. Includes the writer's comments on her novel, information about Chase-Riboud's life, and discussion of the evolution of her thought and art.

Russell, John. Review of *Sally Hemings*, by Barbara Chase-Riboud. *The New York Times*, September 5, 1979, p. III21. A laudatory review that praises the author's ability to vivify the past in her writing.

Carol E. Schmudde

THE SALT EATERS

Author: Toni Cade Bambara (1931-   )
Type of work: Novel
Type of plot: Social criticism
Time of plot: The 1970's
Locale: Claybourne, Georgia
First published: 1980

> *Principal characters:*
> VELMA HENRY, a committed civil rights activist
> MINNIE RANSOM, a community healer, Earth mother, and vehicle
>   for spiritual forces
> JAMES "OBIE" HENRY, Velma's husband, the head of the Academy
>   of the Seven Arts and The Brotherhood
> M'DEAR SOPHIE HEYWOOD, Velma's godmother
> FRED HOLT, a bus driver
> B. TALIFERO "DOC" SERGE, the owner of the Southwest
>   Community Infirmary

The Novel

The Salt Eaters traces the past, present, and alternate futures of the African American inhabitants of Claybourne, Georgia, in the time of two hours. The novel focuses on two women sitting on stools in the Southwest Community Infirmary. On one stool sits Velma Henry, the former activist sparkplug of the community, who has become "uncentered" and has tried to kill herself. On the other stool sits Minnie Ransom, the spiritual center of the community, healer, herb woman, mother of all, in tune with the forces of nature and the universe.

Through Velma's errant mind and psyche, the reader enters the minds of her family and friends: her husband, Obie, and son, Lil James; her godmother, M'Dear Sophie; the Women for Action, a group presided over by Velma until her breakdown; and the Seven Sisters, a performing arts group that includes Velma's best friend, Palma. The Seven Sisters are first seen as passengers on a bus driven by Fred Holt. They are traveling to Claybourne to perform at the black community's annual spring festival.

As he drives, Fred Holt is thinking of his failed second marriage and of his dead friend Porter. Holt apparently follows a suicidal impulse to drive the bus through a railing into swamp water. Two women passengers, however, think the bus back on the road, and it arrives in Claybourne, where Fred goes to the infirmary to await his passengers for the return trip, medical people who have come to watch the unorthodox healing methods practiced at the infirmary under the auspices of its owner, Doc Serge. One of the visitors, Dr. Meadows, an urbanite who has forgotten his roots, grows impatient with watching Minnie and Velma apparently doing nothing, although the battle of their psyches is intense, and goes for a walk that leads him into an impoverished neighborhood, where he meets two "bloods" who put him in touch with his roots.

Meanwhile, trouble seems to be brewing among the Brotherhood, a separatist group inside the Academy of the Seven Arts, and over at the infirmary, the Circle of Twelve, a spiritual group standing around Minnie and Velma and giving support with their thoughts and prayers, begin to tire.

The story weaves in and out of Velma's mind as Minnie's force begins to reach her; Minnie consults with the invisible "Old Wife," her spiritual guide from the Other Side, and remembers her own reluctance when too young to recognize her gifts. Simultaneously, the community begins to position floats and gather at concession stands in preparation for the signal that the Mardi Gras parade is starting.

As Velma's husband, Obie, and Palma make their way to the infirmary, Minnie succeeds in "recentering" Velma, restoring her joy of life. M'Dear Sophie, who had almost given up on Velma, sees that Velma will in her turn be the healer of her generation. Fred Holt has a vision (real or unreal?) of his dead friend Porter crossing the street. The horned Hoodoo Man appears, banging on pans and signaling the beginning of the celebration.

The Characters

The characters in *The Salt Eaters* are not traditional, realistically depicted individuals. They occupy dimensions in time more than space and embody forces of nature and the supernatural.

Velma Henry has perhaps the most conventional background. A committed civil rights activist, she is the heart of the Academy of the Seven Arts, which is in turn the heart of minority education and protest in Claybourne. Having fought on a political and social level for years, she is exhausted and suicidal. Her personal history recapitulates the history of her time.

Velma's husband James, nicknamed "Obie," has been unfaithful to Velma; he is afraid of losing both her and control of his groups, the Academy and the more secret Brotherhood. Like most of the other characters, he is a thumbnail sketch. He illustrates the need of the masculine principle for the creative energy supplied by Velma. His nickname alludes to Obeah, a voodoo-like ritual practice. He exists in the novel to dance around and into the circle containing his wife and her healer, Minnie.

Minnie Ransom, about whom Bambara gives less traditionally novelistic biographical information, is an Earth mother, a community healer, and a vehicle for spiritual forces.

The more peripheral characters whose dance of life coheres around Minnie and Velma serve to recapitulate the African American historical experience in their personal lives: Velma's godmother, for example, thinks of her son Smitty, who has been a paraplegic since he sustained an injury in a civil rights protest.

Fred Holt, the bus driver who brings the Seven Sisters to Claybourne, thinks of events in his life that illustrate the fragmenting of the African American community:

bitter thoughts of his first wife, who left him for a Black Muslim, and his second wife, a white woman who does not understand or care about his black essence, and sad thoughts of his friend Porter, the only other African American employee of the bus company, whose death has left Holt feeling isolated and alienated.

As these characters and others move from fragmentation and isolation toward community, they also represent the need Bambara sees for such unity in the African American community at large. The individual leaders such as Velma, who become burnt out and exhausted, can perhaps be restored by developing such community.

It is significant that the images in Minnie's mind are not of a realistic childhood, of everyday events, but of elemental forces that she at first rejected, not understanding that she was both a channel and a focus of healing. Velma's "uncentered" mind and psyche are cleansed by Minnie's power, which is passed on to Velma; like Minnie, as a child Velma had turned away from the hints and portents indicating that she too was recipient of the gift.

These characters cannot be viewed in the realistic dailiness of their lives. They are containers for psychic energy, perhaps best envisioned as streaks of light on a photographic negative.

Cohesiveness, circularity, completion: If, as Bambara has said, humans are all extensions of the same consciousness, then the reader is expected to participate in creating that circularity. The characters are process, then, not product—and so is the act of reading the novel.

Themes and Meanings

The key to an understanding of *The Salt Eaters* is the realization that the narrative voice and the characters matter-of-factly accept the miraculous as part of living. The characters in *The Salt Eaters* live on more than one plane of reality simultaneously; who is "alive" or "dead" is immaterial. Moreover, in the novel, clock time is not real time; the past, present, and future can exist simultaneously. Nothing is inanimate. Threatening the earth, which is full of living forces inhabiting human beings, animals, trees, and rocks, are the man-made poisons and psychic negativisms symbolized by Velma's splitting off from her whole self and by the Transchemical Company plant in Claybourne, which is poisoning the earth, air, water, and workers and which, in one possible future and novel-ending event, explodes.

Salvation, Bambara seems to say, lies in community, a joining together of people whose selves have become whole, a wholeness of mind and psyche, spirit and logic. From the beginning of the novel, and increasingly toward the end, Bambara invokes names, beliefs, and practices from world religions that share the holistic view, particularly those of Africa and the Caribbean. At the end of the healing process, both plot and metaphor for the meaning of the novel, choices are "being tossed into the street like dice, like kola nuts, like jackstones." Fred sees Porter; the teenager Nadeen acknowledges seeing a true miracle of healing; Sophie, having seen Velma's physical birth, now sees her rebirth and sees that Velma has found her missing other self.

Obie, falling as he races to Velma in the clinic, "couldn't get up so he did get up." At the clinic, "The Lady in the Chair is rising damp but replenished like the Lady Rising from the Sea." ("Don't they know we on the rise?" Minnie has said.) Velma, suddenly knowing the African names for Minnie's jug and bowl without knowing how she knows, rises from her stool, her aura "two yards wide of clear and un-streaked white and yellow," and "throws off the shawl . . . like a burst cocoon." Let the New Age begin.

Critical Context

Toni Cade Bambara's major works of fiction between 1971 and 1980 are variations on a theme—a sense of community and communication—but different in style. *Gorilla, My Love* (1971), a collection of short stories set in Harlem, focuses on the importance of the family as the supportive unit for the principal character, and on the need to create family where there is none. Somewhat autobiographical, perhaps, most of the stories use the first-person narrator, often a young woman going through a rite of passage, as in the title story of the collection. (One of the most often-anthologized stories, however, is "My Man Bovanne," in which the narrator is an older woman whose children, caught up in the Black Power movement, have taken African names and chide her for being "old timey.") The narrators, regardless of age, are funny, strong, honest African American women. Critics and readers re-sponded favorably to it, and it has remained in print. Bambara's second collection of short stories, *The Sea Birds Are Still Alive* (1977), broadens its scope geographically to include women of color in other parts of the world.

Bambara has said that *The Salt Eaters* came from her attempt to find a way to build bridges among differing forces in the black American community, an attempt that is clearly demonstrated in the novel. Although some reviewers found the novel difficult, the reader coming from a prior reading of Toni Morrison's *Beloved* (1987) and Gloria Naylor's *Mama Day* (1988)—and consequently not imposing a linear mindset on the simultaneities of time in *The Salt Eaters*—can find a rewarding experience. Like other contemporary African American writers, Bambara feels no need to, or perhaps sees a need not to, explain African American culture, history, and language to white readers.

Bibliography

Bambara, Toni Cade. "Toni Cade Bambara." Interview by Claudia Tate. In *Black Women Writers at Work*, edited by Claudia Tate. New York: Continuum, 1983. This lengthy, excellent interview elicits Bambara's thoughts on influences on her work and life, on the difficulties an activist finds in making time to write a novel, and on the belief that "we and everything here are extensions of the same con-sciousness."
Burks, Ruth Elizabeth. "From Baptism to Resurrection: Toni Cade Bambara and the Incongruity of Language." In *Black Women Writers, 1950-1980: A Critical Evalua-tion*, edited by Mari Evans. Garden City, N.Y.: Anchor Press/Doubleday, 1983.

Discusses Bambara's short stories and *The Salt Eaters* in terms of the inadequacy of language to impel to action. Velma's spiritual rebirth represents the "beginning of an apocalypse that recognizes that she, just as we, are the light, and the salvation, and the salt which . . . has always seasoned the earth."

Chandler, Zala. "Voices Beyond the Veil: An Interview of Toni Cade Bambara and Sonia Sanchez." In *Wild Women in the Whirlwind: Afra-American Culture and the Contemporary Literary Renaissance*, edited by Joanne M. Braxton and Andree N. McLaughlin. New Brunswick, N.J.: Rutgers University Press, 1990. Bambara says that "organizing is what it's all about," that black Americans must celebrate their ancestors and turn away from disconnectedness and amnesia toward a sense of community and expression of the truth of the African American experience.

Hull, Gloria T. " 'What It Is I Think She's Doing Anyhow': A Reading of Toni Cade Bambara's *The Salt Eaters*." In *Conjuring: Black Women, Fiction, and Literary Tradition*, edited by Marjorie Pryse and Hortense J. Spillers. Bloomington: Indiana University Press, 1985. A perceptive, well-written analysis that clarifies Bambara's handling of time, narrative voice, and symbolism. Argues that a close reading of the novel "should result in personal transformation."

Russell, Sandi. " 'for colored girls . . .' (1970s-present)." In *Render Me My Song: African-American Women Writers from Slavery to the Present.* New York: St. Martin's Press, 1990. Covers briefly black women writers from Phillis Wheatley to Ntozake Shange. Particularly useful to the nonspecialist. Says Bambara's message is that black Americans are divided and should become cohesive and join with Third World peoples.

Traylor, Eleanor W. "The Jazz Mode in the Works of Toni Cade Bambara." In *Black Women Writers, 1950-1980: A Critical Evaluation*, edited by Mari Evans. Garden City, N.Y.: Anchor Press/Doubleday, 1983. This excellent essay compares Bambara's approach to that of a jazz composer examining the "contingencies of time in an examined present moment." Bambara's novel is a "rite of transformation quite like a jam session." Bambara has understandably praised this essay as explanation; it is in its turn a jazz riff on the novel.

Katherine Lederer

SARAH PHILLIPS

Author: Andrea Lee (1953-   )
Type of work: Novel
Type of plot: Domestic realism
Time of plot: 1963-1974
Locale: Paris, France, and the French countryside; Philadelphia, Pennsylvania; and
    Cambridge, Massachusetts
First published: 1984

> *Principal characters:*
> SARAH PHILLIPS, a pretty, twenty-one-year-old black woman
> THE REVEREND JAMES FORREST PHILLIPS, Sarah's late father, a
>   minister
> GRACE RENFREW PHILLIPS, Sarah's mother, a teacher
> MATTHEW PHILLIPS, Sarah's older brother, a law student

The Novel

Sarah Phillips is a novel about the life of the title character and narrator. Sarah, however, is not the kind of black protagonist typically found in fiction. Born of educated parents, she has grown up in a prosperous Philadelphia suburb, sheltered from violence and racism, but confined by the expectations of her parents and her society. After the death of her father, James Forrest Phillips, a well-known minister, and after the completion of her Harvard University degree, Sarah has gone to Europe, ostensibly to study. In fact, however, she is enjoying herself, as she explores a world much larger than that of her childhood.

Although Andrea Lee has termed Sarah Phillips a novel, it is actually made up of a number of short stories, many of which first appeared in *The New Yorker*. The genesis of the work is evident in the fact that each chapter begins without a reference to the action of the previous one, and each ends with the kind of inconclusive conclusion, often symbolic, which is so familiar to readers of that publication. Lee's task of turning the stories into a novel was not as difficult as it might seem, however, since Sarah Phillips was the protagonist in all the stories, and since the subject of each was Sarah's discovery of the world and of her place in it. While in *Sarah Phillips* there is no single movement toward a critical point, such as would be found in a traditional novel, Lee has provided a degree of suspense by having her protagonist make a sudden decision at the end of the first chapter, a decision that one expects will then be explained in the chapters which follow.

The novel begins in 1974, when Sarah is twenty-one. Shortly after she arrives in Europe with the professed intention of studying literature, Sarah becomes involved with a young Frenchman and leaves her school in Switzerland for Paris, where she, her lover, and two of his male friends have moved into an apartment owned by her lover's gay uncle. There, the young people live a carefree, communal existence. There are no limitations on their speech or their behavior. Sarah sleeps with her lover or, out of politeness, with his friends. Sometimes she poses nude, while the young men discuss her body. Sometimes they all throw insults at one another. Their actions are governed by their whims.

Yet Sarah is not as far from her parents and her past as she thinks herself to be. From the first, it has been customary for the friends to allow one another complete freedom of expression, even when that freedom leads to questionable jokes or to malicious attacks on another's family, class, or race. For some reason, Sarah has never been offended; indeed, she has encouraged the use of racial slurs. Nevertheless, when her lover spells out in fanciful detail what he says is her ethnic background, Sarah is surprised by the strength of her own reaction. Even though the young man apologizes, the incident has revealed to Sarah the depth of her attachment to her country, her family, and her heritage. This important first chapter of the novel ends with Sarah's realization that she must go home.

In the eleven chapters that follow, Sarah recounts significant incidents in her life, beginning when she was ten and continuing to her final days in college. Even though each episode is complete in itself, Lee has provided continuity by arranging these chapters in chronological order and, in addition, by both beginning and ending this long section of the book in the New African Baptist Church in Philadelphia. The setting is particularly significant, because to Sarah the church represents her religious heritage, her community, and her beloved father, who was the minister there until his death. The first of these chapters is entitled simply "New African." In it, Sarah is torn between the desire to please Reverend Phillips by volunteering to be baptized, as his congregation expects her to do, and her need to assert herself by adamantly refusing to become a full member of the church. This episode is balanced by the final chapter in the novel, "A Funeral at New African." The funeral is that of Sarah's father, who becomes ill and dies shortly before his daughter's graduation from Harvard. In this chapter, too, Sarah feels conflicting emotions. She must deal with her own guilt, her certainty that by failing to be converted she must have disappointed her father, and with her sense of loss, the realization that she will never again know the love and security that he gave her. Yet she also now feels a new sense of freedom. She is on her way somewhere, though where she does not know.

Appropriately, the third chapter of the book is devoted to the other major influence on Sarah's life: her mother, a complex woman from whom Sarah inherited a stubborn independence. This quality in Sarah is evident throughout the later chapters. Sarah always makes her own observations and draws her own conclusions. She thus learns that racism exists not from television accounts of distant struggles for civil rights, but from her own experience—from hearing words of hatred spoken by envious gypsies, or from being left out of social events at the exclusive girls' school that she attends. At the end of the book, Sarah reports her new insight that it is important for her to flee everything that New African represents. Yet in the initial chapter of *Sarah Phillips*, which follows the final chapter psychologically as well as chronologically, Sarah has already confided an even newer insight: She cannot run away from all that has made her the person she is.

The Characters

The focus of *Sarah Phillips* is on the title character, ˙. sensitive first-person narrator who reports the events that take place around her and her own reactions to those events. Sarah is a born observer. The chapters about her childhood make it clear that at an early age she was already in the habit of noticing the details of her surroundings: the colors, sounds, and scents in a room, the words of others and the expressions on their faces, and the moment-by-moment progress of her own feelings.

Even though the other characters are seen through Sarah's eyes, she does not merely describe them; instead, she brings them to life with the skill of a dramatist. She shows her father, the Reverend James Forrest Phillips, at a service, speaking in powerful phrases, varying his vocal patterns like a musician, glowing with the pleasure he feels when he is preaching. Similarly, she shows her mother, Grace Renfrew Phillips, in action, cooking, talking on the telephone, telling dramatic stories of her past adventures, or going for walks in the shadowy summer night. Sarah notices the significance of details, seeing, for example, that Grace's passionate interests in chicken parts, earthquakes, murders, and suicides are evidence of her delight in the bizarre.

Although far less space is devoted to Sarah's brother, Matthew Phillips, he is important as a foil to Sarah, who adores him but knows from experience that he generally gets her into trouble. Matthew first appears at the baptismal service, playing the role of the good child in contrast to his recalcitrant sister. As Sarah comments, Matthew delights in setting off explosions and then running away, leaving her behind to cope with the consequences. In the hilarious chapter "Matthew and Martha," Matthew delights Sarah and shocks his parents by bringing a white Jewish girlfriend home to dinner. After an uncomfortable meal, Matthew escapes as usual, leaving Sarah to bear the brunt of her mother's fury. In this episode, as throughout the book, an incident is used to support Sarah's analysis of another character as well as to reveal the importance of that character to her own developing understanding.

Themes and Meanings

The first chapter of *Sarah Phillips* ends with a dream, followed by a decision. After a quarrel with her lover and a reconciliation marked by perfunctory sex, Sarah dreams of grappling with an old black woman like those in her father's church; she then wakens to a new awareness of the persistence of her past. The dream may have had an effect on Sarah, reinforcing her desire to go home, but it is more important as a symbol of the conflicts that make up the pattern and the meaning of the novel.

Several of these conflicts involve the rejection of one group by another. The New African Baptist Church itself is evidence of the schism between prosperous blacks and their poor brothers and sisters. Once the center of the community that surrounds it, New African is now an island of well-being in the middle of a slum. On Sundays, well-to-do, conservative church members drive back to their old area for services, then return to the suburbs to which they fled as soon as integration made it possible. Sarah's feelings of dissociation from poor blacks are reflected in her behavior at Miss Prescott's School for Girls when she ignores the greetings of the black cook, even though she finally admits that she might be able to learn something from him.

The same kind of social division is evident when Matthew brings his girlfriend to dinner. Although his parents are officially and sincerely committed to brotherhood, they reject the girl. Reverend Phillips reminds Matthew and Martha that they are too young to make a commitment, while Grace, more forcefully, asks the girl why she does not stick to her own people. Ironically, in "Negatives," Sarah and a black male friend conclude that their being sexually attracted to whites is a fascination with opposites, an admission that they are aware of racial differences even as they might seem to be transcending them.

Although such conflicts involving class, race, and religion may appear to be external in nature, all of them are also part of the internal struggle that Sarah attempts to solve by running away to France. When Sarah goes home, she will have to come to terms with her feelings of alienation toward those who—like the black servants at her girls' school and the black slum children at summer camp—have nothing in common with her except their race. The old woman in the dream symbolizes Sarah's struggles with her own distaste for other blacks; moreover, in her similarity to an old woman who tries to force Sarah to be baptized, she also symbolizes Sarah's struggles with her parents' religious convictions and with their expectations for her.

Ironically, by giving Sarah the freedom to make her own decisions, even about religion, Reverend Phillips makes it inevitable that his daughter will have internal conflicts. The novel's crucial first chapter, however, suggests that in Paris Sarah has learned another lesson besides the importance of the past. She has also realized that there are two kinds of freedom: irresponsible indulgence, which, like her lover's jokes, always goes too far, and freedom to choose the right action, which Sarah accepts as a gift from her father.

Critical Context

When *Sarah Phillips* was published, it was naturally compared to Andrea Lee's earlier work, *Russian Journal* (1981), a diary of a trip Lee and her husband made to the Soviet Union. Although *Russian Journal* was highly praised as a well-written, perceptive work, reviewers were surprised that the author seemed so little interested in race and, in fact, hardly mentioned that she was black.

Unlike *Russian Journal*, *Sarah Phillips* does deal specifically with the difficulty of being African American in a white society. Sarah, though, is a member of a prosperous, conservative black subculture that seems to have more in common with whites of the same social level than with poor blacks; the fact that critics vary so greatly in their assessment of the novel may reflect the varying attitudes toward the class that Andrea Lee describes. While some have lauded Lee for her realism, even for pointing out a cultural common ground between middle-class whites and blacks, others have accused the author of elitism and of indifference toward the black heritage.

Because *Sarah Phillips* is written in the first person, and because the protagonist has the same background as the book's author, it is difficult to distinguish the degree to which the novel is autobiographical. This question is particularly important, because many readers find that Sarah is too detached to be an appealing character. It may be that Lee is pointing out Sarah's passivity; it may also be that Lee shares Sarah's habit of maintaining a distance from her subject. Whatever the case, critics have generally agreed that Lee's first novel is beautifully written and perceptive.

Bibliography
Lehmann-Haupt, Christopher. Review of *Sarah Phillips*, by Andrea Lee. *The New York Times*, December 6, 1984, C22. A generally favorable review, praising Lee's "eloquence and brilliant clarity of detail." Lehmann-Haupt writes that the book is important as a story of "the ambiguities of growing up a member of a proud and privileged minority"; he claims that its only defect is the fact that it is limited to Sarah's memories of the past and does not show her in action after she has come to terms with her heritage.
Obolensky, Laura. "Scenes from a Girlhood." *The New Republic* 191 (November 19, 1984): 41-42. Argues that, despite her knowledge of the world she describes, Lee fails to deal with real issues. Objects to "a tone of detachment often bordering on the sardonic." Reverend Phillips and Sarah are seen as the most successful characterizations; however, Sarah is described as "an elitist snob."
Shreve, Susan Richards. "Unsentimental Journey." *The New York Times Book Review*, November 18, 1984, 13. Comments on the problems of young people such as Sarah and her brother, educated for leadership in the white establishment, yet expected to resist being incorporated into that world. Although Shreve finds flaws in the book's structure and in the characterization of the protagonist, she praises Lee's "simple and yet luminous" style.
Van Wyngarden, Bruce. "Pieces of the Past." *Saturday Review* 11 (January/February, 1985): 74. The reviewer finds the original short-story structure too obvious. Van Wyngarden also expresses disappointment that the book's action stops with Sarah's decision to leave Paris—which, he argues, should have happened in the last chapter instead of in the first.
Vigderman, Patricia. Review of *Sarah Phillips*, by Andrea Lee. *Boston Review* 10 (February, 1985): 23-24. Argues that the novel has taken as its "formal model" the children's novels that are mentioned as Sarah's favorites, in which each chapter "is a separate adventure," but "the book as a whole constructs another world." The reviewer expects the book to be criticized because its characters are so deeply involved in white society, but insists that *Sarah Phillips* is "a very gracefully written book about black identity."
Washington, Mary Helen. "Young, Gifted and Black." *Women's Review of Books* 2 (March, 1985): 3-4. Argues that Sarah Phillips becomes trapped in "a permanent ambiguity," disconnected from her heritage and from her feelings, both as a black and as a woman. Suggests that the "evasions" of *Sarah Phillips* are the result of pressures from the conservative establishment.

Rosemary M. Canfield Reisman

SEASON OF ADVENTURE

Author: George Lamming (1927-   )
Type of work: Novel
Type of plot: Social criticism
Time of plot: The mid-twentieth century
Locale: The imaginary Caribbean island of San Cristobal
First published: 1960

Principal characters:

FOLA PIGGOTT, the protagonist, a beautiful eighteen-year-old
    mulatto girl
"PIGGY" PIGGOTT, a police official, Fola's stepfather of ten years
AGNES PIGGOTT, Fola's mother, an attractive, vivacious woman
    who keeps the circumstances of Fola's conception a secret
CHIKI, Fola's friend and lover, an artist with an unusual past
CHARLOT PRESSIOR, Fola's history teacher, a young Englishman
    fascinated by Caribbean rituals and folk beliefs
VICE PRESIDENT RAYMOND, a friend of the Piggott family
POWELL, the leader of a steel drum band who hates the British
    and those who imitate them
GORT, a man who lives in the Forest Reserve and lives for his
    music

The Novel

Season of Adventure takes place two years after San Cristobal has gained its independence from Great Britain. Divided into two parts, "Arriving and Returning" and "The Revolt of the Drums," the novel traces, through Fola Piggott's life history, the breakdown of colonialism and construction of the new republic.

The novel opens with the native religious ritual of resurrecting the dead, the Ceremony of Souls. Fola, who has been immersed in British culture through her schooling and her home life, attends the ceremony only to please her teacher, Charlot Pressior, who accompanies her. Once there, however, the music of steel drums helps reestablish her connection with her own culture. She becomes dissatisfied with her sheltered upbringing.

Although she has always felt closer to her stepfather than to her mother, she rejects them both in an attempt to become independent and to discover her roots by finding out who her natural father is. Her obsession with learning this information takes her first to lower-class sections of the city, where she meets Chiki in a bar. Hoping that Chiki can help her, she begins visiting him in the Forest Reserve he owns, home to the very poorest of the islanders, many of whom have no education, no work, and no future. These inhabitants isolate themselves from society and wish only to be left alone, away from harassment by the police.

One day Chiki paints a portrait of a man neither he nor Fola has ever seen. Shortly afterward, Vice President Raymond is assassinated. The police arrive, determined to find the murderer among the residents of the Forest Reserve. Constable "Piggy" Piggott, in charge of the roundup of suspects, has allowed his men to beat and handcuff the suspects when Fola appears and announces that she knows who killed the vice president. Lying to save the men of the Forest Reserve, Fola insists that the assassin is her father and that Chiki has painted a portrait of him. The men of the Forest Reserve are released, and copies of the portrait are displayed all over the island. No one, however, can put a name to the face. In the meantime, Powell, the leader of a steel drum band, has disappeared.

Piggott is relieved of his duties because of his family's involvement. He beats Fola and physically throws her out of the house. The Piggotts' servant takes Fola in and notifies Chiki, who then cares for her in his own home. In his absence, Powell appears and tries to kill Fola. To him, she symbolizes hated British authoritarianism. Chiki arrives and saves her, and Powell disappears, never to return.

The government never learns that Powell is the assassin and continues looking for the man in the portrait. He is not found. Frustrated by their inability to solve the case, the government officials connect the assassination to the "backwardness" of their countrymen. In consequence, a proclamation barring the playing of steel drums is issued. Knowing that the lack of music will kill the spirit of the people, Fola and Chiki send word across the island to play the music at an appointed time, in defiance of the edict. Through a quirk on the part of Jim Aswell, the rich distributor of Coca Cola who allows one of his workers to deliver the message of defiance, the islanders believe that this powerful businessman supports the drum boys against the government. With such a sanction, the steel drum bands from all over the island, led by Gort, meet in Freedom Square, play their music, and depart unmolested. Two months later, a new government takes over, led by a man who knows the difficulties of independence and also respects the old ways.

The Characters

Fola Piggott, a strong heroine, has been compared by many critics to Bita Plant, featured in Claude McKay's *Banana Bottom* (1933). Not quite eighteen years old when the novel opens, Fola changes from an obedient young girl to a rebellious, and then finally independent, young woman, paralleling the changes in San Cristobal during its emergence from colony to republic. Fola, through her attendance at the Ceremony of Souls, begins her backward glance at her own past and that of her culture. When she decides that she is Fola and "other than Fola," she starts her exploration into her roots. "Other than Fola" is the name she privately gives herself in order to become an independent woman who is no longer bound by upper-middle-class values. Other than Fola is the person who longs to understand the past.

Her mother's marriage to Piggott and her parents' desire for upward mobility have provided her with a past based on British ruling-class standards. Her rejection of her family also signals her rejection of their values.

The two artist figures, Gort and Chiki, play important roles in the novel. Gort, a drummer, is a folk artist whose art is directly inspired by the peasant community of the Forest Reserve. Chiki, a painter, first provides a political perspective on the role of the artist in a changing society. By the end of the novel, both artist figures make the connection between art and politics, and both become artists who are teachers. Their actions show the rest of the Forest Reserve inhabitants how to live.

Powell symbolizes a part of the peasant community. His rejection of and hatred for all things British (even Fola, simply because she is a product of British-ruled schooling and upbringing) shows what can happen when the will of the people is frustrated. Originally a rebel, he becomes an assassin and escapes from the island.

Agnes Piggott, victim of both the ruling class and of Chiki's brother, who raped her and perhaps fathered Fola, keeps the circumstances of Fola's conception secret, not to further her own ends but for Fola's sake. Her love for her daughter is manifest throughout *Season of Adventure*. She is also instrumental in keeping her husband from sharing in the ill-gotten riches of Vice President Raymond.

Piggott, Agnes' husband, loves Fola unqualifiedly until he learns of her deviation from the imitation of British life-style he has provided for her. A seemingly kind man, his true unpleasantness is revealed in his behavior toward his servants and the men of the Forest Reserve. In many ways, Piggott stands for the nearly inevitable mishandling of the peasant population by the first republic's government. From the servant class himself, he aspires not to share power with others of similar background; instead, he wishes to wield power over them.

Charlot Pressior, the history teacher from Great Britain, seems fascinated with West Indian culture. His fascination leads him to convince Fola to attend the Ceremony of Souls with him, but he looks upon the ritual and the peasants who perform as if he were an anthropologist studying the customs of the natives. Fola's infatuation with him parallels her early infatuation with everything British. Only when he leaves the island can she become free to pursue her own cultural past.

Themes and Meanings

The themes of alienation and exile play important roles in *Season of Adventure*. At the beginning, Fola Piggott is alienated from her heritage. Her experience at the Ceremony of Souls signals her reconnection with her own culture. As the novel progresses, Fola journeys both emotionally and physically from identification with British ways to those of the Caribbean. The theme of the backward glance appears at the beginning of the novel, when Fola attends the ritual ceremony. The theme continues throughout the novel and intensifies in Fola's search for her natural father. This search is also a search for an alternative tradition, the tradition of the past that she has never known.

Chiki embodies both alienation and exile, for he attended the British school for boys, just as Fola attended the school for girls. His alienation increases after his expulsion from the school, as he sails for America as an exile from his native land. After he returns to the Forest Reserve, the theme of the role of the artist in a changing society comes to the forefront. A talented painter, Chiki struggles with his inability to transfer the sound of the Caribbean music made by steel drums onto his canvas. Although Chiki is the first to provide a political perspective on the role of the artist, Gort the drummer eventually realizes the connection between politics and art. Gort is the folk artist whose art is directly inspired by the peasant community. In many ways, *Season of Adventure* focuses on the artist as teacher. Both Chiki and Gort teach others how to live.

Even though the novel is structured around the failure of the first republic, it is organized to underscore the idea that inclusion of the peasant life-style is paramount to creating a sense of shared community on the island. The action of this highly political novel revolves around the attempt to restructure the society of San Cristobal.

Music, throughout the novel, can be identified with the peasant experience. Many varieties of music, such as the music of steel drums, songs, hymns, work songs, and calypsos, foster comprehension of the character of the peasants. The sound of the steel drums and the freedom to play those instruments are shown to be necessities of life to the peasant class of the island. The destruction of Gort's steel drum by the police symbolizes the government's attempt to destroy the peasant class. The motif of the drum music, then, underscores the islanders' rebellion against laws made first by the British and then by the ruling class of their own society. The symbolic importance of the steel drum music to the islanders' heritage and culture is interwoven throughout the novel. The second half of the novel, "The Revolt of the Drums," links the music motif and the theme of revolution.

Images of death and imprisonment permeate the novel. At the end, the possibility for a better life for the people of the Caribbean is symbolized by the election of a new president.

Critical Context

The novel did not emerge as a kind of literature in the English-speaking Caribbean until the twentieth century. After a slow start until the 1930's, West Indian literature began to gain international recognition with the works of Claude McKay of Jamaica, the first Caribbean novelist to write of the experience of the native peoples of the islands. His third novel, *Banana Bottom*, includes the themes of alienation and exile that inform much of the later literature of the Caribbean. In the period between 1949 and 1959, more than fifty novels written by dozens of different Caribbean writers were published. Many of these novels dealt with the themes McKay had first delineated.

Writing twenty years after McKay, George Lamming has dominated the Caribbean literary arena, with six novels published between 1953 and 1972. He garnered strong reviews and a reputation as an important writer with the publication of his first novel, *In the Castle of My Skin* (1953). That novel and his fourth, *Season of Adventure*, have been his most popular and most critically acclaimed works. His other novels include *The Emigrants* (1954), *Of Age and Innocence* (1958), *Water with Berries* (1971), and *Natives of My Person* (1971). Lamming has remarked on several occasions that these six novels make up one long book, beginning with the semi-autobiographical *In the Castle of My Skin*. These novels parallel the social and cultural upheaval involved in changing from a colony to a nation. His acclaimed collection of essays, *The Pleasures of Exile* (1960), traces the cultural and intellectual consciousness inherent in Caribbean literature.

His interest in social issues has linked him with other important black writers such as Langston Hughes, Jacques Roumain, and Richard Wright. All of his works have focused on colonialism and nationhood, dealing with the experiences of the native population of the Caribbean islands. Scholars agree that Lamming's work has been groundbreaking. His influence on later West Indian writers remains unquestioned in critical circles.

Although he works primarily in England and the United States and has accepted invitations from several universities to fill the position of writer in residence, Lamming has kept his ties with his native island of Barbados. He returns to the Caribbean frequently to assist the Barbados Workers' Union, involving himself in various educational and cultural projects.

Bibliography
Birbalsingh, Frank. "George Lamming in Conversation with Birbalsingh." *Journal of Commonwealth Literature* 23, no. 1 (1988): 182-188. Interview with Lamming in which he discusses his first six novels, stating that they can be read as one book, beginning with colonial childhood in *In the Castle of My Skin*. He also credits Rastafarianism with providing the linkage between concepts of Africa and the Caribbean.
Birney, Earle. "Meeting George Lamming in Jamaica." *Canadian Literature* 95 (Winter, 1982): 16-28. Poet Earle Birney reminisces about his initial contacts with Lamming's novels, then describes his unplanned meeting with Lamming. The focus of the article concerns Lamming's political involvement with the Caribbean and how that involvement is demonstrated in Lamming's novels. This piece also includes the author's and Lamming's views of other well-known Caribbean figures.
Cudjoe, Selwyn R. *Resistance and the Caribbean Novel*. Athens: University of Ohio Press, 1979. Discusses Lamming's novels, particularly *Of Age and Innocence* and *Season of Adventure*. Points out that Lamming was the first Caribbean writer to use William Shakespeare's *The Tempest* (1611) as a point of departure for his novels.
Jonas, Joyce. *Anancy in the Great House: Ways of Reading West Indian Fiction*. Westport, Conn.: Greenwood Press, 1990. Examines the related problems of language and perception as thematic motifs in the works of George Lamming and Wilson Harris. Employs the concepts of the Great House and Anancy (a trickster figure of West Indian literature) to present a worldview of opposites in *Season of Adventure*.
Joseph, Margaret Paul. *Caliban in Exile: The Outsider in Caribbean Fiction*. Westport, Conn.: Greenwood Press, 1992. Explores Lamming's novels as parallel to the social and political evolution of Caliban, Lamming's own image of the West

Indian. Concludes that only in *Season of Adventure* does Lamming reach some sense of affirmation.

Maldonado-Diaz, Arturo. "George Lamming: A Descriptive Bibliography of Criticism and Reviews." *Journal of Commonwealth Literature* 16, no. 2 (1982): 165-173. Provides an annotated bibliography, particularly helpful as an introduction to Lamming studies. A complete listing of critical articles and reviews of Lamming's novels and essays up to 1982.

Pouchet Paquet, Sandra. *The Novels of George Lamming.* London: Heinemann, 1982. Discusses Lamming's first six novels, emphasizing their political themes. Underscores Lamming's status as a major novelist, providing a comprehensive overview of his work. Each chapter thereafter concentrates on one of Lamming's novels, providing a close reading. The critic concludes that *Season of Adventure* is Lamming's most positive work, demonstrating the promise of a peasant and middle-class alliance through the characters of Gort and Fola.

Cheri Louise Ross

SEDUCTION BY LIGHT

Author: Al Young (1939-   )
Type of work: Novel
Type of plot: Psychological realism
Time of plot: The last decades of the twentieth century
Locale: Southern California
First published: 1988

> *Principal characters:*
> MAMIE FRANKLIN, the protagonist, a former rhythm-and-blues
>   singer and minor screen actress from Hattiesburg, Mississippi
> BURLEY COLE, Mamie's common-law husband, the father of
>   Kendall and stepfather of Mamie's son, Benjie, and an avid
>   junk collector
> BENJAMIN (BENJIE) FRANKLIN, the son who was conceived out of
>   wedlock by Mamie and Harry Silvertone
> HARRY SILVERTONE, the agent and film producer who helped
>   Mamie start her film career in the 1950's
> THEO, a handsome waiter at the Railroad Croissant cafe; he
>   becomes Mamie's lover
> BRETT TOSHIMURA, a television news reporter

The Novel

Seduction by Light is Mamie Franklin's story of her life and transition to death as she tells it in an exuberant, colloquial style. As if she were speaking in a conversation over coffee between old friends, Mamie often directly addresses the reader: "You must know me well enough by now to know I'm kinda halfway out there mosta the time anyway." Mamie's monologue captures the earthy wit and wisdom of the former actress and band singer from Mississippi, who works until her death as a domestic servant for an eccentric Hollywood couple.

The first part of the novel concerns Mamie's relationship to her common-law husband, Burley Cole, whose death by heart attack in chapter 7 does not end their close relationship or his presence in the novel. Burley appears throughout the novel as a messenger to Mamie from beyond this world. He instructs her about the meaning of her own out-of-body travels, especially after she collapses on the sidewalk outside her house in Santa Monica, California, after the house is destroyed by an earthquake.

The aftermath of the devastating earthquake that rocks Santa Monica is the dramatic focus of the novel's second half. The neck injuries Mamie sustains after being struck by debris as she escaped from her home with her young lover, Theo, cause the physical collapse that leads to Mamie's spectacular travels into the unconscious realm, where she hovers in a dream state that is connected to both life and death. In her out-of-body travels, Mamie realizes important spiritual lessons, such as that her true spirit resides in a place distinct from the shell of her dying body.

Besides using her gift for double-sightedness to stay in contact with her late husband, Burley, and to perform her own out-of-body traveling, Mamie also contacts one of her heroes, the American patriot and inventor Ben Franklin. Mamie realizes that her connection to Ben Franklin stems from his helping to found a new nation, which is, in a metaphorical sense, related to Mamie's enthusiasm for going beyond tired conventions and toward an embrace of new experiences, including the experience of life after death. Franklin tells her in comical but philosophically illuminating passages that he has been "appointed to inform" Mamie of her imminent death. Franklin's role is to welcome Mamie to her "higher self" and to take her time-traveling with him through the ages. They visit France during the Revolution of 1789 and ancient Egypt, where Mamie discovers a resemblance between Ben Franklin and King Tut. Franklin's warning to Mamie that her time on Earth is "severely limited" enables her to live in the moment and to feel a connection to all the people she meets. Ben tells Mamie to "bear in mind that 'now' is the only time there is" and also to "let go of the idea that anyone else is separate from what you like to think of as yourself."

Besides learning about the interconnectedness of all people through Franklin's message, Mamie, in the aftermath of the earthquake that sends the city of Santa Monica into a state of emergency, learns at first hand about the bonds that exist among strangers through the power of television. The instant transmission of images through broadcast journalism disseminates news of Mamie's tragic loss of all of her belongings throughout California via an on-the-scene report and an emotional interview conducted by a local television journalist named Brett Toshimura. Toshimura takes a personal interest in Mamie's troubles and uses her position to publicize Mamie's story. Toshimura's interview leads the former actress, ironically, to a celebrity status well beyond the fame she was able to achieve when she was officially in show business. Her story touches a chord in countless viewers, whose donations to assist Mamie come to more than forty thousand dollars.

Mamie realizes at the end of the novel that she is, finally, on the verge of disconnection from her body for the last time. The last scenes affirm the general humanity of the community in helping Mamie through donations, but the last scenes also allow Mamie the space to settle her personal affairs. Prior to her death, she learns that Benjie, the talented son that she had conceived secretly with her agent, Harry Silvertone, has met with his true father, and that Benjie's career in screenwriting will be assisted through Harry's connections in Hollywood. "The world could do anything it wanted to now; I'd finally gotten my boy and his daddy together. Where they took it from there on out was their business."

The ghost of Burley cannot accept his own death until he sees that his son, Kendall, is taken care of financially. Mamie is able to relieve Burley's burden by helping Kendall to locate a mysterious set of important documents long buried in Burley's trunk. Mamie's mailing of these documents to Kendall just prior to her death helps to ensure his financial well-being.

The Characters

The energy of *Seduction By Light*'s narrative is sustained through the sheer dramatic force, poetic insights, and folk wisdom of the novel's protagonist and overwhelming presence, Mamie Franklin, who is also the novel's first-person narrator. Mamie endures and triumphs over circumstances, including an earthquake that devastates her home and that threatens her physical health, through a spiritual impulse that allows her to perceive a linkage between the living and the dead and an interconnectedness between all persons:

> I dont go to church much anymore—only at Easter and Christmastime—but there's a church in my heart I slip into now and then. The message I get whensoever I turn inside is always the same: There's somethin bigger than me or the world or the whole universe that I'll have to be answerin to by and by.

In spite of the trouble Mamie experiences—an attempted robbery of her home and the death of her beloved common-law husband, the destruction of her worldly possessions, and her death through the injuries incurred during the earthquake—her course is toward a liberation from the worries of the physical world and a heightened perspective from which she can experience a final and lasting peace: "And pretty soon I could tell at last there was nothin left to see but the sea, and nothin left to do but keep on swimmin upstream in that sweet, bright river of light."

Although she is a psychic whose out-of-body travels and conversations with the departed might suggest to some readers that her allegiance is strictly to an extraordinary reality beyond the physical world, Mamie's acceptance of death enables her to embrace life with vigor and intensity. Born on a farm in Mississippi, Mamie still gains a deep satisfaction from gardening, an act that literally connects her to the soil: "When I'm busy gardenin, I wanna be by myself. That's where the happiness starts bubblin up from, from deep down inside nobody but me." Her enjoyment of the physical world is also showcased in her lyrical descriptions of the passion and love she feels for her young boyfriend, Theo.

Mamie's understanding of the interrelationship of life and death, of sadness and of joy, and of the comic and the tragic, as well as her thirst for experience, allows her to overcome the loss of her home and most of her worldly belongings in the earthquake. Her understanding allows her to still consider herself to be lucky because she survived the disaster. As she says, "If you play it right, you might come out with your life, which is all you ever had, anyway!"

Themes and Meanings

The novel's title, *Seduction by Light*, refers to Mamie's philosophical understanding of what happens to filmgoers when they become engrossed in the lives of fictional characters on a screen. Mamie points out that film stars are, essentially, only shadows made out of light projected onto a blank screen. She connects the way audiences become absorbed in the light-induced illusion of life on the screen with the way people become so absorbed in the "reality" of their everyday lives that they cling to a world that is, from her point of view, no more meaningful than the world of sleep or dream.

> Pretty much every last one of us was out here gettin seduced. And by what? Nothin but light, not a thing but light quiverin and makin patterns on a screen. Now that I wasn't worried about losin *anything* anymore, it was all startin to fall together.

Mamie's awareness of the ephemeral, unreal, or absurd quality of life, as well as her faith in the pleasant feelings of weightlessness and brightness she has experienced in her out-of-body travels, allows her to convert depressing experiences into events indicating a promise of a better life. Mamie's ability to overcome depression and loss through faith in a spiritual world after death, and her understanding of the interrelationship of all people on a spiritual plane, illustrate common themes in much of Al Young's imaginative writing. Young has said that "man's effort must be to locate the dance, the song, the rhythm of life even in the mortar and steel of urban living in modern America." With her emphasis on the importance music has played in bringing people together to share a common story and common experience, Mamie, herself a blues singer whose first-person narrative is a sort of extended blues song, embodies Young's message to his audience to locate "the rhythm of life."

Young has also said that he thinks of love as the "ultimate expression of unity" and that God can be "encountered through love." Mamie's intense emotional and physical relationships with Burley and with Theo, as well as her concern for the well-being of her son, Benjie, and for Burley's son, Kendall, illustrate Young's theme of unity through love as Mamie consistently imbues her personal relationships with spiritual significance.

Critical Context

In addition to writing novels, Al Young writes poetry of the African American experience. Part of his literary project, in poetry and in prose, has been to pay tribute not to the African American literary tradition to which his work obviously belongs but to the African American musical tradition from which his creative writing borrows much of its rhythmic language as well as many of its important themes. "That's why I've written poems about [saxophonist] Coleman Hawkins, [blues singer] Ma Rainey, [blues singer and guitarist] Robert Johnson, and [saxophonist] Illinois Jacquet—a whole lot of geniuses," Young has stated. Although Mamie Franklin is a fictional characterization, her story should be placed into this critical context of literary work that stands in praise of the African American performing arts.

One of the important ways in which Mamie Franklin experiences a spiritual identification with other persons is through African American music, dancing, and theater arts. Herself a professional singer in a minor but successful rhythm-and-blues band from the 1950's called The Inklings, Mamie recognized early in her singing career the special role music has played in the lives of many African Americans. "Music, I began to figure out, wasnt exactly what we mostly think it is: entertainment. There was somethin medicinal about it too." The value of blues singing, according to Mamie, should be judged by the degree to which the singer is able to make his or her experience appear universal and recognizable to other listeners.

Young often expresses through his novel the importance other African American performing artists have played in providing role models for African Americans such as Mamie, who grew up under the yoke of Jim Crow laws in Mississippi before the Civil Rights movement of the late 1950's and 1960's brought the possibilities of political, social, and educational advancement to many African Americans. Mamie recalls how important it was for her to see actress Lena Horne in lead roles in quality films that required more of her than to "come on glitterin real slinky and glamorous and sexy to perform some song."

Through Mamie's observations about the healing powers of African American music and through her recognition of the importance of African American visibility in Hollywood films, *Seduction by Light* becomes a powerful homage to the spiritual dimension of the African American performing arts. It is a monument to the influence African American culture has had on national and international culture since the breaking down of racial barriers in the late 1950's allowed the folk, blues, and jazz music of African Americans to be heard throughout the world.

Bibliography
Broughton, Irv, ed. "Al Young." In *The Writer's Mind: Interviews with American Authors.* 3 vols. Fayetteville: University of Arkansas Press, 1989-1990. Young discusses the importance of black rituals, storytelling, the idea of music as a social force, his relationship to the South of his childhood, and the need to "believe in something more all encompassing than one's own limited sense of self."
Fairbanks, Carol, and Eugene A. Engeldinger. *Black American Fiction: A Bibliography.* Metuchen, N.J.: Scarecrow Press, 1978. Includes a thorough bibliography of Young's poetry, novels, short fiction, and jazz criticism, as well as reviews and essays about Young's work until 1978.
Harper, Michael S., Larry Kart, and Al Young. "Jazz and Letters: a Colloquy." *TriQuarterly* 68 (Winter, 1987): 118-158. Young discusses the relationship between poetic language and the rhythms of jazz music, as well as the role of Jack Kerouac in shaping a jazz-inflected American literature.
O'Brien, John. "Al Young." In *Interviews with Black Writers.* New York: Liveright, 1973. Young discusses his theory of poetry as the journey of the self as it seeks unity with other men and nature.
Schultz, Elizabeth. "Search for 'Soul Space': A Study of Al Young's *Who Is Angelina* (1975) and the Dimensions of Freedom." In *The Afro-American Novel Since 1960: A Collection of Critical Essays*, edited by Peter Bruck and Wolfgang Karrer. Amsterdam: B. R. Grüner, 1982. Although this essay focuses on Angelina Green, a hero from one of Young's earlier novels, Schultz's understanding of Angelina's character creates a suggestive reading for the character of Mamie Franklin.

Daniel Charles Morris

SERAPH ON THE SUWANEE

Author: Zora Neale Hurston (1891-1960)
Type of work: Novel
Type of plot: Psychological realism
Time of plot: The early twentieth century
Locale: Rural Florida
First published: 1948

> *Principal characters:*
> ARVAY HENSON MESERVE, the protagonist, a woman whose
> insecurities and irrational fears dominate the novel
> JIM MESERVE, Arvay's husband, an enterprising, handsome man
> of aristocratic but impoverished stock
> EARL DAVID MESERVE, the deformed first-born child of Arvay
> and Jim
> ANGELINE (ANGIE) MESERVE, the beautiful and sensual daughter
> of Arvay and Jim
> KENNY MESERVE, the youngest son of Arvay and Jim
> LARRAINE ('RAINE) HENSON MIDDLETON, Arvay's jealous older
> sister
> CARL MIDDLETON, a preacher who, like Jim Meserve, recognizes
> Arvay's fineness
> JOE KELSEY, an African American loyal to Jim Meserve
> DESSIE KELSEY, Joe's wife

The Novel

Seraph on the Suwanee signals Hurston's departure from her usual subject matter, the African American people and their culture, both of which are inextricably intertwined in her other novels. With the depiction of Arvay Henson Meserve, a poor, white, "cracker born, cracker bred" woman, Hurston focuses on the ambitious poor white class of the South.

When the novel opens, Arvay has spent the last several years retreating into a type of religious hysteria resulting from sexual repression. Believing herself to be in love with her brother-in-law, the uninspired preacher Carl Middleton, she alternates between feelings of guilt and erotic fantasy. Perceived by the poor white community of Sawley as "odd," Arvay finds herself alienated. She constantly compares herself with her voluptuous, flirtatious sister 'Raine, Carl's wife, and comes up wanting.

When Jim Meserve, the attractive, ambitious newcomer to the "teppentime mill," decides to court Arvay, she is distrustful. Jim sees her as a woman of beauty and character. Arvay sees only her lack of sexual attractiveness as defined by the Sawley community. She views her mental adultery with her brother-in-law as a reason she is not fit to be the wife of Jim Meserve. In an effort to cleanse herself of her guilty thoughts, she leads Jim to the old mulberry tree, a "cool green temple of peace." Instead of being purged of guilt, Arvay is raped by her suitor under this natural temple. Seeing his chance now that Arvay has been deflowered—and therefore "ruined"—he sweeps her off to the justice of the peace to cement their bond legally and properly.

The enterprising Jim knows that the turpentine mill offers no financial security or social mobility. He makes plans to make a new start in the Florida citrus groves but must delay the family move when Arvay becomes pregnant with their first child, the mentally and physically deformed Earl David. Arvay, believing that Earl David represents some sort of divine retribution for her mental adultery, becomes overprotective of the child, refusing to acknowledge his violent outbursts.

In Citrabelle, Jim becomes the premier citrus grower in the area. He builds a fine home for his wife and growing family on his carefully cleared and cultivated land. Only one detail mars Arvay's happiness over such affluence: The house is built in front of a swamp that Arvay instinctively fears because it represents her own dark, guilt-ridden subconscious.

Arvay constantly judges by outward appearances, rather than looking at the realities of life. This injects constant tension into her marriage. During her third pregnancy, Jim teasingly commands Arvay that she must make sure that the child will be a boy. Arvay takes him at his word and is tormented for months by what she imagines might happen to her if the child were to be another girl. She finally confesses the source of her ongoing anxiety. Jim, horrified, astutely realizes that "there was not sufficient understanding in his marriage. . . . It could not keep on like this. He was panging and paining far too much. What help for it except by parting from Arvay?"

The child is a boy, whom Jim names Kenny. Kenny, like his older sister Angeline, is a winsome, intelligent child. Both children provide a sharp contrast to Earl, who has grown more uncontrollable with age. Jim knows that Earl must be put away, but Arvay refuses to see the danger in allowing Earl to remain at home. After Earl viciously attacks a local girl, he hides in the swamp but is killed by a posse.

Years later, Jim decides to leave Arvay and move to the Florida coast. He admonishes her that if she wants to save their marriage, Arvay must make the offer of reconciliation. Instead, she draws upon her secret pride in her "cracker" heritage and decides to move back to Sawley.

When she returns to her hometown, she finds her mother neglected and dying in the filthy, ramshackle Henson home. 'Raine, Carl, and their ugly, mean-spirited children are firmly ensconced within. For the first time, she is able to see past imagined appearances and recognize the truth. After her mother dies, Arvay, in an act of renunciation, burns down the house that has become for her a symbol of evil and stagnation. The mulberry tree is spared because it is where she "had triumphed, and with nothing more than her humble self, had won her a vivid way of life with love. This tree was a sacred symbol." At last Arvay has made peace with her past and her heritage. She now realizes how clinging to the past had poisoned her marriage. Much wiser, she travels to the coast to find Jim and save their marriage.

The Characters

Arvay Henson is a puzzling female protagonist, one beset by irrational feelings of guilt and inferiority. Hurston admitted to her editor that she, too, found Arvay's clinging tendencies to be irritating, yet she vowed that Arvay would grow into a self-confident woman. Unlike other Hurston protagonists, Arvay finds self-actualization only in relation to her husband. She discovers her worth only when she realizes that her husband is dependent upon her as a Madonna figure.

Conversely, Arvay is probably the most ambitiously conceived character Hurston ever created. The story is her story, filtered through her own troubled misconceptions. She is a haunted figure. Somewhat shadowy, she is most likely the "Seraph on the Suwanee," a woman whose ethereal looks inspire her husband but repress her sense of self-worth.

Her husband is another matter. The symbolic significance of Jim Meserve's name can be interpreted two ways, as serving himself and as one who serves others. Jim is a man burdened by chauvinistic views toward women, views reinforced by his friend Joe Kelsey's advice that "women folks will love you plenty if you take and see to it that they do. Make 'em knuckle under. From the very first jump, get the bridle in they mouth and ride 'em hard and stop 'em short. They's all alike, Boss. Take 'em and break 'em." Both men, black and white, hold dominating and self-serving views toward women.

Despite this flaw, Hurston depicts Jim sympathetically. During the novel's climax, when Arvay does not make a move to save her husband from a rattlesnake that has entwined itself around his body, Jim instinctively knows that unless she changes, Arvay cannot give him the type of love that he needs: "I feel and believe that you do love me, Arvay, but I don't want that stand-still, hap-hazard kind of love. I'm just as hungry as a dog for a knowing and a doing love. You love like a coward. Don't take no steps at all. Just stand around and hope for things to happen out right." Essentially, both characters become victims of their own twisted sort of thinking. Arvay has allowed her "cracker" heritage to dictate her life. Jim, enslaved by chauvinistic ideas and by his stoic insistence on maintaining silence, locks his wife out of his life, thus not permitting or encouraging her to offer "a knowing and doing love."

The other characters in *Seraph on the Suwanee* are one-dimensionally limned, serving as representations of other types of Southern personalities or symbols. Angeline, the "angel" figure who is a daughter of the "seraph," is a sensualist. Unlike her mother, she does not suffer pangs of inferiority or harbor feelings of guilt. She is a true Meserve, self-assured, sensual, and clearly focused on obtaining what she desires. Her pursuit of Hatton Howland is as painstakingly planned and executed as her father's courtship of her mother was twenty years earlier. The character of Angie signifies what a woman, freed from sexual repression and feelings of inadequacy, can achieve: a knowing and doing love.

Kenny Meserve represents not only the best traits of both of his parents but also the best of Southern culture. Handsome, loving, and generous, he has a firm commitment to his family. He even sends money and gifts to his seldom-seen grandmother, Maria Henson. Furthermore, as an artist figure, he represents what has been identified as Hurston's artistic intent when writing *Seraph on the Suwanee*: to depict the shared language and culture of black and white Southerners. Kenny is a successful musician because he has skillfully blended the music of the African American into a white medium, just as the novel was to serve as an illustration of the similarities between the white and black Southern experiences.

The peripheral characters become symbolic, both in the novel and in Arvay's mind. Earl David, twisted and unnatural, becomes a living reminder of Arvay's guilt over Carl Middleton. She is unable to relinquish her hold on Earl because she is unable to free herself from her youthful feelings of sexual guilt. 'Raine, Carl, and their monstrous children symbolize the spiritual stagnation of those who cannot or will not aspire to a better life. To his credit, Carl realizes that Arvay would have inspired him to become a better preacher and a better man. Instead, he is easily duped, partly because of his own feelings of inferiority, and forsakes Arvay in favor of her older sister. Thus the novel offers a complex look at the psychological and metaphysical motivations of poor white Southerners. Although the ending somewhat dubiously validates Arvay's sense of self, both husband and wife are enveloped within a feeling of peace and harmony, as symbolized by the mulberry tree.

Themes and Meanings

The story of Arvay Meserve is the story of a woman's quest for self-fulfillment, a quest fraught with self-imposed obstacles. A victim of her social class's mores and values, Arvay is not a woman in charge of her own destiny. Two symbols, one natural, the other constructed, exemplify the two warring halves of Arvay's psyche: the mulberry tree and the Henson house.

Throughout the novel, the mulberry tree grows in mythic proportions in Arvay's mind. As a child, the tree took on an idyllic significance for Arvay. The center of her childhood play, the mulberry tree also became the vehicle for her pondering the mysteries of the universe. Peering through its strong, life-affirming branches, Arvay cannot see the heavenly figures she strains to envision. She learns then that heaven is not in the realm of her perception, that it is a long way off.

As an adolescent, the tree becomes a refuge from what Arvay thinks is an unbearable situation. She indulges in her fantasy that Carl Middleton will realize the mistake he has made by marrying 'Raine and will come back to her, kissing the hem of her garment as an act of contrition. Under its ever-blooming branches, Arvay renews her hope that she will be freed from the guilt and repression that have imprisoned her soul. Eventually, the tree becomes a sacred respite, a temple where she knows that she can find peace and spiritual sanctuary. When her sexual feelings are reawakened with the appearance of Jim Meserve, she brings him to this sacred place in an effort to purge herself from her wanton, and therefore unworthy, thoughts of Carl Middleton. Her rape may seem like an act of desecration, but in Arvay's mind it is an emancipation of sorts. Out of this violent act, Arvay's slow movement away from her "cracker" ties begins.

When she returns as a middle-aged woman, the tree brings back Arvay's most pleasant memories. The rape now marks the beginning of her new life. The mulberry tree thus again becomes a sacred place. Appalled at the sight of the dilapidated house and its sinister appearance, Arvay sets fire to it. She recognizes that her heritage, symbolized by the house, has stifled her: "It had soaked in so much of doing-without, of soul starvation, of brutish vacancy of aim, of absent dreams, envy of trifles . . . that it was a sanctuary of tiny and sanctioned vices." Her soul purged by the fire, Arvay is free to seek the peace and harmony the tree symbolizes. She donates the land to the town of Sawley, stipulating that it be used as a park and that the mulberry tree be cared for in perpetuity. The Henson home, which stood for the pettiness of Sawley, is transformed into a metaphorical sacred grove. Now that she has vanquished the house, she is able to embark on her newfound quest for happiness and marital bliss.

Critical Context

Hurston's last extant novel has been viewed as a valiant effort to prove to the white literary establishment that an African American writer was artistically and intellectually capable of transcending the race issue. Other African Americans writing at this time, notably Ann Petry, Willard Motley, and Chester Himes, had achieved moderate success depicting white characters.

Hurston's own motivations for undertaking this divergent turn are threefold. First, she wished to see one of her novels turned into a Hollywood screenplay. Second, she would contest the supposition that African American writers were only capable of dealing with black subjects. Third, she would challenge the assumption that the white and African American experiences in the South were divergently opposed. Her subject matter may be different, but her milieu remained the same.

Granted, the words of the Meserves echo the cadences and musicality reminiscent of Hurston's more memorable African American characters, reflecting Hurston's premise that there is no white or black dialect, merely a Southern dialect. Even though the characters are white, the themes present in this novel mirror those in her earlier works that had dealt solely with the African American folk experience. Arvay Henson, like other Hurston female protagonists, is searching for fulfillment and love. Women, black and white, in this novel are viewed as lesser creatures than men, creatures whose spirits must be tamed. In addition, *Seraph on the Suwanee* shares the focus of her other fiction; that is, love, marriage, personal growth, and exploration of the feminine psyche predominate the work.

Bibliography

Carby, Hazel V. Foreword to *Seraph on the Suwanee*, by Zora Neale Hurston. New York: HarperCollins, 1991. Offers a historical overview of Hurston's writing of the novel as well as a comparison/contrast analysis to Hurston's *Their Eyes Were Watching God* (1937).

Coleman, Ancilla. "Mythological Structure and Psychological Significance in Hurston's *Seraph on the Suwanee.*" *Publications of the Mississippi Philological Association* (1988): 21-27. Sees a parallel between the Psyche/Cupid myth and the story of Arvay and Jim Meserve.

Glassman, Steve, and Kathryn Lee Seidel, eds. *Zora in Florida.* Orlando: University of Central Florida Press, 1991. A collection of essays that deal with the major phases of Hurston's life in Florida in relation to her work.

Hemenway, Robert. *Zora Neale Hurston: A Literary Biography.* Urbana: University of Illinois Press, 1977. The standard biography of Hurston. Argues against the view that *Seraph on the Suwanee* is assimilationist.

Howard, Lillie P. *Zora Neale Hurston.* Boston: Twayne, 1980. Addresses and explores the chauvinism issue. Questions Arvay's decision to rejoin her husband.

Anita M. Vickers

THE SHADOW BRIDE

Author: Roy A. K. Heath (1926-   )
Type of work: Novel
Type of plot: Psychological realism
Time of plot: The 1930's
Locale: British Guiana
First published: 1988

Principal characters:
  BETTA SINGH, a young medical doctor of East Indian descent
  MRS. SINGH, Betta's wealthy widowed mother
  MEENA SINGH, the beautiful, sensual woman whom Betta marries
  AJI, an ancient female family retainer
  MULVI SAHIB, a Muslim religious teacher
  THE PUJAREE, a Hindu religious teacher
  RANI, an orphan adopted by Mrs. Singh
  LAHTI, another orphan adopted by Mrs. Singh
  SUKRUM, a vicious, scheming opportunist

The Novel

Like most of Roy Heath's novels, *The Shadow Bride* deals with the disintegration of a single character. In this case that character is Mrs. Singh, a woman born in India but brought to British Guiana as a bride when still an adolescent. The novel's title suggests that Mrs. Singh has left part of herself back in India and remains a "shadow" of herself throughout her life. She symbolizes the problems of all East Indian immigrants living in Guiana, and in a certain sense she symbolizes all first-generation immigrants everywhere, including Heath himself.

The protagonist of the novel is not Mrs. Singh but her son Betta, who has been studying medicine in England. Contrary to his mother's wishes, he goes to work as a government official supervising the health of workers on a big colonial estate that is engaged in the business of growing sugar cane for export. The time is the 1930's, and the country is still under British rule. Such estates played a major part in Guiana's history, because the British imported large numbers of indentured workers from India to do the backbreaking, poorly paid labor in the fields. The East Indians became the dominant racial group in Guiana, which is the reason Heath, himself of African descent, is writing about them.

The British overseers were as heartless in their treatment of the indentured workers as the slave owners in the Deep South of the United States were to their slaves before the Civil War. The biggest scourge in Guiana was malaria, which was transmitted by mosquitoes and not well understood at that time. Betta is appalled at the living and working conditions of the people he is called upon to treat, but he quickly runs afoul of the overseers when he tries to hospitalize men who are obviously too sick to work under the equatorial sun. An attempt is made on Betta's life by thugs acting on orders from the estate's top management. By this time, Betta is married and has a child; he quits his post because he does not want to endanger his family.

When Betta tries to move back into his mother's house with his family, he finds that the gates have been padlocked to keep them out. His mother has fallen under the influence of a holy man of the traditional Hindu faith who, under the guise of teaching her to free herself from worldly attachments, is actually destroying her relationships with relatives and friends.

While Betta struggles to build a medical practice and support a growing family without his mother's assistance, she becomes a helpless thrall to the Pujaree, who eventually becomes her husband and lord and master of her household. At last she realizes what has happened to her and manages to evict her hateful husband, only to fall into the hands of Sukrum, a loathsome household servant with no religious pretensions whatever. When Sukrum tries to assert his complete dominance by raping Mrs. Singh, she accepts the final humiliation of running back to her son and the daughter-in-law she has repeatedly scorned. She begins to lose her mind completely and finally frees her son and daughter-in-law of her demanding, disruptive presence by committing suicide.

The Characters

Roy Heath's greatest strength as a fiction writer is in his characterization. He creates characters who seem to be real people. In *The Shadow Bride*, he tells his story from many different viewpoints, including those of Mrs. Singh, Betta, Betta's wife Meena, Rani, Lahti, Sukrum, the Pujaree, and several others. He displays adroit craftsmanship in constructing scenes in which different characters are paired for purposes of contrast. Almost every character will interact at some point in the story with every other character, and the interactions are always appropriate to what is known of their personalities and motivations.

Heath writes good dialogue that suggests the intellectual, educational, and moral level of his characters; he never uses dialogue in a heavy-handed manner for the purpose of conveying plot information to the reader. Like real people, Heath's characters do not always say what they think and feel because they do not always know what they are thinking and feeling. Moreover, they often have reasons to conceal their true thoughts or feelings.

Heath shares one quality with the world's greatest creative writers: He is able to project himself into all of his characters. Betta reflects that there is something in himself of all the people he has encountered over a period of about ten years. It should be noted that Heath himself has obvious points in common with both Mrs. Singh and Betta. Like Mrs. Singh, Heath is an expatriate who feels he has left an important part of himself behind in his native land. Like Betta, Heath is strongly motivated to find his true identity and be useful to society, but he is hopelessly perplexed by the enormity of humanity's problems. Heath feels guilty about running away from the seemingly insurmountable troubles of Guiana in the same way that Betta feels guilty about abandoning the sick and dying workers. There are many such autobiographical projections in Heath's major and minor characters.

Heath, like many other West Indians, emigrated to England. It is evident from his published writings that he feels alienated in that cold northern land with its predominantly white population; however, he also feels alienated in his native Guiana, because, like the great American novelist Henry James, he has been an expatriate for so much of his life. In writing about Mrs. Singh's chronic unhappiness, Heath is actually writing about himself. In one revealing passage, Betta muses that the book's other characters "were all mirrors in which he had glimpsed something of himself, admirable or repugnant, according as he rejected or welcomed what he saw."

Themes and Meanings

Heath's major theme has to do with the difficulty of adjusting to a new environment. Mrs. Singh never feels at home in Guiana and is always dreaming about her native India. Her son Betta is a first-generation Guianan and does not have his mother's memories of India or her fantasies about its superior culture. He is forced to come to terms with the land where he was born and to face its multifold problems like a pioneer hacking his way through the dense Guiana jungles. His mother feels alienated from the Guianese people because she comes from a different culture; Betta feels alienated because his European education has made it nearly impossible to relate to the majority of the ignorant, superstitious, impoverished people of his homeland.

There are three principal religions represented in *The Shadow Bride*: Islam, Hinduism, and Christianity. Conflicting religious faiths keep the different ethnic groups divided. The African Americans of Guiana are predominantly Christian, while the East Indians are either Hindu or Muslim and are divided among themselves by religious differences. Betta tries to believe in each of the religions in turn, and he even toys with the idea of converting to Christianity, but he finds that his scientific education has made it impossible for him to accept any religion purely on faith.

Heath's message is that there are no easy solutions to the problems that beset the people of his native land. Each individual has to attempt to work out his own salvation without any reliable set of guidelines to follow, and many people, like Mrs. Singh, will find themselves helpless to make the psychological adjustment required to deal with the chaotic conditions that exist in multiracial, multicultural Guiana.

Heath himself, it bears repeating, did not stay to try to understand or cope with Guiana's problems but moved to well-ordered, deep-rooted Great Britain at an early age. There he encountered a different set of problems as an African American living in a predominantly white, highly class-conscious society.

Heath seems to be saying that it is hard enough for the individual to cope with his own problems without trying to solve the problems of an entire nation. He believes that people are at the mercy of vast historical forces that they cannot understand or control. As an expatriate, Heath sees that Guiana's problems reflect the whole world's problems in a microcosm. Toward the end of the novel, the thoroughly disillusioned idealist Betta Singh reflects on what he has observed and experienced since returning home from abroad:

> It occurred to him that he, and perhaps others, rarely made any conscious decisions, that his actions were dictated by a series of images so brief, he was almost entirely unaware of them. The act of passing the unlit house in Regent Street had left in his mind a retinue of unfulfilled longings, and he was to question whether his life had been his own.

Critical Context

Roy Heath has been given little attention in books about Caribbean writers. He moved away from his homeland and has lived in England since 1951, returning to Guiana only for occasional visits; thus, many books about Caribbean writers do not even mention his name in a footnote. He is considered by many critics to be a British writer rather than a Caribbean writer.

Those critics who have discussed Heath's books invariably note that he is more concerned with the past than the future and with the individual than society. He is often called an "expatriate" author, and his harshest critics say that he does not truly understand the problems of his native land because he has been away from it for so long. He has been accused of lacking social conscience and national and racial identity.

Yet Heath's situation gives him a broader perspective than is available to writers who are immersed in a single familiar environment. He can be usefully compared to Henry James and Vladimir Nabokov, two great novelists who suffered by being cut off from their roots but whose suffering gave them a deeper understanding and tolerance than was exhibited by many of their stay-at-home contemporaries.

The Shadow Bride is generally considered to be Heath's best novel. It is an important work that avoids giving easy answers to problems of race relations and personal alienation. Instead of offering salvation through politics or religion, the novel places the burden of existence upon each individual. Heath is too intelligent a writer to believe, or to attempt to convince his readers, that the enormous problems of his native land can be solved overnight by any quick fix. Through his protagonist, Betta Singh, he shows that the only hope for the future can be found in the patient, diligent, self-sacrificing dedication of many such intelligent individuals. He does not cast blame, even on the brutal colonial exploiters of the East Indian workers; he recognizes that human beings are complex mixtures of good and bad.

Bibliography

Boxill, Anthony. "Penetrating the Hinterland: Roy Heath's Guyana Trilogy." *World Literature Written in English* 29, no. 1 (1989): 103-110. A mainly favorable evaluation of Heath's novels *From the Heat of the Day* (1979), *One Generation* (1981), and *Genetha* (1981). Boxill discusses Heath's life and work, pointing out that Heath has never been especially interested in race relations, Guianese nationalism, the colonial heritage, or the search for a unique West Indian identity, all of which are characteristics of most Caribbean literature.

Dasenbrock, Reed Way. Review of *The Shadow Bride*. *World Literature Today* 63, no. 1 (Winter, 1989): 151-152. Gives a brief history of the settlement of Guiana and calls Heath's novel "the epic of malaria" because this dreaded scourge of the tropics is central to *The Shadow Bride*. Compares the book to V. S. Naipaul's classic Caribbean novel of "creolization," *A House for Mr. Biswas* (1961).

Heath, Roy. *Shadows Round the Moon: A Caribbean Childhood*. London: William Collins Sons, 1990. The author relates the story of his early life in what was then British Guinea. His personal history is interwoven with many amusing anecdotes about his multiracial homeland under colonial rule.

Jaggi, Maya. "Promising Secrets." *The Times Literary Supplement*, September 14, 1990, 979. A review of *Shadows Round the Moon*. Jaggi points out some of the autobiographical elements that found expression in fictional form in such works as *The Shadow Bride*.

McWatt, Mark A. "Roy A. K. Heath." *Fifty Caribbean Writers: A Bio-Bibliographical Critical Sourcebook*, edited by Daryl Cumber Dance. New York: Greenwood Press, 1986. An informative discussion of Heath's life and work, highlighting his ambiguous position as an expatriate.

Rubin, Merle. "A Marriage Tie That Binds." *The Christian Science Monitor*, February 17, 1993, 15. A review of the American edition of Heath's *From the Heat of the Day*, originally published in Britain in 1979. Focuses on the complexities of marital relationships and praises Heath for his refusal to provide simple solutions to his characters' complex family problems, many of which are taken up again in *The Shadow Bride*.

Bill Delaney

THE SIGN IN SIDNEY BRUSTEIN'S WINDOW

Author: Lorraine Hansberry (1930-1965)
Type of work: Play
Type of plot: Protest drama
Time of plot: The early 1960's
Locale: Greenwich Village, New York
First produced: 1964, at the Longacre Theater, New York City
First published: 1965

> *Principal characters:*
> SIDNEY BRUSTEIN, the protagonist, an idealistic Jew in his late
>   thirties who runs a newspaper
> IRIS PARODUS BRUSTEIN, Sidney's wife, a pretty woman in her late
>   twenties
> GLORIA PARODUS, Iris' younger sister
> MAVIS PARODUS BRYSON, Iris' older sister, in her thirties
> ALTON SCALES, Sidney's friend and helper with the newspaper
> DAVID RAGIN, Sidney's neighbor, a homosexual playwright
> MAX, a middle-aged artist who helps with Sidney's newspaper
> WALLY O'HARA, a politician

The Play

The Sign in Sidney Brustein's Window, Lorraine Hansberry's second Broadway play, is set in New York's Greenwich Village in the early 1960's. Although its action arises out of the early ferment of the 1960's phase of the American Civil Rights movement, the play seems only indirectly connected with that movement. *A Raisin in the Sun* (1959), Hansberry's first Broadway play, deals with lower-class African American life in Chicago after World War II and directly presents key African American issues of the period, such as the ways African Americans are shut out of and yet tantalized by the materialistic American Dream as well as class, ideological, and intergenerational conflicts within African American communities. One of the main themes of *A Raisin in the Sun* is the potential loss of spiritual and moral strength if African Americans assimilate into the materialistic, dominant "white" culture. By contrast, *The Sign in Sidney Brustein's Window* offers a portrait of what Hansberry saw as a vanguard of American society, a social elite of artists and intellectuals struggling to achieve multicultural and multiethnic harmony. The central characters are not African Americans but instead an American Jew and his wife, Iris, who is of Greek, Irish, and Cherokee descent. Hansberry's second play, while presenting several issues present in her first, such as problems of racial prejudice and sexism, has a broader focus. One effect of this is to reveal the larger social context of prejudices and struggles for justice. Nevertheless, like *A Raisin in the Sun*, this play is centrally concerned with the combination of ignorance, intolerance, and the corrosive materialism of American culture as driving forces of social injustice.

The main action of the play concerns Sidney's political involvements and his marriage. In the opening scene, Sidney has withdrawn from political action, believing it
to be ineffectual. Instead, he will concentrate, in his newly acquired newspaper, on
supporting artistic activities. The first scene also reveals tension in his marriage,
resulting mainly from his thinking of Iris as a creature of his idealistic fantasies. She
is growing into herself, albeit somewhat clumsily, and he is unwilling to face this. A
week later, in the second scene, the sign in Sidney's window has gone up. It supports
Wally O'Hara as a reform political candidate. Sidney has decided to commit his
newspaper to political reform.

The remainder of act 1 and the three scenes of act 2 continue to introduce and
then mix the fairly large cast of supporting characters who make Sidney's apartment
a center of discussions about a variety of contemporary issues. These characters
divide into several groups. The Parodus sisters—Mavis Bryson, Iris, and Gloria
(who does not appear until act 3)—form what their Greek surname implies, a kind
of chorus of the commentary of ordinary people on the activities of artists and intellectuals. The artists and intellectuals divide between those who have withdrawn from
social action, David Ragin and Max, and those who are committed to bringing about
social change, such as Alton Scales and Wally O'Hara. As these characters converse
during a period of about six months, the Brustein marriage comes apart and the
political campaign enjoys unexpected success. By the end of act 2, Iris has left Sidney. As she leaves, she informs him that everyone knows that O'Hara has sold out to
organized crime to win his election.

The first scene of act 3 shows Sidney's descent into despair. The scene ends with
Gloria, David, and Sidney sharing a poetic, nihilistic nightmare vision, part of it in
rhymed verse, of a materialistic and hedonistic wasteland America, with *Playboy*
magazine as the ultimate reflection, showing philosophy, fine art, and pornography
as equally valued cultural products, packaged together between the same covers. Out
of this despair comes the suicide of Gloria, a prostitute, reflecting her refusal to
continue being a commodity. Out of this suicide comes Sidney's realization that he
still cares, that he wants to save his marriage and to fight the forces of compromise
that, in the end, will kill everyone "who believes that death is waste and love is
sweet . . . and that people wanna be better than they are."

Themes and Meanings

Hansberry believed that all plays have ideological content, that all contain a thesis
or central idea about what sort of social order is best. Some plays may seem not to
have such content, because nearly everyone who sees them accepts the main ideas.
Only when a play contains ideas that challenge majority opinion do those ideas tend
to become visible and to draw direct commentary. *The Sign in Sidney Brustein's
Window* contains many ideas that set viewers to arguing in 1964. The play also
contains ideas that remain highly controversial, such as those regarding homosexuality. The quantity of intellectual conversation and the range of issues discussed

might make the play seem mainly a drama of ideas. The center of the play, however, is human action. Many of the ideas flow from the nature of the main characters, people who are passionately concerned about how to live according to their best ideas and who, therefore, talk incessantly about those ideas. Accounts of the Broadway production, which ran for one hundred one performances, suggest that on stage the play was lively and engaging, despite initial doubts about the audience appeal of its intellectual tone.

The human action of the play points to the center of its meanings. Sidney Brustein wants to improve his world in some clear way. Most of the characters believe that suffering and stupidity are much more common than enlightenment and happiness. Sidney's stomach ulcer becomes symbolically associated with this hard reality. The world would be better, Sidney thinks, if people were more tolerant of differences, if people treated each other as individual human beings rather than as stereotypes, if people never compromised with the forces that manipulate social differences for power or profit or with the forces that encourage the sale of personal integrity to achieve independence and success. Sidney believes that the arts, more than any other social force, can help people see how to better themselves and their world. Sidney lives in a society in which people debase and destroy individuals and groups in order to gain and keep power and wealth, and he continues to find in himself the weaknesses and limitations he deplores in others. He wavers between despair of making any significant change and desire to help bring about the world he dreams. This play chronicles one of his swings, from mild despair, to high hope, to deeper despair, and finally back again to a chastened and perhaps more mature hope.

As Sidney moves through this cycle, he also moves through a counterpointing cycle in his marriage. This movement highlights a feminist theme. In *A Raisin in the Sun*, feminism is an unresolved theme. Men believe that in the proper social order, women are subordinate and obedient, and even the rebellious Beneatha Younger seems finally to accept this view, though she insists upon a larger field of female action than the traditional wife and mother roles. This view of women also appears in *The Sign in Sidney Brustein's Window*. One of Sidney's main flaws is his failure to consider the individuality of his wife. Caught up in his political activities and accepting uncritically the assumption that Iris is his intellectual inferior, he insists that she conform to his dream of her as the pure mountain girl, the spirit of his idealized, transcendental wilderness. The first scene of act 2 is given to a critique of this dream. In one of several dreamlike scenes in this realistic play, Sidney envisions his mountain paradise, and it becomes visible to the audience. Into this scene comes his visionary Iris, who lets her long hair down and dances for him, embodying his dream of America. This dance is qualified by the parallel realistic dance scene in act 1, described this way: "She snakes out promptly, hissing, in the dance steps of the Greek Miserlou—which turns into a jig and then into the usual stereotyped notion of some Indian war dance, concluding with a Marilyn Monroe freeze." This reality parodies Sidney's dream of Iris' dance, and so in the later scene, when the real Iris enters Sidney's visionary world, she is unhappy, resisting, and skeptical.

She confides to Sidney that she has come to wish to make a mark on the world, just as Sidney wishes to do.

Another main theme concerns the complexity of the characters and their concerns. Alton Scales, a mulatto Marxist, is deeply concerned about racial justice, but when he learns that Gloria is a prostitute, he finds that even though he loves her and knows he is wrong to abandon her, he cannot get past the pain of his racial history. This history is reflected in his light skin, one of the badges of his family's prostitution to white power. In a similar way, each character in turn discovers that his or her personal integrity fails or can be bought. Iris will advertise inferior hair products in order to break into television. Sidney, who despises O'Hara for selling himself to win the election, finds that in order to save his marriage with Iris he is willing to try to bribe David to write Iris a part in one of his newly successful plays. David, who will not prostitute his writing, later asks Gloria to prostitute herself to help him in his current homosexual affair. Each of these episodes interacts with and comments upon Sidney's progress in politics and marriage. For example, Alton's failure to overcome his personal pain and forgive the woman he loves immediately follows and comments upon Sidney's exuberant new faith in people's ability to overcome the inertia of the past, when he knows that O'Hara has won the election but does not know how.

Examples of heroism come from Iris, who will risk her soul and her security in order to do something that can make a difference; from Gloria, who chooses death rather than continued prostitution; and from Mavis, who has worked out a generous if limited way of living after her husband took a mistress and ended her dreams of an ideal middle-class life. Finally, Sidney finds that, like Mavis, he wants to live in the world without being of it. This conviction leads him toward provisional resolutions of the main conflicts in his politics and marriage.

Sidney is in some ways a model of toleration and openness to difference. For example, like Hansberry—herself a lesbian—Sidney believes that homosexuality is just another kind of sexuality and that there should be no legal discrimination on this basis. Sidney is, however, blind to the misogynist prejudices that confine Iris and to the intolerance in his needling Mavis about her middle-class values and racism. Similar complexities appear in every other major character, and as they appear, the audience is encouraged to learn along with Sidney to see every individual as like himself in aspiring—however imperfectly—to goodness, integrity, dignity, and making a difference for the better in the world.

Critical Context

The importance of *The Sign in Sidney Brustein's Window* to American drama and to African American writing is unclear. Critics disagree about the quality of the play and about its influence on other dramatists, but most agree that Hansberry's compassionate humanism shines through it.

Hansberry was dying of cancer when the show opened to mixed reviews on October 15, 1964. Hansberry's friends and associates in theater raised money to keep the show running until her death on January 12, 1965. This series of events has influenced the play's reputation both negatively and positively, some critics believing that the play, though weak, did reasonably well because of the outpouring of sympathy for a promising young playwright cut off so early in her career, and others arguing that the play equals the quality of *A Raisin in the Sun*. Some have argued that the play is intellectually above most audiences and, therefore, doomed to few revivals.

The play was controversial because, though written by an African American, it has only one African American character in its fairly large cast. James Baldwin, in his essays, often discusses the peculiar position of African American intellectuals and artists. They are expected to represent their race and to speak for it. Hansberry resisted categorization as an African American writer insofar as this meant she had a duty or a limitation to write only about African American life and themes. On her own behalf and along with many in her generation of African American artists, Hansberry claimed all of her experience of life as potential subject matter for her plays. Good plays, she thought, change for the better the ways people see themselves and one another, and when this happens the subject is relatively unimportant. Whether or not this play is finally judged as good, it has encouraged African American writers to claim a similar freedom of subject.

Most important to Hansberry was that people recognize one another's humanity, even when they disagree. Critic Steven Carter wrote, "Perhaps the most remarkable of Lorraine Hansberry's qualities was the depth of her determination to understand all sides of a conflict, with compassion for what shapes and motivates everyone involved, while firmly deciding where justice lay—and acting on that decision." This statement characterizes both of her best-known plays, *A Raisin in the Sun* and *The Sign in Sidney Brustein's Window*.

Bibliography

Carter, Steven R. *Hansberry's Drama: Commitment Amid Complexity*. Urbana: University of Illinois Press, 1991. An informative study of Hansberry's plays and life. The book includes a brief chronology of her life and much other biographical information. The first chapter is an overview of Hansberry's life and opinions. Subsequent chapters discuss various works. The final chapter considers Hansberry's legacy to American drama.
Cheney, Anne. *Lorraine Hansberry*. Boston: Twayne, 1984. A study of Hansberry's life and works, including her extensive nondramatic works. This book contains a brief chronology of her life, followed by a more detailed examination of her career. There is a chapter on *The Sign in Sidney Brustein's Window* that includes a summary of the play. Includes a useful annotated bibliography.
Hansberry, Lorraine. *The Collected Last Plays*. New York: New American Library, 1983. In addition to the three plays on which Hansberry was working at her death, this volume contains important discussions of Hansberry and her work by Margaret B. Wilkerson and Julius Lester.
_____. *"A Raisin in the Sun" and "The Sign in Sidney Brustein's Window."*

New York: New American Library, 1987. In addition to the texts of both plays, this edition contains essays on each, including an important review of *The Sign in Sidney Brustein's Window* by John Braine, and a detailed account of the circumstances surrounding its Broadway run.

_____. *To Be Young, Gifted, and Black.* New York: New American Library, 1970. An autobiography compiled from Hansberry's writings, drawings, and artworks by her former husband, Robert Nemiroff. This readable and informative volume includes several photographs as well as short essays by Nemiroff and James Baldwin.

Terry Heller

THE SIGNIFYING MONKEY
A Theory of Afro-American Literary Criticism

Author: Henry Louis Gates, Jr. (1950-   )
Type of work: Cultural criticism
First published: 1988

Form and Content

After an informative introduction, Gates divides his study into two parts. Part 1, "A Theory of the Tradition," includes three chapters that set the background against which part 2 is to be read. Part 2, "Reading the Tradition," first treats five early narratives of slavery or captivity and then analyzes in separate chapters three novels by twentieth century African American writers.

The preface acknowledges a strong debt to two works: Ralph Ellison's critical study *Shadow and Act* (1964) and Ishmael Reed's novel *Mumbo Jumbo* (1972). Gates states his purposes as "to show how the black tradition has inscribed its own theories of its nature and function within elaborate hermeneutical and rhetorical systems" and "to argue, implicitly, that the central questions asked in Western critical discourse have been asked, and answered, in other textual traditions as well."

The introduction makes important points about the analyses to come. The black vernacular has been a source of great power to African Americans, standing out as their "ultimate sign of difference." It is the relationship of this vernacular tradition, with its African roots, to the African American literary tradition that constitutes the heart of this study.

The book begins with Esu-Elegbara, a "divine trickster figure" of the Fon and Yoruba cultures of Benin and Nigeria, with counterparts in Brazil, Cuba, Haiti, and the United States. Numerous carved representations of him exist. Esu's powers are set forth in numerous poems as well as in prose narratives about the origin of the world and the gods. Esu is especially identified with the power of figurative language and its interpretation, and he is traditionally double-voiced, an attribute identified with textual indeterminacy. He is, in a sense, a god of rhetoric. Among the Fon, he is "the divine linguist" who speaks all languages. In the Yoruba tradition, he often holds a calabash containing *ase*, a slippery word that Gates translates as *logos*, the divine reason.

Esu is the interpreter of Ifa, the sacred knowledge of the Yoruba. The texts with which Esu works are a set of sixteen palm nuts that are shaken up on a wooden divination tray. The arrangement into which the nuts settle is read by Esu to reveal to humans the message of Ifa. Even though Esu is depicted as masculine, he can be understood as genderless; his sexual ambiguity is matched by his double-voicedness.

The historical details cannot be filled in, but evidence suggests that Esu survived the Middle Passage—the Atlantic crossing of the slave ships—and was reborn in the New World in the rhetorical genius of the Signifying Monkey. Gates is succinct: "The Signifying Monkey is the figure of the text of the Afro-American speaking subject, whose manipulations of the figurative and the literal both wreak havoc upon and inscribe order for criticism in the jungle."

The Signifying Monkey originates in the playful, usually coarse, language rituals found in such typically male settings as barrooms and pool halls. The characters in these ritual stories are the Monkey, the Lion, and the Elephant. The Monkey repeats to the Lion some insult supposedly uttered by the Elephant, but this insult, meant figuratively, is taken literally by the Lion. The Elephant will not apologize to the Lion but whips him instead, whereupon the Lion, now realizing his mistake, goes back and thrashes the Monkey. The Monkey in this drama is a disingenuous master of rhetorical deceptions, as is Esu, the Yoruba personification of indeterminacy.

The Monkey is said to "Signify" on the Lion in these rituals; that is, he is working on the Lion any of a number of complex verbal ruses that can make fun of, cajole, deceive, irritate, or otherwise befuddle a victim. "Doing the dozens" is probably the best-known version of Signifyin(g), which also has obvious close relations with rapping. (The spelling "Signifyin(g)" denotes a set of African American rhetorical devices, with many examples given in chapter 3.)

Part 2, "Reading the Tradition," begins with an engrossing chapter on "The Trope of the Talking Book," a figure of speech that apparently appeared originally in Gracilasso de la Vega's *Historia General del Peru* (1617), translated as *The Royal Commentaries of Peru* in 1688. Gracilasso recounts a confrontation between the Inca chief Atahualpa and Friar Vincente de Valverde in which Atahualpa holds a Bible to his ear and, not hearing anything, hurls it to the ground. This trope ("the ur-trope of the Anglo-African tradition," Gates calls it) captures poignantly the image of the slave who seeks to master the written word as the embodiment of divine reason (the *logos*, or the Yoruba *ase*).

This trope then appears in five slave narratives that Gates summarizes with commentary. A key passage from James Albert Gronniosaw's narrative makes the trope vivid:

> [My master] used to read prayers in public to the ship's crew every Sabbath day; and when I first saw him read, I was never so surprised in my life, as when I saw the book talk to my master, for I thought it did, as I observed him to look upon it, and move his lips. I wished it would do so with me. As soon as my master had done reading, I followed him to the place where he put the book, being mightily delighted with it, and when nobody saw me, I opened it, and put my ear down close upon it, in great hopes that it would say something to me; but I was very sorry, and greatly disappointed, when I found that it would not speak. This thought immediately presented itself to me, that every body and every thing despised me because I was black.

This story is the primal scene of black self-consciousness of color.

Gates's chapter on the Talking Book is splendid literary history. More than that, the accounts by the five authors are moving to read.

In separate chapters, Gates explicates three well-known novels in terms of their "Signifyin(g)": Zora Neale Hurston's *Their Eyes Were Watching God* (1937), Ishmael Reed's *Mumbo Jumbo* (1972), and Alice Walker's *The Color Purple* (1982). The word "Signifyin(g)" hums through these chapters like a mantra, with the (g) symbolizing the "black difference." "Whatever is black about black American literature is to be found in this identifiable black Signifyin(g) difference." Thus Hurston, Reed, and Walker share a difference that unites them, and their works embody a tradition derived from that (g). Writing with others in the Signifyin(g) tradition in mind, they create a uniquely African American canon. At the same time, Gates insists, this Signifyin(g) quality of texts is not limited to African American literature, for in the postmodernist fashion of intertextuality "the implicit premise of this study is that all texts Signify upon other texts."

Analysis

The main argument of this book is best summed up in several parts. First, there is a tradition built around Esu-Elegbara that characterizes him as the double-voiced god of indeterminate rhetorical meaning, a feature that renders him particularly attractive to the practices of postmodernist criticism. Second, although the connection cannot be proved, Esu-Elegbara can reasonably be seen as the inspiration for the Signifying Monkey, that imaginative imp, mimic, mischief-maker, and rhetorical genius of African American lore and legend. Third, the introduction into print by Gracilasso de la Vega of the trope of the Talking Book provided the authors of slave narratives with a figure that evokes movingly their hunger for "the Word," and in their preoccupation with this word they create a tradition of African American narrative rich in Signifyin(g). Fourth, the three modern novels examined reveal a considerable network of influences, as twentieth century African American writers have gone about their creative business with their predecessors on their minds.

The main point of Gates's analysis of Zora Neale Hurston's *Their Eyes Were Watching God* is to explain her resolution of the long debate over "how an authentic black voice should be represented in print." Hurston's answer was to employ neither the third-person omniscient point of view that Richard Wright later used in *Native Son* (1940) nor the first-person voice that Ralph Ellison would use in *Invisible Man* (1952), but instead to compose a "speakerly text" that derives from an oral literary tradition and that suits the search for self that is the central character's challenge. Hurston's "bivocal" text incorporates elements of both first- and third-person narrators, achieving exposition by a third-person narrator in the idiom of the milieu represented.

Gates's brilliant chapter on Ishmael Reed's novel *Mumbo Jumbo* is virtually unsummarizable in its intricacy. The title—"On 'The Blackness of Blackness': Ishmael Reed and a Critique of the Sign"—points to what Gates sees as Reed's central theme, that there is no preordained eternal blackness, only the idea called up by the word. In working out this critique, Reed is Signifyin(g) upon those African American writers and critics, specifically Ellison and W. E. B. Du Bois, who expound a "repeated trope of dualism." That is, they see the African American as both American and black, thereby consenting to a transcendental blackness. Reed speaks for an African American tradition (he resists the primacy of what he calls "the so-called oral tradition") that is part of the Western tradition and just as encrusted with convention as the rest of it.

Compared to the discussion of *Mumbo Jumbo*, the chapter on Alice Walker and *The Color Purple* is strained and insubstantial. The thesis is that in Signifyin(g) on Hurston's *Their Eyes Were Watching God* and its "speakerly text," Walker collapses direct and indirect discourse into one voice such that "we can never be certain whether or not Celie is showing us a telling or telling us a showing." This slight point abets a reading of *The Color Purple* that liberates its characters from both white sensibility and male domination and makes "Walker's boldest claim about the nature and function of the black tradition and its interpretation."

Critical Context

The Signifying Monkey continues a discussion that Gates began in *Figures in Black: Words, Signs, and the "Racial" Self* (1987). These works will clearly constitute a monument to African American literature and its history and theory. *The Signifying Monkey* adds to the story of Esu-Elegbara and his many-faceted nature, bringing the Monkey himself front and center in American culture. The protean figure of the Monkey, whatever its origin, vitalizes African American literature with a trope that helps link the works of a living corpus. Ironically, Gates devotes his subtlest, most satisfying explication to Reed's *Mumbo Jumbo*, explicating that complex novel as a rejection both of the theory of a double-voiced African American, at once American and black, and of the notion of a transcendental blackness.

Gates has done truly groundbreaking work in slave narratives, and the section on that genre and its trope of the Talking Book will be for many readers the most valuable. No theory is necessary to account for the power of the passages quoted: The speakers reach out with human voices that command respect for their courage and longing. The accounts of the slave writers, moreover, are free from the mostly gratuitous postmodernist jargon that frequently gnarls the other chapters.

As for the explications of the novels by Hurston, Reed, and Walker, the chapter on *Mumbo Jumbo* has an impressive substantiality to it that the other two discussions lack. The whole analysis in *Mumbo Jumbo* is built on a foundation of the theory of the sign conjured by the Swiss linguist Ferdinand de Saussure; hence Gates's subtitle "A Critique of the Sign." Briefly, Saussure defined a sign as an alloy of a signifier (the vocalization of the word) and a signified (the idea named by the signifier). Gates's interpretation of Reed is that Reed accepts a signifier (the word blackness) and a signified (the idea of blackness) but will not allow any transcendental blackness that gives the signified meaning. Not every student of African American literature will assent to Gates's dense argument about *Mumbo Jumbo*.

To find a "speakerly text" in *Their Eyes Were Watching God* seems fair enough, but it remains to be proved that Hurston invented it. As Gates interprets Hurston's intentions, the "speakerly text" solves the problem of an authentic voice that Hurston faced, and she undeniably used it well.

The Signifyin(g) of African American writers on one another is a phenomenon that nobody would deny, but sometimes Gates's unraveling of relationships seems too fine. Perhaps the steady focus on black writers Signifyin(g) on other black writers blurs their considerable Signifyin(g) on whites as well, although Gates himself points to several examples of that. How, for example, does Ernest Gaines's admiration for Anton Chekhov, William Faulkner, and Eudora Welty get assimilated into the tradition?

An inevitable impulse is to start finding parallels suggested by Gates's research into Esu-Elegbara and the tradition of the Signifying Monkey. How does the divination practiced by Esu compare to the transactions carried out at the Oracle of Delphi? What does Signifyin(g), as it occurs in "doing the dozens," share with the Anglo-Saxon flyting? Was Zora Neale Hurston Signifyin(g) on Katherine Mansfield's story "Bliss" (1918) in her symbolic use of the pear tree in *Their Eyes Were Watching God?* Doesn't Ishmael Reed in *Mumbo Jumbo* seem to be Signifyin(g) on Vladimir Nabokov's *Pale Fire* (1962) more than on any African American work? These are the kinds of questions that occur naturally in reading *The Signifying Monkey*, a complex and rewarding study that will certainly invigorate the future study of African American literature.

Bibliography
Abrahams, Roger D. *Deep Down in the Jungle: Negro Narrative Folklore from the Streets of Philadelphia.* 1st rev. ed. Chicago: Aldine Publishing, 1970. One of the earliest studies of black signifying; still a valuable source study.
Abrahams, Roger D., and Rudolphe C. Troike, eds. *Language and Cultural Diversity in American Education.* Englewood Cliffs, N.J.: Prentice-Hall, 1972. Section 5 contains six essays on "Black English," including the seminal study "The Relationship of the Speech of American Negroes to the Speech of Whites" by Raven I. McDavid and Virginia Glenn McDavid.
Baker, Houston A., Jr. *Blues, Ideology, and Afro-American Literature: A Vernacular Theory.* Chicago: University of Chicago Press, 1984. A powerful and well-written study that, Gates explains, does for the blues what he tries to do for Signifyin(g).
Cuddon, J. A. *A Dictionary of Literary Terms and Literary Theory.* 3d ed. Cambridge, Mass.: Blackwell Reference, 1991. *The Signifying Monkey* is rife with the special language of postmodernist critical theory, most of it not on the tip of the common reader's tongue. Cuddon explains the jargon as lucidly as anyone can.
Pelton, Robert D. *The Trickster in West Africa: A Study of Mythic Irony and Sacred Delight.* Berkeley: University of California Press, 1980. Indispensable study of the tradition of Esu-Elegbara and his variants. The final chapter summarizes theories about the trickster's significance.
Smitherman-Donaldson, Geneva. *Talkin and Testifyin: The Language of Black America.* Boston: Houghton Mifflin, 1977. A study of African American dialect that asserts for it a unique rhetorical style rooted in its African origins.

Frank Day

SLAVERY AND SOCIAL DEATH
A Comparative Study

Author: Orlando Patterson (1940-   )
Type of work: History
First published: 1982

Form and Content

  Slavery and Social Death: A Comparative Study reflects Orlando Patterson's West Indian background and his experiences as a resident of the United States since 1970. Stylistically, the work owes much to Patterson's European training and the European philosophical tradition, but the book's emphasis is clearly a New World one. Readers may note themes from Patterson's earlier sociological works as well as a restatement of concerns from his novels such as *Die the Long Day* (1972). A major strength in Patterson's work has always been his keen awareness of the psychological and political dynamics of slave systems and his attention to the complexities and ironies of the master-slave relationship.

  Patterson himself sees this book as a response and a correction to the enormous growth in the quantitative analysis of slavery. Prior analyses, he accurately points out, centered primarily on the Atlantic slave trade and patterns of slavery in the Americas. The author rejects these concerns and attempts to broaden the framework to include both a qualitative and quantitative assessment of the institution of slavery across time and space. Patterson emphasizes that no global analysis of the institution had been attempted since H. J. Niebor's classic study in 1910.

  This volume is a product of twelve years of concentrated historical research (mainly from secondary sources) preceded by six years of archival research in Jamaica. Patterson draws on his earlier studies, most notably *The Sociology of Slavery: An Analysis of the Origins, Development, and Structure of Negro Slave Society in Jamaica* (1967). *Slavery and Social Death* also anticipates Patterson's arguments in *Freedom, Volume 1: Freedom in the Making of Western Culture* (1991).

  Slavery and Social Death is in three parts. A brief introduction provides an overview of Patterson's argument and outlines what he considers to be the constituent elements of slavery. Slavery, he asserts, is a form of social death, originated as a substitute for physical death. The author also introduces the theme of natal alienation of the slave and explores elements of violence and dishonor as they are brought into play in slave societies.

  Part 1 deals with the internal dynamics of slavery. Subsections (chapters 1, 2, and 3) outline idioms of power and the connection between property and slavery. Patterson rejects the notion of the slave as property and seeks to develop a definition of slavery independent of property idioms. He contends that the commonly accepted emphasis on property is misplaced and suggests that researchers should see slaves not only as legal entities but as symbolic entities as well.

  The next subsection deals with notions of authority and alienation. Borrowing from British social anthropology—most notably the works of Meyer Fortes, Raymond Firth, and Victor Turner—Patterson makes a case that the slave is a liminal person. Slaves do not belong to any kin group. The problem, then, becomes: How do ordinary people relate to the living who are dead? This theme, a most intriguing one, has been taken up by Wade Davis in his study of the process of zombification in Haiti, *Passage of Darkness: The Ethnobiology of the Haitian Zombie* (1988).

Patterson also pays particular attention to the rituals and marks of enslavement. He notes name-changing and shaving of heads as well as the physical branding of slaves. Color, he contends, is not as important in most cultures as hairstyle in differentiating slaves from nonslaves. This subsection ends with an erudite presentation of Hegelian dialectics and the master-slave relationship.

Part 2 deals with slavery as an institutional process. The author discusses the complex and varied process by which free persons become slaves. He notes that captivity in warfare has historically been the major means of enslavement. Yet there is need to differentiate between the original and current mechanisms and rationalizations for enslavement. In most societies, the significance of warfare declines as the proportion of the slave population enslaved through birth increases. The author also observes that the most common fate of prisoners of war was ransom, not slavery. Other mechanisms for procuring slaves have included kidnapping, tribute and tax payment, debt, punishment for crimes, abandonment and sale of children, and self-enslavement as a means to escape poverty. Later subsections (chapters 5 through 10) deal with the conditions of slavery, the status of freed persons, and patterns of manumission.

Part 3 focuses on the dialectics of slavery itself, with special attention to elite slaves in Rome and China and to palatine eunuchs in imperial Byzantium. Such elite slaves—with their important political, administrative, and military functions—have not usually been included in the scholarly analysis of slavery. The Byzantine case constitutes what Patterson believes to be the cornerstone of his argument. He considers eunuchs to have been the "ultimate slaves" due to their ritual impurity and—borrowing from anthropologist Mary Douglas' classic study *Purity and Danger: An Analysis of Concepts of Pollution and Taboo* (1966)—explores the complex interrelationship of ritual impurity and power. Slavery, Patterson concludes, is nothing less than a form of human parasitism.

Analysis

Slavery and Social Death is not a history of slavery, and despite its attention to statistical data, it is more interpretive than empirical. Historians have had difficulty with some of Patterson's uses of historical records and have noted that some of his historical evidence has been taken out of context.

Patterson is mostly interested in the process and meaning of slavery, not its substance. In this respect, his approach is essentially sociological. He borrows elements of Marxist theory and adopts models from symbolic anthropology. Ultimately, though, Patterson structures his argument along the lines of Émile Durkheim's classic sociological study *Le Suicide: Étude de sociologie* (*Suicide: A Study in Sociology*, 1951).

The author cogently puts slavery into worldwide perspective. He demonstrates effectively that slavery is not a "peculiar institution." It has existed from the dawn of human history and seems to have thrived in those areas and periods of the world where it would least be expected. Patterson points out that slavery was the base of the economic structures in ancient Greece and Rome and explores the association between high civilization and slavery. His bold assertion that Rome's reliance on slavery has been unsurpassed by any other society's casts new light on previous perspectives on the rise of so-called Western civilization.

The author's style is dense; Patterson's narrative flow is interrupted by myriad examples. This becomes all the more problematic for the reader, since Patterson's basic argument, the author admits, is a "dialectical" one. Again, it is helpful to compare Patterson's book's style and structure of argument with Durkheim's work. A major difference is that Durkheim relied on quantitative data exclusively, and for that reason Durkheim's use of data is more consistent. Nevertheless, there are many parallels between these two works.

Patterson's tone is philosophical. He is not so much telling a story as making a case. He summarizes a prodigious amount of material (111 pages of footnotes alone incorporate findings from highly specialized and often inaccessible sources). *Slavery and Social Death* has been highly praised for its mastery of secondary sources.

Critical Context

Patterson's studies have sparked controversy because he finds in slavery not an aberration from the Western ideal of freedom but a necessary condition of the notion of freedom itself. This is a theme taken up again in his National Book Award-winning *Freedom, Volume 1: Freedom in the Making of Western Culture* (1991). For many readers, Patterson's argument is made all the more difficult because it is hard to acknowledge freedom as a peculiarly Western value. That is, freedom is not inherent, as many Westerners like to believe. Freedom, for Patterson, is a noble sentiment with a less-noble progenitor. The reader is forced to grapple with the interdependence of good and evil.

Concerns of the book reflect Patterson's background as a native of Jamaica who took his early education in the West Indies. In addition, his comparative approach reflects his further training at the London School of Economics as well as his anthropological sophistication. His methods and presentation, however, reflect his training as a sociologist; in reading this book, one must keep in mind that Patterson is neither a philosopher nor a historian.

Slavery and Social Death offers a single coherent theory that challenges deeply rooted assumptions in Western culture. It provides new points of departure for future research, and it speaks to contemporary social issues in Europe, the Caribbean, and the United States. The book raises fundamental issues concerning human psychology and the potentials of social organization. The author is to be commended for his skillful use of the past to explicate the present. He has provided a new and creative synthesis that forces the reader to see both past and present from a new and often radically different perspective.

Bibliography

Davis, David Brion. Review of *Slavery and Social Death*, by Orlando Patterson. *The New York Review of Books*, February 17, 1983. A thoughtful, sometimes critical review by an eminent historian of slavery. Points out some of the historical shortcomings in Patterson's book. Takes Patterson to task for taking some historical evidence out of context.

Davis, Wade. *Passage of Darkness: The Ethnobiology of the Haitian Zombie*. Chapel Hill: University of North Carolina Press, 1988. Takes Patterson's argument one step further by suggesting that there is a category beyond slavery ("social death")—namely, that of the zombie ("the living dead").

Douglas, Mary. *Purity and Danger: An Analysis of Concepts of Pollution and Taboo*. London: Routledge & Kegan Paul, 1966. Classic anthropological study of the relationship between unclear categories and notions of taboo in preliterate societies.

Durkheim, Émile. *Suicide: A Study in Sociology*. New York: Free Press, 1951. An excellent introduction to the style of sociological argumentation. Durkheim's classic study inspired the form and structure of Patterson's presentation in *Slavery and Social Death*.

Patterson, Orlando. *Die the Long Day*. New York: William Morrow, 1972. Novel dealing with the psychology of the master-slave relationship.

_____. *The Sociology of Slavery: An Analysis of the Origins, Development, and Structure of Negro Slave Society in Jamaica*. Madison, N.J.: Fairleigh Dickinson University Press, 1967. Anticipates many of the arguments in *Slavery and Social Death*, with attention to the Jamaican case. Good use of archival materials.

Stephen D. Glazier

A SOLDIER'S PLAY

Author: Charles Fuller (1939-   )
Type of work: Play
Type of plot: Mystery
Time of plot: 1944
Locale: Fort Neal, Louisiana
First produced: 1981, at Theatre Four in New York City
First published: 1981

Principal characters:

SERGEANT VERNON C. WATERS, the murder victim whose killing is the genesis of the plot

CAPTAIN RICHARD DAVENPORT, the lawyer sent to investigate Waters' murder

PRIVATE C. J. MEMPHIS, a popular and talented black soldier

PRIVATE FIRST CLASS MELVIN PETERSON, the murderer

The Play

A *Soldier's Play* exposes the institutional racism of the Army in the 1940's and explores the psychological effects of oppression on African Americans. Although set in 1944 in a segregated barracks at Fort Neal, Louisiana, the play shows the pervasive effects of racism by utilizing the detective mystery form. Ironically, the all-black company is eager to fight for justice in World War II, but has not yet been deployed because of discrimination.

The play begins with Sergeant Vernon C. Waters' murder; the setting then immediately shifts to the barracks of Company B. The white commanding officers, Captain Charles Taylor particularly, are fearful that Waters' murder may cause a violent racial confrontation between the company and whites in nearby Tynin, Louisiana. Captain Taylor's anxiety increases when he meets the black lawyer sent to investigate the case, Captain Richard Davenport.

Davenport's investigation consists of interviews with soldiers who knew Waters, and these interviews allow the audience to form a composite characterization of Waters. Each interview is an incident dramatized on stage as it happened in the past; for example, the first interview, with Private Wilkie, reveals Waters' uncompromising standards: He demotes Wilkie because Wilkie was drunk on duty.

The next interview, with Private First Class Peterson, reveals more clearly Waters' unreasonable expectations and his seemingly racist bias. Despite their winning an important baseball game, Waters orders his men to paint the officers' club; when his men complain, he tells them, "I'm the kinda colored man that don't like lazy, shiftless Negroes!" His frustration and rage is especially directed at C. J. Memphis, a talented baseball player and a blues singer. When Melvin Peterson attempts to defend C. J., Waters challenges him to a fistfight, which is interrupted by Captain Taylor, who condescendingly compliments the men on their baseball game.

The interviews are diverted by a red herring: Taylor reveals to Davenport that two racist officers, Byrd and Wilcox, were the last to see Waters alive. The audience is led to believe that Byrd and Wilson killed Waters. Because Taylor thinks that only he, as a white liberal, could prosecute whites for the murder of a black, he requests that Davenport be relieved of his duties. The interview with Byrd and Wilcox reveals the profound division in Waters' spirit. Waters fully believed that by operating within a white supremacist's definition of success, he himself could provide an example of African American achievement. Such commitment to the white power structure, however, took its toll by inducing in him a contempt for his own race: "I hate myself!" Waters tells Byrd and Wilcox. Yet when Waters says, "I've killed for you!" he discloses the clue that will ultimately solve the case for Davenport.

In his next interviews, Davenport discovers that an unforeseen consequence of Waters' self-hatred was C. J.'s death. Waters, in his effort to cleanse the race of people he considers undesirable, had trumped up charges against C. J., provoking C. J. to assault him. When he is imprisoned in the stockade, C. J. despairs, again with Waters' provocation, and commits suicide. Davenport realizes whom Waters had "killed"—C. J. The tension between Captain Taylor and Davenport then erupts: Taylor too wants to punish those responsible for Waters' death, and the primary suspects are whites. Once again, he argues with Davenport over control of the case. When Davenport interviews Byrd and Wilcox again, however, he suddenly understands that neither murdered Waters. Davenport asserts his authority, and Taylor relents, allowing Davenport a free hand.

The final interview, with Private Smalls, reveals the mystery's solution. Both Smalls and Peterson were on guard duty when Waters was murdered, and Smalls confesses that he witnessed Waters' murder. Peterson, enraged with Waters, had accused Waters of a racism as vicious as Adolf Hitler's and Hideki Tojo's. Drunken and filled with despair, Waters had told Peterson that it "doesn't make any difference! They still hate you!" At that, Peterson had fired twice, killing Waters.

In the play's denouement, Davenport discloses the men's destiny: Peterson is captured and jailed, Waters' murder is misreported, and the entire company is later killed in a surprise German advance. Davenport laments the split caused by "the madness of race in America."

Themes and Meanings

A Soldier's Play explores the corrosive effects of racism by focusing on the tragedy of one man, Sergeant Vernon C. Waters. Although he has distinguished himself in World War I—and has risen in the ranks by his own effort and against an entrenched racism, his vision of himself extends far beyond his own career. His action reflects another purpose, one grander than simple personal success: Waters has taken upon himself the role of savior of all African Americans in a racist society. Like Hamlet, Waters takes it upon himself to set things right. Waters' sinister side, however, is that he attempts to eliminate any black he considers inferior. By dramatizing the story of Waters, Fuller creates a powerfully moving tragedy.

Waters' identity as tragic hero is revealed to the audience slowly, through Fuller's use of the mystery plot vehicle. The investigating officer, Captain Richard Davenport, conducts a series of interviews in which characters summarize incidents involving Waters. Complicating the understanding of Waters is the fact that the soldiers interviewed themselves do not understand him. Wilkie, the first soldier interviewed, respects Waters because he earned his rank and is faithful to his wife and children; the second, Peterson, despises Waters because he sees him as a black bigot. The whites are even more divided on Waters: Captain Taylor thinks of him as a simpleton who does his job adequately, but the two bigots, Byrd and Wilcox, are threatened by his "uppityness." Racial stereotypes continually interfere with the characters' perceptions. The audience must infer Waters' character with Davenport as the guide; Davenport acts as a chorus, explaining the action while being involved in it.

The actual Waters, as disclosed in composite, is a failed idealist, a messianic African American who wants the best for his race but is uncertain about how to achieve it. "I don't intend to have our race cheated out of its place of honor and respect in *this* war," he tells Wilkie. Waters' tragedy is a consequence of his terrible miscalculation, his fateful error in judgment. Because he is convinced that "the only thing that can move the race is power," and that empowerment means becoming white, he chooses to deny his own racial identity and emulate white racists. This choice, however, commits him to a power dynamics that only conceives of the oppressed and the oppressor. If he accepts the assumptions of black inferiority from a racist society, his purpose is doomed to failure. Unable to relate to his men as brothers, he transforms them into objects to be rescued; Waters willingly destroys their self-respect and integrity in order to save them. His vision is clouded by his purpose until the end of his life. His own words "They still hate you!" begin and end the play, testifying to his own recognition that he has failed both himself and his race.

Waters is a sympathetic character because he suffers deeply over the wrongs committed against him and his race. More sensitive than other characters, he has withheld his rage, choosing instead to direct it, he supposes, against a vicious system that denies him his humanity. Ironically, his actions redound against him and his men, for his efforts to inspire them to achievement only alienate them and make them despise him. Even more important, he is alienated from himself; as C. J. says, "I feel kinda sorry for him myself. Any man ain't sure where he belongs must be in a whole lotta pain." C. J., whom Waters victimizes relentlessly, knows Waters best of all. Waters tells C. J., "Them Nazis ain't all crazy—a whole lot of people just can't fit into where things seem to be goin'—like you, C. J. The black race can't afford you no more." His unconscious use of a mercantile vocabulary, as if some human beings were more "costly" than others, summarizes where he went wrong in trying to help African Americans.

C. J. provides an alternative mode of consciousness to Waters' dichotomous vision of the races. Waters hates C. J. because C. J. represents what Waters thinks blacks must abandon to achieve success: Southern roots, African American spiritualism, and the blues (Waters himself listens only to symphonies). The play shows that C. J.

accepts his own diversity; he is unashamed of his dialect, his music, his beliefs, and his background. Fuller places C. J. at the center of historical African American self-expression by making him a blues singer, and his songs inevitably draw a response from the company. His baseball heroics also function as an affirmation of community, for he is a true team player. In C. J., then, Fuller advocates pluralism, the acceptance of diversity as good in itself and as the only solution to the "madness of race in America."

The murderer, Peterson, is a fully developed character, though he only appears onstage momentarily. Peterson, like the other soldiers, misunderstands Waters as the "new boss—shoutin', orderin' people aroun'." Yet Peterson does not see that Waters is a reflection of his own hidden self. Although Waters is equally demanding of everyone, it is Peterson who kills him, for Peterson senses his connection with Waters. Like Waters, Peterson tries to conceal his Southern roots, preferring to call Hollywood, not Alabama, his home; his ambition to rise in the Army (his early enlistment reveals his illusions) mirrors Waters' own. Finally, Peterson, like Waters, insults C. J. "Justice," Peterson says as he kills Waters. The murder, though, is his symbolic self-destruction, Peterson executing his own despised, hidden identity.

The white Captain Taylor also presents a complex, though economical, character study. Taylor represents the white liberal, pragmatic in his pursuit of justice. His unconscious racial prejudice is revealed when he meets Davenport, since he admits he cannot accept blacks in positions of authority. Thus, Taylor assumes that Davenport will fail in his investigation, and that he should allow Taylor to take control. The play suggests that liberal pragmatists, though well-meaning, may be as much a hindrance to racial justice as Southern bigots are.

As chorus, Davenport represents an ideal in the play. He is an oracular commentator, narrating the action from a detached and Olympian perspective, but he also understands C. J.'s dislocation, Waters' misguided quest, and Peterson's rage. He derives self-definition from his profession, but he is not limited by it; he symbolizes in his character the acceptance of diversity that the play itself promotes.

Fuller's use of the detective form to dramatize a tragedy is itself worthy of consideration. The detective genre usually represents crime as an aberration in a well-ordered society (often the crime occurs in an isolated setting). The solution to the crime, a result of the detective's rationality applied to evidence, assumes the restoration of a benign social order, and justice reasserted reassures the audience.

Fuller, however, reverses the typical detective-story pattern. The crime, Waters' murder, is in fact a logical extension of a society that is itself corrupt and unjust. That men must suffer for the color of their skins renders ironic America's war against Hitler's Final Solution and Tojo's race-consciousness. Although the setting is isolated, Fuller makes clear that racism is institutionalized throughout America.

Fuller's use of the stage is also highly inventive. The entire set resembles a courtroom, implying that the play is in reality an interrogation of American justice. Dominating the set is a poster of boxing champion Joe Louis—as a private. The implication is that even black superstars have a very low ceiling in the segregated Army.

Critical Context

Aesthetically and politically, Charles Fuller's plays occupy a middle ground between the more conservative, conventional dramatic narratives of black playwrights such as Lorraine Hansberry and the politically radical, Absurdist drama of writers such as Amiri Baraka (LeRoi Jones). Fuller's first major success was with *The Brownsville Raid* (1976), based on a true incident. In that play, he re-creates the story of the dishonorable discharge in 1906 of an entire black regiment from the Army on the orders of President Theodore Roosevelt. Like *A Soldier's Play, The Brownsville Raid* is organized along the lines of a mystery, slowly revealing the psychic torments that racism inflicts on African Americans. The play's focus is on a black sergeant's subsequent crisis of faith.

A Soldier's Play won immediate acclaim as a portrait of human relations, winning three Obies, an Audelco award, a New York Drama Critics Circle Award, an Outer Circle Award, and the 1982 Pulitzer Prize for Drama. In 1984, the play was adapted to film by Norman Jewison as *A Soldier's Story*, and Fuller wrote the screenplay, which won the 1985 Mystery Writers of America Edgar Allan Poe Award for screenplay. Fuller has received a Guggenheim Foundation fellowship, a Rockefeller Foundation grant, a National Endowment for the Arts grant, and a Creative Artists Public Service grant.

Fuller has engaged in writing a five-part dramatic history of African Americans from the Civil War to 1900. The first play, *Sally*, opened at the First National Black Arts Festival in Atlanta in 1988, and the second play in the series, *Prince*, was produced in 1989.

Bibliography

Bygrave, Mike. "A Soldier's Story." *Sight and Sound* 54 (Winter, 1984-1985): 17-19. Discusses the problems involved with producing the 1984 film. Includes insightful comments by Fuller about his experiences with racism.

Kunz, Don. "Singing the Blues in *A Soldier's Story*." *Literature Film Quarterly* 19, no. 1 (1991): 27-34. Focuses on the film's score. Kunz argues that the film reproduces the play and that both affirm racial progress in American society.

Peterson, Bernard L. *Contemporary Black American Playwrights and Their Plays: A Biographical Directory and Dramatic Index*. New York: Greenwood Press, 1988. Contains useful factual information on Fuller's career. Bibliography, indexes.

Sanders, Leslie Catherine. *The Development of Black Theater in America: From Shadows to Selves*. Baton Rouge: Louisiana State University Press, 1988. Provides a helpful context for interpreting Fuller's work.

Storhoff, Gary. "Reflections of Identity in *A Soldier's Story*." *Literature Film Quarterly* 19, no. 1 (1991): 21-26. Examines the reflection trope that organizes both film and play. In contrast to Kunz, Storhoff argues that the film oversimplifies the play and compromises its artistic integrity.

Gary Storhoff

SOLEDAD BROTHER
The Prison Letters of George Jackson

Author: George Jackson (1941-1971)
Type of work: Autobiography
Time of work: 1964-1970
Locale: California
First published: 1970

>*Principal personages:*
>GEORGE JACKSON, an African American who spent much of his
> life in prison
>JONATHAN JACKSON, George's brother, who became a revolutionary
> and died at the age of seventeen
>(ROBERT) LESTER JACKSON, the father of George and Jonathan
> Jackson
>GEORGIA JACKSON, the mother of George and Jonathan Jackson
>ANGELA DAVIS, a black instructor accused of supplying Jonathan
> with guns used in an assault on a courthouse

Form and Content

   Soledad Brother is a collection of George Jackson's letters to relatives and friends, written from California prisons. At the age of eighteen, Jackson was given an indeterminate sentence of one year to life for stealing $71 from a gas station. Despite his two prior convictions for armed robbery, his rage at serving eleven years in prison for stealing only $71 is understandable. What made it worse was his belief that he might spend the rest of his life in prison. This real-life event has been compared with Victor Hugo's classic novel *Les Misérables* (1862), in which the hero, Jean Valjean, serves nineteen years as a galley slave for stealing a loaf of bread.

   While in Soledad Prison, Jackson incurred the enmity of prison guards because of his defiant spirit and his outspoken advocacy of Black Power politics. Eventually Jackson and two other black inmates were accused of murdering a white guard during an uprising. They came to be known as the Soledad Brothers. All were held in isolation cells awaiting trial. Conviction for murdering a prison guard would bring automatic death sentences.

   Jackson undertook a grueling course of self-education in politics, economics, history, philosophy, languages, and other subjects. His letters reveal the evolution of a remarkable intelligence. He became an ardent Marxist-Leninist, advocating violent revolution as the only means of correcting the injustices of the capitalist system in the United States. He blamed all the problems of African Americans on capitalism.

   Jackson was killed in a riot in San Quentin Prison in 1971, a riot in which three guards and two other inmates were also killed. Jackson's many sympathizers claimed that he was deliberately murdered because he threatened to become too dangerous an insurrectionary leader. In many of his letters, he predicts that he will never leave prison alive.

All of Jackson's incoming and outgoing letters were read by prison censors. He had to be circumspect in expressing himself because objectionable letters would not be delivered, and there was a danger of correspondence privileges being terminated for any individual who was considered a security threat. This makes it all the more extraordinary that the contents of Jackson's letters are still so hostile and militant. Regardless of political sympathies, one is compelled to admire the strength of character of a helpless individual who refuses to bow his head in defeat and who realizes that anything he writes in his letters may be used against him at his parole hearings.

The reader can sense the much greater anger seething behind the words that appear on the printed page. Jackson's rage at the mistreatment of African Americans for more than three hundred years provided the motivation for him to survive physical and mental abuse by guards and white prisoners, as well as to pursue his remarkable program of self-improvement.

The letters are dated from June, 1964, to August, 1970. Most are arranged in chronological order, although the first section, which provides biographical and other background information, contains letters written in 1970. Each letter in the volume is headed with a date and the first name of the addressee. An introduction by the colorful French author, career criminal, and revolutionary Jean Genet is included.

Jackson describes his day-to-day existence inside a cell, his views on prison life in general, his efforts to improve his mind with reading and his body with strenuous physical exercise, his memories of growing up in the slums, and his gradually evolving political awareness.

Many of Jackson's letters are addressed to his mother and father. He blames them for educating him to be humble and subservient like themselves. He blames his mother especially for sending him to Catholic schools, where he believes he was indoctrinated with false beliefs from which he is making a painful effort to free himself. He attempts to argue his political and philosophical ideas with his parents, even though his reading and solitary thinking have obviously elevated him to a sophisticated level of thought that his parents are unable to comprehend.

Part of the irony of his torment is that he finds it increasingly difficult to communicate with the people he loves the most. Like most autodidacts, his self-education suffers from lack of dialogue with intellectual equals. He writes: "I feel no love, no tenderness for anyone who does not think as I do." He describes himself as a "monster" bent on violent revenge. The more dangerous he makes himself appear in his rigorously censored letters, the more he antagonizes his guards and undermines his chances of parole. His rage blinds him to the fact that he has had anything to do with his own suffering.

None of the replies he receives from his parents or any of his other correspondents are included in the book. The reader is forced to guess the nature of these replies from the ways in which Jackson responds. Jackson's father Lester is an intelligent man but has an extremely conservative attitude, as can be seen in his article published in *Ebony* after both of his sons had met violent deaths. Judging from Jackson's letters to his mother, she is a devoutly religious woman who tries to persuade her son to emulate the conciliatory, nonviolent Martin Luther King, Jr., instead of revolutionaries such as Eldridge Cleaver and Malcolm X. Rather pathetically, Jackson threatens to break off correspondence with his parents, but he writes to them again because his list of approved correspondents is strictly limited.

As the years pass and Jackson grows older, his letters become increasingly objective. At first he thinks mainly of his own unhappiness and writes often about his hopes for parole. Gradually, however, he becomes aware that the only way he can hope to get released is by proving to the custodians and the parole board members that he has been broken in spirit, like so many other convicts. This his courageous character will not allow him to do; he is marked down as a troublemaker and a Communist revolutionary. He believes that his life is in imminent danger, either from the guards or from white prisoners encouraged by the guards with the promise of parole or at least special privileges. Jackson's description of prison conditions in Soledad and San Quentin makes the reader realize how bad things were and how much they have improved in some important respects, partly as a result of prisoners' rights protests.

After the Soledad Brothers had attracted worldwide attention, Jackson came into contact with young radicals who were far more in sympathy with his ideas than were his early correspondents. Chief among these was Angela Davis, a beautiful young black revolutionary who seemed almost the perfect female counterpart to the fiery Jackson. Jackson makes it clear how much he suffers by being deprived of heterosexual companionship. His letters to Davis and other young women are often tender and poetic. They are in sharp contrast to his attitude toward the prison authorities, the police, the justice system, and the white power structure in general. One forms the mental picture of a black panther pacing back and forth in a narrow cage, building up a seething hatred for the system that put him there and dreaming of revenge.

Analysis

Jackson was surprisingly explicit about his ideas in spite of the fact that he was a helpless prisoner whose well-being and hopes of freedom were dependent upon the goodwill of his captors. He believed in the armed overthrow of the American government and the establishment of a socialist state. In some letters, he suggests that African Americans should have their own independent nation in North America. He distrusted white people and did not see any possibility of sharing power with them. Like Malcolm X, Jackson believed that the white race was inherently evil. It is interesting to observe his rapidly expanding vocabulary and the increasing abstractness of his ideas over the years of his imprisonment.

He frequently refers to the fact that Europeans had been at war among themselves and against the nonwhite peoples of the world for hundreds of years. It was his contention that African Americans were a "colonial" people treated almost exactly like most of the people who had lived under European rule in Africa. He thought that since black Africans had been brought to North America against their will, they were entitled to reparations for their pain and suffering. He believed that it was the historic mission of African Americans to lead an armed revolution against U.S. capitalism and imperialism, and it was his contention that some of the best revolutionaries were to be found in U.S. prisons.

Jackson sympathized with the North Vietnamese, who were engaged in a bloody war against a reactionary South Vietnamese government supported by the might of the United States military machine. He strongly believed that African Americans should not participate in such hostilities because they were only helping to strengthen the American "fascist" establishment, which was bent on dominating the world and prolonging white capitalist exploitation of nonwhites everywhere.

Jackson joined the Black Panther Party during the last year of his life in prison and was appointed a field marshal. His views were nearly identical with the Black Panthers' program, which included the right of African Americans to control public institutions in their own areas, right to trial by all-black juries, exemption of African Americans from military service, and financial compensation for past and present exploitation by the white majority.

Jackson had many female admirers, and he addresses some of them in his letters with great affection and sensitivity. He also displays a male chauvinistic attitude that is in striking contradiction to the Marxist-Leninist egalitarianism in which he professes to believe. For example, in a letter of July, 1967, he writes:

Women like to be dominated, love being strong-armed, need an overseer to supplement their weakness. . . . For this reason we should never allow women to express any opinions on the subject [of racial discrimination], but just to sit, listen to us, and attempt to understand. It is for them to obey and aid us, not to attempt to think.

The content and tone of Jackson's letters increasingly reflect the influence of his favorite writers, including Karl Marx and Fredrich Engels, authors of *The Communist Manifesto* (1848); Frantz Fanon, the black West Indian author of books on race relations; Ho Chi Minh, venerated leader of the North Vietnamese anti-imperialist struggle; and Malcolm X and Eldridge Cleaver.

Jackson's unique contribution to the radical thought of the period was that he wanted immediate violent action rather than mere rhetoric. Many sympathizers thought him crazy to contemplate armed rebellion against the police, National Guard, Army, Navy, Marines, and Air Force, but he was ready to begin an underground guerrilla campaign against the establishment as soon as he got out of prison. It was his stated ambition to organize the entire population of approximately thirty million African Americans into a revolutionary party inspired by the tactical principles described in the writings of Mao Tse-Tung, leader of the Communist revolution that had transformed China into one of the world's great powers.

Critical Context

Jackson's book was a best-seller and won the nonfiction book award from the

Black Academy of Arts and Sciences for 1971. It attracted both critical praise and condemnation, depending largely on the political sympathies of the critic. Julius Lester, writing for *The New York Times Book Review*, called it the most important single volume from a black writer since *The Autobiography of Malcolm X* and added that Jackson made the volatile Eldridge Cleaver "look like a song-and-dance man on the Ed Sullivan show."

Many commentators, including Angela Davis, Eric Mann, and Bobby Seale, have openly charged that Jackson was murdered in a conspiracy because he was too dangerous to be released from prison and too dangerous to be kept inside. Jackson's book appeared during a turbulent period in American history, when the war in Vietnam was raging and the United States was threatened with violent revolution. *Soledad Brother* was regarded as a book of antiwar protest because of its contention that domestic racial oppression and involvement in wars against former European colonies were both motivated by the same fascist principles being displayed by Americans in Vietnam. Jackson's book has been credited with helping to force the United States to terminate hostilities against the North Vietnamese because Jackson specifically advised African Americans not to participate in foreign wars. Because a large percentage of American troops in Vietnam were black, his book had an adverse effect on American military morale. This was a powerful factor in motivating the government to find a way out of the unpopular and divisive conflict.

Beyond the racial question, the letters were regarded as a blanket indictment of the penal system. It was easy for critics to identify with Jackson's rage. He seemed to be living proof that if men are treated like wild animals they will become like wild animals. Many writers asserted that, regardless of Jackson's crimes against society, society for its own protection should learn to deal with prisoners more humanely.

Since Jackson's death, there have been numerous politically inspired prison riots, such as the spectacular one at Attica State Prison in New York in 1971. Largely because of activists such as Jackson, prison conditions have improved in many important ways, including better food, better living conditions, better educational facilities, and better communication with the outside world. Widespread attempts have been made, for example, through the recruitment of nonwhite prison guards, to ameliorate racist abuse of nonwhite prisoners.

Jackson became a self-taught, articulate spokesman for African Americans in general and African American prisoners in particular. His eloquent letters and essays published in *Soledad Brother* and posthumously in *Blood in My Eye* (1972) had an incalculable influence in improving the lives of African Americans both in prisons and in urban ghettos. Although the majority of African Americans did not subscribe to a program of violent action, they did recognize the truths that inspired his emotionally charged writings.

Bibliography
Cleaver, Eldridge. *Soul on Ice*. New York: McGraw-Hill, 1968. Jackson was influ-

enced by this autobiography of Cleaver, who became one of the leaders of the Black Panthers. Like Jackson, Cleaver found his identity and mission in life while in prison and became an articulate spokesman of Black Power principles through a strenuous process of self-education.

Davis, Angela Yvonne, et al. *If They Come in the Morning.* New York: Third Press, 1971. A collection of essays, letters, poetry, and articles dealing mainly with African Americans' experiences with courts and prisons in the United States. A section of the book is devoted to the Soledad Brothers. The consensus of the articles is that the American prison system is racist and that Marxism can be used to explain the cause as well as to prescribe the cure for this social malady.

Jackson, George L. *Blood in My Eye.* New York: Random House, 1972. This posthumously published collection of letters and miscellaneous writings by Jackson focuses intensively on his ideas about history and politics, in contrast to most of the letters in *Soledad Brother,* which dealt more with personal relations and life in prison.

Jackson, Lester. "A Dialogue with My Soledad Son." *Ebony* 27 (November, 1971): 72-74. The author describes his experiences visiting his son George in prison. He recalls his many arguments with George over politics and religion. The father states his belief that the country's racial and other troubles can be dealt with by working through the existing political system. Illustrated with many interesting photographs.

Lester, Julius. "Black Rage to Live." *The New York Times Book Review,* November 22, 1970, 10. The longest and most informative review of Jackson's book to appear at the time of its publication. Contains some explanation of the background events and compares the book with *The Autobiography of Malcolm X* (1965) and *Soul on Ice.*

Mann, Eric. *Comrade George: An Investigation into the Life, Political Thought, and Assassination of George Jackson.* New York: Harper & Row, 1974. As its title suggests, this book is heavily biased in favor of Jackson and his ideals. It contains much information about his life that is helpful in understanding the thoughts, feelings, and personal references contained in his letters, most of which assume considerable background knowledge on the part of the letters' recipients.

Seale, Bobby. *Seize the Time: The Story of the Black Panther Party and Huey P. Newton.* Baltimore, Md.: Black Classic Press, 1991. The former chairman of the Black Panther Party tells the history of the organization in dramatic terms from a firsthand perspective. Vivid profiles of many prominent black revolutionaries of the 1960's, including Eldridge Cleaver and Huey P. Newton. Contains the Black Panthers' program for revolutionary reform.

Bill Delaney

SOME SOUL TO KEEP

Author: J. California Cooper
Type of work: Short stories
Type of plot: Social realism
Time of plot: The late twentieth century
Locale: The United States
First published: 1987

> *Principal characters:*
> SUPERIOR, the heroine of "Sisters of the Rain," a big, strong, homely girl
> JEWEL, a sexy girl in contrast to Superior
> GLENELLEN, the only major character in this collection of stories who is white
> MOLLY, the narrator of "The Life You Live (May Not Be Your Own)"
> ISOBEL, Molly's childhood friend who becomes her next-door neighbor after they are both married
> BIRDIE, the narrator of "Red-Winged Blackbirds"
> REVA, a "Cinderella" whom Birdie meets by accident when the girl is fifteen years old
> BESSIE, the protagonist of "About Love and Money"
> MAVIS, Bessie's foil
> CHRISTINE, the heroine of "Feeling for Life"

The Stories

Some Soul to Keep is made up of five stories, all of which are sufficiently long and eventful to seem like miniature novels. All are told by female narrators and are intended to be read aloud so that the subtleties of the black dialect can be fully appreciated. These narrators are strongly opinionated and frequently interrupt their narratives to interject philosophical observations. Cooper violates many sacrosanct conventions of modern story writing. It might be more accurate to call these five short works "tales," because they have an episodic quality that is rather refreshing to readers who have become accustomed to tight, calculated, inhibited modern short stories in which conflicts are mainly internalized.

"Sisters of the Rain" is narrated by two women who are not characters in the story but are observers. The first is an elderly schoolteacher. Halfway through the story, the narration is taken over by the schoolteacher's daughter, who grew up with the characters Superior, Jewel, and Glenellen. The story contrasts the lives of those three women between their early teens and their mid-forties. Two of them have tragic lives because they lacked worthy female role models. Only Superior, the least attractive and least intelligent, is successful, because her mother inspired her to make the most of her limited talents. The schoolteacher narrator uses her part of the story to illustrate her guiding principle: "You know, life goes a long way, don't it? Just is all around you . . . filling up all the tiniest places, so you got to watch round you and keep it all together. Watch it, so to take care of it best you can, with whatever you have to work with."

"The Life You Live (May Not Be Your Own)" is narrated by Molly, who is also the main character. She and her childhood friend Isobel live as hostile next-door neighbors for twelve years with each believing that the other hates her. It is not until Isobel's husband Tolly dies and Molly's husband leaves her that the two women realize how maliciously they have been deceived. Both resolve to lead their own lives and never to trust men or to become financially or emotionally dependent upon them again. Molly states the point of her story at the beginning: "It's like you got to be careful what life you live, cause it may not be your own! Some love, marriage or friend done led you to the wrong road, cause you trusted em."

"Red-Winged Blackbirds" is another story about a young girl who is born into poverty and manages to achieve success and happiness through her own courage and determination. Twelve-year-old Birdie is almost raped by the son of her father's white employer. Both of her parents are murdered by Klansmen when her father accuses the young man of attempted rape. She grows up an orphan but achieves financial success as proprietor of a bordello. She is terrified of sex because of her childhood experience but yearns for a child of her own. Eventually she vicariously "adopts" a teenage girl who is the victim of her mother's abuse.

"About Love and Money" takes one of Cooper's young "Cinderellas" into a different milieu. Bessie goes to work for a black dentist and his lazy wife. Eventually she displaces the wife in his affections. She marries the dentist and enjoys a life of luxury beyond that experienced by any of Cooper's other heroines. When her husband begins cheating on her, however, she realizes that money is not everything. She obtains a divorce and finds true love with a husband who earns a humble living as a garbage collector. Cooper moralizes at the end of her story that love is more important than money but that there is nothing wrong with having both.

Cooper places "Feeling for Life" at the end of her collection as if to underscore her dominant thesis that any handicap can be overcome with courage and persistence. The heroine of this story starts in what appears to be an impossible situation: She is totally blind and, as the title suggests, has to feel her way through life. She is abandoned by her brother and sister, then raped by the minister to whom she goes for help. When a social worker tries to persuade her to give up her baby for adoption, Christine refuses. She learns to read braille, raises her own child, eventually finds true love from a man who respects her for her strength of character, and ends up providing a home for her selfish brother and sister, who have been failures.

Themes and Meanings

In all the stories in *Some Soul to Keep*, as well as in two earlier collections, Cooper does not attempt to be subtle, indirect, or ambiguous in illustrating her themes and meanings. She uses female first-person narrators who make no pretense of being "literary" and feel free to interject their comments at any point in the story. Her narrators, who are often major characters themselves, invariably have strong feelings about the situations they discuss. It is clear that Cooper is a feminist who admires and advocates hard work, self-reliance, and independence. Her heroines have all led such hard lives that they have lost all illusions. They know which things have real value and are willing to fight hard for them. Their values invariably include such tangible things as real estate and cash in the bank, but they also include love of children, friendship between women, and genuine love between women and men.

Cooper wants to encourage women to think for themselves, to stand on their own two feet, to make the best of any talents they possess, and to refuse to be passive objects manipulated by men. Her stories make it clear that wholesome relations between men and women, including sexual relations, can only be maintained under conditions of equality. Dependent love is not true love; a weak person cannot really love anyone else and should not expect true love in return for dependency.

Cooper has little to say about black-white relations. Few white people appear in her stories, and those who do are not always identified as being white. In other words, she believes that people are good or bad, strong or weak, kind or cruel, generous or selfish, and that these attributes are not exclusive to any ethnic group. She accepts racial prejudice as a fact of life but does not think that it justifies apathy or despondency.

Cooper not only expresses her philosophy directly through her female narrators but also illustrates it in the life histories of her characters. Those who succeed in life are the ones who accept their handicaps and endure hardships. Those who fail are the ones who whine and complain, who are lazy and lacking in ambition, and who expect others to provide for them. All the stories in this collection might be described as variations of the Cinderella fairy tale. Cooper departs radically from modern storytelling trends by writing stories with strong morals that she underlines through her narrators, through what happens to her characters, and through what her strong characters say to her weak ones. The life stories of all of her heroines suggest that Cooper believes that hardship, rejection, loneliness, and even physical handicaps can be sources of strength because they often force people to work harder to overcome their disadvantages.

Cooper's attitude toward men often sounds quite militant. Although she presents a few male characters who are humble, hard-working, generous, and affectionate, the major male characters in her stories are selfish, predatory, and unscrupulous. These include such despicable males as the minister who rapes the blind, helpless Christine, her worthless brother who makes his mother and sisters support him even though he is fully capable of working, and the ruthless Tolly, who spreads wicked lies about his own wife in order to keep her dependent and submissive.

Critical Context

Cooper has received widespread praise for her short stories in *Some Soul to Keep* and in previous collections. The qualities most often singled out are her optimism, her sincerity, her earthy humor, and her obvious desire to encourage her female readers—black female readers in particular—to assert themselves. She is an important writer mainly because of her philosophy opposing dependency. As novelist Terry McMillan wrote in an article in *The New York Times Book Review*, "After reading *Some Soul to Keep*, you feel lucky to have entered the worlds of a few poor black women and their families who don't cry or whine about their condition, but are set on figuring out how to get on with their lives."

Some critics have complained that Cooper is too didactic. It is true that Cooper drives home moral arguments by shaping her plots to illustrate them. She also uses the same narrative technique in every story: A first-person female narrator tells a person's life story in black dialect and frequently intrudes on her narrative to moralize about the characters and events she is describing. Cooper's interjections are frequently striking in their commen sense, but they threaten to destroy the illusion of reality. Some critics complain that all the female narrators sound exactly the same and that this becomes monotonous.

Cooper, however, is comfortable with the style she has worked out for herself and seems impervious to this type of criticism. She is definitely not an advocate of "art for art's sake" but has strong opinions that she insists on expressing in the most effective way available. Her indifference to modern trends in short fiction writing, such as minimalism, sets an important example for younger writers because it deliberately violates inhibiting rules. She might be described as a "primitive." Like most primitive artists, she injects refreshing new life into her medium. Her style, like her subject matter, is a protest against timid conformity and an affirmation of freedom and individuality.

The stories in *Some Soul to Keep* are crammed with people and events. Some critics have complained that the stories violate the cardinal rules formulated by Edgar Allan Poe that a short story should be designed to produce a "single effect." Cooper's stories in *Some Soul to Keep* read more like miniature novels because of the plethora of incidents and the lengthy philosophical commentaries by the narrators. Cooper has moved steadily in the direction of becoming a novelist because she realized that she needed the larger canvas to depict her vision of life. In 1991, she published her first novel, *Family*, which received generally favorable critical attention.

Bibliography
Ames, Carol. Review of *Some Soul to Keep*, by J. California Cooper. *Los Angeles Times Book Review*, December 27, 1987, 4. The reviewer criticizes Cooper's stories as being too long for stories and not long enough for novels. She says the stories have "neither the concision and focus of stories, nor the amplitude of detail and incident of a novel." She acknowledges that they are often "lusty, touching and wise."
Carter, Patricia A. Review of *Some Soul to Keep*, by J. California Cooper. *Essence* 18 (September, 1987): 34. The reviewer believes that the common denominator of Cooper's stories is her "strong yet sensitive heroines who find the inner power to

survive the poverty of the rural South or the cold indifference of the North."

Cooper, J. California. *Family.* New York: Doubleday, 1991. Cooper's first novel deals with slavery and conditions in the South after emancipation. Many of the stylistic devices developed in her short stories are evident in this historical novel, particularly the use of a first-person female narrator.

_____. *Homemade Love.* New York: St. Martin's Press, 1986. A collection of short stories in which Cooper continues to develop her unique method of using a narrator who interjects personal observations and bits of folk wisdom.

_____. *A Piece of Mine.* Navarro, Calif.: Wild Trees Press, 1984. An early collection of Cooper's short stories, with an informative introduction by Alice Walker. These stories are much shorter than those in *Some Soul to Keep* but display Cooper's moral and artistic values in miniature.

Kirkus Reviews. Review of *Some Soul to Keep,* by J. California Cooper. 55 (August 15, 1987): 1178. The reviewer praises Cooper's simplicity and sincerity, saying that her message in both *Some Soul to Keep* and her earlier collection *Homemade Love* is essentially that "goodness wins out in the end, and love conquers all."

McMillan, Terry. "Life Goes on, and Don't You Forget It." *The New York Times Book Review,* November 8, 1987, 23. This review of *Some Soul to Keep* acknowledges Cooper's sincerity and forcefulness but criticizes her on several points. McMillan objects to the didactic nature of the stories as well as to the fact that the narrators are too intrusive and always seem to be the same voice under different names.

Oliver, Stephanie Stokes. "J. California Cooper: From Paper Dolls to Paperbacks." *Essence* 22 (May, 1991): 52. This profile discusses Cooper's works in relation to her personal life. Cooper is portrayed as a woman not unlike many of the heroines of her stories.

Schumacher, Michael. Review of *Homemade Love,* by J. California Cooper. *Writer's Digest* 67 (February, 1987): 21. Schumacher discusses modern short stories in general and uses Cooper's stories as examples of good short fiction that is still entertaining in the traditional way. He describes the pleasure of hearing Cooper read her work in person and points out that she writes for the ear as well as for the eye.

Bill Delaney

SONG OF SOLOMON

Author: Toni Morrison (1931-   )
Type of work: Novel
Type of plot: Bildungsroman
Time of plot: The mid-twentieth century
Locale: The urban North and rural Virginia
First published: 1977

> *Principal characters:*
> MACON "MILKMAN" DEAD, the protagonist, who goes on a
>   journey to discover his real roots, his personal and family
>   identity
> PILATE DEAD, Milkman's tall and imposing aunt
> MACON DEAD, Pilate's brother and Milkman's father
> RUTH FOSTER DEAD, Milkman's unfulfilled, submissive mother
> GUITAR BAINES, Milkman's best friend and alter ego
> HAGAR DEAD, the pampered but unhappy granddaughter of Pilate
> CIRCE, the midwife who delivered Macon Dead and Pilate

The Novel

   Song of Solomon is the account of Milkman Dead's physical and spiritual journey to maturity. The quest for his Aunt Pilate's gold leads him to his ancestral home in Virginia and the far more significant wealth of his personal and family history. Milkman's journey is paralleled by Pilate's long search for her father's body and the meaning of his ghostly words. The novel turns on the conflict between two estranged households: that of Milkman's parents, who embody materialism, and that of his aunt, who represents family.

   The novel begins on February 18, 1931 (Morrison's birthdate), with the disastrous flight of a man from the roof of "No Mercy" Hospital, triggering the labor of Milkman's mother in the crowd below. Thus Milkman's birth becomes a kind of secular miracle, that of the first African American baby to be born at the hospital.

   He is twelve before he ventures with his friend, Guitar, to Pilate's house to meet his father's sister, of whom Macon will not speak. Milkman is struck by the regal bearing of his tall, powerful aunt and by the comfort of the simple house. Later, he is attracted to his cousin Hagar, Pilate's granddaughter, and carries on an affair with her for nearly fifteen years. Eventually, Hagar becomes "the third beer. . . . the one you drink because it's there," and Milkman decides to break off the relationship, causing Hagar to pursue him in a luckless attempt to kill him. Later, stricken with grief over his rejection of her, she dies.

   Meanwhile, Milkman is learning more than he wishes to know about his family. When he steps in to prevent his father from striking his mother, he is confronted with her unhealthy love for her father, Doctor Foster, and discovers her secret pilgrimages to the doctor's grave. He also learns of the murder of his paternal grandfather, the first Macon Dead, by white men in Pennsylvania who wanted his rich farmland. Eventually, Milkman's father urges him to take his grandfather's gold, believed to be in a green sack hanging from Pilate's ceiling. Milkman and Guitar agree to steal it so that Milkman can get away from his family and so that Guitar can share the rest with the underground organization he has joined. Instead of gold, however, they find a sack filled with rocks and bones.

Milkman travels alone to Danville, Pennsylvania, in search of the gold he believes that Pilate has hidden there; what he finds instead is acceptance. "I know your people!" cries the town's minister, whose father had fashioned Pilate's eccentric snuffbox earring. Milkman discovers more about his powerful grandfather from the aged but oddly seductive Circe, living now in the ruined house of her former masters.

Convinced that Pilate must have taken her father's gold back to Virginia, Milkman seeks the hamlet of Shalimar, from which his grandparents originally emigrated. At Shalimar he soon feels wonderfully at home and gradually leaves behind his suitcase, watch, and other trappings of civilization. After Milkman is invited to join a hunt, a night journey with the men of Shalimar that initiates him into a primal knowledge and sensitivity he has never known, he finally begins to take responsibility for his own actions. Nor does he blame Guitar, who follows Milkman and tries to kill him, believing that Milkman is double-crossing him with the gold.

No longer interested in gold, Milkman seeks to know more about his father's people. He finds not only the lost identity of his Indian grandmother, Singing Bird, but also learns through a children's game the name of his great-grandfather Solomon, for whom Shalimar (originally "Shalleemone") was named. Many years ago, Solomon leaped triumphantly into the air and flew away from slavery, back to Africa, leaving behind twenty-one sons, the youngest of whom was Pilate's beloved father and Milkman's grandfather. Milkman has discovered his past, and through that, who he really is.

He returns to the North to tell Pilate what he has learned. She now realizes that she has unknowingly carried the bones of her father with her for years, and she determines to bury him in Virginia. At the rocky outcropping of Solomon's Leap, however, Pilate is shot by Guitar, who has followed them there. "You want my life?" Milkman cries to him. "You need it? Here." The ambiguous ending leaves Milkman leaping into the air, selfless rather than selfish, and now fully human.

The Characters

Song of Solomon is the first novel in which Morrison uses a male protagonist. She has said that she chose a man because "he had more to learn than a woman would have," but she also noted that she was "amazed at how little men taught one another in the book." Most of Milkman's teachers are women, especially Pilate and his mother, but he also learns from Hagar and his two sisters, Lena and Corinthians, who turn on him after enduring years of his indifference. Pilate tells him that "if you take a life, then you own it," and Milkman eventually accepts his responsibility for Hagar's death.

Milkman's moral imperfection is suggested by his shortened left leg, which creates a barely noticeable limp. After the communal hunt, in which he is initiated by the men of Shalimar into comradeship and respect for life and nature, he ceases to limp. The cold, self-centered Milkman matures into a sympathetic, caring man through the discovery of his own past, his ancestors' suffering, and their struggles against poverty, racism, greed, and pride.

At the same time, Guitar, who is at first wiser and more aware than Milkman, becomes narrower and more fanatical as he immerses himself in the zeal of the Seven Days, a group organized to avenge the murders of blacks with the killing of whites. Guitar loses perspective, locked into a mathematical balance of life that must be maintained without any degree of mercy for either side. Yet enough is seen of his past—for example, sugar makes him sick, because his childhood grief for his dead father was stifled with a stick of candy—to allow him to be a sympathetic character rather than a stereotyped terrorist.

Morrison's women characters still remain her strongest suit, and the best of these is "wide-spirited" Pilate. She is the ancestor, the guide, the pilot, one of the free-walking dark women of Shalimar, wise and unafraid. Pilate is also given mythic overtones. She birthed herself, expelled from the womb after the death of her mother, and she has no navel. Pilate's knowledge of herbs and magic helps Ruth to conceive Milkman by means of a powder mixed into Macon's food, and her juju doll warns Macon against harming his wife or the child he does not want. It is Pilate who carries the burden of the past with her in her green tarpaulin, and Pilate who is equally at home in the present.

Ruth, the lemon-skinned daughter of the first African American doctor in town, is a child of privilege but is far less capable of dealing with life than Pilate is. She worships her father in life and death, but she bravely confronts Hagar, who is trying to murder her son.

Hagar, the child-woman whose name means "to forsake," has had everything she wanted and has been spoiled by the love of her mother and grandmother. Yet she cannot have Milkman, and it destroys her. Guitar warns her that, if she has so little regard for herself, she cannot expect Milkman to have more, but she cannot hear him. She is an outcast almost by choice, childish and emotionally immature—indeed, Pilate's "baby."

Morrison uses the warm, omniscient voice of the storyteller for the novel. This voice, which enables her to move into the minds of her characters whenever she wishes, also echoes the oral tradition that is so much a part of African American history. Moreover, the past is an integral part of her characters' lives.

Themes and Meanings

A primary theme in *Song of Solomon* is the journey or quest for identity. Milkman is assisted by a number of guides as he seeks and discovers community, including Circe, who helps him in a symbolic return to the womb, and the men of the hunt, who serve as elders guiding a youth to manhood. In the course of his journey, Milkman is initiated into knowledge. One critic has written that he "journeys from spiritual death to rebirth . . . symbolized by his discovery of the secret power of flight."

Morrison acknowledges that flight, her central metaphor, is everybody's secret dream. Flight, symbolizing freedom or escape and found frequently in African American writing, is seen in the Flying African, Milkman's great-grandfather, who embodies the many folktales of the escaped slave. The novel opens with the failed flight from the hospital roof of a man wearing blue silk wings and closes with the triumphant flight of Solomon and the redemptive flight of Milkman, who has finally learned to "ride" the air.

As a child, Milkman longs to fly; at age five, he feels uncomfortable riding while facing backward on a train because "it was like flying blind." This comment also suggests that he does not want to look at the past. Later, as he and Guitar are planning to steal Pilate's sack of gold, they notice a white peacock with a "tail full of jewelry," apparently escaped from the zoo, and try to catch it. Milkman notes that the bird "can't fly no better than a chicken," and Guitar tells him that is because of the weight of its tail; in order to fly, Guitar says, one must give up the things that weigh one down. After he visits Shalimar, Milkman is able to give up the material things that weigh him down, and finally he, like his ancestor, is able to soar.

Character names are used both symbolically and ironically. Milkman—a name that suggests his immaturity and also his symbolic hunger—is emotionally and spiritually "Dead." Guitar, through his desire for social justice, becomes an instrument of vengeance. The Dead women's biblical names are allusive and sometimes ironic. The biblical Ruth is famed for her steadfast companionship; Morrison's Ruth is a companion only to her father, for her husband shuns her. Hagar, named for Abraham's outcast slave, is cast aside by her lover Milkman. Pilate, named by her illiterate father, who liked the way the name looked in the Bible, does not, like Pontius Pilate, abdicate authority but instead embraces it; she is also the "pilot" who guides both Ruth and Milkman, though Macon rejects her.

The ancient midwife Circe is an ironic counterpart to the beautiful enchantress of Greek mythology; in *Song of Solomon*, she is surrounded not by swine but by dogs with the eyes of children. The scent of ginger and sweet, spicy perfume, symbolic of Africa and the past, lingers around Circe, Shalimar, and the bones of Pilate's father.

Critical Context

Although early critical reaction was somewhat muted, *Song of Solomon*, Morrison's third novel, won the 1977 National Book Critics Circle Award for Fiction and became the first novel by a black writer chosen as a main selection for the Book-of-the-Month Club since Richard Wright's *Native Son* (1940). In this book, Morrison seems to have found her true voice as a storyteller, although from the beginning of her career she has included in her work features of the oral tradition.

Morrison has always been aware of her audience. Her first novel, *The Bluest Eye* (1970), was written because she saw no stories about black girls growing up, and she decided to write a book that she would have wanted to read. She has frequently stated that her writing is an attempt to present the world from an African American perspective. Morrison uses many characteristics of African American art in her writing, stressing the importance of involving the reader directly in the work, and including a chorus, "meaning the community or the reader at large, commenting on the action," and always an ancestor-figure as a guide. She believes that a historical connection is essential for awareness. "When you kill the ancestor you kill yourself," she has written.

Song of Solomon includes numerous references to civil rights figures of the 1950's and 1960's. Emmett Till, murdered in Mississippi, and the four girls who died in the 1963 bombing of a Birmingham church are specifically mentioned, as are Malcolm X and Arkansas Governor Orval Faubus. Morrison believes strongly that "black people have a story, and that story has to be heard." Morrison's receipt of the 1993 Nobel Prize in Literature provided clear evidence that "that story" was being heard—and appreciated—around the world.

Bibliography
Bakerman, Jane S. "Failures of Love: Female Initiation in the Novels of Toni Morrison." *American Literature* 52, no. 4 (January, 1981): 541-563. Explores women characters' search for love and self-worth in Morrison's first three novels. Notes that each woman defines herself by "the standards and desires of a beloved man," which results in her incomplete initiation and failed integration into the community.

Lee, Dorothy H. "*Song of Solomon*: To Ride the Air." *Black American Literature Forum* 16, no. 2 (Summer, 1982): 64-70. A study of the novel's mythic foundation, including folktales of the Flying African, whose flight is always triggered by the utterance of a secret, now-forgotten word and a signal given for the leap into the air. Incorporates a discussion of Egyptian, Greek, and biblical symbolism.

Mickelson, Anne Z. *Reaching Out: Sensitivity and Order in Recent American Fiction by Women.* Metuchen, N.J.: Scarecrow Press, 1979. Examines the woman character who breaks away from established society to create her own life. Pilate's successful independence signals "a growth in the author's feminist consciousness" not seen in previous novels. Parallels Pilate's odyssey with Milkman's picaresque journey, where each event tests character and brings knowledge. Unlike novelist Richard Wright, who "finds no sustaining values in the past of black people, Morrison celebrates the past."

Morrison, Toni. "Rootedness: The Ancestor as Foundation." In *Black Women Writers, 1950-1980: A Critical Evaluation,* edited by Mari Evans. Garden City, N.Y.: Anchor Press/Doubleday, 1983. Interview on the importance of the ancestor, the community, reader participation, and the oral tradition in Morrison's work. The author explains that in her novels, an elder is always present "whose relationships to the characters are benevolent, instructive, and protective, and . . . provide a certain kind of wisdom."

Royster, Philip M. "Milkman's Flying: The Scapegoat Transcended in Toni Morrison's *Song of Solomon.*" *College Language Association Journal* 24, no. 4 (June, 1982): 419-440. Analyzes the novel as a *Bildungsroman* depicting Milkman's literal and figurative journey to manhood. Milkman is seen as an "unconscious scapegoat" by virtue of his sex and race, "victim of his burdensome past, blind to his future, and unable to assert himself" in the present until he is ultimately made whole at Shalimar.

Joanne McCarthy

SOUL ON ICE

Author: Eldridge Cleaver (1935-   )
Type of work: Autobiographical essays
First published: 1968

Form and Content

Soul on Ice is a collection of autobiographical essays and notes on the black experience in the ghetto, in prison, and in the larger society. Eldridge Cleaver experiences great anguish as he constructs a philosophy capable of making sense of his life and of the inferior status of black people in America and throughout the world.

The book's topics reflect a life shaped by events outside Cleaver's control. Cleaver's intellectual unfolding is mapped by his inner toiling to fathom himself and what is occurring around him. Eldridge Cleaver's autobiography is, therefore, a testament written by an outcast. *Soul on Ice* describes Cleaver's endeavor to understand a world painted in black and white, a world in which poverty and powerlessness exist in the midst of plenty. It is, however, more than a personal account of one African American's plight in a racist society; it is a narrative of all oppressed people in American society.

Cleaver pored through Greek classics, American history, and the works of Sigmund Freud and Carl Jung. He read insatiably from the works of African American writers such as Richard Wright, who inspired him, and James Baldwin, whom Cleaver found full of hatred for black people and confused about his own sexual identity. In *Soul on Ice* Cleaver takes Baldwin to task.

Cleaver's account of himself is revelatory. A man with many burdens and demons, Cleaver claims to be too many things; it is left to the reader to decide what he was, and when he was that way, from tidbits scattered through his book.

Soul on Ice shows Cleaver attempting to merge several philosophies: Black Muslim teachings, the attitudes of the Civil Rights movement, and the doctrine of the latter-day Black Power movement rooted in revolutionary struggles in Third World countries. The synthesis thus fashioned by Cleaver offers an accurate insight into his mental evolution and acts as a commentary on black struggle in the late 1950's and throughout the 1960's.

In places, Cleaver echoes Frantz Fanon: "We shall have our manhood. We shall have it or the earth will be leveled by our attempts to gain it." In other instances, he jabbers much like a pimp on the make or boasts about his "rod," which, he claims defines him and nearly all black men as "the Supermasculine Menials" who possess mostly bodies in search of their minds.

Cleaver has a problem with women. Black women are described as "bitches," and so are white women; black women are humiliated by black men, who cower before white power or act the buffoon in order to beat a traffic infraction or to escape a lynch mob's knotted rope. Black women, writes Cleaver, are like granite and steel; they break their men without remorse and covertly desire white men, whom Cleaver refers to as "Omnipresent Administrators." Black women are "Amazons," and in union with the Omnipotent Administrators, Cleaver claims, they fuse mind and body.

Cleaver's problems with white women are even more severe. He hones his skill as a rapist by practicing on black women; when he feels he is prepared, he assaults white society by attacking white women, whom he sees as the antithesis of the black man.

In time, Cleaver matures and places his rape rampage into perspective: Rape is violence and, therefore, wrong, but such violence is fostered among blacks by white racism. He comes to see occupations as a means of defining black human beings throughout the earth as a servile people.

The author's Marxist leanings are apparent and mark, perhaps, his last stage of development in *Soul on Ice*. Cleaver stands Marxism on its head by applying it as an analytical tool to understand white racism and black self-hate. Cleaver also embraces Fanon's theories in his explanation of his attempts to become less black through sexual intercourse with white women.

The book, though, winds its way through a tangled course: A street hood in the Los Angeles slums, a transplanted Arkansan, becomes a convict of long standing, a writer, an orator, and a theorist for the Black Panther Party, and later, beyond the scope of *Soul on Ice*, a fugitive from justice, a terrorist in residence in Algeria, and, by the early 1980's, a preacher who had seemingly come to terms with the white power structure. At the conclusion of *Soul on Ice*, Cleaver is further along the path than seems possible at the beginning of his trek.

Analysis

The book is divided into four parts, with several subparts. The essay format allows Cleaver to focus on specific topics. One essay, "On Watts," has Cleaver describing the August, 1965, riot there as an abortive uprising. Within the walls of Folsom Prison, blacks mill around congratulating each other for the intrepid fighters in Watts. Riot was therapy, a catharsis, a rebuttal to the myth of the submissive Negro.

In "Soul Food," Cleaver criticizes middle-class blacks for their failure to uplift their brothers. Soul food, pork, is "counter-revolutionary." The piece is too short to call an essay, a few paragraphs; nevertheless, Cleaver thinks if blacks became beef eaters, they might become revolutionaries, too. At least, they would realize the foibles of capitalism.

A more illuminating and longer essay is Cleaver's "Initial Reactions on the Assassination of Malcolm X." Cleaver tells of his transformation before Malcolm X's assassination from racism to nonracism; he no longer considered whites to be blue-eyed devils but rather fellow human beings with a multiplicity of possibilities for good and for evil. After his momentous pilgrimage to Mecca, Malcolm had written of his conversion to true Islam: He had supped with men whose eyes were the bluest of blue and whose skin was the whitest of white and believed that they, too, were his brothers. Malcolm X's conversion to "true" Islam shocked Black Muslims and deepened the rift between the followers of Malcolm X and Elijah Muhammad. Elijah Muhammad's racial supremacy doctrine was a heavy burden for blacks to carry. Cleaver found that rejecting it was liberating; so did, in time, the majority of Black Muslims at Folsom Prison.

Whites, Cleaver saw, had proven their capacity for humanity beyond denying. The bigot in Cleaver died some when he embraced Malcolm X. Malcolm X represented the best in blacks and in any man; this was the secret to his charisma.

Another essay that embodies the new Cleaver is pulpy and sunny, a love sonnet, perhaps: "Prelude to Love—Three Letters." Beverly Axelrod was his white damsel. Axelrod was a San Francisco lawyer to whom Cleaver had written for legal assistance. Axelrod had visited Cleaver three times before the exchange of letters. Cleaver was impressed and clearly in love with her; out of respect for her, he stopped calling women "bitches." He was impelled to write her; her reply was cryptic but revealing: "What an awesome thing it is to feel oneself on the verge of the possibility of really knowing another person. Can it ever happen?" Axelrod also wrote of the difficulty of stripping themselves naked and facing the fear of rejection.

In his second letter to Axelrod, Cleaver is enraptured, speaking of her letters as "chunks" of her, the most important things in his life. His metamorphosis is thus completed—from hatred of whites to a kind of love, albeit euphoric and remote, for one of them.

The next essay is full of anger and misery. Cleaver uses "The Allegory of the Black Eunuchs" to describe and debunk the stereotype that older blacks were Uncle Toms. "I asked you why you aren't dead?" says one of Cleaver's henchmen to "Lazarus," an elderly black, beginning an interesting exchange between two generations.

The elderly black man tells Cleaver and his cohorts of his relations with a black woman who had a "hook like Sugar Ray Robinson." He could not be gentle with her; she relished fighting on Saturday nights. When he was tired of fighting, he sought to show his affections, and all went well for a time; however, she left him for another man, one more given to that kind of strife. The new duo fought a lot; eventually, she shot him "like a dog." The courts ruled the shooting was justifiable homicide. In time, the former girlfriend of Lazarus ripened her voice and became a famous singer. She soon married a white man, and Lazarus claims that a white is the dream man of all black women. The chasm between black men and white women is vast and deep, and it is the fault of white racism.

In Cleaver's last essay, "To All Black Women, from All Black Men," he endeavors to unravel the tensions between black men and black women. Despite the black man's culpability through compromise and complicity, he has endured with his woman, according to Cleaver, through suffering and death; together, they will build a new city on the wreckage of slavery and oppression in American society. Cleaver finds his answer, and a cerebral peace.

Critical Context

Soul on Ice gained international recognition and became an icon among black radicals. In his essays, Cleaver scrutinized numerous aspects of racism in the United States, not least of all the strain and induced self-hatred of blacks, specifically represented by rape and sexual abuse among blacks and by black-on-black violence. Cleaver, though self-taught and mostly a caged observer of the events of the 1960's, exhibited a simplicity and insight that fated his book to be of great value.

Soul on Ice sold more than two million copies. The sheer volume of sales was significant and had a wide influence on black radicals and even moderates in the Civil Rights movement.

Eldridge Cleaver redirected the rhetoric of the Civil Rights movement in the immediate aftermath of the assassination of Martin Luther King, Jr. Cleaver remains an enigmatic personality of the 1960's. It is difficult to explain why he has endured, larger than life, when after all he was a theorist; when he undertook to become an activist, he failed and ended up fleeing the country for a safe haven in Cuba and then in Algeria.

Soul on Ice was his most conspicuous attainment, if not his only consequential bequest to black radicalism. After prison and his involvement with the Black Panther Party, Cleaver bade farewell to the political scene, only to return in the 1980's as a symbol of the 1960's. He proclaimed on his return that he was a born-again orthodox Christian. His search continued for his identity and that of his people, but with less fanfare for both.

A history of the times is incomplete without mention of *Soul on Ice*. Cleaver's impact on the black bourgeoisie, whom he loathed, was perhaps greater than on any other constituency: It was the black youth, relatively affluent and educated, who read *Soul on Ice* and appropriated Cleaver's dreams for themselves.

Bibliography
Cleaver, Eldridge. *Soul on Ice.* Waco, Tex.: Word Books, 1978. The born-again Cleaver's memoirs, written after his prison conversion to fundamentalist Christianity.
Lockwood, Lee. *Conversation with Eldridge Cleaver.* New York: McGraw-Hill, 1970. An overview of Cleaver's philosophy, published at the height of his fame. Contains remarks made by Cleaver while he was an expatriate fugitive from the U.S. legal system.
Parks, Gordon. "What Became of the Prophets of Rage?" *Life,* Spring, 1988, 32. Special issue. Devoted to a retrospective look at the activists of the 1960's (including Cleaver) and their subsequent evolution.
Rout, Kathleen. *Eldridge Cleaver.* Boston: G. K. Hall, 1991. A thorough overview of Cleaver's life and writings. Bibliography, index.
"Whatever Happened to . . . Eldridge Cleaver?" *Ebony,* March, 1988, 66-68. America's leading black magazine looks at Cleaver's career from the vantage point of two decades.

Claude Hargrove

THE SOULS OF BLACK FOLK

Author: W. E. B. Du Bois (1868-1963)
Type of work: Essays
First published: 1903

Form and Content

The Souls of Black Folk is a collection of essays that focus upon the post-Reconstruction reality of African Americans in the South, where local white rule and Ku Klux Klan terrorism had erased a decade-long effort to bring democracy to all Americans. W. E. B. Du Bois, a Northern-born graduate of Harvard University, sought to make a scientific analysis of the problems besetting African Americans as a necessary first step in the resolution of the American racial dilemma. Du Bois envisioned a series of scientific studies of African Americans that would provide reliable data for policymakers to end discrimination and injustice; he considered that the lack of scientific information on the African American was the root of the race problem in the United States. In addition to performing these scientific studies, Du Bois sought to reach intelligent white readers by writing articles in prestigious magazines of the day such as *The Atlantic Monthly* and *The Dial*. Du Bois collected nine such published pieces, revised them, and added five new essays to make up the contents of *The Souls of Black Folk*. Du Bois had already published *The Suppression of the African Slave Trade to the United States of America, 1638-1870* (1896) and *The Philadelphia Negro: A Social Study* (1899), a pioneering work in the field of urban sociology. As the first African American to receive a doctorate from Harvard University, he was a leading intellectual in the United States.

Born in Great Barrington, Massachusetts, at the beginning of Reconstruction, Du Bois was the son of a Civil War veteran who had fought with the Massachusetts Fifty-fourth Regiment, a black unit (led by white officers) that had garnered praise for its valor. This was one of the factors that gave Du Bois a sense of racial pride. He represented the "new" African Americans born in the freedom of Reconstruction and imbued with a sense of destiny; Du Bois hoped to set a new course for African Americans. Although reared in the free atmosphere of abolitionist Massachusetts, he had not many African American contacts. This situation was remedied when he attended Fisk University in Nashville, Tennessee, one of the institutions founded during Reconstruction to educate the children of freed slaves. After finishing his studies at Fisk and going on to receive another bachelor's degree and a doctorate from Harvard, Du Bois went to Ohio to teach at Wilberforce University, the African Methodist Episcopal Church flagship institution for young African Americans. From Wilberforce University, he moved to the Deep South to teach at Atlanta University in Georgia.

In Atlanta, Du Bois came into contact with the experiment in vocational education of African Americans being conducted in the neighboring state of Alabama, where Booker T. Washington reigned at the Tuskegee Institute. In "Of Mr. Booker T. Washington and Others," the most famous essay in *The Souls of Black Folk*, Du Bois spells out his differences with Washington, then the most powerful African American political and educational leader in the United States. Supported by Northern business magnates and stressing the need of the newly freed African Americans to prove their loyalty to the South by repudiating the political and social gains of Reconstruction, Washington represented a powerful threat to the emergence of the "new" African Americans that Du Bois championed. Washington asserted that he represented the mass of untutored peasants who needed to learn about hygiene, citizenship, and agricultural technology rather than about foreign languages, political economy, and sociology. Washington emphasized the practical aspects of living in the South, maintaining that the survival of African Americans depended on their ability to demonstrate their fealty to values held dear by white Southerners. African Americans must demonstrate, Washington declared at a meeting of Southern white businessmen, that they could function alongside whites like the fingers of a hand, "separate but equal."

Du Bois thought Washington's power was being used for shortsighted and parlous ends. In his essay on Washington, Du Bois decries the surrender of hard-earned rights for which generations of African Americans had fought. In effect, Du Bois challenges Washington's right to engineer a compromise involving the loss of the right to vote, the end of civic equality, and the surrender of intellectual development in favor of vocational training. Du Bois urges the thinking elite—the "Talented Tenth" of African American society—to oppose Washington at every turn on these questions.

Another of the most compelling essays in *The Souls of Black Folk*, "Of the Meaning of Progress," renders the experience of Du Bois as a schoolteacher in the rural South teaching poor and illiterate African Americans. Living in primitive conditions, Du Bois was able to learn experientially about the actual lives of the mass of African Americans residing in the South and to know how fragile were the conditions of freedom. The world of postslavery poverty is graphically depicted in the essay. Du Bois describes returning to the area ten years after he had left to find his star pupil dead and the hopes of the little community crushed by poverty.

The Souls of Black Folk contains a number of types of essays. Perhaps Du Bois' essay on the death of his young son reaches an emotional apogee, but there is a dispassionate analysis of African American spirituals and folk tunes in his essay entitled "Of the Sorrow Songs." An essay on Alexander Crummell, the respected African American educator and missionary leader, prefigures Du Bois' later commitment to pan-Africanism. His sense of the importance of education for young African Americans was almost a crusade call.

Analysis

The Souls of Black Folk is a manifesto of the new class of educated African Americans. With degrees from Harvard University and the University of Berlin, Du Bois had the best education Europe and America could offer. That he was able to master this world and yet retain affection for the untutored masses gave an example to other educated African Americans of how to handle the problem of the "Veil" that divided the worlds of whites and African Americans. The metaphor of the "Veil" unifies the disparate themes Du Bois explores in these essays; showing how to survive with the knowledge of this duality is one of the significant contributions of *The Souls of Black Folk*.

Each chapter is prefaced by a quotation from a famous writer, sometimes in the language of the original, and below each quotation is a bar of music from a spiritual (Du Bois called such music "Sorrow Songs"). Du Bois' alma mater, Fisk University, was famous for making the world aware of these songs by having its choir tour Europe and the United States singing what had been the expression of slaves; the inclusion of even a bar of this music in a written form was thus an assertion of cultural consciousness. The ability of the new African American intelligentsia to use the oral tradition of slavery in a written form alongside the writings of Europeans and Americans was also new.

While he acknowledges the significance of the African American folk tradition, Du Bois also develops the theme of encouraging African Americans' aspirations to greater intellectual achievement. Rather than accepting the prevailing belief of African Americans' mental inferiority to whites, Du Bois saw his own life as a refutation of that fallacy and emphasized the importance of encouraging African Americans to work to attain educational parity and civil equality with whites. In the essay entitled "Of the Training of Black Men," he develops his concept of the "Talented Tenth"—that portion of African American society capable "by character and talent" to be trained as teachers, clergymen, and business professionals, and who would, as a result of higher education, become community leaders dedicated to the improvement of their race. Self-improvement alone was not enough; cultivation of these leaders was of paramount importance, according to Du Bois, because

> while it is a great truth to say that the Negro must strive and strive mightily to help himself, it is equally true that unless his striving be not simply seconded, but rather aroused and encouraged, by the initiative of the richer and wiser environing group, he cannot hope for great success.

Although he lived in the South during the rollback of civil rights for African Americans and through the terror of the Ku Klux Klan, Du Bois thought that information would cause change. He wrote for highbrow Northern magazines and academic journals and thought that if he could influence the few who ran the country, life would become better for the former slaves. He considered the cause of prejudice to be ignorance on the part of whites. If they only knew, he averred, things would change. Du Bois was a believer in rationalism, and he clearly underestimated the power of emotion and class. In his final autobiography, published in 1968, he admitted that he had underappreciated the role of class in society. Despite this admission, his faith in rationalism remained unshaken—nowhere in his writings is there any significant consideration of the power of the nonrational.

What one finds in *The Souls of Black Folk* is the overriding sense that African

Americans had a history worth knowing. Although the book was aimed at a popular audience, it was also aimed at educated African Americans. In a sense, Du Bois showed what one could do with education. He demonstrated that it could be another weapon in the struggle of African Americans for racial equality. People whose ancestors had been used for their labor, their brawn, now could see a proud African American mind on display.

Critical Context

The Souls of Black Folk is a seminal work about the roots of modern African American life. The book anticipates many of the central questions of the twentieth century and makes the reader aware that current problems have their roots in the failed effort to bring equality and justice to African Americans after the Civil War. Africans and African Americans who encountered the book felt uplifted by the assertion of the organic reality of a black culture. While African Americans were the predominant readers who savored this work, *The Souls of Black Folk* was also well received by some white American scholars. William James was impressed by it and sent a copy to his brother Henry, who considered it the only book of distinction from the South in some time.

Emerging at a time when the rights of African Americans were being heavily eroded and, in some cases, eradicated, Du Bois' work was also an essay in faith and hope. J. Saunders Redding, an African American critic, deemed *The Souls of Black Folk* more "history-making than historical." The armoring of black peoples with a sense of themselves provided a foundation for the rise of independent African states and the emergence of the Civil Rights movement. Generations of African Americans who sought leadership roles in the United States were buoyed by the message in *The Souls of Black Folk* and by the rousing call to arms that Du Bois issued in the work. Each succeeding generation has had to cut its intellectual teeth on the substance and questions raised by this work. In African American studies programs across the country, *The Souls of Black Folk* is still used with great success to provide a sense of the roots of the African American struggle for freedom and dignity.

Bibliography

De Marco, Joseph P. *The Social Thought of W. E. B. Du Bois.* Lanham, Md.: University Press of America, 1983. A useful overview of Du Bois' philosophy.

Du Bois, W. E. B. *The Autobiography of W. E. B. Du Bois: A Soliloquy on Viewing My Life from the Last Decade of Its First Century.* New York: International Publishing, 1968. Du Bois' classic life story, covering the many events of his long career. Essential reading for Du Bois scholars.

_____. *Du Bois: Writings.* Edited by Nathan Huggins. New York: Literary Classics of the United States, 1986. A useful compilation of Du Bois materials from 1890 to 1958. Contains *The Souls of Black Folk.*

Essien-Udom, E. U. *Black Nationalism: A Search for an Identity in America.* New York: Dell Books, 1964. Focuses on Du Bois as a major advocate of pan-Africanism.

Notes that he differed from other black activists of his time by calling for full political participation and racial unity as a response to racism.

Green, Dan S., and Edwin D. Driver, eds. *W. E. B. Du Bois: On Sociology and the Black Community.* Chicago: University of Chicago Press, 1978. Discusses Du Bois' sociological contributions. Contains a brief biographical sketch and excerpts from his writings.

W. A. Jordan III

THE SPEECHES OF MARTIN LUTHER KING, JR.

Author: Martin Luther King, Jr. (1929-1968)
Type of work: Speeches
First published: A Testament of Hope: The Essential Writings of Martin Luther King, Jr., 1986; *Martin Luther King, Jr., I Have a Dream: Writings and Speeches That Changed the World*, 1992

The sermons and speeches of Dr. Martin Luther King, Jr., mirrored the Southern black preaching tradition that surrounded his childhood in Atlanta. King's father, the Reverend Martin Luther King, Sr., was the pastor of Ebenezer Baptist Church and a seminal influence in shaping his son's commitment to racial justice and his confidence that carefully chosen words were crucial to attaining it.

As a boy, King witnessed many occasions when his father and mother refused to be intimidated by segregationist policies; his parents always linked their resistance to moral values. Above all, young King developed a passion for learning to express himself with "big words" such as his father and his maternal grandfather, the Reverend Adam Daniel Williams, before him, delivered from the pulpit at Ebenezer. The cadence and forceful tones of this Southern black preaching style stimulated the future civil rights leader's mind before he could read and remained a decisive element in his public career. Although he did not plan to become a minister, his experience at Morehouse College changed his thinking and led him to further study in theology and philosophy at Crozer Theological Seminary and Boston University and prepared him for his first pastorate in Montgomery, Alabama. There, he emerged as an effective civil rights spokesman during the historic bus boycott of 1955-1956. One major result was a long series of speeches and sermons, including several that have been published in many languages that are considered to be models of rhetorical effectiveness and important contributions to African American social thought.

King's first speech to a national audience was his "Give Us the Ballot" address during the Prayer Pilgrimage to Washington, D.C., in May, 1957. By then King was taking an important place among such familiar civil rights leaders as Asa Philip Randolph, Roy Wilkins, and the Reverend Charles Kensie Steele; the "Give Us the Ballot" speech propelled him further as a major advocate of civil rights. Although some considered its judgment premature, after the speech New York's *Amsterdam News* hailed King as the "number one leader of sixteen million Negroes" and said that "the people will follow him anywhere."

His rhythmic repetition of the phrase "give us the ballot" had counterparts in several of his most influential addresses of the following decade. In August, 1963, during the massive March on Washington by some 250,000 people in behalf of jobs and freedom, King delivered his best-known speech. This time the pivotal phrase was "I have a dream," as King surveyed the broad landscape of African American history in the United States and expressed his hope for a better future. The next year, he modified his style somewhat in his speech in Oslo, Norway, as he accepted the

1964 Nobel Peace Prize, but his quintessential rhetorical form was reflected in his thematic emphasis upon peace both as a possibility and as a necessity for survival of the human race. It was a speech marked by King's frequent proclamations of faith in his vision for the world, modified at each change of topic to fit the specific point such as world peace or economic justice. "I refuse to accept the cynical notion," he affirmed, "that nation after nation must spiral down a militaristic stairway into a hell of thermonuclear destruction." With equal fervor, he told the crowd of marchers who gathered in Montgomery on March 25, 1965, after their fifty-mile trek from Selma, Alabama, in behalf of voting rights that "Confrontation of good and evil compressed in the tiny community of Selma generated the massive power to turn the whole nation to a new course." In each case, content and method revolved around a central concept based on a synthesis of historical black experience and faith in the power of idea-charged words as a catalyst for change.

All King's major speeches were historical sermons, focusing on the moral dimensions of the struggle for human equality and the nonviolent method that he believed essential to its success. Frequently, he drew illustrations from religious writings and experiences, as well as from quotidian details of the life of the poor and oppressed.

After the passage of the 1965 Voting Rights Act, he retained his earlier style but increased his emphasis upon socioeconomic problems and the escalating Vietnam War. In April, 1967, at New York's famed Riverside Church, he delivered a controversial speech in which he looked "Beyond Vietnam" and the destructive conflict he now openly opposed. King clearly saw his criticism of the war as consistent with his earlier position of nonviolence, but he had yet to learn just how much it would damage his previously amicable relationship with President Lyndon B. Johnson, who strongly supported the war, and even many of his associates in the civil rights struggle. In that sense, King's later speeches were more divisive politically than before. He averred at Riverside that needed social programs were being destroyed by the heavy cost, both moral and economic, of the conflict in Southeast Asia.

The year following the Riverside speech was a difficult one for King. He was losing support among highly visible black leaders who feared, as indeed was true, that his stance on the Vietnam War would alienate the Johnson Administration and thus reduce its support for civil rights reform. His speeches and sermons inevitably echoed his discouragement over the erosion of the consensus that had produced the Civil Rights Act of 1964 and the Voting Rights Act a year later. His plans to lead a Poor People's March on Washington were ended by his assassination in Memphis, Tennessee, where he had gone to help striking sanitation workers, on April 4, 1968. Yet even there, just before his death, King delivered a somber, but typically hopeful, final address often called "To the Mountain Top." In it, King virtually predicted his own death without losing confidence that black Americans would reach that better condition he called "the promised land." "I may not get there with you," he told a stunned audience, "but I want you to know tonight that we, as a people, will get to the promised land."

The contents of King's major addresses are varied, since they were delivered over a period of more than a decade and in shifting contexts. All of them were signposts of the nonviolent Civil Rights movement and the prevailing concerns of many black Americans. The "Give Us the Ballot" speech addressed the rising interest among black organizational leaders and grassroots support groups in obtaining the right to vote. That, said King, was pivotal for any future gains. If African Americans could attain the unhampered opportunity to vote, they could remove segregationist officials from office and thus facilitate other reforms. In Washington in 1963, his "I Have a Dream" speech reflected the uncertainty about the Birmingham campaign recently completed; black leaders had attained an agreement with local officials and business leaders to increase employment of blacks and to remove other racial barriers, but the agreement was not yet secured by enforceable laws. The elusive goal of enlarging employment and educational opportunities was basic to the Birmingham effort and very much on King's mind in the nation's capital.

King recognized in himself the dual and sometimes contradictory roles of a black man struggling for his own freedom and a public figure created in part by the press. After King received the 1964 Nobel Prize, this dichotomy was widened as he became a global figure. His increased stature can be seen in the broadening content of his speeches and writings, which increasingly incorporated issues of world peace and justice. If this seemed to burden King with an impossible task, it also reinforced his commitment to nonviolence as the key to creating communities freed from racial and other artificial barriers. Those concepts were fundamental premises of his Riverside and Memphis speeches of 1967 and 1968.

The linkage in King's speeches between African American history and broader American and global experience is both visible and complex. Frequent quotations from poems, biblical passages, and seminal figures in intellectual history such as Thomas Aquinas and Reinhold Niebuhr echoed not only his particular educational experience but also his belief that politics, faith, and freedom were all intricately connected. In Oslo in 1964, he told the audience of world leaders that the African Americans' struggle in the United States was actually part of a global movement for justice. He accepted the prize not for himself, he said, but for a movement still short of having "won the very peace and brotherhood which is the essence of the Nobel Prize." As usual, he would not claim full victory. The tension between reality and possibility, a characteristic feature of his speeches, was obvious, yet neither would he yield to pessimism even about prospects for genuine human community. "I refuse to accept the view," he insisted, "that mankind is so tragically bound to the starless midnight of racism and war that the bright daybreak of peace and brotherhood can never become a reality."

Most of his later speeches contained a similar blend of growing concern over the post-Selma decline of multiracial support and an ardent expression of the need to continue the movement on its nonviolent course. His final address in Memphis in 1968 was the clearest expression of this polarity. That his presence in Memphis was a detour from the planned Poor People's March on Washington to revitalize public support by focusing on the urgent needs of poor people of all races reflects the complexities of the time. He and others hoped that the march and related lobbying of government offices in Washington would engender the kind of positive response witnessed after the 1963 march, but fatigue, repeated threats on his life, and public criticism of his statements were taking their toll. King's last speech in Memphis was stunning to his aides, as they watched him virtually collapse into his chair after talking pointedly about the possibility of dying soon. Yet as he had done so often in the past, he spoke of hope and practical steps that could be taken to alleviate social inequities. He urged blacks not to do business with companies that practiced racial discrimination and called for building a "greater economic base" for black Americans.

The most familiar part of his Memphis speech remains the closing section, which clearly demonstrates that King sensed his impending death. "Well, I don't know what will happen now," he reflected in a serious tone that long haunted his close friends,

> We've got some difficult days ahead. But it doesn't matter with me now. Because I've been to the mountaintop. And I don't mind. Like anybody, I would like to live a long life. Longevity has its place. But I'm not concerned about that now. I just want to do God's will. And He's allowed me to go up to the mountain. And I've looked over. And I've seen the promised land. I may not get there with you. But I want you to know tonight that we, as a people, will get to the promised land. And I'm happy, tonight. I'm not worried about anything. I'm not fearing any man. Mine eyes have seen the glory of the coming of the Lord.

Early the next evening, King was shot to death as he stood on the balcony of the Lorraine Motel in Memphis, preparing to attend yet another rally.

King's speeches were shaped by his background, his education, and his distinctive synthesis of Gandhian nonviolence and the black religious experience. He saw himself and his message as rooted in the prophetic tradition of social criticism grounded in the eternal truths of divine revelation. Frequently, he quoted biblical passages such as "Let justice roll down like waters and righteousness like a mighty stream" and echoed Christ's emphasis on preaching good news to the poor and freedom to prisoners.

Instinctively and by training, King preferred nonviolent persuasion, but he understood the need for nonviolent coercion through such means as boycotts, litigation, and pressure on legislators. An interesting blend of these elements can be seen in several of his addresses. In 1963, he frequently drew the audience's attention to what he called the "promissory note" of the Constitution and Declaration of Independence. That debt, he said, had not been honored. Millions still lived on an "island of poverty" amid an ocean of plenty. Nor did he fail to warn of possible negative repercussions if the promises of the Constitution and the Emancipation Proclamation were not realized in the future. "This sweltering summer of the Negro's legitimate discontent will not pass until there is an invigorating autumn of freedom and equality," he predicted.

In key respects, King's oratory bore resemblance to the poetic expressions of African American discontent seen in Harlem Renaissance writers such as Langston Hughes and Claude McKay. Hughes's "The Negro Speaks of Rivers" was not unlike most of King's works in that it frankly acknowledged the pain of African American history while holding out hope for future fulfillment of the American dream. McKay, too, expressed this kind of realism-optimism as he nostalgically reviewed love, nature, and faith and subtly reminded his readers of the promises of American democracy in such poems as "If We Must Die" and "America."

Thus, King was not an isolated modern innovator or revolutionary in his orations, but rather a modern prophet with substantial linkage to the African American literary theme of struggling from internalized values to a better external world. King drew upon the African American cultural legacy as well as his training in mainstream Euro-American thought, the Social Gospel philosophy of Walter Rauschenbusch, and his own middle-class upbringing under the shadow of the Ebenezer Baptist Church in Atlanta.

As literature, several of King's speeches stand out as paradigmatic. The "I Have A Dream" speech has often been used in speech classes to demonstrate effective technique, and its content has been reviewed in countless books and articles. The metaphor of a "dream" to express the almost ineffable concept of a community at harmony with itself and the world has had an impressive impact even upon the organizational identity of the movement. The Southern Christian Leadership Conference (SCLC) under King's successors found the idea of keeping the "dream" alive to be its most effective theme for maintaining some continuity with the heyday of the Civil Rights movement. Other nonviolence oriented organizations such as the Congress of Racial Equality (CORE) and the National Association for the Advancement of Colored People (NAACP) have also found this imagery and other King rhetorical symbolism useful to their efforts. The reason seems to be that King clearly articulated both the needs and hopes of African Americans.

There is clearly an institutional as well as historical orientation in King's speeches that is consistent with African American literary tradition. The black church, the family, hard work, and the variegated network of adjustment mechanisms are all emphasized. If there is a high degree of Gandhian influence, there is also much that is distinctively African American. If there is paradox in King's juxtaposition of a midnight of racism and a dawn of hope, there is also much realism, discipline, and measured optimism. Perhaps the most effective expression of their confluence can be seen in the stirring conclusion of "I Have a Dream":

> So let freedom ring from the prodigious hilltops of New Hampshire; let freedom ring from the mighty mountains of New York; let freedom ring from the heightening Alleghenies of Pennsylvania; let freedom ring from the snowcapped Rockies of Colorado; let freedom ring from the curvaceous slopes of California. But not only that. Let freedom ring from Stone Mountain of Georgia; let freedom ring from Lookout Mountain of Tennessee; let freedom ring from every hill and molehill of Mississippi. From every mountainside, let freedom ring.

"And when this happens," he continued, people of all races and faiths will cooperate in bringing about the kind of just community envisaged by the founders of the United States and be able "to join hands and sing in the words of the old Negro spiritual: 'Free at last. Free at last. Thank God Almighty, we are free at last.' "

Bibliography

King, Martin Luther, Jr. *I Have a Dream: Writings and Speeches That Changed the World.* Edited by James Melvin Washington. San Francisco: Harper, 1992. Washington's compilations of King materials is premised on the epoch-making quality of the civil rights leader's work. King, argues Washington, was a paradigm for action; there was an integral connection between his writings and speeches and participation in voting, education, and wider employment opportunities.

_____. *A Testament of Hope: The Essential Writings of Martin Luther King, Jr.* Edited by James Melvin Washington. San Francisco: Harper & Row, 1986. A compendium of King's writings and speeches from the early days of the nonviolent Civil Rights movement to his last days in Memphis. Offers the reader a convenient sampling of King's major works.

Peake, Thomas R. *Keeping the Dream Alive: A History of the Southern Christian Leadership Conference from King to the Nineteen-Eighties.* New York: P. Lang, 1987. Contains numerous references to King's nonviolent theory and to specific addresses and sermons that emphasize the concept. Extensive coverage is given to the 1963 "I Have a Dream" speech that mirrored the full spectrum of elements of King's nonviolence and its relevance to African American experience.

Schulke, Flip, ed. *Martin Luther King, Jr.: A Documentary, Montgomery to Memphis.* Text by Penelope McPhee. New York: W. W. Norton, 1976. A pictorial survey that is much more. Schulke, a photographer who viewed firsthand much of the story, provides the drama missing in many accounts. Photographs, especially of major speeches, are extraordinarily focused on the intensity of the moment. Useful narrative with considerable historical detail accompanies the photographic coverage.

"Speeches by Dr. Martin Luther King, Jr." *Negro History Bulletin* 31 (May, 1968): 22. A brief but useful commentary on King's power as an orator who embodied the African experience in modern America. Sees King as a catalyst who defied the odds against making significant progress in a short period of time.

Thomas R. Peake

THE SPEECHES OF MALCOLM X

Author: Malcolm X (Malcolm Little, 1925-1965)
Type of work: Speeches
First published: Malcolm X Speaks, 1965; *Malcolm X on Afro-American History*,
1967, 1970 (expanded), 1990 (new ed.); *The Speeches of Malcolm X at Harvard*,
1968; *By Any Means Necessary: Speeches, Interviews, and a Letter by Malcolm X*,
1970; *The End of White World Supremacy: Four Speeches by Malcolm X*, 1971;
Malcolm X: The Last Speeches, 1989; *Malcolm X Talks to Young People: Speeches
in the United States, Britain, and Africa*, 1991

Malcolm X, by virtue of his charismatic personality and his dynamic speaking,
joined the small group of major black orators of the twentieth century that includes
Martin Luther King, Jr., Booker T. Washington, W. E. B. Du Bois, Marcus Garvey,
Thurgood Marshall, and A. Philip Randolph. He was different from the others in
several respects: He was not an educated person, he was not a representative of the
mainstream African American organizations, and he was not content to work within
the bounds of gradualism, amelioration, desegregation, and legislation. Although he
came from a rather orthodox Christian family background, he lived the life of the
streets and of crime. He became a convert to the Nation of Islam and was a minister
of that black American adaptation of the Islamic faith until he became disillusioned
with its leader, Elijah Muhammad. He later founded his own group, the Organization of Afro-American Unity (OAAU), which replaced his initial enterprise, the
Muslim Mosque, Inc., an umbrella group that envisioned black community development through social, economic, political, and religious cooperation. He was assassinated at the height of his influence, just as he was about to deliver another of his
fiery speeches, on February 21, 1965.

Malcolm's career as a speaker and leader was undoubtedly influenced by his father, who was an influential Baptist preacher in Omaha, Nebraska, where Malcolm
was born. The Reverend Earl Little was a tall black man, an elementary-school
dropout from Georgia who had married Louise Norton, a well-educated mulatto
from Grenada, in the West Indies. In Philadelphia, the Littles encountered both
the virulence of segregationist attitudes and the philosophy of Marcus Garvey, the
Jamaica-born founder of the Universal Negro Improvement Association. Garvey proposed a solution to the racial problem that existed in the United States: a return to
Africa and the establishment of black states with high self-esteem and enviable cultural achievements. Unfortunately, Garvey's efforts came to little end, and Garvey
lived his later life in exile in Jamaica.

The Reverend Earl Little's emotional preaching style, typical of black Baptists,
and his espousal of the Garvey doctrine of self-improvement and separatism certainly influenced the young Malcolm's later social and political agendas. Harassment
from white supremacist groups in both Wisconsin and Michigan hardened the attitudes of both father and son. After Malcolm's father was killed by a streetcar and his

mother was committed to a mental hospital, he was separated from his siblings and placed with foster parents. These were all wrenching experiences that may well have accounted for his subsequent antisocial, anti-Christian, antiwhite attitudes that were expounded in speech after speech. Although he liked English and history in school, he was seldom academically interested or successful. Although he was intent upon influencing the larger black population, he was never an able or fluent writer, and his knowledge of history—even of black and African history—was sketchy and approximate at best. His life experiences provided him with great enthusiasm for the correction of injustices and affronts, but his intellectual background was no match for that of most leaders of black groups.

After entering the hustling world of Roxbury, a Boston suburb, Malcolm moved to Harlem, where he commenced his encounter with the underworld, selling and using drugs, soliciting for prostitutes, selling bootleg liquor, and committing robbery. He returned to the Boston area and organized a robbery gang. In 1946, at the age of twenty-one, he was sent to Charlestown State Prison. It was there that he was introduced to the Black Muslim sect headed by Elijah Muhammad. He quickly became an outspoken advocate of its racist viewpoint, uncritically endorsing the view that "white devils" and the "white man's Christian world" were the source of all the problems of the black folk. After his release from prison, Malcolm soon became the most popular and notorious of the Black Muslim spokesmen. As assistant minister of a mosque in Detroit, Michigan, Malcolm increased its membership tremendously.

On March 24, 1961, Malcolm achieved some stature and publicity by giving a speech before the Harvard Law School Forum. This was at the beginning of a decade of civil unrest in the United States. The war in Vietnam divided the country politically, civil rights agitation disturbed the peace, and city after city burned in riots. Malcolm advocated revolution. He advocated a separate black state or states, though this was clearly a constitutional impossibility. He espoused black conversion to Islam, though not by mass migration to Islamic countries, where American blacks would be alien in culture, language, and social behavior. He predicted that Armageddon would see the white race extinguished and the black race resplendent and supreme. Further, he extolled Elijah Muhammad as "divinely taught and sent to us by God Himself," as the Black Muslims' "divine leader and teacher," and as savior of the twenty million African Americans. Finally, he maintained that the world was approaching its end and that the white world should repent for its treatment of African Americans.

The vision of this speech is clearly apocalyptic, yet the speaker proposes ameliorative or corrective steps that would take millennia to implement. As in most of his subsequent speeches, Malcolm ignores the fact that slavery was endemic to African societies—the European slave trade would have been impossible without African cooperation—and as widespread in Islamic nations as in Christian societies.

In his speech of November 10, 1962, at the King Solomon Baptist Church in Detroit (now generally called the Grass Roots Speech), Malcolm delivered one of his last statements before severing his connection to the Nation of Islam. He objected to the term "Negro" and reiterated that the common enemy of black people is the white man. He stressed that there is no such thing as a bloodless revolution. He denigrated Martin Luther King, Jr., and other desegregationists, gradualists, and members of the Southern Christian Leadership Conference as fallen idols, as failures, as persons being used against the black revolution. He concluded by suggesting that the national leaders of the black cause should be given awards for "the best supporting cast" for the status quo and white supremacy.

The speech represents a transition in Malcolm's thinking. Although there are occasional dutiful allusions to Elijah Muhammad, there is no explicit iteration of the Black Muslims' platform and demands. Malcolm identifies with the "field Negroes" rather than the "house Negroes" of America, and he stresses the difference between his violent, revolutionary program and that of the mainstream, acknowledged national leaders of the African American community. The speech is noteworthy for its rhetorical characteristics. There is extensive use of analogy (the Russian and French revolutions are compared to the one that he proposes); there are numerous stressed points; there are frequent metaphors ("He's a wolf—and you're sheep"); and there is effective use of triads (words, phrases, and clauses in groups of three). It is this repetition that suggests the influence of the Baptist preaching of Malcolm's father. Some examples of effective triads are these: "a desegregated theater, a desegregated park, and a desegregated public toilet"; "The black revolution is sweeping Asia, is sweeping Africa, is rearing its head in Latin America"; and "They control you, but they have never incited you or excited you. They control you, they contain you, they have kept you on the plantation."

"The Ballot or the Bullet," one of Malcolm's major addresses, was delivered in Cleveland, Ohio, on April 3, 1964, ten days after he broke with the Nation of Islam, primarily because he had become disillusioned with Elijah Muhammad for having committed non-Islamic sexual and personal acts. He had begun to enunciate the tenets of the Muslim Mosque, Inc., his new organization that was precursor to the OAAU. The speech was delivered at the Cory Methodist Church as part of a symposium, "The Negro Revolt: What Comes Next?," organized by the local chapter of the Congress of Racial Equality (CORE). The title of the speech was Malcolm's own.

The basic premise of the speech is that equal rights legislation, as propounded by President Lyndon B. Johnson, was unnecessary, since post-Civil War laws, if enforced, would suffice. As he says, "Civil rights, for those of us whose philosophy is black nationalism, means: 'Give it to us now. Don't wait for next year. Give it to us yesterday, and that's not fast enough.'" Later in the speech, he explains that black nationalism means simply that, with the vote, the black man should control the politics of his own community. That is, he no longer subscribes to the belief that some states should be handed over to black people as "homelands." He maintains some ambivalent positions. For example, he maintains that he does not believe in any kind of segregation, but that a school that is all black is not segregated, and he addresses the problems of "Negroes" though he considers the word "Negro" to be offensive. His economic philosophy can be summed up as small scale, involving ownership and operation of stores and businesses. His social philosophy is to forget about trying to join white social groups and to remove vices, alcoholism, drug addiction, and other evils that beset black communities. Clearly, these goals are not radically different from those long held by mainstream black associations. He maintains that black nationalism does not mean a threat to any existing organization, making an analogy between black nationalism and the Billy Graham crusades: Each merely wants to uplift. His message is not pacifist: "If it's necessary to form a black nationalist army, we'll form a black nationalist army. It'll be the ballot or the bullet. It'll be liberty or it'll be death." The paraphrase of Patrick Henry's famous speech cannot be missed.

Parallelisms, doubled elements, and triads are again used, and the speech has a literary tone to it, even though it is also vehement and hortatory. Malcolm asserts his authority on behalf of the African American cause, but he tends to reduce his credibility by conceding—in a moment of unguarded candor, perhaps—"I'm not a student of much of anything."

Malcolm was active as a speaker overseas as well as in the United States. In 1964 and 1965, he addressed student audiences in Ghana and in Great Britain. In Accra, Ghana, he described himself as a "victim of Americanism" rather than as an American. At the University of Oxford, he said that he supported "any means necessary to bring about freedom" (which he defined in his own way). At the London School of Economics, he expressed his belief that black people throughout the world would unite against "the common oppressor." He did not live to see the horrendous internecine oppression in the new African states, the abuse of human rights, and the replication of the worst examples of Western capitalist oppression.

During 1964 and 1965, it became apparent that Malcolm's break with the Nation of Islam was becoming fraught with dangers for him. He was a clear threat to the hegemony of Elijah Muhammad, who had never achieved any success as an orator and who had depended in great measure on the remarkable facility that Malcolm possessed at public discourse, whether to small groups or to large, enthusiastic, supportive, and encouraging audiences. Malcolm's message became more tempered. At a Harvard Law School Forum on December 16, 1964, he stressed his two pilgrimages to Mecca and his commitment to prayer, charity, fasting, and the brotherhood of all men, stressing that the OAAU was "a peaceful organization based on brotherhood." His anticapitalist position increasingly became democratic socialist. His religious position became more cooperative than exclusive, more accommodating than exclusive. Because of these changes, he thought it necessary to hold a series of three informational meetings at the Audubon Ballroom in Harlem on Sundays. The first was scheduled for January 24, 1965, the second a week later, and (because he had been invited to speak in Europe) the third for February 21. As he commenced this third speech, he was gunned down.

Malcolm's speech of January 24 is essentially an expository one. Its subject is African American history. In it, he acknowledges that the main thing that separates black people from other groups is that they know little of their past. He proposes that black unity is not racism and opposes Black History Week because it stresses black achievement in the West under white tutelage. He suggests that ancient black civilizations were dominant from Africa to the Middle East, India, and southern Europe and that black people excelled in mathematics, building, and music. The speech is loosely organized, uses many antiwhite epithets ("cracker," "Charlie," "big white ape," "Sam," "the man"), is prolix and repetitive, and shows little concern for history as a discipline based on facts rather than fictions, partial truths, and assertions. It is of interest, however, because it restates the basic beliefs underpinning Malcolm's philosophy and policies. In a way, it is a concise statement of his basic ideas. As did his previous speeches, it displays his penchant for triads, doubled elements, antitheses, and provocative and riveting statements.

Throughout his speeches, Malcolm stressed the advantages of education. His frequent allusions to black historians suggest his own feeling of inadequate education, especially in terms of black history. His knowledge of street life was firsthand, but his understanding of black sociology was more anecdotal than thorough. His knowledge of Islam and its history was far from expert.

Perhaps the greatest shortcoming in Malcolm's movement was the lack of a well-defined agenda. There have been many black messiahs in the United States, particularly in Harlem, where Sufi Abdul Hamid and Marcus Garvey promised the imminent arrival of the black millennium. Malcolm can be seen in that tradition. He articulated problems known to all and promised a route to the goal but disappeared before any change had been effected. He did manage to convince many that self-help, in the true American tradition, was the most feasible means to immediate improvement. He persuaded many that voting was a useful first step to greater self-esteem through self-government. His ideas were in constant flux, however, and the Malcolm X that one person remembers may well be quite different from the Malcolm X that another recalls.

Malcolm never engaged a ghost writer. He most frequently spoke extemporaneously. He spoke in the language of his people, with the gestures, rage, humor, and repetition of the traditional black preacher, and with the appearance of learning. He had immediate effects on his audiences. He drew from them thoughtful questions, which he answered with ease and with grace, though sometimes, if he sensed antagonism, with vitriol and insult. By almost universal consent, he was one of the most dynamic and rousing speakers of his age and cause. The large number of books and articles about him suggests that he will remain among the pantheon of black speakers.

Bibliography
Clarke, John Henrik, ed. *Malcolm X: The Man and His Times.* New York: Macmillan, 1969. Perhaps the most valuable collection of essays about Malcolm, including excerpts from his speeches and documents relating to his petition to the United Nations. The essayists tend to be less critical than adulatory, and many seem, in retrospect, to have been unjustifiably optimistic or convinced of Malcolm's significance in international affairs.

Davis, Thulani, ed. *Malcolm X: The Great Photographs.* New York: Stewart, Tabori, and Chang, 1993. More than one hundred duotone photographs by some of the world's principal photographers document Malcolm's major public appearances and speaking situations with visual force.

Frady, Marshall. "Reflections: The Children of Malcolm." *The New Yorker* 68 (October 12, 1992): 64+. An excellent biographical summary and interpretive essay that proposes that Malcolm's legacy is an awareness that his goal—a nation in which all races can coexist and progress—must be met.

Gallen, David, comp. *Malcolm A to X: The Man and His Ideas.* New York: Carroll & Graf, 1992. Excerpts from Malcolm's many speeches give a convenient overview of his philosophy as it impinges on a wide range of subjects, arranged alphabetically. Copiously illustrated.

Grimes, Nikki. *Malcolm X: A Force for Change.* New York: Ballantine, 1992. Rather elementary in its style, this is nevertheless a good introductory book. Tends to be rather uncritical.

Johnson, Timothy V. *Malcolm X: A Comprehensive Annotated Bibliography.* New York: Garland, 1986. Wide-ranging and balanced in its annotations, it covers books, journals, magazines, and alternative newspapers. The scope and comprehensiveness reveal the extent and intensity of the public debate about Malcolm and his messages.

Malcolm X, with the assistance of Alex Haley. *The Autobiography of Malcolm X.* New York: Grove Press, 1965. One of the major autobiographies by an African American. It is difficult to understand Malcolm's philosophy and speeches without having read this work. The literary touches are likely those of Alex Haley, but the substance is Malcolm's.

Wood, Joe, ed. *Malcolm X: In Our Own Image.* New York: St. Martin's Press, 1992. A collection of essays by fourteen African Americans that investigates the contribution of Malcolm to the black cause in the United States. Many of the contributors offer sober reassessments of Malcolm's role and achievements.

Marian B. McLeod

THE SPOOK WHO SAT BY THE DOOR

Author: Sam Greenlee (1930-　　)
Type of work: Novel
Type of plot: Social criticism
Time of plot: The 1960's
Locale: Chicago, Illinois; Washington, D.C.; New York City; and Langley, Virginia
First published: 1969

> *Principal characters:*
>   DAN "TURK" FREEMAN, the protagonist, an idealistic black man
>   who infiltrates the Central Intelligence Agency
>   PETE "DAWS" DAWSON, a friend from Freeman's youth, now a
>   Chicago police detective
>   JOY, Freeman's college sweetheart, now a buyer for a Chicago
>   department store
>   THE DAHOMEY QUEEN, Freeman's nickname for a Washington
>   prostitute in whom he tries to instill pride in her African roots

The Novel

Dan Freeman's elaborate plot against a racist society is set in motion by Senator Gilbert Hennington's willingness to do anything to win reelection. Concluding that he cannot win without the black vote, he decides to campaign for the integration of the Central Intelligence Agency (CIA), figuring that the CIA is vulnerable after the Bay of Pigs and U-2 disasters. This cynical maneuvering for public attention works, and Hennington is reelected.

Freeman is one of the twenty-three black men chosen for training, with the understanding that only one will complete the program. The CIA plans to make the training so difficult that no one will last. Freeman, the only candidate without a typical middle-class African American background, survives because disadvantage has given him the strength of will to prevail. His biggest test comes in the hand-to-hand combat sessions taught by the racist Calhoun, whom he defeats and disgraces. Hennington himself is indifferent to the fruits of his protest. He had won his election, and for another six years he was safe.

Having learned how to be a spy, Freeman employs these skills in the CIA not toward his country's enemies but against his employers, playing to their racist expectations and manipulating them. He is given a menial desk job at CIA headquarters in Langley, Virginia, as "top secret reproduction section chief," a job that simply entails operating a ditto machine. He is asked to give a tour to a Senate committee, including Hennington. After seemingly flattering Hennington, he is promoted to special assistant to the CIA director. His job was "to be black and conspicuous as the integrated Negro of the Central Intelligence Agency of the United States of America. As long as he was there, one of an officer corps of thousands, no one could accuse the CIA of not being integrated." Since this tokenism is his primary function, Freeman fails to receive another promotion over the next four years, but he takes advantage of his position to study guerrilla tactics in Algeria and other Third World countries and sees such warfare in action when he accompanies his boss, known only as "the general," on four trips to South Vietnam. Greenlee based Freeman's CIA experiences in part on his eight years as a U.S. Information Agency officer in Asia, Europe, and the Middle East.

Having learned all he needs, Freeman resigns after five years in the CIA and becomes a social worker in his old Chicago neighborhood for the South Side Youth Foundation, an organization run by white liberals. He concentrates on the most volatile of the street gangs, the Cobras, whose warlord he had been when he was a teenager known as Turk. Freeman masks his true intentions by convincing his boss that he is a hedonist motivated more by materialism than by idealism.

Believing that the Cobras hold potential for learning guerrilla tactics, Freeman studies them from a distance before getting their attention by coming onto their territory and effectively defending himself when attacked by their three leaders. He promises to train them to "mess with" white people. Freeman theorizes that although it ordinarily would take three to five years to build an underground fighting force, the Cobras have always been an underground organization. He expects them to form the core of a five-hundred member Chicago revolutionary group and hopes to recruit similar forces in other major cities, all the while pretending to be working to subdue the gangs. The Cobras camouflage their intentions by feigning having retreated into the passivity of heroin addiction.

The Cobras put Freeman's training into practice and equip themselves by robbing a bank and an armory. When a policeman kills a fifteen-year-old boy and civil unrest spreads, Freeman's troops slowly begin taking advantage of the situation. Soon, they blow up the mayor's office to emphasize their seriousness of purpose and sophistication of attack. Freeman identifies himself to the press as "Uncle Tom, the official spokesman for the Black Freedom Fighters of America." The attack then shifts to sniper shootings of police and soldiers, and units in twelve cities are ordered into action. After being betrayed by one of the women in his life, Freeman is confronted by Pete Dawson, a policeman and friend of his youth, and they fatally wound each other. Dying, Freeman knows that the revolutionary movement he set in motion will be successful without him.

The Characters

The Spook Who Sat by the Door is primarily a portrait of the complex personality of Dan Freeman, and his is the only fully developed character. A football star at Michigan State and a Korean War veteran, Freeman remains a product of the slums. During the CIA training, he sets himself defiantly apart from his fellow candidates, all bourgeois blacks: "Only Freeman was not middle class, and the others knew it. Even had he not dressed as he did, not used the speech patterns and mannerisms of the Chicago ghetto slums, they would have known."

Freeman's most significant skill is his chameleonlike ability to change his public persona to accomplish his purposes, becoming an unobtrusive middle-class African American while working for whites, Turk the warlord to gain the respect of the Cobras, and Uncle Tom the terrorist to frighten whites, all the while keeping his true identity to himself. His adoption of a down-home pose during the CIA training makes his black classmates consider him less of a threat to their plans for success. As for those judging the candidates, "Whitey will be more likely to ignore a nigger who approaches the stereotype than these others who think imitation the sincerest form of flattery." His method works, as the director of the training school tells the general: "I somehow forgot that the man existed. He has a way of fading into the background. You can't remember his face, or what he looks like, or what he has said, even minutes after you have spoken to him."

The real Freeman prides himself on his intelligence and sophistication, exulting, when on his own, in his taste in literature, music, art, and clothes. While working for the CIA, he escapes to New York occasionally, shedding his Tom disguise for the trappings of a hipster. He had pondered the danger of leading a double life and decided that "the strain of squaredom would have to be eased somehow from time to time." The novel's title underscores the double nature of Freeman's existence, since "spook" is both a racial epithet applied to African Americans and a slang term for spies. Undercover in several senses of the word, Freeman realizes that he must allow himself to be himself to protect his true sense of identity.

Nevertheless, Freeman allows no one to surmise what he really is, not even Joy, the college sweetheart he wants to marry. With her, he assumes the role of integration pioneer, sacrificing his integrity by performing menial tasks at the CIA for the advancement of his race. Joy refuses to marry him until he can promise her economic security, but he refuses to sell out to white expectations: "A showpiece spade is a showpiece spade, no matter how many times he gets his picture in the papers or how much bread he makes."

Freeman sees himself as a modern Prometheus, as both hero and martyr "who had stolen the secret of fire from Olympus by the Potomac and was teaching its use to his people. . . . How long before they chained him, to let the black and white vultures tear at his liver?" He must suffer before achieving his goal, primarily by living constantly in a mask. He recognizes the psychological risks of such a burden and strives to subdue delusions of being a black messiah. Summarizing his desire to avoid labels and stereotypes, to be himself, Freeman asks one of the Cobras, "Why can't I just be a man who wants to be free, who wants to walk tall and proud on his own turf as a black man?"

Greenlee could easily have made Freeman an omnipotent superhero, a black James Bond, but his protagonist is plagued by insecurities and doubts. He admits to a Cobra that he abhors the violence he plans to unleash. He feels guilt about wanting to use his friend Dawson to achieve his ends. He does not even enjoy deceiving the liberal whites for whom he works. Freeman worries about the stability of his identity during his CIA years: "Had his mask become him? . . . Had he really put them on, or had he been putting himself on for half a decade?"

The other characters are mostly two-dimensional. Dawson serves to create an almost equal antagonist for Freeman. Joy and the prostitute Freeman calls "the Dahomey queen" reveal his tender side. Greenlee gives the leaders of the Cobras— Do-Daddy Dean, Sugar Hips Scott, Stud Davis, and Pretty Willie—a few distinctive attributes to show that they have the potential to be more than gang members.

Themes and Meanings

As an attack on racism, *The Spook Who Sat by the Door* emphasizes, for the most part, the subtler forms of prejudice practiced by whites who falsely consider themselves enlightened and tolerant. The liberals at the South Side Youth Foundation are far more interested in the prestige of their work than in actually improving conditions in the slums. Instead of seeing concrete evidence of progress, they merely want to be told that their efforts are useful.

The general says that African Americans are incapable of "the highly specialized demands of intelligence work" because "a gap simply exists between the races which is a product of social rather than racial factors." He also claims that African Americans are too childlike to be effective spies. Greenlee clearly shows that the opposite is the case, since African Americans have traditionally played roles to survive in a society that expects certain behavior from them. Freeman's every action illustrates how he understands the demands of a life undercover far better than do his ostensible mentors.

Greenlee frequently expresses outrage at the consequences of racism. Freeman is constantly angered that the Cobras have not been allowed to develop their talents and intelligence. In the ghetto, Freeman sees "people born to the sun but forced to live in the sunless garbage heap of a sad, sunless, sick society." He does not think that his revolution will automatically improve matters and does not seriously consider overthrowing a racist society. He wants to force white leaders to quit playing international political games, such as the war in Vietnam, at its height when the novel appeared, and pay more serious attention to social problems such as racism. Freeman simply wants African Americans to be given the opportunity to share in the fruits of the American economic system.

Greenlee balances his overt anger with a satirical portrait of the foolishness of whites. He underscores their deficient sense of humanity by having them believe fully whatever computers tell them. African Americans make insufficient social progress in part because fickle whites are bored with civil rights. His supervisor at the youth foundation wants Freeman to succeed with the Cobras primarily so that the foundation will win a Ford Foundation grant. On the other hand, liberals want him to fail so that he will turn to them for help. When the revolution begins, white officials waste considerable energy trying to prove that Communists are behind it, since they believe that blacks are incapable of creating such an organized effort.

Freeman tells the Cobras, "The white man can handle a put-down, but a put-on hangs him up." Greenlee therefore also employs humorous ridicule in attacking racism. When Senator Hennington tells Freeman that he favors a national study of juvenile delinquency "among the culturally deprived," Freeman replies, "Excellent idea, Senator. We certainly need another study of that problem." When the general attempts to compliment blacks by praising their skill as athletes, Freeman observes, "we can sing and dance, too." He often insults whites in the guise of agreeing with them.

The Cobras stage their bank robbery disguised as whites. When the riots start, they kidnap the racist Colonel "Bull" Evans, paint him in blackface, and feed him LSD. When found, the colonel says he has met the "most wonderful niggers in the world."

Greenlee reserves ridicule as well for African Americans who strive for success by imitating whites. Carter Summerfield, Senator Hennington's adviser on black issues, is "a professional Negro" incapable of correcting white misconceptions. Freeman sneers at his black CIA competitors for many reasons, including the fact that nine of them were chosen to receive training because they were relatives of civil rights leaders or politicians. The most important questions they have for each other are what jobs their fathers hold, what fraternities they belonged to in college, and what kinds of cars they drive. They drop the names of "Great Negro Leaders" they have known and the brand names of expensive products they covet. Freeman saves some of his harshest vitriol for civil rights leaders: "They don't give a damn about any niggers except themselves and they don't really think of themselves as niggers."

He attempts to combat such superficial, self-serving progress by instilling pride in the Cobras in their black heritage, teaching them about African American writers and artists and about black jazz and blues musicians: "Somehow, they had attained a pride in themselves as human beings based on their contempt and hatred of the white man and stubborn pride in their toughness and defiance. Now he told them that theirs was a history and tradition of which they could be proud." More important, he teaches them that black people have a moral responsibility for one another.

Critical Context

The Spook Who Sat by the Door, appearing at the end of a decade in which Ian Fleming's James Bond novels were extremely popular, is on one level a parody of the spy genre, showing how easily an outsider can manipulate the espionage establishment when it thinks it is putting him in his place. Freeman's snobbish tastes in cars, clothes, and music recall those of Fleming's 007. More significant, however, Greenlee's novel grows out of the black fiction tradition of the 1960's, sharing the angry seriousness of James Baldwin and John A. Williams, the satirical thrust of Ishmael Reed, and the thriller elements of Chester Himes.

Greenlee's novel was published the same year as two other tales of black avengers with revolutionary intentions: Williams' *Sons of Darkness, Sons of Light* and Edwin Corley's *Siege*. All three books capture the black militant fervor of the period and represent a departure from the approach of a writer such as Baldwin, who had appealed in his fiction to whites, trying to touch their hearts and coax them into supporting social change. A writer such as Greenlee, on the other hand, makes it clear that African Americans must be the authors of their own liberation and must be willing to triumph by any means necessary.

The violent, militant tone of his book resulted in its being rejected by several American publishers before being accepted in England. Upon its American publication a few months after it appeared in England, its combination of action, humor, and political commitment helped it develop a following as a cult novel.

Bibliography

Burrell, Walter. "Rappin' with Sam Greenlee." *Black World* 20 (July, 1971): 42-47. In this interview, Greenlee explains how *The Spook Who Sat by the Door* is aimed not only at educated African Americans but also at ordinary black people who rarely read. He discusses why he made no concessions for white readers, arguing that fiction pleading for whites to understand blacks had not worked. Greenlee also offers his views on the treatment of African Americans in films and on television.

Gould, Mark. "Through the Front Door with Sam Greenlee." *Biography News* 1 (January, 1974): 39. In this interview, reprinted from *Chicago News*, Greenlee discusses the difficulty of getting *The Spook Who Sat by the Door* published and a similar difficulty facing the production of the 1973 film version, which he cowrote and coproduced. Greenlee answers charges that the film is irresponsible.

Schraufnagel, Noel. *From Apology to Protest: The Black American Novel.* Deland, Fla.: Everett/Edwards, 1973. In a short analysis, *The Spook Who Sat by the Door* is placed in the context of African American protest novels, showing the influence on Greenlee of the writings of Richard Wright and James Baldwin. Argues that the novel succeeds primarily as propaganda and that in spite of such flaws as authorial intrusions and caricatured characters it is an effective exposé of American racism.

Starke, Catherine Juanita. *Black Portraiture in American Fiction: Stock Characters, Archetypes, and Individuals.* New York: Basic Books, 1971. Includes a brief analysis of the character of Dan Freeman. Discusses how he contrasts with middle-class blacks. Explains how he is a double agent in several senses.

Van Deburg, William L. *New Day in Babylon: The Black Power Movement and American Culture, 1965-1975.* Chicago: University of Chicago Press, 1992. The anger of *The Spook Who Sat by the Door* is considered briefly in the context of the larger social, political, and cultural issues of its day.

Michael Adams

THE SPORT OF THE GODS

Author: Paul Laurence Dunbar (1872-1906)
Type of work: Novel
Type of plot: Naturalism
Time of plot: The last quarter of the nineteenth century
Locale: The South and New York City
First published: 1902

> *Principal characters:*
> BERRY HAMILTON, the loyal servant of the Oakley family
> FANNIE HAMILTON, the wife of Berry Hamilton and housekeeper
>   to the Oakleys
> JOE HAMILTON, the son of Berry and Fannie
> KITTY HAMILTON, the daughter of Berry and Fannie
> MAURICE OAKLEY, the wealthy white employer of Berry and
>   Fannie
> FRANCIS OAKLEY, the half-brother of Maurice Oakley, an artist
> LESLIE OAKLEY, the wife of Maurice Oakley
> MR. SKAGGS, a muck-raking journalist for the *New York Universe*
> HATTIE STERLING, a showgirl who becomes Joe Hamilton's
>   girlfriend

The Novel

The Sport of the Gods is Paul Laurence Dunbar's last novel and in many aspects his best. It is the story of the destruction of the Hamilton family, who fall from their status as a relatively wealthy African American family in an unnamed Southern city to imprisonment and degradation in New York City. The novel combines the conventions of naturalism and sentimental fiction to give the reader one of the first descriptions of the effect of city life on African Americans.

The first chapters of the novel describe the idyllic life of Berry and Fannie Hamilton and their two children, Joe and Kitty. Berry and Fannie are the trusted servants of the wealthy white Oakley family, former slaveowners who have managed to regain the wealth they lost during the Civil War. The happy arrangement is soon lost, however, when Francis Oakley, the dilettante artist half-brother of Maurice Oakley, reports the theft of nearly a thousand dollars from his room. Suspicion immediately falls on Berry, who has recently deposited a large sum of money in the bank. The narrator reports caustically the observations of many of the local whites, who believe that African Americans could only become wealthy through theft. After a speedy trial, Berry is sentenced to ten years of hard labor in prison.

This sudden overturning of the Southern romance plot is continued through the relocation of the three remaining family members, Fannie, Joe, and Kitty, to New York City. Hoping to escape the persecution associated with being related to a convict, they rent rooms in a boardinghouse and attempt to hide their family history. Things go well at first; Joe Hamilton finds employment in his trade as a barber, and Kitty Hamilton soon finds that her singing talents secure her a prominent role in a musical revue. Despite Fannie's protests against her children's habits, Joe and Kitty's first impression of New York is positive.

Things begin to fall apart, however, when Joe falls under the sway of the hedonistic crowd associated with the Banner Club, a biracial social club and watering hole. True to the tenets of naturalistic fiction, Joe soon changes from a competent young man to an alcohol-soaked parasite tutored by a character named "Sadness" Williams. He eventually begins living with an over-the-hill performer named Hattie Sterling. Even Fannie Hamilton begins to fall under the morally relativistic influence of the big city. She remarries without even informing Berry, and she watches in horror as Joe finally strangles Hattie during a fit of alcoholic rage.

The only positive outcome of the family's move to New York is their acquaintance with a white reporter, Mr. Skaggs, another frequenter of the Banner Club. He decides that he will research the decline of the family after Joe is sentenced to life in prison. He soon discovers that Berry was innocent and that there was no robbery. Francis Oakley had gambled away the money in an attempt to support his Parisian mistress, a fact covered up by the Oakley family. Mr. Skaggs publishes his findings in the *New York Universe*, and the subsequent furor leads to Berry's release from prison. Berry and Fannie eventually remarry, spending their last years back on the Oakley plantation, happy to escape from the horrors of the city.

The Characters

The characters of *The Sport of the Gods* are a mixture of stereotypes and innovative new characters. The Oakleys, the primary white characters in the text, are mostly stereotypical Southerners who value family name and image above all else. Maurice Oakley is somewhat unusual because he welcomes the Reconstruction period and sees it as an opportunity to recoup the wealth lost in the Civil War. His half-brother Francis is also the stereotypical dilettante Southern artist typical of post-Civil War fiction. His artistic talent is sacrificed in order to fulfill his sensual nature, and he spends his money on a Parisian mistress instead of his art.

The Hamilton family presents a more interesting group of characters. Berry Hamilton is the stereotypically loyal servant until he is accused of stealing money from his employers. He then begins to express some of the more radical sentiments concerning racial relations often found in African American novels of the 1930's and 1940's. Likewise, his passive nature is changed into an active one after he is released from prison. When he discovers that his wife has remarried during his incarceration, he decides that he will murder the second husband, an action that the old Berry would never have contemplated.

The Hamilton children also represent significant departures from the characters typically represented in turn-of-the-century novels. Joe Hamilton might be considered a stock character from a nineteenth century temperance story except for his gradual and detailed descent into alcoholism and murder. Joe's decline is based on both internal and external factors: His vanity and general weakness of temperament contribute to his problems. Kitty Hamilton becomes a hard-hearted performer after her move to the city. Beginning as a singer in a church choir, she soons turns her talents to the secular arena. Surprisingly, she is one of few characters who is neither ground down over the course of the novel nor punished for her material success.

The secondary characters show Dunbar at his best and demonstrate why the novel is generally thought to be his most promising work of fiction. "Sadness" Williams is a likable rogue who makes his living conning people out of alcohol and food. It is his role to initiate the unwary provincials into the fast ways of the big city. He drops his mask only when he contemplates the significance of Joe's murder of Hattie Sterling. Sadness concludes, after having seen Joe, that it would be better if Joe were sent to the electric chair. Mr. Skaggs, the reporter who discovers the truth concerning the alleged robbery, is another well-developed character. Skaggs will stop at nothing, including robbery, to get his story before the public. His interest in justice is based more on profitability than morality.

Themes and Meanings

The Sport of the Gods serves a double purpose in its treatment of its subject matter. First, it provides a naturalistic treatment of the line from William Shakespeare's *King Lear* (1605) that serves as a source for the paraphrased title: "As flies to wanton boys, are we to th' gods,/ They kill us for their sport." Second, the novel counters the popular romantic tradition of plantation fiction. Dunbar sets forth this purpose in the opening paragraph of the book, which places his text in an antagonistic relationship to the popular fiction of the day:

> Fiction has said so much in regret of the old days when there were plantations and overseers and master and slaves, that it was good to come upon such a household as Berry Hamilton's, if for no other reason than that it afforded a relief from the monotony of tiresome iteration.

Thus Dunbar's text opens a dialogue with the reader's expectations and immediately sets itself in opposition to the treatment given to African American characters by white writers.

Dunbar applies the techniques of naturalism to his treatment of the subject matter, but he places his text thoroughly in the American tradition of naturalism rather than in the European tradition. Here he differs from later African American writers such as novelist Richard Wright. Dunbar's style is both more sentimental and melodramatic, and it bears resemblance to the texts popular in the late nineteenth century. In particular, Dunbar includes the appealing temperance theme, a motif common in American writing from the 1830's onward. Joe Hamilton is a successful young man until he falls under the influence of alcohol, and he becomes so besotted that he kills his girlfriend in a fit of alcoholic rage. Dunbar also includes several digressive passages concerning the corrupting effects of the city, in this case New York. Yet he avoids lapsing into pastoral idealism by making the ending, which features a return to the countryside, an unhappy one.

Dunbar instead emphasizes the importance of fate, or at least some indifferent natural force, in the manipulation of his character's lives. As in much African American writing, the whites who control the unnamed Southern city in which the Hamiltons reside also act as a kind of uncontrollable natural force. Berry Hamilton, who has never transgressed against whites in his life, find himself defenseless when he is accused of stealing money from his employer's brother. The local African Americans appear to contribute to this fate by helping to ostracize the Hamilton family after Berry is sent to prison. Joe is denied a job at any of the black barbershops in the area, and the rest of the family is likewise denied employment by blacks and whites alike. Once the Hamiltons arrive in New York City, the importance of white society almost disappears until Berry Hamilton is rescued by Skaggs.

Finally, one of the subjects addressed in the text is the subject matter of popular fiction itself, particularly Southern plantation literature. Dunbar, as the first paragraph of the novel indicates, went to lengths to show an African American family who did not want slavery to return and who were not nostalgic about the good old days. Berry and Fannie prospered during Reconstruction and its aftermath by working conscientiously and saving their money. That their thrift draws the envy of both blacks and whites is one of the most significant points addressed in the early chapters of the novel. Though the Oakleys attempt to re-create the façade of plantation life and gracious living, Dunbar reveals it to be based on deception and prejudice. He adds one last twist to the master/slave dialectic at the end of the novel by having the Hamiltons return to their old home next to the Oakley mansion. The former masters have by now become totally dependent on their former servants. Maurice Oakley, driven mad from remorse, must be cared for by his wife and the Hamiltons. The final uncertainty rests in the question of the cause of Oakley's madness: Has he been driven insane because of what happened to Berry or by the shame of exposure?

Critical Context

As one of the first popular African American writers of fiction and poetry, Paul Laurence Dunbar necessarily found himself reliant upon the aid of white benefactors. His most influential literary friend, the novelist and editor William Dean Howells, helped to promote Dunbar's image as a humorist. Howells, the influential editor of *The Atlantic* magazine, was also more interested in Dunbar's poetry than his fiction. Early negative reaction to the novel thus resulted, in part, from audience expectations based on Dunbar's reputation as a poet and humorist.

The reference made by Dunbar in the opening paragraph of the work to plantation fiction alludes to the popularity of a number of writers such as the rabidly racist Thomas Dixon, author of the turn-of-the-century works *The Leopard's Spots* (1902) and *The Clansmen* (1905), the latter of which served as the source for the 1915 D. W. Griffith film *The Birth of a Nation*. Dixon's novels unvaryingly depict African Americans as pathological thieves, liars, and killers. Dunbar answers these charges by showing a prosperous family of African Americans who live a comfortable life even in the bitterly racist South of the time. The family's fall is caused not by their own deeds but by the prejudice of the ignorant whites who surround them.

The greatest significance of the novel rests in its strength of voice and its tone, which make it a pivotal text in the history of African American novels. In the first section of the book, Dunbar is outspoken in his indictment of Southern prejudice and oppression. The mask of the entertainer is dropped and is replaced, for at least a few moments, by the outspoken voice of indignation. This use of realism and naturalism helped to make possible the work of the Harlem Renaissance in the 1920's, particularly the fiction of Claude McKay and Langston Hughes. It likewise helped to lay the foundation for the great novels of city life written by Richard Wright in the 1940's and 1950's.

Bibliography
Best, Felton O. "Paul Laurence Dunbar's Protest Literature: The Final Years." *The Western Journal of Black Studies* 17 (Spring, 1993): 54-64. Argues that Dunbar's use of plantation settings was done to help counteract the plantation myth that was prevalent at the turn of the century. Also argues that Dunbar was more active in the protest movement than some critics have given him credit for being.
Candela, Gregory L. "We Wear the Mask: Irony in Dunbar's *The Sport of the Gods.*" *American Literature* 48 (1976): 60-72. An important reassessment of the novel, placing it in the tradition of protest literature. Candela argues that Dunbar's use of irony undercuts his occasional resort to stereotypes.
Gayle, Addison, Jr. *Oak and Ivy: A Biography of Paul Laurence Dunbar.* Garden City, N.Y.: Doubleday, 1971. A critical biography that deals equally with Dunbar's life and works. Gayle writes extensively of the tragic results of Dunbar's efforts to free his work from racial stereotypes while dealing with powerful white publishing firms.
Larson, Charles R. "The Novels of Paul Laurence Dunbar." *Phylon* 29 (Fall, 1968): 257-271. An essay that places all Dunbar's novels in a critical context. Places *The Sport of the Gods* in the category of protest novel.
Revell, Peter. *Paul Laurence Dunbar.* Boston: Twayne, 1979. Part of the Twayne series on American writers, this critical biography covers all Dunbar's poetic and fictional works. Revell emphasizes the naturalistic elements of Dunbar's fiction and discusses Dunbar's work in relation to French naturalism. Revell states that *The Sport of the Gods* is Dunbar's most successful novel and places it at the center of the African American tradition of novel writing.

Jeff Cupp

THE SPYGLASS TREE

Author: Albert Murray (1916-   )
Type of work: Novel
Type of plot: Psychological realism
Time of plot: The 1910's to the 1930's
Locale: Southern Alabama
First published: 1991

Principal characters:

SCOOTER, the otherwise unnamed narrator, a young African American boy who grows up in Mobile County, Alabama

LITTLE BUDDY MARSHALL, the narrator's best friend while growing up

LUZANA CHOLLY, a blues singer, master of the twelve-string guitar, and mentor to the two boys

LEXINE METCALF, a teacher at the Mobile County Training School

B. FRANKLIN FISHER, the head of the Mobile County Training School

T. JEROME JEFFERSON, Scooter's eccentric college roommate

GILES CUNNINGHAM, the owner of a group of jazz and blues clubs in the vicinity of the college attended by Scooter

HORTENSE HIGHTOWER, a jazz singer at Giles Cunningham's clubs

DUDLEY PHILPOT, a white businessman and owner of a check-cashing operation

The Novel

The Spyglass Tree is the story of a young African American who grows up in Gasoline Point, Mobile County, Alabama, and who attends a famous African American college, identifiable geographically as Tuskegee Institute (now Tuskegee University) in Tuskegee, Alabama. The story is a continuation of Murray's first novel, *Train Whistle Guitar* (1974), which follows Scooter from the ages of ten to fourteen. This novel is told in a series of flashbacks, dealing alternately with Scooter's days at the Mobile County Training Academy and at the university, ending with his full entry into the African American adult world after he spends a night riding shotgun as the bodyguard of Miss Hortense Hightower, a singer.

The early teen years of Scooter and Little Buddy Marshall are driven by their two ruling passions, blues and baseball. They are torn between the world of respectable people—the one that Scooter finds at school—and the unrespectable realm of bad men, exemplified by legendary local blues player Luzana Cholly, master of the twelve-string guitar. The two inseparable companions become distant, however, when Scooter is chosen as one of the "talented tenth" by his teacher, Miss Lexine Metcalf, at the Training Academy. With Scooter spending an increasing amount of time after hours at school, Little Buddy soon decides that he will take to the road in emulation of Luzana Cholly.

Scooter finds the distinction between the respectable and unrespectable worlds to be present at college as well. His eccentric roommate from Chicago, T. Jerome Jefferson, who is alternately known as Geronimo, Doctor Faustus, Snake, or Snake Doctor, embodies both worlds. Although his family was originally from Lowndes County, Alabama, Snake plans to spend two years studying at Tuskegee, after which he will transfer to an Ivy League or Big Ten university. His two-sided greeting card, or "reversible escutcheon," as he terms it, posted on the door of the dormitory room, illustrates the dual personalities of the occupants. "Atelier 359" is printed on both sides of the card. One side features a monk with a T square and the warning "CAUTION . . . work-in-progress." The other has a top-hatted satyr playing a trumpet and dancing on a keyboard; it says "WELCOME . . . mischief afoot."

The crisis of the plot occurs in the second half of the novel, entitled "The Briarpatch." Scooter is introduced to the briarpatch of race relations through his relationship with Hortense Hightower, a local jazz singer, dancer, and music aficionado. He spends many afternoons at Hortense's house listening to a collection of what seems to be every blues and jazz recording made. Hortense's employer, Giles Cunningham, is a successful African American businessman and one of the few locals who is willing to come into conflict with the white establishment. Giles antagonizes one white businessman, Dudley Philpot, when he cashes a check for a client and deprives Philpot of the customary "percentage" taken for check-cashing privileges. When Philpot threatens to run Giles out of town, Giles enlists the aid of Scooter, Giles's business associates, and three Thompson submachine guns that he keeps in a locked trunk in one of his clubs. The crisis is averted, however, when Giles is able to work out a deal with an influential white family, which in turn keeps Philpot from attempting any violent acts. Scooter's reward for riding shotgun with Hortense is a bass fiddle that he takes back to room 359, a place that has by now become his own personal spyglass tree.

The Characters

Scooter as a narrator serves two functions in the plot. At one level, he is the older narrator who has escaped from the briarpatch to become one of those who are qualifying instead of just signifying, to paraphrase the character Dewitt Dawkins. Thus Scooter as narrator brings a sophisticated understanding to the plot as well as a perspective on the significance of the events that occur. Secondarily, Scooter is the teenager and young man who manages, unlike many others, to avoid all the hazards that await an African American male growing up in the South in the 1930's. Scooter exhibits this double perspective through his fascination and interest not just in the intellectual life, but also in the active popular culture, of Gasoline Point, consisting mainly of blues, baseball, and nicknames.

The young Scooter is chosen by the teachers at Mobile County Training Academy as one of the academically talented elite. While he is going through the transition from adolescence to adulthood, he is aided by a wide-reaching network of supportive adults in Gasoline Point. Miss Tee, who is revealed to be Scooter's biological mother, aids him in his education by making him promise to fulfill his potential. Scooter's adoptive parents also urge him to become somebody "worthwhile." Even Luzana Cholly, the itinerant blues musician, makes Scooter promise not to follow in his tracks, riding the rails from town to town, but to place all of his attention on his education.

Lexine Metcalf, the teacher given credit for discovering Scooter's talent, and B. Franklin Fisher, the principal of Mobile County Training Academy, are also representative of the adults who help Scooter to overcome the obstacles that would otherwise have prevented him from achieving academic success. These are not just stereotypical heroic educators; they are reasonably well-developed characters with idiosyncrasies of their own and a not unreasonable pride in the achievements of their students. They each give Scooter a present to take with him to college, as does Slick McGinnis, the sophisticated lady who initiates Scooter into the adult sexual world. Through each of these characters, Scooter gains some knowledge of the world outside Gasoline Point. Unlike his friend Little Buddy Marshall, he is able to escape all the traps, as Slick calls them, that wait for the talented but unwary.

At college, these two different character types merge to help mold a talented but adult Scooter. His roommate for the first two years, T. Jerome Jefferson, combines the traits of the juke joint blues players with the intellectual abstractions of the Mobile County educators. Jefferson, who intends to study architecture at a nationally prominent university, is a phenomenal student who also gains a reputation for his sexual exploits. Scooter nicknames him Dr. Faustus to reflect what he sees as Jefferson's flexible moral standards and unnatural ambition. Jefferson also becomes known as Snake and Snake Doctor, all elaborate puns on his mental and physical capabilities.

The two most important characters outside the university community in Tuskegee are Hortense Hightower and Giles Cunningham. Both are prospering in spite of the hostile surroundings in Macon County and rural Alabama, primarily because of their strength of character. Hortense, a jazz singer, is known to the band as "Boss Lady," and she is able to take control of any situation with little apparent effort. Giles is definitely the male counterpart of Hortense. His successful group of clubs is guarded with ferocity and cunning. Scooter is highly impressed by Giles when, during a conflict with businessman and stereotypical white Southerner Dudley Philpot, Giles shows Scooter a closet full of various weaponry, including three Thompson submachine guns.

Themes and Meanings

Like the jazz and blues that are among the major subjects of the novel, *The Spyglass Tree* revolves around the issues of discourse, expression, and practice. The style of the novel is based on the endless improvisations of African American music and on the interplay and conflict between different orders of verbal codes. An equal, and potentially more violent, conflict results from the differing methods of cultural practice that accompany these modes of discourse.

The most important of these styles of discourse are "signifying" and "woofing," both of which are practiced in Gasoline Point and Tuskegee. Signifying, or verbal gamesmanship, was introduced as a literary term by the African American critic Henry Louis Gates, Jr. In the novel, signifying is used by characters in a usually humorous attempt at one-upmanship. The barbershop is the most common place to encounter signifying, as in the following lecture given by Fred Douglass Whatley, better known as Deke Whatley, on the importance of playing politics properly:

> That's all it is. Everybody getting their little taste and that other fellow getting his little taste, too. That's what the king and them aristocrats forgot and that's how come so many of them wound up losing their hat, ass, and gas mask. You don't have to have no Ph.D. to dig that. Me, all I ever had was a little old country RFD [Rural Free Delivery; a mailbox address] myself, and I damn sure know it.

Deke's signifying on politics sets up the conflict not only between black and white cultures but also between the different varieties of discourse practiced within the African American community itself. Deke represents those who are not trained in academic discourse but believe that their mode of understanding is not inferior to that of the professors at the university. His commentary is in some ways analogous to the blues, a form invented by the African American working class. Deke's commentary, however, also reminds Scooter of something that he learned from Dewitt Dawkins, baseball umpire extraordinaire, about the dangers of relying too much on rhetoric and not enough on practice. Dewitt comments, with some irony, that there were already too many people signifying and not enough qualifying.

A more extreme example of conflict of discourse takes place between Scooter and some local gamblers in Tuskegee when he stumbles upon a craps game. As Scooter describes it, when one citizen begins "woofing," or insulting him, he, who is becoming a master of all discourses, is able to reply in kind, much to the astonishment of his interlocutor:

> I said, Sounds to me like somebody is just about to let his big loud snaggle mouth get his bony ass kicked raw. . . . I said, If you looking for somebody to cut you a new asshole, I'm just the son-of-a-bitch to oblige you.
> That was when he seemed to decide that moral outrage was the better part of valor. Hey, y'all hear this, y'all heard him, supposed to be some kind of high-class college boy and listen what kind of language he using.

Scooter relies on the shock value of the discourse to extricate himself from the situation, and the return "woofing" has the desired effect. The idea of a university student using such morally reprehensible language gives both of the characters an opportunity to escape but maintain their honor.

The last of the conflicts between modes of discourse and practice comes when Giles Cunningham, owner of several jazz clubs, infringes upon the business practices of local white businessman Dudley Philpot. Philpot approaches Cunningham with some woofing of his own and tells him, in so many words, that he has twenty-four hours to get out of the county. Giles, who refuses to participate in such games, replies by sending examples of his impressive array of weaponry to each of his clubs. A last-minute truce arranged by Giles and an influential white friend helps to avert exposure in one last form of discourse, the white newspaper headline. In an example of signifying of his own, Scooter imagines a headline similar to the mock headlines featured in many of Richard Wright's works: "ALABAMIANS MOWED DOWN IN WILD TOMMY GUN MASSACRE BY CRAZED, RAMPAGING BLACK RENEGADES."

Critical Context

Albert Murray, a longtime resident of Harlem, first became known as a music scholar and essayist before he began writing novels. His interest in blues, jazz, and African American popular culture combines with his erudite sense of literary and intellectual history in his two novels *Train Whistle Guitar* and *The Spyglass Tree*. In one review of *The Spyglass Tree*, musician Duke Ellington referred to Murray as "the unsquarest person I know."

Murray's views on African American culture first became widely known when a collection of his essays from the 1960's, *The Omni-Americans: New Perspectives on Black Experience and American Culture* (1970), was published. He argued that writers, African Americans among them, who pictured African American culture primarily from a sociological point of view were ignoring the strength and vibrancy of the culture, particularly its musical and oral forms. It is these oral and musical traditions that Murray depicts through his character Scooter, a semi-autobiographical figure. Scooter speaks of the heroes of his adolescence as members of an oppositional culture: Luzana Cholly, a hard-living, twelve-string guitarist; Gator Gus, the original free agent baseball pitcher who would change teams between games; and the slaves who helped to organize and maintain the underground railroad.

Even Murray's description of his alma mater, Tuskegee Institute, differs from that given by his close friend and classmate Ralph Ellison. Ellison, in *Invisible Man* (1952), presented a now-famous scathing description of Tuskegee as a repressive institution run by a Machiavellian Uncle Tom administrator, funded by guilt-ridden white liberals who were so emotionally disturbed that they could not face the realities of life in the South. Murray, on the other hand, presents Tuskegee as a place where young African Americans could receive the academic and social training they needed to succeed beyond the Jim Crow world of the South. The Tuskegee section of the novel is called "The Briarpatch," and Murray's sentiments match those of Uncle Remus' famous rabbit: It may look bad from the outside, but it is home for those who are accustomed to its geography.

Bibliography

Gates, Henry Louis, Jr. *The Signifying Monkey: A Theory of Afro-American Literary*

Criticism. New York: Oxford University Press, 1988. Contains detailed descriptions of Gates's concept of "signifying," using three novels and several slave narratives to provide examples.

Jones, Malcolm, Jr. "An Old Grad Aces the Course." *Newsweek* 118 (December 9, 1991): 71. A positive review of the novel, emphasizing the second half of the book. The reviewer concludes that Scooter is on his way to becoming the wise man who wrote the novel.

Karrer, Wolfgang. "The Novel as Blues: Albert Murray's *Train Whistle Guitar.*" In *The Afro-American Novel Since 1960: A Collection of Critical Essays*, edited by Peter Bruck and Wolfgang Karrer. Amsterdam: B. R. Grüner, 1982. A complete survey of the influence of the blues on the prequel to *The Spyglass Tree.* Karrer concludes that Murray's views are too "middle class" to do justice to the blues tradition.

Mercier, Vivian. "Gasoline Point Blues." *Saturday Review/World* 1 (May 4, 1974): 51. A negative review of the novel, comparing the author Murray to Uncle Tom, the fictional character from Harriet Beecher Stowe's *Uncle Tom's Cabin: Or, Life Among the Lowly* (1852).

Schiff, David. "Blues and the Concrete Truth." *The New Republic* 206 (February 3, 1992): 39-41. An extended positive review of the novel, presenting an overview of Murray's career along with a review of the novel. Schiff places Murray in the context of the debate over African American art forms since the 1960's and outlines theories of the roles of blues and jazz music in American and African American culture. He concludes with a comparison of Murray's description of Tuskegee Institute to that of Murray's friend and classmate Ralph Ellison.

Jeff Cupp

STARS IN MY POCKET LIKE GRAINS OF SAND

Author: Samuel R. Delany (1942-   )
Type of work: Novel
Type of plot: Science fiction
Time of plot: The distant future
Locale: The planets Rhyonon and Velm
First published: 1984

> *Principal characters:*
> RAT KORGA, the only survivor of the destruction of the planet
>   Rhyonon
> MARQ DYETH, an industrial diplomat who becomes involved in a
>   homosexual relationship with Korga

The Novel

Stars in My Pocket Like Grains of Sand traces the lives of two characters born on planets light-years apart but drawn together by forces beyond their control. The intersection of their lives and the lives of those with whom they interact forms the central thrust of the novel.

The novel opens on Rhyonon, where Rat Korga, a social and sexual misfit, has undergone Radical Anxiety Termination (RAT) and been placed in institutional slavery. For years, Rat Korga labors in menial jobs, demeaned by employees of the organization that owns him. Sold illegally into personal slavery, Korga is captured and returned to what would have been a life of unremitting manual toil had not Rhyonon been completely destroyed, perhaps by the Xlv, an alien race with whom humankind has yet to establish any communication.

Rat Korga's rescue by the Web, an intergalactic organization, and his return to higher cognition through the use of the rings of Vondramach Okk seem to fit some larger pattern. The wealth of Dyethshome, the huge ancestral residence of the Dyeth family, is owed in large part to the service of Marq's ancestor Mother Dyeth to Vondramach Okk, a ruler of many worlds, including Velm. There is a sense of appropriateness, then, when Korga appears wearing these rings at Dyethshome as part of a new group of students who regularly engage in research at that historic landmark. Immediately, Marq Dyeth is drawn to Korga; the Web's determination of their erotic compatibility is accurate. A willing student ready to be introduced to his new world, Korga carries with him an aura of mystery and reserve. The brief stay on Velm presents Korga and the reader with an introduction to an alien culture.

Velm is home to both humans and evelm, an indigenous race. The evelm, six-legged and multitongued creatures bearing vestigial wings, have established an uneasy relationship with humans. The southern sectors of Velm are known for the positive social climate that has developed between evelm and humans; the north has only recently legalized sexual acts between humans and evelm. The Dyeth family has maintained one of the more progressive interspecies relationships, its family, or "stream," being made up of both humans and evelm. Marq himself has both human and evelm siblings and parents. Rat Korga is introduced to this extended family and takes his first steps at understanding this complex fusion of human and evelm culture.

Korga is introduced as well to a new world of sexuality on Velm. Both he and Marq Dyeth appear to have finally achieved emotional and sexual fulfillment together. Yet normal sexuality is not shown as an exclusive relationship between two individuals. The cultural complexity of sexuality on Velm is demonstrated in the sexual "run" through which Marq Dyeth takes Rat Korga. There, both humans and evelm may engage in various combinations of sexual activity. Separate runs exist to fulfill different sexual interests, and any erotic combination is possible, including heterosexual or homosexual encounters within one species or between humans and evelm partners.

Another important event in Rat Korga's cultural education takes place when Dyeth suggests that Korga might enjoy taking part in a dragon hunt, a hunt that Korga and the reader expect will end with the death of the dragon prey. Actually, the hunt is conducted with radar-guided bows, but rather than killing the beasts, hitting the dragon allows one to share consciousness with the creature for a brief moment. Both characters succeed at the hunt, sharing their experiences later in songs, the traditional cultural conclusion to this activity. News, however, of Rat Korga's presence in the hunting grounds draws a large crowd of people intent on speaking with or touching the sole survivor of Rhyonon.

The evening of the dragon hunt, as Rat Korga and Marq Dyeth attend a formal dinner party at Dyethshome, a huge crowd begins to grow outside. Korga's presence seems to be exerting a mysterious force, drawing thousands of curious people to see him. Finally, because the Dyeth family fears that the steadily increasing crowd may become a danger to itself, Marq Dyeth and Rat Korga project their images to the crowd and ask them to return to their homes. Afterward, representatives of the Web take Korga away; spaceships of the Xlv (possibly drawn by Korga) are circling Velm, perhaps intending to destroy it. Dyeth is emotionally devastated by the loss of Korga, about whose future the Web has chosen not to communicate. The events in the novel do not achieve closure, as the novel is only half of what Delany refers to as a "science-fiction diptych" to be concluded in the projected *The Splendor and Misery of Bodies, of Cities.*

The Characters

Rat Korga, the only survivor of the destruction of the planet Rhyonon, is an individual Delany first empties of character, then shrouds in mystery. While a teenager, Korga chose to undergo Radical Anxiety Termination (RAT), an operation that destroys the brain cells that produce violence and antisocial behavior, rendering him incapable of anger and destructive emotion. Korga, now called Rat because of this surgical procedure, has become a slave of the RAT Institute, for which he must work in a series of unskilled jobs, directed by abusive supervisors. After years of slave labor, including an illegal sale to an individual who sexually abuses him, Korga is the sole survivor after a fireball hits the planet. Delany uses a third-person point of view in the opening section of the novel to help portray Rat Korga as a dehumanized slave, a subhuman owned and used by others. Readers enter his mind only briefly, adding to the mystery of his character.

Eventually discovered by relief members of the Web, an intergalactic organization dedicated to maintaining a communications network among the six thousand inhabited worlds, Korga is healed of his physical wounds and fitted with special rings that reintegrate much of the cranial short circuiting that RAT effected. Now capable of communication and sophisticated social interaction, Korga seeks a new world to replace Rhyonon, the home he never really understood. Korga is brought by the Web to the planet Velm, where he is introduced to Marq Dyeth, an individual whom the Web has identified as his perfect erotic object. Korga and Marq Dyeth begin a homosexual relationship almost immediately. When Velm is in danger of being destroyed, perhaps by the alien race Xlv, the Web chooses to remove Korga from the planet.

Delany contrasts the mysterious Korga with the other main character, Marq Dyeth, an industrial diplomat, through chapters using a first-person point of view. Unlike the introverted and enigmatic Korga, Dyeth is drawn as a culturally sensitive and open individual. A member of the historically powerful Dyeth family, he travels between worlds easing the difficulty of trade between various cultures and planets. While on a trade mission, he is contacted by the Web and told of the discovery of Rat Korga amid the charred ruins of Rhyonon. The Web intends for them to meet, · indicating that the high level of sexual compatibility between them should make their relationship mutually rewarding. Upon his return to his home planet Velm, Dyeth is united with Rat Korga at Dyethshome, the huge ancestral residence of the Dyeth family. While at Dyethshome, Dyeth attempts to introduce Korga to the culture of Velm, providing him with a new world to replace the one he has lost. Together, they discover their erotic compatibility, engage in a traditional Velmian dragon hunt, and take part in a large formal dinner at Dyethshome. Inexplicably, large crowds begin to gather in order to view the survivor of the destroyed planet, first in the urban complex of Morgre, then inside the dragon hunting ground, and finally around Dyethshome. The crowds appear to be drawn by some compulsion to come in contact with Korga. When Korga is spirited away from the planet by the Web, Dyeth is left brokenhearted. Critics anticipated that the mystery of Korga's destiny would be revealed in the novel's sequel.

Themes and Meanings

In Marq Dyeth, Delany creates an open and forthright character to contrast with the enigmatic Rat Korga. Dyeth's education, privileged background, and nurturing family life serve as a foil to the ill-educated, abandoned social misfit Rat Korga. Even physically, the two are at odds: Dyeth is short and clean-favored; Korga is well over seven feet tall and disfigured. Perhaps most significant, Dyeth's successful career is based on his understanding not only of his home world but also of the myriad cultures of other planets, while Korga has never understood his home world and knows virtually nothing about any other. That these opposites are still strongly attracted to each other underscores Delany's cross-cultural and cross-racial themes.

Korga's life on Rhyonon has been one of institutional and personal servitude and exploitation. Misled by the RAT Institute to believe that he would be happy after undergoing the surgical procedure, Korga loses his freedom to an institution that strips away his dignity and profits from his mistreatment. As if his economic exploitation were not bad enough, Korga is illegally purchased by a woman—on Rhyonon only institutions can legally own slaves—and experiences sexual exploitation. Required to fulfill his new owner's erotic desires, the homosexually oriented Korga is obliged to imagine his female owner a man in order to perform sexually. Later, she sadistically abuses him for her own sexual satisfaction. These predestruction scenes on Rhyonon comment pointedly on the institution of slavery, reinforcing Delany's position that slave systems abuse the individual economically and sexually.

Rat Korga's relationship with Marq Dyeth contrasts with the social and sexual slavery on Rhyonon. The Web's determination that each is the "perfect erotic object" of the other is validated by the intense physical relationship they establish when they meet on Velm. Unlike the backward sexual restrictions on Rhyonon, where both homosexual relationships between those younger than twenty-seven and any sexual relationship between those of varying heights are proscribed, custom on Velm promotes a relaxed sexual atmosphere where erotic encounters between humans and evelm are culturally sanctioned. The capacity to see "the other" as erotic object is shown as a cornerstone for healthy individual relationships, fostering cross-cultural and cross-species understanding. Delany's sexually repressed Rhyonon may correspond to Earth, where gay and interracial relationships continue to face legal and social obstacles.

Delany has acquired a reputation for writing difficult books, and *Stars in My Pocket Like Grains of Sand* is no exception. Some critics suggest that Delany writes "quantum fiction," reflecting the radical uncertainty of quantum physics in his worldview and fictive discourse. Certainly, the choices Delany makes in providing the reader with cultural background information increase the difficulty. Midway through the novel, for example, Delany explains the rules governing his characters' pronoun usage. Intelligent creatures are referred to as "she," no matter the gender, and those for whom there is sexual interest as "he." Obviously, the novel heightens some confusions, with male characters drawn to each other referring to themselves and others as "she," then "he." Nevertheless, this complexity yields rewards, as it allows Delany latitude to investigate not only issues of sexuality and gender but also issues of language itself.

The nature of science fiction as a vehicle to explore the here and now in the guise of the distant in time and space is amply rewarded in the novel. The worlds Delany creates allow him to observe and comment on human diversity and the difficulty of cross-cultural communication. In addition to an analysis of power politics and the control of information, the novel presents a futuristic critique of slavery and its economic and sexual implications. Issues of gender, sexuality, and culture are presented in a way that allows readers to apprehend Delany's sometimes-controversial positions without the confusion and out-of-hand rejection that individuals with twentieth century expectations and assumptions might bring to the consideration of those issues.

Critical Context

Long awaited, *Stars in My Pocket Like Grains of Sand* had been drafted in 1979 and expected for publication in 1981 or 1982. The novel was enthusiastically received by critics when it was first published in December, 1984. The book's publication signaled a return to science fiction for Delany, who had previously published a series of fantasy novels. Delaney was recognized early as a talented writer, and two of his early novels, *Babel-17* (1966) and *The Einstein Intersection* (1967), won Nebula Awards while Delany was still in his mid-twenties. Delany's reputation as a serious novelist has continued to grow, not only in the United States and England but also on the European continent, where he has won the praise of critics and fellow artists, among them Umberto Eco.

Delany has repeatedly acknowledged his interest in issues of gay, women's, and civil rights. *Stars in My Pocket Like Grains of Sand* reflects these interests and extends them into a fictive future world. Delany's investigation of institutional slavery and cross-racial barriers to communication reveals his intention to translate many of the issues of the present-day African American experience to a future universe. No doubt the completion of his science-fiction diptych will occasion even greater critical study of his novels.

Bibliography

Bartter, Martha A. "The (Science Fiction) Reader and the Quantum Paradigm: Problems in Delany's *Stars in My Pocket Like Grains of Sand.*" *Science-Fiction Studies* 17 (November, 1990): 325-340. Suggests that Delany's fiction reflects a worldview representative of quantum physics, as opposed to Newtonian or Einsteinian physics. Characters in his novel experience quantum leaps in understanding, The uncertainty that describes states in quantum physics effectively describes the reader's relationship with the novel.

Delany, Samuel. *The Motion of Light in Water: Sex and Science Fiction Writing in the East Village, 1957-1965.* New York: William Morrow, 1988. Describes Delany's early experiences as a science-fiction writer and provides some autobiographical background useful in understanding the themes of his fiction.

Fox, Robert Elliot. *Conscientious Sorcerers: The Black Postmodernist Fiction of Le-Roi Jones/Amiri Baraka, Ishmael Reed, and Samuel R. Delany.* New York: Greenwood Press, 1987. Discusses *Stars in My Pocket Like Grains of Sand* as a postmodern text, connecting Delany's vision with the work of Amiri Baraka and Ishmael Reed. Science fiction becomes a method by which the concept of otherness can be extended and investigated in a "fantastic" future. Delany's novel posits the belief that only through physical desire can the possibility for understanding "the other" take place.

Peplow, Michael W., and Robert S. Bravard. *Samuel R. Delany: A Primary and Secondary Bibliography*. Boston: G. K. Hall, 1980. Provides a brief biography of Delany, establishing three periods in his literary career. Thorough annotated bibliographies list Delany's fiction and nonfiction and critical studies of his work from 1962 to 1979.

Weedman, Jane. *Samuel R. Delany*. Mercer Island, Wash.: Starmont House, 1982. Adapted from Weedman's doctoral dissertation. Discusses Delany's work through the novel *Dhalgren* (1975), emphasizing biographical and social elements in his fiction that continued to appear in later works. Includes bibliographies of Delany's fiction and of works about Delany.

Kenneth B. Grant

THE STORIES OF TONI CADE BAMBARA

Author: Toni Cade Bambara (1939-　)
Type of work: Short stories
First published: Gorilla, My Love, 1972; *The Sea Birds Are Still Alive,* 1977

Toni Cade Bambara was one of the first writers to approach the search for black identity from a feminist perspective. In her fiction, as in the anthologies she has edited, Bambara explores the world of black women, encouraging them to defeat sexism and social injustice through the exertion of their own powerful wills within a larger community.

While she was still in elementary school in New York City, Bambara was already writing stories, skits, and plays. As a student at Queens College in New York, she essayed everything from novels to film scripts. After graduation in 1959, Bambara pursued various interests, studying theater in Florence and Paris, holding various positions in areas of social work and community service, and, after receiving her master's degree in 1964 from the City University of New York, teaching on the college level.

Throughout those years, Bambara also continued to write, producing and publishing many of the stories later collected in *Gorilla, My Love.* Bambara describes the works in this collection as "on-the-block, in-the-neighborhood, back-glance pieces," which she says were inspired by a specific concern, the need to "insure space for our children." What Bambara means by space, of course, is much more than playgrounds, which in high-rise ghettos have disappeared or turned into no-man's-lands; she means also room for the spirit, room for children to dream and, most important, to achieve the sense of self-worth that will enable them to realize those dreams.

In these early stories, Bambara's abiding interest in black women is already evident. Typically, her protagonist is a young girl who lives in the ghetto, and the barricades to her full development have been erected not only by a white-ruled establishment but also by the black males within her own society. For example, "Sweet Town" (1959), the first story of this collection to have been published, dramatizes the disillusionment of the narrator, Kit, who in her fifteenth spring had been swept away by a Dionysian ecstasy, diagnosed by her mother as simply "sex." With her equally mad companions, the handsome B. J. and his friend Eddie, Kit races through the summer, unaware that as a female she is not a full member of their little group. She participates fully in their dreams of going to California. Then B. J. awakens Kit, literally and symbolically, to tell her goodbye. B. J. and Eddie are going west; Kit will be left behind. At this point, she can find no consolation in knowing that she is intellectually superior to most of her friends, including these boys, or even in looking forward to college. She feels that she has been betrayed, as women are so often betrayed by the men who enjoy them and abandon them.

Betrayal is also the theme of another early story, "The Hammer Man" (1966). Again the narrator is a young black girl, and again the situation involves her involvement with a boy. From the first line of the story, in which the narrator expresses her happiness about his fall from the roof, one might think that she hates Manny, who, as she says repeatedly, is crazy. Yet her fights with him are clearly just a part of her tomboy existence, a kind of life that is far more interesting than the girlish conduct her mother keeps urging upon her. Her real admiration for Manny becomes evident when she describes his skill with a basketball. Then, when the police interrupt his play and insult him, she defends Manny, all the while expecting him to bring out his hammer and fight, undoubtedly getting them both shot. After a brief resistance, however, Manny proves to be docile, and he permits the policemen to haul him away. Later, the narrator hears that he is in a mental institution, but she never sees him again. Thus, the boy who had almost mythical stature in his neighborhood has been first emasculated in her presence, then imprisoned. If Manny has been destroyed by white society, however, the narrator has been just as surely betrayed by her own society, which finally has confined her within its narrow definition of what a woman should be. She has given up her struggle for independence, discarded her blue jeans for dresses, and set her mind on an upcoming fashion show.

The adult world's offenses against its children may be sins not of commission but of omission. In "Happy Birthday" (1969), no one intends to mistreat the orphan girl, Ollie. It simply happens that her birthday falls on a summer day when her usual haunts are deserted and her adult friends away or too busy to talk to her. The two authority figures who might have been expected to take an interest in her both fail her. Her grandfather has passed out, and she knows that he will be drunk for days, while the minister, who hates children, chases her away from the church. Even Miss Hazel dismisses Ollie's unhappiness, shutting out the child's howls in order to hear her television.

The title story of Bambara's volume, "Gorilla, My Love" (1971), illustrates the fact that adults often underestimate a child's capacity for moral outrage. Instead of the film that he has advertised on his marquee, the manager of a theater shows a religious film. When the children whom he has cheated protest, he threatens them; when they demand their money back, he raises the sound level to drown out their voices. Yet he has not reckoned with the narrator, young Hazel. She may not get her refund, but she does set a fire that causes the theater to close down for a week. As Hazel says, she has been taught to believe that a person's word should mean something.

Although Hazel does avenge herself on the theater manager, however, she can do nothing when her beloved uncle breaks his word to her. Unfortunately, she has taken seriously his promise to marry her when she grows up, and when he announces that he is in love with another woman, Hazel can only interpret his action as a betrayal. She is not deceived by the specious argument with which the adults attempt to placate her—that because he is no longer "Hunca Bubba" but "Jefferson Winston Vale," her uncle is not the person who made the promise. To Hazel, this proves that adults are liars.

In part, it is their very howls of anguish and anger that makes Bambara's girl children so appealing. Unlike male characters such as Manny, they argue and protest. Moreover, while, like the protagonist in "The Hammer Man," some of these very young women eventually submit to their mothers and to society, it is obvious that others, such as Hazel, will always maintain their independence. Of course, Hazel is lucky in having a role model such as her mother, who is the terror of P.S. 186 when she walks in "with her hat pulled down bad and that Persian lamb coat draped back over one hip." It is such strong black women that Bambara offers as role models for the young people who may be reading her stories. Though they may be as different as the ebullient Miss Hazel in "My Man Bovanne" (1971) and the activist Miss Moore in "The Lesson" (1972), these characters are determined not to submit to life but, through their strength and their determination, to attain some power over it.

From their first appearance, Bambara's short stories were praised for accurately capturing the realities of black life. It is not only the facts that the author has right, it is the language. The everyday speech of Bambara's ordinary African Americans has the richness, the repetitiveness, and the exhortatory effectiveness of the spiritual, the thematic complexity of improvisational jazz. As the critic Eleanor W. Traylor points out, in a jam session the jazz musician may refer to all of the ways a melody has ever been heard and then present a new version of the theme. In language, Bambara's characters do much the same thing. Their words and their thoughts are full of fits and starts, rapid changes in direction and mood, colorful chords and dissonances. For example, in "The Hammer Man," the narrator describes not only the event that is taking place—Manny's harassment by a police officer—but also the maternal warnings that go through her mind ("Oh God here I am trying to change my ways, and not talk back in school, and do like my mother wants") and the tragic scenario that she can imagine, "getting shot in the stomach and bleeding to death in Douglas Street park." She alternates between concern for "poor Manny" and for herself: "It just wasn't no kind of thing to happen to a small child like me." With such accurate use of language, Bambara seems to efface herself as an author, producing the immediacy of oral history.

Two stories in *Gorilla, My Love* forecast the direction that Bambara was to take in her later work. In "The Johnson Girls" (1972), women of various ages gather to help a family member make a decision about a philandering man. In "The Lesson," a woman activist and teacher teaches a group of children how unjust their world is. The first of these stories reflects Bambara's feminism, the second her social activism. In their different ways, however, both of these stories suggest that a group can achieve far more than an individual can. Furthermore, both stories show women not as followers but as leaders, demanding change. This synthesis of feminism and activism, which was suggested in Bambara's early stories, was firmly established in *The Black Woman*, the important and influential anthology that Bambara published in 1970. In her second collection of short stories, *The Sea Birds Are Still Alive*, the political and social messages are explicit.

According to Bambara, many of the stories in this collection are "both on-the-block and larger-world-of-struggle pieces." One of the works she mentions in this connection is "The Apprentice" (1977), which tells the story of a part of one day in the life of a black woman revolutionary, as seen through the eyes of her admiring but apprehensive young woman trainee. The revolutionary, Naomi, is not only courageous but canny. For example, when she sees a police officer harassing a black man, she stops and very politely offers to make any necessary telephone calls for her brother, making it evident that the two women will remain as witnesses until the matter is resolved. Then Naomi shows her apprentice how to make a record of the incident, including a description of the police officer, and even how to leave the scene safely. Throughout the story, Naomi continues to teach in this way, showing the narrator how to function and punctuating her own actions with a running commentary, like a master mason showing an apprentice how to lay bricks.

Naomi, however, is doing more than merely transmitting skills; she is also transforming her student in spirit and in will. Whenever the narrator complains, Naomi pulls her up, sometimes shaming her by pointing out that others have sacrificed their lives for the cause, sometimes frightening her with a glimpse of a horrifying future, and sometimes simply hugging her to remind her that she is not alone but is one member of a sisterhood and of a resolute people. Like Bambara herself, Naomi is an educator in the most comprehensive sense. Even her methods are important. Since her student will eventually be tested not on paper but in action, Naomi, like her predecessor in "The Lesson," teaches not by lecturing but by questioning and commenting. Her goal, like Bambara's, is not simply to transmit ideas but to produce new leaders for the revolution.

Bambara says that the force that keeps her telling stories is the need to preserve the past and to transmit the values of her people to future generations. This pattern of preservation and transmission is reflected in "The Apprentice," when Naomi and her young friend go to a senior citizens' complex. As the narrator notices, Naomi does not simply burst in and tell the old people what kind of action they should take. Instead, she first listens to them and learns from them. Only after that does she make her expertise available; thus, the pattern is established. As in Bambara's later novel *The Salt Eaters* (1980), each generation passes on its wisdom to the next. Here, the middle-aged Naomi listens to the old people, and in turn her apprentice listens to her. Finally, like Miss Moore in "The Lesson" and Dada Bibi in "A Girl's Story" (1977), who "even hugged the dirty kids from Mason Street," the strong young women schooled by the Miss Moores of the movement will touch the lives of the young, giving them a sense of their own worth within a worthy community.

Another of the stories in *The Sea Birds Are Still Alive* that Bambara points to as an example of her changing direction is "Broken Field Running" (1977), which shows teachers as the leaders of ghetto children. The scene is a real war zone, an area dominated by bullies, thieves, and drug dealers. The narrator, Lacey, and her fellow teacher regularly escort a group of children from school to their homes in the projects. As they proceed through the snow, the two voice a number of Bambara's own ideas, for example deploring the fact that the high-rise ghettos have made it impossible for community members to watch over their own, as they could in neighborhoods with park benches, front stoops, and unobstructed views. Bambara's teachers also speak of the change in families, which no longer provide their children with love, security, and a real sense of value but now are merely "cargo cults" in a materialistic society, teaching children to believe that everything and everyone has its price.

Ironically, although in "The Lesson" and "The Apprentice" Bambara shows her teachers transmitting their ideas by indirection, in works such as "Broken Field Running," the author herself comes close to sermonizing, to telling rather than to showing. When she permits her characters to live rather than to lecture, as in "The Organizer's Wife" (1977), her stories are more interesting and her messages are more effectively delivered. Although it has important political implications, Bambara calls "The Organizer's Wife" a love story. Certainly, Virginia is deeply in love with her husband Graham. She also, however, sees marriage to this highly educated, intelligent leader as a way out of her prison of poverty and ignorance. It is no wonder that Virginia is disappointed at finding herself still trapped in the country, her life relatively unchanged, except for the addition of a baby, a garden for which she is responsible, and a group of people for whom she must care as long as her husband remains in jail for his activities. The turning point of the story comes when Virginia learns that their preacher has sold the land that Graham has been trying to save. Although Virginia had been hoping that Graham would lose his battle—since then he and she could leave the area—she becomes furious when she is faced with the preacher's perfidy. Then she discovers that she, too, is dedicated to her husband's cause—in other words, that she loves not only Graham but also his people and his dream. Significantly, because she makes this new commitment independently, not after prompting from her husband or even because of her love for him, at the end of this story Virginia has become not less but more of a person. "The Organizer's Wife," then, is an example of the fusion of feminism and activism.

Bambara concludes her essay "Salvation Is the Issue" by saying that her fiction poses the question of whether people can safely "violate the contracts/covenants we have with our ancestors, each other, our children, our selves, and God." Since the obvious answer is "no," Bambara's brilliant short stories have a further purpose: to show her readers how humanity can be saved, not only by listening to the old and nurturing the young but also by making the most of "our tradition of struggle and our faculty for synthesis." This task can be achieved only if resolute black women take the lead within the black community and in the larger struggle for survival, which involves not only African Americans but also the entire planet.

Bibliography
Bambara, Toni Cade. "Salvation Is the Issue." In *Black Women Writers, 1950-1980: A Critical Evaluation*, edited by Mari Evans. Garden City, N.Y.: Anchor Press/ Doubleday, 1983. Explains Bambara's didactic purpose and outlines her artistic development, with useful comments on the changing form and content of her short stories.
_____. "What It Is I Think I'm Doing Anyhow." In *The Writer on Her*

Work, edited by Janet Sternburg. New York: W. W. Norton, 1980. An informal commentary on the writer's intentions in which she explains her partiality for the short story.

Burks, Ruth Elizabeth. "From Baptism to Resurrection: Toni Cade Bambara and the Incongruity of Language." In *Black Women Writers, 1950-1980: A Critical Evaluation*, edited by Mari Evans. Garden City, N.Y.: Anchor Press/Doubleday, 1983. Argues that Bambara's fiction shows the "inadequacy of language and the powers of the spirit" in the tradition of African American religious practice. Burks supports her thesis with references to many of the short stories. Interesting.

Butler-Evans, Elliott. *Race, Gender, and Desire: Narrative Strategies in the Fiction of Toni Cade Bambara, Toni Morrison, and Alice Walker*. Philadelphia: Temple University Press, 1989. The chapter devoted to "Desire, Ambivalence, and Nationalist-Feminist Discourse in Bambara's Short Stories" is particularly useful. Essential reading.

Traylor, Eleanor W. "Music as Theme: The Jazz Mode in the Works of Toni Cade Bambara." In *Black Women Writers, 1950-1980: A Critical Evaluation*, edited by Mari Evans. Garden City, N.Y.: Anchor Press/Doubleday, 1983. Argues persuasively that jazz is basic to Bambara's fiction, both in form and content. A fascinating study.

Vertreace, Martha M. "Toni Cade Bambara: The Dance of Character and Community." In *American Women Writing Fiction: Memory, Identity, Family, Space*, edited by Mickey Pearlman. Lexington: University Press of Kentucky, 1989. Concentrates on the relationship between community and identity in Bambara's writing. The strength of her heroines is not inborn but is developed in communal interaction. Helpful bibliographical references.

Rosemary M. Canfield Reisman

THE STORIES OF HENRY DUMAS

Author: Henry Dumas (1934-1968)
Type of work: Short stories
First published: Ark of Bones and Other Stories, 1970; *Rope of Wind and Other Stories,* 1979; *Goodbye, Sweetwater,* 1988

Henry Lee Dumas has become increasingly recognized, in the years following his tragic death in 1968, as one of the most significant voices of the Black Arts movement of the 1960's. Dumas was born in Sweet Home, Arkansas, on July 20, 1934, the son of Appliance Watson and Henry Joseph Dumas. In the mid-1940's Dumas moved to Harlem, where he was graduated from Commerce High School in 1953. After briefly attending City College, Dumas entered the Air Force. He served until 1957. In 1955, he married Loretta Ponton; together the couple had two sons.

Following his discharge from the Air Force, Dumas enrolled at Rutgers University, attending variously as a full-time and a part-time student before leaving the university altogether in 1965 without completing requirements for a degree. During the early 1960's, Dumas became deeply involved in the Civil Rights movement, journeying to the Deep South on several occasions to take clothing and supplies to those on the front lines of the struggle. In the meantime, he continued to work, write, study, and provide for a growing family.

Little of Dumas' work was published during his lifetime, although he had written poetry and short fiction, as well as the draft of a novel, in the years preceding 1968. It has been largely through the efforts of Eugene B. Redmond, who became the executor of Dumas' literary estate, that the various collections of Dumas' work have been published. At Redmond's behest, Southern Illinois University Press published collections of Dumas' poems and short stories posthumously (Dumas had been associated with the university's Upward Bound Program shortly before his death); Redmond's continued efforts resulted in subsequent publication of Dumas' work by major publishing houses.

For the traditional folk artist, value, be it cultural, political, economic, or aesthetic, must be grounded in a preexisting concept of community. In the short stories of Henry Dumas, the concept of community is both a refuge from a hostile world and a microcosm of that hostility; it is both a reservoir for creativity, social activism, and political consciousness and the very embodiment of destructiveness, social stagnation, and moral conservatism. Published posthumously, all of Dumas' short fiction concerns, to one degree or another, the precarious relation of an individual black male, or black males, to a black community. Some of these communities are rural, others are urban; some are working class and poor, others are middle class and relatively solvent. Yet poor or comfortable, the community is never a homogenous source of support or compassion. Nevertheless, Dumas proffers a higher or transcendent community as an alternative to the real-life community. The implications of the necessity of positing an other community, located outside space and time, outside history, in the ethereal realm of the mythic, underlines the central dilemma of all folk artists in general, and black folk artists specifically: How does one valorize community "values" when some of those values call into question or block not only the folk artist's remedies to community problems but also the folk artist's individual vision that inspires those remedies? For a black folk artist like Dumas, the dilemma is compounded by the debilitating effects of slavery and racism: How does one valorize community values constituted as both an effect of and a reaction to oppression?

Dumas responds to this problem by invoking myth: More often than not, the heroes of his short fiction (they are exclusively male) find their identity in an idealized ahistorical community of blacks, transcending the contingencies of moment and place. Thus, African magic, supernaturalism, and religion serve as the fulcrum on which many of these short stories teeter, always about to tumble into the caricatures of sentimentality. Since all Dumas' short fiction was collected after his death, it is not clear if the order of the stories represents Dumas' vision of his work. Nevertheless, despite the fact that most of the stories from *Ark of Bones and Other Stories* can be categorized as "social realism" while the majority of those in *Rope of Wind and Other Stories* (both collected in *Goodbye, Sweetwater*) are highly charged allegories or parables, there is a strong continuity between the early and late stories. In both collections, one finds the overtly mythic ("Ark of Bones" and "Rope of Wind"), the political ("Strike and Fade" and "Harlem"), and the allegorical ("Fon" and "The Marchers"). Naturally, these genres overlap in many of the stories. What gives them their coherence is Dumas' insistent but varied interrogation of the black community.

The title story of the first posthumous collection, "Ark of Bones," exemplifies the tension between communities set in history and those placed outside history. As in almost all the stories collected in *Ark of Bones*, the tension between the two communities is represented by two male protagonists—here, Head-eye and Fish-hound. As the narrator, Fish-hound is the voice of convention, spokesman for the community; he is the everyday, normal person. Head-eye, though, is uncommon. As the narrator says, he is "bout the ugliest guy I ever run upon" and "bout the smartest nigger in that raggedy school." More important, Head-eye follows his mojo to an Ark that majestically and magically rises from the Mississippi River, bearing within its hull all the bones and spirits of enslaved Africans. The allusion to Noah's Ark is deliberate; in Judaic-Christian theology, Noah's Ark is an emblem of God's mercy and grace, an island of life surrounded by a sea of death. The Ark of Bones is, for Head-eye and, eventually, for Fish-hound, a sign of a promise more radical than the Judaic covenant. For them, the Ark of Bones is an island of life-in-death surrounded by a sea (the community) of death-in-life. Rather than the simple disruptive discontinuity symbolized by the Flood and Noah's Ark, the Ark of Bones allows Head-eye and Fish-hound to end the isolation of a black community uprooted from the soil of its ancestry. At the story's end, however, Head-eye leaves the community for parts unknown, while Fish-hound is completely transformed by the experience. Suddenly, people in the community view him as strange, like Head-eye, they say. Fish-hound has severed his ties with the historical living and bound himself to the mythical living dead. The story ends with the implication that Fish-hound, like Head-eye, will soon disappear, perhaps after "converting" yet another community member the way Head-eye converted him. Continuity with the past becomes a possibility for the individual, not a privilege of the community.

The conversion of the skeptic through the intercession of the believer, and their subsequent disappearance, suggests that Dumas may not have always been optimistic about the possibility of community—as opposed to individual—regeneration through the affirmation of heritage. This theme gets repeated in the story that follows "Ark of Bones," "Echo Tree." Once again, Dumas deploys the framework of myth to underscore the limits of knowledge. In this brief parable and allegory (it is both), two unnamed young male friends confront their spirituality and mortality in the form of a tree that serves as a kind of border between the worlds of the dead and the living. Indeed, the only character given a name, Leo, the best friend of one of the boys and the brother of the other, is dead. Leo's brother is the skeptic, the one who doesn't "believe" in the power of the tree. His friend, however, is a believer, having been taught by Leo to believe in the magical power of the tree. Once again, Dumas demonstrates the power of the mythic community over the historical community, the power of spiritual relations over blood relations: Though the young skeptic is Leo's brother, he is not as close to Leo as is his best friend. Just as Fish-hound is "awed" into conversion by the spectacle of the Ark of Bones, however, so Leo's brother is terrified into belief by the natural elements, the howl of the wind through the echo tree. Thus, Dumas links nature and myth, the continuity between the human and nonhuman, life and death. For Dumas, the survival of black communities depends on nature as a channel to an entire history always on the verge of being lost, denied, or forgotten; the mythic community channeled through nature overcomes time and history.

The linking of this mythic community with nature provides the frame for two other Dumas stories, "Fon" and "Will the Circle Be Unbroken?" "Will the Circle Be Unbroken?" concerns the attempts of young white jazz lovers to crash a black nightclub to hear a new African horn, despite the warnings from the doorman. Insisting upon their rights, they enter as the musician—a friend of one of the whites—is about to play the new horn for the first time. He puts the horn to his lips, blows, and, in a scene deliberately reminiscent of the Biblical story of Jericho, watches as the white patrons crumble to the floor, dead. In "Fon," white racism, which is linked to the culture of the city, is foiled by a black heritage exemplified by the title character and his "brother." In this story, Nillmon, a white man, is driving along a deserted country road when a "fragment of black rock about the size of a fist" crashes through his rear window. Enraged, Nillmon gets out of the car, sees Fon sitting on a billboard, grabs his gun, forces Fon down, and stuffs him into the car. Fon denies throwing the rock. He claims he was simply sitting on the billboard with his brother, though when Nillmon looks, he sees no one else. Fon tells Nillmon he was teaching his brother "how to shoot arrows." On their way to town, they almost run into a herd of cows crossing the road; Nillmon is so distracted that Fon is able to slip away. Here, the culture of the city (which, for Dumas, is the culture of whites) is opposed to nature, which Dumas links to black culture: car/cows, gun/bow and arrow. The minor triumph of Fon's temporary escape—he is captured again by Nillmon and two of his buddies—foreshadows the story's conclusion; Nillmon and his cohorts, about to shoot Fon, are cut down by arrows from above, presumably from Fon's "brother" (whom the reader never sees). In short, Fon's brother is the symbol of the mythic, transhistorical community, as opposed to Fon's own historical community (symbolized by the church congregation), which proves itself helpless and ineffectual when confronted by Nillmon and his comrades.

Taken as a whole, Dumas' fiction links a white, mechanistic racist culture of the city with the black skeptic. Refusing to believe in the magical powers of nature as articulated by African cultures, refusing to see beyond the immediate and tangible world of contingency, the black skeptic implicitly, like the white racist explicitly, denies the validity and interconnections of the natural world, black cultures, and black histories. Thus, even the black urban landscape becomes, for Dumas, the site of intraracial hostility at worst ("A Harlem Game") and interracial combat at best ("Strike and Fade"). "A Boll of Roses" also deals with this theme, but on a grand scale. Here, black rural life confronts black urban life in the persons of Layton, a young Southern sharecropper, and Rosemarie, a Northern Freedom Rider trying to register voters. The story opens with the familiar paradigm: Layton, the young believer who expresses more than a casual interest in this Rosemarie, and Floyd, his cynical friend, who tells him in no uncertain terms, "Man you crazy! That girl ain't thinkin about no cotton pickin nigger like you!" Though Layton remains determined to meet Rosemarie with roses, his already shaky self-confidence is systematically broken by his encounters with his mother, Floyd, and the other sharecroppers, who all, to one degree or another, question his worthiness to a girl like Rosemarie. Thus, when Layton finally does get an opportunity to speak with her, he becomes the no-good, foul-mouthed "cotton pickin nigger" everyone has implied he is. At the story's end, he decides to give the rejected roses to his mother, symbolizing, perhaps, his reconnection to his rural heritage. The urban world of Rosemarie—she is accompanied by a young white woman—is precisely what Layton must shun if he is to remain true to himself, to his community.

While the stories in *Ark of Bones* are primarily marked by the symbolic, those collected in *Rope of Wind* are extensive allegories. The opening story, "The Marchers," sets the tone; it is an excoriating parable about the domination of the group over the person, the facile preference for abstraction and sloganeering over active and difficult struggle. In a white dome, a black prisoner sits, "shackled to inertia by a great chain of years." Suddenly he hears the roar of a crowd gathering at the great door of the dome. The crowd shouts, "OPEN THE GREAT DOOR OF THIS NATION AND BRING OUT THE PAST." Eventually, after several such proclamations, the crowd crashes the door, trampling "the sentiments, the truths, the lies, the myths, the legends of the past in a frenzied rush to lay hold of freedom." They drag the prisoner out, still in chains, and more speeches and slogans follow. The prisoner, barely able to whisper, begs for water, for the loosening of his chains, but the crowd, caught up in its own spectacle, ignores him. For Dumas, the question of individual responsibility in relation to a community is a moot one, since responsibility presumes self-motivation; yet the prisoner is "shackled to inertia by a great chain of years." The community must shoulder the burden of motivating and inspiring, yet here it fails in its responsibility.

In the four stories that follow "The Marchers," individuals are abandoned or ignored by a rebelling community ("Harlem"), are forced to abandon the community in order to understand fully wisdom and knowledge ("The University of Man"), and sacrifice their lives for the sake of the community ("Rope of Wind" and "Devil Bird"). What is distinctly absent is any sense of an effective, supportive historical community.

The group of stories that conclude *Rope of Wind* share a certain attitude toward religion and money. Specifically, these stories reject the lure of traditional Christian explanations of experience as well as traditional American norms for earning money. For Dumas, both American Christianity and capitalism attempt to yoke blacks to systems that are intrinsically antithetical to black, or rather African, values. The problem is that the community has adopted these norms, so individual dissenters are forced to walk a fine line between rejection of the norms (which implies rejection of the community values) and acceptance of the norms (which implies rejection of alternative African values). Yet if these stories show the individual attempting to meet the community halfway, they rarely show the opposite: the community attempting to reach out for and understand the peculiar needs and desires of the black iconoclast.

On balance, Dumas appears to endorse iconoclasm over conformity, if what is at stake is a continuity with a mythic, ahistorical community. This is why memory plays such a crucial role in many of his stories. At the same time, Dumas never rejects the historical black community out of hand, since he sees in it, in his best and most optimistic moments, the potential for historical understanding and responsibility. This potential remains, for Dumas, ever present, since even the best that white culture offers blacks is a mechanistic, inhuman value system in which profit and competition are valued at the expense of charity and cooperation. In their own way, the short stories of Henry Dumas presage the antiestablishment critiques of the Black Power movements that would rise from a number of black communities in the 1960's.

One of Dumas' last works was an elegy written upon the assassination of Martin Luther King, Jr., in April, 1968, "Our King Is Dead." Ironically, this poem became a prophecy, for some six weeks after King's death, Dumas himself was dead, killed by a white police officer in a New York subway under suspicious circumstances. The incident was officially described as a case of mistaken identity. Henry Dumas was only two months short of his thirty-fourth birthday.

Bibliography

Baraka, Amiri. "Henry Dumas: Afro-Surreal Expressionist." *Black American Literature Forum* 22 (Summer, 1988): 164-166. Explores the connection of Dumas' work to the Black Arts movement, the Civil Rights movement, and the black liberation movement of the 1960's.

Baytop, Adrianne. " 'Into the dawn light/ the shadow walks behind you': Henry Dumas." *Black American Literature Forum* 22 (Summer, 1988): 171-174. Discusses the importance of blues music and water images as sources of spirituality and comfort in the lives of African Americans.

Collier, Eugenia. "Elemental Wisdom in *Goodbye, Sweetwater*: Suggestions for Further Study." *Black American Literature Forum* 22 (Summer, 1988): 192-199. Focuses on what the author believes are the fundamental structures of Dumas' fiction: allegory and archetype.

De Jongh, James L. "Notes on Henry Dumas's Harlem." *Black American Literature Forum* 22 (Summer, 1988): 218-220. Examines the multiple rhetorical function of Harlem in Dumas' fiction.

Halsey, William. "Signify(cant) Correspondences." *Black American Literature Forum* 22 (Summer, 1988): 238-240. Explores the African tradition of naming as a method of linking individuals separated by history. Shows how naming-as-link connects Dumas with such other African American writers as Richard Wright, Ralph Ellison, Margaret Walker, and Toni Morrison.

Mitchell, Carolyn A. "Henry Dumas and Jean Toomer: One Voice." *Black American Literature Forum* 22 (Summer, 1988): 297-309. Argues that Dumas' fiction descends directly from Jean Toomer's poetic novel *Cane* (1923) in terms of both writers' attempts to establish the basis for a new spirituality for African Americans.

Traylor, Eleanor. "Henry Dumas and the Discourse of Memory." *Black American Literature Forum* 22 (Summer, 1988): 365-377. Explores the function of memory in Dumas' work and its influence on Toni Morrison's novel *Beloved* (1987).

Werner, Craig. "Dumas, Nationalism, and Multicultural Mythology." *Black American Literature Forum* 22 (Summer, 1988): 394-399. Attempts to construct Dumas as a postmodern descendant of the modernist Langston Hughes by showing how not only Hughes's but also T. S. Eliot's, James Joyce's and Ezra Pound's modernism is undermined and revised by Dumas.

Tyrone Williams

THE STORIES OF JOHN HOLMAN

Author: John Holman (1951-   )
Type of work: Short stories
First published: Squabble: And Other Stories, 1990

Squabble: And Other Stories is the first collection of John Holman's short fiction. The title story is about a young professor who loses his teaching job because of budget cutbacks and ends up tending bar at a dive where customers have to be searched for weapons before being allowed to enter. He meets an assortment of unusual characters, including a vivacious young woman with whom he contemplates having a love affair. The point of the story seems to be that upward mobility for African Americans is fraught with danger.

In "Peso Street," another young intellectual type is thrown in with a group of unusual characters at a house party. Some of the characters seem to have underworld connections. They talk about a recent funeral that degenerated into a brawl. The very pointlessness of the story seems to underline the alienation of the characters involved.

In "Presence," two young black friends are working on a car at their apartment complex. A young white truck driver tries to make friends with them by bringing a six-pack of beer. He tells them a story of a violent family feud. The two friends feel uncomfortable with his "presence" and obviously wish he would go away. The story symbolizes the difficulties blacks and whites have relating to one another, even when they have the best intentions.

In "I and I," three young men are delivering cocaine to various dealers in the state of Mississippi. They stay high on alcohol, marijuana, and cocaine. They pick up a couple of young local women and stage an impromptu party in a deserted house. All three men seem to realize that they are trapped in a trade that will inevitably lead to prison or death. The story reflects the fatalism of many modern African American men.

"On Earth" is the story of a sensitive young man who leaves home because he realizes that his parents have gotten old, and he cannot bear to see them die. He ends up going to college in another city and renting a furnished room from a toughminded landlady who shares the house with her daughter and young grandson. The young hero becomes a part of this family, but his landlady suddenly dies of a stroke and he realizes that he will soon have to move on again. The story illustrates the omnipresence of death and suffering "on earth."

"Scuff" is one of Holman's many stories that contrast upwardly mobile African Americans with African Americans who seem doomed to remain ignorant, impoverished, and confined to the ghetto. Sarah, a smart, ambitious young professional, is saddled with an irresponsible younger brother who camps in her apartment, eats all of her food, breaks her possessions, and refuses to look for a job. In the meantime, she is carrying on a hopeless affair with her boss, who is married.

In "The Story of Art History," a young college professor visits a shopping mall and is accused of stealing some junk jewelry. Even though a body search proves that he is innocent, he is asked to leave the mall. This is the only overt incident of racial discrimination in Holman's stories. The young professor goes to visit some friends and dances with a pretty coed who is majoring in art history, but his whole day has been darkened by his humiliating experience.

"Yard Lights, Water, and Wink" is an impressionistic story about the long-term relationship between a young woman and an old man. His renegade attitude toward life has inspired her to retain her individuality as she is exposed to the homogenizing influence of higher education. The story symbolizes the relationship between modern African Americans and their indomitable ancestors who survived slavery, poverty, and repression to make a better life possible for future generations.

"I Did That" is composed of six very brief memoirs of a man's childhood. He seems to have been exceptionally sensitive, lonely, and in need of love. The six episodes convey an expressionistic picture of the segregated neighborhood in which he grew up and the type of people who lived there.

"Pimp" is another story that contrasts an upwardly mobile African American with one who seems doomed to failure because of race and environment. A young woman who is headed for college meets a former childhood sweetheart after he has been away for six years. He drags her into an unsavory adventure that makes her painfully aware of how incompatible they have become.

"Monroe's Wedding" is yet another story that contrasts middle-class and lower-class African Americans. A middle-aged, divorced, lonely college graduate who is building a profitable gardening business is coerced by an improvident employee to be the best man at the employee's upcoming wedding. While shopping for a wedding gift, the best man impulsively invites an attractive white saleswoman to attend the wedding with him. She seems tempted to accept but then declines. He thinks about her afterward, wishing he could get to know her better and realizing that her feelings were similar to his. The story symbolizes the evolving relations between blacks and whites in the South.

All of Holman's stories belong unmistakably to the minimalist school. The common denominator of minimalist fiction is that it puts the reader in the position of being a combination of voyeur and eavesdropper. The relation of the reader to the story is similar to that of the viewer to many French "New Wave" films. No effort is made to orient the reader or viewer regarding the background to the story. The reader of a minimalist story is forced to do a lot of guesswork because he or she is usually dropped right into the middle of the story, with the author never bothering to introduce the characters or perhaps even failing to mention where the story takes place.

Holman does not mention that his principal characters are African Americans, perhaps because white authors do not think it necessary to mention that their characters are white. The racial identity of Holman's characters, along with much other factual information, has to be deduced from what the reader can see and hear.

Minimalism is effective because it forces the reader to grope for clues to understand what is going on. This forces active participation and ideally engages and absorbs the reader in the action of the story, even if the story does not contain any intensely dramatic events. Minimalism is also a sort of hyperrealism: It rarely deals with spectacular events, because such events are the exception rather than the rule in life and hence are unrealistic.

It is not common practice for minimalist authors to highlight their themes and meanings. These too have to be deduced from what the reader sees, hears, and vicariously experiences. Minimalist authors are frequently accused of writing mere "slices of life" or "vignettes," terms that used to be anathema in critical circles but have lost some of their sting with the appearance of such fine minimalist writers as Raymond Carver, Ann Beattie, and Holman.

It is significant—and amusing—that reviews of Holman's *Squabble: And Other Stories* offered many different interpretations of the author's themes and meanings. It seems as though the reader is free to make an independent assessment of what Holman is trying to communicate, which is probably exactly the way Holman wanted it. He is not dealing specifically with the problems of racism and segregation. The best description of his goal in these short and often cryptic stories is that he is trying to paint a living picture of contemporary reality without being obvious in communicating a message. He leaves it up to the reader to make moral judgments. All of his stories seem to say, "This is what life is like for African Americans in the South in the last decade of the twentieth century."

That life seems to have improved since the Civil Rights movement of the 1960's but still involves segregation and deprivation. There are opportunities for economic advancement, but upwardly mobile African Americans may feel unwelcome in a predominantly white middle-class milieu and at the same time cut off from their own social roots. Racism is no longer blatant but still is omnipresent. The subtlety of racial prejudice that exists in the "new" South is appropriately conveyed by the subtlety that characterizes Holman's short stories. Many African Americans, like Americans in general, feel alienated and bewildered by the accelerating changes taking place in contemporary America. They are victims of what author Alvin Toffler termed "future shock."

Nothing much happens in any Holman story; the stories portray static situations. Like most minimalists, Holman is more interested in conflicts than in resolutions. He writes stories that symbolize characteristic human predicaments and contemporary social problems. He looks for the tiny details that convey meaning, such as the scuff marks made all over Sarah's apartment by her irresponsible brother in the story "Scuff." The most frequent theme in Holman's stories is that contemporary African Americans in the South are uncertain about their identities and are tempted to regress to traditional ways of behaving.

The fact that Holman rarely mentions whether a character is white or black forces the reader to recognize unconscious racial stereotypes. Frequently the implicit meaning of a story is that there is no difference between people except skin color; it is as if Holman is saying, "Color is destiny."

What is particularly significant about Holman's short stories is that he has demonstrated how the techniques of minimalism can be applied to dealing with the experiences of African Americans. At the time of publication of *Squabble: And Other Stories*, he was the leading black minimalist author in the United States. His work has shown other African American writers that there are effective alternatives to literature of protest, which is belligerent, strident, and propagandistic. His stories provide striking contrast to the plays of Amiri Baraka (LeRoi Jones) and the speeches of Malcolm X, for example, even though he is dealing with similar matters.

Most criticism of Holman's stories has been favorable, although some critics have expressed antipathy toward his minimalist style. In her review of *Squabble: And Other Stories* in *The New York Times Book Review*, fiction writer Margot Mifflin, obviously a member of the antiminimalist camp, complained that Holman sounded too derivative. Her only praise went to the story "Yard Lights, Water, and Wink," which she called "an astonishing departure from a plodding impressionism into a perfect explosion of expressionism." She expressed the hope that Holman would write more such stories if he would "stop echoing his teachers' voices and find his own."

Holman actually took writing courses with two of the most famous minimalist short-story writers, Raymond Carver and Frederick Barthelme. The resemblance between Holman's and Carver's stories is particularly striking; Holman even has a wry humor that strongly resembles Carver's. Holman's humorous attitude to the perplexities of modern life is a feature often singled out by critics who have discussed his stories. Although it is undeniable that Holman often "echoes his teachers' voices," it is a moot question whether he should abandon minimalism, since he has demonstrated such mastery of its techniques that he might be considered Carver's natural successor.

Bibliography

Barth, John. "A Few Words About Minimalism." *The New York Times Book Review*, December 28, 1986, 1. This article makes it easy to understand the heated controversy concerning minimalist fiction. An understanding of minimalism is indispensable to an understanding of Holman's stories. Barth is definitely not a minimalist himself but displays an open-minded attitude in his discussion.

Carver, Raymond. *Where I'm Calling From*. New York: Atlantic Monthly Press, 1988. Carver, who died in 1988, was the foremost minimalist writer of his time and had a powerful influence on Holman's literary career. Reading Carver is essential to understanding minimalism in contemporary American fiction, just as understanding minimalism is essential to understanding Holman's work.

Cecil, Vicki. Review of *Squabble: And Other Stories*, by John Holman. *Library Journal* 115 (May 15, 1990): 94. Holman's stories receive enthusiastic commendation for their sense of humor and generally realistic portrayal of contemporary young African Americans. Cecil is one of few critics to call attention to Holman's compassionate attitude toward social misfits.

Hemingway, Ernest. *The Short Stories of Ernest Hemingway.* New York: Scribner, 1966. Two early Hemingway stories, "The Killers" and "Hills Like White Elephants," are among the earliest examples of American minimalism. Reading them is indispensable to understanding the aims and methods of contemporary minimalists such as Carver and Holman.

Hempel, Amy. "Young Blacks in the 'New' South." *Los Angeles Times Book Review,* August 5, 1990, 13. Hempel analyzes each of the stories included in *Squabble: And Other Stories.* Her main focus is the influence of Raymond Carver and Frederick Barthelme.

Kirkus Reviews. Review of *Squabble: And Other Stories,* by John Holman. 58 (March 15, 1990): 365. The reviewer displays a prejudice against minimalism in general and describes the stories as "unfinished" and "anorexic" while conceding that Holman has considerable talent.

Lemon, Lee. Review of *Squabble: And Other Stories,* by John Holman. *Prairie Schooner* 65 (Summer, 1991): 129. Lemon believes that all Holman's stories have to do with "gamesmanship" and "makeshift survival strategies" that have evolved from traditional African American tactics for surviving in a hostile environment.

Mifflin, Margot. Review of *Squabble: And Other Stories,* by John Holman. *The New York Times Book Review,* July 22, 1990, 20. Mifflin's review is unusual in its strongly negative attitude toward Holman's literary style. She thinks that the common denominator of his stories is the "existential impotence" of his African American characters.

Nelson, E. S. Review of *Squabble: And Other Stories,* by John Holman. *Choice* 28 (November, 1990): 484. This enthusiastic reviewer praises Holman's "ironic gentleness" and "remarkable subtlety."

Bill Delaney

THE STORIES OF LANGSTON HUGHES

Author: Langston Hughes (1902-1967)
Type of work: Short stories
First published: The Ways of White Folks, 1934; *Simple Speaks His Mind,* 1950; *Laughing to Keep from Crying,* 1952; *Simple Takes a Wife,* 1953; *Simple Stakes a Claim,* 1957; *The Best of Simple,* 1961; *Something in Common and Other Stories,* 1963; *Simple's Uncle Sam,* 1965

Langston Hughes was already an accomplished poet when he began writing short stories. Though he had previously published several stories in a Harlem magazine, it was not until 1933 (while sitting in a hotel room in Moscow, after having read D. H. Lawrence's *The Lovely Lady*) that he decided the short story was another genre he could master. Hughes became proficient in such a short time that his first collection of stories, *The Ways of White Folks,* was published in 1934. Despite this initial success, there was a delay of sixteen years before another collection appeared, though after the drought came seven extensive volumes of short stories published between 1950 and 1965. Five of these feature Hughes's most famous fictional character, Harlem "folk" philosopher Jesse B. Semple, who holds forth on subjects ranging from his landladies to former first lady Eleanor Roosevelt. Hughes's short stories in general can be divided into two categories: early ones that follow Hughes's adapted version of a traditional Aristotelian short-story form, and later ones, most of which utilize a more flexible and generally more entertaining dialogue form. Both categories feature Hughes's incisive commentary on race relations and demonstrate Hughes's career-long search for a form flexible enough to accommodate both his high aesthetic principles and his political interests.

The title of Hughes's first book of short stories, *The Ways of White Folks,* is a homage to W. E. B. Du Bois' classic of African American sociology, *The Souls of Black Folk* (1903). Du Bois' work makes the bold claim that the history of the twentieth century will be the history of the color line; Hughes's work investigates the psychological and sometimes physical consequences of an individual character's relationship to the color line. Two stories, "Little Dog" and "Father and Son," show, respectively, the white and black sides of customary and legal segregation. In "Little Dog," the protagonist, Miss Clara Briggs, a forty-five-year-old Manhattan-dwelling spinster, suddenly decides to adopt a pet. Miss Briggs chooses a little white dog that she names Flips, only to find that her decision brings her into daily contact with Joe, the broad-shouldered African American janitor of her building. Miss Briggs soon becomes enamored of Joe and organizes her schedule around his daily delivery of dog bones. She will not, however, allow her emotions to take any public form; she represses her feelings for Joe and eventually moves to another apartment building in an attempt to escape her socially unacceptable desires. The structure of the story, as in much of Hughes's best work, reinforces spatially the structure of Miss Briggs's emotions. Joe and his family are kept down in the basement, just as Miss Briggs's feelings for him and sympathy for his family are denied. Her "white flight" becomes an emblem of the connection between spatial relationships and her inability to control the color line in her own mind.

In the concluding story of the collection, "Father and Son," Hughes offers some of his most trenchant criticism of Southern race relations. "Father and Son" is the story of Colonel Thomas Norwood, a wealthy Georgia planter, and his illegitimate mixed-race son, Bert Lewis. Colonel Norwood obviously overcame the customary problem of sexual relations between the races, having fathered several children by his servant Cora Lewis. He also has some affection for these children, for he is willing to pay for their education (if they agree to go to Atlanta). Like Miss Briggs, however, the Colonel is unwilling or unable to cross the color line and admit that Bert is his son. Where Miss Briggs can literally move away from her problems, Colonel Lewis cannot avoid seeing his son when Bert returns from a year at the "Negro college" to visit his mother and family who remain on the plantation. Bert, who is said to have inherited his father's stubborn character, refuses to work in the fields and in general gives the impression that he is "uppity." In 1930's Georgia, the combination of intelligence and character in an African American does not go over well with the local white population. In an ending that foreshadows the work of Richard Wright in *Uncle Tom's Children* (1938), the conflict is resolved in an orgy of violence. Bert strangles his father after the Colonel refuses one last time to recognize him as his son; the ensuing manhunt ends with a double lynching, as both Bert and his Uncle Tomish brother Willie are made victims of the Jim Crow traditions. Both "Little Dog" and "Father and Son" show the ways in which whites refuse to face the truth of their feelings about African Americans and attempt, sometimes forcibly, to put them back on their side of the color line.

Laughing to Keep from Crying, which appeared in 1952, offers a more lighthearted approach to racial issues. The stories tend to be more flexible in form and more simplified in subject matter. Conflict is often reduced to its simplest form, and the function of the characters involved is often that of comical and ironic opposition. Stories of exceptional merit include "Who's Passing for Who?," a story of disguised racial identity; "Something in Common," the title story of a later collection of selected stories; "Little Old Spy," an ironic story of prerevolutionary Cuba; and the concluding story of the collection, the powerful and moving "Big Meeting."

In "Who's Passing for Who?," Hughes tells the story of a group of Harlem artists who let guilt-trip white liberal tourists foot all of their nightly bar tabs. It is only when a group of Iowans pass through town that they get their comeuppance. The artists begin to impress upon the Iowans, in a good-natured manner, the magnitude of the cross-racial disguise problem. According to the artists, thousands of African Americans throughout the country are passing for white. In an ironic ending typical of Hughes's stories from the 1950's, the Iowans reveal that they indeed belong to the group of African Americans who are passing for white, though only for the reason that they make more money as white people. The confession leads to all parties dropping their pretensions and enjoying the evening on an equal footing. As the story ends, however, the Iowans leave with one last parting shot—they reveal that they are in fact whites who are passing for "colored," just for the sake of having fun. The narrator is left musing about the racial identity of the Midwesterners and can only conclude that the evening's entertainment has been at his expense.

"Something in Common" is one of a group of Hughes's stories that are set in exotic locations, in this case Hong Kong. This "defamiliarization" of the reader allows Hughes to represent the conflict in its simplest terms. The dialogue between a stuffy and pretentious Kentucky colonel and a radical Midwestern African American allows the reader direct access to the story in a manner similar to the Semple dialogues. Both characters carry their conception of the color line with them to Hong Kong, and they soon begin arguing about Jim Crow (segregation) laws in the United States. They can come to agreement only when confronted by a common enemy, the Cockney bartender who throws them out of the bar for fighting. "The Little Spy" is another of the stories set in a foreign locale; this time, the Havana location features a Cuban pimp who has been hired by the government to spy on a visiting African American artist. Again the plot is resolved only after the artist and the spy enter into a dialogue about race and sex over a bottle of Bacardi (provided at the artist's expense). The ironic twist at the conclusion concerns the delivery of a secret message from the artist to his revolutionary comrades—all accomplished while the pimp/spy is suffering from the consequences of too much talk and drink.

"Big Meeting" is the concluding story of the collection and is Hughes's most complicated story that utilizes the dramatic dialogue form. The story revolves around three sets of interwoven dialogues: one between the preacher and worshippers at a tent revival, one between two youths who have skipped the meeting but remain within earshot, and one between a white couple who have decided to use the meeting as a form of entertainment. The two youths, Bud and the narrator, are the only characters who are in a position to overhear what is said by all the others, and they therefore serve as a bridge between the reactions of the whites and the African American worshippers. As the story proceeds, the skepticism of the boys and the voyeuristic enjoyment of the whites give way to a profound feeling for the proceedings of the big meeting. Reverend Duke Braswell repeats the story of Jesus' crucifixion in terms of black-white conflict. Christ is "lynched" because of his support of the poor and downtrodden (a theme repeated by Jesse B. Semple in the story "Simple Prays a Prayer"). It is only a black man named Simon who is willing to bear the cross before Christ is left on Golgotha with the two thieves. The reverend is stressing the point of Christ's abandonment on the cross when the whites decide to leave, the evening's entertainment having suddenly turned serious. The narrator attempts to stop the whites by saying that the part of the service where sinners are called upon to confess is approaching. The whites, however, have no interest in entering into any dialogue at this point and drive off in an effort to avoid any contact. The color line is redrawn, but all have been changed in some way. The boys are drawn back into the meeting by the persuasiveness of the reverend's oratory, and the whites have been exposed and affected by the power of the dialogue between the preacher and his congregation.

The last and most famous of Langston Hughes's fictional creations is Harlem "folk" philosopher Jesse B. Semple. The "Simple" stories began as a column for the African American newspaper *The Chicago Defender* and soon acquired national attention. Semple, like Ishmael Reed's character Jes Grew, is a signifying creation, though Jesse B. Semple's folkloric home is a modern, urban one. Semple provides colorful commentary on every topic from politics to landladies, usually from his second home, the Wishing Well bar. His constant interlocutor is the college-educated narrator, who serves as the perfect straight man in the dialogues. Semple's "signifying" (or verbal gamesmanship, to use the term popularized by Henry Louis Gates, Jr.) always concerns the issues of sex, race, and class, all complicated by Semple's Southern upbringing. On the issue of sex, Semple's life is governed by his ex-wife in Baltimore and his two present-day loves. Zarita, his former girlfriend and still sometime companion, also spends a great deal of time at the Wishing Well bar and fits in the Semple category of "nighttime" women. Joyce, Semple's wife, is a thoroughly respectable and hard-working woman who conveniently fits in the category of "daytime" women. Not coincidentally, Joyce supports Semple during many of the early stories. In fact, when Hughes decided to stop writing the column, instead of killing Semple off (as many writers have done when retiring their most famous characters), he moved him to a house in the suburbs bought by Joyce.

Semple is most eloquent on the subject of race relations, especially when he recalls his early life in Virginia. In fact, Semple can never forget about his Southern past, because his Virginia cousins F. D. and Minnie come to live with him for brief periods of time. The narrator, who is always on the side of moderation and understanding, is regularly shocked and appalled by Semple's views. Semple's comments on race are very simple; in the story entitled "Semple Prays a Prayer," Semple comes to the conclusion that Christ should come back as avenger and smite down white folks. The narrator, somewhat taken aback at Semple's radicalism, asks Semple if he really means all white folks should be smitten. Semple's reply is no, not all of them: He hopes Christ leaves Eleanor Roosevelt alone. Likewise, in the story "There Ought to Be a Law," Semple has another radical idea after watching a nature film. In addition to a nature preserve where there is a sign that reads "NO HUNTING," Semple would like to see a game preserve for blacks where the sign would read "NO LYNCHING."

The last and one of the most telling of Semple's criticisms of society concerns the class system. In many respects the class system coincides with the race problem, the exception, in Semple's mind, being Harlem landladies. His encounters with landladies have all been problematic, usually with his landladies winning the verbal battle, as in the story "Landladies," in which Semple has to rewrite all the signs he has removed from an apartment house. To Semple, however, monetary barriers are the spirit of Jim Crow reborn, and they keep him from finding the high-paying job he wants. All is related to the confluence of race and class: When Semple is told by his white coworkers in "Apple Strudel" that he can stay in the Waldorf-Astoria hotel if he wants to, his reply is that he cannot because he does not have the money.

Semple claims that he would have the money if he were not black.

The stories of Langston Hughes show a progression from a relatively traditional short-story form to a flexible, dialogic structure. As Hughes became more adept at exploiting the conventional beginning-middle-end formula, he also realized its short-comings in the presentation of his subject matter. His conversion to the dialogue approach, first in the short stories of the 1950's and then in the Semple stories, proves the success of his efforts to create a narrative form through which the truth of African American experience could be told.

Bibliography
Blake, Susan L. "Old John in Harlem: The Urban Folktales of Langston Hughes." *Black American Literature Forum* 14 (Fall, 1980): 100-104. Examines Hughes's Simple stories and how they function as folktales in a black urban society. Shows how the stories, functioning as folktales, tend to unite the black population through recognizable past and present experiences.
Emanuel, James A. "Bodies in the Moonlight: A Critical Analysis." *Readers and Writers* 1 (November-January, 1968): 38-39, 42. A critical examination of one of the first of Hughes's published short stories. This brief analysis emphasizes an "innocence" theme that is set in a seafaring environment. Does not include notes.
Jemie, Onwuchekwa. *Langston Hughes: An Introduction to the Poetry.* New York: Columbia University Press, 1976. Explores the African American, political, and musical experiences of Hughes's life and shows how these areas affected his works. Jemie's conclusion is that these experiences proved to Hughes that there was a "black existence," or a distinctly separate black culture, in America. It was this "black existence" that developed into the incessant African American themes used in Hughes's writings, including the fiction. Extensive notes.
Klotman, Phyllis R. "Jesse B. Semple and the Narrative Art of Langston Hughes." *Journal of Narrative Technique* 3 (January, 1973): 66-75. Klotman's essay establishes a theory that Hughes's narrative technique in the Simple stories cemented the popularity of those stories with black and white audiences alike. Klotman successfully proves her theory by a detailed analysis of four literary devices used by Hughes.
Mullen, Edward J., ed. *Critical Essays on Langston Hughes.* Boston: G. K. Hall, 1986. Reprints reviews, essays, and articles on Hughes's poetry, prose, and drama. Contains a thorough introduction by Mullen that includes a brief biography of Hughes, a bibliographic overview, and analyses of Hughes's poetry, prose, and drama. Extensive notes.
Rampersad, Arnold. *The Life of Langston Hughes.* 2 vols. New York: Oxford University Press, 1986, 1991. The definitive biography of Hughes. Rampersad provides an extensive account of Hughes's decision to begin writing fiction and offers a fascinating version of the history behind the Simple stories.

Jeff Cupp

THE STORIES OF JAMES ALAN McPHERSON

Author: James Alan McPherson (1943-   )
Type of work: Short stories
First published: Hue and Cry, 1969; *Elbow Room,* 1977

James Alan McPherson was immediately recognized for his talent as a writer. In the same year that he was graduated from Harvard Law School, his first collection of short stories, *Hue and Cry,* was published. McPherson was twenty-five at the time, and a year later he was awarded an O. Henry Prize for the volume's title story. Less than ten years later, his second collection, *Elbow Room,* was published and received the Pulitzer Prize for fiction. In 1981, McPherson was honored with the prestigious MacArthur Foundation Award.

Such prompt and extensive praise has resulted from McPherson's penetrating examination of themes of racial differences, as in the story "On Trains," in which a plump, matronly woman boards a train in Chicago. She spends the entire afternoon in the dining car until she is asked to leave so the waiters can prepare the next table setting. The porters and stewards gossip that she does not tip though she receives good service. Alone in the club car with the bartender, she grows uncomfortable and leaves in a hurry when he comes from behind the bar to wipe tables. The woman moves on to the Pullman car, where she learns that the Pullman porter stays in the car overnight in case passengers need him. She complains to the Pullman conductor that the porter is black and should not be allowed to stay in the car. Told that it is the porter's job, the woman decides to sleep in the coaches instead of the Pullman, while the porter falls asleep, feeling guilty and ashamed despite his innocence.

"On Trains" demonstrates the themes of difference and separation that characterize much of James Alan McPherson's work. It is clear from the start that the woman who boards the train in Chicago and the workers on the train are different in more ways than simply their status as passenger and crew. In addition to her portrayal as plump and matronly, the woman is described as "colorless," an intimation that she is white. She is also called an "old Southern gal," implying that she represents the old South. While the train continues on its journey, difference is magnified as the woman moves from one car to the next, always escaping the train crew. Finally, when there are no more cars to which the woman can move, she is forced to reveal that, in her mind, she and the porter are forever incompatible, no matter what the circumstance, because of their different skin colors.

In McPherson's two collections of short stories, the plots, like that of "On Trains," primarily revolve around the distinctions that exist between two main characters who are at once together within a particular setting or time frame yet separate because of their differences. Each story lies in how the characters contend with the situation those differences present. McPherson's heroes and heroines are immediately identifiable within any community. Barbers, custodians, porters, widows, post-office clerks, and shopkeepers are the people he writes about. Even when they represent the underside of life, they are affable. The fact that McPherson worked his way through college as a waiter aboard the Great Northern Railroad could account for his skill in portraying in a natural, unassuming voice the ordinary people who inhabit *Hue and Cry* and *Elbow Room*. Most of his characters have migrated from the small towns of New England, Southern backwoods, or Midwestern prairies to the larger cities of the American landscape. Places such as Boston, New York, Cleveland, Chicago, and San Francisco are the settings for most of the stories (and, incidentally, the major stops of the railroad).

Because readers can easily recognize such characters, McPherson's stories are particularly unsettling. Throughout both collections, distinctions between people ultimately prove irreconcilable and forever condemn them to be at odds with one another. In "Gold Coast," for example, the custodians of a building off Harvard Square are opposites in terms of economic, educational, and professional stature. Robert, a Harvard student, takes a job as an apprentice janitor under James Sullivan. Whereas Robert aspires to be a writer and uses the job for its story potential, James has worked in the same building his entire life. Robert mines the garbage cans for bits and pieces of information to use in his stories, while James lives vicariously through insignificant associations he has had with the Harvard elite.

In the end, Robert avoids James, who constantly pesters him for company, especially during late-night drinking sessions in the basement. When Robert finally gives up his job in the building, unable to find value in the trash of those who live there, he is so alienated from James that he cannot even help him on the street one day when he sees him struggling with two heavy shopping bags. Robert is close enough to touch James, yet because James is conscious only of how heavy his bags are, Robert passes him by and never looks back. Though Robert is black and James is white, differences unrelated to race give Robert an advantage over James and prevent him from caring for James.

This is not to say that McPherson ignores the adversity that racial differences cause among people. In fact, when his stories revolve around issues of race, particularly in the title stories of both collections, McPherson is at his best. In keeping with the bleak resolutions of the majority of pieces in McPherson's corpus, in "Hue and Cry" and "Elbow Room" the two main characters' racial distinctions either thwart their relationships with one another entirely or constantly run as undercurrents, preventing them from existing in a context where difference is not problematic. As in "On Trains," McPherson, in "Hugh and Cry" and "Elbow Room," masterfully infers and alludes to widely held beliefs ingrained within American culture that ultimately give rise to the racial tensions in both stories. This same technique can be found in "An Act of Prostitution" and "Problems of Art." Because racial stereotypes get in the way of two couples' love in "Hue and Cry" and "Elbow Room," though, the racism portrayed is all the more evil.

In "Hue and Cry," Margot Payne's and Eric Carney's involvement is hampered by the stereotypes associated with their racial differences. Margot is black and Eric is white. In order to counter beliefs that black women are promiscuous, Eric refrains from kissing Margot for the first three weeks of their relationship. A conversation that Margot has with Eric's African American roommate, Jerry, also alludes to the racist innuendo that surrounds the story. Jerry tells Margot that he is a better lover than Eric, flaunting the idea of black male prowess. Like Margot and Eric, Virginia Valentine and Paul Frost, the two main characters of "Elbow Room," must also contend with racist assumptions. Virginia is black, Paul is white. Paul is particularly troubled by such beliefs and spends much of his time learning about them in a constant effort to disregard them.

Ironically, both Margot and Eric and Virginia and Paul are involved in the social movements of the late 1960's and early 1970's. In fact, their individual commitment to social reform is the basis for their attractions. Eric worked in the South during the civil rights marches for a semester and summer. When he returns to school in the fall and meets Margot, he recruits her to work alongside him. In "Elbow Room," Virginia is involved in the Peace Corps, and Paul is a conscientious objector to the Vietnam War. The greatest contribution that both couples make toward political change, however, is their personal involvement with one another despite their differing racial backgrounds. Through such private circumstances, McPherson speaks to the larger racial anxieties present within the subtexts of both stories and powerfully demonstrates the difficulties in overcoming such obstacles when they are so deep-seated that they intrude upon personal lives.

In both "Hue and Cry" and "Elbow Room," the couples' parents, particularly the white parents, function as emissaries of the cultural standards that all but deny interracial relationships. When Eric takes Margot to New Hampshire to meet his parents, his father is mysteriously away in the woods hunting, while Eric's mother nearly breaks into tears when she looks at Margot. Soon after the visit, Margot and Eric split up. Virginia and Paul, on the other hand, get married; Paul, however, must perpetually contend with his father's badgering him to desert Virginia.

Not all of McPherson's stories that deal with racial difference end in despair. In "A Loaf of Bread," Harold Green, a Jewish shopkeeper, and Nelson Reed, a black assembly-line worker, resolve their conflicts with each other, and in "Problems of Art," Mrs. Mary Farragot, a black spinster, triumphs over a court system that pronounces her guilty until proven innocent. The fact that "Hue and Cry" and "Elbow Room" end with unresolved racial conflicts, however, makes the conclusions of both stories all the more unnerving. The intrusion of the omniscient narrator in both "Hue and Cry" and "Elbow Room" also expands the pain of irreconcilable racial forces to include and involve the reader in a resolution. The narrator forces the reader to have a stake in the stories' scenarios and outcomes.

In "Hue and Cry," after Margot and Eric's breakup, the storyteller asks, "If this is all there is, what is left of life and why are we alive?" The question thrusts the racial tensions that Margot and Eric tragically succumb to toward the reader, demanding consideration. The narrator's intrusion underscores the futility of Margot and Eric's existence, leaving the reader alone to ponder the possibility of life in the world that Margot and Eric sought but were ultimately unable to grasp. Likewise, the narrator of "Elbow Room" intrusively announces throughout the piece that he is in search of a new story in which differences are not threatening. In fact, it is with this hope that the storyteller pursues a relationship with Paul and Virginia in the first place, hoping to advance his own writing career with the novel idea of a successful interracial relationship. The narrator is especially enamored of Virginia, who tells him that she has made "elbow room" within her head, meaning she has made a space for herself that allows for differences between people. Though the story ends with the description of a picture of Paul, Virginia, and their newborn son in Kansas at Paul's parents' house, the narrator regrets that he lacks the insight to tell if Paul and Virginia's story is a successful one. The narrator is of this world, still largely unable to make "elbow room." He does wager his reputation on the boy's story, giving some hope for the future. McPherson raises the possibility of change but cleverly leaves the reader in control of deciding the destiny of Paul, Virginia, and their son.

Bibliography

Beavers, Herman. "I Yam What You Is and You Is What I Yam: Rhetorical Invisibility in James Alan McPherson's 'The Story of a Dead Man.'" *Callaloo* 9 (Fall, 1986): 565-577. Though the narrator in "The Story of a Dead Man" is like other McPherson narrators in that he is visible both as storyteller and character, Beavers discusses how he is different because of his innocence and naïveté, lacking the usual all-knowing authority that legitimizes his role as storyteller.

Gervin, Mary A. "Developing a Sense of Self: The Androgynous Ideal in McPherson's 'Elbow Room.'" *College Language Association Journal* 26 (December, 1982): 251-255. Discusses the androgynous implications of "Elbow Room," wherein Paul and Virginia assimilate the strongest character traits of the other into their own self-concepts, subsuming their masculine and feminine attributes.

McPherson, James Alan. "Interview with James Alan McPherson." Interview by Bob Schacochis and Dan Campion. *Iowa Journal of Literary Studies* 4, no. 1 (1983): 6-33. A rare opportunity to read what McPherson himself has to say about his career as a writer within the African American literary tradition, about classifications in regard to writing and writers, about the publishing industry, about writing workshops, and about the craft of storytelling.

Wallace, Jon. "The Politics of Style in Three Stories by James Alan McPherson." *Modern Fiction Studies* 34 (Spring, 1988): 17-26. Discusses the ways the narrators of "The Story of a Dead Man," "The Story of a Scar," and "Just Enough for the City" seek a space within themselves antithetical to the "elbow room" of Virginia Frost, in that they want to defend themselves from human intimacy, involvement, and personal history.

_____. "The Story Behind the Story in James Alan McPherson's 'Elbow Room.'" *Studies in Short Fiction* 25 (Fall, 1988): 447-452. Considers the story's real meaning to be the narrator's search for a storytelling form that will let Paul and Virginia exist despite their interracial relationship.

Patricia J. Ferreira

THE STREET

Author: Ann Petry (1908-   )
Type of work: Novel
Type of plot: Naturalism
Time of plot: The 1940's
Locale: Harlem, New York, and suburban Connecticut
First published: 1946

> *Principal characters:*
> LUTIE JOHNSON, a young, divorced African American mother
> JONES, the superintendent of Lutie Johnson's apartment building
> JUNTO, a slumlord
> BOOTS SMITH, the leader of Junto's band
> MRS. HEDGES, a tenant of Lutie Johnson's apartment building
> MIN, a woman who lives with Jones
> BUB, Lutie's young son
> THE CHANDLERS, a suburban family

The Novel

  The Street relates the difficult education of Lutie Johnson, the protagonist; she has not yet learned to read the mythical signs and symbols of American culture with the disbelieving irony required by the conditions of her race and gender. At the opening of the novel, Lutie is intoxicated by such commonplace American images as Benjamin Franklin, self-made individuals, and white picket fences. By the conclusion of the novel, however, Lutie is filled with a new vision of herself, of the society around her, and of her place in that society—a society in which she had formerly fully invested her faith and her imagination. To this end, one of Lutie's final thoughts in the narrative is the recollection of the words of a grammar school teacher who once proclaimed to her: "I don't know why they have us bother to teach your people to write." Lutie understands the rejected position in which she is placed by the views of the dominant society. In a similar vein, the final images of the novel are those of the garbage that lines and defines the Harlem streets, images with which the novel also began but which now recur with a stirring resonance. By the end of the narrative, Lutie begins to reconcile herself to the manner in which she is seen by those who control the signs, symbols, and opportunities of American culture.

  The narrative begins with Lutie's quest to find an apartment for herself and her son, Bub. Having inspected an apartment in the building superintended by Jones, Lutie puts aside her disappointment with the building; she is certain that she will eventually be able to better her lot. Once Lutie has settled into life in the building, her imagination releases her much of the time from the depression and oppression of her surroundings. She recalls the happy, early moments of her former marriage as well as her tenure working as a maid in suburban Connecticut, a tenure during which she was both enamored of and ambivalent concerning "model" surburban life. Lutie's imaginings are interrupted by the bleakness of her surroundings, and much of the early tension of the novel revolves around this tension between her hopes of a promising future and the bleakness around her that apparently denies the possibility.

Much of the novel is concerned with this type of tension, and soon the narrative point of view takes up the bleak perspective of Jones, the superintendent, who has been battered and cowed by his environment and circumstances. Somewhat like Lutie, Jones leads a life of fantasy, but fantasy that is much more lively, grotesque, and blinding than that of Lutie. His fantasy life and sexual desires prompt him to try to rape Lutie and, ultimately, to entice Bub to steal letters from mailboxes so that he is arrested by the authorities.

In turn, the narrative point of view also embraces the bleak perspectives of Min, the timid woman who lives with Jones as his lover, of Bub, Lutie's fearful and impressionable son, of Mrs. Hedges, the madame in the employ of Junto, and of Boots Smith, the co-opted bandleader also in Junto's employ. Hence, much of the action of the novel is psychological, action that multiplies the tension between the mental life of the many characters and the bleak physical, social, and economic realities confronting them. This tension is first introduced and is most powerfully maintained within the perspective of Lutie Johnson.

Nevertheless, the action of the plot accelerates when, seeking more than imaginary relief from the pressures facing her, Lutie enters Junto's corner bar and casually sings along with the blues song playing on the jukebox. Boots Smith both sees and overhears Lutie and offers her the opportunity to sing with his band. After her first performance with Smith's band, and as her sense of success and a promising future grows, Lutie's prospects turn for the worse. When she comes in late in the night from her performance, Jones attempts to rape her, and she is rescued only by the equally questionable Mrs. Hedges. Almost simultaneously, Junto communicates to Smith his own desire for Lutie and the ultimatum that Smith must secure Lutie for him. Accordingly, Lutie is never paid for her singing, so that her sexual favors may be extorted from her. What is more, Bub is eventually arrested by post office authorities. In short, Lutie Johnson's circumstances, environment, and community quickly conspire against and overwhelm her.

By the conclusion of these events, Lutie turns to Boots Smith for cash in order to retain a lawyer to defend Bub. In the moments when she faces him in his apartment, waiting for him to decide her fate, however, she begins to see herself as a beleaguered pawn manipulated by him as well as by others and by an overwhelming set of circumstances. These circumstances, she begins to understand, are largely premised by the social realities of race, gender, and class in America. In her sudden rage, Lutie bludgeons Smith and thus ensures, it seems, her exclusion from the mythical American life and suburbs she has so long desired to enter. Lutie Johnson flees her former life and former home, leaving behind even her incarcerated son.

The Characters

Lutie Johnson is characterized by independence of spirit. Lutie is greatly enamored of cultural myths of the self-made American—a figure symbolized for her by the suburban Chandlers, for whom she worked as a maid, and by the larger-than-life image of Benjamin Franklin. While preoccupied with notions of "pulling oneself up by the bootstraps," Lutie finds herself prey to the desires of those around her—the sexual fantasies of the apartment superintendent, the practiced eye of the resident madame, the lust of the white slumlord. She survives an attempted rape at the hands of Jones, the superintendent, and by happenstance is presented the opportunity to escape her environment and realize her dreams by singing. Apparent happenstance is revealed as a plot on the part of Junto, slumlord and ubiquitous presence, to sacrifice Lutie to his sexual appetite. Faced at the conclusion of the novel with having to solicit money from Junto's middleman, Lutie is consumed with rage at those who manipulate her and at the patent falsehood of American cultural myths in relation to herself and those who share her circumstances. Faced with an imminent rape attempt, Lutie, in her rage, murders Boots, Junto's middleman, and flees Harlem, leaving behind her son—in whose name she had so often fashioned her "American" dreams.

Jones, the superintendent of Lutie Johnson's apartment building, has spent his life on ships and in basements and boiler rooms. He views women almost exclusively as instruments for fulfilling his sexual fantasies. In his life of confinement in the basement of tenements working for men like Junto, Jones has become an almost subhuman figure. He begins to resemble his alternately cringing and aggressive dog.

Junto, the presiding slumlord, controls the economies of both finance and desire in the environment in which Lutie discovers that she is trapped. In addition to owning the building in which Lutie lives, Junto owns the house of prostitution on the first floor of the apartment building, the bar at the corner where she seeks a momentary respite, and the band and dance hall by means of which it seems that Lutie will realize her dreams after all. Much of the latter half of the plot is driven by Junto's desire to possess Lutie.

Boots Smith, the leader of Junto's band, is ultimately co-opted into attempting to procure Lutie for Junto, despite the fact that he too desires Lutie. Boots is provided with a life-style and financial security that he finally will not risk in defiance of his employer. He has escaped the environment that Lutie wishes to escape, but, ironically, is the very figure that Lutie must kill in order to make her own tattered escape of sorts at the conclusion of the novel.

Mrs. Hedges is an unflappable tenant of Lutie's apartment building who seemingly maintains an omniscient watch over the street and its people and events. Mrs. Hedges is employed as a madame by Junto, who owns the apartment building, and the two have maintained a long and mutually beneficial business partnership.

Min, the meek, subdued woman who lives with Jones, is thankful foremost for having secured a rent-free situation. She seems to possess little of the mythical American determination and ambition "to better oneself" that is so central a preoccupation for Lutie. She lives meekly in fear of Jones, seeking protection from his brutality from a conjure man. By the end of the novel, she gains the courage to leave Jones.

Bub, Lutie Johnson's young son, in many ways inherits her uncritical fixation with the American Dream. Once Lutie's downfall occurs, he is abandoned.

The Chandlers are the emotionally troubled and sterile suburban family for whom Lutie Johnson worked for a time as a live-in maid. It is from the Chandlers and their constant pursuit of increasing wealth that Lutie learns her most enduring lessons concerning the American Dream. Lutie learns to imitate uncritically their hopes and ambitions, although she also witnesses the shallowness of their lives.

Themes and Meanings

Ann Petry's character Lutie Johnson is one of the most independent and self-reliant African American women in fiction. Petry's naturalist and psychological portrait of Lutie Johnson is closely and intensely drawn, and it is this facet of the novel that to an important degree renders the novel so remarkable. Lutie's psychological life is detailed and sustained to a point virtually unique in fiction. From Lutie's perspective, the exigencies of race in America are compounded and intensified by those of gender. One is unable to forget that the issue of race is profoundly transformed when considered in tandem with the issue of gender. Moreover, one understands that the two must be considered together in order to understand fully the dynamics of African American presence in America. Similarly, Lutie Johnson's determination and perseverance, her sense of pursuing and controlling her own destiny, provide a portrait of an African American woman that is relatively rare in the African American literary tradition up to the time of the novel's publication.

In addition to the powerful consideration of gender and intense psychological realism that Petry brings to African American fiction, her manipulation of narrative structure and chronological sequencing bears noting. As much as she relies on the sequential action of traditional plot construction, Petry deviates from this traditional construction. That is, rather than moving forward in time, much of the narrative expends itself recapitulating events already introduced to the reader. As the narrative perspective shifts from character to character, readers find themselves once again considering moments and events already narrated, but from an alternative perspective. Each successive perspective and each successive narration of familiar events heightens the sense of constriction and confinement characterizing the situation and psychic realities of the novel's characters. Petry's readers discover that in "the street" each moment is as fully and suffocatingly occupied as are the relatively small spaces into which masses of people like Lutie Johnson are confined. The refusal of narrative or chronological time to move forward as expected begins to suggest that the confined people in the environment described by the novel lack a future. In short, their future seems destined to repeat the desperation of their past. Much to Petry's credit, this theme is cunningly worked out in terms of the complex time-line of the story, the structure through which the events of the story are conveyed.

Important symbols in *The Street* include signs and other means by which information is widely circulated in the culture and society in which Lutie Johnson finds
herself. One of the first such signs to appear in the text is one that advertises the
apartment Lutie will eventually take, and Lutie proves adept at decoding the euphe-
mistic language obscuring the true condition of the tenement. It is this type of acu-
ity, however, that she has not yet developed in consideration of more beguiling and
widely disseminated signs and symbols in American culture. Post offices, mailboxes,
movies, movie theaters, and newspapers (which can alter and reinvent actual events)
bear similar symbolic weight in the text. These are the places that prove most beguiling and most misleading for Lutie Johnson and her son. They bear messages of the
dominant society that, at best, must be read ironically or, at worst, must be guarded
against entirely. Also important to the symbolism of the novel is the issue of "rooms."
The novel begins with Lutie's search for appropriate rooms, and it is through numerous descriptions of rooms that Lutie's dreams and disappointments are regis-
tered.

Critical Context

Anne Petry's *The Street* made a somewhat sensational appearance in 1946. This
novel was the first by an African American woman to sell in excess of one million
copies. Moreover, the book's naturalist orientation, attention to urban reality, and
understanding of the explosiveness of violence in urban environments reserved for
African Americans led to Petry's being regarded as a writer within the Richard Wright
orbit. While one might certainly see similarities between the work of Petry and
Wright, Petry's work attains a psychological depth and closeness of portraiture never
quite pursued or attained by Wright. Narrative drama is often much more psychological for Petry than it is for Wright.

Despite the avidness with which the novel was first received and acclaimed, Petry's novel, unlike the work of Wright, remained out of print for several decades.
With the increasingly high profile of black feminist criticism in academic circles in
the late 1970's and early 1980's, interest in Petry's work was rekindled, and the novel
was reissued in 1985 by Beacon Press. *The Street* is one of only three novels written
by Petry, although she has also written short fiction and children's stories. *The Street*
remains perhaps Petry's most gripping and intense work, a work she hoped would
be "a book that was like an explosion inside the head of the reader."

Bibliography

Bell, Bernard W. "Ann Petry's Demythologizing of American Culture and Afro-
American Character." In *Conjuring: Black Women, Fiction, and Literary Tradition*, edited by Marjorie Pryse and Hortense Spillers. Bloomington: Indiana University Press, 1985. Bell attempts to free Petry's work from stifling, traditional
comparisons to the works of Richard Wright and Chester Himes, two of Petry's
notable contemporaries. He contends that these longstanding comparisons over-
shadow and misrepresent Petry's talent and that, in contrast to Wright and Himes,

Petry moves beyond a mere naturalist vision in order to probe pervasive cultural myths and the intricacies and complexities of character.

Christian, Barbara. *Black Women Novelists: The Development of a Tradition, 1892-1976.* Westport, Conn.: Greenwood Press, 1980. Christian places Lutie Johnson, the protagonist, within the tradition of the "tragic mulatta," the beautiful and ill-fated heroine commonplace early in the tradition of African American women's fiction. Christian sees the novel as exposing the falseness of governing American myths in addition to exposing the inevitability of crime given the hostility of urban environments for African American communities.

Hernton, Calvin C. *The Sexual Mountain and Black Women Writers.* New York: Anchor Press, 1987. Hernton praises Petry as the first African American writer to portray strikingly and forcefully the multiple oppressions facing African American women. Junto, Jones, and Boots Smith are explicated in the essay as oppressors of Lutie, and Min is contrasted to Lutie in their roles as victims of the multiple oppression facing African American women. Hernton singles out the novel as a pioneering example of the "womanist/feminist protest" that would later emerge from African American women novelists.

Pryse, Marjorie. " 'Pattern Against the Sky': Deism and Motherhood in Ann Petry's *The Street.*" In *Conjuring: Black Women, Fiction, and Literary Tradition*, edited by Marjorie Pryse and Hortense Spillers. Bloomington: Indiana University Press, 1985. Pryse explores the significance of the novel's references to Benjamin Franklin in order to consider the determinist, or deist, narrative world in which Lutie Johnson struggles. Having established the nature of the narrative world, Pryse then considers the characters who provide visions of the community in which Lutie Johnson lives. Pryse's footnotes provide important bibliographical data concerning earlier criticism on *The Street.*

Washington, Mary Helen, ed. *Invented Lives: Narratives of Black Women, 1860-1960.* Garden City, N.Y.: Doubleday, 1987. Discusses Petry's development of the female characters in her novels.

Lindon Barrett

SUDER

Author: Percival L. Everett (1956-   )
Type of work: Novel
Type of plot: Picaresque
Time of plot: The second half of the twentieth century
Locale: Fayetteville, North Carolina; Seattle, Washington; and the Cascade mountain range, Oregon
First published: 1983

>*Principal characters:*
>
>CRAIG SUDER, the protagonist, a black third baseman for the Seattle Mariners
>
>CATHY SUDER (MA), Craig's mother, whom his father one day pronounces "crazy"
>
>BEN SUDER, Craig's father, a physician
>
>MARTIN SUDER, Craig's brother, who shares Craig's distress over their mother's condition
>
>BUD POWELL, a real-life jazz pianist introduced into the fictional narrative
>
>LOU TYLER, the white manager of the Seattle Mariners
>
>SID WILLIS, a retired baseball player and "black Indian"
>
>DOCTOR MCCOY, a bigoted white man who runs a "Christian" dental practice that uses prayer rather than pain killers
>
>FAT THOMAS, a three-hundred-pound gay Chinese vending machine serviceman
>
>NAOMI WATKINS, the daughter of the local undertaker
>
>JINCY JESSY JACKSON, a nine-year-old white girl who runs away from her abusive mother

The Novel

This short novel follows two narrative threads: baseball player Craig Suder's quixotic adult adventures and his childhood memories. Each contemporary moment is informed by some action in the past; chapters shift from one narrative line to the other.

The first story line begins with a strikeout, but Craig Suder's problems in batting are only the beginning of his worries. His poor performance on the field is letting down his team and embarrassing his son; his poor performance in bed is driving his wife Thelma to her exercycle and perhaps to another man. After he is conveniently put on the disabled list, not for any physical injury but for his supposed jinx on the team, Craig uses his long leave of absence to examine his life. He does not like what he sees. Only with his discovery of what he assumes is Thelma's infidelity does he decide to abandon his responsibilities. He leaves, taking only his baseball bat, saxophone, record player, and a recording of Charlie Parker's "Ornithology."

Herein begins a series of episodic, seriocomic experiences. First, Craig asks Sid

Willis if he can stay on Willis' boat. During his short sojourn with the renegade Willis, Suder becomes the unknowing accomplice to a drug-smuggling scheme. Unhappy with his implication in criminal activities and wary of Willis' offer to do him a favor by ending his "miserable, pathetic life," Suder pushes Willis and the drugs overboard. He then adds a suitcase full of money to his list of movable property.

Willis' paraphrase of Austrian mathematician Kurt Gödel's theory that "you need a dash of illogicalness to make your life complete" seems to apply to much of Suder's life. After his adventure at sea, he lands in Portland, Oregon, where he rents a room in a boardinghouse in the Chinese district, unaware that its residents are gay. He also unwittingly inspires the affection of Fat Thomas, who helps him escape from Willis, who has followed Craig to the city. Taking Thomas' station wagon, Suder heads for manager Lou Tyler's cabin in the Cascade mountain range. Along the way, he acquires an elephant by making a wager at a suburban shopping mall. Once in the mountains, he takes in a nine-year-old runaway white girl named Jincy Jessy Jackson.

Up to this point, Suder's saxophone has replaced his baseball bat as his principal mode of self-expression, but because the sax hurts Jincy's ears and makes Renoir, the elephant, bellow, Suder turns to a new outlet: self-propelled flight. Long interested in birds and their assumed freedom from earthly responsibility, Suder announces his intention of flying by his own power off the edge of Willet Rock, more than two thousand feet above the surface of Ezra Pond. In preparation, he tries to become more like a bird, catching a fever to raise his body temperature, doing exercises to become more flexible, and, on one occasion, eating a worm. As the book ends, a bewinged Suder runs naked from a host of pursuers until he jumps from the rock. After a long dive, he masters the air currents and truly flies.

The second narrative line, tracing Suder's childhood memories, offers commentary on the main plot and illuminates the character of the protagonist. It begins with Suder's recollection of when he was ten years old and his father announced to him and his brother Martin, "Boys, your mother is crazy." This statement turns Suder's childhood world upside down, making him question himself and his place in the scheme of things. Concerned about his mother's public instability, Suder begins to wonder if he himself carries the seeds of madness.

His father's sober presence is a stabilizing factor in his life. He is also comforted by the counsel of Bud Powell, a celebrated jazz pianist who is staying with the Suder family during a hiatus from his musical journeys. Powell interests the boy in jazz and in travel; he talks of going to France, where "people are free."

In its own way, Powell's restlessness complements Cathy Suder's. At one point, when he unties Craig's pet dog Django (named for jazz guitarist Django Reinhardt), even though it is likely that an irate neighbor will shoot the animal, Powell asserts, "That's called a chance. Nothing is fair, and nobody knows anything."

After Suder hits his mother on the head with a china bowl to knock "sense into her," as his brother had suggested, she takes the event as a revelation from God and plans to join a Bible study group led by a bigoted dentist, Doctor McCoy. "If you fellows believed more strongly in God, maybe you wouldn't be colored," McCoy announces to the Suder family at the dinner table. Against her husband's wishes, Cathy Suder continues to seek McCoy's company, until he treats her ambition to run around the boundaries of the city as a great joke.

When she is not obsessed with her husband's imagined infidelity, Cathy Suder wages a campaign to preserve her sons' chastity. She badgers Martin about his masturbatory activities and catches Craig experimenting with Naomi Watkins.

The second narrative thread ends with both Ben and Cathy Suder successfully running around Fayetteville, to the applause of the city's black citizens. This event parallels Craig's flight in the first story line.

The Characters

Craig Suder is an unusual combination of victim and victor. On one hand, he appears to be the archetypal dupe; in fact, Sid Willis asserts, "Luck has decided you're the greatest patsy since the Jews." On the other hand, his flight from adversity seems to propel him forward to experiences that are life-affirming both for himself and for others.

The character and fate of Craig Suder validate Bud Powell's contention that he resembles Charlie "Bird" Parker. The now-legendary jazz saxophonist led a hapless, rootless existence marked by drug abuse and living on the edge of his endurance. Parker, however, wrote and performed music that could be both energetic and exuberant; his music gave shape and coherence to his private emotional turmoil. Craig Suder's life is characterized by much the same pattern: stunning reversals and an ultimately triumphant transcendence of his problems when he takes flight.

Much of the frantic propulsion of the story is derived from its first-person narration, which is marked by short sentences and the active voice. In some ways, Suder's clipped narrative voice emulates the pacing of bebop jazz. Having worked as a jazz musician, Everett has intimate knowledge of the art form that pervades this novel, especially the staccato phrasing of Charlie Parker's "Ornithology." "I could feel the push of the song, a tension," Suder admits as a young boy hearing Powell play the tune. Much the same can be said of the plot of his own life. It is full of twists and turns, abrupt changes of direction, and unpredictable complexities.

The other characters in the novel, even the most minor, are easily remembered. All of them, such as gay lovers Mike and Larry, who read—in the nude—their individual copies of Mao Tse-tung's little red book, or Ugly Marsha, the barfly whom Suder kisses to catch a fever and raise his body temperature to birdlike levels, contribute to the zany world through which Suder moves.

In the final analysis, it is Craig Suder's character that dominates the book. The narrative centers on his mad dash to define himself, to be himself. Beyond the labels of "black man" or "ballplayer," Suder insists on being true to his own unique identity. It is not surprising that, at the novel's end, when a university zoologist witnesses the flight and the protagonist imagines the professor labeling him with the classifying term "homo sapiens," Suder utters the last words of the book, the affirmative, individualizing response "Craig Suder."

Themes and Meanings

Suder's twin obsessions with birds and jazz come together in the person of saxophonist Charlie "Bird" Parker. As a musician, Parker epitomizes the power of art to transcend the earthbound self and the everyday world. Like a bird in flight, Parker in performance soared above the cares of his world on the wings of jazz.

In youth and adulthood, Craig Suder had the same impulse. As a child, he collected the dead sparrows that his brother Martin shot with a BB rifle. He says that he "imagined the lives of those birds passing up through the box spring and the mattress and into me." When Bud Powell introduces Craig to Parker's composition "Ornithology," the boy's attraction to the freedom of birds merges with the freedom of jazz improvisation. Powell argues, "Jazz is one step beyond, one giant step." Besides the obvious bird reference in its title, "Ornithology" draws its basic chord progression from the earlier pop standard "How High the Moon." Thus, the work derives its inspiration from the desire to reach beyond one's grasp; it is the musical embodiment of the spirit of aspiration.

This same desire transforms Suder into a modern-day Daedalus. Unlike his unfortunate son Icarus, Daedalus successfully escaped his problems on the island of Crete by fashioning his own pair of wings and flying to the sanctuary of Sicily. Like his mythological role model, Suder masters the air currents and flies.

The fact that he flies with an erection calls attention to another major image pattern in the novel, a concern about male potency. At the very beginning of the book, Suder's problems with his batting performance affect his success in the bedroom. A linkage between baseball bat and male phallus is made. In Craig's youth, his mother also makes this connection when she calls out to Martin at a church league game, "Clench that bat, Martin! Wrap those nasty fingers around it. Is that how you hold it, Martin?"

Cathy Suder polices her two sons rigorously and relentlessly in regard to their masturbatory activities, and this obsession seems almost justified in light of the interest most of the neighborhood boys seem to take in the matter. Even Virgil Wallace, an older, mentally retarded boy who appears from time to time in the narrative, seems to be concerned about little else. It is Virgil who provides the key to the larger meaning of this act. When he finally asks Virgil why he "pulls" on himself, Craig Suder receives the one-word answer—"Life." This equation of sexual potency with the affirmation of life pervades the novel. Suder is physically aroused not by the prospect of sexual release but by its sublimation; he gets excited when listening to "Ornithology" or by flying naked under his own power.

As a counterpoint to these matters are the references to death and dead things. As a boy, Suder is fascinated by the Pernell Watkins Funeral Home and Hair Parlor and the rumors that Mr. Watkins recycles coffins and uses dead people's hair for his wig business. Suder is also traumatized by the prospect of kissing the suture-sewn mouth of his dead grandmother during the viewing of her mortal remains. At the funeral home, Suder experiences a moment of paralysis when he is left alone with the cadavers one night after following his brother Martin into the building.

This acquaintance with death and dead things continues into Suder's adult life. At one point, he is forced to drive Lou Tyler on one of his quests for road kill to take home to stuff and mount. "You're not filling up my trunk with dead dogs," Suder tells his taxidermy-mad manager. There is nothing that Tyler does not want to stuff, and he will go as far as killing an animal himself in order to obtain a specimen, trying to run over deer as they cross the road and, near the novel's end, trying to kill Suder's elephant with a chain saw. Ironically, his fate is to die at the hands of a motorist while standing in the middle of a rural road with a dead dog in his arms. In some ways, motion is the antidote to death. There is life in movement, whether it is the motion of a musical phrase or Suder's frantic travels on water, on land, and in the air.

Critical Context

Suder is Everett's first novel. Subsequent works were not greeted with as much popular enthusiasm and critical praise. The book has been contrasted to the fiction of other modern African American novelists such as Richard Wright and James Baldwin, whose vision of the African American experience can be labeled nothing less than somber. *Suder*, on the other hand, has been hailed by such critics as Carolyn See as a happy work of "sustained and glittering incandescence."

In the opposite camp, however, are critics who believe that the novel is nothing more than escapist fare that fails to tackle the important issues confronting the main character. In this regard, some reviewers assert that flight, real or imagined, is not a valid option for real people in the real world.

Bibliography

Atlantic. Review of *Suder*, by Percival Everett. 252 (September, 1983): 124. The narrative does not live up to initial expectations, and the ending is especially unsatisfactory. "Even daffiness provides no escape from a daft world."

Gray, Paul. "Laugh Track." *New York* 122 (August 22, 1983): 70. The novel abandons its promising beginning, Craig Suder's many-layered professional and personal predicament, and opts for jokes at the expense of character development.

Hoffman, Alice. "Slumps and Tailspins." *The New York Times Book Review* (October 2, 1983): 9, 26. Describes the novel's humor as often overstated. Calls "redeemingly evocative" the flashbacks involving Suder's youth, wherein the author captures the "terrors of childhood."

See, Carolyn. "Suder." *Los Angeles Times Book Review*, July 31, 1983, 1, 8. The novel is a comic masterpiece that tells how an individual can achieve transcendence over problems.

Stuewe, Paul. "Late Night Thoughts." *Quill and Quire* 50 (January, 1984): 33. An inventive plot and imaginative characters are undercut by prosaic language.

S. Thomas Mack

SULA

Author: Toni Morrison (1931-   )
Type of work: Novel
Type of plot: Social realism
Time of plot: 1919-1965
Locale: A neighborhood in Medallion, Ohio, called "the Bottom"
First published: 1973

Principal characters:
SULA PEACE, one of the two protagonists
NEL WRIGHT, Sula's quiet complement, the other protagonist
EVA PEACE, Sula's grandmother, the one-legged matriarch of the
    Peace family
HANNAH PEACE, Eva's daughter and Sula's mother
HELENE WRIGHT, Nel's mother, the daughter and granddaughter
    of New Orleans prostitutes
SHADRACK, a World War I veteran who suffers from shell shock
PLUM PEACE, Eva's son who returns broken after serving in
    World War I
THE DEWEYS, three unrelated boys who are summoned to live in
    Eva's house
AJAX, a strong young man who loves airplanes and women

The Novel

Sula traces people's lives in "the Bottom," a neighborhood of Medallion, Ohio, begun as "a nigger joke." When a white farmer had promised a slave rich bottom land in exchange for his labor, the slave was given "hilly land, where planting was backbreaking, where the soil slid down and washed away the seeds," and where the white people in the next century longed to live, far from the farms and factories of the valley. Readers follow the lives of the community's central figures for half a century. The prologue states that the people of the Bottom have three concerns: "what Shadrack was all about, what that little girl Sula who grew into a woman in their town was all about, and what they themselves were all about."

What Shadrack was all about was control. Having survived death in World War I, he had to find a way to survive life. In the hospital, his fingers "began to grow in higgledy-piggledy fashion like Jack's beanstalk" so that he had to hide "his huge growing hands under the covers." Released in such a mental state, he is taken home to the Bottom, where he declares January 3 to be National Suicide Day, "to order and focus experience. It had to do with making a place for fear as a way of controlling it. He knew the smell of death and was terrified of it, for he could not anticipate it." If he knew when it was coming, however, then there was nothing to fear. "If one day a year were devoted to it, everybody could get it out of the way and the rest of the year would be safe and free." Each year, beginning in 1919, he walked the streets with a cowbell and a hangman's rope, offering people the opportunity to meet death. No one takes up his offer until 1941.

Sula Peace is about self-possession and relationships. Both she and Nel Wright are "solitary little girls whose loneliness was so profound it intoxicated them." When they found each other, it changed everything. Sula was the brave one, once slicing off the tip of her finger to prove to neighborhood Irish bullies that if she were that strong, she would not be afraid of them. Nel, however, "seemed stronger and more consistent than Sula, who could hardly be counted on to sustain any emotion for more than three minutes." They complete and love one another.

Just as important in Sula's life are her mother and grandmother. In her mother, Sula sees a woman's delight in pure sensuality: "Hannah simply refused to live without the attention of a man." Her grandmother Eva has only one leg, but it is a beautiful leg donned with expensive stockings and a fashionable shoe to show all the men who called on her. "Although she did not participate in the act of love, there was a good deal of teasing and pecking and laughter." The affection that the Peace women give to men is not shared with one another. Eva's love expresses itself through actions, not words. She saves Plum as a baby and then takes away his life as an adult, soaking him in kerosene and setting him on fire because she cannot stand what he has become since returning from World War I. When Hannah asks her mother why she killed him, Eva says, "he wanted to crawl back in my womb and well . . . I ain't got the room no more even if he could do it. . . . I had room enough in my heart, but not in my womb, not no more. I birthed him once. I couldn't do it again." No gesture can reach Sula. Because her grandmother's strength frightens her, Sula does the unforgivable in the eyes of everyone in the Bottom: She places Eva in a nursing home.

For Sula, as for Hannah, sex and love have nothing in common. Seducing Nel's husband is nothing personal, but it drives a wedge in the women's friendship. Years later, when Nel knows Sula is dying, she comes to her friend expecting an apology only to receive a rebuke. When Nel insists that Sula's selfishness has left her alone in the world, Sula will have none of it: "my lonely is *mine.* Now your lonely is somebody else's. Made by somebody else and handed to you." Twenty-five years later, when Nel visits Eva in the nursing home, Eva confuses her with Sula. Eva remembers the girls' friendship and tells Nel: "You, Sula. What's the difference?" Nel realizes that there is none.

What the people of the Bottom are all about is community. These people sustain each other. They can accommodate Shadrack and the could-be white man, Tar Baby, who lives at Eva's house for years as he tries to drink himself to death. They even incorporate National Suicide Day into their lives, remembering births and planning marriages in relation to it. They find solace in one another when white Medallion will not hire strong young black men to work on the New River Road. Unable to display their masculinity in their jobs as hotel waiters while wearing their thin-soled black shoes, they stand in front of the Time and a Half Pool Hall and Reba's Grill calling out to the girls. The community respects Eva, mourns Hannah's death, and castigates Sula when, first, she puts Eva in a home, then takes Nel's husband Jude, and finally sleeps with other women's husbands. Sula as the source of sorrow causes wives to love their husbands more, mothers to care for their children, and neighbors to find solidarity with each other. Such unity also leads to many of their deaths, when Shadrack leads them on National Suicide Day in 1941 down to the New River Road tunnel.

The Characters

Toni Morrison has said of Sula and Nel that "the two of them together could have made a wonderful single human being." They need and love each other, though neither recognizes that fact until it is too late. As little girls, the two are polar opposites. Sula is headstrong, independent, and courageous; Nel is quiet, obedient, and thoughtful. Together they are wildly happy—proud when Ajax and his friends in front of the ice cream parlor utter the words "pig meat" in their direction, excited when discovering their woman's bodies for the first time under the trees by the river, and curiously joyful as Sula lets go of Chicken Little's hands as he flies out over and into the water, to become "something newly missing." He is a secret that closes the gap opened up between the girls at his funeral: "They held hands and knew that only the coffin would lie in the earth; the bubbly laughter and the press of fingers would stay aboveground forever."

Nel and Sula grow into very different women. Nel represents women who choose selflessness, devoting their lives to bolstering their insecure husbands and rearing children. Nel becomes what Sula calls "one of *them*. . . . Now Nel belonged to the town and all its ways." Sula, on the other hand, chooses herself. She has been to college, lived in various cities, and been with many men, only to return home as a stranger.

Nel appears to be the good woman and Sula the evil. A plague of robin deaths and a warm winter are all the proof the people in the Bottom need of Sula's character. Morrison does not allow such easy categories. When Nel attempts a reconciliation near Sula's death, Sula asks, "How you know? . . . About who was good. How you know it was you? . . . I mean maybe it wasn't you. Maybe it was me." Sula, in effect, makes Nel question all of her assumptions about her own innocence and about Sula's guilt. The matriarchal Eva Peace is drawn in strength. Morrison says of her: "Eva is a triumphant figure, one-legged or not. She is playing God." She is a dignified survivor who commands respect. Seated in her rocker atop a child's wagon, she rules her eclectic household.

The men in this novel, with the exception of Ajax, are presented as helpless, absent, irresponsible, or dead. Shadrack and Plum are casualties of war, driven by violent social forces to an orderly madness or drugs. Tar Baby—possibly "high yellow," possibly white; no one seems to know—drinks his life away on cheap wine. Emasculated by a white racist society that will not employ black men in well-paying, respectable, and meaningful work, Jude too is victimized. He is incomplete and needy. Sula's father is dead, Nel's always away. Only Ajax appears strong. In a 1976 interview, Toni Morrison observed, "Although in sociological terms that is described as a major failing of black men—they do not stay home and take care of their children, they are not there—that has always been to me one of the most attractive features about black male life." When Sula wants to possess Ajax, he follows the airplanes he loves. The negative expression of this impulse is Eva's husband BoyBoy, who leaves her and three children for fast women and the city.

Themes and Meanings

Sula is a novel about self-creation, about women, about men, and about a culture. The girls, Sula and Nel, realize early on that the world does not easily accommodate people such as them: "Because each had discovered years before that they were neither white nor male, and that all freedom and triumph was forbidden to them, they set about creating something else to be." They would be black women. That means something different to each of them. For Nel, it means becoming a wife and mother, sustaining the values of the community. For Sula, it means living an "experimental life," rejecting commonly held values. Nel tells Sula, "You *can't* do it all. You a woman and a colored woman at that. You can't act like a man. You can't be walking around all independent-like, doing whatever you like, taking what you want, leaving what you don't." Sula will not accept such limitations. When Nel demands to know what Sula has gained from her choices—having no husband and no children; her grandmother put away in a nursing home; her mother, father, and uncle dead; residents of the Bottom all despising her—Sula responds, "Girl, I got my mind. And what goes on in it. Which is to say, I got me." Nel, on the other hand, has loneliness, an empty space that Jude used to fill, and another one Sula formerly occupied. Sula's self-knowledge and Nel's connection to other people are both essential to human existence. Each woman, even if only momentarily, comes to understand that.

Fire and water are recurrent themes throughout the novel, demonstrating the destructive forces always threatening the individual self. Two of Eva Peace's children die by fire. Plum burns in a kerosene conflagration, and Hannah, her beautiful skin burned and melted, dies while Sula watches. Eva "remained convinced that Sula had watched Hannah burn not because she was paralyzed, but because she was interested." Water also proves to be an agent of death for Chicken Little, who disappears in the river after flying from Sula's hands while Nel watches. The warm January thaw and the soft, water-soaked ground lead to the deaths of many Bottom residents who follow Shadrack to the New River Road tunnel to be crushed or drowned. Some are victims of the powerful forces that can overwhelm human beings while others watch. Shadrack watches a little boy drown; he watches his neighbors die. Morrison has commented that " 'watch' is something different from 'saw.' You have to be participating in something that you are watching. If you just saw it, you just happened to be there." Eva, Sula, Nel, and Shadrack all watch the destruction of others.

Morrison uses the image of a gray fur ball to symbolize Nel's indistinct anxiety that grows into gradual self-awareness. It begins after Sula commits adultery with Nel's husband, Jude. It is a gray ball hovering, "a ball of muddy strings, but without weight, fluffy but terrible in its malevolence." This ill-defined feeling remains with Nel for more than twenty-five years as she struggles to know herself and understand her friendship with Sula.

Such discovery and affirmation, however, must be personal and individual, as the residents of the Bottom also come to know. Waiting for the larger white society to provide validation through jobs, social status, or recognition only leads to self-destruction. Scores of people who die on Shadrack's National Suicide Day at the site of the Bottom's hope for a better life, the New River Road tunnel, demonstrate the futility of social redemption. Only the personal is possible.

Critical Context

Toni Morrison's reputation has risen with the publication of each of her novels. Her first novel, *The Bluest Eye* (1970), gained little public attention. *Sula*, her second novel, was given more serious consideration and praised, though some early reviewers focused on issues peripheral to its main intent. These two novels, along with Morrison's succeeding works—*Song of Solomon* (1977); *Tar Baby* (1981); *Beloved* (1987), for which Morrison received the Pulitzer Prize; and *Jazz* (1992)—established her firmly as one of America's finest writers. In 1993, Morrison's standing as a major author was confirmed by her receipt of the Nobel Prize in Literature.

Sula holds a special place in African American literature for its depiction of young women coming of age. It can be placed alongside such important works as Morrison's own first novel, *The Bluest Eye*, Zora Neale Hurston's *Their Eyes Were Watching God* (1937), Paule Marshall's *Brown Girl, Brownstones* (1959), Louise Meriwether's *Daddy Was a Number Runner* (1970), and Maya Angelou's *I Know Why the Caged Bird Sings* (1970). It is also a powerful story of female friendship and of female courage and survival. Finally, it speaks of belonging to a family, to a home, to a place, and to a community.

Bibliography

Bakerman, Jane S. "Failures of Love: Female Initiation in the Novels of Toni Morrison." *American Literature* 52 (January, 1981): 541-563. Presents Morrison's first three novels as accounts of female initiation. Maintains that they show female characters looking for love and self-worth but ultimately failing in their search.
Bryant, Cedric Gael. "The Orderliness of Disorder: Madness and Evil in Toni Morrison's *Sula.*" *Black American Literature Forum* 24 (Winter, 1990): 731-745. Maintains that in the worlds of Morrison's novels, the community not only tolerates but also integrates individuals whom the larger world would deem insane or evil.
Christian, Barbara. "The Contemporary Fables of Toni Morrison." In *Black Women Novelists.* Westport, Conn.: Greenwood Press, 1980. Argues that Morrison's first two novels "chronicle the search for beauty amidst the restrictions of life, both from within and without." Her main characters in both novels search for meaning

through connection with the greater world.

De Weever, Jacqueline. *Mythmaking and Metaphor in Black Women's Fiction.* New York: St. Martin's Press, 1992. Examines contemporary black women writers as part of the "return to myth" tradition in letters. Insists that the experience of black people in the New World cannot be told through realism or naturalism and that Morrison and others use myth to order that experience.

Stepto, Robert B. " 'Intimate Things in Place': A Conversation with Toni Morrison." *Massachusetts Review* 18 (Autumn, 1977): 473-489. A wide-ranging discussion of Morrison's life and work, with special attention given to *Sula*.

Laura Weiss Zlogar

SWEET WHISPERS, BROTHER RUSH

Author: Virginia Hamilton (1936-   )
Type of work: Novel
Type of plot: Social realism
Time of plot: The 1970's, with flashbacks to a decade earlier
Locale: A small Midwestern city and southwestern Ohio
First published: 1982

> *Principal characters:*
> SWEET TERESA "TREE" PRATT, a fourteen-year-old black girl
> DABNEY "DAB" PRATT, Tree's mildly retarded brother
> VIOLA "MUH VY" SWEET RUSH PRATT, Tree and Dab's mother
> SYLVESTER WILEY D. SMITH (SILVERSMITH), Muh Vy's boyfriend
> MISS CENITHIA PRICHERD, an elderly cleaning woman

The Novel

Sweet Whispers, Brother Rush is a ghost story with a purpose. Through the supernatural intervention of Brother Rush, Tree Pratt comes to understand something of her family's past, which helps her to deal with her present problems and work out the identity that she will carry into a hopefully happier future.

Tree is fourteen and has just "begun growing into a woman," which is why the "street dudes" she passes on her way home from school have started to notice her. Yet Tree is no typical teenage girl; in some ways, she is the mother of the family, at least to her seventeen-year-old brother Dab, who is mildly retarded and cannot set the table without frustration. Tree lives an isolated, friendless life of school and Dab, and has for some time. Tree has such a life and such enormous responsibilities because her mother, Muh Vy, is a practical nurse who must live at her jobs, at least during the week.

The novel opens not with any of Tree's family problems in the present but with her discovery of Muh Vy's brother's ghost. One Friday afternoon after school, in the little room where she often goes to draw, Tree sees him. "Brother was in the middle of the table. Not standing on the top of it in the middle, but through the middle." Brother Rush holds "an oval space shaped like a mirror," and Tree is able to enter this "shining space" into her own past. At first she does not realize it is her past. She becomes her own mother a decade earlier—when Muh Vy was younger and had two small children—and she experiences Muh Vy's rural Ohio world through her mother's eyes. On this and subsequent trips with Brother Rush, Tree will witness his death and see her mother beat Dab. Tree learns her family history—and its tragedies.

The present, however, is as insistent as the past in the novel. During this weekend, Dab has been getting progressively sicker, and when Muh Vy returns home late Saturday night, she, Silversmith, and Tree must take him to the hospital. Dab dies from his inherited porphyria, and the family must try to recover. In a typically adolescent fashion—in her anger over Dab's death, her resentment at the changes her mother is going through, her jealousy at her mother's new boyfriend—Tree lashes out. In many ways, Tree is a normal adolescent (although one with abnormal problems), and *Sweet Whispers, Brother Rush* is a young adult initiation novel showing her progress toward adulthood.

Viola Pratt is the second-most important character in the novel. Although she does not appear—at least in the present—until the novel is nearly half over, her presence is felt from the very beginning. Viola's life has not been an easy one: She has been abandoned by her husband with two young children, one of them retarded; her own family has been struck with a rare, fatal disease, and she has seen three of her brothers die. She has carved out a life for herself and her children in the best way she can, within her own limitations; although she has to live apart from her children most of the time, she has stressed to Tree that discipline had kept the family together. She has also been working for the future: She and Silversmith have been talking about starting a catering business together. In hiring Miss Pricherd to clean and then to live in the house with Tree after Dab dies, she is trying to help not only her daughter but also someone less fortunate at the same time. Muh Vy is a composite character whose faults and strengths both are present before the reader and who can admit her past mistakes. She abused her children when they were younger, and she has ignored them in the present, but she is clearly now headed on a better path.

Not everything has been resolved by the end of *Sweet Whispers, Brother Rush*. Tree still wants to go and find her father, who, she has learned during this intense week, did not die but abandoned his family. Moreover, Muh Vy wants Tree tested for porphyria; although Muh Vy is sure that the women in this family do not have the disease, the test will reassure Tree. In the end, Tree has gained, through all this pain and trouble, a new identity.

The Characters

While *Sweet Whispers, Brother Rush* is an exciting reading experience because of its occult elements and dramatic plot, the backbone of Virginia Hamilton's novel is its characterization. The protagonists here are three-dimensional with a vengeance: Contrary and contradictory, they act in ways that reveal their true humanity.

Minor characters, understandably, have less depth. Brother Rush only speaks when he appears in the past, but his warmth and pain come through clearly in those trips. Dab is retarded and therefore limited as a character, but Tree's devotion to her quiet brother is moving. Miss Pricherd is also a minor character, but in the course of the novel, she is transformed from an old lady interfering in Tree's routine into Tree's means of getting out of her own anger and resentment. Finally, Silversmith is a strong, gentle man whose good qualities come through in a number of ways.

Muh Vy is a unique character in young adult fiction, and Virginia Hamilton presents her in a unique way, warts and all. For one thing, readers see Tree's mother from several perspectives. She is not merely visible action and dialogue; in the trips Tree takes back into her own past, she becomes her mother, giving readers a double view of Muh Vy's character.

Muh Vy's strengths are clear, but it is her imperfections that make her so human. She has abused Dab as a baby, both by hitting him and by tying him to a bedpost to keep him in one place. When confronted by the knowledge Tree has gained through Brother Rush, Muh Vy can admit her mistakes to herself. As she explains to Tree, her abuse of Dab was her defense against something she could not deal with as a young mother. Now she has compounded that earlier crime by ignoring Dab's possible porphyria until it is almost too late. Certainly, Dab's drug dependence comes in part from the fact that Muy Vy is gone so much. At the end, Muh Vy does act; although it is too late, readers admire her attempts to save her son. In hiring Miss Pricherd to clean and then to live in the house with Tree, Muh Vy is trying to help not only her daughter but also someone less fortunate at the same time. Muh Vy is a complex character, a "gray" lady whose faults and strengths are equally evident.

Tree has a similar complexity, and just the same kind of contradictions, and her characterization is a subtle psychological portrait of the young adolescent—confused, self-doubting, dreamy. Tree loves her mother but, at the same time, she resents her, both because she feels unloved and ignored and because, irrationally, she resents the loss of freedom she feels when Muh Vy actually does come home. Tree's feelings conflict, and she must act them out against her mother. The same thing happens with Silversmith: Tree loves having this strong father figure at home, but she also resents someone stepping into her life and taking over. Silversmith, fortunately, has the sense to understand Tree's dilemma: "You can turn me out, Tree," he says to her, "I'm still gone like you."

Tree's contradictory complexity is not limited to her relationships. Throughout the novel, she demonstrates the kind of ambivalence adolescents often feel. On the way to the hospital with Dab, for example, Tree cannot help thinking about the fact that she is in a new car; in the midst of Dab's tragedy, Tree is fantasizing about finding her real father. Tree, in short, is wonderfully human. While the novel ends on a positive note—Tree has thrown her running-away bag back into the closet and is accepting her new family—readers know that, in this realistic family situation, the problems will have to be worked out for some time. It is the complex and subtle characterization that helps to carry the weight of this knowledge.

Themes and Meanings

Sweet Whispers, Brother Rush is a novel about family—about its complex evolution, about the relationship between its past and its present, and about the identity that one person can gain through that multilayered history.

Tree Pratt is already older than her years when the novel opens, for she is almost totally responsible for her brother in her mother's absence. She still has a lot of growing to do, however, and she does much of it in the short course of this novel. Brother Rush gives her the family history she never had, and through her trips with him, Tree learns about her mother's early life. In the midst of the crisis over Dab, though, Tree is not able to process everything that is happening to her, and she lashes out in a typically childish way, getting angry at Muh Vy and threatening to run away. Through the intervention of Rush, Muh Vy, Miss Pricherd, and Silversmith, Tree is able to work her way out of this emotionally difficult place and to feel better about her emergent family. Readers should feel good about Tree's future as well, for she has navigated the shoals of adolescence and seems headed for a happier adulthood with a real identity and real strengths.

Yet this is also a novel about family and family relationships. Few young adult novels have such realism or depth about family life and history. Readers witness the pain of Tree's aloneness but also experience the joy of the new family beginning together at the end. Muh Vy's love for her children is apparent, but so too is the abuse she was driven to as a younger woman. Likewise, Tree's devotion to her brother is admirable, but she is also capable of selfishness, even in the moments of Dab's sickness and death. The novel, in short, gives readers family life with all its warts, but not a few of its wonders. Here is a family unique in young adult fiction: single-parent, with a dramatic history, and with a future. The intensity of the relationships—the love between Tree and Dab, the struggles between Tree and Muh Vy—creates a powerful psychological realism.

Finally, the story of Tree and her family is also a story of roots, of the search for, and discovery of, one's own lost family past. "Tree and Dab never had time to find out about the past; they had so little of the present," Hamilton says. Brother Rush, as Muh Vy explains, has come to correct that ignorance about the past, to show Tree where she came from, in the technicolor trips back to rural Ohio. Like Alex Haley's *Roots* (1976), the story of *Sweet Whispers, Brother Rush* is the story of that discovery of one's own past. This is an important theme not only for the black family here that experiences it but also for all readers cut off from their own history. Silversmith says to Tree at one point, "You can't separate your skin from what's inside it"—including its biological history. Yet the past can also become a way of dealing with the present, and the future. On her last trip, Tree witnesses Brother Rush and Dab driving into death, and thus is reconciled.

Other themes touch the story—death, drugs, the supernatural, mothers and daughters—and other lessons. Yet the initiation of Tree Pratt is the major meaning of the novel; it is tied up with the story of her family identity and, finally, her roots, the family history that she slowly acquires through the course of the novel.

Virginia Hamilton's use of language and imagery is truly impressive, particularly for a young adult novel. *Sweet Whispers, Brother Rush* is extremely tactile, for readers actually feel much of the experience here: Dab's being struck with a switch as a child, for example, or the pain he and Brother Rush feel if their skin is touched (one symptom of porphyria). Many of the descriptions are fully detailed (especially in the trips back to Ohio), and the colors, textures, and sounds of the novel give it added force.

As part of this use of language, the black dialect in the novel must also be noted, for it may give some readers a little trouble at the beginning. Virginia Hamilton captures black speech in an easy way, for characters here speak as a Midwestern urban black family in the late 1970's might speak. Hamilton describes Brother Rush as "The stone finest dude Tree had ever seen in her short life of going-on fifteen years." Of Dab, Tree says, "Think he home cause he don't have no place else to go. . . ." Part of the realism of the novel, and not a little of its power, comes from this accurate rendition of how people speak and think.

Critical Context

Sweet Whispers, Brother Rush is one of the best examples of the "new realism" genre of young adult fiction, in which—as in Robert Cormier's *The Chocolate War* (1974) or the novels of S. E. Hinton—the problems of adolescents are realistically portrayed. The book is at the same time a ghost story, and thus an example of the supernatural genre. The fact that the two genres do not usually reside together is a tribute to Virginia Hamilton's ability to fuse them in fiction, to make them work for each other.

The novel is also in some ways a culmination of what Virginia Hamilton has been doing successfully for several decades. The writer of two juvenile biographies of important black figures (W. E. B. Du Bois and Paul Robeson), she is also the creator of other popular young adult novels, including *M. C. Higgins, the Great* (1974). Further, Hamilton is the author of *The People Could Fly: American Black Folktales* (1985), a children's collection. *Sweet Whispers, Brother Rush* thus combines her several interests: It is an exciting young adult novel that keeps readers glued to their seats, but at the same time it gives important information about black life, black history, and folklore. The fact that *Sweet Whispers, Brother Rush* is a young adult novel is almost irrelevant. Better to say that, like Toni Morrison and Alice Walker, Virginia Hamilton uses black life, language, and history to weave a powerful story of the ways the past and present intersect. The many prizes that went to *Sweet Whispers, Brother Rush*—including a John Newbery Honor Book Award, the Coretta Scott King Award, and an American Book Award nomination—are evidence enough of this view.

Bibliography
Farrell, Kirby. "Virginia Hamilton's *Sweet Whispers, Brother Rush* and the Case for a Radical Existential Criticism." *Contemporary Literature* 31, no. 2 (Summer, 1990): 161-176. Argues that the novel's "apparent celebration of black solidarity overlays a regressive vision of relentless sadistic competition."
Guy, David. "Escaping from a World of Troubles." *The Washington Post Book World*, November 7, 1982, 14. Guy comments that *Sweet Whispers, Brother Rush* "could vaguely bore me and utterly astound me within the space of a single chapter" and wishes that Hamilton would "release her remarkable imagination from the contrived situations of the conventional young adult novel."
Heins, Ethel L. Review of *Sweet Whispers, Brother Rush*, by Virginia Hamilton. *The*

Horn Book Magazine 18, no. 5 (October, 1982): 505-506. Praises the novel's characters as "complex, contradictory, and ambivalent as is life itself: sometimes weak, sometimes attractive, always fiercely human."

Paterson, Katherine. "Family Visions." *The New York Times Book Review*, November 14, 1982, 41, 56. A highly laudatory review of *Sweet Whispers, Brother Rush.* Paterson challenges readers to read the first paragraph of the book and "then stop—if you can."

Townsend, John Rowe. "Virginia Hamilton." In *A Sounding of Storytellers: New and Revised Essays on Contemporary Writers for Children.* Philadelphia: J. B. Lippincott, 1979. A thorough overview of Hamilton's early fiction.

David Peck

THE SYSTEM OF DANTE'S HELL

Author: Amiri Baraka (Everett LeRoi Jones, 1934-   )
Type of work: Novel
Type of plot: Bildungsroman
Time of plot: The early 1960's
Locale: Newark, New Jersey, and the American South
First published: 1965

Principal characters:
ROI, also known as Dante, the protagonist and narrator
PEACHES, a youthful prostitute, the only other fully developed
    character in the novel
BEVERLEY, one of the girls in Roi's Newark neighborhood
LEON WEBSTER, one of Roi's numerous friends and acquaintances

The Novel

Discussing *The System of Dante's Hell* in the light of conventional expectations regarding fictional form and content is misleading, since one of the fundamental effects the work seeks to achieve is to abolish such categories by showing them to be inadequate, suggesting thereby that they are irrelevant to the world that the author desires to depict. Rather than being a reliable narrative, the work reads as a series of variations on a scattered network of themes. As a result, the appeals to conflict and resolution that novels usually make are overridden in favor of appeals to more immediate experiences that the reader will find less easy to incorporate into an overall pattern of development. The avowedly experimental nature of Amiri Baraka's *The System of Dante's Hell* is not only a fundamental fact of its character but also a crucial expression of an attempt to call into question the basis of familiar fictional discourse. The novel's method also attempts to render what might be called the presentness of the material, drawing attention thereby to the texture rather than to the lessons of experience.

Although it moves at an unusual pace, articulates itself in an unusual rhythm, and possesses a challenging structure, *The System of Dante's Hell* is by no means consumed by its own artifice. On the contrary, its experimental elements make unavoidable the author's clear desire to be heard and to have the distinctiveness of what he has to say appreciated. Much of what he has to say draws less on individual experience than on a sense of the common experience in which individuality finds its social and cultural foundations. Although the voice of the narrator in the novel reflects upon his own experience, it also presents that experience as both part of, and resistant to, the common run of human activity.

Much of the novel is centered on certain areas of the author's home town of Newark, New Jersey. The city is not represented in a conventionally accessible way, and the author is clearly at pains not to provide the reader with a road map. What for the reader are simply street names and other purely nominal tokens of the urban landscape are for the author countersigns and landmarks of experience. Through their repetition, however, the urban landscape becomes for the reader a tissue of associations and possibilities that reflect the potential of experiencing without ever attaining the concrete finality of fully achieved experience. The names and other elements that compose various Newark neighborhoods are articulated as a matrix of desire, striving, and various other related processes of consciousness rather than reproduced as the lapidary emplacements of an objective reality.

  The System of Dante's Hell does not have a plot. Instead, it has a pattern of experiencing, the features of which are repeated with variations throughout. From the protagonist's perspective, it is misleading to point out a pattern, since none exists for him. He appears to be caught in the flow of urban experience, which may be erratic in its rhythm but is incessant in its pace. From the reader's point of view, it emerges that Roi's experiences not only are confined to a relatively narrow section of Newark but also are restricted to a small number of psychological and cultural areas consisting of having sexual encounters, restlessly walking the streets, being with his peers, playing basketball and baseball, recollecting or witnessing acts of violence, reading, and being self-absorbed to a degree predictable for an adolescent. The problematic influence on development of many of these areas is brought into critical focus when, toward the end of the novel, Roi leaves Newark, joins the United States Air Force, and is stationed somewhere in the Deep South. His encounter with Peaches, a prostitute, operates as an incisive critique of the codes of manhood that he learned on Newark's streets and also, as a result, of the identity that those streets conferred on him.

  Rather than recount a specific and individuated process of development, *The System of Dante's Hell* dwells on the fluctuating and irresolute energies of its protagonist, Roi. Seen in that perspective, *The System of Dante's Hell* is a *Bildungsroman*, a novel of growth and development. Once again, however, this novel deviates from the conventions of its genre. Instead of growth and development, the author stresses growth without development. Roi becomes increasingly well-versed in the ways of the world, and the range of his experiences broadens. These attainments do not give him greater access to a wider world. Rather, they seem to confirm how confined he is to a certain repetitive sequence of experiences, as though not only his social existence but also his consciousness must be confined in a ghetto.

The Characters

  The method of characterization in *The System of Dante's Hell* is as radical as are the novel's style and structure. Although this is a highly populated work, none of its characters, with the exception of Roi and Peaches, is in any way developed. Rather, they are human analogies of the city's various fixtures, occurring and recurring throughout. They are names more than they are people. They are zones of energy instead of being persuasively or engagingly individual. They seem to resemble members of a tribe, their social existence determined by rituals of self-assertion and self-protection, as opposed to being members of a complex, modern society. They flit in and out of Roi's narrative as though they are sites of his experience rather than autonomous agents in their own right.

The kinds of work they do, their relationship to social institutions, their family lives, and their psychological and intellectual makeup are not directly emphasized by Baraka. Instead, the insistent stress is on the fact of their presence, as though the most important statement that can be made on their behalf is that they cannot be overlooked, avoided, or otherwise relegated to making a merely colorful, or minor, contribution to the problematic matter of Roi's growth and development.

Roi's peer group is presented as if it consisted exclusively of foreground and immediacy. This approach prevents the reader from presuming to know any of these numerous minor characters with any degree of intimacy. The apparent irrelevance of their background keeps them at a distance and maintains them in Roi's keeping. They are his people rather than members of a world that the reader shares with them. By fabricating conditions of ignorance and remoteness in the reader, Baraka successfully encodes the different reality that the large number of minor characters inhabit. The sheer reality of population density in *The System of Dante's Hell* registers the inescapable press of context and the manner in which the context encloses even as it enriches the individual attempting to locate and take possession of a space of his or her own within it. The originality of this fluid and dynamic method of representing the life of a community is one of the novel's most original and challenging features.

Keeping pace, and coming to terms, with the community's shifting ground and multiple personalities is not simply what Roi has to accomplish. To describe his status in the novel in such a way would infer that he was somehow distinct, if only in principle, from his community. The separation between self and world, a standard feature of the modern novel, is not the basis of Roi's distinctive presence. That separation occurs only in the sequence with Peaches, when Roi has already removed himself from Newark and has taken on a very different set of loyalties and affiliations as a member of the United States Air Force. Such an assertion of citizenship turns out to compromise his manhood and the possibility of belonging to the unseemly environment to which Peaches belongs. Up until his Southern sojourn, however, far from being isolated and on trial for his manhood, Roi functions as a delighter in, meditator upon, and spokesman for his Newark community. His personality achieves presence by virtue of its capacity to absorb and divulge the energies of his community. He is not prepared to rank those energies in order, or to place specific values on them, or to differentiate between them in any way, so that what is bad in the community, or unworthy of it, is depicted with the same force as is what is attractive and beneficial. Life is not a system of priorities but a continuum of whatever happens to be happening. The events, thoughts, circumstances, and attitudes of the community make Roi what he is, so that his consciousness is an extension of what the community at large feeds it. Character is considered to be synonymous with a capacity for experience, not the capacity to organize experience.

Themes and Meanings

The form of *The System of Dante's Hell* is consistent with its radical treatment of narrative and character. The most obvious element missing from the novel's form is a sense of time. This absence makes problematic such considerations as growth and development, the historical background to Roi's and the other characters' existence, and a coordinated sense of forward movement. The novel does contain time signatures, referring to the seasons, times of day, and the like, but these occur in their own right, in relation to an overall immediacy of which they are part, and do not serve to give the novel a regulated pace or structure. The effect is to make *The System of Dante's Hell* resemble less a piece of literature than a statement by a modern jazz ensemble, a resemblance that receives a certain amount of plausibility from the fact that Amiri Baraka has written prolifically on African American music.

Such a perspective suggests a characterization of Roi as soloist among a legion of sidemen and other spontaneous contributors to the social and cultural jam session that the novel could be described as. Roi's, and the novel's, elliptical and contracted language, and the cultural shorthand with which many of its references and resonances are conveyed, can also be seen to be inspired by jazz. The perspective also suggests the way in which Baraka adapts the conceptual underpinnings of Dante Alighieri's concept of hell. The author puts under the conceptual microscope of his own narrative tradition work that has been taken as central to European humanism, a cultural outlook that has made a decisive contribution to the formation of the American social conscience. The ironies resulting from this investigation are multiple.

Particularly noteworthy, and fundamental to Baraka's ambitious project, is the manner in which he inverts Dante's system, or rather, the way in which he dismantles the ethic of the systematic in Dante. Dante's hell consists of a taxonomy of sin and places certain offenders in specific circles of the inferno. Baraka toys with this design, retaining its numerical sequence while rejecting any other manifestation of its coherence, such as the theological. Instead, as a reflection of the nature and social behavior of his fellow African Americans, a conception of structure is installed that is fluid, spontaneous, vocal, protean, and all-embracing. This alternative to order, which evinces an ethic of coherence at odds with a Eurocentric one, is one of the most far-reaching suggestions of *The System of Dante's Hell.*

Along with courageously attempting to dismantle the conventional conception of the systematic, Baraka also detaches hell from its traditional theological and eschatological associations. The concluding pages of the novel provide the beginnings of a gloss and guide to what the author was attempting to achieve. It becomes clear that his understanding of hell is the set of social conditions in which African Americans are obliged to function. This raises serious questions concerning some of hell's key connotations, such as pain, deprivation, damnation, and incrimination. These are terms that have frequently structured the discourse about race in America. To find them reproduced in the stark emotionality of some of the novel's scenes is to perceive the cultural relevance of a work that superficially may seem to be an exercise in deviant literary revisionism. The disorder to which Dante's themes and

systems are subjected articulates the challenge to find interpretive schemes to illuminate the meaning of African American reality.

Critical Context

The System of Dante's Hell represents an early effort in the postwar period to
appropriate a classic of Western civilization for the cultural use of a non-Western
audience and culture. Although it may be neither accurate nor productive to consider
African Americans outside the domain of Western or Anglophone culture, it must
be acknowledged that the status of these people and the works of their imagination
as either contributing to or dissenting from those of the dominant culture remain
matters of intense debate. Some of the intellectual and artistic energy fueling that
debate and some of the debate's ultimately political implications are given significant expression in the form, technique, and revolutionary conception of *The System
of Dante's Hell.*

In addition to its cultural and perhaps ideological self-consciousness, the novel
seems to owe some local artistic debts. Its decision to construct an artistic reality
based on an ethos of community energies seems to draw, without specific acknowl-
edgment, on the example of William Carlos Williams, the influential New Jersey
poet and man of letters. It would be surprising if Baraka, whose reputation rests on
his poetry and drama rather than on his fiction, were not aware of both Williams'
fidelity to place and his artistic experimentalism. The status given the New Jersey
city of Paterson in Williams' long poem "Paterson" (1946-1951) is comparable to
that given Baraka's Newark in *The System of Dante's Hell.* In that sense, the novel
has a perhaps paradoxical, even marginal, but nevertheless revealing place in the
American tradition of radical aesthetics.

An additional factor that must be included in any assessment of this novel's significance is its date of publication. The history of the mid-1960's in the United States
is to a considerable extent the history of the African American and the adjustments
made to accommodate the African American struggle for an adequate model of
citizenship. That struggle took many forms, not the least of which were artistic. The
public expression of a critical African American consciousness during this period
provides a standpoint from which the revolutionary artistic character of *The System
of Dante's Hell* can be evaluated, particularly as the novel's psychological tropes,
community dynamics, and radical form identify energies and anxieties within the
African American experience that are far from being fully acknowledged.

Bibliography

Brown, Lloyd W. *Amiri Baraka.* Boston: Twayne, 1980. Contains a chapter devoted
    to analysis of *The System of Dante's Hell*, which is examined from various per-
    spectives, including its relationship to the works of James Joyce, T. S. Eliot, and
    Dante Alighieri, its debt to existentialist philosophy, and its formal character.
Dieke, Ikenna. "Sadeanism: Baraka, Sexuality, and the Perverse Imagination in *The
    System of Dante's Hell.*" *Black American Literature Forum* 19 (Winter, 1985):

163-166. An examination of the treatment of sexuality in the novel, seen through the framework of the writings of the Marquis de Sade.

Jackson, Esther M. "LeRoi Jones (Imamu Amiri Baraka): Form and the Progression of Consciousness." *College Language Association Journal* 17 (September, 1973): 33-56. An elaborate examination of some of the philosophic underpinnings of *The System of Dante's Hell*. Particular emphasis is placed on Baraka's debt to the aesthetic philosophy of G. W. F. Hegel. The novel's relationship with the thought of the American Transcendentalists is also discussed.

Munro, C. Lynn. "LeRoi Jones: A Man in Transition." *College Language Association Journal* 17 (September, 1973): 57-78. An analysis of *The System of Dante's Hell* largely devoted to the work's relationship to Dante's *Inferno* (1802).

Pennington-Jones, Paulette. "From Brother LeRoi Jones Through *The System of Dante's Hell* to Imamu Ameer Baraka." *Journal of Black Studies* 4 (December, 1973): 195-214. An account of the development of Baraka's cultural and artistic consciousness, drawing attention to the pivotal place of *The System of Dante's Hell* in the evolution of the author's thought.

Ward, Jerry. "The System of Dante's Hell: Underworlds of Art and Liberation." *Griot* 6 (Summer, 1987): 58-64. Considers the novel in relation to Dante's *Inferno* and to other treatments of the underworld. The pertinence of these to the work of African American novelists is also discussed.

George O'Brien

THE TAKING OF MISS JANIE

Author: Ed Bullins (1935-   )
Type of work: Play
Type of plot: Social criticism
Time of plot: The 1960's
Locale: Principally California
First produced: 1974, at the New Federal Theatre, New York City
First published: 1981

> *Principal characters:*
> MONTY, a black student in his early twenties attending a West
>   Coast university
> JANIE, a white student in her early twenties
> RICK, a black man in his early twenties
> LEN, a roommate of Rick and Monty
> SHARON, a young white woman who marries Len
> PEGGY, a young black woman who needs and searches for love
> FLOSSIE, a woman who, like Peggy, turns to other women for love
> LONNIE, a white male who seeks association with blacks
> MORT, a leftover hippie struggling to find a niche

The Play

   The Taking of Miss Janie begins in Monty's California apartment. Lights come up
on Janie sitting on the side of the bed while Monty, exhausted from their sexual
encounter, lies beside her. She tearfully expresses her confusion and disappointment. Monty, whom she has always thought of as a friend, has raped her. He counters by stating that she always knew their relationship would culminate in sex. He
calls the love and caring of their relationship wasted and, in spite of her objections,
continues his sexual domination of her.

   A quick shift in time shows the two characters at their first meeting on the campus
of a college in Southern California during the late 1950's. She compliments him on
his "black poetry" and asks to hear more; he invites her to a party at his apartment.
The tension between them is clearly indicated in this first meeting, as he refers to
her as "Miss Janie," a pejorative reference to a white woman who was mistress of a
plantation. Janie is unaware of the sarcastic import of the name.

   The action shifts to the party as Len and Rick, Monty's roommates, are interrupted in the midst of a lively discussion of political strategies and philosophies by
the entrance of Janie, who is soon followed by Peggy. There is immediate rapport
between Rick, Len, and Peggy, but Janie is clearly an outsider, the recipient of
sarcastic comments from both Rick and Peggy. Others gather, and the play's dynamic is clearly established. Between these people there is no common ground.

   The play continues as, through a series of monologues and dialogues, the various
characters portray events—past, present, and future—that summarize not only their

lives but the times as well. With the arrival of Mort, the mood of the party becomes increasingly antagonistic. He is an addict in need of a fix and unable to control his anger. He insults and provokes Monty, and a fight ensues. Monty is beaten to the point of unconsciousness and thrown into the alley.

The action shifts back to the time and place of the opening scene, where the taking of Miss Janie is still in progress. This time, however, it is clear that Janie is a cooperative, if not willing, participant. When Monty asks her if she will fight or scream as he rapes her, she states that she and Monty know each other too well. The lights dim as he removes her clothes and pushes her onto the bed.

Themes and Meanings

The Taking of Miss Janie is the story of a decade as experienced by its youth. It presents a group of college students who are struggling to find their place in society. Some of the characters face the problems of interpersonal relationships; others try to find a viable way of causing political and social change. All begin the decade with hope and energy, a sense of purpose, but these qualities are quickly dissipated as each confronts the personal responsibility for whatever change there is to be.

Bullins' work is a powerful exploration of an important era. The 1960's, suggests the play, presented the country with a missed opportunity to cure itself of racism and other political and social ills. The attitudes resulting from years of separation make it impossible for the people in the play to come together and attack the injustices they see with such clarity. They desire a better world but lack the commitment to fight for it. Coupled with this failure in commitment is confusion. Like Monty and Janie, America's youthful revolutionaries are simultaneously drawn to and repulsed by the issues they attack. They begin the struggle filled with youthful optimism and end in complete disillusionment. Finding that she can never have Monty, Peggy refuses involvement with all men. Mort, pushed to the brink, can no longer maintain the mask of jovial partnership with blacks and betrays his true allegiance to things as they are and were. Janie, who for years was sustained by the belief that she and Monty could maintain a relationship that ignored the inherited ugliness of racism, must finally confront the fact that both she and he are its victims and, therefore, destined to destroy each other.

Rather than a conventional story, *The Taking of Miss Janie* is the exploration of an event. The event is the party, and the action is in the interplay of the various characters that triggers the monologues through which they reveal themselves. Structurally, the work owes more to music than to drama, as it moves from ensemble, with all the characters together, to solo and duet, as the various characters, separately or in pairs, share their thoughts with the audience in direct addresses.

Critical Context

Ed Bullins was among the most prolific playwrights of the late 1960's and 1970's. As the principal writer for the New Lafayette Theatre, he created a panorama of characters never before seen on the American stage. These were not upwardly mobile blacks who struggled to present their frustrations in standard English but people of the street, whose every gesture and utterance expressed the intense anger of the disenfranchised and powerless. Bullins, however, was not content merely to show black lives made to seem unimportant by racism; he challenged his audience to view itself through them.

The plays of this early period include *In the Wine Time* (1968), *The Fabulous Miss Marie* (1971), and *Goin' a Buffalo* (1968). Some critics, black and white, were affronted by the harshness of Bullins' vision and his use of profanity. Others described his work as powerful and uncompromising in its criticism of America's political and social issues.

The Taking of Miss Janie is, in some ways, a departure from those early works. The New Lafayette plays were very definite attempts at mirroring the lives and concerns of black Americans in the 1950's and 1960's, but *The Taking of Miss Janie* expands its focus to attack those issues facing the whole of America during that period. When viewed in relation to Bullins' earlier work, *The Taking of Miss Janie* demonstrates the author's continued commitment to theater as political statement.

Bibliography
Bigsby, C. W. E. *A Critical Introduction to Twentieth-Century American Drama.* New York: Cambridge University Press, 1982-1985. Contains an article focusing on the sources of Bullins' work, using interviews and commentary by the playwright. Also offers interpretive comment on Bullins' early works, stressing the importance of its relationship to the Black Arts movement and the New Lafayette Theatre.
Bullins, Ed. *The Hungered One: Early Writings.* New York: William Morrow, 1971. A collection of early works, short stories, and sketches by Bullins. Although many of the pieces appear incomplete, they offer insight into the more mature works to follow.
_____. *The Reluctant Rapist.* New York: Harper & Row, 1973. The playwright's first published novel, introducing various characters and themes found in his plays.
Fabre, Genevieve. *Drumbeats, Masks, and Metaphor: Contemporary Afro-American Theatre.* Translated by Melvin Dixon. Cambridge, Mass.: Harvard University Press, 1983. Helpful commentary on the works of Bullins and other African American playwrights.
Peterson, Bernard L. *Contemporary Black American Playwrights and Their Plays: A Biographical Directory and Dramatic Index.* New York: Greenwood Press, 1988. Contains useful factual information about Bullins and his work. Bibliography, indexes.
Sanders, Leslie Catherine. *The Development of Black Theater in America: From Shadows to Selves.* Baton Rouge: Louisiana State University Press, 1988. Provides a helpful context for the interpretation of Bullins' plays.

Donald T. Evans

TAR BABY

Author: Toni Morrison (1931-   )
Type of work: Novel
Type of plot: Social criticism
Time of plot: The late 1970's
Locale: The Caribbean, New York City, Florida
First published: 1981

> *Principal characters:*
> JADINE CHILDS, an African American model with a degree in art
>   history from the Sorbonne
> WILLIAM GREEN (SON), an African American wanderer
> VALERIAN STREET, a rich, retired white industrialist
> MARGARET STREET, Valerian's young wife
> SYDNEY CHILDS, Jadine's father
> ONDINE CHILDS, Sydney's wife
> GIDEON (YARDMAN),
> THÉRÈSE, and
> ALMA ESTÉE, locals who perform odd chores

The Novel

Tar Baby traces the quest for self-identity of Jadine Childs, the protagonist. Jadine does not seem to have rebelled against the constructs of the white society in which she is enmeshed; in fact, she has accepted and embraced the white culture without question. Because she was orphaned at the age of twelve, a break with her African American heritage occurred. Ondine and Sydney, the aunt and uncle who assumed responsibility for the orphan, unwittingly enlarged this gap by sending her to exclusive private schools and later to the Sorbonne. The adult Jadine feels equipped to deal successfully with the white world; she is a part of it. It is the African American world, represented by her nightmares, her disagreements with Son, and the feelings of otherness that overwhelm her in his hometown of Eloe, Florida, that disturbs her. Set in the late 1970's, Toni Morrison's *Tar Baby* explores the sexual, racial, familial, and social tensions associated with the individual's journey to self-autonomy and self-actualization.

The novel begins with Son (William Green) escaping from a merchant ship to a yacht that Margaret Street and Jadine have borrowed. He hides in the Streets' home for days until Margaret Street discovers him in her closet a few evenings before Christmas. This discovery initiates the crumbling of Valerian Street's world.

Valerian, a wealthy, retired businessman, has created and ordered his own world on his Caribbean island. He controls his wife Margaret, his servants, Sydney and Ondine, the natives who work for him, and even Jadine, quietly manipulating her choices. A god-like figure, he is relatively beneficent to but also distant from his subjects; he is comfortable in the artificially natural world of his greenhouse.

The discovery of Son, coupled with Valerian's calm acceptance of him, causes tension in Margaret, who feels Valerian is indifferent to her needs; in Jadine, who is attracted to and repelled by Son at the same time; and in Sydney and Ondine, who feel slighted because Valerian treats Son better than he treats them, whom he has known for years. Son also feels tension, not only because of what happens within the Street household but also because he sees that the Streets and Childses treat Gideon, Thérèse, and Alma Estée, whose names they do not bother to learn, as chattel, not as individual human beings. Perhaps most significantly, Son also resents the fact that Jadine acts more like the Streets than like the African American women of his childhood.

All tensions erupt at Christmas dinner after Valerian casually announces that he has fired Gideon and Thérèse for stealing apples, without previously notifying Sydney and Ondine. Verbal blows between Valerian and Son, Valerian and Ondine, Valerian and Sydney, and Ondine and Margaret ensue, with Jadine trying to smooth everything over. The climax occurs when Ondine reveals the reason for her bitterness toward Margaret: Margaret had abused the Streets' son, Michael, when he was a baby. This revelation renders Valerian virtually helpless and provides redemption for the emotionally disturbed Margaret.

In the resultant numbness, Jadine and Son grow close and decide to meet each other in New York, where Jadine has a modeling job scheduled. Son, who arrives in the city first, feels uncomfortable in New York, but for Jadine, it is a welcome change. The two close themselves off from the outside world for weeks, living only for and through each other. Finally, Son persuades Jadine to visit his family and friends with him in Eloe. Jadine feels like an outsider during their entire stay and feels especially threatened by the women in Son's background. She does not fear their repossession of Son as much as she fears their claims upon her and her own identity. When the two return to New York, their differences escalate. Jadine looks toward the future, wanting Son to make something of himself in the real world. Son looks toward the past, wanting Jadine to imbibe the traits of the women in his community who mothered him. Both want to rescue the other from "misguided" worldviews. The relationship ends after Son emotionally and physically assaults Jadine. She returns to the Streets' Caribbean island for a brief visit and to retrieve her belongings. During the visit, Ondine criticizes Jadine for not feeling and acting like a daughter. Jadine refuses to let guilt subordinate her to someone else's wishes and leaves for Paris alone, determined to face her future and her past on her own terms. Meanwhile, Son, after realizing that Jadine is more important to him than his past, flies to the Caribbean to find her. He is sidetracked by Gideon, Thérèse, and Alma, who lies to him about seeing Jadine with a man. Thérèse agrees to row Son to the island but takes him to the swampy side, not to the Street home. Disoriented and confused, Son leaves the boat to join mythical blind horsemen rumored to haunt the island. Whether he reaches his destination remains a mystery.

The Characters

Jadine is a well-educated professional model. Orphaned at twelve, she was taken in by her aunt and uncle, Ondine and Sydney. Their employer, Valerian, helped them send Jadine to private schools and to the Sorbonne. Partially because of this upbringing, Jadine experiences conflict between the white society in which she is entrenched and the black culture represented by her uncle and aunt and Son, her lover. Jadine refuses to submit to the traditional image of womanhood that both Ondine and Son want to impose upon her. When, at the end of the novel, she returns to her own life in Paris, she is determined to face her fears alone.

Son is a wanderer from Eloe, Florida. At the beginning of the book, he escapes from a ship in the Caribbean and slips onto the boat Jadine and Margaret have borrowed. Son represents everything that Sydney and Ondine have tried to shield Jadine from, and everything that she herself seems to have rejected. To them, he seems to have the qualities of the stereotypical black male—he is shiftless, wild, and unrefined—yet he reveals an honest, direct way of looking at the world. Son, unlike Jadine, seems too nostalgic for the past.

Valerian, the rich, retired white industrialist from Philadelphia, does not interact well with other people, preferring plants instead. He treats his employees fairly well—better than he treats his wife—but never relinquishes his superior status.

Margaret, Valerian's wife, is a beauty queen from Maine who married the much older Valerian and got pregnant soon after. She lacks emotional stability and often feels that her husband is closer to Sydney and Ondine than he is to her.

Sydney, Jadine's father, is a domestic employee of the Streets. Very proud of his "Philadelphia Negro" breeding, he seems to be even-tempered, appreciative of and even friendly toward his employer until Son appears. After that, the novel reveals Sydney's resentment of Valerian, and, at the end, the balance of power between the employer and employee shifts.

Ondine, Sydney's wife, is also a domestic employee of the Streets. She represents the traditional African American female in the novel, feeling more like the "woman of the house" than Margaret does because of Margaret's inability to nurture her son. Ondine both resents and takes pride in Jadine, praising her accomplishments but wishing that Jadine were more like her; that is, more family-conscious. Also, like her husband, she is very proud of who she is and patronizes those whom she considers to be beneath her (Son and the local islanders) just as Valerian patronizes her.

Gideon, Thérèse, and Alma Estée, locals who often perform odd chores at the Streets' home, are less clearly drawn. These three characters, however, serve as catalysts for the major action of the novel.

Themes and Meanings

With *Tar Baby*, Morrison traces the struggle of an African American woman to find and keep her identity and individuality despite the efforts of her lover, who would domesticate her like the ladies of his childhood, her mother figure, who would chain her to the past, and her white patron, who would subtly bind her to his worldview.

With careful skill, Morrison creates characters realistic in their complexities; not one of the characters can be easily typed or categorized. The reader is never allowed to judge a character because Morrison gives such insight into each one that absolute judgments are impossible. There are no good or bad characters in the novel, only human characters.

Jadine Childs is the most complex character in the book. Jadine feels cut off from her culture and her family. She grew up in boarding schools and then moved to Europe; she has no hometown, no place that she belongs, nor does she feel that she belongs to any other people, even though her aunt and uncle became responsible for her when her mother died. Jadine feels gratitude to her aunt and uncle for their help, as well as to the Streets for paying for her education, yet she does not equate gratitude with duty, for which some readers might fault her. She also refuses to see herself as an African American first or even as a woman first. Jadine insists on defining herself using her own codes. She does not want to subscribe to the roles that communities, groupings, and labels often force on individuals.

Jadine has to endure great pain before she realizes that this is her way of meeting the world. She tries to establish closeness with her aunt; she tries to protect Valerian's world; she even tries to enter Son's Southern community. Women of her past and of Son's past haunt her constantly, trying to draw her into their group, and she just as constantly resists this pull so that she might keep her self. The price she pays for holding on to that self is high: She loses Son, she weakens the relationship with Ondine, and she flies off alone, determined to make it without Valerian's help. Some might see this as a defeat, yet the story of the soldier ants Morrison narrates near the novel's end, in which the queen of the ants is the dominant force, reveals Jadine's power and strength, making the ending full of possibilities rather than defeat.

Morrison's skill extends to the other characters as well. Son is more than an African American wanderer; he is a man scarred by the recent past yet yearning to return to the home of his childhood for the safety and insulation it represents. Though he tells Jadine he could be successful in the world if he wished, no evidence is given to prove this, and the reader wonders if his love of the past is connected to a fear of the future. Valerian, too, is multifaceted. His past insecurities, his lonely childhood, and his failed marriage all haunt this master of the house. The greatest guilt he faces, though, is his knowledge that he was too insulated, too distant from his family to realize that his wife was abusing their young son. Margaret, too, though she is the least likable character in the book, is presented sympathetically. Morrison uses her to show how early pregnancies can damage the emotional growth of women. Finally, Ondine and Sydney, though they fill roles traditionally set aside for African Americans and other minorities, subvert the stereotype by being the proudest characters in the book, and by demonstrating that power comes in different forms.

By creating these characters that defy traditional, stereotypical roles, Morrison is voicing a theme that permeates the form and content of this novel: Polarized thinking, dichotomous thinking, is ineffective for living in the real world. Defining people as black or white, male or female, educated or uneducated, logical or emotional, rich or poor, or as other polar opposites, and subscribing to these categories, limits the individual and, ultimately, the world. Individuals must rely on the authority within themselves to define their roles. By having her characters confront such issues as racism, sexism, classism, and regionalism, and by merging and converging conflicting cultures and myths into her unified narrative, Morrison demonstrates that one can organize one's world and one's understanding of it without binary thinking.

Critical Context

Like her previous novels—*The Bluest Eye* (1970), *Sula* (1974), and *Song of Solomon* (1977)—*Tar Baby* showcases Toni Morrison's talents. She creates magical narratives, glittering with flowing descriptions, ancient myths, and folklore. *Tar Baby* also continues Morrison's analysis and critique of society and the roles African Americans play in that society. Like her precursor Ralph Ellison's *Invisible Man* (1952), however, Morrison's *Tar Baby* transcends the question of race to examine the human identity. Her ability to create strong characters, and to reveal those characters' struggles to realize their strength in spite of external and internal barriers, places Morrison firmly in the canon of respected American novelists.

Bibliography

Lange, Bonnie Shipman. "Toni Morrison's Rainbow Code." *Critique* 24 (Spring, 1983): 173-181. Discusses Morrison's use of color in her first four novels, arguing that her color imagery works consistently throughout the novels. Of particular importance to *Tar Baby* are the discussions of red, green, yellow, silver, and gold.

Lepow, Lauren. "Paradise Lost and Found: Dualism and Edenic Myth in Toni Morrison's *Tar Baby*." *Contemporary Literature* 28 (Fall, 1987): 363-377. Argues that one of the primary themes of *Tar Baby* is the unfulfilling, destructive nature of dualistic or binary thinking. As a result, unlike many other critics, Lepow views the ending of the novel as positive for Jadine, who flies out on her own.

Mobley, Marilyn E. "Narrative Dilemma: Jadine as Cultural Orphan in Toni Morrison's *Tar Baby*." *Southern Review* 23 (Autumn, 1987): 761-770. Argues that with *Tar Baby*, Morrison attempts to realize two conflicting goals: to affirm the autonomy of the self and to emphasize the importance of one's heritage.

Samuels, Wilfred D., and Clenora Hudson-Weems. "Folklore as Matrix for Cultural Affirmation in *Tar Baby*." In *Toni Morrison*. Boston: Twayne, 1990. Discusses Morrison's use of folklore and myth to describe and portray the theme of finding one's identity or true self.

Wagner, Linda W. "Mastery of Narrative." In *Contemporary American Women Writers: Narrative Strategies*, edited by Catherine Rainwater and William J. Scheick. Lexington: University Press of Kentucky, 1985. Discusses Morrison's narrative strategies. Argues that Morrison's skillful mixing of dialogue and dense prose accentuates her theme of the importance of cultural identity.

Lauren Chadwick

TECHNICAL DIFFICULTIES
African-American Notes on the State of the Union

Author: June Jordan (1936-   )
Type of work: Essays
First published: 1992

> *Principal personages:*
> GRANVILLE IVANHOE JORDAN, the author's father, an immigrant
>   from Jamaica
> MARTIN LUTHER KING, JR., a social visionary and political leader
> JESSE JACKSON, a political activist and social commentator
> ANITA HILL, a lawyer and witness at confirmation hearings for
>   Clarence Thomas
> CLARENCE THOMAS, the second African American to be appointed
>   to the Supreme Court
> MIKE TYSON, a professional boxer and convicted rapist

Form and Content

In 1981, June Jordan published her first collection of essays, *Civil Wars: Selected Essays 1963-1980*, a pioneering volume described by the publisher as the first book of political essays to be published by a black woman in the United States. Perhaps best known as a poet and anthologist/critic, Jordan has also been very active politically as a commentator, teacher, organizer, and witness. Despite her national reputation, she has never had the kind of forum available to political writers who are less critical of conventionally accepted ideas and policies. "If political writing by a Black woman did not strike so many editors as presumptuous or simply bizarre," she wrote in 1985, "I might regularly appear, on a weekly or monthly schedule, as a national columnist." Instead, she has been publishing her work in periodicals sympathetic to the challenging or unconventional view, magazines such as *The Village Voice* in New York City and *The Progressive* in Madison, Wisconsin. Even with these forums available, her second collection, *On Call: Political Essays* (1985), and *Technical Difficulties* contain essays that have not been published previously. She has explained the necessity for these collections by saying that books "must compensate for the absence of a cheaper and more immediate" print outlet and emphasized the need "to pose our views in the realm of public debate" as the major impetus behind her books. Against what she describes as "American censorship," which she identifies as the restrictions imposed by all the positions of power across the political spectrum, she sees herself as "a dissident American poet and writer" who is determined to work toward the betterment of "my country, my home." Explaining further that her politics are an expression of "my entire real life," she asserts that nothing in her writing or thinking "reflects any orthodox anything" and lists as the goal of her work "my political efforts to coherently fathom all of my universe, and to arrive at a moral judgement that will determine my further political conduct."

The essays gathered in *Technical Difficulties* were written between 1986 and early 1992 and express Jordan's extremely critical judgments about the direction of governmental policy and social expectancy during that time. Continuing the coverage of the issues of race, gender, and class from her previous collections, Jordan combines reflections on her own experiences as a single parent, a professional African American writer and educator, and a person gradually discovering all the dimensions of her sexuality. Her reportorial technique employs statistics, factual information, and a carefully developed, logical argumentation to present a powerful, openly personal perspective on the "State of the Union." As she did in her earlier essays, Jordan juxtaposes essays on the virtues of American democracy in theory and practice, often concentrating on exemplary people whose lives exhibit these qualities in action, with the worst examples of what she considers to be the most serious impediments to the realization of these ideals and principles. She writes about Martin Luther King, Jr., and Jesse Jackson in *Technical Difficulties*, focusing on the kind of political activist, one who stands for principled, outspoken, determined resistance to undemocratic tendencies, whom she wishes to emulate in her writing, teaching, and public pronouncements. Her work as a poet is not necessarily secondary. She uses all the dynamics of poetic language to charge her essays with a fervor that demands attention and response.

Like other American artists whose love for what they believe their country can be has led them to speak forcefully about their disappointments, Jordan is sensitive to the accusation that she is merely a malcontent. Her initial essay is a loving recollection of her father and other members of her family who believed in the American Dream and whose lives were expressions of a dedication to its promises and obligations. These people, along with King and Jackson, are the measure of citizenship and its responsibilities that Jordan uses to condemn prominent politicians such as past presidents Ronald Reagan and George Bush. The fact that her examples of excellence and standards for achievement are black men and women emphasizes the importance of African American experience in building a just society in the United States. Similarly, in an essay about her family and in an essay called "Park Slope: Mixing It Up for Good," which is the only essay in the collection originally published in what might be considered a nationally prominent publication (*The New York Times*), Jordan offers a description of a community in which a multicultural ethnic mix provides for a level of tolerance as well as a spirit of exuberance and vitality that might stand as a model both for the small "town" within a larger urban setting and for the entire country.

The organizational pattern for the contents of the book is generally chronological, following Jordan's own thoughts and personal development during the time period under examination. After the essay written in admiration of her family, there is a very personal essay entitled "Waking Up" in which the dark side of the American Dream, the nightmare/shadow looming over the light of optimism and hope, is evoked in terms of an ever-present sense of danger from which a vulnerable member of Amer-

ican society (that is, almost everyone, but particularly an independent African American female artist) is never really free. The alternation of a positive position with its
points of weakness, or a negative situation with a possible solution, is a mode that
continues throughout the book, not specifically in the bracketing of contiguous entries but in the elements linking several essays, or within an oppositional context in a
specific one. This technique is an echo of the classic Afrocentric style of the "call
and response." It suggests by implication that there is a complexity in human affairs
that defies the simplistic proscriptions of those who wish to defend a single approach to literature, education, sexuality, or artistic endeavor as the only correct
one. Consequently, an essay such as "No Chocolates for Breakfast," which considers
the aloneness of a single female parent, is answered by "Don't You Talk About My
Momma!," which is a defense of and tribute to black women who are the heads of
families. The viciousness decried in "Alternative Commencement Address" is counterposed with the healing instincts of people responding to the San Francisco earthquake in "Unrecorded Agonies." The immoral actions of the United States government in Nicaragua ("Where Are We and Whose Country Is This, Anyway?") and
the foreign policy that led to the Gulf War ("On War and War and War and . . .") are
counterposed with many examples of individual acts of conscience against oppression.

The most prominent thread of these intertwined essays is the political one, centered on the essay "Inside America," which carries the explanatory subtitle "An
Essay on Blackfolks and the Constitution." Jordan explicitly details the disparity
between the principles set out in the documents that describe the ideals of the founding fathers and the actual conditions of life in the United States for many African
Americans. She then extends this cleavage to the academic curriculum in practice in
many American universities, one that is exclusionary and narrow, and thus inappropriate for and inapplicable to the lives of the majority of the population who are
not male and not white. This division between two conflicting positions is brought to
a dramatic conclusion in the last two essays, as the elements of contention are located within the African American community. In a blistering discussion of the
Clarence Thomas confirmation hearings and the Mike Tyson rape trial, Jordan concludes the book with a stunningly candid critique of the failures of many black
people to move beyond positions of power and privilege to speak out for the kind of
justice that is at the heart of her entire political philosophy.

Analysis

Jordan's essays illustrate one of the more serious social concepts to emerge from
the furor of the 1960's, the insistence that the political is personal and that to attempt
any kind of disengagement is deceptive. Jordan does not present herself as either a
spokesperson or a pundit. Rather, she writes in the spirit of an alert citizen of a
democratic state trying to refine what she has called "the starter tablet of laws" that
is the American Constitution. In the "Alternative Commencement Address" delivered at Dartmouth College, she declares that the history of the United States is "the

history of a democratic republic under torturous but steadfast construction" and that attacks on the protections and rights guaranteed by the Constitution and its amendments are assaults on "the basis for liberty and the well-being of all of our lives." One of the most crucial points of the entire book is that African American citizens have responded to and worked for these essential rights as steadfastly as any other Americans. Contrary to the inaccurate depiction of black people as somehow outside the process of American life, she describes her parents as living in America "full of faith," "eager Black immigrants . . . as grateful and loyal" as any other arrivals "whose trust in the democratic promise of the mainland has never been reckoned with, fully, or truly reciprocated." Her goal in these essays is to keep the faith in the possibilities of American democracy and to work toward the inclusion of all the citizens of the country in a vision of America defined and evoked by its hopeful immigrants in the most expansive terms.

Recognizing the power inherent in the employment and control of language, Jordan uses the entire range of her skills as a writer to speak for those denied a voice as a result of any "technical difficulty." She has claimed for herself the role of celebrator of the heroes of her culture, like an ancient epic poet, and the role of a "conscience of a generation" in the tradition of British essayist George Orwell, whose progressive politics placed him in opposition to powerful forces in the political establishment of his country. The union of these tasks has led her to an examination of the contradictions between the isolated individual artist and the committed social activist. After drawing some revealing parallels between the arrogance of an artist's "illusions of autonomy" and the "misbegotten American dreams . . . about you and me as gloriously rugged, independent individuals" that have deterred the "simplest capabilities for cooperation" necessary for a just, decent society, Jordan explains how (in the essay "Of Those So Close Beside Me, Which Are You?") she decided that the aim of art is to "comfort and to empower the possible victims of evil" and to "impart all that we can of our inspired, our inherited humanity."

The strategy she follows for empowerment is based on a reasoned, logical exposition of the techniques of control and suppression employed by "self-selected patriarchs." Control began in the United States with a founding document. The Declaration of Independence implicitly excluded all those who were "never the 'Men' . . . never the People" referred to by that document. Her plan is not to reject the philosophical underpinnings of the founding proclamations but to widen their scope to include all the people of the country. Essays on the necessity of expanding and redefining the canon of approved authors and the materials of the standard curriculum at many American universities are based on the need to hear "the variegated sounds of multiple languages spoken by so many truly different Americans" so that the "teachings of public education in America" become a "sane basis for our multicultural, multiracial, and two-gendered lives on this infinitely multifaceted, multilingual planet." The compelling but abstract formulation of this proposal is balanced by the other element of her artistic ambition—to provide an account of those inspirational but fully human figures who have been the leaders of "a tender and powerful company of others struggling as we do." The essays on Martin Luther King, Jr., and Jesse Jackson, as well as the "letter" addressed to Anita Hill ("Can I Get A Witness?") are written with a lucidity and fervor that fuses passionate involvement with the clarity of historical judgment. The essay on King is built on the foundation of classical rhetorical repetition. Jordan repeatedly asserts that "He was not a god" but shows that with his common human frailties, he was "one man trying to do good" whose legacy is "the astounding persuasion of . . . moral appeal." In the rhythms of the biblical cadences King used, Jordan reanimates the "colossal courage" behind the specific accomplishments and the lofty expectations of his dream of America.

The tribute to King is cast in the reflective terms of a recollection of a figure already partially a mythic presence. The letter of support and gratitude to Anita Hill is Jordan's declaration of righteous anger after seeing a woman "isolated, betrayed, abused" by a political process, then ridiculed by hate-inflamed representatives of the ruling forces decried throughout the book. Jordan's sympathy for Hill, "a good black woman in this America" acting out of "her earnest commitment to do right," is expressed in a poetic eloquence matched by the devastating invective directed at Clarence Thomas. She sees Thomas as "a virulent Oreo phenomenon" whom she regards with distinctive disdain because of his self-serving, self-abasing collaboration with the "incredibly powerful and hypocritical and sneering" men of the Senate Committee. Stripping away the relatively polite language addressed to Thomas, Jordan turns the tables, delivering a condemnation of "this Uncle Tom calamity of mediocre abilities . . . this bootstrap miracle of egomaniacal myth and self-pity" that balances the "slandering suppositions" and "malevolent speculation" Hill had to endure. There is a cathartic release in this, but the purpose of the essay is to present a brief for Hill in her torment, to be her "witness" before the country and the judgment of history. The form that Jordan's address takes is a series of questions pointed toward the conscience of the country and toward all those people and organizations who failed to stand and be counted. Anticipating the election of November, 1992, when African American women won seats in the Senate for the first time, Jordan presciently announces, "If this government will not defend us . . . we will change the government."

The concluding essay, "Requiem for the Champ," ends the book on a somber note. Recalling her childhood on the same mean streets in Brooklyn where Mike Tyson grew up, Jordan—while in no way excusing Tyson's brutal sexual assault—presents a kind of a brief for Tyson. There is a deep mood of sorrow in her examination of the conditions that deprived Tyson of nearly everything he needed to learn before he could treat a woman with love and respect. "Mike Tyson comes from Brooklyn," Jordan observes, "and so do I." This bleak landscape, which she likens to Berlin immediately after World War II, brutalizes and shatters the possibilities of a civilized world in which people respect each other's basic humanity. Although she agrees with the jury's guilty verdict, she does not "rejoice" in it. In response to the query of whether she would like to "see Mike Tyson a free man again," her succinct statement that "He was never free!" is an expression of her disappointment in the glorification of desperately flawed figures pathetically presented as "heroes" as a distraction from the enormous problems that African Americans still face.

Critical Context

The fact that Jordan was the first black woman to publish a collection of political essays in the United States is interesting and important as a register of the historical constraints placed on both women and African Americans. As John Thompson, the basketball coach at Georgetown, remarked when his team won the National Collegiate Athletic Association championship, he would not have been the first black coach to achieve this honor if similarly capable people had had similar opportunities. Jordan joins other pioneering black writers finding means to speak, but her work is clearly within a tradition of commentary. What is more significant is that her work has an enduring power that satisfies Ezra Pound's definition of literature as "News that stays news." While still firmly grounded in the specific experiences of her life as a poet and professor of African American studies, and as a woman of color in the United States in the late twentieth century, Jordan's concerns are those of all responsible Americans, and her writing has a relevance that American citizens ignore at the nation's peril.

Bibliography

Hooks, Bell. *Black Looks: Race and Representation.* Boston: South End Press, 1992. Twelve essays on images of race in popular culture, including a discussion of the Thomas-Hill hearings.

Jordan, June. *Civil Wars: Selected Essays 1963-1980.* Boston: Beacon Press, 1981. Jordan's first collection of political essays.

——————. *On Call: Political Essays.* Boston: South End Press, 1985. Jordan's second collection, with many connections to *Technical Difficulties.*

——————. *Things That I Do in the Dark: Selected Poetry.* New York: Random House, 1977. A representative group of poems illustrating the strengths of Jordan's grasp of language and style.

Madhubuti, Haki. *Black Men: Obsolete, Single, Dangerous?* Chicago: Third World Press, 1990. Incisive essays and poems discussing the same issues Jordan covers but from a masculine perspective.

Wallace, Michele. *Black Macho and the Myth of the Superwoman.* New York: Routledge, Chapman, Hall, 1990. An examination of the relationship between black men and women, paralleling some of the concerns Jordan addresses.

Leon Lewis

THEIR EYES WERE WATCHING GOD

Author: Zora Neale Hurston (1891-1960)
Type of work: Novel
Type of plot: Psychological realism
Time of plot: The first half of the twentieth century
Locale: Rural Florida
First published: 1937

> *Principal characters:*
> JANIE CRAWFORD, the protagonist, a light-skinned African
>   American woman
> NANNY CRAWFORD, Janie's grandmother, a maid to a wealthy
>   white family
> LOGAN KILLICKS, Janie's first husband, a farmer
> JOE STARKS, Janie's second husband
> VERGIBLE "TEA CAKE" WOODS, Janie's third husband
> PHEOBY WATSON, Janie's friend and the audience for her narrative
> MRS. TURNER, a business owner who worships Janie's light-
>   skinned features

The Novel

  Their Eyes Were Watching God is the story of Janie Crawford's quest to fulfill her ideals of life and love during a thirty-year period beginning soon after the turn of the century. The novel is framed by a narrator's description of a conversation between Janie and Pheoby Watson that takes place on Janie's back porch in Eatonville, Florida. The point of view soon shifts to Janie's perspective, and she tells Pheoby the story of her life, beginning with her sheltered childhood in western Florida. The two points of view merge to become one perspective, carrying the narrative through to its violent climax and eventual return to the placid back-porch setting.

  The first conflict that Janie recalls concerns her differences with her grandmother, Nanny Crawford. Nanny, a former slave, attempts to keep Janie as sheltered as possible and thus becomes alarmed when she sees Janie kissing a boy over the gatepost. Nanny consequently arranges a marriage between Janie and local farmer and landowner Logan Killicks, believing that she can thus keep Janie from suffering the fate of other African American women, who become "de mule[s] of de world." Janie has no desire for that kind of protection, however, and the bony Logan little fits her image of a romantic partner.

  Janie soon leaves Logan for the attractive Joe Starks and moves to the newly founded all-black town of Eatonville, Florida. At first Janie thinks that Joe might be the man for whom she is looking. She soon discovers, however, that the basis for their relationship is "foot kissing" rather than "mouth kissing" and that Joe wants her to be set above the rest of the black folk in town. Janie has once again fallen into the trap of settling for security, only this time she has done it of her own volition.

When she goes to work in Joe's store, she is forced to wear a headrag to cover her long, straight hair. As she becomes more alienated from Joe, she withdraws further from her dream of self-fulfillment through romantic love.

Joe dies an embittered man, leaving Janie with the store and the big white house he had built for her. She instantly becomes the object of attention from many suitors, but she spurns them all, preferring her independence to the security of marriage. She finally meets a younger man, Tea Cake (Vergible Woods), and becomes romantically involved. She leaves the security of the store and house for the adventure of traveling to the "muck" of southern Florida to spend the season among migrant farm laborers. Here Janie is finally able to come into contact with both herself and the "folk" from whom she has been separated all of her life. The idyllic life is cut short, however, by a hurricane that floods the region and scatters her and her friends. Tea Cake is bitten by a rabid dog during their escape, eventually contracting the disease and becoming increasingly violent and paranoid. He bites Janie and shoots at her, and she kills him in self-defense. After she is acquitted by an all-white jury, she returns to the security of her home to tell her story and contemplate the significance of having her dream fulfilled.

The Characters

Janie Crawford, the central character in the novel, is one of the strongest female figures in American literature. Unlike her counterparts in many of the African American novels influenced by European realism and naturalism, her quest is fulfilled and her desire is celebrated.

Janie's idealism forms the core of the novel. She desires not only romantic love but also connection with the natural and folk life that surrounds her. Hurston vividly illustrates this motif with the image of the blossoming pear tree kissed by singing bees, which is Janie's picture of romantic love. Hurston elaborates the point by providing Janie with three husbands, each of whom reflects a part of Janie's character and demonstrates the perils of the quest she has undertaken.

Logan Killicks, Janie's first husband, embodies the dangers of passivity and the search for security. Nanny Crawford's choice for Janie's husband, Logan is the type of new African American envisioned by Booker T. Washington. He is a perfectly safe and secure man, a relatively prosperous small farmer who works his land with a mule. When it appears to Janie that she is also expected to work like a mule, she moves out of the passive mode instilled in her by her grandmother and escapes with the romantic Joe Starks. Starks, however, represents another of the possible traps on Janie's quest for self-fulfillment.

Starks originally appeals to Janie's sense of adventure and romance when he tells her of his plans to become a successful politician and businessman. She soon finds, however, that Joe intends to use her as an emblem of his success. Joe desires the status that comes from having a light-skinned wife; however, he commands Janie to keep her long straight hair hidden in a headrag whenever she is in public. Thus he controls the envy of his neighbors and Janie's ambition to become one of the folk.

Janie believes that Joe's desire is to be like the whites for whom he once worked. He eventually builds a large white house for Janie that she compares to those of wealthy Southern whites.

Joe's materialism is nicely balanced by the egalitarian qualities represented in Tea Cake. Tea Cake is literally a man of the people, for he spends a majority of his time each year as a migrant farm laborer in southern Florida. He also has no desire to keep Janie above people; instead, he asks her to do what she wants. She decides of her own volition to work with Tea Cake out in the fields; he reciprocates by helping her with the housework after they both return from work, and he does his share of the cooking as well. He has his faults, including a fondness for gambling and knife-fighting, but to Janie even his faults add to his romantic appeal.

The townspeople of Eatonville and the migrant workers on the "muck" add yet another dimension to the range of characters Hurston represents in the novel. The Eatonville folk are out of reach of Janie as long as Joe is alive; their "signifying" ways serve as entertainment and culture in which Janie is not allowed to participate. The migrant workers and their bluesy style are Janie's antidote to years spent caged by Starks in Eatonville, but even this group comes to resent her independence. Only when Janie returns to her home in Eatonville does she find fulfillment.

Themes and Meanings

The novel begins with a statement of its central subject:

> Ships at a distance have every man's wish on board. For some they come in with the tide. For others they sail forever on the horizon. . . . That is the life of men. Now women forget all those things they don't want to remember, and remember everything they don't want to forget. The dream is the truth. Then they act and do things accordingly.

The differences between the reactions of men and women form the core of the novel. Janie, the protagonist, is able to live her dream after two false starts. At the novel's end, Janie is left with her memories, and her gift to the community at large is her willingness to share her story with others.

The horizon is a metaphor to which Hurston returns to describe the characters and their relation to their dreams. Nanny Crawford, Janie's grandmother and protector, is described as a woman who has a limited and limiting dream. She wants protection for Janie; Janie, however, comes to think of Nanny's dream as a noose that is slowly strangling her and depriving her of her own dream.

Other characters share Nanny's dream of material wealth as a safety net that helps to buoy their position in society. Logan Killicks represents the completely practical man whose ship has come in with the tide. Likewise, Joe Starks wishes that "his people" would spend less time playing and more time attending to their business. Janie comes to reject this materialistic philosophy as a masculine dream; however, her later adventures are underwritten by the wealth she inherits from Starks.

Arrayed against the materialists are a group of characters loosely defined as the "folk." Hurston's anthropological work, particularly her folklore collection *Mules and Men* (1935), serves as the basis for the folk characters depicted in the novel. Though they are despised and exploited by characters such as Starks, the "folk" are noteworthy for their "signifying," or verbal gamesmanship. Signifying may take the form of jokes, putdowns, or storytelling, and the stories may be truthful or fabulous.

Janie's growth as a character is closely related to her ability as a master storyteller. At first she is prevented from telling stories by Nanny Crawford and Logan Killicks, who want to keep her isolated from the world. Joe Starks wants her to enter the world, but in a limited role: She is to serve as a nonspeaking ornament to his success. When she does attempt to join in the storytelling and signifying that goes on at the store, she is rebuked by Starks and told to stay in her place. Only Tea Cake allows her the choice of joining into the dialogue of the culture. As a blues musician, Tea Cake realizes the importance of the audience and its response, and he and Janie soon join in a symbiotic, nonhierarchical relationship of storyteller and audience. Tea Cake and the crew down on the muck help to give Janie the confidence that she needs to live and tell her own story. By the time that she returns to Eatonville, Janie has acquired the ability to become the narrator of her own story; Pheoby comments that she has grown simply from having heard Janie's story.

Critical Context

The original publication of *Their Eyes Were Watching God* in 1937 brought a less than positive response. Richard Wright, who would become the best known African American novelist with the publication of *Native Son* (1940), harshly criticized the novel as being irrelevant to the struggles of the African American community. Wright was particularly critical of Hurston's portrayal of race relations in the South, arguing that Hurston considered the repression of African Americans to be irrelevant. The critical consensus has recently come full circle; novelist Alice Walker, for example, has written that "there is no book more important to me than this one."

Hurston's strained relations with other African American writers may account for the negative reactions to the novel. She was one of the youngest writers to be associated with the Harlem Renaissance, though most of her work was done after its heyday. She had alienated particularly the leader of the movement, poet and short-story writer Langston Hughes, by claiming sole authorship of a play they had written together. Her politically conservative views and cultivation of wealthy white patrons also angered some writers, Wright in particular.

The critical consensus on the novel changed after its reprinting by the University of Illinois Press in 1965. The novel subsequently gained an underground following and became one of the most successful books in the history of academic publishing. It was not until the feminist movement of the 1970's, however, that the book gained the status of an American classic, on the level of the works of Wright and William Faulkner. Hurston's influence continued to be widely felt in the 1970's and 1980's, particularly in the works of younger African American novelists such as Alice Walker and Toni Cade Bambara.

Bibliography
Bloom, Harold, ed. *Zora Neale Hurston's "Their Eyes Were Watching God": Modern Critical Interpretations.* New York: Chelsea House, 1987. A collection of selections and essays on the novel written by critics of African American literature. Bloom's introduction places the novel in the world tradition of novels and discounts its role in the genealogy of African American writing. Bloom argues as well that Hurston's writing transcends the limitations of feminist and racial political ideologies.

Callahan, John F. "'Mah Tongue Is in Mah Friend's Mouf': The Rhetoric of Intimacy and Immensity in *Their Eyes Were Watching God.*" In *In the African-American Grain: The Pursuit of Voice in Twentieth-Century Black Fiction.* Urbana: University of Illinois Press, 1988. Callahan's essay examines the most controversial aspect of Hurston's novel, the role of narrative voice in the telling of Janie's story. He emphasizes the novel's utilization of African American folk forms of storytelling, which promote a democratic conception of culture.

Cooke, Michael G. "Solitude: The Beginnings of Self-Realization in Zora Neale Hurston, Richard Wright, and Ralph Ellison." In *Afro-American Literature in the Twentieth Century: The Achievement of Intimacy.* New Haven, Conn.: Yale University Press, 1984. Cooke highlights the movement from materialism to self-fulfillment in the work of three very different African American writers.

Davies, Kathleen. "Zora Neale Hurston's Poetics of Embalmment: Articulating the Rage of Black Women and Narrative Self-Defense." *African American Review* 26 (Spring, 1992): 147-160. Davies argues that Hurston's own relationships with abusive men are glossed over in her biography and the novel by her reliance on the ideology of love.

Hemenway, Robert. *Zora Neale Hurston: A Literary Biography.* Urbana: University of Illinois Press, 1977. The standard biography of Hurston; helped to establish her as a major writer. Includes material on her life as well as critical analyses of her novels and other work.

Woodson, Jon. "Zora Neale Hurston's *Their Eyes Were Watching God* and the Influence of Jens Peter Jacobsen's *Marie Grubbe.*" *African American Review* 26 (Winter, 1992): 619-636. Woodson traces the similarities in the plot of *Their Eyes Were Watching God* and Jens Peter Jacobsen's *Fru Marie Grubbe* (1876). He argues that Hurston turns the basic plot in Jacobsen's tragic novel into the affirmative plot of *Their Eyes Were Watching God* in order to counteract the negative stereotypes of women in fiction.

Wright, Richard. "Between Laughter and Tears." *New Masses* 25 (October 5, 1937): 22, 25. A diatribe against *Their Eyes Were Watching God* by the soon-to-be-famous African American novelist. Wright accuses Hurston of contributing to almost every stereotype concerning African Americans and also accuses her of accommodating her wealthy white audience.

Jeff Cupp

THERE IS A TREE MORE ANCIENT THAN EDEN

Author: Leon Forrest (1937-   )
Type of work: Novel
Type of plot: Psychological realism
Time of plot: The mid-twentieth century
Locale: Primarily the fictional Forest County
First published: 1973

> *Principal characters:*
> NATHANIEL (TURNER) WITHERSPOON, the main protagonist of the
>   novel
> MAXWELL "BLACK-BALL" SALTPORT, a close friend of Nathaniel
>   who becomes a Black Muslim minister
> JAMESTOWN FISHBOND, a talented artist who struggles with
>   alcoholism and drug addiction
> JERICHO WITHERSPOON, the mulatto grandfather of Nathaniel
> HARRIET BREEDLOVE WORDLAW, a matriarch whose presence
>   infuses the novel with religious and moral meaning
> SWEETIE REED, Nathaniel's grandmother by adoption

The Novel

There Is a Tree More Ancient Than Eden is an experimental novel depicting the growth and development of Nathaniel Witherspoon. Narrated from a central image of Nathaniel Witherspoon riding in a Cadillac with Aunty Breedlove to his mother's funeral, the novel ranges in time. His mother's death in the late 1950's, while Nathan is a teenager, ignites a personal search for meaning in life and leads him to a deeper understanding of his African American family and consciousness.

The novel consists of six chapters: "The Lives," "The Nightmare," "The Dream," "The Vision," "Wakefulness," and "Transformation." It uses various narrative devices such as sermons, letters, poetic monologues, and dialogues to tell the story. For example, "The Lives" depicts the partial biographies of the main fictional characters as well as giving thumbnail sketches of historical figures such as Louis Armstrong, Abraham Lincoln, and Harriet Tubman. Within this section, some of the characters speak to Nathaniel, telling their stories in stream-of-consciousness prose. The last chapter contains a long letter to President Lyndon Baines Johnson by Nathaniel's grandmother, Sweetie Reed. With the help of Nathaniel, who types out her long-winded oration, Sweetie outlines poignantly the progress of her people while indicting the American government for its injustices to the black race. The final section of the novel contains a sermon concerning Martin Luther King, Jr.

The body of the novel also uses more traditional narrative techniques to outline the life of Nathaniel Witherspoon from infancy to adulthood. By cleverly combining stream-of-consciousness narrative with character sketches, evocative vignettes of youth, and snatches of realistic dialogue, Forrest builds a convincing portrait of the Witherspoon family. Nathan's inward journey is described in poetic prose. Surrealistic episodes give the reader a portrait of the black community of Forest County, which may be modeled on the South Side of Chicago. With interjected passages in single-spaced prose, Forrest immerses the reader in the richly symbolic lives of his characters and the consciousness of his race. Long dark passages evoke feelings and fears associated with the Great Flood, the Middle Passage, and migrations by African Americans, in boxcars, to northern cities.

Nathan's recollection of an old wagon from which watermelons are sold launches an acute reverie concerning the atmosphere of downtown, with its House of Soul Bar-Be-Que restaurant, the Joe Louis Theater, and the House of the Brown-Skinned Goddess Salon. The atmosphere of his community and the influence of his family are presented in a number of ways. Religious images echo throughout the novel as Nathaniel struggles between despair and redemption. He is attracted to the dynamic power of black Baptist storefront preaching. Jericho Witherspoon and Sweetie Reed, as two forebears of Nathaniel, demonstrate through their longevity and their strong characters a tenacity of spirit common to the African American experience.

The chapter entitled "The Vision" contains perhaps the most harrowing image in the book. Nathaniel witnesses in a dreamlike fashion the crucifixion and dismemberment of a black man in front of a huge crowd of people, who fight over his remains. The internal conflict between communities separated by a blood-red river mirrors the misunderstandings and hate depicted in other episodes of the book. The novel is rich in symbolic language and images of both a biblical and a mythic nature. One of the most important visions is of a black madonna under a tree that is more ancient than Eden. This symbolic pairing suggests the ancestral strength and continuity of the African American people. It is this legacy of survival and vernacular strengths that finally gives Nathaniel the ability to continue.

The Characters

Nathaniel Witherspoon is the central character in the novel, which chronicles the Witherspoon family as well as the neighborhood of Forest County. Nathan's inward search begins as he sits in a Cadillac with his Aunty Breedlove on the way to his mother's funeral. In his late teens, Nathaniel is a troubled youth searching for meaning in his existence, torn in different directions by members of his family and the influences of life in an American city. Nathaniel's journey transcends the bonds of time and space. The exploration of his consciousness reaches far back, to the memory of his grandfather, Jericho Witherspoon, who was born a slave. It also reaches to his immediate future, when he attends college. It is through his consciousness that the voices of the past speak as he weighs the lives and influences of his ancestors against the troubles of the present. Nathaniel's own development is illustrated through a number of vignettes that show his attachment to as well as conflict with his family. His father is strongly outlined in the first part of the novel. As a man who works as a cook, he is considered to be a failure by the more successful Dupont side of the family. Nathaniel recognizes his father's appreciation of the small wonders of life; that appreciation influences Nathaniel to develop his own poetic strengths.

The Duponts provide a more sinister influence. The family has made a fortune on skin bleaching cream. Nathan feels the pull of their mercenary power. In the end, the voices of his ancestors who struggled out of slavery and built a community enliven his spirit and point the way to redemption.

Jericho Witherspoon, Nathaniel's paternal grandfather, is a major character in the story, even though he died in 1944. Branded with his initials on his left shoulder, Jericho is representative of the mythic black bad man in African American oral tradition. He is armed constantly and hates the master race with a passion. Having escaped slavery by running away, Jericho vows that he will never be caught alive. Jericho is a mulatto, born of a white slave master and an unknown woman. To keep his freedom, he learns to imitate accents and pose as different characters. Jericho leaves a cruel, unmerciful legacy to the Witherspoon family. As a hard drinker, gambler, and wanderer, he represents a rebellious secular force that flies in the face of religious tradition.

Aunty Hattie Breedlove Wordlaw is the voice of religious sanity in the novel. Her counsel is always laced with biblical allusions. She manifests through her righteous soul the healing qualities of forgiveness and moral strength.

Jamestown Fishbond is one of Nathaniel's closest friends and represents the passage of the black man into the second half of the twentieth century. Born in 1929, Jamestown is an extremely intelligent artist whose artistic ambitions are stifled at an early age. He is forced by a teacher to paint a sentimental version of Abraham Lincoln embracing a slave rather than the scene he wanted to paint—a black man surrounded by the evils of drink and drugs that are destroying his life. Ironically, Jamestown falls into the same trap. Jamestown is wanted dead or alive for gun running and high treason. His early desires to succeed have been frustrated. After being decorated in the Korean War, he turns to a life of crime. Like Jericho, he is a dedicated revolutionary who will allow no restrictions on his freedom. A hard drinker, insomniac, and restless traveler, Jamestown is found shot dead in Mozambique in 1971, apparently killed while fighting for the liberation of that country.

Forrest is particularly good at presenting in surrealistic prose the madcap and often tragic progression of friends and family. Sweetie Reed, Nathaniel's adopted grandmother, emerges at the end of the novel as the matriarchal black voice, summing up the Witherspoon legacy while indomitably contributing her own unique perspective to the narrative.

Themes and Meanings

There Is a Tree More Ancient Than Eden blends realistic passages with sections consisting of poetic monologues, surreal episodes, sermons, and letters. The novel contains many aspects of the African American vernacular tradition in its concentration on language, music, and religion. Within the oral tradition of black Americans, the text can be seen as one long piece of signifying or verbal play on the theme of a collective black identity. Through a combination of memory, imagination, and multiple narrative techniques, Forrest presents a spectrum of African American voices that create a cohesive worldview of black America.

With language that often resonates with biblical images and Shakespearean eloquence, the narrative takes the reader on an intense journey. The kernel of this journey is the maturation process of Nathaniel Witherspoon. In this sense, it functions as a traditional *Bildungsroman*, pinpointing important episodes in a young man's life that lead to his growing up. Many of the sections turn inward into Nathaniel's consciousness, illustrating through the use of symbol and archetypal images his legacy and connection with a mythic past.

The narrative of Nathaniel's story is fragmented by the entry of other voices into the narrative. These voices amplify his story by introducing the reader to ancestral figures as well as members of his surrounding black community. Readers learn of Nathaniel's troubled upbringing and his need to mend a spiritual and cultural schism within his soul. Forrest's concentration on the ancestral past is orchestrated through mythical images that convey the collective consciousness of Nathaniel's race. Echoes of ancient civilizations reverberate through the text, as scenes of rebirth and renewal conflict with passages of death and destruction.

The sacrificial aspect of black slavery lies at the center of the novel. Many of the characters are old enough to remember slavery. Nathaniel sometimes becomes the conduit for voices from the past. This ancestral counsel helps him to develop a perspective on his personal history. The novel works both as a chronicle of a family and as a history of the trials and tribulations of the African American people.

The rich legacy of the black vernacular tradition is intimately connected with the narrative. The folk religious images of the river of salvation blend with passages devoted to the train, a trope often used in blues songs. The biblical language of storefront preaching intermingles with street-smart descriptions of inner-city life. In this way, Forrest touches upon the panorama of African American culture in a narrative based on the oral and musical traditions of African Americans.

The novel deals with the 1960's as well as connecting to the past. Through Sweetie Reed's letter to the president of the United States, the reader is introduced to issues such as the War on Poverty and student revolts. The final section contains a dynamic sermon of many different hues eulogizing Martin Luther King, Jr., and at the same time presenting a whole era of black American concerns.

The novel's poetic prose refigures oral tradition and represents jazz idioms in its improvisational style, which mimics the rhythms and sounds of black life. The surrealistic episodes evoke a mythic world of the collective unconscious. These combinations of narrative ploys depict a personal journey toward self-identity as well as a comprehensive overview of black America's progress from slavery to contemporary times. By emphasizing the power of language in the African American tradition, commenting on the importance of ancestral counsel, and by structuring the narrative around religious and moral imperatives, Forrest has written a novel that flows and floods like a mighty river washing through the mind.

Critical Context

There Is a Tree More Ancient Than Eden is the first novel of three that Forrest devotes to the Witherspoon family saga. *The Bloodworth Orphans* (1977) and *Two Wings to Veil My Face* (1983) contain many of the same characters introduced in the first novel. Critics generally praise this ambitious undertaking and laud Forrest for his innovative use of poetic language and image. They recognize that the experimental nature of these novels is primarily focused on creating a verbal music that leads to a deeper understanding of the collective consciousness of the black race. The oral testimony of the books comes from both religious and secular sources. The expressive force of the narratives has been compared to jazz in its creative reworking of common meters. At the core of each novel lies Nathaniel Witherspoon's search for a new spiritual identity.

Many critics suggest that Forrest has been influenced by white writers such as James Joyce and William Faulkner and black writers such as Jean Toomer and Ralph Ellison. Forrest's creation of Forest County, a mythical landscape, is suggestive of Faulkner, while his expressive language and imagery connects with Ellison. Other critics also recognize the influence of Carl Jung's psychological theories of the collective unconscious and archetypal images. Many of the images of the novel have a biblical cast to them, suggesting a deep spiritual battle waged within the text concerning the nature of African American redemption.

With its episodic structure, surrealistic passages, and use of a variety of narrative ploys, the novel falls definitively within the modernist literary tradition. It extends the classic *Bildungsroman* by using language that is like music to create powerful passages. The evocation of collective consciousness through family history and black cultural creations makes this novel outstanding.

There Is a Tree More Ancient Than Eden uses the traditional folk methods of legend, tales, religion, and music to present a comprehensive view of African American vernacular strengths. The novel uses the past to make a bridge to the present. Some characters in the novel were born into slavery; Nathaniel is able to go to college. Nathaniel Witherspoon's understanding of self is intimately connected to his exploration of his family heritage. By placing his family chronicle in the context of American history, Nathaniel creates a living testimony of African American survival techniques. Furthermore, by merging his family history with that of the black community, the novel makes an important statement on the progress of black people into the twentieth century.

Bibliography

Bell, Bernard W. *The Afro-American Novel and Its Tradition.* Amherst: University of Massachusetts Press, 1987. Discusses Forrest in the section on fabulation, romance, and fantasy. Considers Forrest as part of a tradition of black fabulators who use dream visions and other linguistic forms to present personal and spiritual journeys.

Byerman, Keith E. "Orphans and Circuses: The Literary Experiments of Leon Forrest and Clarence Major." In *Fingering the Jagged Grain: Tradition and Form in Recent Black Fiction.* Athens: University of Georgia Press, 1985. Praises Forrest's use of stream-of-consciousness techniques and believes that within the stylized and surreal episodes lies a cultural wealth of material carried by black Americans.

Jones, Gayl. *Liberating Voices: Oral Tradition in African-American Literature.* Cambridge, Mass.: Harvard University Press, 1991. Jones stresses the blues, jazz, spiritual, and sermonic rhythms of the text as it attempts to redefine the oral tradition of black Americans.

Lee, A. Robert. "Making New: Styles of Innovation in the Contemporary Black American Novel." In *Black Fiction: New Studies in the Afro-American Novel Since 1945.* New York: Barnes & Noble Books, 1980. Comments on Forrest's strengths in making symbolic connections between generations while expressing mythic racial truths of American history.

Mootry, Maria K. "If He Changed My Name: An Interview with Leon Forrest." *The Massachusetts Review* 18 (Winter, 1977): 631-642. The author comments on his own goals, interpretations of his novels, and his writing style.

Stephen F. Soitos

THE THIRD LIFE OF GRANGE COPELAND

Author: Alice Walker (1944-   )
Type of work: Novel
Type of plot: Social realism
Time of plot: From 1920 to the early 1960's
Locale: Rural Georgia and New York City
First published: 1970

Principal characters:
GRANGE COPELAND, a poor black sharecropper in rural Georgia
MARGARET COPELAND, Grange's wife
BROWNFIELD COPELAND, the son of Grange and Margaret
MEM COPELAND, Brownfield's wife
JOSIE COPELAND, Mem's aunt, Brownfield's lover, and Grange's
    second wife

The Novel

The Third Life of Grange Copeland, a three-generational account of the Copeland family, begins in rural Georgia in the 1920's and ends during the early stages of the Civil Rights movement in the early 1960's. The novel records the impact of racism and poverty on one family by emphasizing what it does to individuals and by showing what individuals must do to keep alive kinship, the strongest weapon black people have to fight injustice.

Using a conventional chronological plot and an omniscient third-person narrative point of view, Walker begins by detailing the life-styles of Grange and Margaret Copeland. Grange and Margaret work hard to make a life for themselves and their son, Brownfield, but they are unsuccessful in rising above what Walker documents as almost absolute poverty and degradation.

Grange works as a sharecropper, planting, chopping, and picking cotton for a white man named Shipley. No matter how hard he works, he can never get out of debt to Shipley. Grange responds to his cycle of poverty by keeping his best self secret. He never smiles at his son or his wife. He rarely even talks to them, and when he does it is to say something harsh. The immediate consequences of Grange's reaction to poverty and oppression are that his son and wife fear him. Brownfield develops a barely suppressed hatred for his father, and Margaret goes out of her way to please Grange. As a result of the fights and arguments that invariably crop up between Grange and Margaret over his affair with Josie or his inattention to Margaret and Brownfield, Grange feels inadequate, unhappy, and empty. He resolves to leave his wife and son.

His leaving, however, only means that his wife and son are left to fend for themselves, and neither fares very well. Margaret, who has had an affair with Shipley and given birth to Shipley's son, cannot go on without Grange. She kills herself and the baby. After his mother's death, Brownfield strikes out on his own, thinking that if he can get to the North he might yet have a chance of having a happy life. With no family support, he only gets as far as a neighboring county, where he meets and is temporarily supported by Grange's old flame, the prostitute Josie.

Brownfield falls in love with the gentle and kind Mem, Josie's niece. He marries her and initially has high hopes of creating a warm and loving family. Walker makes it clear that Brownfield has not seen or learned how to love, how to be a good husband and father. Brownfield and Mem soon have several children, and the only way Brownfield can support his family is by hiring out as a sharecropper. Like Grange, Brownfield hates himself because he is unable to escape the cycle of poverty associated with sharecropping. Like Grange, he takes his own inadequacies and frustrations out on his wife.

While Brownfield is bent on destroying his own wife and family, Walker lets the reader know that Grange is in New York City trying to piece his life together. In New York, he feels better when he directly confronts those who oppress him, and he learns that as one man he cannot do battle against all white people. He returns to Georgia to find a place of his own where he can be left alone. Josie, who owns her own business—a juke joint—and has money, is the financial key Grange needs to buy his own farm. He marries Josie and tries to be a grandfather to Brownfield's daughters.

Grange reasons that Brownfield is beyond help, but he tries to help his grandchildren and Mem. After Brownfield murders Mem, Grange vows to accept responsibility for raising his granddaughter Ruth. His two other granddaughters go to live with Mem's relatives in the North. Grange becomes the sort of paternal figure he should have been with Brownfield.

The Characters

Although Grange is the title character, the majority of characters in the novel are black women, and the novel progresses as an account of the women in Grange's life and what he has done directly or indirectly to them. In structuring major parts of the novel around Grange's struggles to find himself and to be a responsible man, Walker presents his character primarily from an interior perspective. Although the external conditions of racism and poverty are important to the novel's meanings, how Grange responds to those conditions is the key to his character presentation.

In his first life, when he thinks of himself as a victim of injustice, he responds to his condition by taking his frustrations out on those closest to him, his wife and his son. He treats both cruelly, because expressing his love outwardly and in positive ways would mean acknowledging his inability to do anything for his family that might change their condition. Beyond his abuse of his family, he retreats into himself and avoids who he is through excessive drinking and by having an affair with Josie. Walker depicts Grange as a coward, a man afraid to face up to his kinship responsibilities. This point is made when Walker has Grange use the occasion of his wife's affair with Shipley as a rationalization for leaving his family.

Grange, however, is not a static character. He confronts new experiences and a second life in New York City, and he begins the process of coming to terms with who he is and what he might do to make up for his failures in his first life. A growing sense of a new self marks his reentry to the South, where he assumes the responsibility for rearing his granddaughter Ruth in his third life.

The early depiction of Grange shows how his lack of parental concern for Brownfield makes Brownfield the hard and cruel man that he becomes. Brownfield carries forward Grange's legacy of abuse to family.

Margaret, Josie, and Mem are victimized and thwarted in their self-development both by society and by Grange and Brownfield. These women's lives show what happens when little kinship is present.

Margaret only wanted to be loved. She used to wait for Grange to come home, dressing up for him and hoping he would notice her, but he never did. The sharecropping system oppresses Grange, but Margaret has to contend with oppression and debasement not only from without but from within her own family. By the time Brownfield is fifteen years old, she has long since given up. Only in her sexual affairs does she find arms that temporarily comfort her.

Josie has similar experiences. On the surface, she is not passive like Margaret and Mem. Josie hides her reaction to a lifetime of abuse by men in her loud and vulgar behavior and in her profession as a prostitute, in which she relishes taking money from men and debasing them. Like Margaret, she wanted somebody to love her. Her father rejected her and publicly humiliated her when she was a pregnant teenager. Grange uses her even in his third life, marrying her for her money and ignoring her while he showers all of his attention on Ruth. Brownfield uses her in his attempt to get revenge on his father.

Only Mem's youngest daughter, Ruth, has the opportunity to not be a victim. Unlike her mother, whom Brownfield beat and finally killed, Ruth receives only the best part from her family, her grandfather Grange. He teaches her to be independent, proud, and strong. He shows her how to defend herself, even to use a gun if she must. She is the only Copeland woman posed to deal effectively with racism and oppression, and to be healthy in the process. At the novel's end, she challenges segregated schools and racist history books, and she joins the emerging Civil Rights movement.

Themes and Meanings

The Third Life of Grange Copeland, Walker's first novel, is a poignant preface to her fictional canon. In this novel, published when Walker was only twenty-six years old, many of her later artistic concerns are present, including the creation of "real" black women, the sexual and racial oppression of black women, the preoccupation with the inner lives of characters, the repressed or thwarted creativity of black women, the exploration of the effects of racism and discrimination on individuals from an inside perspective, the legacy of parental values transmitted to children, and the use of African American history and cultural traditions. More than anything, the novel is the story of the individual's relationship to community.

The novel privileges the idea that in African American experience the individual has a responsibility to the group, whether the group is family or the larger black community. In working with this idea, Walker charts the toll on individual lives when kinship or the communal self is absent or seriously undervalued.

The history of the Copeland family is a record of the difficulties African Americans face in keeping the notion of kinship alive in a racist world. Walker's narration of the effects of the sharecropping system, a metaphor for America's overarching racism and discrimination, on Grange and Margaret reveals that kinship has a precarious future. If black people do not struggle to maintain it, awful events can happen to them, events more terrible than racism itself.

Grange responds to his lack of power to combat racism by taking his frustration and anger out on his wife and child. Margaret responds to the same environment and to Grange's treatment of her by neglecting Brownfield. Brownfield, in turn, responds to this parental neglect by becoming even more cruel than his father. Thinking that no one loves him, he cannot love himself. He reasons that the only thing he has to give people, whether family or friends, is hate. Brownfield, as an adult entrapped in the same sharecropping system, treats his family with more venom than Grange had treated his. Walker suggests that with each generation the bonds of kinship are potentially lessened, and more damage to black people may occur.

In New York City, Grange begins to understand that what he did to his family was wrong. When he returns to rural Georgia, he does so to atone for his previous sins against the tribe, his family. To underscore the idea that the bonds of kinship must not be transgressed, Walker prevents the new Grange from having any positive effect on Brownfield. In other words, Grange and Margaret's neglect of Brownfield and the damage it caused was permanent. Grange might still be able to make up for his past mistakes with Ruth, and that is what he does.

In Ruth's story, Walker notes the good that can come from a lived kinship. Grange takes part in Ruth's growing up, sharing her frustrations and joys, never letting her forget that she is deeply loved. He also expands her knowledge of black history and culture so that she will have a base to help her deal with racial discrimination. He teaches Ruth how to use a gun and how to drive a car, and he encourages her to read so that she can become self-sufficient, strong, and resourceful. At the novel's end, Grange says: "Survival was not everything. *He* had survived. But to survive *whole* was what he wanted for Ruth."

The Third Life of Grange Copeland shows that the survival of black people depends as much on tribal love and responsibility. Although this theme informs the novel, Walker is sensitive to the fact that black women apparently suffer more when kinship is absent than do men, particularly in her examination of the destroyed and wasted lives of Margaret, Mem, and Josie Copeland.

The novel exposes those parts of black experience that subvert kinship and delete its life-giving potential. Targets of Walker's exposition and criticism are male-female relationships, motherhood, and sexism. Walker's message, contained within the Copeland family chronicle, is that any destruction of black people, from within or from without the black community, must stop. African Americans must accept responsibility for saving one another's lives, as Grange finally does when he becomes close to Ruth.

Critical Context

As Walker's first novel, *The Third Life of Grange Copeland* announces and launches her discerning and complex fictional examination of African American life and culture, especially the experiences of black women in the South. The novel addresses issues and themes Walker would explore in her later fiction with more daring and inventive narrative techniques. Black women and black people, their history and culture, and how they must all learn to get along and to be responsible for one another are major concerns in all of Walker's writing.

The Third Life of Grange Copeland, published in 1970, also began the creative efforts of black women writers to respond to the 1960's, a decade of political and civil rights struggles that did not always address the issues in black history and culture that related to black women. The novel bears comparison to other works published in 1970 by black women writers. Sonia Sanchez, Carolyn Rogers, Mari Evans, and Alice Walker, for example, infused their poems with black women's issues, conditions, and images. In 1970, Toni Cade Bambara edited the groundbreaking collection of short stories *The Black Woman*, and Toni Morrison published her first novel, *The Bluest Eye*, detailing the growing up experiences of several black girls. As the decade unfolded, fueled by both black cultural ideology and the women's liberation movement, black women were seeing more of their work published.

Walker's first novel, moreover, emphasizes a major thrust of her creative vision: The world must change, and black people must also change. Grange Copeland learns to change even as the events around him are slow to do so. As he changes, the possibilities for political change are offered. His acceptance of his role as provider for and teacher of Ruth helps Ruth to be the kind of woman who can join the Civil Rights movement without any reservations. Walker's subsequent fiction made use of this strategy as a corrective both for her characters and for African Americans, as can be seen in *In Love and Trouble: Stories of Black Women* (1973), *Meridian* (1976), *You Can't Keep a Good Woman Down* (1981), *The Color Purple* (1982), *The Temple of My Familiar* (1989), and *Possessing the Secret of Joy* (1992).

Bibliography

Banks, Erma, and Keith Byerman. *Alice Walker: An Annotated Bibliography.* New York: Garland Press, 1989. Collects the major and minor material written on Alice Walker from 1968 to 1986.

Bloom, Harold, ed. *Alice Walker.* New York: Chelsea House, 1989. Major critics from a variety of critical and theoretical perspectives discuss the majority of Walker's fiction, nonfiction, and poetry.

Gaston, Karen C. "Women in the Lives of Grange Copeland." *College Language*

Association Journal 24 (March, 1981): 276-286. Positions the women characters' lives as Walker's major thematic concern.

Harris, Trudier. "Fear of Castration: A Literary History." In *Exorcising Blackness: Historical and Literary Lynching and Burning Rituals.* Bloomington: Indiana University Press, 1984. Argues that Grange and Brownfield attempt to flee the symbolic castration and lynching of the sharecropping system. Only Grange is able to resurrect his dignity.

Hogue, W. Lawrence. "History, the Feminist Discourse, and *The Third Life of Grange Copeland.*" In *Discourse and the Other: The Production of the Afro-American Text.* Durham, N.C.: Duke University Press, 1986. Demonstrates how Walker uses a period of black history to represent a largely feminist story.

Charles P. Toombs

THIS CHILD'S GONNA LIVE

Author: Sarah E. Wright (1928-   )
Type of work: Novel
Type of plot: Social criticism
Time of plot: The late 1920's
Locale: The eastern shore of Maryland
First published: 1969

Principal characters:

MARIAH UPSHUR (RAH), the protagonist, a young African
    American woman
JACOB UPSHUR, Mariah's husband
PERCY UPSHUR, Jacob's father
BERTHA ANN UPSHUR, Percy's wife and an antagonist to Mariah
HORACE UPSHUR (RABBIT), Mariah's son, who suffers from a
    harelip and who dies from roundworms and tuberculosis
BARDETTA TOMETTA UPSHUR, Mariah's daughter by Dr. Albert
    Grene
BANNIE UPSHIRE DUDLEY (MISS BANNIE), a mail carrier, white
    landowner, and lover of her relative, Percy Upshur
VYELLA, Jacob's adopted sister and mother to his child Ned
DR. ALBERT GRENE, Percy and Miss Bannie's son, a respected
    physician and father to Mariah's Bardetta Tometta
HAIM CRAWFORD, a red-faced, racist patriarch of a powerful
    family

The Novel

Although *This Child's Gonna Live* consists of the stream-of-consciousness narrations of both Mariah and Jacob Upshur, the novel begins and ends with Mariah's thoughts, conversations with God, and actions as seen from her perspective. Since most of the chapters belong to Mariah, it becomes her story, a tale of attempted flight from poverty, racism, and religious hypocrisy.

As the story begins, a distraught, pregnant Mariah worries about whose child— Dr. Albert Grene's or Jacob's—she will bear. She becomes determined to escape the poverty, racism, and religious hypocrisy of the African American community of Tangierneck. If "this child's gonna live," she believes that she must flee north, although she is aware that none of Jacob's brothers have survived their exodus to Baltimore. Since her thoughts flow by association, the present is inextricably related to the past as well as to the future. The loss of Mary, her first daughter, the scars on her father's back, and Jacob's exploitation by Miss Bannie all suggest the futility of life in Tangierneck. Jacob is equally upset, but his concerns involve the impending loss of land to Miss Bannie, whom he blames for his troubles.

Both Mariah and Jacob confront past and present humiliations. At a prayer meeting, the Committee of Judgment denounced Mariah for being pregnant out of wedlock, and Bertha Upshur protected Jacob's reputation. Jacob learns about Bannie's involvement in the death of Bard Tom, his grandfather; and Mariah hears that Aunt Cora Lou, who was going to get help for Mariah, has been run down by a carload of white teenagers. When Mariah meets Miss Bannie, who has been attacked by Percy, she sympathizes with her until Miss Bannie utters a string of racial insults. Mariah and Jacob, whose minds are preoccupied by death, both intend to kill Miss Bannie. Jacob is easily persuaded to go home, while Mariah succeeds in getting Miss Bannie to the Gut, where she plans to drown her. She cannot follow through, but when she accompanies Miss Bannie to her home, she gives her the pills that cause her death.

Miss Bannie's death is followed by Mariah's giving birth to a light-skinned daughter. Her father asks, "Well, what in the name of God has the Master sent us here?" Mariah links the death and the birth when she bargains with God about dying for her sins but allowing her child to live. Although she considers suicide, she resolves to live when the "Messenger" absolves her of guilt in Miss Bannie's death. Even in death, Miss Bannie precipitates trouble. Her will poses problems for the white power structure. Jacob's queries about the will cause more violence, including visits by the Paddy Rollers (a white vigilante group), a beating, the burning of the local school, and the arrest and subsequent lynching of Percy Upshur, who had revealed the truth about Dr. Grene and Bannie. When Mr. Nelson lays claim to the Upshur land, Jacob has to leave Tangierneck to "seek his fortune" and regain the land.

Jacob moves his family to Chance. Here Wright abandons her practice of modifying real place names to take advantage of the irony in "Chance," a "real" Eastern Shore town where the family lives in squalid quarters. In this part of the novel, Wright focuses on the exploitation that migrant laborers suffered, whether working in a canning factory in Chance or picking strawberries on Kyle's Island, where Rabbit gets tuberculosis and dies. During its migrant odyssey, the family returns three times to Tangierneck to attend funerals. These returns suggest that the Upshur family cannot escape from Tangierneck and that death ties it to the land.

The funeral of Vyella, Jacob's adopted sister and Mariah's best friend, is the most significant of the three because Mariah has to confront her feelings about her best friend, her family, and her fate. Mariah, who was putting money aside for her escape from Tangierneck, had entrusted her savings to Vyella. Shortly before her death from cancer, Vyella had written to Mariah and revealed that Jacob was the father of Little Ned. At the funeral, Mariah, the last one to speak, is torn between exposing the preacher woman and remaining silent and true to her friend. Ultimately she decides not to exact revenge. Instead, she takes on the responsibility for Vyella's children and those of Aunt Cora Lou, for whom Vyella had been caring. She even gives Jacob her savings so that he can purchase the twenty acres of land he needs for a fresh start. The pressures of caring for her extended family and the realization that escape is now impossible are almost too much for her, and she returns to the Gut, wading in and almost yielding to the desire to drown. Her decision to live represents affirmations of self, of life, and of commitment to family.

The Characters

Wright reveals Mariah's character through the stream-of-consciousness technique, which involves Mariah's thoughts, her conversations with God, and her reactions to and evaluations of the events that unfold before her. Because she has been judged, she herself judges; she is harsh on white society, Jacob, African American men, and herself. Unlike the other characters, with the possible exception of Jacob, Mariah develops, changes, and emerges as a complex human being. She is religious, but her chatty God-talk suggests that her concern is with the present, with the survival of her children, rather than with an afterlife. Her superstitions put her at odds with the religious women of the community. Her statements to others, particularly Jacob and her children, are usually at odds with her thoughts and behavior. Unable to express her love verbally, she vents her frustrations and anger but immediately regrets her words and actions and then blames herself, as with Rabbit's death.

With the exception of Vyella, who seeks Mariah's forgiveness, the other women in the novel tend to be flat, one-dimensional characters who serve as background to the action. Aunt Saro Jane is more interested in avoiding trouble at the funeral than in discovering the truth; Bertha Upshur is devoted to protecting the public image of her husband and son; Miss Bannie is a cowering pathetic racist alone in the woods; and Mrs. Cranston at the welfare office is a smug, officious white bureaucrat. There is little "sisterhood" in this novel.

The African American men are the target of some scathing comments in the novel, but Wright allows Jacob, through his stream-of-consciousness chapters, to defend himself. Vyella states, "ain't none of our men worth enough to worry yourself over," and Mariah describes Jacob as "a wind-beaten, life-beaten going-nowhere man" who is "always hiding behind the Lord." Jacob has been conditioned by his father, much as he influences his sons, and he dreams of being "master of all I survey," the land his ancestors owned. His power is limited, however, as he discovers when the Paddy Rollers invade his house and terrorize his family. Jacob wants to answer his son Skeeter's question in the affirmative: "Ain't I something, Daddy?" Land is Jacob's answer, but he cannot have it without Mariah's money.

Like his father, Jacob has committed adultery and fathered an illegitimate son, but unlike his father, Jacob is tormented by guilt and loves his wife. Percy's transgression also has more grievous results—his relationship with Miss Bannie costs the Upshurs their land. When Mariah confronts him, he becomes physically abusive. Patriarchal, abusive, morally flawed, and weak, Percy is a negative stereotype, but when he asserts his rights to the white establishment, he dies as his father, Bard Tom, did. Bard Tom is a legendary rebel whose memory Mariah perpetuates in Bardetta Tometta, but the legendary rebel himself and those who emulate him die.

Themes and Meanings

As its title implies, *This Child's Gonna Live* concerns survival in a hostile environment. In addition to experiencing life-threatening diseases with almost no access to health care, coping with a legal system that supports the white power structure and ignores the criminal activities of white vigilantes, and enduring the judgments of the self-righteous African American religious community, Mariah must deal with the obstacles posed by African American men and by the land itself. In such an environment, death is a recurring motif, in the form of conversations with the Grim Reaper, superstitions, and the loss of loved ones.

In this novel, whites probate wills, staff the legal system, control welfare regulations, prohibit African Americans from holding mill jobs, and restrict access to health care. Unfortunately, whites also control the attitudes of the African American community, which believes that it must please, even emulate, the white power structure. When Rosey dies at the camp meeting and Mariah is humiliated, both pregnant young women are condemned by Bertha not so much for their "sin" as for their visibility: "We had a lot of white people on this campground today . . . and wasn't this a sight for them to see!"

Sexual politics and sexual stereotyping also pose problems for Mariah, who describes sex in violent, graphic terms and regards it in terms of power. Her problems with Jacob stem from his assumption that he should and will control her. Her father assumes the right to criticize her conduct as a woman, and she fears facing him if she escapes Tangierneck. He lectures her about the future, foresees the eventual dominance of "the black nation's overcoming all," but warns Vyella and Mariah that women are "supposed to obey their men." When women invade the masculine space, as Mariah does when she confronts Percy, they are subject to physical abuse.

Mariah's reference to taking "the plow in my own hands," her premonitions about the "green winter," and her frequent references to the land and sea suggest the close relationship between survival and her physical environment. Jacob's beloved land almost seems to be unwilling to yield a harvest, and the storms they endure destroy a cemetery. Even in death, those harvested by the "Grim Reaper," grimly ironic in this sense, are subject to further violation. Mariah's assertion that a green winter produces a "fat graveyard" reinforces the link between the environment and death, a subject that pervades Mariah's thoughts. The affirmation of life that concludes the novel has tremendous significance in the light of the omnipresence of death.

Critical Context

When *This Child's Gonna Live* appeared in 1969, it was hailed as an impressive achievement. The reviewer for *The New York Times* wrote, "The canon of the American folk-epic is enriched by this small masterpiece." Its initial success was a result of two factors: its stylistic brilliance, including handling of stream of consciousness, dialect, and speech rhythms, and its indictment of a racist society. Despite its promising debut, the novel eventually lapsed into relative obscurity and was out of print until 1986, when the Feminist Press reissued it. Its later popularity was, in part, a result of the feminist movement. Mariah's determination to maintain her dignity and humanity in a world hostile to women and their causes speaks to contemporary women who face the same problems.

Feminists have called attention to the relevance of Wright's themes and noted the importance of gender in the telling of stories. Although Jacob has his say, this is Mariah's story, a familiar but seldom-told story of both racism and sexism. Contemporary African American novels are, in large part, written by women who employ women as storytellers who use folk tales, superstition, dialect, and humor to express their perspectives on life.

In a sense, Wright's novel is mainstream, similar in style and content to the works of Alice Walker, Zora Neale Hurston, and Paule Marshall. All these writers use folk culture and folk heritage, but their works surely transcend the canon of the American folk epic, a genre identified with African American literature.

Bibliography
Harris, Trudier. "Three Black Women Writers and Humanism." In *Black American Literature and Humanism*, edited by Baxter Miller. Lexington: University Press of Kentucky, 1981. Contrasts the hypocritical Christianity practiced in Mariah's African American community with the humanistic, individualistic values of African American folk culture and folk heritage. Sees the novel as the tale of Mariah's evaluation and rejection of Christianity, her struggle to retain her humanity, and her ultimate acceptance of her own folk heritage.
Hollis, Burney J. "The Race and the Runner: Female Fugitives in the Novels of Waters Turpin and Sarah Wright." In *Amid Visions and Revisions: Poetry and Criticism on Literature and the Arts*. Baltimore: Morgan State University Press, 1985. Discusses Mariah as a "runner" who rejects and flees from the injustice to which her birth and environment subject her. In her primarily mental flight, she is hindered by her paranoia and by the African American men whose romanticized definitions of themselves keep them bound to their circumstances.
Howe, Irving. "New Black Writers." *Harper's* 239 (December, 1969): 130-131. Reviews several African American novels, among them *This Child's Gonna Live*. Considers Mariah not only the central character but also the surrogate voice for Wright. Praises local color but faults characterization, suggesting that Wright needs "disciplined removal from her materials."
Schraufnagel, Noel. *From Apology to Protest: The Black American Novel*. Deland, Fla.: Everett/Edwards, 1973. Considers the novel part of the "apologetic protest" in the 1960's for its focus on exposing the effects of white racism. Calls attention to the sexual aspects of racism as reflected in the economic exploitation of African Americans by their white relatives. Praises the novel's stream-of-consciousness narrative and asserts that the novel does not revert to pure propaganda.
Whitlow, Roger. *Black American Literature: A Critical History*. Totowa, N.J.: Littlefield, Adams, 1974. Compares Wright favorably to Zora Neale Hurston in terms of style, citing Wright's use of dialect, her merger of humor and seriousness, and her diction. Also calls attention to Wright's criticism of the vicious behavior of self-righteous African Americans who punish social "sins" and encourage conformity to "white" Christianity.

Thomas L. Erskine

THROUGH THE IVORY GATE

Author: Rita Dove (1952-   )
Type of work: Novel
Type of plot: Psychological realism
Time of plot: From the 1950's through the early 1970's
Locale: Akron, Ohio, and Arizona
First published: 1992

> *Principal characters:*
> VIRGINIA KING, the protagonist, a college-educated puppeteer, musician, and actress
> BELLE KING, Virginia's embittered mother
> ERNEST KING, Virginia's father, the first African American chemist to work for Goodyear
> CLAUDIA KING, Virginia's younger sister, a rebellious teenager
> ERNEST KING, JR., Virginia's brother and ally
> AUNT CARRIE, Virginia's "short aunt with the big bosom"
> GRANDMOTHER VIRGINIA EVANS, Virginia's namesake and the matriarch of the family
> CLAYTON EVERETT, a handsome, tall, talented cellist whom Virginia meets in college
> TERRY MURRAY, an educated, handsome, sensitive, available bachelor whose son is one of Virginia's students
> TODD WILLIAMS, Virginia's handsome high-school boyfriend
> RENEE BUTLER, a quiet, musically talented student of Virginia
> KAREN, Virginia's white elementary-school friend

The Novel

Although *Through the Ivory Gate* focuses on Virginia's brief tenure at Washington Elementary in Akron, Ohio, the novel spans most of Virginia's life, beginning with Virginia's memory of Grandmother Evans' anger at an African American doll with stereotypical features and ending with her grandmother's "benediction and farewell." In a sense, the novel concerns Virginia's journey to knowledge about her parents, her racial identity, and herself; her memories and dreams of the past interrupt and influence the flow of ongoing events.

Virginia's memory of a scene at the Akron train station is incomplete. She remembers the external action but does not know why the family moves to Arizona, why her mother calls her Aunt Carrie "lovely," and why her father is near tears. The Arizona years are unhappy ones, characterized by her mother shutting out the outside world, her father's obsessive quest to learn about other cultures, and her own desire to belong to the predominantly white high-school culture.

She majors in dramatics in college, pursues her cello playing, and meets Clayton, a homosexual musician with whom she has an affair. The affair ends, though she has illusions about Clayton returning to her. When she meets his homosexual lover, she accepts the situation and throws herself into drama, mime, and music. During her college years, which she calls a "refuge," her progress with the cello becomes a kind of measure of her development, as both her music and her life lack passion. Significantly, she conquers the music of Bach at the same time she has her affair with Clayton. After graduation she joins, in spite of her mother's disapproval, a mime troupe, Puppets and People. Because of her dramatic background and education, she is hired as an arts consultant to work in a variety of public schools in Ohio.

Her first assignment is in Akron at Washington Elementary, her own school, now racially integrated. Using her puppets, particularly Gina, her puppet alter ego, she reaches the students and encourages them to express themselves indirectly through the puppets. Renee Butler, who reminds Virginia of herself at an earlier age, becomes a devoted fan. Kevin Murray, another student, improves academically and socially as a result of the puppetry and attempts to get Virginia interested in his father, Terry, who helps her with the puppet stage and falls in love with her.

Akron is also the home of Virginia's grandmother and her aunt Carrie, who hold the key to understanding the scene at the train station. Because she both wants and fears to know the truth, Virginia postpones her visits to her relatives, but they force the issue. When she finally goes to Grandmother Evans' apartment, she listens to a long story about her grandfather. The point of the story—that secrets cannot be hidden—has special relevance for Virginia, who subsequently learns from Aunt Carrie that Virginia's father, Ernest, moved to Arizona after her mother found out about incest involving Carrie and Ernest.

The climax of the story occurs at a puppet show the students stage at the school. A story about a football player successfully courting a girl is a success with the audience, but its aftermath—Renee jumping from some stairs and injuring her ankle—forces Virginia to reexamine her priorities and relationships. She again visits Grandmother Evans, who tells her that Carrie has been healed by the truth and that people can benefit from examining the damage in their lives. Virginia seems determined to try the New York City stage. The novel ends with a drama in Akron itself, so New York may not be necessary.

The Characters

Dove uses a third-person limited point of view, with all information filtered through Virginia's perspective. The characters in *Through the Ivory Gate* are therefore presented as Virginia sees them. Because she is at a pivotal point in her life, some particularly relevant characters from her past appear in dreams and memories that shape her current decisions about characters in the present. Her reservations about Terry Murray, for example, are the result of her relationship with Clayton Everett, and her willingness to benefit from Grandmother Evans' advice stems from the beginning of the novel, when her grandmother asserts herself as an authority figure.

With the exception of Belle, the African American women are presented favorably. Virginia's grandmother, who speaks from her "throne," is the storyteller matriarch whose clear moral vision absolves her children of their incest, understands Belle's pain, and guides Virginia on her journey to discovery. Despite her sin, Aunt Carrie emerges as a strong, nurturing woman, cursed by being unattractive, isolated and alone as a young widow, and devoted to her brother's children, particularly Virginia.

The only two white females from her past both serve to reflect on Virginia's somewhat ambivalent feelings about race. Karen, the second-grade friend who defines her as "Nigger," not only makes her aware of prejudice but also seems to spur her to act "white" by straightening her hair and becoming the only African American majorette. Kelly, her white university friend, "imagined they were nearly sisters" but did not understand the real dimensions of racism at the university. Both white women function essentially to make points about racism.

Terry Murray is the romantic male lead in the novel, but his character is inextricably linked to the men who precede him. Virginia wonders why she is so "skittish" around Terry, but one page later the reader has the answer: "Todd—what a failure *he* had been." Clayton seemed to be the answer, a perfect soulmate, but his homosexuality made her even more cautious and less impulsive. Parker, a puppeteer colleague, terms her "My Lady of the Immaculate Name," a pun on her name but also a comment on her emotional withdrawal from men. In Terry, Dove has created a character who is too good to be real: an educated, handsome, sensitive, caring man who is, incidentally, a gourmet cook. That Virginia can remain "skittish," can ponder the reasons for his divorce, and can retreat to her cello indicates the depth of her emotional problems.

Virginia's problems dealing with her family are caused by the emotional aridity of the Arizona home, but the immediate family members seem fairly superficial: Ernest, Jr., her ally; Claudia, the rebellious teenager; Belle, the embittered, critical mother; and Ernest, "Rubber Smoke from the Far Hills Kachina." The nickname she and her brother give their father significantly labels him, defines him in terms of his Akron home and chemist occupation, and distances him from them. The term also has historical roots: "When a Hopi man puts on a Kachina mask, his troubles disappear." When Virginia learns the truth about her father—when she removes the mask—he becomes real again, a guilt-ridden man, one of the "damaged," as Grandmother King describes him.

Virginia's students appear to be the most complex minor characters in the novel, perhaps because she feels more at home with them, less prone to treat them as stereotypes. Kevin, Terry's son, is a case in point. He both worships Virginia and resents her relationship with his father. It is Renee, however, who is the most fully developed minor character. Because she reminds Virginia of herself in musical ability, withdrawn manner, and penchant for jumping the stairs, Virginia takes a keen interest in Renee, who is dealing with her mother's miscarriage—she had counted on having a sister. Although Virginia comes to fill the void in Renee's life, she ignores Renee when her relationship with Terry preoccupies her. Renee's accident prompts Virginia to do some soul-searching.

Themes and Meanings

Through the Ivory Gate begins with a conversation about a child's doll and ends with children in Halloween costumes, assuming new roles and identities. In the course of the novel, there are recurrent references to dolls, puppets, and masks, all of which relate to Dove's focus on the theme of identity. Virginia's childhood selection of dolls reflects her attitude toward race. She keeps and identifies with her white Penelope doll and rejects the African American doll her grandmother gives her. Grandmother Evans senses the unconscious motive for Virginia's choice: "Your daughter is ashamed of being a Negro."

When the family visits a Hopi reservation, Dove returns to the theme of identity. Donning a mask, a Hopi man loses his identity, "forgets his name," and assumes the identity of a god. Virginia puts on metaphorical masks, assumes different roles (majorette, for example), and changes her hair to become someone else. She repeats this tendency in college, where she majors, appropriately, in drama. She is more interested in mime and cello, neither of which involve verbal expression. Although she can express herself through music, her playing is the expression of someone else's composition.

Believing that there are few roles for black actresses, she decides to use her talents in a puppet troupe. The puppet becomes the channel for the puppeteer's emotions. Virginia even creates Gina, a puppet alter ego that lacks Virginia's inhibitions, caution, and "skittishness." Just as she succeeds in getting shy, reserved students to express themselves through the puppets, she occasionally relies on Gina to handle a situation she cannot. Virginia cannot deal with Renee's leap because she sees the fallen Renee not as a child but as a "tossed-out doll, a splintered configuration." Earlier she threw her grandmother's black doll out the window.

Virginia's decision about Terry also concerns her identity as a wife or as a musician or actress. Although the choices are not mutually exclusive, she initially sees them that way. Much of the novel traces her developing personality through her maturing musical ability. A telephone call from New York narrows the choice to Terry or the theater, and she chooses the latter. After she talks with her grandmother, however, she encounters costumed Halloween revelers who seem to suggest that "theatrical" experiences are not limited to the stage.

Dove's title suggests that there has been a passage, that Virginia has gained insight that will enable her to express herself directly, rather than through surrogates. A puppeteer identifies the "ivory gate" in a line from Homer's *The Odyssey*: "Issuing by the ivory gate are dreams of glimmering illusion, fantasies, but those that come through solid polished horn may be borne out, if mortals only know them." The line both testifies to the power and magic of art (music, theater, even fiction) and identifies reality or life as superior, if accompanied by self-knowledge.

Critical Context

Dove is known primarily as a Pulitzer Prize-winning poet and as the poet laureate of the United States (1993), but she has published, in addition to *Through the Ivory*

Gate, a collection of short stories, *Fifth Sunday* (1985). Even her fiction reveals poetic cadences and rhythms, especially in Virginia's lyrical outbursts about the puppet shows she attends and stages.

Although her novel has many of the staples of contemporary works by African American women, it is not primarily about race. The storytelling matriarch, the slights and wounds inflicted by a racist society, the sisterhood of black women, and some stereotypical black males are all featured in the novel, but they are background to the action. Unlike many novels by black women, the novel accepts rather than protests the society in which the characters function. It is more romantic and social than political, and it stresses healing and happiness more than pain and suffering. Although Virginia has some psychological problems, they are not insurmountable, and she is a coping, happy woman more than a victimized survivor.

In its narrative, protagonist, and style, however, Dove's novel closely resembles the work of other black women writers. Although many of these novels use the first-person point of view, the third-person limited point of view also provides the reader with a woman's perspective. The plot, moreover, is not linear. Associations dictate content, so that the reader may go from the present to the past, or even experience flashbacks within flashbacks. The effect is a blurring of time in which the present is tied irrevocably to the past through memory and dream. As is the case with most contemporary African American novels, Dove's protagonist ends the novel on an affirmative note.

Bibliography
Hoffert, Barbara. Review of *Through the Ivory Gate*, by Rita Dove. *Library Journal* 117 (August, 1992): 146. Quibbles about the need for "tighter" prose but praises the images and the poetic quality of the novel.
Kitchen, Judith, Stan Sanvel Rubin, and Earl G. Ingersoll. "A Conversation with Rita Dove." *Black American Literature Forum* 20 (Fall, 1986): 227-240. Although the interview focuses on Dove's poetry, many of her remarks also concern her fiction. She notes that "language does shape our perceptions" and comments on the results of carelessness with relationships. The interview is followed by "The First Suite," described as "from a novel in progress," which is *Through the Ivory Gate*.
Prose, Francine. "Pulled by the Strings of the Past." *Washington Post Book World* 202 (October 11, 1992): 5. Focuses on the theme of returning to the past. Maintains that there are no villains, just "fallout" from human frailty, in the novel, which she faults for its long lectures on music and puppetry.
Ryman, Geoff. Review of *Through the Ivory Gate*, by Rita Dove. *The New York Times Book Review*, October 11, 1992, 11. A lengthy, sympathetic review that notes that Virginia's quest for a male partner has a larger social dimension. Finds a slight but effectual treatment of race relations. Observes that the novel is essentially happy and criticizes Virginia's character as too perfect.
Schneider, Steven. "Coming Home: An Interview with Rita Dove." *Iowa Review* 19

(Fall, 1989): 112-123. Discusses Dove's Akron roots but is most valuable for her comments about the literary establishment being unfair to black writers and about the necessity for revising the literary canon to include more female and minority writers.

Taleb-Khyar, Mohamed B. "An Interview with Maryse Condé and Rita Dove." *Callaloo* 14 (Spring, 1991): 347-366. Dove's discussion of her family, especially her chemist father at Goodyear, identifies the autobiographical nature of *Through the Ivory Gate.* Dove also talks about black militancy, the "trauma of color," and the notion that African Americans are "bilingual" in their possession of two sets of cultural values. Although she describes herself politically as a feminist, she opposes didactic or propagandistic fiction.

Thomas L. Erskine

TRAIN WHISTLE GUITAR

Author: Albert Murray (1916-   )
Type of work: Novel
Type of plot: Bildungsroman
Time of plot: Primarily the 1920's
Locale: Rural Alabama
First published: 1974

> *Principal characters:*
> SCOOTER, the boyhood nickname identity of the adult narrator of
>   the novel
> LITTLE BUDDY MARSHALL, Scooter's best friend
> LUZANA CHOLLY, a fearless blues hero who plays the twelve-string
>   guitar
> MISS TEE (EDIE BELL BOYKIN), Scooter's favorite aunt
> DELJEAN MCCRAY, Scooter's first, continuing, and last lover
>   during his youth

The Novel

Train Whistle Guitar offers a story of a black boy's preadolescent and adolescent seasons in a small town deep in the South during the decade after World War I. The story is told by the man whom the boy has become, recounting his memories after he has gone away to college, served in World War II, and made somebody out of himself, as he was born marked to do. He has also been marked for life by his education in that small-town community and culture. The events of the story are the remembered highpoints in a daily dialogue, one carried out between the child and his community and between the conscious and unconscious (or spontaneous and reflective) selves of that child. The story implies a dialogue between the narrator's childhood self and adult self, the facts of his growing and the art of his telling of it— what, in memory and crafted language, can now be made of that growing. As memory and art thus valorize life, the feature that emerges as most meaningful is the boy's daily education, partly in school but most clearly out of school.

Like many novels of the early education of a heart, *Train Whistle Guitar* is episodic in its plot structure. What is remembered and told is what was felt as adventure by the boy. The story therefore moves as the boy felt life to move, from worthy time to worthy time, with only a sense of lull filling in the time between, like the steady rhythm of a drum or heart. Those experiences were intuited by the boy to be charged with meaning, but the full revelatory quality of their meaning has come to be known only later, in their telling as story.

The story is told in the first person, in the past tense. Often the voice that the reader hears and the language in which that voice speaks are the boy's, but occasionally the voice of the adult narrator reminds the reader that memory is occurring, so that persons, places, and events are doubly distanced, taking on the heightened reality of names of things that are evoked but are not actually present, except in their essences, and may have never existed in any simple, fixed form.

The novel opens with an introduction of the chinaberry tree that stood in the front yard of the boy's home. As in a fairy tale, often the boy would climb to the top of this "spyglass tree" and look out to the horizon. The point of view from which the story is told, especially in the early chapters, is that of a child's privileged position vis-à-vis adult life and a child's interpretation and reinterpretation of the life that he observes, as his awareness expands with experience, study, status, and reflection.

The story moves outward from the tree to the fields and the town, to the boy's earliest sense of a hero on whom he might model himself for finding meaning in the larger, outer world, to his sense of himself as having a destiny (perhaps even heroic) in that world. Then come, chapter by chapter, the boy's adventures, with each one suddenly presenting a lesson to be learned: the premature attempt to hop a freight train north; the celebration of athletic heroes; discovery of a corpse in the swamp; rhythms of family, school, and town; visions of a living history and geography; observations of obsessive romance and of racist hostility; adolescent experiences of sex; and discoveries about kinship. These experiences teach the value and fragility of human well-being and what can be done to protect and nourish it: lessons of love, courage, responsibility, and sacrifice; the mystery of violence and death; appropriate pride and humility; imagination and possibility; style and grace. The story of each adventure is told in the language and spirit of the blues, of signifying, and of incipient jazz. It is the language of play and of art. Each lesson includes a further insight into the blues as a mythologizing perspective on life.

The Characters

Early in the novel, Scooter remarks that his hero, Luzana Cholly, "was forever turning guitar strings into train whistles which were not only the once-upon-a-time voices of storytellers but of all the voices saying what was being said in the stories as well." These are also the voices of the characters in Murray's novelistic storytelling, a cross section of the "blues people" (to borrow a phrase from the contemporary African American writer Amiri Baraka) whom Murray knew in the rural South of his boyhood—ordinary people who spoke with extraordinary wisdom in an extraordinary new style of American English as they composed a heroic life and heritage. The artistic style of these voices, as exemplified in the novel's narration, is a major device used by Murray for characterization. Another device is the content spoken by these voices, as Scooter talks about the members of his family and the people of his town and as they talk about one another and about him.

Characterization is accomplished mainly through talk, especially as Scooter relates and comments upon conversations among persons around him, discussing conversational styles and attitudinal content. He also reports, interprets, and sometimes explains people's clothing styles, gestures, food, habits, achievements or failures, reputations, special acts and responses, histories, and stories they are known for telling about their own lives. Scooter's characterizations of persons are corroborated by remarks by Little Buddy Marshall and by other observers and storytellers in the community, or sometimes by white folks. Some of the characters in the novel, like some of the scenes, conversations, and language, are types, but these are the ones that Scooter knew at greater distance and that would exist as types for any child, and even these are given individualizing touches of detail. Those that he knows closely are portrayed lovingly and extensively enough to take on multifaceted and urgent identities in the reader's imagination.

Scooter, a child with definite but mysterious parentage, emerges as a product of this entire community of talkers. By his own representation and his later adult assessment, and by the remarks of others, Scooter is revealed as having the flaws and making the mistakes that are common to his age group. He is also revealed, in contrast to his friend and foil, Little Buddy Marshall, as having been known all along, and having known himself, to be destined for a larger life. He is a learner and spirited articulator of all that is most vital in what comes his way. As such, he is taught (and the reader is taught) by every character in the novel, from blues musicians and relatives to jive interloper and sheriff. Scooter personifies the heart's imagination, finding the beauty of compassionate and truthful expression of the full range of persons and events that life presents to him.

Gasoline Point, Alabama, becomes a collective character of the novel, given physical form by Scooter and given personality by the stories that its citizens tell about themselves and one another. A reader of the novel, hearing or overhearing through Scooter the details of characters' lives and their responses to their own lives and the lives of others, perceives a collective spirit of communal caretaking, realistic acceptance of human foibles and catastrophes, exceptional daily competence and courage to survive and even triumph in the face of racist oppression, and profound appreciation of the best features and accomplishments exhibited by humans.

The language of that community—flowering with enthusiasm in the voice of the boy as he learns his own variation of its syncopated, signifying style, now remembered lovingly by the adult narrator and thereby released by the novelist like the notes from a guitar or a piano—has a life of its own, performing for the reader like an over-character who is the embodiment and spirit of the novel's plot and themes.

Themes and Meanings

In *Train Whistle Guitar*, Murray takes his reader into the center of the briarpatch of post-Reconstruction confederacy, Alabama in the 1920's, and draws on that canvas a portrait of the human spirit overcoming its environment of adversity and absurdity to make life good. His message, like that of the storytelling voices in the train-whistle guitar of Luzana Cholly, is that happiness, although provisional and mixed with pain, is achievable, and therefore so is a life without illusion but in which hope is nevertheless a justifiable and nourishing emotion.

Within the context of restrictive and destructive pressures of racism, the citizens of Gasoline Point construct a culture that is so realistic about life and so beautiful that within the context of its richness racism can be seen to be merely one of the grosser of humanity's limitations. This visionary and expansive perspective on life creates possibilities for growth and fulfillment by developing and constantly reinforcing a strong and affirmative sense of selfhood on the part of individuals and of the community as a self-identifying whole.

As seen in the lives of Scooter and his friends, the community moves to encourage its young to go in quest of such an identity, directly through schooling that prepares individuals to fully realize their potentials in ways that will also contribute to the progress of the entire community, and indirectly through the modeling and contextual support of family and church. Scooter exemplifies those individuals who look outward, with curiosity, confidence, and imagination (as he does from his lookout at the top of the chinaberry tree) and those individuals who apply themselves with purpose and discipline to overcome obstacles to their full self-development. Scooter remembers, from his earliest reading with Miss Tee, that the littlest engine tried and did. When he returns to his hometown as a college graduate and soldier, his girlfriend Deljean tells him that one thing that Miss Tee never had to worry about was "you trying your best to make somebody out of yourself."

The most effective and vivid means by which the community educates its members, young and old, while at the same time entertaining them and reinforcing their shared identity, are its talk and its music. Scooter remarks that "it was the very best of all good times to be where grown folks were talking." Some of the most important aspects of talk that Murray presents are naming, rhythm and rhyme, extemporizing and improvisation, voice inflection, and individual stylistic wizardry. Names are functional identities that attach both public and personal dimensions of symbolic meaning and value to the one named. Because an individual plays many roles, he or she may have more than one name and thereby acquire a sense of multiple layers of worth. The protagonist of the novel, for example, is called Scooter in celebration of his mobility in the briarpatch of his societal environment. He also sometimes thinks of himself, in connection with his cultural heritage, as Jack the Rabbit; any boy can claim that name. At home he is called by a name of affectionate mother-child bond, and at school he is called by the legal name by which he will someday converse with society at large.

All the aspects of talk can be, and should be, used by each individual in the daily process of forging the fully developed personal identity that bears its many names. The larger the repertoire of verbal techniques, the more successfully the individual will play the game of skill that is his or her way of understanding and influencing the world. One's life then is a give-and-take dialogue (with oneself, family, friends, associates, strangers, and enemies) that gradually plots the story of one's life—the signification of one's history, functional mythology, and personal frame of reference.

Storytellers and blues guitarists, then, play a heroic role of telling or playing personal journey into mythic quest. By skillfully describing and shaping life into an aesthetic experience, they conceptualize life into a beauty that confronts and counters both indifferent chaos and hostile forces. In their community's own language they offer moving and clarifying new imaginations of life that heal and enrich the community. In their artistry, as Murray illustrates through Scooter, Luzana Cholly, and many other characters, probably the single most important technique is improvisation. Because life is characterized by constant change and by tension between disparate elements such as construction and destruction or freedom and restriction, spontaneity in language, music, or any area of action is the key to an individual's, and a community's, ability to adapt a traditional pattern into an immediate possibility for triumph over adversity and for enjoyment of the good life.

Critical Context

It is useful to read *Train Whistle Guitar* beside *Black Boy* (1945), in which novelist Richard Wright autobiographically presents his boyhood in small-town Mississippi. His story takes place at the same time as Murray's quasi-autobiographical story of Scooter in neighboring Alabama. Wright wrote vividly of the saving power of the imagination in a highly intelligent and questioning boy. His tale is bleak, with its emphasis on the presence of racist whites and on the cultural as well as physical poverty of a black peasant class. Wright's seminal and still powerful novel *Native Son* (1940) also provides a meaningful critical context for Murray's novel. In that story, set in Chicago in the 1930's, Wright emphasizes the same conditions of black life as in *Black Boy* and shows resulting acts by the young black protagonist that are monstrous and lead to his death, although, at the end, he mentally and spiritually transcends both racism and the impoverished culture of his black community. In its psychological and sociological analysis, *Native Son* lodges a strong protest against racism and prejudiced capitalism in the United States. It is clear that Wright conceived his readers to be, like the jurors who convicted his protagonist, white and prejudiced. His novel solidly established the concept of "protest literature" as a valuable kind of writing by African American authors.

Ralph Ellison, in essays and in his novel *Invisible Man* (1952), expresses the position that in writing protest literature a black author kneels before a jury of white readers and pleads for recognition of the humanity of black Americans. Ellison proposes that African American novelists should begin from an assumption of the full humanity of black Americans and strive from there toward meeting the highest universal artistic standards in the clarification of human life for all readers.

The matter of universality is itself a part of the critical context for the present novel. In 1974, when it was published, white literary critics could still belittle a work by a black author by claiming that since it portrayed the understandably limited lives of African Americans, it could not represent the universality of human life and therefore could not achieve the status of high art. Meanwhile, however, the black aesthetic movement was proposing that African American writers should take as their audience exclusively African American readers and write with the assumption that white American culture rendered white readers less than fully human by its pervasive racism.

Murray's aesthetic and ethical position is closer to Ellison's. Stating that in America cultural differences are more important than are differences of race, he assumes the full humanity of both blacks and whites and writes for any open-minded reader. Racists in his novel are portrayed as fools and enemies of humanity, and racism does not dominate the content of the novel. Murray goes beyond protest by establishing an irresistibly large, humane perspective in which racism is rendered impotent by its own blind pettiness. Racists are unattractive. African American culture is triumphantly beautiful in its creation of life-enhancing possibilities out of chaos and absurd social divisiveness. Murray sees the creation of a culture to be primarily an aesthetic endeavor of transforming experience into strong mythic selfhood.

Bibliography

Berry, Jason. "Musical Literature." *The Nation* 224 (January 15, 1977): 55-57. Because of this novel's derivation from blues perspective and idiom, its content and style contrast with those of traditional black realism and social protest literature, as well as with white Southern regional fiction.

McPherson, James Alan. "The View from the Chinaberry Tree." *The Atlantic Monthly* 234 (December, 1974): 118, 120-123. Participating in a rediscovery and reaffirmation of black cultural and spiritual roots in the South, the novel expresses the complexity of relationships between illusion and ever-changing American reality that form essential parts of both black American consciousness and the literary burden of transforming history into art.

Murray, Albert. *South to a Very Old Place.* New York: McGraw-Hill, 1971. Murray's stream-of-consciousness chronicle of his journey through the South, which included interviews with contemporary black and white Southern authors and with residents of the Alabama town in which he spent his boyhood.

O'Meally, Robert G. Foreword to *Train Whistle Guitar,* by Albert Murray. Boston: Northeastern University Press, 1989. With his uses of naming, storytelling, counterstatement, and call and response, Murray has invented "ways to write the blues," thereby expressing themes of everyday heroism, possibility, and *joie de vivre* while presenting types of people and places of a Southern blues community.

Schultz, Elizabeth. "Albert A. Murray." In *Afro-American Writers After 1955: Dramatists and Prose Writers.* Vol. 38 in *Dictionary of Literary Biography,* edited by Matthew J. Bruccoli. Detroit: Gale Research, 1985. By examining content and style in each of Murray's books, Schultz presents Murray's general philosophy of aesthetics and ethics, especially as related to blues music and the blues hero. Throughout his work, Murray's major subject is the triumph of African American people in creating a life-enhancing culture.

Wideman, John. "Stomping the Blues: Ritual in Black Music and Speech." *American Poetry Review* 7, no. 4 (1978): 42-45. This review of Murray's study of the history and nature of blues music, *Stomping the Blues* (1976), provides context and insights for understanding and appreciating Murray's musical use of African American speech patterns in his prose style in *Train Whistle Guitar.*

Tom Koontz

TROUBLE IN MIND

Author: Alice Childress (1920-   )
Type of work: Play
Type of plot: Problem play
Time of plot: 1957
Locale: New York City
First produced: 1955, at the Greenwich Mews Theater, New York City
First published: 1971, in *Black Theater*

> *Principal characters:*
> WILETTA MAYER, a mature actor who loves the theater
> AL MANNERS, the volatile director of *Chaos in Belleville*, his first
>   Broadway show
> SHELDON FORRESTER, an elderly actor who plays stereotypical
>   poor blacks
> MILLIE DAVIS, an attractive black actress who dresses stylishly
> JOHN NEVINS, an idealistic African American youth
> JUDY SEARS, a young white actress
> BILL O'WRAY, a white character actor

The Play

   Trouble in Mind takes place on a Broadway stage where a group of actors are rehearsing a predictable Southern melodrama, *Chaos in Belleville*, written and produced by whites and filled with racial stereotypes. Wiletta Mayer enters, speaking kindly to an elderly doorman who recognizes her from a musical in which she played years ago. A moment later John Nevins appears, thrilled with this opportunity. Wiletta advises the young man from her experience in white-dominated theater: He must not acknowledge he has studied drama, which might sound presumptuous, but should say that he appeared in *Porgy and Bess*, although he did not. She tells John to play the role of subservient black in order to succeed, and never to let director Al Manners know how much he really wants this job. The play, she admits, "stinks." John, however, is sure that he will be a star, and she realizes that her advice is wasted.

   Other cast members drift onstage. Millie Davis enters in a mink coat, commenting that she does not care if she works or not. Sheldon Forrester and Judy Sears follow. Sheldon has been ill and laments his loss of work. Judy, who is white, has just graduated from Yale; this is her first professional role, and she is enthusiastic but awkward. To demonstrate that she is not prejudiced, she ventures her belief that "people are the same," unaware that others see this as a denial of their experience as African Americans.

   Manners, who directed a Civil War film in which Sheldon and Wiletta appeared, enters. He exhibits unconscious racist and sexist attitudes by ordering coffee and Danish for the cast but ignoring Sheldon's request for jelly doughnuts. Noticing Judy, Manners moves too close to her; when she backs away, he takes offense. He praises John for his dramatic training (which has not been mentioned), but Judy, who volunteers her Yale background, is dismissed. When she makes a mistake, he parades her forcibly around the stage, then throws paper on the stage in a tantrum. Although others jump to retrieve the paper, Manners orders Wiletta to pick it up. Wiletta, startled, responds, "I ain't the damn janitor!" Embarrassed, Manners tries to pretend that all of them have been acting.

In *Chaos in Belleville*, Wiletta and Sheldon play John's sharecropper parents. Wiletta tells Manners that she knows what he wants from her song (Ruby, her character, sings whenever she is worried), but he insists that she probe Ruby's motivation and think about what she is feeling. Ruby's son Job is about to be lynched because he dared to vote, and Ruby refuses to help him, which seems unnatural to Wiletta. Soon she can neither sing nor read the way Manners wants. He forces her to get angry, then is appalled by the depth of her emotion.

After Manners leaves the stage, Wiletta struggles with a headache from the tension. Sheldon tries to comfort her, saying that they should not mind humiliation because they are trying to accomplish something. Yet Wiletta insists that she does mind. "Yeah, we all mind," Sheldon admits, echoing the play's title, "but you got to swaller what you mind."

In act 2, Bill O'Wray rehearses his big speech as Renard, the white landowner. His plea for racial tolerance sounds impressive, but it is filled with platitudes. Job's parents wait anxiously for his arrival. Wiletta, as Ruby, sings and prays for her son; Sheldon, as Job's father, whittles and prays; both are symbolically impotent. Ruby orders Job, who has voted against her wishes, to kneel: "Tell 'em you sorry, tell 'em you done wrong!" She directs him to give himself up to the oncoming mob.

Wiletta, still trying to make her role work, questions why a black woman would knowingly send her son to his death. Why can't the boy escape? "We don't want to antagonize the audience," Manners explains. "We're making one beautiful, clear point . . . violence is wrong." Then Sheldon, the only person who has actually seen a lynching, talks about it in simple and terrible detail. Wiletta reverses herself: "John, I told you everything wrong." Passive agreement is no longer possible for her.

After a lunch break, Manners charges Wiletta with deliberately sabotaging the play by showing anger. Ignoring the stage directions, Wiletta as Ruby tries to raise John as Job off his knees. She challenges Manners: "Tell me, why this boy's people turned against him? . . . I'm his mother and I'm sendin' him to his death. This is a lie. . . . The writer wants the damn white man to be the hero." She demands, "Would you do this to a son of yours?"

Manners responds with self-pity, telling her that the American public is not ready for what she wants. He suggests that making the white audience feel sorry for the black characters is a worthy goal. When Wiletta repeats her question, he flares, "Don't compare yourself to me! . . . Don't compare [John] with my son, they've got nothing in common," and rages off. Millie tries to make peace, urging everyone to go out for coffee and talk.

Wiletta is consoled by the doorman. She knows there will be no phone call for her for tomorrow's rehearsal, but, she says, "I'm gonna show up. . . . He'll have to fire me." At the play's end, the doorman listens admiringly as Wiletta quotes Psalm 133 in a ringing voice: "Behold how good and how pleasant it is for brethren to dwell together in unity." There has been chaos on the stage this day, but now Wiletta stands firm and steady.

There are at least three versions of *Trouble in Mind*. The two-act published version discussed here incorporates material added after the original performance, specifically references to the 1955-1956 bus boycott in Montgomery, Alabama, and the 1957 school integration in Little Rock, Arkansas. Critic Doris E. Abramson also cites a three-act manuscript that Childress considers "definitive." The three-act version ends on a more hopeful note as Manners comes to negotiation: "I, a prejudiced man, ask you, a prejudiced cast, to wait until our prejudiced author arrives tomorrow. I propose that we sit down in mutual blindness and try to find a way to bring some splinter of truth to a prejudiced audience." This speech also gives him more depth and complexity.

Themes and Meanings

Childress identifies herself as a "problem writer," and her play treats issues of racism and sexism in the theater and in society. She is obviously concerned with the ways in which African Americans are invalidated as persons. Manners silences his cast by ignoring them, gesturing impatiently, or telling them not to interrupt. He patronizes Wiletta by informing her that the black characters of *Chaos in Belleville* are human beings, although the fictional white playwright depicts them as ignorant shufflers. Manners likewise invalidates the women in his cast, mocking Judy as "Yale" and warning Wiletta, when she continues to question the actions of her character, that "you are going to get a spanking."

Playwright-critic Elizabeth Brown-Guillory notes another consistent theme in Childress' work, that of women making sacrifices. Wiletta is ready to risk her professional life because she must speak out against someone who threatens her human dignity. Millie also sacrifices dignity for the money she needs.

Several characters symbolically unmask. Manners, self-proclaimed friend of the Negro, betrays his own prejudice. Sheldon, who says he cannot read well yet who always knows his lines, reveals himself as an angry survivor, doing the only thing he knows how to do well. Millie, who has played the pampered darling, admits that she is desperate for a job. Wiletta drops her compliant mask and reclaims her pride, anger, and true majesty.

Trouble in Mind uses the common theatrical device of the play within a play to reveal a truth about the struggle of blacks in America. The line between inner and outer play effectively blurs as the actors move in and out of their roles. Wiletta unconsciously repeats one of Ruby's lines in answer to a question from Manners, and Sheldon's whittling while his "son" prepares to die mirrors his real life—going through empty motions.

The play's irony is effective. Wiletta begins by advising John to survive by pretense, but as he grows more adept, she becomes less capable. Judy winces at the word "darkies" in her script, but the black actors insist that the word does not bother them. Method acting becomes a paradox for Wiletta. By searching for the truth of her role, she finds a truth she did not expect.

In several places, the dialogue separates into simultaneous conversations, usually with the white characters discussing one subject and the black characters another. As an example, Manners praises the hackneyed script of *Chaos in Belleville* while Sheldon, John, and Millie discuss the Montgomery bus boycott, underscoring the serious breakdown in communication between the races.

Critical Context

Childress, an actor and an original member of the American Negro Theater company, co-directed *Trouble in Mind*, her first full-length play, which ran for ninety-one performances. The work earned Childress an Obie Award for the best original Off-Broadway play, the first ever won by a black woman. An important statement of the play is its attack on the white retelling of African American experience and the refusal of blacks to insist on the truth. Thus, when *Trouble in Mind* was scheduled for Broadway, Childress refused to execute script changes that would make the play more palatable to a white audience, a decision strongly supported by her colleagues, and the project was canceled.

Childress, the great-granddaughter of a slave, has been hailed as "the mother of professional black theater in America." Her fourteen plays include the one-act *Florence* (pr. 1949, pb. 1950), and *Just a Little Simple* (pr. 1950), a musical-revue adaptation of Langston Hughes's book *Simple Speaks His Mind* (1950). *Just a Little Simple* and *Gold Through the Trees* (pr. 1952) were the first plays by a black woman to be professionally produced with unionized actors. Childress has also written four books; her young adult novel *A Hero Ain't Nothin' But a Sandwich* (1973) was nominated for the National Book Award.

In a theater that has historically excluded women and blacks, Childress has established new ground and made possible the emergence of many black women playwrights. As an African American, she commands the attention of black audiences and also of whites. Her concern for plain speaking has never wavered. She has vowed that "I will not keep quiet, and I will not stop telling the truth."

Bibliography

Abramson, Doris E. *Negro Playwrights in the American Theatre, 1925-1959.* New York: Columbia University Press, 1969. A good overview, by decade, of African American playwrights and plays produced in New York's professional theater. Includes an analysis of *Trouble in Mind*. Abramson praises Childress for refusing to compromise her ideals but regrets her tendency to sermonize.

Brown-Guillory, Elizabeth. *Their Place on the Stage: Black Women Playwrights in America.* Westport, Conn.: Greenwood Press, 1988. An extensive study of the pioneering work of Childress, among others, and of the unique vision of black women playwrights. Brown-Guillory views Childress as "a writer of great discipline, power, substance, wit, and integrity."

Childress, Alice. "A Candle in a Gale Wind." In *Black Women Writers, 1950-1980: A Critical Evaluation,* edited by Mari Evans. Garden City, N.Y.: Anchor Press/ Doubleday, 1983. Discusses her early life, motivation ("the Black writer explains pain to those who inflict it"), themes, and subject matter. Childress notes that being a woman does not present as much difficulty for her as being black does.

Hay, Samuel A. "Alice Childress's Dramatic Structure." In *Black Women Writers, 1950-1980: A Critical Evaluation,* edited by Mari Evans. Garden City, N.Y.: Anchor Press/Doubleday, 1983. An analysis of the structure of four of Childress' plays. Notes that she uses a traditional structure of beginning-middle-end in *Trouble in Mind* but allows theme rather than character to dominate, and she reveals this theme not through her characters but through argumentation.

Mitchell, Loften. "The Negro Writer and His Materials." In *The American Negro Writer and His Roots: Selected Papers.* New York: American Society of African Culture, 1960. Reports comments made by Childress in a panel discussion. She expresses the general resentment against being told to write universally, without regard to race or controversy. African American writers "have much to say about white society 'and we must say it. . . . For they cannot write what we see.'"

Joanne McCarthy

TWO TRAINS RUNNING

Author: August Wilson (1945-   )
Type of work: Play
Type of plot: Psychological realism
Time of plot: 1969
Locale: A restaurant in a Pittsburgh, Pennsylvania, ghetto
First produced: 1990, at the Yale Repertory Theater, New Haven, Connecticut
First published: 1991, in *Theater* magazine

> *Principal characters:*
> MEMPHIS LEE, a restaurant owner who came to the North after
>   whites forced him off his Mississippi farm
> WOLF, one of Memphis' customers, a numbers runner
> RISA (CLARISSA) THOMAS, Memphis' lethargic employee
> HOLLOWAY, another of Memphis' regular customers
> HAMBONE, a retarded man in his late forties
> STERLING JOHNSON, a thirty-year-old ex-convict
> WEST, a funeral director

The Play

 Two Trains Running is a two-act drama consisting of eight scenes that unfold over a period of one week in Memphis Lee's restaurant in Pittsburgh. As in many of August Wilson's plays, there is a minimum of action: Many of the drama's key events occur offstage and are discussed by the characters. The emphasis is on dialogue— the rich musical language of the street and the harsh urban reality it explores.

 As the drama opens, urban renewal has gradually (and ironically) brought a once-vibrant neighborhood under the wrecker's ball, and Memphis' once-thriving business has been reduced to the few patrons who constitute the play's cast. Moreover, the dying neighborhood and restaurant are matched by Memphis' moribund marriage. His wife has left him, tersely stating that "she was tired."

 In scene 1, the talk of the neighborhood is concerned not so much with the turbulent events that characterized the 1960's but with economic issues. Wolf, Holloway, and Memphis all play the numbers game in the hope of staving off the enervating effects of poverty. Even Memphis, whose business once provided a steady income, admits: "It wasn't till I hit the numbers eight or nine years ago that I got to the point where I could change my clothes every day." The sense of unfairness is reflected in the discussion of Prophet Samuel, a deceased preacher who enriched himself at the expense of the poor. Prophet (perhaps a pun on "profit") maintained a harem of sorts and lived a life of luxury in this otherwise impoverished neighborhood. As people crowd into West's funeral home to view him, Holloway states: "He got hundred-dollar bills . . . got diamonds on all his fingers." The location of Prophet Samuel's remains is appropriate, for West, the funeral director, has repeatedly conned his nearly penniless neighbors into purchasing expensive funerals.

As Memphis anxiously waits for word from his lawyer regarding the city's payment for his soon-to-be-demolished restaurant, two more poverty-stricken figures enter the scene: Hambone and Sterling. Hambone, a middle-aged retarded man, talks continually about a debt owed to him by Lutz, the white owner of a meat market who, years earlier, cheated Hambone out of a ham. While he voices his demand for his long-delayed payment, Sterling receives some advice from Holloway. He tells the ex-convict that he can change his luck by visiting Aunt Ester, a true prophet: "Aunt Ester give you more than money. She make you right with yourself."

In scene 2, Memphis, Wolf, and Holloway watch Hambone enact his daily ritual of demanding from Lutz the payment of a ham. Nearly ten years after he painted the meat-market owner's fence, Hambone still awaits compensation; again and again, he repeats the lines, "He gonna give me my ham. I want my ham." Though Memphis dismisses this obsession, Holloway grasps the true significance of Hambone's persistence. Holloway believes that Hambone "might have more sense than any of us." Instead of accepting the chicken that Lutz offers him, Hambone has taken the difficult but nobler course of demanding what is rightfully his. Memphis, however, reveals his own painful past. He intends to reclaim the Jackson, Mississippi, farm that whites stole from him in 1931. Memphis reveals his determination to get his fair share when he turns down West's offer of fifteen thousand dollars for his restaurant.

In scene 3, the growing relationship between Sterling and Risa (he invites her to a rally, and she gives him what she predicts will be a winning number) is contrasted with their bleak environment. As Wolf observes, African Americans are "always under attack." The pervasiveness of this harsh reality is underscored by both Hambone and Memphis. Sterling is unable to change the former's chant to "black is beautiful," and the latter must contend with a city government that tries to utilize a contract clause to deprive him of a fair price for his property. Predicting victory in his fight, Memphis declares, "They don't know I got a clause of my own."

Scene 1 of act 2 is significant for what Memphis, Holloway, and West reveal about themselves. When Memphis refuses another offer of fifteen thousand dollars from West, he explains why he is so intent on reclaiming his farm. He abandoned his property when whites gave him a clear warning: They disemboweled and castrated his mule. Memphis was forced to flee for his life, but he declares, "once I know the rules, whatever they are, I can play by them."

West firmly states that "life ain't nothing. . . . But death . . . you can't blow away death. It lasts forever." West once asked Aunt Ester, the local mystic, to help him determine whether his wife was in heaven, but his greed prevented him from following her instruction to throw twenty dollars into a river. Holloway, on the other hand, complied with her request and was relieved of his desire to kill his grandfather, a notorious Uncle Tom. With these stories in mind, Sterling vows again to visit Ester and to marry Risa if his number wins.

Events progress rapidly toward the end of the play. Memphis indicates that he is seeking Aunt Ester's advice: Tomorrow he is to learn the amount of his compensation from the city. The third scene is notable for the manner in which Hambone's death serves to crystalize the characters of West, Risa, and Sterling. When Risa pleads with West for something better than the usual pauper's burial, the mortician refuses to make the financial sacrifice. For West, money is the only object. Sterling, however, recognizes that one needs more than just money and sex: "I know if you get the surface it don't mean nothing unless you got the other." This bond between Sterling and Risa is sealed when the former tells of his visit to Aunt Ester, who gives her opinion that Risa was sent to Sterling by God in lieu of an angel.

When the final scene opens, it is the day of Hambone's funeral and Memphis' final court appearance. Again, the concepts of injustice and just reward clash. Though Hambone's wake draws only a handful of visitors, Memphis enters the restaurant triumphant: He has followed Aunt Ester's advice and emerged a thirty-five-thousand-dollar winner in his fight with city hall. As Memphis promises to celebrate his victory, a bloodied Sterling emerges from Lutz's meat market with a ham for the coffin—the long-sought-after payment that eluded Hambone in life.

Themes and Meanings

The overriding theme of *Two Trains Running* is the bitter economic reality of urban life and the need to preserve African American culture amid such conditions. For Wilson, the primary means of maintaining and celebrating African American culture is the blues. Calling it "a philosophical system," Wilson claims that, with the blues, "You get the ideas and attitudes of the people as part of the oral tradition." Understanding the importance of the African American musical heritage is crucial to any analysis of Wilson's drama. Not only is the title taken from an old jazz tune, but the narrative structure itself is also derived from the blues. The pace of the play is slow and its tone melancholy; the drama is language-oriented, not action-driven. As part of the blues and the oral tradition, such characters as Memphis, Holloway, Wolf, and Sterling become storytellers—storytelling being both an act of memory and a means of communion in this otherwise fragmented urban landscape.

In keeping with Wilson's belief that the great migration of Southern blacks to the North was a mistake, the play explores a powerful economic theme: specifically, a series of broken or unfulfilled contracts, with African Americans on the losing end. Most important is the clause that the city government tries to use to deprive Memphis of a fair price and his claim that he has a clause of his own. The play's exposition, however, reveals an earlier contract dispute: Memphis lost his farm because the deed stated that the discovery of water on the land would nullify the sale. In addition, there is the contract dispute that left Hambone unpaid. Holloway succinctly articulates the problem: "If it wasn't for you the white man would be poor. . . . He give you three dollars a day for six months and he got him a railroad for the next hundred years. All you got is six months' worth of three dollars a day." These broken or unfulfilled contracts imply a flawed social contract. In other words, manumission did not end economic slavery for African Americans.

Two Trains Running is noteworthy for its episodic structure and for the ensemble quality of its characters. Wilson, though, exploits the symbolic nature of two figures both to unify the drama and to explore the African American experience. The first such figure, Hambone, is an African American everyman, one who dies without receiving his just reward. Though it is true that his dialogue is limited to only a few lines, he is arguably the most important person in the play. Hambone is more than just a cardboard character; as a dramatic device, he is the catalyst who generates the storytelling and the economic discussions in this memory play. For example, it is only after observing Hambone's daily ritual that Memphis tells of his life in Jackson and Holloway gives his discourse on economic slavery.

In addition, both Memphis and Sterling resemble Hambone in that they, too, are waiting for what is rightfully theirs. Like Hambone, Memphis claims that whites have not paid him his due. Though Memphis ironically rejects Hambone throughout the play, in the final scene Memphis imitates him, demonstrating the correspondence between the two. Sterling, moreover, shares with Hambone a passion for chants and recognizes the fact that Hambone's sense of purpose gives him an advantage. His daring theft of the ham at the end is an effective dramatic device that confirms his identification with Hambone.

Though Aunt Ester never appears onstage, her role as the unseen prophetess is central to Wilson's explorations of economic reality and of African American culture. As Holloway notes, Aunt Ester gives her clients something more valuable than money: tradition. She is the spiritual antidote to the economic enslavement of the community. She is allegedly 349 years old, and her life thus encompasses the entire African American experience, stretching back to its African roots. Appropriately, Memphis, Sterling, and Holloway all find satisfaction in following her advice. West's failure to do so accounts for his empty philosophy of money and death.

Critical Context

Two Trains Running is the fifth published drama in August Wilson's decade-by-decade chronicle of the African American experience in the twentieth century. Previous entries in the series include *Ma Rainey's Black Bottom* (pr. 1984), *Fences* (pr. 1985), *Joe Turner's Come and Gone* (pr. 1986), and *The Piano Lesson* (pr. 1988). Like the other plays in the cycle, *Two Trains Running* made its premiere at the Yale Repertory Theater and underwent revisions while being performed at regional theaters. Thus, the first edition of *Two Trains Running* that appeared in *Theater* magazine in 1991 differed slightly from the version that was published in 1993.

In a very real sense, all these plays are historical dramas. Wilson, however, examines characters who are marginalized by society, people who indirectly feel the effects of "great events" but do not participate in them. In chronological terms, the cycle traces the great migration and its aftermath from the turn of the century (*Joe Turner's Come and Gone*) to the time of the Civil Rights movement (*Two Trains Running*). Wilson seeks to highlight the African American experience and create what he characterizes as "a world in which the black American [is] the spiritual center."

Critical reception for Wilson's plays has been generally enthusiastic. Both *Fences* and *The Piano Lesson* won the Pulitzer Prize. Following the Broadway premiere of

Two Trains Running in April, 1992, *Time*'s William H. Henry III praised Wilson's ability to "embed subtle and complex political commentary within the conversational riffs of fully realized characters." Recognizing the play's ability to re-create a sense of time and place, Frank Rich of *The New York Times* praised Wilson's "penetrating revelation of a world hidden from view to those outside it." There have, however, been some dissenting voices on the drama scene. In *The Hudson Review*, Richard Hornby rejected the play's "slow and erratic" pacing. Moreover, *The New Yorker*'s Mimi Kramer condemned Wilson's creation of characters who "rant and speechify themselves out of existence."

Bibliography

Ching, Mei-ling. "Wrestling Against History." *Theater* 19, no. 3 (Summer/Fall, 1988): 70-71. Discusses how the characters Herald Loomis (*Joe Turner's Come and Gone*), Troy (*Fences*), and Boy Willie (*The Piano Lesson*) must struggle with history and the reality of being African American in a white society. Ching argues that Boy Willie's contest with a ghost is an exorcism that reconciles him with his sister.

Glover, Margaret E. "Two Notes on August Wilson: The Songs of a Marked Man." *Theater* 19, no. 3 (Summer/Fall, 1988): 69-70. Examines the role of music in *The Piano Lesson*, *Joe Turner's Come and Gone*, and *Ma Rainey's Black Bottom*. Notes that though the plays' songs represent a kind of personal freedom, the characters "must open themselves to be consumed by this music."

Harrison, Paul Carter. "August Wilson's Blues Poetics." In *Three Plays*, by August Wilson. Pittsburgh: University of Pittsburgh Press, 1991. Explores the role of the blues in *Ma Rainey's Black Bottom*, *Fences*, and *Joe Turner's Come and Gone*. Claims that Wilson invokes the blues through such devices as anecdotes, "polyrhythm and repetition, choric call 'n' response, double entendre and improvisation," and a "text that resists closure." Harrison's findings can be applied to all Wilson's dramas.

Reed, Ishmael. "In Search of August Wilson." *Connoisseur* 222 (March, 1987): 92-97. Provides important biographical material on the reclusive playwright. Places Wilson in the context of the African American literary and oral traditions.

Shannon, Sandra G. "The Good Christian's Come and Gone: The Shifting Role of Christianity in August Wilson's Plays." *Melus* 16, no. 3 (Fall, 1989-1990): 127-142. Contends that Wilson's male characters have abandoned Christianity in favor of the blues as a means of communication and healing. Shannon asserts that the African American men in Wilson's dramas have rejected the concept of God.

Wilde, Lisa. "Reclaiming the Past: Narrative and Memory in August Wilson's *Two Trains Running*." *Theater* 22, no. 1 (Winter, 1990-1991): 73-74. Holds that Wilson uses language to reconstruct the past; through storytelling and memory, the characters reclaim the past from the pain associated with it. Liberation comes by way of a supernatural agency; in *Two Trains Running*, the agent is Aunt Ester.

Cliff Prewencki

TWO WINGS TO VEIL MY FACE

Author: Leon Forrest (1937-   )
Type of work: Novel
Type of plot: Magical Realism
Time of plot: From before the Civil War to the mid-twentieth century
Locale: The Deep South
First published: 1983

Principal characters:

NATHANIEL (TURNER) WITHERSPOON, a young black man who
    transcribes family reminiscences
SWEETIE REED WITHERSPOON, the great storyteller of the novel
AUNT FOISTY, an ancient black conjure woman
I. V. REED, the father of Sweetie Reed, a slave
JERICHO W. WITHERSPOON, an escaped slave who went north to
    become a lawyer and a judge

The Novel

Two Wings to Veil My Face is a cleverly woven tapestry of a novel detailing the family chronicle of the Witherspoon family. Ranging in time from the slavery period into the twentieth century, the novel focuses on the history of one family but in so doing draws parallels with the saga of all African American people.

The novel takes the form of an oral reminiscence interlaced with dialogue, sermons, dreams, and incantations. Nathaniel writes down his grandmother's memories and forms a link between the great folk and oral traditions of the past and the modern period. Sweetie Reed's "backwater time" is a fantastic interwoven tale of slaves and masters, betrayals, rapes, and racial violence played out against the backdrop of African American survival in the United States. The novel depicts the family's origins in slavery, the illegal miscegenation of its forebears, and its survival against all odds.

The initial chapter sets the scene of Sweetie Reed's bedchamber as she is visited by her son Arthur and her grandson Nathaniel. Thereafter, the novel unravels a fresh interpretation of the past, filtered through Sweetie Reed's inexhaustible and detailed memory. Inspired by her special brew of sassafras tea and brandy, Sweetie Reed lies in bed and summons up mystical revelations in poetic prose. She allows the voices of her ancestors to speak through her, giving different viewpoints on key episodes from the past.

Through Aunt Foisty's voice, readers learn of Africa, the Middle Passage, early survival in the Colonies, and the wonders of hoodoo. From I. V. Reed's voice, readers learn of the plantation and the terrible truth of his parentage. Through Sweetie Reed's voice, readers complete a picture of hope and loss among the African American slave community. There is Sylvia Reed, who as the white mistress of the house forces Angelina to hide diamonds in her hair at the end of the Civil War. Angelina, Sweetie Reed's mother, is almost raped by three white Union soldiers who steal the diamonds and later is raped and murdered by patrollers. Sylvia Reed commits suicide by biting the gold key to the household, a key that contains poison.

I. V. Reed stays on the plantation, serving Rollins Reed after the slaves are freed. Although Sweetie Reed hates her father, I. V., many of her verbal skills are inherited from his great gifts of mimicry and masking. I. V. Reed learns all that Aunt Foisty knows, adds his own knowledge, and passes this down to Sweetie Reed. Sweetie Reed is almost killed by patrollers, but Jericho Witherspoon saves her.

Sweetie Reed leaves the plantation in 1882 to flee to the North with Jericho. They have an unhappy and childless marriage, but Jericho gives Sweetie his illegal son Arthur to rear as her own. As Sweetie Reed's memories move into the present time, she continues to repeat the motifs and refrains that resonate throughout the novel; among these are mirrors, magic, hoodoo, dreams, and biblical imagery.

Although primarily about one African American family whose blood has been mixed with white slaveowners, the novel takes on universal significance in its use of archetypal images and situations. In many ways, Sweetie Reed's spirit, wisdom, and voice reflect the long line of black women who have passed before her. Her story redeems their suffering and neglected past as it transcends the misery of the world with incantatory prose and miraculous power.

The Characters

Nathaniel Witherspoon, a college dropout, twenty-one years old at the time of the novel, writes down his grandmother's memories. His recrafting of his family history forms the structure of the novel as he interlaces sermons, tales, and memories. From this experience he shapes a worldview that gives meaning to his existence.

Sweetie Reed Witherspoon relives in detail her family history, giving a picture of pre- and post-Civil War life in the Deep South. Her tales of the horrors of slavery and the triumph of the black spirit bring alive the distant past. Sweetie Reed's mother, Angelina, and father, I. V. Reed, were married as slaves in 1855. Sweetie Reed marries Jericho W. Witherspoon in 1882, when she is fifteen years old and Jericho is fifty-five. Barren, she has one adopted son named Arthur. After Jericho Witherspoon and Sweetie Reed get a divorce, she becomes a preacher. Sweetie Reed is an oral historian who uses all the rhetorical tricks at her disposal to give a complete picture of the past.

Aunty Foisty, the ancient conjure woman, forms the second primary link to the past. Aunt Foisty's history stretches back to Africa. She is rumored to have clawed her way out of the bottom of a slave ship. With her African retentions in language and folk religion, she is the primary image of the African mother figure who gave birth to a great race. Aunty Foisty possesses powerful magic. She controls the Praise Shack, to which the slaves come to worship. She is an oral historian who passes her remembered wisdom to I. V. Reed.

Mistress Sylvia Reed and Rollins Reed are cruel white plantation owners. Rollins

Reed is guilty of raping his female slaves, and I. V. Reed is one of his sons. Sylvia Reed dominates and punishes the household slaves. Both of the Reeds are evil and capricious.

I. V. Reed forms the third important link to the past. After emancipation, he stays to serve on the Reed plantation. Because of his fidelity to the slave past, he is disliked by his family. His stormy dialogue with his daughter Sweetie on his deathbed forms one of the great passages of the novel. I. V. Reed is a complicated blend of guile and cleverness. A great actor and mimic, he keeps the early tradition of African American music alive. He is also a trickster figure.

Jericho W. Witherspoon is the one character in the novel who spans the period from slavery well into the twentieth century. He flees slavery to live in the North and becomes a lawyer and a judge. He is tough, argumentative, and intolerant of injustice. Self-educated and indomitable in will and spirit, he brings to Sweetie Reed a child of his born out of wedlock. Jericho Witherspoon's funeral is one of the focal points of the novel, inspiring an extended verbal reminiscence from Sweetie Reed, who comes to the funeral on her own.

Merlin Spottswood, the black Master's Magician, brings an antic spirit and a trickster flair to the plantation house. Merlin Spottswood combines magic with black dignity as he entertains the Reed household. As an inspiration to I. V. Reed, he brings out the trickster side of Reed's personality as well as reflecting important aspects of magic seen elsewhere in the novel.

Themes and Meanings

The novel is composed with a frame story about Nathaniel's attempts to write his grandmother's memories of her past. Within this frame there is a circle of interconnected recollections revolving around three main testaments, those of Aunt Foisty, I. V. Reed, and Sweetie Reed. The novel uses a variety of techniques in its chronicle of the past. Poetic monologues, dialogues, dreams, and passages of surrealistic prose knit a complex overview of the origins of African American culture.

Sweetie Reed's fabulous narration of her family's history establishes through a blend of legend, memory, and dream the intense saga of her ancestors. Certain key refrains and incidents form the nucleus of the novel. One recurring refrain is the fragment of a spiritual containing the lines "Angel got two wings to veil my face/ Angel got two wings to fly me away." Other motifs include the use of masquerade, mirrors, and magic.

The first important incident is the funeral of Jericho Witherspoon, which inspires Sweetie Reed to deliver a commanding eulogy over her dead husband's coffin. This in turn launches a more comprehensive recitation of her ancestors' past. By returning to Aunt Foisty's life on the Reed plantation, Sweetie Reed reaches far back into the origins of slavery. Aunt Foisty is the repository of ancient wisdom and the vernacular tradition. Her perfect memory records the passage of all the slaves of the plantation. She keeps the complete genealogy of the Witherspoon family intact.

Sweetie Reed's father, I. V. Reed, adds a different perspective as witness to another key episode in the progress of the Witherspoon saga. He uses a slingshot to hit Rollins Reed in the head with a rock. Rollins Reed is magically revived from death by Aunt Foisty and undergoes a spiritual rebirth. The horrors of slavery, its destruction of families and the rape of its women by white slaveowners, are dramatically presented through the person of I. V. Reed, himself a bastard child of Rollins Reed.

Sweetie Reed's memories of the freeing of the slaves, the rape and murder of her mother, and the suicide of Sylvia Reed provide knowledge of key incidents. Her recollections of her life with Jericho move the history into contemporary times. As Nathaniel records the words of his grandmother, he is transformed into a complete black man. It is Nathaniel who forces the last important revelation from the lips of Sweetie, concerning the date of his father's birth and his actual parentage.

Two Wings to Veil My Face is a tour de force of language and imagery that depicts a tumultuous tale of loss, betrayal, and redemption. The novel uses the basic conceit of oral testimony to present a complete family saga that educates in important ways. The horrors of slavery are revealed in subtle and psychologically convincing ways while portraying the indomitable spirit of African American survival.

Critical Context

Two Wings to Veil My Face is the last novel of three that Forrest devotes to the Witherspoon family saga. *There Is a Tree More Ancient Than Eden* (1973) and *The Bloodworth Orphans* (1977) complete the trilogy. These books contain many of the same characters and cover some of the same territory, particularly in the use of black vernacular and folk traditions such as music, language, and religion. *Two Wings to Veil My Face* is a supreme triumph of signifying experimentation, developing techniques initiated in the other two books.

The realistic social document of the text is amplified by use of poetic prose, imaginative episodes, and surrealistic description. The unusual verbal dexterity of Sweetie Reed is reflected in other characters' voices. She is an outstanding example of the traditional strong black woman in African American history and literature.

Through the intimate and detailed exploration of one African American family, Forrest has created a deeper understanding of the collective consciousness of the black race. In *Two Wings to Veil My Face,* he has created a text that in itself demonstrates the strength of black cultural creations. The technique of the novel mimics other black cultural expressions such as jazz solos and extemporaneous language testifying. Forrest also shows the influence of the modernist tradition, echoing James Joyce and William Faulkner. Surreal episodes suggest Ralph Ellison, while the exhaustive examination of character and motive have an almost Proustian elegance.

The fabulous quality of many of the passages bears a relation to the Magical Realism of Gabriel García Márquez. By logically extending real characters and situations through poetic prose, Forrest creates a fantastic landscape of dreamlike intensity. At the same time, he builds a magical universe of masquerade, madness, and collective transformation.

Like the two other novels in the series, *Two Wings to Veil My Face* uses the traditional folk methods of legend, tales, religion, and music. The Witherspoon family tree extends and makes relevant the past. It moves beyond historical fiction by bridging two worlds through the union of Sweetie Reed and her grandson Nathaniel. By skillfully combining the fragments of the narrative, Nathan re-creates his past and remakes himself.

Bibliography
Bell, Bernard W. *The Afro-American Novel and Its Tradition.* Amherst: University of Massachusetts Press, 1987. Discusses Forrest in the section on fabulation, romance, and fantasy. Considers Forrest as part of a tradition of black fabulators who use dream visions and other linguistic forms to present personal and spiritual journeys.
Byerman, Keith E. "Orphans and Circuses: The Literary Experiments of Leon Forrest and Clarence Major." In *Fingering the Jagged Grain: Tradition and Form in Recent Black Fiction.* Athens: University of Georgia Press, 1985. Praises Forrest's use of stream-of-consciousness techniques and suggests that within the stylized and surreal episodes lies a cultural wealth of material carried by black Americans.
Jones, Gayl. *Liberating Voices: Oral Tradition in African-American Literature.* Cambridge, Mass.: Harvard University Press, 1991. Jones stresses the blues, jazz, spiritual, and sermonic rhythms of Forrest's texts.
Lee, A. Robert. "Making New: Styles of Innovation in the Contemporary Black American Novel." In *Black Fiction: New Studies in the Afro-American Novel Since 1945.* New York: Barnes & Noble Books, 1980. Comments on Forrest's strengths in making symbolic connections between generations while expressing mythic racial truths of American history.
Mootry, Maria K. "If He Changed My Name: An Interview with Leon Forrest." *The Massachusetts Review* 18 (Winter, 1977): 631-642. The author comments on his own goals, interpretations of his novels, and his writing style.

Stephen F. Soitos

UP FROM SLAVERY
An Autobiography

Author: Booker T. Washington (1856-1915)
Type of work: Autobiography
Time of work: 1856-1915
Locale: Virginia, West Virginia, and Alabama
First published: 1901

Principal personages:

BOOKER T. WASHINGTON, the author, an African American born in slavery, founder of Tuskegee Institute

FANNIE N. SMITH WASHINGTON, his first wife, who died in 1884 after two years of marriage

OLIVIA DAVIDSON WASHINGTON, his second wife, from 1885 until her death in 1889

MARGARET MURRAY WASHINGTON, his third and last wife

W. E. B. DU BOIS, the leader of the Niagara movement, a principal critic of the Tuskegee Institute's gradualist approach

SAMUEL CHAPMAN ARMSTRONG, a Civil War army officer who founded Hampton Institute

Form and Content

A statue on the campus of Tuskegee Institute illustrates the historical impact of Booker T. Washington, the school's founder. The memorial shows the famous African American educator removing a covering from the head of a black male student. Below are inscribed these words: "He lifted the veil of ignorance from his people and pointed the way to progress through education and industry."

Sometimes called the "great accommodator," Washington made his mark on history by establishing Tuskegee Institute as the foremost black vocational institution in the United States. His method was to teach young black people to improve themselves through hard work and learning a trade of marketable value: "I think that the whole future of my race hinges on the question as to whether or not it can make itself of such indispensable value that the people in the town and the state where we reside will feel that our presence is necessary to the happiness and well-being of the community."

Washington's educational philosophy was the product of his own difficult road upward from a childhood lived in slavery. His "Atlanta Compromise" address on September 18, 1895, to the Cotton States Exposition, delivered just seven months after the death of Frederick Douglass, established him as the leading public spokesman for African American interests. There was little in his early life to suggest that he would become such a powerful influence that poet Langston Hughes would say, "Booker T. Washington was the Roy Wilkins, James Farmer and Martin Luther King of his day rolled into one."

Up from Slavery is Washington's account of his life and the Tuskegee movement. In seventeen chapters, Washington traces his life, from the modest cabin in Virginia where he was born to a black cook and a white father, to sumptuous Parisian hotels and stately homes of English noblemen he visited four decades later.

Carefully worded to reflect his gradualist approach, Washington's autobiography is both highly readable and absorbing. Like his life in general, his book elicited little controversy and tended to confirm his position as Frederick Douglass' successor. It is a self-effacing story that consciously avoids an image of egocentrism and is thus consistent with his effort to inspire his race to advance by self-help. Any affirmation and praise is presented in the form of letters and speeches about him by others. This is not to say that *Up from Slavery* is disingenuous. On the contrary, Washington seems quite sincere in his self-denying account. His purpose in writing the book, it seems, was to reinforce his educational work by seeking larger public support for the concept of racial cooperation and mutual respect.

By his own admission, Washington did not know the exact date of his birth. "I was born a slave on a plantation in Franklin County, Virginia," he notes in his opening chapter. "As nearly as I have been able to learn, I was born near a cross-roads post-office called Hale's Ford, and the year was 1858 or 1859." Scholars later estimated that his birth year was 1856. His earliest memories included living in slave quarters. Known simply as "Booker" (although, as he discovered later, his mother had named him Booker Taliaferro), the embarrassed young boy added Washington when he started school and noticed that the other children had family names.

His early interest in education shaped Washington's childhood and permanently influenced his life. Opportunities for young black people were severely limited and often dependent on their willingness to take advantage of whatever doors were opened. In his case, several white people who were impressed by his good manners and ambition helped him with his education and encouraged him to make something special of his life. Just after the Civil War, his mother and his stepfather, Washington Ferguson, moved to Malden, West Virginia, where he worked in a coal mine and as a houseboy in the home of General Lewis Ruffner. The Ruffners took an interest in Booker and were impressed by his willingness to "stay in his place" as he pursued his learning. Viola Ruffner, in particular, aided his quest for learning. Fearing her at first, he came to view her as a friend. Viola Ruffner helped him collect his first personal library and to attend Hampton Institute in Virginia.

Up from Slavery gives much attention to Washington's studies and teaching at Hampton Institute. Founded and directed by General Samuel Chapman Armstrong, Hampton provided basic education to Native and African Americans, always emphasizing personal discipline, character development, and useful skills. Armstrong's influence continued through Washington's life, shaping the curriculum and educational philosophy of Tuskegee Institute. Washington entered Hampton in 1871. After his graduation in 1875, he spent one year at Wayland Seminary in Washington, D.C., before returning to Hampton as a member of the faculty from 1876 to 1881.

With the help of Armstrong, Washington went to Tuskegee, Alabama, in June,

1881, to establish and direct a planned normal school for Macon County. With only a small legislative appropriation for teachers' salaries and no money for land or buildings, Washington began to raise additional money for the project that would become the center of his career. The result was the Tuskegee Normal and Industrial Institute, which secured its campus on an abandoned plantation just three months after its opening. Washington and his supporters raised the $500 necessary to buy the estate and began equipping it with the necessary facilities. Washington proved to be a remarkable fund-raiser. His nonconfrontational approach endeared him to many white contributors. Soon Tuskegee was widely known around the country and was supported by a host of philanthropists and businessmen who liked its approach to racial advancement.

Throughout the remainder of his book, Washington demonstrates his commitment to self-help as the best hope for African Americans. As his reputation grew, so did his base of support. He knew how to charm an audience and includes a chapter on "Success in Public Speaking." Washington enjoyed captivating an audience and knew what to say at any given moment. With the help of a dedicated faculty, which eventually included the famous agricultural scientist George Washington Carver, and three wives, Washington made Tuskegee the leading vocational and normal school for African Americans in the United States.

There were detractors, but Washington gives little attention to them in his autobiography. He does briefly mention W. E. B. Du Bois, a well-educated African American from Massachusetts. Du Bois had a radically different view from Washington's, preferring "freedom now" and political rights over the more accommodationist Tuskegee goals. Each had a network of informers to keep watch over the other as their rivalry deepened.

Washington became a national figure in September, 1895, when he was a featured speaker at the Cotton States Exposition in Atlanta, Georgia. There he reviewed his race's long commitment to America and its loyalty to the South. He tried to calm fears of black uprisings and even political aspirations. He asked that white people give African Americans the chance to advance on their own. "Cast down your bucket where you are," he urged fellow blacks, meaning that they should stay in the South rather than migrate to the North.

After this "Atlanta Compromise" address, Washington was even more widely known and respected by white leaders. He refers to many honors bestowed upon him, none more cherished than an honorary master's degree from Harvard University in 1896.

> [I]t was hard for me to realize that I was to be honoured by a degree from the oldest and most renowned university in America. As I sat upon my veranda, with this letter in my hand, tears came into my eyes. My whole former life—my life as a slave on the plantation, my work in the coal-mine, the times when I was without food and clothing, when I made my bed under a sidewalk, my struggles for an education, the trying days I had had at Tuskegee, days when I did not know where to turn for a dollar to continue the work there, the ostracism and sometimes oppression of my race—all this passed before me and nearly overcame me.

Occasionally in his book, Washington shares highly personal feelings that humanize him. One particularly interesting example is his account of a trip to Europe given by supporters in 1899. At first reluctant to go, he thoroughly enjoyed sleeping late on the ship and meeting famous Americans and Europeans in Paris, London, and other places. The trip was one of the highlights of his life. Another memorable personal experience was a visit by his old benefactor General Armstrong, who came to Tuskegee in 1893 just before his death. Unable either to speak or to walk, the former Civil War officer visited for two months in Washington's home, enjoying the company of his prize student and reaffirming his support for the self-help approach to education. Washington wrote, "I resolved anew to devote myself more earnestly than ever to the cause that was so near to his heart."

Analysis

At one level, *Up from Slavery* is an interesting autobiography by a prominent African American educator, perhaps the most influential ever. Washington certainly believed in, and unceasingly supported with time and resources, the Tuskegee philosophy that bore the imprint of Hampton Institute. The book is also an apologetic for that educational and race relations theory. Throughout its coverage, the reader is constantly reminded of both the difficulties confronted in building and maintaining Tuskegee and the supportive response by the American public, especially the political and economic leadership. Washington sought in the book to solidify and expand that support, always giving a positive note even in the most problematical times.

Washington's account is also a valuable history of Tuskegee Institute from 1881 to 1915. Threading through the personal vignettes and commentaries, a fairly coherent historical summary of the institute's development can be discerned. From modest beginnings, it grew into a major university by the mid-twentieth century.

In Washington's time, it was largely a teacher training institution and a vocational school devoted to training African Americans in the requisite skills in an economic sphere that Washington assumed, not entirely accurately, would be the best source of jobs for many decades. As it turned out, the vocational training Tuskegee emphasized would not be sufficient to meet the job needs of future generations of black Americans. In that sense, W. E. B. Du Bois' criticism was valid. Du Bois argued for cultivating what he called the Talented Tenth, those African Americans who could attain the highest levels of professional education. Tuskegee was so good at what it did that it grew from a one-building school with about thirty students to a major complex with six schools that included one of the best agricultural and veterinarian programs in the world. Eventually more than three-fourths of African American veterinarians would be graduates of Tuskegee. In his memoir, Washington stresses the early formative days, when his school gradually attracted the attention of wealthy supporters and countless people of modest means who sent their children there to study. In 1898, President William McKinley visited the Tuskegee campus, fulfilling one of Washington's dreams that one day an American president would walk on the grounds of the institute.

    Up from Slavery has a distinctive place in the history of African American litera-
ture. In its own time, it was a best-seller that aided the Tuskegee cause, and it continues as an item of interest to scholars and the general public. What it lacks in
critical analysis it compensates for with its optimism and theme of racial cooperation. Washington has been underestimated as an activist in racial advancement. His
views are easily labeled accommodationist, but he was hardly accepting of the status
quo. In his own way, he was attempting a revolution that would give black people a
sense of pride while equipping them for practical success through developing skills
and social graces.

    Washington's study also includes several documents or parts of documents—among
them the full text of the Atlanta address and numerous personal items, most of them
letters and citations—that are helpful in reconstructing Washington's and the Tuskegee Institute's history. Few books have been written with a clearer goal, in this case
to promote the image of the school that was the quintessence of his career.

Critical Context

    It has been noted that *Up from Slavery* elicited little controversy; indeed, the book
was carefully shaped to avoid it. Written at the height of Washington's career, although a time when some were questioning the wisdom of both his gradualist approach and his vocational emphasis in education, his book mirrored the author's
perennial commitment to the growth and influence of the famous Alabama institute.

    There are no formal references to other books or articles. Thus it is not, in the
usual sense, a scholarly account. Neither is it superficial or trivial. Washington wrote
it during one of the most critical periods of American social history. In the wake of
Reconstruction came disfranchisement, lynchings, systematic segregation, and widespread poverty in the African American population. Washington's philosophy was
only one of several alternative paths to liberation proffered by various black leaders.
His voice was different from the powerful one of Frederick Douglass, whose death
in 1895 thrust Washington into the limelight, and his differences with the more activist W. E. B. Du Bois were deep and intense. *Up from Slavery* is a product of the
critical period between Reconstruction reformism and the interwar period of racial
tension.

    In the broader spectrum of African American social thought of that period, Wash-
ington occupied a more conservative position than either his predecessor Douglass
or his long-lived contemporary Du Bois. Du Bois gave his energy first to the Niagara
movement, a small group founded in 1905 to promote immediate political and social
gains for black people and other minorities, then to the more durable National Association for the Advancement of Colored People (NAACP). In the Niagara movement
and the NAACP, the emphasis was on politics, public education, and the courts. At
Tuskegee, it was more a matter of getting better equipped to speak, work, act, and
think in a disciplined way. Regardless of one's estimation of the relative merits of
these roads to liberation, Washington's book stands as an important landmark in
both American social evolution and African American literary history.

Bibliography

Cain, William E. "Forms of Self-Representation in Booker T. Washington's *Up from Slavery.*" *Prospects* 12 (1987): 201-222. Cain deals effectively with an often-neglected aspect of *Up from Slavery*, its literary style. Washington deliberately and carefully crafted the wording of his book in a conscious attempt to avoid seeming ego-centric. According to Cain, Washington consciously used a literary counterpart to the typical self-effacement acts used by black people of that period to avoid clashes with white people.

Daniel, Pete. "Up from Slavery and Down to Peonage: The Alonzo Bailey Case." *Journal of American History* 57 (December, 1970): 654-670. An interesting adden-dum to typical coverage of Washington. Daniel discusses in detail the case of Alonzo Bailey, an Alabama laborer who had received a monetary advance for a job he did not complete. The state law imposed punishment on offenders as if they had stolen money from the prospective employer and was used to control African Americans as though they were slaves. Washington supported the eventually suc-cessful effort to get the U.S. Supreme Court to overturn the Alabama law.

Fitzgerald, Charlotte D. "The Story of My Life and Work: Booker T. Washington's Other Autobiography." *The Black Scholar* 21 (Fall, 1991): 35-40. Unknown to many people is an earlier version of Washington's *Up from Slavery*, published a year earlier. Fitzgerald reveals that it was poorly written by an incompetent ghostwri-ter. It is significant that he said more in the original version about self-help and less about those things that made him appear accommodationist. It is suggested that he was trying in his second edition to avoid offending former slaveholders.

Horton, James O., and Lois E. Horton. "Race and Class (Contemporary America)." *American Quarterly* 35 (Spring/Summer, 1983): 155-168. A succinct connected narrative on the work of W. E. B. Du Bois, Martin Luther King, Jr., Booker T. Washington, and William J. Wilson in challenging the rigid racial and class bar-riers in the United States. Each functioned within a distinctive historical setting but was part of a continuum.

Howard-Pitney, David. "The Jeremiads of Frederick Douglass, Booker T. Washing-ton, and W. E. B. Du Bois and Changing Patterns of Black Messianic Rhetoric, 1841-1920." *Journal of American Ethnic History* 6 (Fall, 1986): 47-61. A valuable discussion of the messianic-prophetic dimension of black leadership in the late nineteenth and early twentieth centuries. Although more accommodationist than Douglass or Du Bois, Washington appears as a genuinely prophetic voice in the black quest for liberation.

James, Jacqueline. "Uncle Tom? Not Booker T." *American Heritage* 19 (1968): 50-63, 95-100. A fresh approach to a traditional theme. James shows that "Uncle Tom" is an inappropriate rubric to define Washington, since he was always fighting in his own way for racial equality. Washington realized, she stresses, that an overt challenge to the system would only result in worsening conditions.

Thomas R. Peake

A VISITATION OF SPIRITS

Author: Randall Kenan (1963-   )
Type of work: Novel
Type of plot: Psychological realism
Time of plot: April 29-30, 1984, and December 8, 1985
Locale: North Carolina
First published: 1989

> *Principal characters:*
> HORACE THOMAS CROSS, a sixteen-year-old undergoing a severe psychotic episode
> REVEREND JAMES ("JIMMY") MALACHAI GREENE, a minister of the Southern Baptist Church
> ANNE GAZELLE DUBOIS GREENE, Jimmy Greene's deceased wife
> EZEKIEL CROSS, Horace's grandfather
> GIDEON STONE, a highly intelligent and artistic adolescent

The Novel

A Visitation of Spirits is essentially a novel about homosexuality. Young Horace Cross finds himself irresistibly attracted to men and has been having one affair after another. He finds that his attraction to males does not recognize racial barriers; he has love affairs with virile white actors who are playing in summer stock in his rural area, and he prefers to associate with a group of rowdy young white males who are considered renegades and dropouts at his high school. Horace is exceptionally bright and has been getting top grades up until the time of this adolescent crisis. Now his grades have plummeted, and all of his relatives, including his doting grandfather, are pressuring him to change back into the polite, ambitious, well-behaved boy he had been.

Horace goes to his cousin, the Reverend Jimmy Greene, with his problem, asking him in confidence what he can do, if anything, to renounce his homosexual tendencies. Jimmy has been through the same crisis himself and is ashamed to discuss it openly. He simply tells Horace he will outgrow it. It becomes evident, however, that Jimmy himself has never outgrown his own homosexual proclivities and that denying them has turned him into a sort of spiritual and sexual eunuch. His failure to help Horace causes him to begin to reevaluate his entire life.

Jimmy serves as a foil to Horace, more or less the way Leopold Bloom served as a foil to Stephen Dedalus in James Joyce's classic novel *Ulysses* (1922). While Horace is wandering around town nearly naked, struggling with his repressed sexual desires, Jimmy is going through the motions of being a small-town preacher and interacting mainly with the older African Americans of the community. Through Jimmy's eyes, the reader gets a thorough picture of the small-mindedness, the provinciality, and the xenophobia of the older generation, with its lip service to moral rectitude and its actual selfishness, spitefulness, and ignorance of everything outside its isolated, small-town world.

Throughout the novel, Horace is wandering around the North Carolina town of Tims Creek carrying his grandfather's rifle. He is experiencing severe hallucinations, thinking that he is being manipulated by demons he has read about in the esoteric literature he favors. He visits various places in town and experiences vivid memories of significant events that occurred in each of them. It is sometimes difficult for the reader to distinguish between what is really happening and what is happening only in Horace's mind. He recalls his various homosexual encounters and feels that he was a helpless victim of the demons who have been manipulating his mind since puberty. He is uncertain whether he wants to use the rifle to kill the demons, to kill himself, or to kill some living acquaintance.

The novel moves backward and forward in time, and many of the subsections are headed with specific dates to give the reader some much-needed grounding. The author relies heavily on interior monologues to delineate character and advance the story, although the monologues are not italicized or written in such a way as to make the reader feel trapped in any character's mind. There is more flexibility to Kenan's style of storytelling than to those used, for example, in Joyce's *A Portrait of the Artist as a Young Man* (1916) or William Faulkner's *The Sound and the Fury* (1929), works that Kenan's book resembles.

Many readers will find *A Visitation of Spirits*, Kenan's first novel, to be strongly reminiscent of *The Sound and the Fury.* Horace Cross resembles young Quentin Compson, the intelligent, neurotic Southern youth who commits suicide after a long day of aimless wandering and reminiscing. Horace eventually confronts Jimmy with the rifle and, now obviously totally out of his mind, threatens to kill the minister. In the end, he turns the rifle on himself.

The confrontation between Horace, the lost young rebel, and Jimmy, the minister who represents all the traditional, conventional values of African Americans in the South, is symbolic. The message of the book is that society is wrong in trying to force people to conform to rigid standards of sexual behavior or any other conventional moral dogma. The author does an excellent job of showing how African Americans are changing in rural America, particularly how the younger generation, to the consternation of its elders, is seeking out radical new directions. Sensitive, intelligent young African Americans, many of whom are receiving educations denied to their elders for centuries, are groping for new values and new beliefs in a rapidly integrating, rapidly homogenizing world.

The Characters

Kenan contrasts the older and newer generations of African Americans in order to highlight their differences. His younger characters are being drawn into mainstream America through their better educational and vocational opportunities, their exposure to the mass media, their access to better transportation, and, to some extent, their integration with their white neighbors. The older people simply cannot understand what is happening. They complain about the behavior of the younger people and give them advice that often falls on deaf ears. In *A Visitation of Spirits*, the older characters such as Ezekiel Cross serve as a sort of Greek chorus commenting on the real action of the story, which inevitably involves the young people; they are the only ones whose activities are of real significance.

The younger characters, particularly Horace Cross and Jimmy Greene, are portrayed from the inside, whereas the older characters are portrayed from the outside, from their behavior and their conversation. Kenan describes Horace's and Jimmy's thoughts and feelings in such detail that the novel in many places comes close to stream-of-consciousness writing.

Throughout the novel, Horace is cut off from everyone else by his psychosis. He is by far the most important character in the novel, which is essentially the story of his mental breakdown. His characterization, therefore, presents the greatest creative challenge to the author, and it is here that the author displays the full range of his talent. Not only does the reader experience Horace's present hallucinations of demons and monsters, but the reader, through Horace's memories, also experiences important episodes in the unfortunate young man's past. Horace becomes so caught up in his hallucinations that he actually loses all awareness of his real identity; he becomes completely possessed by some nameless, malevolent spirit.

Kenan's younger characters are remarkably taciturn in comparison to his loquacious older characters. The author uses his gift for dialogue to characterize the members of the older generation and manages to convey the unique flavor of their North Carolina dialect without resorting to bizarre orthographical constructions. It is through the conversations and monologues of the older characters that the reader is made to appreciate the rich history and traditions of the Old South.

Kenan obviously favors the young in the conflict between young and old, but he does not set his older characters up as straw figures to be knocked down. The reader is made to feel the same respect for the older generation that is felt by Horace and Jimmy themselves, even while it is made clear that the older generation is becoming a quaint curiosity in the New South.

Themes and Meanings

Like William Faulkner and many other Southern writers, Randall Kenan seems to be obsessed with history. His characters struggle in a web of history and usually fail to extricate themselves. *A Visitation of Spirits* is a story about homosexual conflicts, but it is also a story about the conflict between the young and the old, between the new generation of African Americans and their ancestors reaching all the way back to the earliest days of slavery. Kenan seems to be suggesting that, sooner or later, a radical change is going to have to take place in the New South. That change will ultimately entail complete racial integration and the forgetting of old grievances. While his young characters struggle to arrive at a new understanding of the present, his old characters cling desperately to the past because of their fear of change.

The deliberate ongoing contrast between the old generation and the new generation is obviously designed to make the reader feel the inexorability and the necessity of change. The characters who represent the old order cause unnecessary pain and confusion by their insistence on clinging to old habits and prejudices. The characters who represent the new order are caught between past and present; they are unable to accept their parents' and grandparents' values but, at the same time, are unable to conceptualize the new consciousness that is needed by their society.

Kenan's principal concern is with the ways in which the South is changing. He demonstrates these changes by illustrating their effects on the lives of his characters. Neither his young nor his old characters can see that their problems are not personal but universal; Kenan, however, manages to present that broader perspective to the reader. His intelligence, sensitivity, and compassion distinguish him as one of the most important writers to emerge from the New South.

Critical Context

A Visitation of Spirits received exceptionally favorable reviews for a first novel by a previously unknown young author. Kenan has been compared to James Baldwin, who introduced the subject of homosexuality among African Americans in his novel *Giovanni's Room* (1956) and later elaborated on the subject in his autobiographical novel *Just Above My Head* (1979). Whereas Baldwin was a New Yorker and a cosmopolitan, however, Kenan writes about the rural South. Critics have been especially appreciative of the younger author's precocious insight into human character and his ability to demonstrate how the New South is being shaken by such powerful forces as civil rights activism, the so-called electronic revolution, and the educational and professional opportunities opening up to African Americans.

The only serious complaint made by critics has had to do with the format of Kenan's novel. Some have felt it is unnecessarily obscure because it moves backward and forward in time and shifts points of view unexpectedly. Kenan, however, has chosen to cover a very broad subject in a relatively short work of fiction. While focusing on a single incident in the life of his young protagonist, Kenan is trying to suggest the influence of all the history of the Deep South on a new generation of African Americans. His book of short stories *Let the Dead Bury Their Dead and Other Stories* (1992) shows that he is widely read and deeply immersed in the history of his native state of North Carolina. His published writings suggest that he is ambitious to produce the same type of panoramic mural of his native state as William Faulkner did in his many novels and stories about Mississippi.

Kenan is an important writer because he is able to show how younger African Americans in the New South are becoming radically different from their forebears. At the same time, Kenan and his characters do not lose sight of what they owe to the millions of anonymous men and women who toiled and suffered and fought to give them the opportunities they are now beginning to enjoy.

Bibliography

Gingher, Robert, ed. *The Rough Road Home: Stories by North Carolina Writers.*

Chapel Hill: University of North Carolina Press, 1992. A large collection of stories by contemporary North Carolina writers that shows the impact of this relatively small state in the revival of the American short story. Contains Kenan's
"The Virtue Called Vanity," which was not included in *Let the Dead Bury Their
Dead.*

Kenan, Randall. *Let the Dead Bury Their Dead and Other Stories.* San Diego: Harcourt Brace Jovanovich, 1992. A collection of twelve short stories by Kenan all
dealing with life in rural North Carolina. These stories are all set in the fictional
village of Tims Creek, the same setting that was used in *A Visitation of Spirits,*
and deal with some of the same characters. The stories suggest that Kenan is
trying to create an imaginary world not unlike William Faulkner's Yoknapatawpha
County.

Kirkus Reviews. Review of *A Visitation of Spirits,* by Randall Kenan. 57 (May 1,
1989): 650. Calls attention to Kenan's stylistic daring, which is judged extraordinary for a young writer in his first novel. Highlights the dramatic changes in the
New South as a result of the cultural implosion taking place in contemporary
America.

Mosher, Howard Frank. "The Ghosts on Main Street." *The New York Times Book
Review,* June 14, 1992, 12. An enthusiastic review of Kenan's *Let the Dead Bury
Their Dead.* Mosher points out that "inexorable sexual entanglements and the
preternatural" are two of Kenan's favorite subjects.

Virginia Quarterly Review. Review of *A Visitation of Spirits,* by Randall Kenan. 66
(Winter, 1990): 22. An entirely favorable review. Points out the paradoxical truth
that the only bigotry in Kenan's depiction of the New South seems to be demonstrated by older blacks, who cling to their old grievances because they provide a
sense of security.

Bill Delaney

VOICES IN THE MIRROR
An Autobiography

Author: Gordon Parks (1912-   )
Type of work: Autobiography
Time of work: 1912-1979
Locale: The United States
First published: 1990

> *Principal personages:*
> GORDON PARKS, a prominent African American artist who has
> distinguished himself as a photographer, composer, novelist,
> journalist, poet, and filmmaker
> SARAH PARKS, his mother, who died when he was still a child but
> remained an inspiration to him
> JACKSON PARKS, his stern but devoted father, who taught him the
> values of industry and responsibility
> SALLY PARKS, his first wife
> ELIZABETH PARKS, his second wife
> GENEVIEVE PARKS, his third wife

Form and Content

Voices in the Mirror is a full-length autobiography of an African American who achieved spectacular success in a number of fields that had previously been open almost exclusively to whites. Gordon Parks distinguished himself as a photographer, a painter, a journalist, a poet, a novelist, an author of nonfiction books, a musician, a composer, and a motion-picture director. He received more than fifty honorary doctorates and awards, including the National Medal of Art, which was presented to him by President Ronald Reagan in 1988.

Parks's autobiography reads like an exciting novel because he had such an eventful life, rising from the depths of poverty to the heights of fame and fortune. Because Parks is a photographer and a painter, he cannot help writing in a visual, metaphorical style, with many vivid descriptions of people, places, and things. His book consists largely of a string of anecdotes intended to highlight different periods of his life.

The twenty-six chapters carry the reader in steady chronological order from Parks's earliest childhood up until the death of his son Gordon Parks, Jr., in 1979. In an epilogue written when he was in his late seventies, Parks states that he still has a passion for living and still retains big dreams about future accomplishments.

The book that *Voices in the Mirror* most closely resembles is *The Autobiography of Malcolm X* (1965). Parks, like his eloquent and charismatic friend Malcolm X, grew up in poverty and lived in slums as a youth. He could easily have become a dangerous criminal, like the young Malcolm X, were it not for the fact that Parks possessed unusual artistic talent. After flirting with a criminal career, which he describes in interesting anecdotes, he became interested in photography.

The camera proved to be his salvation. It not only became a means to earn a good living and to achieve social status but also served as a "weapon" against the forces of racial bigotry and economic discrimination. Parks paints vivid word-pictures of conditions in the black ghettos during the 1930's and 1940's, when African Americans were restricted to the most menial occupations and could not even aspire to be taxi drivers or elevator operators, much less policemen, firemen, or construction workers.

In the epilogue to his autobiography, Parks writes that all his life he has been called "Mr. Dreamer," "Mr. Striver," and "Mr. Success." These three nicknames characterize him effectively. Because of the strength instilled in his character by his devoted mother, Parks has exhibited an amazing degree of courage and self-confidence. He relates many anecdotes about his enterprising behavior. For example, without having any experience in fashion photography, he asked for a job taking pictures of the latest gowns for one of the most prominent designers in New York—and, largely because of his cockiness, he got the job.

Parks did all kinds of work with a camera during his long career. The biggest turning point came when he managed to get a job as the first African American ever to become a staff photographer for the prestigious *Life* magazine, which sent him all over the world to work on many different kinds of stories. He became one of the world's best photojournalists, using both words and pictures to capture the essence of a particular story or situation. His experience in writing prose to accompany his photographs gave him the confidence to try writing poetry and fiction. His life is a story of looking for new challenges and then succeeding with distinction.

Parks was able to do stories for *Life* that no white reporter or photographer would have dared to try. One of Parks's earliest accomplishments as a photojournalist was his article on Red Jackson, a young Harlem gang leader. He was able to win the confidence of a gang of violent young African Americans because he could talk their language. He went on to do articles on Southern segregation, the Black Muslims, the Black Panthers, and black civil rights leaders. For many years, he was *Life's* only black photographer, and the magazine was happy to have him, because he could be counted on to handle such sensitive assignments judiciously.

Parks was involved in the Civil Rights movement of the 1960's and became personally acquainted with many of its most important figures. His photojournalism helped to make the American public familiar with the names and faces of such leaders as Malcolm X, Huey Newton, Stokely Carmichael, Eldridge Cleaver, and Martin Luther King, Jr.

Parks also became a trusted friend of the fearlessly outspoken heavyweight boxing champion Muhammad Ali. Many of Parks's most interesting anecdotes in *Voices in the Mirror* contain revealing looks at famous African Americans of the twentieth century. His book is illustrated with some of his own best photographs of celebrities, revealing how he was able to use his camera to condense an entire story into a single powerful image.

Parks knew a great deal about still photography but next to nothing about motion-picture making when he agreed to direct a film adaptation of his own 1963 novel *The Learning Tree*. He eventually agreed to write the screenplay for the film and the musical score as well. His success led to more filmmaking assignments, including the cult classic *Superfly* (1972) and the highly successful *Shaft* (1971), which, according to Parks, gave black youth "their first cinematic hero comparable to James Cagney or Humphrey Bogart."

Parks loved the motion-picture medium because it called upon many of his creative talents. He also directed several documentary films and the feature film *Leadbelly* (1976), a dramatized biography of the African American composer and folk singer Huddie Ledbetter. Parks identified with Leadbelly because both had used their creative talents to rise above poverty and social injustice.

Voices in the Mirror is made colorful by its vivid descriptions of places such as Paris, Manhattan, and Rio de Janeiro, as well as by anecdotes about such famous people as Richard Wright, Ingrid Bergman, Gloria Vanderbilt, Winston Churchill, Dwight Eisenhower, King Farouk, and the Duke and Duchess of Windsor. As sophisticated as he became, Parks is nevertheless clearly impressed by many of the celebrities he met during his adventurous lifetime.

One of the most striking aspects of Parks's autobiography is the dynamic way in which he balances anecdotes about his personal life with anecdotes about his travel experiences and encounters with celebrities. Parks was married three times and had four children. His first marriage lasted the longest; it broke up in 1961 because his wife resented the fact that her husband was leading an exciting life and achieving fame while she was confined at home with their children. His second marriage was to a much younger woman who attracted him physically but could not relate to him on an intellectual level; they were divorced in 1973. In his third marriage, he felt that he had at last found a real soul mate and intellectual equal; however, that marriage disintegrated after ten years. He candidly admits that his driving ambition and itinerant life-style made marriage difficult for his wives.

His autobiography contains many anecdotes about his wives and offspring. It concludes with the tragic story of the death of his son, Gordon, Jr., who died in an airplane crash while taking photos for a motion picture set in Africa. The last pages of *Voices in the Mirror* have a somber tone, in contrast to the optimism and sense of high adventure conveyed even in the early chapters. He acknowledges that he has made many mistakes. In old age, he writes, "You are left wondering if you are all you set out to be; if what was to be done is finally done. . . . By then you are locked into your fate, and you are whatever you are, waiting for the final door to slam shut."

Analysis

Parks intended his autobiography to be an inspiration to young people in general and to young African Americans in particular. His message might be summarized as "there is hardly anything you cannot accomplish if you try hard enough." He records the important incidents of his long, eventful lifetime as illustrations of the ways in which success can be achieved by a person who is motivated to succeed and not afraid of occasional failures.

One of the themes recurring throughout Parks's autobiography is that of white racism. Every time he faced a new challenge in his life, he was met with reminders that African Americans could not expect the same opportunities as whites. Parks steadfastly refused to listen to words of discouragement and tried many things that African Americans had never tried before. He was the first African American to achieve success as a fashion photographer, the first African American photographer to work for *Life*, and the first African American to direct a feature film for Hollywood.

Parks knew many of the most prominent African American revolutionaries of the turbulent 1960's, including Malcolm X and Eldridge Cleaver. He never, though, subscribed to doctrines of armed rebellion or separatism, because his life experiences had shown him that although the doors of opportunity might have been closed to African Americans, they certainly were not locked and bolted. He repeatedly states and illustrates that no race has a monopoly on bigotry or injustice. He found too much friendship and encouragement from members of other races to be able to believe that African Americans were faced with nothing but prejudice and hatred.

Parks regards himself as living proof of his message that bigotry is motivated by ignorance and fear and that it does not have to be a crippling influence if the intended victim refuses to accept it as such. His attitude toward life throughout his autobiography is positive, aggressive, and enthusiastic. He states that the United States, in spite of its history of racial intolerance, is still the best place in the world for African Americans to live.

Parks's early experiences with poverty left him with feelings of deep compassion for all the impoverished people of the world. He chose photography as his "weapon" to fight against poverty and the conditions that breed it. He believed that society would find ways to correct social injustices if such injustices were exposed through the light of publicity and the emotional impact of art.

His life work may be regarded as an alternative to the radical teachings of men such as Malcolm X, Huey Newton, and Stokely Carmichael. Parks believes in the principles upon which the United States government was founded, including liberty, justice and the pursuit of happiness. He regards his record of successes as proof that American ideals are not mere platitudes but powerful truths that apply to all humankind.

Implicit in every chapter of his life story is the belief that hard work brings recognition and builds strength of character. Parks does not brag about how hard he worked to achieve what he did; however, the reader cannot fail to appreciate the amount of time and effort that went into acquiring all the different skills Parks needed to distinguish himself in so many different fields of endeavor.

On a more personal level, Parks is concerned with fulfilling his ambitions to explore his own potential: to find out who he is and what he can do. He has an existentialist attitude toward life and is skeptical in matters of religion. He believes that self-realization in the here and now is far more important than possible rewards in the hereafter. At the same time, he admits that success does not always bring happiness and can create as many problems as it solves. He emphasizes that human love is the most important value in life. He speaks with pride and pleasure of the women in his life and of his many children and grandchildren.

Every good biographical work contains a "key" to the subject's character and life story. In Parks's case, that key is his mother's love. Throughout his book, he reiterates not only that his mother gave him the self-confidence to test himself to the fullest possible extent but also that his love for her inspired him to achieve recognition that would honor her memory.

Critical Context

Parks's photographs, paintings, poetry, books, musical compositions, and films have met with critical acclaim throughout his multifaceted career. *Voices in the Mirror* was no exception. Critics were practically unanimous in calling it an interesting book because it was expertly written by a man who was himself his most fascinating character. Critic Phoebe-Lou Adams called Parks's autobiography "a superb example of what talent, courage and determination can accomplish against odds." Michael Eric Dyson's review in *The New York Times* commented that "through the power of his words, this intelligent and sensitive interpreter of human experience has now turned the mirror toward us as well as himself; we, like Mr. Parks, must be judged by the integrity of our response to what we hear and see. Let us hope that we are half as successful as he has been."

Parks's autobiography demonstrates to readers of all races that African Americans have no reason to feel inferior to anyone. Even the most bigoted reader is forced to acknowledge that Parks's record of successes in a wide variety of difficult endeavors has been rivaled by few whites. Parks writes from an elevated standpoint; his own life is proof of the principles he preaches.

For African Americans, Parks's message is clear. Even the most disadvantaged has no cause to despair; the doors of opportunity can be forced open if one is willing to work hard, to learn the skills needed for success, and to refuse to be intimidated by hostility, ridicule, or rejection. Above all, Parks's autobiography demonstrates that young African Americans can accept any challenge life has to offer and can share equally in the cultural riches of the entire world.

Bibliography

Berry, Skip. *Gordon Parks.* New York: Chelsea House, 1991. A brief biography of Parks, liberally illustrated with black-and-white photographs taken by Parks and others. Part of Chelsea House's Black Americans of Achievement Series.

Parks, Gordon. *Born Black.* Philadelphia, J. J. Lippincott, 1971. A collection of essays mainly about Parks's impressions of famous black leaders, including Malcolm X, Muhammad Ali, Martin Luther King, Jr., Stokely Carmichael, Eldridge Cleaver, and Huey Newton. Illustrated with some of Parks's best photographs.

Many of the essays and photographs originally appeared in *Life.*

——————————. *A Choice of Weapons.* New York: Harper & Row, 1966. An earlier autobiographical work covering the author's difficult life in Kansas, Minnesota, Chicago, New York, and Washington, D.C., up until the year 1944, when he went to Harlem. The title of the book refers to his choice of the camera as a "weapon" against racial and economic injustice.

——————————. *Flavio.* New York: W. W. Norton, 1978. A true account of an impoverished Brazilian boy and his family whom Parks befriended during a photographic assignment for *Life* magazine. Illustrated with Parks's emotionally stirring photographs of slum conditions in Rio de Janeiro.

——————————. "Freedom's Fearful Foe: Poverty." *Life* 50 (June 16, 1961): 86-98. This article about Flavio da Silva and his family is an excellent example of Parks's photojournalism. For many years *Life*, like its sister publication *Time*, was a powerful shaper of opinion, and the magazine was of vital importance to Parks's career.

——————————. *In Love.* Philadelphia: J. J. Lippincott, 1971. A collection of Parks's poetry, illustrated with his own impressionistic color photographs. Displays another side of Parks's multifaceted personality.

——————————. *To Smile in Autumn: A Memoir.* New York: W. W. Norton, 1979. An earlier autobiographical work by Parks illustrated with his own distinctive black-and-white photographs. Covers his life and work during the period from 1944 through 1978.

Bill Delaney

WAITING TO EXHALE

Author: Terry McMillan (1951-   )
Type of work: Novel
Type of plot: Social realism
Time of plot: 1990
Locale: Phoenix, Arizona, and Denver, Colorado
First published: 1992

> *Principal characters:*
> BERNADINE HARRIS, a woman struggling with the breakup of her marriage
> SAVANNAH JACKSON, a friend and former college roommate of Bernadine
> ROBIN STOKES, an underwriter for a major insurance company
> GLORIA MATTHEWS, a hair-salon owner who derives much of her meaning in life from eating
> RUSSELL, Robin's most important recent lover
> MICHAEL KING, an upper-level employee at Robin's company who falls in love with her
> MARVIN KING, a warm, generous man who moves into Gloria's neighborhood
> JOHN HARRIS, Bernadine's former husband

The Novel

Waiting to Exhale tells the story of four college-educated, middle-class black women who rely on one another to overcome a number of personal and professional crises. As a record of a year in these women's lives, the novel goes back and forth in time to chart the paths that have led each woman to Phoenix and to become the sort of woman each is. In addition to telling the story of the women, the novel explores the social and cultural contexts of African American life in the 1990's. McMillan focuses on a number of political and social issues that are in the background of these women's lives.

Through the story of Savannah Jackson, McMillan provides some sense of the struggles many black women must endure to have successful careers. Savannah often telephones her mother and sister, who live in Pittsburgh. Her mother lives on Social Security benefits and food stamps. Savannah's sister endures a troubled marriage and has often been on the run, taking her children to cheap motels but always returning to her husband, on whom she is dependent but whom she perhaps does not love. Savannah, knowing the difficulties her family faces, often does not tell them of her own problems, and she of all her siblings is the only one to send her mother money every month to supplement the meager Social Security benefits.

Robin Stokes's relationship with her family creates an additional burden for her.

Her father suffers from Alzheimer's disease, and her mother remains firm in her resolve to care for him in her Tucson home. Robin's experiences with her sick father show how the disease takes him away from her; eventually, she and her mother have no choice but to admit him to a nursing home, and McMillan shows how painful that choice is. Other choices by Robin also illuminate the novel's context. Before they first have sex, for example, Robin asks Michael if he has a condom, and she lets him know that she does. Practicing safe sex is important to these women, particularly since they unfold a history of many sexual partners.

The need for safe sex hits Gloria Matthews' home when one of the stylists at her hair salon develops acquired immune deficiency syndrome (AIDS). When Gloria's son acknowledges to her that he is having sex, sexually transmitted diseases and teenage pregnancy become family issues.

Other social concerns the novel addresses in its background include scholarships for black students, the problems of single mothers, and opportunities for professional and personal networking among African American women. This last topic is a major concern of the main characters; all are members of an organization called Black Women on the Move, in which Gloria serves as a member of the board of directors. All the women agree to vote to make Martin Luther King, Jr.'s birthday an official Arizona state holiday.

While McMillan takes note of the contexts that surround and invade these characters' lives, the four women remain the focus and *raison d'être* of the novel. Each struggles with a number of difficulties, and all are there to support one another. Yet, although Bernadine, Savannah, Robin, and Gloria are mutually supportive, the novel's record of their friendship is far from a fairy tale. They argue and disagree, and they laugh at and judge one another. To a large extent, what any one woman is able to offer to the others depends on how she is dealing with her own problems. At the novel's end, some crises have been met and conquered, and others are yet to come. The women, however, know that their friendship will see them through.

The Characters

McMillan's strategy for character creation is closely aligned with her narrative choices. The novel employs omniscient and first-person points of view to reveal characters and their conflicts. When McMillan uses omniscient narration, she brings out her characters' individuality through their speech, which ranges from Standard English to street-level dialect. When the author uses first-person narration, the characters tell their own stories in their own ways. McMillan's introduction of the four main characters emphasizes the close connection between form, content, and character that is a hallmark of *Waiting to Exhale*.

First-person narrative point of view is used to make clear that Savannah, level-headed and confident, already has the voice to tell her story. She is planning to make big changes in her life. She moves from Denver to Phoenix and changes jobs, giving up her position as director of publicity at a major public utility to take a job in the publicity department at a television station, with a huge cut in pay. Savannah is depicted as in control of most of the issues in her life. When she talks about finding a shortage of "decent" black men in Denver and then reveals that she has not been successful with men in the last few years, however, she highlights an area of her life that she does not control. Indeed, as she prepares to drive to Phoenix, her errors in selecting men become evident; she allows Lionel, a man she hardly knows, to drive with her to Phoenix, where he attempts to sponge off her.

Robin also introduces herself in the first person; like Savannah, Robin has made an intelligent analysis of her personal and professional life. She is a successful insurance underwriter, and she has the money to dress the way she wants (she is given to purchasing expensive hairweaves), but she knows what she does not have control over—the men in her life. As she tells her story, her first topic is her breakup with Russell, her boyfriend of the last few years. She understands that Russell lies to her and uses her, and she knows that she should be glad their relationship has ended— but she also notes the regret she feels at not being a part of his life. She even understands that he was willing to give her only a good time, not a commitment, and she knows that she has a weakness for good-looking men. Although Robin, too, is able to state her problem, she, like Savannah, has yet to take control over it.

Bernadine and Gloria are introduced through the use of omniscient narration. Their initial stories are interspersed with dialogue, so a sense of their voices is present. The fact that they lack the authority to tell their own stories, however, is indicative of the self-analysis, and action to go with it, that neither has performed. Although Bernadine has mused over her discontent with her husband and the compromises she has made for him, she has done nothing about either, and she is shocked when he calls off their marriage. She is so upset that for several days she is in an alcohol- and drug-induced stupor. Gloria, too, has been going through the motions of living. The narrator records the principal things that occupy Gloria's time: her son Tarik, her eating, and her hair-salon business. Gloria senses that she needs to make changes; she knows that her son will soon leave home for college. Gloria, however, has not analyzed her life and developed a course of action to improve her future.

All four women experience troubles with men. Bernadine's husband leaves her for a young white woman, and he uses the divorce proceedings to wear her down emotionally so that he can steal their community property—much of it acquired because Bernadine had worked hard to make his business succeed. While she deals with the divorce, Bernadine is not always the best listener when Robin and Savannah discuss the new men in their lives. Gloria tires of listening to the women talk of their relationships with men, because for almost seventeen years she has not had a healthy relationship with a man. She tells the other three to spend less of their time concentrating on sex and men.

The women sometimes get testy with one another when they talk about men, but they are more tolerant when discussing other subjects, such as Robin's father's illness, Bernadine's legal affairs, Savannah's career moves, or Gloria's high blood pressure. Although the women share a common space—their friendship—they are highly individualized.

Themes and Meanings

Waiting to Exhale is an odd yet brilliant fictional representation of issues and concerns affecting middle-class African American women in the late twentieth century. The novel is odd in that the four protagonists are so intensely preoccupied with their relationships with men. Yet because McMillan explores in minute detail what is on the minds of these educated and successful women, no matter what it is—men, careers, families, or the African American community—the characters' preoccupation with their relationships helps to tell their stories. Black men are important to them; in this sense, the novel, beyond merely presenting the women's frustrations and heartaches, presents a blueprint for what healthy and committed relationships between black women and black men must be.

Moreover, *Waiting to Exhale* is not about black women in general. It is, rather, about four particular middle-class black women whose friendship, as far as the narrative space is concerned, takes place within a specific locale. These four black women are not necessarily representative of anyone other than themselves. The narrative denies readers the luxury of easy generalizations.

Personal and social struggle intermingle in the novel, as the four women use one another for support both in their personal ups and downs and in their efforts to make the world a little better for other African Americans. Affirmation, of self and other, is present at every turn in the novel. The women struggle to achieve, as Savannah says, peace of mind and a warm home, and they know that if all else fails, they have one another. The women's friendship unites them and connects them to larger moments in the African American experience, in which the existence of a communal "self" has often been essential to the cultural survival of the race. The novel makes this point poignantly after Gloria has a massive heart attack that has been caused by an adult lifetime of overeating and by a family history of hypertension. When Gloria awakes in her hospital bed, her friends are present, as are her son and Marvin King, a sympathetic older neighbor of Gloria. All tell the doctor that they are her family. Bernadine, Savannah, and Robin tell the doctor that they are Gloria's sisters, and Marvin, who is in love with Gloria, says that he is her husband. All, by tacit agreement, accept responsibility for assisting Gloria through her recovery.

If the meaning of the novel is not entirely contained within the women's friendship, then a part of it resides in the book's setting in the urban landscape of Phoenix. McMillan shows that it is more than possible for African Americans to be successful and upwardly mobile and still to find time to have a collective consciousness that recognizes that life in America is not always good for the masses of African Americans.

Critical Context

McMillan explored the dilemmas facing other black women in her first two novels, *Mama* (1987) and *Disappearing Acts* (1989). In her first novel, McMillan beautifully rendered the difficulties and joys of Mildred Peacock, a poor, alcoholic single parent. Mildred fights many battles and manages, often with the assistance of her women friends and daughters, to affirm her existence at every chance. *Disappearing Acts*, which uses alternating interior monologues to trace the stages of a couple's relationship, is one of the few novels by a contemporary black woman writer to give equal attention to the perspectives of black women and black men.

Waiting to Exhale combines two of McMillan's earlier fictional concerns. She creates credible black women and also includes a variety of black male characters. Some of these, such as Bernadine's husband and Robin's Russell, are shown in a bad light, but many, such as Marvin and Michael, are decent, loving, and strong black men. Nevertheless, McMillan shows that some of these men are simply not suitable for these particular women, regardless of the men's redeeming or unredeeming qualities. McMillan suggests strongly that these women know what makes them happy, and their friendship affords them the opportunity to have their individual choices supported and respected.

McMillan's third novel received a number of accolades. Many reviewers suggested that McMillan, at the pinnacle of her craft, was now the equal of her more celebrated contemporaries Toni Morrison and Alice Walker. During the summer of 1992, all three novelists had works on *The New York Times*'s best-seller list—and McMillan remained on the list in the number-one position for the longest time of the three.

If McMillan invites comparison to Morrison and Walker, her work should also be juxtaposed to that of a long line of black women writers who have explored the urban terrain and how black characters adjust to it. Ann Petry's *The Street* (1946), for example, presented the dilemma of a black woman who wants to have a successful relationship and who also wants to have a successful career. Unlike the women in *Waiting to Exhale*, however, *The Street*'s Lutie Johnson has no circle of women friends to help her through her personal and social problems. Comparing *Waiting to Exhale* to the Petry novel demonstrates both how far black women writers have come and how much America has changed.

Bibliography

Gates, Henry Louis, Jr., ed. *Reading Black, Reading Feminist: A Critical Anthology.* New York: Meridian Books, 1990. Several essays in this important collection address ways of responding to black women's literature.

Henderson, Mae Gwendolyn. "Speaking in Tongues: Dialogics, Dialectics, and the Black Woman's Literary Tradition." In *Reading Black, Reading Feminist*, edited by Henry Louis Gates, Jr. New York: Meridian Books, 1990. Emphasizes how black female subjectivity helps to structure many texts in the black women's literary tradition.

Johnston, Tracy. Review of *Waiting to Exhale*, by Terry McMillan. *Whole Earth Review* 78 (Spring, 1993): 84. Johnson praises *Waiting to Exhale* as a "wonderful mix of black, urban, female voices"; however, she finds McMillan's portrayal of the book's "good men" somewhat unconvincing.

Smith, Wendy. "Terry McMillan." *Publishers Weekly* 239, no. 22 (May 11, 1992): 50-51. An incisive overview of McMillan's career, written on the eve of *Waiting to*

Exhale's publication. Largely based on an interview with the author, who energetically defends her book's depiction of black men.

Wall, Cheryl A., ed. *Changing Our Own Words: Essays on Criticism, Theory, and Writing by Black Women.* New Brunswick, N.J.: Rutgers University Press, 1989. Major black feminist critics analyze the black woman's literary tradition.

Willis, Susan. *Specifying: Black Women Writing the American Experience.* Madison: University of Wisconsin Press, 1987. Considers the many alternative creative visions black women writers contribute to American literature, African American literature, black women's literature, and women's literature.

Charles P. Toombs

WALK ME TO THE DISTANCE

Author: Percival L. Everett (1956-   )
Type of work: Novel
Type of plot: Bildungsroman
Time of plot: The Vietnam War era
Locale: Savannah, Georgia, and Slut's Hole, Wyoming
First published: 1985

> *Principal characters:*
> DAVID LARSON, an aimless young Vietnam veteran in search of a
>   purpose in life
> CHLOE SIXBURY, an elderly woman rancher
> PATRICK, Sixbury's mentally handicapped son
> HOWARD DALE, a veterinarian who becomes David's closest male
>   companion
> JILL, David's sister
> BUTCH, a seven-year-old Eurasian girl abandoned by her
>   Vietnamese family
> JOSHUA LOWE, a local rancher who functions as David's surrogate
>   father
> REVEREND DAMON ZACKS, a traveling preacher
> OLIVIA, a twenty-year-old prostitute
> KATY STINSON, a pretty young woman who becomes the focus of
>   David's yearnings

The Novel

Returning from the Vietnam War to his native Savannah, Georgia, David Larson feels as "unremarkable" as when he left. This general sense of detachment is evidenced by his unemotional response to the loss of his parents in a traffic accident during his absence and the subsequent ease with which he distances himself from his sister because of her antiwar sympathies.

Purchasing a used car, David motors west. Chance lands him in Slut's Hole, Wyoming, after he damages the car's radiator while shooting at a jackrabbit. Forced to spend two weeks in town until his car is repaired, David acquires, in quick succession, a job and a place to stay. His time is largely divided among his undemanding caretaker chores at a highway rest area, his forays into Laramie with his new friend Howard Dale, and his life on the Sixbury ranch.

At the rest area, David engages in largely mindless tasks punctuated only by the daily arrival of the red-haired, gold-toothed prostitute Cecile, who offers entertainment to truckers, and by the short stopovers of highway motorists such as Damon Zacks, a preacher fascinated by the view from the cliff at the edge of the parking lot. David's periodic trips to the city of Laramie are marked by barhopping and brawling and by an emotionally empty relationship with Sarah Newman, a counselor in the Bureau of Indian Affairs.

The heart of his existence, however, is the Sixbury ranch. David develops a close, comfortable relationship not only with Chloe Sixbury, the ranch's elderly owner, but also with the land. "He liked the people and he loved the terrain," Everett writes. In addition to helping out with the chores, David involves himself more and more in the affairs of Chloe and her son, Patrick. After discovering Patrick's use of sheep as a sexual outlet, he convinces Sixbury to drive with him to the town of Casper to hire a prostitute for Patrick. Although she fails to stir Patrick's interest, Olivia does become the temporary object of David's concern and of his misdirected desire to redeem a wasted life.

His quest is interrupted by Patrick's brief scuffle with his mother after she catches him in a sex act in the barn. Patrick runs away, and despite a hasty search, he is not found for some time.

Only after the inclusion of the abandoned child Kyongja, renamed "Butch," into the Sixbury fold does Patrick reappear. He abducts the little girl, setting off an extensive search. A party of five men find the naked and molested Butch in a deserted cabin, and they chase after Patrick's fleeing form. David shoots him in the right arm in an attempt to impede his flight, and the men, with the exceptions of Deputy Quinn Rutland and Howard Dale, conduct an impromptu lynching.

Although the men tell Sixbury that they never discovered who raped Butch, Sixbury seems to sense the truth. Nevertheless, David alternates between interpreting the lynching as "somehow beautiful" and thinking of himself as a criminal. He is comforted by a sermon delivered at the town's only church, where the minister speaks of how a "bad thing need not be evil" if the intention is good.

Deciding that he needs some time away, David flies to Georgia to visit his sister and her husband. On the plane, he meets Katy Stinson, who becomes the object of his subsequent interest.

Back in Savannah, he is uncomfortable; he is depressed by the conformity of suburban life, upset over changes made to his parents' house, and disoriented by the crowds and urban energy. David is touched only by some of the people whom he encounters, including a woman trapped in an early marriage and an elderly man who suffers from Parkinson's disease but who is still interested in people and life. David returns to Wyoming without having become reconciled with his sister.

Once back, David makes the rounds in order to become reacquainted with familiar faces, and he hears that the police are asking questions about the night of Butch's disappearance. David punches Howard Dale, whom he suspects of having told the authorities about what happened; he also courts Katy Stinson and thinks of going back to college to study ranch management.

This period of suspense and anticipation is interrupted by Sixbury's stroke. David learns that she may never walk again, but the crisis puts an end to his feelings of being trapped by his new family; he realizes that he loves the elderly woman and the Eurasian child. Katy visits twice to cook meals, but she is overwhelmed by the situation. The police arrive, but Sixbury tells them that she had seen Patrick raid the pantry the night before. This lie puts an end to their inquiries.

While massaging Sixbury the next day, David spies a pistol in the drawer of her nightstand. Knowing that she cannot endure her current helplessness, he senses that she is contemplating suicide, for much the same reason that she had earlier bought a deformed sheep at auction with the sole intention of putting it out of its misery. Sixbury has already made a will leaving her ranch to David.

As in the case of the lynching, David does not intervene. He sits at the bottom of the stairs, with Butch half asleep on his lap, as the narrative ends.

The Characters

The novel's protagonist is David Larson, an alienated young man in search of a purpose. Some reviewers expressed concern that the main character is not an African American, as was the case in the author's first novel *Suder* (1983); Everett, however, seems to be avoiding the issue of racial identity for the sake of creating a generalized portrait of displacement.

The reader must look to sources in Western literature for some clue as to authorial intention in regard to the creation and development of this character. At one point in the narrative, David spends time at his desk reading a copy of *The Virginian* (1902) by American author Owen Wister. In Wister's novel, the first serious fictional treatment of the American cowboy, the title character makes a place for himself in the town of Sunk Hole, Wyoming. Like David, the Virginian becomes one with the people and the landscape of his adopted state, and he must face a difficult moral decision when he participates in the hanging of a cattle rustler who had been his friend. As in *The Virginian*, the setting of *Walk Me to the Distance* underscores the main character's development and defines the community that he encounters.

The landscape of Wyoming is depicted as a living presence. Having himself worked on a sheep ranch, Everett knows the country he describes. For example, in the pivotal sermon from which David derives so much consolation after the lynching, the minister asserts, "The thing about this country is—well, it's relentless. It doesn't let up. It goes on and on, with this enormous sky for a face." Furthermore, the minister makes a connection between the land and its inhabitants by arguing that the people need to trust the land: "We have no choice. We are alone here."

This sense of collective identity, which one character summarizes by saying "it's like we're a tribe here," is the central quality that draws David to consider the place as home and the people as his family. It is this collective identity that makes him a participant, however passive, in the lynching of Patrick and the imminent suicide of Sixbury and then reconciles him to those events, which have, like the landscape, their own "oppressive beauty."

The land itself demands of the people who dwell there a kind of strength, a determination to make their own way, to dispense their own brand of justice. Some of that inner strength and assuredness can be seen in the laconic speech of the region, a verbal reticence that Everett himself tries to emulate in his narrative style. These are a people who live by deed and not by word. The decision to lynch Patrick, for example, is made without conversation; the men act almost by nature.

On the whole, Patrick is an object of sympathy even at the moment of death. Initially, it is his sexual passion, his use of sheep to satisfy his lustful urges, that makes David think of him as human. It is this same passion, however, that when misdirected toward a child impels the men to eliminate Patrick as they would any animal predator.

At one point in the narrative, David picks up a copy of *The Hamlet* (1940), by American novelist and short-story writer William Faulkner. This work also includes an idiot boy whose physical affection for livestock is sympathetically portrayed; Isaac Snope's love for a cow, Faulkner would have the reader believe, is at least evidence that he can feel and that he shares this one important characteristic with the rest of humanity.

Such sympathy, however, is tempered by the necessity for autonomy. There is a premium paid for self-determination and self-sufficiency. Shortly after David first meets her, for example, Sixbury wonders aloud about what will happen to Patrick when she is dead. Her worries are amplified not by Patrick's inability to cope after he runs away but by his reversion to predatory, animal behavior. Sixbury adjusts to Patrick's ultimate fate as naturally as she seems to cope with her own physical dilemma. Hers has been a life of grim determination after many setbacks: four miscarriages, two stillborn children, the birth of Patrick, the death of her husband, and the loss of her independence as a result of her stroke. It is only with the last of these personal tragedies that she comes to the end of her resources. "I'm pretty tired," Sixbury tells David on what is presumably her last night. She has walked the distance, and all Larson and Butch can do is stand by her until the end.

Themes and Meanings

The title itself is a key to unlocking the meaning of the text. At one point in the narrative, Butch, referring to the horizon, asks, "Can we walk to the distance?" Sixbury replies, "We can try, but, no, we can't get there." This possible allusion to the poem "I Saw a Man Pursuing the Horizon" by the American poet Stephen Crane offers commentary on the characteristic human longing to chase after the unattainable. Like the speaker in Crane's poem, Sixbury knows that the horizon is an imaginary line.

This is a realization that also comes to David Larson, who, after spending much of his free time at the rest area assembling plastic model cars—an act symbolic of his urge to be in motion—comes finally to throw these toys away and settle for the given.

Yet one must not confuse the horizon with the edge. Butch uses the term "edge" to mean "horizon," but she is corrected by Sixbury. The term "edge" has two important meanings in the novel. First, there is the edge of Montgomery Cliff upon which the highway rest area is perched. Damon Zacks, while climbing over the rail to get closer to the rim, tells David, "The edge is where you should be, brother!"

In a very real sense, David has already made such a choice. The West is still the "edge" of America, and classic frontier values are still evident in the behavior of its people. This is another aspect of the title's meaning—one is not asked to walk alone. The title can be seen as an invitation to accompany another to the edge, to confront the extremities of experience with a companion, a family, a community.

In this way, even the edge can be home. The epigraph at the beginning of the first section of the novel, a quotation from Grayson Silas, reads, "Home is always recognizable, though eyes may never have been set upon it."

By contrast, the novel abounds in images of transitoriness. The come and go of the highway rest area, the quick coupling of prostitutes and their clients, and David's own family past and sexual history all speak of mutability.

It is only with the recognition that there are certain fixed values to be derived from an acceptance of place and people that David stops running from himself and others. Not long after his arrival in Slut's Hole, Larson remarks, "Staying here just feels like the right move." Only after he has fully bonded with the community, however, does his personal understanding catch up with his feeling.

Critical Context

In the wake of his first novel, the much-praised, humorously picaresque *Suder* (1983), Percival Everett made a dramatic shift when he published the more traditional, more serious *Walk Me to the Distance*. In some ways, the second novel may be regarded as an answer to his first: *Suder* offers flight as an option in dealing with life's problems; *Walk Me to the Distance* offers the antidote of home and family.

Walk Me to the Distance has not benefited from the positive critical reception of Everett's first, most popular novel. Many reviewers, for example, have missed the comic creativity of *Suder.* Even those who felt at times moved by Everett's second novel nevertheless reacted negatively to what they saw as a narrative style that was too terse, a brevity of expression that perhaps masked a shallowness of content. At least one reviewer, moreover, lamented that the main character was not African American and that Percival Everett, though an African American writer, had chosen not to confront the issue of racial identity.

Bibliography

Brown, Rosellen. "The Emperor's New Fiction." *Boston Review* 11 (August, 1986): 7-8. While praising the novel for its skillful organization and its essential hopefulness, Brown laments the fact that Everett has avoided the issues of African American identity, both personal and societal.

Hemesath, James. *"Walk Me to the Distance." Library Journal* 110 (March 1, 1985): 102. After a rather thin but pleasing first half, Hemesath writes, the novel turns serious and ugly. Unfortunately, he claims, the characterization, description of setting, and general tone lack the weight sufficient to maintain the author's sober purpose.

Kirkus Reviews. Review of *Walk Me to the Distance.* 52 (December 15, 1984): 1156-

1157. Although praising *Suder* as "intriguing but strained," the review finds *Walk Me to the Distance* hard to enjoy and hard to believe. Argues that there is "emotional power" in the "David/Sixbury/Patrick triangle," but that the rest of the narrative is encumbered by clumsy plotting and dialogue marked by "Gary-Cooper-ish grunts."

Publishers Weekly. Review of *Walk Me to the Distance.* 226 (December 21, 1984): 81. States that *Walk Me to the Distance* is hampered by a spare prose style that leaves too much to reader interpretation. Notes that the novel nevertheless provides an evocative treatment of one veteran's "repatriation."

Smith, Wendy. *"Walk Me to the Distance." The New York Times Book Review*, March 24, 1985, 24. Argues that the novel can be read as a cautionary tale concerning the misplaced desire to escape the problems of the modern world, including the increasingly problematic relationships between men and women, by seeking some imagined frontier. Asserts that the book's theme and characterization, however, are undercut by a "terseness that verges on blankness."

S. Thomas Mack

THE WINE OF ASTONISHMENT

Author: Earl Lovelace (1935-   )
Type of work: Novel
Type of plot: Social realism
Time of plot: The 1940's and 1950's
Locale: Bonasse, Trinidad
First published: 1982

> *Principal characters:*
> EVA, the narrator, the wife of the leader of the Spiritual Baptist
>   Church in Bonasse
> BEE, Eva's husband of twenty-three years
> BOLO, the warrior turned "badjohn," the champion stick fighter
>   of the area
> IVAN MORTON, the village scholar and hope of the village
> PRINCE, the policeman who is relentless in his pursuit and
>   suppression of the Baptist religion in Bonasse

The Novel

The Wine of Astonishment is the story of the struggle of a Spiritual Baptist community, from the passing of the Prohibition Ordinance in 1917 until the lifting of the ban in 1951. It is told by one of the members of the church. Eva begins her narrative of the trials and sufferings of those of the Spiritual Baptist faith with the notion that there is a purpose behind it all.

The only hope for the villagers of Bonasse, as they see it, lies in Ivan Morton, a teacher turned politician, the new man in the legislative council of the country. They would like Morton to intervene on their behalf to lift the ban so that they can be free to worship in the way that they choose. Morton disappoints them and reveals his loyalty when he abandons the "house that his father build with his own two hands." With his wife, he leaves the village, taking nothing, to live in the big house "on top of Bonasse hill looking over the sea and the whole village." The house, which some say is haunted, has itself been abandoned by the Richardsons, colonials who have returned to England.

Meanwhile, the village undergoes significant changes with the coming of the war. An American base is established in the country, resulting in prostitution and the corruption of the youth. At the same time, the Spiritual Baptists suffer persecution at the hands of the police and government. At the center of this harassment is the cruel and relentless Corporal Prince, whom Bolo, the warrior and champion stick fighter, suggests should be killed. Bolo challenges Prince as Prince takes the worshippers to jail, but he is beaten and arrested by the police while the others look on passively. For his action, Bolo is sent to jail for three years of hard labor.

While the warrior Bolo is in jail, the people of Bonasse, believing this to be the time of the intellectual, work to elect Morton to the legislative council, seeing him as "a man to plead [their] cause, to change the law, to right the wrong that is going on against [them] for those long years." Bolo returns from jail only to find his efforts at making an honest living frustrated by the bureaucracy.

Contemptuous of the community, Bolo challenges the stickmen to do battle with him, but no one obliges. From this point on, the warrior in Bolo degenerates into the "badjohn." He terrorizes the Bonasse community "with his recklessness and vexation and wickedness boiling up in him." The community's outrage reaches a limit when Bolo takes the two daughters of one of the villagers to live with him. Determined to show him "we is a people," Bee, the leader of the Spiritual Baptists, decides that they "have to go against him with strength and anger." They must take up their "manhood challenge that [they] turn away from for too long." Bolo is finally killed by the police in a showdown.

Shortly thereafter, with the approach of elections, a law is passed allowing the Baptists the freedom to worship in their own way. When the church congregation gathers to celebrate its freedom, however, the "Spirit just wouldn't come," in spite of the impassioned preaching, incense burning, and candle lighting. The sadness that Eva, Bee, and the others experience at this realization is assuaged by the music of the steel pans that they hear on their way home. They are convinced that the pan music has in it "the same spirit that we miss in our church."

The Characters

Since all the characters in the novel are presented through the eyes of Eva, it is important that she is presented as a credible character. A member of the Baptist church herself and an ordinary peasant woman, she is capable of insightful thinking and profound analysis of her society. Lovelace's effective use of dialect in Eva's mouth makes her that much more reliable in her judgment of people and events.

Bolo, the warrior turned "badjohn," represents rebelliousness within the society. As warrior, he is both admired and feared. He is the only one to stand up to the police and proclaim the rights of the people, but when the people refuse to support him and fail to stand up for their rights, he turns to terrorizing them, forcing them to find their "peoplehood."

Bee, on the other hand, represents the voice of moderation and patience. Unwilling to challenge the authorities directly, he seeks to use the political and legal machinery to change things. His slow approach results in a falling off of the church's membership and the loss of the Spirit in the church. Bolo tries to show Bee the inadequacy of this approach. In time, Bee echoes Bolo's sentiments: "We . . . shoulda never stop worshipping in the true Baptist way" and "we shoulda fight them, we shoulda kill Prince." Eva, with her commonsense approach to survival, reminds him of the wisdom of his decision.

Ivan Morton's character is used to discuss a phenomenon within Caribbean society, that of the self-seeking politician who takes the people for fools, bribing them at election time but doing nothing for them for the rest of his term. Morton is the typical neocolonial puppet who seeks to take over from the colonial overlord while perpetuating all the bad habits of his predecessor.

Armed with his colonial education, Morton thinks of himself as the natural leader of the people, but when he is elected, he abandons his village, rejects the dark-skinned Eulalie whom he had made pregnant, and goes to live in a colonial mansion overlooking the village. From this vantage point, it is easy for Morton to betray the interests of the community.

The lack of third-person narration in the novel places limitations on the depth of characterization, since it is from Eva's restricted knowledge that the characters are presented. Moreover, characters are presented as types or symbols; they are one-dimensional. Each one represents a specific type or mode of social behavior. No one changes except Bolo, who moves from being a warrior to being a "badjohn" with respect for no one.

Themes and Meanings

Lovelace is consistently focused on the powerlessness of the black masses in the Caribbean and the consequent struggle they must go through to achieve dignity and peoplehood. In *The Wine of Astonishment*, the Spiritual Baptists are powerless against colonial law, which defines them as "illegal and illegitimate." The result is that they cannot worship in the "true Baptist way." They cannot ring their bell, burn their incense, and light their candles; nor do their ministers "have the authority to marry anybody."

Refusing to exercise the power that rightfully belongs to them, the people in their collective impotence look upon the scholar, intellectual, and politician—in this case, Ivan Morton—to fight for them. In an obvious criticism of Caribbean political leadership, Lovelace depicts Morton as a man who alienates himself from his community and finally betrays that community as he promotes his self-interest.

The betrayal makes him one with the colonial overlord in the eyes of the village. He comes to the people only when he is seeking their votes, but once he is elected, he has no use for them. In time, the people come to see through these election gimmicks and begin to realize that "this sudden rush to answer applications for land, this sudden rush to put up crash programs to give a man a job for a week or two is just a trick for election."

Lovelace suggests that it is only when the people realize that the power is with them, only when they look inward to themselves, will they be able to achieve their dignity as a people. Eva, clear-sighted woman that she is, reveals this notion to her husband when he seeks to lay the blame for their predicament on Ivan Morton: "For if we didn't have the strength, if we didn't have the power, if we wasn't standing up on our own as a people, what was he there standing up for? We is a lot of people but we ain't a people." This is Lovelace's way of criticizing the people of the Caribbean for placing too much emphasis on their political leaders and insufficient emphasis on themselves as a people.

Lovelace knows that the struggle for peoplehood demands sacrifice, for which the people must accept full responsibility. In the novel, Bolo embodies that sacrifice. He must die so that the people can survive. Very early in the novel, Eva observes that "the warrior was dying in the village as the chief figure." The change in focus from warrior to scholar means that the people are ready to do away with one while embracing the other. Once Bolo performs his role, there is no use for him, but he must first challenge the people to locate their power within themselves by standing up for their right to worship in the "Baptist way."

Bolo shows them how, but they refuse to take heed. He alone must bear the brunt of the beating by Corporal Prince and his men. Bolo loses respect for them, concluding that they are not prepared to challenge the law in order to continue worshiping in their way. It is no wonder that he confronts the whole community of Bonasse in his deterioration from warrior to "badjohn." It is only at the very end that Bee understands that Bolo's role is "to be the sacrifice. To be the one terrible enough and strong enough and close enough to our heart to drive us to take up our manhood challenge that we turn away from for too long." Bolo's role is to push the people until they "have to stand up against him." Only then can they redeem themselves, but he has to die in the process.

The Wine of Astonishment celebrates more than the people's struggle for freedom. It also celebrates the culture that nurtures that struggle and that in turn is created out of the struggle. As in *The Dragon Can't Dance* (1979), Lovelace is principally concerned with the culture that the masses of African people of the Caribbean have been able to develop. Whether it is through stick fighting, playing "mas," worshiping in the Baptist faith, or playing in steel bands, Lovelace is fascinated by the manner in which black people have been able to use their retention of African culture, adopting and transforming that culture in the process.

The stick fighting that Bolo excels in "was more the dance, the adventure, the ceremony to show off the beauty of the warrior." Bolo's skills are the skills of the people. He wants them to know, through his skill, that they are "people too, with drums and song and warriors." As the society undergoes changes, the culture changes as well. Some aspects are lost altogether; others are transformed. The warrior tradition that sustains and gives impetus to Bolo disappears as the society welcomes education "as the way to win the battle to be somebody."

Similarly, the Baptist church, which represents the syncretism of African and Christian religious beliefs and practices, is a living testimony to the black culture of the people. The religion is testimony of the adaptability of the people's culture, and it is precisely the African elements in it that the authorities seek to repress. They condemn the form of worship, and they forbid the singing of hymns, the lighting of candles, and the burning of incense. The result is that the church gradually loses the Spirit, central to making it a black church.

All is not lost, however; the Spirit missing in the church has gone over to the steel band. Both Eva and Bee recognize it as "the same Spirit." As they pass the steel band tent, with music being played by "some young fellows, bare-back and with tear-up clothes," they get the feeling that they are "passing in front of something holy." In typical Lovelace style, the sacred and the secular have been brought to-gether. The struggle has been painful, but there is hope at the end. The people and their culture survive, making their struggle for dignity, for their peoplehood and their freedom, a realizable objective.

Critical Context

Fourth among his published novels, *The Wine of Astonishment* shares with Love-lace's other works his continuing concern for the black oppressed people of the Caribbean. Lovelace is not afraid to confront the social issues of the day. The preva-lence of political corruption, the destructiveness of misguided warriorship, the West-ern and class bias against African culture (in this case a religion), and betrayal by black middle-class intellectuals are issues that plague the postcolonial societies of the region.

Lovelace, unlike other writers who address the problems of the society, is not altogether hopeless in his prognostication. The ills of the society and the corrupt-ibility of individuals and institutions are balanced by the ability of the people to adapt and survive, constantly creating new cultural forms to ensure their dignity and personhood. The "spirit" may leave the church, but the steel band is created to inherit that spirit.

Another achievement of Lovelace's *The Wine of Astonishment* is his ability to deliver his narrative through Eva, herself a Spiritual Baptist. He captures both the language and the sentiments of the Baptist community with a sensibility that sug-gests a deep understanding of that religion. That he can sustain both for an entire novel is truly a mark of great skill as a writer. In the introduction to the 1986 edition of his text, critic Marjorie Thorpe notes that this linguistic skill "from the outset, encourages the reader to believe that he is in fact listening to the artless, unstruc-tured narrative of a simple peasant woman."

Just as he had infused the rhythm of the steel band and calypso into the language of the ordinary folk in *The Dragon Can't Dance*, Lovelace infuses the rhythm of the Trinidad dialect and the Baptist sermon into the language of Eva in *The Wine of Astonishment*. At times, this language reflects the spirit possession characteristic of the Baptist church. As he had done in his previous novel, he eschews grammatical convention and chooses to focus on capturing the rhythm of the Baptist religious service in his writing.

Bibliography

Cudjoe, Selwyn. "A Critical Analysis of the Works of Earl Lovelace." *Trinidad and Tobago Review* 6, no. 10 (1982): 14-15. Contends that the thrust of the novel is to counterpose the badjohn/warrior tradition to the intellectual/scholarly tradition. Criticizes Lovelace for not making a more comprehensive analysis of the social forces that cause the breakdown of the society. Faults the text for not adopting a socialist perspective to the problems of the society.
Green, Jenny. "Lovelace's *Wine of Astonishment*." *Trinidad and Tobago Review* 6,

no. 4 (1982). Points out that Lovelace deals with the significance of history and roots as well as the implications of social reliance on the intellectual. Lovelace is able to capture the voice of the people in his use of the language. Green sees the characters as symbols of forces at work in Trinidadian society.

Lowhar, Syl. "Ideology in *The Wine of Astonishment*: Two Views." *Trinidad and Tobago Review* 10, nos. 11-12 (1988): 41-43. Taking a historical approach to the novel, Lowhar sees the major events of the novel as having their parallels in the actual history of the society and explores the implications of these events.

Thorpe, Marjorie. "In Search of the West Indian Hero: A Study of Earl Lovelace's Fiction." In *Critical Issues in West Indian Literature: Selected Papers from West Indian Literature Conferences, 1981-1983*, edited by Erika Sollish Smilowitz and Roberta Quarles Knowles. Parkersburg, Iowa: Caribbean Books, 1984. Argues that the "search for a hero-figure establishes the basis of Earl Lovelace's four published novels." Insists that Lovelace makes the distinction between false heroes, whom the society esteems, and true hero-figures, whom the novelist celebrates.

——————. Introduction to *The Wine of Astonishment*, by Earl Lovelace. London: Heinemann, 1986. Notes the literary advantages of choosing Eva as a narrator of his novel. Argues that Lovelace focuses on the theme of betrayal. *The Wine of Astonishment* celebrates a people's struggle for freedom and dignity as human beings. It speaks to "the oppressed everywhere."

Roosevelt J. Williams

THE WOMEN OF BREWSTER PLACE

Author: Gloria Naylor (1950-   )
Type of work: Novel
Type of plot: Psychological realism
Time of plot: The second half of the twentieth century
Locale: The South and an unnamed Northern city resembling Boston
First published: 1982

> *Principal characters:*
> MATTIE MICHAEL, the protagonist early in the novel
> EVA TURNER, Mattie's mentor, the kindly woman who welcomed
>   Mattie to her home
> ETTA MAE JOHNSON, a friend of Mattie who gives her money and
>   supplies when she and her son are destitute
> KISWANA BROWNE, a college dropout and liberal activist
> LUCIELIA TURNER, Eva's daughter
> CORA LEE, a woman whose fixation on dolls is transferred to a
>   large number of children
> LORRAINE and THERESA, "the two," lesbians who attempt to find
>   in Brewster Place a refuge from prejudice
> BEN, an alcoholic janitor in Brewster Place
> C. C. BAKER, the macho leader of the alley gang

The Novel

The Women of Brewster Place is an unusual novel because of its structure. It consists of a prefatory Langston Hughes poem, a prologue ("Dawn") and epilogue ("Dusk"), six stories featuring a character through whose eyes readers see the action unfold, and a seventh story, "The Block Party," that brings many of the characters together in the violent destruction of a wall. The destruction, which occurs only in Mattie's dream, is followed by a short description of the day of the block party. Naylor has described the book as a collection of interconnected short stories, but they do form a novel. The short stories, which are connected by recurring characters, concern the principal characters who come together for Mattie's dream about the block party.

"Mattie Michaels," the first story, concerns her seduction by Butch Fuller, by whom she becomes pregnant; her beating by her father when she will not identify Butch as the father of her child; and her betrayal by Basil, her son, who skips bail, costing her the house she had put up for bond. The story, however, also concerns Eva Turner, her benefactor; Lucielia Turner, who is reared with Basil; and Etta Mae Johnson, her friend in Rock Vale, Tennessee, and in Brewster Place. Mattie's story concerns the events that led her to Brewster Place, and Etta's story provides a short summary of her life, including a series of affairs, flight from the law, and her drive to

Brewster Place in a stolen car. It focuses on her abortive romance with the Reverend Moreland Woods and the disillusioned aftermath. The two stories complement each other: In the first story, Etta helps Mattie, and in the second, Mattie heals Etta.

Kiswana's story provides a change of pace. Rather than coming from the South by necessity, she leaves her nearby suburban home of Linden Hills and chooses to live with "the poor," whom she plans to mobilize and help. Her mother's visit proves to be a revelation for her. Her mother provides her with "real" African American family history as opposed to the fashionable Ashanti print and name change that "Kiswana" has adopted. At the end of the story, she stares "at a woman [her mother] she had been and was to become." The mother-child bonding that occurs at the end of Kiswana's story is paralleled by the nurturing Mattie provides for Lucielia in the next story. After the accidental death of her child, Lucielia is intent upon death, but Mattie "rocks" Lucielia and heals her pain.

In Cora Lee's story, a well-intentioned but naïve Kiswana attempts another kind of healing, in this case intellectual, when she encourages Cora Lee to take her children to a Shakespeare play in order to uplift the family, to expose them to the "finer things in life." After the play is over, however, Cora Lee must return to Brewster Place and the "shadow" men who provide "the thing that felt good in the dark." "The Two" also concerns sexual exploitation, but in harsher, more graphic, violent terms. Lorraine and Theresa, two lesbians intent on escaping prejudice, threaten some of the women in Brewster Place, and Lorraine becomes the victim of rape by a local gang. Brutalized and near death, she mistakes Ben, her janitor friend, for one of the rapists and kills him.

These stories lead to the violence of "The Block Party," Mattie's dream about the Brewster Place women's violent destruction of the bloodstained brick wall where Lorraine was raped and fatally beaten. It is a symbol for the patriarchal oppression and violence that pervade the book. The reader discovers that the story is a dream when Naylor describes Mattie waking up and looking forward to the block party. The ending is enigmatic: Will the dream become a reality? Is retribution possible only in dreams?

The Characters

As the title suggests, Naylor's novel is about a community of women. Naylor writes of them, "Brewster Place became especially fond of its colored daughters as they milled like determined spirits among its decay, trying to make it a home." Although the undisputed leader of this community is Mattie, the women are presented as sisters who mentor, nurture, guide, and heal one another. With the exceptions of Kiswana and "the two," the women are refugees from the South, women for whom Brewster Place is both a literal and a figurative dead end.

Mattie holds the community and the novel together. Hers is the first story, and her dream concludes the novel. In her story, she is impregnated by Butch, beaten by her father, and betrayed by a son she had spoiled. What she learned from Eva, her mentor and benefactor, sustains her when she loses her home and moves to Brewster

Place. Naylor likens her situation to that of her plants: "All the beautiful plants that once had an entire sun porch for themselves in the home she had exchanged thirty years of her life to pay for would now have to fight for life on a crowded windowsill." Rather than feeling self-pity, Mattie fights for life but also aids the other women in Brewster Place.

She heals Etta, but her most significant act involves Lucielia, who seems determined to die after her baby's death. Mattie rocks her as a mother rocks a child, but the rocking transcends physical movement. It becomes a historical journey that traces the suffering of mothers and their children and finds Lucielia's hurt to be a "slight silver splinter" which, nevertheless, leaves a gaping hole when it is removed.

Although Mattie is the central character in the novel, she is not a major character in all the stories. Naylor seems intent on presenting a variety of women rather than a single character who would serve to represent all African American women. There are straight and lesbian women, lower- and middle-class women, rural and urban women, and young and old women in Brewster Place. These women minister to one another: Kiswana, for example, attempts to help Cora Lee and her children. Their dreams unite them in sisterhood: All, regardless of age, dream of Lorraine, "the tall yellow woman in the bloody green and black dress." Lucielia, who had been away, returns when she dreams of Ben, the wall, and "a woman who was supposed to be me, I guess." Lucielia's statement also refers to the identification of the women with each other. They all, through their own histories, empathize with Lorraine; and they all, even though in a dream, attack the wall.

Because the novel focuses on women, the men are essentially flat minor characters who are, with the exception of C. C. Baker and his gang, not so much villains as the product of selfishness and weakness. Eugene, the Reverend Woods, Butch, and Cora Lee's "shadow" men sexually exploit women without making any commitment. Basil betrays his mother and jumps bail because he is selfish. Even Mattie's father, who savagely beats her, is capable of physically tending to her when she is ill with scarlet fever. Although he loves her, he selfishly cannot accept what she has done to him. The members of C. C. Baker's gang are depicted differently, as vicious hoodlums able to deal with women only sexually and as disenfranchised youths with nothing to lose. Their violence is only the latest manifestation of the violence all the women have endured at the hands of men.

Themes and Meanings

Naylor's novel begins with a prologue, "Dawn." It is a short introduction to Brewster Place, which she personifies so that it almost becomes a character, an antagonist as well as the setting. Brewster Place is the "bastard child" of politicians and realtors, who "conceive it" in a "damp smoke-filled room." It is born just three months later (Naylor implies that its premature birth has malign long-term results), and its "baptism" occurs two years later. Cut off from the rest of the unidentified city by a wall, it "became a dead-end street." Both the wall and Ben, its first African American resident, become "fixtures," so that when Ben dies, the wall's destruction almost inevitably follows in Mattie's dream.

In the cramped space between the last building on Brewster Place and the brick wall is the alley that C. C. Baker and his gang consider to be their territory, their "stateroom, armored tank, and executioner's chamber." There Lorraine is brutally raped. Naylor's description of the gang implies that the rape, terrible as it is, pales in comparison to the violations perpetrated by a patriarchal political system. The gang will not be asked to bayonet Asian farmers, "scatter their iron seed from a B-52," or "stick a pole in the moon." All these images involve penetration, and one concerns ejaculation.

The women of Brewster Place are driven into a "dead end." There is no further refuge, so survival in the decaying neighborhood is the only viable course of action. People cannot endure passively forever, and Lorraine's death serves as the catalyst for Mattie's dream of retribution and revenge. In her dream, only the women participate in tearing down the wall, which has come, through the bloodstains, to represent violence against women. The likelihood of such action occurring other than in a dream is small. Etta's last words, "We're gonna have a party," may be an affirmation, but Naylor's epilogue, "Dusk," describes the abandonment of Brewster Place.

Critical Context

The Women of Brewster Place, Naylor's first novel, won the National Book Award in 1983. Employing what critic Kathryn Palumbo calls "female-defined imaging," the novel presents a circumscribed and circumscribing world from the perspective of several women, although one woman, Mattie, seems to exercise some control over the characters and over the narrative itself. The interconnecting stories foreshadow Naylor's larger structural concerns, as Naylor's novels themselves seem to be interconnected. Kiswana is from Linden Hills, the title of Naylor's second novel, about an African American neighborhood where middle-class people have sold themselves out to pursue the American Dream. Naylor's treatment of these two African American neighborhoods, so close geographically and so distant attitudinally, is unusual.

Several scholars have cited the many ties between *The Women of Brewster Place* and Ann Petry's *The Street* (1946), and in her emphasis on setting, Naylor resembles Toni Morrison. Besides the literary influences, there are political and cultural influences reflected in Naylor's work. In the years before the publication of *The Women of Brewster Place*, African Americans responded to patriarchal society's devaluation of women by affirming female virtues and the central position of women in their communities; in the years before the publication of *Linden Hills* (1985), social historians depicted the rise of an African American middle class. Naylor's novels reflect literary trends, contemporary social concerns, and changing racial attitudes.

Bibliography

Christian, Barbara. "Gloria Naylor's Geography: Community, Class, and Patriarchy in *The Women of Brewster Place* and *Linden Hills*." In *Reading Black, Reading Feminist: A Critical Anthology*, edited by Henry Louis Gates, Jr. New York: Me-

ridian, 1990. Contrasts the two worlds of Brewster Place and Linden Hills, regards Kiswana as the link between the novels, and places Naylor in a literary
context.

Fraser, Celeste. "Stealing B(l)ack Voices: The Myth of the Black Matriarchy and *The Women of Brewster Place.*" *Critical Matrix* 5 (Fall/Winter, 1989): 65-88. Reads Naylor's novel as a refutation of conservative political theory that calls for break-ing the power of the black matriarchy. Cites Naylor's refusal to depict a single uniform image of black women or black families in opposition to the monolithic image white politicians describe. Considers the novel to be an attack on patri-archy.

Kelly, Lori Duin. "The Dream Sequence in *The Women of Brewster Place.*" *Notes on Contemporary Literature* 21 (September, 1991): 8-10. Focuses on the blood on the brick wall, finding the blood to be a symbol of female experience (birth, menstruation, loss of virginity). Sees the dismantling of the wall as an expression of rage at women's collective experience with males.

Matus, Jill L. "Dream, Deferral, and Closure in *The Women of Brewster Place.*" *Black American Literature Forum* 24 (Spring, 1990): 49-64. Relates the novel to Hughes's prefatory poem about the "dream deferred," seeing the marginalized women in the last story as experiencing a cathartic dream of resistance followed by an affirmation of personal dreams.

Naylor, Gloria, and Toni Morrison. "A Conversation." *The Southern Review* 21 (Sum-mer, 1985): 567-593. Naylor maintains that she "bent over backwards not to have a negative image come through about the men" and that she focused on telling women's stories that had not been told enough in literature.

Pearlman, Mickey. "An Interview with Gloria Naylor." *High Plains Literary Review* 5 (Spring, 1990): 98-107. Concerns space and memory in Naylor's novels. Dis-cusses her graduate work at Yale and the conflict between writing and attending school.

Saunders, James Robert. "The Ornamentation of Old Ideas: Gloria Naylor's First Three Novels." *The Hollins Critic* 27 (April, 1990): 1-11. Compares *The Women of Brewster Place* to Ann Petry's *The Street* and notes that in both novels three gener-ations of men fail the protagonist. Observes that the two novels differ in their treatment of "sisterly love." Naylor's is the more optimistic portrait.

Wells, Linda, Sandra E. Bowen, and Suzanne Stutman. "'What Shall I Give My Children?' The Role of Mentor in Gloria Naylor's *The Women of Brewster Place* and Paule Marshall's *Praisesong for the Widow.*" *Explorations in Ethnic Studies* 13 (July, 1990): 41-60. Asserts that Naylor uses a series of mentors who are linked to other mentors by healing communal experiences. Sees Mattie Michael as the central consciousness and the moral agent in the novel. The negative image of men is seen as a product of their selfishness.

Thomas L. Erskine

THE XENOGENESIS TRILOGY

Author: Octavia E. Butler (1947-   )
Type of work: Novels
Type of plot: Science fiction
Time of plot: 250-350 years after a fictional holocaust on Earth
Locale: Space and Earth's Amazon Basin
First published: Dawn, 1987; *Adulthood Rites,* 1988; *Imago,* 1989

> *Principal characters:*
> LILITH IYAPO, the protagonist of *Dawn,* a black woman in her late
>   twenties who is selected as the mother of a new breed
> NIKANJ, a member of a third gender (an ooloi) who as a child is
>   assigned to instruct Lilith and to gather information from her
> AKIN, the protagonist of *Adulthood Rites,* the son of Lilith,
>   Nikanj, Joseph, and their Oankali mates, Ahajas and Dichaan
> AUGUSTINO (TINO) LEAL, a Hispanic human who in *Adulthood
>   Rites* becomes the mate of Lilith and Nikanj
> JODAHS, the protagonist of *Imago,* a construct child of Lilith,
>   Tino, and Nikanj
> AAOR, the pair-sibling of Jodahs, born of an Oankali mother

The Novels

In the *Xenogenesis* series, Octavia E. Butler tells a story of confrontation and accommodation between cultures. One of these cultures is made up of human beings; the other, of far more advanced extraterrestrials called Oankali. After a war devastated Earth and killed most of its inhabitants, the Oankali transported the survivors to their spaceship, where they observed the humans for some two and a half centuries, finally concluding that human nature is so badly flawed that human beings will destroy any world they inhabit. Sensibly, the Oankali refuse to let human beings reproduce their own kind. They are willing, however, to absorb the human species by mating with human beings, removing human flaws through genetic alteration, and using human genes in the production of new life forms. This means that the human beings in these novels are faced with a difficult choice: either to breed with aliens or to become extinct.

The first human to be offered this choice is a young black Californian, Lilith Iyapo. *Dawn* is her story. Even though it is a third-person narrative, the novel is dominated by Lilith's consciousness; the plot is moved and governed by her changes in attitude. The four parts of the novel, "Womb," "Family," "Nursery," and "The Training Floor," describe the major stages in Lilith's development.

After being reborn, or awakened from her drugged sleep, Lilith must learn to discard her human prejudices. Her first test is to learn to see beneath the reptilian exterior of her Oankali instructor Jdahya to his real wisdom and kindness. Then she can venture out to meet other members of his family, in particular his child Nikanj, who is an ooloi, a member of a third gender that heals illness and genetic defects as well as linking mates for sexual pleasure and generation. When Lilith helps Nikanj through its metamorphosis, she becomes even more closely bonded to it. Eventually, she becomes its mate.

The last two sections of the novel deal with Lilith's attempt to select and train other humans, persuading them to follow her example and mate with the Oankali. The experiment is not successful. Lilith's recruits attack her, wound Nikanj, and kill the gentle human Joseph Li-Chin Shing, whom both she and Nikanj love. Lilith manages to save Nikanj, but she is forced to realize that by expanding her own understanding she has alienated her own people.

The protagonist of *Adulthood Rites* is Akin, the first son born to Lilith, the dead Joseph, Nikanj, and her two Oankali mates. Akin is the first male human-born construct. Again, Octavia Butler tells her story in the third person, but as in *Dawn*, she concentrates on a single consciousness, in this case Akin's.

Adulthood Rites is divided into four sections, each of which is named for the place where the action occurs. In the first, "Lo," set in Lilith's colony on Earth, Akin is born and begins to gather knowledge. He meets the human Augustino Leal (Tino), a resister to the Oankali who changes his mind after meeting Lilith and Akin. Unfortunately, Akin is carried off by a raiding party, to be sold to childless humans.

In Phoenix, a settlement of resisters, Akin is bought by a kindly couple that cherishes and protects him. Akin becomes sympathetic to the humans and comes to believe that they should have their own colony and their own children.

After his family turns up to claim him, they send Akin to a third location, the homeship Chkahichdahk, so that he can learn about his Oankali heritage. There Akin persuades the Oankali to let humans settle on Mars, and when he goes back to Earth in "Home," he immediately takes his news to Phoenix, only to meet hostility from the hard-line resisters. At the end of the novel, Akin and his human friends escape from Phoenix and start off toward Lo, the embarkation point for the new colony on Mars.

Like *Adulthood Rites*, *Imago* is a tale of conflict and adventure. The protagonist and first-person narrator, Jodahs, is another of Lilith's children, an ooloi with Tino as the human father. While *Adulthood Rites* was a story of childhood and youth, *Imago* focuses on the passage into adulthood, which for Jodahs and its pair-sibling Aaor is destined to be particularly difficult.

When they realize that Jodahs is a human-born ooloi, Lilith and her family go into exile in the forest, where they can supervise Jodahs' development. They also hope to encounter humans who will agree to mate with Jodahs and with the Oankali-born Aaor, who is also an ooloi. Jodahs finds its humans easily, and after it cures them of their genetic disorder, they become bonded. In order to find mates for Aaor, however, the family members must enter a settlement of hostile humans. What could have been a massacre is avoided: When Jodahs heals them, the humans are won over. At the end of the novel, Jodahs is asked by the Oankali to plant a new town in the mountains of Earth.

The Characters

Butler's handling of characterization is particularly interesting because she deals not only with humans of all backgrounds but also with nonhumans. In fact, there are more sympathetic nonhumans than humans. Even Lilith, who has been chosen to be the mother of the new species, begins as a prejudiced and belligerent person. Because she is open-minded and sensitive, however, she eventually comes to understand beings so different from her own kind. Moreover, because she is at heart a nurturer, Lilith can love anyone who needs her. It is no accident that the Oankali assign to her an ooloi who is still a child or that she is allowed to help Nikanj through its metamorphosis. Her love for Nikanj, with a sound basis in her maternal response, later turns to passion and pleasure.

The most sympathetic humans in Butler's trilogy share these characteristics so marked in Lilith. All are willing to listen to reason, and all are sympathetic to the needs of others. They include Lilith's mates Joseph and Tino; her recruits, later Akin's foster parents, Gabriel and Tate Rinaldi; and Jesusa and Tomas Serrano y Martin, who give their loyalty and their love to Jodahs and Aaor.

On the other hand, the unsympathetic humans are closed-minded, self-centered, aggressive, and prone to violence. These are the qualities that cause Lilith to refuse to mate with Paul Titus, who hits her when he is rejected. These are also the characteristics seen in the predatory raiders who kidnap Akin and in the armed gangs that roam the forest, shooting everything and everyone they see. Perhaps the most revolting human character is the woman who is determined to have the tentacles cut off of captured girls so that she can think of them as her human children.

Because Butler's male and female Oankali are by definition perfect, they are not particularly interesting characters. Their function seems to be to explain and to reflect their society. It was important for Butler to make the ooloi Nikanj an appealing character so that Lilith's sexual commitment to it would be plausible and the Oankali system of mating acceptable to her readers. The author succeeds in making Nikanj one of the most sympathetic characters in the trilogy, as well as one of the most complex. Butler's technique is to show Nikanj first as a vulnerable child, then as an adult who, like the humans in the novels, must cope with new and puzzling situations. In *Dawn*, for example, Nikanj must discover how to please a human woman and, later, to entice a human man into its bed. In *Imago*, by having a same-sex child, it emerges from the loneliness that supposedly is the inevitable condition of its gender, and it must also find a way to keep that child from being removed from it, as Oankali law dictates.

The protagonists of the second and third books in this trilogy are fascinating because they both manage to overcome whatever defects of character might have come from their human ancestry. Both are on probation. Both prove to be courageous leaders who, because they have the Oankali intelligence, can think and argue clearly, but because they are part human, can understand the lesser species. Thus both the Oankali Akin and the ooloi Jodahs serve as bridges between the two cultures of their mixed heritage.

Themes and Meanings

In *Xenogenesis*, the author's ideas are stated explicitly, in the form of instruction to the uninformed, either by Oankali characters or by informed humans such as Lilith who agree with the Oankali point of view. The central theme of the trilogy is the existence of a flaw in human nature. This flaw is defined as possession of two irreconcilable characteristics, intelligence and a passion for hierarchy. Because they are hierarchical by nature, humans always try to exert their authority. Because they are intelligent, they are capable of doing great damage.

This drive for domination makes humans a violent people. Butler illustrates this human habit throughout the trilogy, for example in Paul Titus' physical attack on Lilith; in the raids, vandalism, and shootings; even in the sounds of threats and blows that are always heard in human villages. Despite the fact that violence destroyed Earth, humans do not seem to have changed. In sharp contrast is the Oankali's reverence for all living things.

The aggressiveness of humans also explains their dislike of anyone or anything that looks or acts different from them. Their answer to difference is either to destroy it or, like the would-be mother who wishes to cut off girls' tentacles, to force it into conformity. In *Adulthood Rites*, Akin recalls Lilith's explanation of a basic difference between humans and Oankali. Humans, she told him, fear difference, while Oankali search for it and embrace it. As a result, it is implied, humans stagnate while the Oankali constantly improve themselves and their lives. Their use of human cancer cells illustrates the Oankali method of absorbing the defects of others and putting them to positive use. Instead of rejecting the cancer cells they found in humans such as Lilith, the Oankali channeled them into a healing function, the reconstitution of destroyed or damaged body parts.

As conservative as they are, it is not surprising that humans are shocked by the three-gender sexual system of the Oankali. Butler's ingenious invention has important thematic implications. In her system, there is no male sexual domination. Instead, an enlightened ooloi controls both the male and the female, making impossible the manipulation, intimidation, and rape so common among humans. It is also notable that the Oankali family system, in which five adults serve as parents, provides the same kind of shared responsibility and emotional stability that is now often found in extended families in one location.

Finally, the author makes it clear that even the most considerate, least violent humans could learn intellectual flexibility from the Oankali, who are always willing to consider new suggestions, to modify their ideas, even on occasion to reverse their decisions. Their flexibility is illustrated by their agreeing to the colony on Mars. Even though they fear that humans will once again destroy themselves, the Oankali would rather give them another chance than close out the possibility of good. In a similar position of power, Butler's humans would hardly have been so generous.

Critical Context

Since the publication in 1976 of her first novel, *Patternmaster*, Octavia Butler has steadily gained in readership and in reputation. Venturing into a genre that, as she commented in an interview, originally was directed to adolescent white males, Butler uses her works to make serious statements not only about male-female relationships but also about power, slavery, and the African American experience.

Inevitably, the *Xenogenesis* trilogy has been compared to Butler's earlier Patternist series, which included *Patternmaster, Mind of My Mind* (1977), *Survivor* (1978), and *Wild Seed* (1980). The works have a number of themes in common; however, in *Xenogenesis* the mutations of the Patternist works are replaced by deliberate genetic alteration. Critics disagree about the implications of this difference. It may be related to what most agree is Butler's pessimism about the future of humanity, which seems doomed by what she admits is its inborn tendency toward hierarchical systems.

Feminist critics are also troubled with what they see as an approval of rape in *Xenogenesis*, pointing out that Lilith is invaded by the ooloi. In fact, she is also impregnated without her consent. The entire Oankali mating system is so exotic, however, that it is hard to classify the ooloi's function. It may well be that it is meant to substitute for assertive human males. In the sexual context, there is also some discussion of the absence or presence of homosexuality in the trilogy, but again, the unusual nature of the system Butler has invented makes it difficult to make any good argument on that matter.

Critics do agree that *Xenogenesis* is an admirable work. Its characters are memorable, and its themes are thought-provoking. It presents an experience not unlike a real visit to an unfamiliar culture, which one leaves as a somewhat different person.

Bibliography

Beal, Frances M. "Black Scholar Interview with Octavia Butler: Black Women and the Science Fiction Genre." *The Black Scholar* 17 (March/April, 1986): 14-18. A crucial interview in which Butler denies that her fiction is utopian, since she does not "believe that imperfect humans can form a perfect society," stressing their lethal combination of intelligence and hierarchical behavior. Butler comments extensively on the recent emergence of women as science fiction writers and also cites examples of the prejudice with which a black science fiction writer must deal.

Bonner, Frances. "Difference and Desire, Slavery and Seduction: Octavia Butler's *Xenogenesis.*" *Foundation: The Review of Science Fiction* 48 (Spring, 1990): 50-62. Although this essay has a feminist emphasis, it is a thorough and thoughtful analysis. Bonner discusses each theme of the series at length, comments on the relative importance of gender and race in the works, and argues the rape/seduction question intelligently and fairly. Includes helpful endnote references. Essential reading.

Newson, Adele S. Review of *Dawn* and *Adulthood Rites*, by Octavia E. Butler. *MELUS* 23 (Summer, 1989): 389-396. Comments that the works are important reading for African Americans, since the primary theme is the results of prejudice. Lilith is a prototype of the admirable African American woman, surviving in a situation not of her making. Unlike the first novel, Newson notes, *Adulthood Rites* has serious flaws such as weak characterization and prosiness.

Shinn, Thelma J. "The Wise Witches: Black Women Mentors in the Fiction of Octavia E. Butler." In *Conjuring: Black Women, Fiction, and Literary Tradition*, edited by Marjorie Pryse and Hortense J. Spillers. Bloomington: Indiana University Press, 1985. A good essay on the feminine archetypes in Butler's early work, arguing that her African American women provide hope for the future of humankind. Through them, society can learn to change its attitudes toward differences and toward power and politics.

Zaki, Hoda M. "Utopia, Dystopia, and Ideology in the Science Fiction of Octavia Butler." *Science Fiction Studies* 17 (July, 1990): 239-251. Disagrees with Butler's denials of feminism and utopianism made in the 1986 interview with Frances M. Beal and argues that there are both utopian and, admittedly, dystopian elements in Butler's fiction. Her feminism differs from that of female science fiction writers who are not black; at times her works seem more a critique of most feminist utopian science fiction than an affirmation of it.

Rosemary M. Canfield Reisman

YEARNING
Race, Gender, and Cultural Politics

Author: Bell Hooks (Gloria Watkins)
Type of work: Essays
First published: 1990

Form and Content

Writer Bell Hooks has been in the forefront of African American feminist theory since the early 1980's, and she continues with her groundbreaking work here. *Yearning* is the fourth of her feminist theory books, following *Ain't I a Woman: Black Women and Feminism* (1981), *Feminist Theory: From Margin to Center* (1984), and *Talking Back: Thinking Feminist, Thinking Black* (1989). She wrote her first volume while an undergraduate at Stanford University. It was the result of research she did when she found little about black women in her women's studies courses. *Yearning* is an outgrowth of her involvement with cultural criticism and her concern that African American women are not significant in this field. She believes that cultural criticism is vital: It is interdisciplinary, and the best of its feminism includes perspectives of race and class.

The title *Yearning* suggests a "longing" across lines of race, class, gender, and sexual practice. All groups, believes Hooks, share a desire for radical social change. This shared "yearning" opens up a common ground where all people might meet and engage one another. For epigrams for her book, Hooks quotes four writers, all of whom speak of "yearning": Lydia, a Salvadoran woman; Cornel West, a male African American cultural critic who teaches at Princeton; Robert Duncan, a white male poet; and Tayeb Salib, an Egyptian writer. Neither separatist nor exclusive, Hooks has thus included Third World women and men as well as white and African American men.

Most of these short essays were published previously in such alternative magazines as *Zeta*, *Sojourner*, and *Emerge*. Publication in this volume brings a wider audience. Many of the essays are reviews of films or dramatic productions—the 1988 television production of Lorraine Hansberry's *A Raisin in the Sun* (1959), Spike Lee's film *Do the Right Thing* (1989), Euzan Palcy's film about South Africa, *A Dry White Season* (1989), the film version of Alice Walker's *The Color Purple* (1985) and the controversy it sparked in the black community about the sexism of black men, and Isaac Julien's 1989 short film *Looking for Langston*, about Langston Hughes's closeted homosexuality. In all of these, Hooks takes a "counter-hegemonic" (or oppositional) view of the work. Throughout, she is concerned to note that African Americans must work on their own self-actualization, their own autonomy. They must no longer be objects or "Others." They must be subjects.

Hooks's manifesto, which lays out her political agenda, is found in two succinct paragraphs buried in her essay "Radical Black Subjectivity." The characteristics are these: She believes in leftist politics and ending domination wherever it exists in the world, and she believes in remaining on the margins, the borders, of various cultures, but she is not afraid of losing her "blackness." She is "one of the people, while simultaneously acknowledging our privileges." She is working class and continues to claim her ties and roots to that part of the population. She believes in the primacy of identity politics, but she rejects essentialist notions that make assumptions on the basis of birth. She is in solidarity with both black men and black women but wants dialogue, so that dissent can be accepted without violating anyone. She believes in living simply and is concerned about the planet. She wants to conserve traditional black aesthetics.

Censorship, not in terms of First Amendment rights but in terms of ideological, political, and market factors, is a constant theme. She worries that manuscripts are rejected on the basis of not being able to sell, on the basis of being too radical, or for being concerned with "feminist stuff" or "the race thing." These kinds of censorship are never acknowledged as such in American society.

Black writers should be able to use different styles in their own way. She describes Cornel West's scholarly presentations, often given in the style of black preachers. He involves nonacademic members of the audience, making central "a marginal aspect of black cultural identity." She herself often gives presentations in the black storytelling mode. Both she and West have been criticized for presenting "mere" entertainment. She says, "*WE must determine* what style to use; we must not utilize just the methods of the majority." Speakers and writers must choose practices from their own identities and heritage. She would like to make her abstract, fragmented, nonlinear style central in her own work, but this kind of writing is constantly rejected by editors and publishers, who say that it will not sell or that this is not what they think black women should be writing.

Hooks insists, especially in the essay called "Postmodern Blackness," that "racism is perpetuated when blackness is associated solely with concrete gut level experience" that is not connected to abstract thinking. White male intellectuals are those doing most of the publishing and speaking in the field of cultural criticism. This is partly because the Black Power movement of the 1960's had mainly a "modernist universalizing agenda" that assumed single explanations.

Another and more important reason for the lack of African Americans in this dialogue, says Hooks, is that Third World elites and white critics, both male and female, have assumed to speak for underclass people of color. According to Hooks, the postmodernist antagonism to identity politics is misplaced, and the "master narratives" need to be replaced by listening. An example is rap music, which is a kind of critical voice, a form of empowerment. The hopeful side of postmodernism is that many other groups share with black people "the sense of 'deep alienation, despair, uncertainty, loss of sense of grounding.'" Hooks wants to give credence to multiple black identities and challenge one-dimensional colonialist attitudes that reinforce stereotypes of "the primitive" and "the natural." "Not black enough," "Miss White," "has no soul"—these denigrations assume an essentialism that Hooks decries. Why can we not as black people, she asks, accept different black identities?

Her assessment of cultural critics' discussions about "difference" is related. She asks who controls this new "difference" discourse (as it is called). Who gets hired? Who gets published? Who gets the grants? She maintains that the discussion of "difference" and "Otherness" is always from the perspective of "Whiteness." Why not interrogate whiteness? she asks. "Otherness" is always "that which is not white"; it is never discussed from the perspective of the "not white." The work of white scholars, she maintains, is overvalued. Few nonwhite scholars are being awarded grants for work on "difference"; they are passed over as being "too angry." It must be noted, however, that since the publication of *Yearning*, Hooks has been recognized by a mainstream publisher and has signed a three-book contract with Routledge. Thus, she will be able to publish her autobiography and other less scholarly works.

Many readers will respond most positively to the essays that narrate her early childhood in rural Kentucky, even when her point is the conservative one of showing how school desegregation destroyed black community and black culture, the world of black schools. Why didn't we, she asks, talk about what we would be losing in the discussions over desegregation in the South? The "chitlin' circuit"—that network of black folks who knew each other and supported each other—was broken in the black community by desegregation, urbanization, and the establishment of government programs.

"Homeplace: A Site of Resistance" uses her grandmother's house as a metaphor. Black women for generations have made their homes the place of resistance, the spot that enables everyone to go back out and face the racism of society. "Homeplace" is a place for renewal and self-recovery. This locus of struggle is shared with women of color elsewhere in the world, most especially in South Africa. Only in the 1960's did the strong black woman first begin to be denigrated in the struggle over "black matriarchy" as the "cause" of the breakdown of the black family and a threat to black manhood. This idea was taken up by parts of the black community, with calls for black women to be submissive to black men, not only in the Nation of Islam but also within the Black Power movement.

The essay "Sitting at the Feet of the Messenger: Remembering Malcolm X" is a spiritual tribute, based on a rereading of *The Autobiography of Malcolm X* (1965). Hooks does not review the 1992 film *Malcolm X*, with its emphasis on politics and the "great man theory of history." The passage in the book that describes Malcolm's struggle over kneeling to Allah is much more powerful in the text than in the film; this is one passage that Hooks analyzes. Her emphasis is on spirituality, not plot and action. Still, she must be pleased by the media attention given to this hero nearly three decades after his death.

In "Third World Diva Girls," Hooks discusses the politics of feminist solidarity. She claims that female scholars from India, Africa, or East Asia play the role of "interpreter" from African Americans to the white world and often demean African Americans in the process. Without naming names, Hooks calls for a positive critique (called "signifying" in the black community); she abhors both trashing on one hand and uncritical acceptance of every negative point on the other.

Analysis

The analysis of sexism in the black community is one of Hooks's strongest themes. She observes that black male sexism is analyzed differently from white male sexism; popular assumptions in the "liberal" establishment that racism is more oppressive to black men than to black women are based on the acceptance of patriarchal notions of masculinity. These, she notes again and again, are life-threatening to black men. The continuing argument over sexism versus racism misses the point of the interlocking nature of oppressions: They cannot be ranked.

Her stance between various points of view—between black and white, between positions in the black community, between positions in the feminist community—is a foundation of her political belief. This view has characterized her work at least from the time of *Feminist Theory: From Margin to Center*. In *Yearning*, however, she is clearer about the choice to stay on the boundary: "Understanding marginality as position and place of resistance is crucial for oppressed, exploited, colonized people."

The critique of *Writing Culture: The Poetics and Politics of Ethnography* (1986), edited by James Clifford and George Marcus, provides a practical example of the kind of analysis done by cultural critics. Hooks's assessment, which focuses on the omission of articles by non-Western or feminist theorists, spotlights the cover as an ironic visual metaphor for the position of the book. The cover reproduces a photograph of a white male fieldworker taking notes on darker-skinned people who watch him from a distance. Although the brown man seems to be watching with admiration, the brown woman's face is blocked by the graphics of the cover. Although the book itself critiques the traditional exploitative stance of the anthropologist, the cover seems to undercut that critique by reinscribing or reinforcing the colonialist power position.

The cover of *Yearning* also lends itself to analysis, especially considering Hooks's critique of the cover of *Writing Culture*. The image on *Yearning*'s cover appears to be a portion of a nineteenth century etching, in which a barefoot darker-skinned woman, seated on an oriental carpet, tells the fortune of a white woman, lying on a couch above her. The darker-skinned woman is wearing a loose jacket, open to show her cleavage; loose pants with her legs crossed above her bare feet; scarf; and earrings. She is holding out a card to the lighter-skinned woman. More cards are spread around her. The lighter-skinned woman, dressed in white, reclines on pillows. In this image, the darker-skinned woman is made to seem a sexual object (on the floor, breasts showing, begging), while the lighter-skinned woman's position is literally higher (arms and chest covered, eyes downcast, passive). But to whom is the darker woman a sexual object? To the white woman? Or to the audience of the etching, playing out a stereotyped notion of the exotic Other? The lighter woman is no less stereotyped: The passive lady, on a couch instead of a pedestal, constricted by corsets and clothing, is taking no active role in public life. Although the cover almost certainly shows a colonial scene from Turkey or Egypt, it could just as likely stand

for the situation of the Southern United States during slavery—house slave entertaining plantation mistress.

Read in a different way, the cover could also be saying that the darker woman is
prophesying a different future to the white woman, a more egalitarian one in which
the colonial world of which the white woman is a part will be overturned by the
"underside of history." Perhaps both women are "yearning" for a radical change to
their very different oppressive situations.

In all this discussion of cover images undermining ideas of the book, Hooks has
not recognized the market forces that usually preclude the author's choice or even
approval of the cover. Thus, seeing significance in the cover should perhaps be prefaced by a recognition of the prevailing system. In this particular case, according to
South End Press's editorial department, Hooks herself helped to choose the cover.

Critical Context

Yearning is unique among African American feminist works in its understanding of
the necessary many-sidedness of African American women. Hooks "firmly resists,"
says P. Gabrielle Foreman in her important review in *The Women's Review of Books*,
"any homogenizing notion of black essence." Hooks manages to stay on the boundary
("choosing the margins," she would say) in the various controversies among African
Americans and among cultural critics of whatever race about identity politics and
essentialism. Refusing to espouse only one position—that race is constructed by social and historical context or that race is a biological reality—she forces all sides,
including the academic cultural critics and the political cultural nationalists, to participate in dialogue. Her work continually refuses absolutes; she therefore has been
dismissed as assimilationist. As she clearly says, however, "We cannot participate in
dialogue that is the mark of freedom and critical agency if we dismiss all work
emerging from white western traditions."

A second reason for the importance of Hooks as an African American theorist is
her insightful judgment of those who continue to read African American writers
only for race issues, "while whiteness remains," says Susan Bordo in *Feminist Studies*, "unproblematized, unexamined, constructed as *no* race at all." The ability of
Hooks to understand and use the language of the postmodern theorists while at the
same time pointing to their weaknesses is one of her greatest strengths. Although
Hooks reiterates Audre Lorde's assertion that "The master's tools will never dismantle the master's house," it may be necessary to use the master's discourse to
move to the place where different tools (style, language, genre) will be usefully
heard. This is the meaning of Hooks's repeated call for a new aesthetic of blackness,
one that arises from the history and culture of African Americans, that calls on the
rich traditions of storytelling, preaching, and "signifying" (positive criticism) in the
black community.

Bibliography

Bordo, Susan. "Postmodern Subjects, Postmodern Bodies." *Feminist Studies* 18

(Spring, 1992): 159-175. An important scholarly review essay that relates Hooks's work to that of other academic postmodernists and shows how she is both participant and observer of the contemporary condition.

Burford, Barbara. "Review of *Yearning.*" *New Statesman and Society* 3 (November 30, 1990): 39. Reviews the book's "black womanist" perspective from the vantage point of England.

Donovan, Josephine. *Feminist Theory: The Intellectual Traditions of American Feminism.* New York: Frederick Ungar, 1985. Puts Hooks's early feminist theory in the context of other radical feminists.

Foreman, P. Gabrielle. "The Racism of Postmodernism." *The Women's Review of Books* 8 (September, 1991): 12-13. Analyzes the importance of Hooks's critique of postmodernism and her refusal to succumb to strident diatribes against identity politics and anti-essentialism. Critiques her occasional deference to white feminists.

Hooks, Bell, and Cornel West. *Breaking Bread: Insurgent Black Intellectual Life.* Boston: South End Press, 1991. Chapters on Hooks give much biographical information as well as exploring Hooks's scholarly and activist goals, her intellectual influences, and her hopes and dreams.

Walker, Rebecca. "A Political Homeplace." *Ms.* 1 (January/February, 1991): 62-63. Applauds Hooks for her "critical yet supportive" model of understanding diversity and analyzes the book's varied audiences, both scholarly and activist.

Margaret McFadden

YELLOW BACK RADIO BROKE-DOWN

Author: Ishmael Reed (1938-   )
Type of work: Novel
Type of plot: Satire
Time of plot: Primarily the nineteenth century
Locale: The imaginary town of Yellow Back Radio, near Video Junction
First published: 1969

Principal characters:
> LOOP GAROO KID, the plot's "hero," who battles relentlessly
>   against the forces of conventionality and orthodoxy
> DRAG GIBSON, a wealthy white landowner
> BO SHMO, a vigilante leader and Loop's ruthless enemy
> CHIEF SHOWCASE, the Indian who befriends Loop
> MUSTACHE SAL, a parody of a middle-class white feminist
> SKINNY MCCULLOUGH, a cowpoke who sells his soul for part of
>   Drag's power

The Novel

Yellow Back Radio Broke-Down is at once Reed's revelation of his new aesthetic, called "Neo-HooDooism," and his answer to some of his most acerbic critics, both white and African American. Reed constantly averts generic expectations in the novel, so it is difficult to define the work with any precision. It is a cowboy story that overturns the traditions of the television Western, a science-fiction/fantasy novel about real-life politics during the 1960's, and a historical novel that denies the accepted meanings of Euro-American history. Reed's novel shocks the reader into revising entirely a traditional worldview founded on conventional assumptions about race, art, sex, and morality.

The incident that generates the plot occurs when the nefarious Drag hires assassins to attack the children who have gained control of Yellow Back Radio. The children dream of the Seven Cities of Cibola, the utopian paradise that lured Spanish conquistadores in the fifteenth century. Drag, concerned that the profoundly democratic dreams of the children will disrupt his regime, orders his men to slaughter them. They also kill Zozo Labrique, a member of a visiting carnival and the HooDoo priestess that founded the HooDoo church. Before she dies, she gives her friend Loop a "mad dog's tooth." She has taught him all he knows about "wangols" (spells and enchantments), so it is his responsibility to avenge her death.

At this point, the novel's action dissolves into a bewildering series of incidents in which Loop is challenged to demonstrate his heroism within a HooDoo context. In essence, the characters fight a war of ideas. For example, Loop is immediately contested by Bo Shmo. Bo's quarrel with Loop concerns the political significance of art, not the importance of property, yet Bo and Drag are alike in seeking absolute power. The contest, then, is between Loop's imaginative freedom and Bo's regimented control. When Loop refuses to yield to Bo's demand for a politicized, mundane, "realistic" novel, Bo buries him in sand. Loop is rescued by Chief Showcase, who in Euripidean fashion appears in the sky as a *deus ex machina* in his helicopter. Showcase becomes Loop's secret ally for the rest of the novel, as he, like Loop, rejects a Eurocentric worldview.

Back at the ranch—Reed's novel is replete with such clichés of the Western melodrama—Drag is sadly contemplating the dissolution of his marriage, wishing for heirs—"nice obedient progeny." His wife, a ghastly parody of science-fiction characters, is a "Various Arrangement of Dead Parts," so Drag cannot expect progeny from her. She is a parody of the American middle-class wife. He shoots her, then advertises for a new wife who enjoys variety in sexual practices.

As Loop's chief antagonist, Drag has two main motivations in the novel: to find a wife who will give him children and to destroy the threat that both Loop and children represent. Drag's chief value in the novel is stability ("law and order") that will solidify his vast property holdings. He therefore frustrates the vital powers of life that Loop, as an African American experimental artist, and "flower children" represent. As proof of legality, Drag continually prints "stiffycates" (certificates) that provide bogus evidence of ownership, marriage, and authority; these only rationalize his domination.

The first signal of Loop's mystical power in his war against the rancher is the intense itching that Loop inflicts upon Drag. Loop gradually destroys Drag's power. Before he escalates his war, however, Loop performs a "micro-Hoo-Doo mass," in which he calls on Legba, a *loa* (African spirit), to end "two thousand years of bad news." His prayer summarizes the artistic goal of Reed's Neo-HooDooism: "please do open up some of these prissy orthodox minds so that they will no longer call Black People's American experience 'corrupt' 'perverse' and 'decadent.' "

As Drag's illness increases in severity, he weds his second wife, Mustache Sal, who is eventually seduced by Chief Showcase. Next, he meets two longtime associates, Lewis and Clark, who are busy exploring western America and who report to Drag on drums that seem to be a threat to his ranch. Drag confides to them that he is under a hex from Loop, and his resolve to stop Loop intensifies.

Loop, however, is invincible. He defeats both the town marshal and the preacher, Drag's "establishment" conspirators, using only his whip. Loop's next opponent is the legendary killer John Wesley Hardin, who is on a religious crusade against black America. Loop kills him with a white python. Loop warns Drag that he cannot win with mercenaries and slowly rides out of town, his white python in his saddlebags.

Drag's final mercenary, called in desperation, is the pope. The pope has his own purpose for stopping Loop, since Loop represents a threat to the wealth of Christendom. The pope reveals the HooDoo source of Loop's power and recommends to Drag that they bribe Loop's friends to betray him. Loop is captured and taken to Drag for the final showdown. In a jailhouse interview, the pope pleads with Loop to join forces with Catholicism. When Loop refuses, the pope in dejection returns to the Vatican.

The novel's climax occurs, as in many Westerns, at the gallows, where Loop is to die. Drag gloats, confident in his victory, and calls all the villagers of Yellow Back Radio to witness Loop's final humiliation. Reed's conclusion parodies the traditional Western rescue scene. The children arrive in a Chicken Delight truck, announcing that the Seven Cities of Cibola have been discovered, then Theda Blackwell, the government leader, proclaims the arrest of Drag Gibson. Drag's men, paralyzed by the ray guns drawn by government officials, cannot help, so Drag challenges Theda to a gunfight. Drag accidentally falls off the scaffold to his death, eaten by "greedy and unnatural" pigs that await him.

With Drag dead, the government destroyed, and all the "common folk" gone to the Seven Cities of Cibola, Loop feels "cheated out of his martyrdom." He rides away on Drag's green horse, in an effort to catch up with the pope.

The Characters

A reader expecting a conventional set of characters will be disappointed. Although the plot seems to be fashioned after the conventional "horse opera," Reed twists and turns the action so as to make the traditional outline of the Western almost indecipherable. It is as if by caricaturing the basic premises of an indigenous narrative form Reed also calls into question fundamental ideas about American culture.

The two main characters, Drag Gibson and Loop Garoo, are the "bad guy" and "good guy." Their characterization depends upon the categories of meanings they represent rather than on their intrinsic, "realistic" personal traits. The two characters act in ways consistent with the sets of values they symbolize. Drag is villainous because he represents a constellation of values antithetical to Reed's Neo-Hoodooism. Drag symbolizes property, capitalism, legalism, materialism, rationality, and hypocritical restraint, identified by Reed with the white establishment. Everything that Drag does or says, then, must be seen in the context of Reed's argument against establishment values.

In contrast, Loop symbolizes the liberation Reed posits in Neo-Hoodooism: imagination, freedom, creativity, and joy. Loop's magic (his art) is dependent upon his intuitive sense of life's possibilities and upon his connection to African religion. Significantly, his *loa* (spirit) is Legba, "master of the crossroads," who was given the gift of languages and who acts as an intermediary between God and humanity.

The pope's character is also defined by his symbolic significance. He represents not only Reed's sense of the dogmatic inflexibility of the church but also the immense wealth the Vatican controls, thus linking him to Drag's character. Reed satirically implies a Mafia connection with the Vatican. In the pope, spirituality is depleted; force and deception are his only attributes. Loop, the priest of African religion, is presented as an obvious alternative to Christianity, which Reed sees as corrupt and lifeless.

As might be expected, Reed's characterization is highly controversial. Many readers, for example, are offended by his novel's women, who are mindlessly searching for sexual gratification, or by what appears to be Reed's homophobic denunciation of gay life. Other readers defend Reed on the grounds that he is writing a satire, not "realistic" fiction, and that to interpret Mustache Sal, for example, as Reed's definitive comment on women is to misunderstand the novel.

Themes and Meanings

Early in the novel, when Loop debates Bo Shmo, Reed makes Loop his mouthpiece:

No one says a novel has to be one thing. It can be anything it wants to be, a vaudeville show, the six o'clock news, the mumblings of wild men saddled by demons.

This statement encapsulates Reed's central theme: A work of art must not be restricted by any a priori concept of the "poetic"; art can be "anything." Because all experience has a poetic dimension, the novelist can include virtually any material in a novel. Reed himself says that his novel was partly inspired by a poem about plumbing repair manuals. The novelist—particularly the African American, who is often told by others what to write—should feel no obligation to choose a specific subject or political theme.

As if to demonstrate his theme, the narrative is controlled not by probabilities and likelihoods established by characters and action, as in realistic plots, but by Reed's imaginative quirkiness. His novel resembles the "ready-mades" of Dadaist art: new and unexpected combinations of objects. His narrative shifts according to unpredictable and startlingly improbable moments in the action. For example, Bo says that Loop "can't create the difference between a German and a redskin"; as if to prove Bo wrong, Germans, acting much like film "redskins," attack and burn down Yellow Back Radio. In another example, Drag says a thing is "not worth a green horse's dream"; soon, the narrative point of view plunges into the nightmare of Drag's green stallion. Later, giant sloths stampede Drag's cattle herd. The entire plot advances Reed's theme that anything, from giant sloths to green mustangs to man-eating pigs, can be considered aesthetically pleasing.

Related to Reed's aesthetic theme is his satiric attack on Western culture. Drag and Loop's conflict symbolizes a confrontation between white culture, which often denies the validity of African American experience, and Reed's "Neo-HooDooism." From Reed's perspective, white culture attempts to disqualify black art as meaningful because it lacks "universality" and "beauty" according to an exclusively Euro-American standard. In contrast, Reed's Neo-HooDoo hero delights in the wonderful potential of language, of invoking through language a sense of the mysterious presence of the immanent divinity of humanity. Loop's power as artist transcends Drag's dependence on "mainstream" culture. When Loop defeats Drag, Reed by implication celebrates a greater inclusivity in America, an openness that recognizes the beauty of any experience, regardless of race.

Critical Context

This novel is an important transitional work between Reed's *The Free-Lance Pall-bearers* (1967), which sketches the outline of the Neo-HooDoo aesthetic, and *Mumbo Jumbo* (1972), in which he presents a mythic history of African American culture.

Reed has been judged harshly by several African American critics, and in many ways his novels are his response. Bo Shmo, for example, is a thinly disguised embodiment of the Black Arts movement of the 1960's. Bo says, "All art must be for the end of liberating the masses. A landscape is only good when it shows the oppressor hanging from a tree." This alludes to Amiri Baraka. Because Reed rejects the prescriptive nature of Baraka's criticism, he and Baraka have waged critical battles throughout their careers.

Reed is also attacked by feminists, especially African American feminists. Believing that black women writers too often portray black men negatively, Reed retaliates by making his female characters either lesbians or sexually promiscuous, a strategy that feminists understandably find deplorable.

Yellow Back Radio Broke-Down must be seen in the historical context of the 1960's, when African American literature was "rediscovered" by academia, when the Black Arts movement insisted on the political functionality of black literature, and when feminists protested the outrage of male chauvinism. Also significant for the novel are the "law and order" administration of President Lyndon Johnson and the "Flower Power" and Free Speech movements of Berkeley, California. Reed satirizes all these targets.

Bibliography

Fabre, Michel. "Postmodernist Rhetoric in Ishmael Reed's *Yellow Back Radio Broke Down."* In *The Afro-American Novel Since 1960: A Collection of Critical Essays,* edited by Peter Bruck and Wolfgang Karrer. Amsterdam: B. R. Brüner, 1982. The best discussion of the novel to date. Fabre scrupulously analyzes the rhetorical strategies Reed employs in the novel. Fabre also links the novel to a discussion of postmodernist experiments.

Fox, Robert Elliot. "Blacking the Zero: Toward a Semiotics of Neo-HooDoo." *Black American Literature Forum* 18 (1984): 95-99. Although this is a difficult article because of the technical language of contemporary literary criticism, Fox's discussion of the African background of Reed's Neo-HooDooism is valuable. Fox explains that Reed's motif of the blackened circle beside the empty circle is central to Reed's artistic vision.

——————. *Conscientious Sorcerers: The Black Postmodernist Fiction of LeRoi Jones/Amiri Baraka, Ishmael Reed, and Samuel R. Delany.* New York: Greenwood Press, 1987. Fox places Reed in the context of recent African American experimental novelists and gives a brief discussion of *Yellow Back Radio Broke-Down.* Fox argues that Loop's real adversary is the pope and discusses the pope's function in the novel.

Martin, Reginald. *Ishmael Reed and the New Black Critics.* New York: St. Martin's

Press, 1988. Martin places Reed within the context of African American literary history, especially the conflict between Reed and the "black aesthetic" of Amiri Baraka. Martin also defines Reed's Neo-HooDoo aesthetic.

Reed, Ishmael. "Ishmael Reed on Ishmael Reed." *Black World* 23 (June, 1974): 20-34. An essential article for understanding Reed's perspective. The interview focuses on the literary intentions of *Yellow Back Radio Broke-Down*. Reed explains that the meaning of "Yellow Back," for example, derives from nineteenth century Eastern hack writers who wrote "dime Westerns," called "yellow backs."

Schmitz, Neil. "Neo-Hoodoo: The Experimental Fiction of Ishmael Reed." *Twentieth Century Literature* 20 (April, 1974): 129-138. Schmitz discusses Reed's experimental fiction and argues that *Yellow Back Radio Broke-Down* degenerates into polemics. The proselytizing for HooDooism unacceptably slows the novel's action.

Gary Storhoff

YOUR BLUES AIN'T LIKE MINE

Author: Bebe Moore Campbell (1950-   )
Type of work: Novel
Type of plot: Social realism
Time of plot: The 1950's through the 1980's
Locale: Rural Mississippi and Chicago, Illinois
First published: 1992

> *Principal characters:*
> ARMSTRONG TODD, a fifteen-year-old African American boy from
>   Chicago
> DELOTHA TODD, his mother
> WYDELL TODD, his father
> LILY COX, a young white woman from a poor family
> FLOYD COX, Lily's husband, owner of a pool hall and bar
>   patronized by African Americans
> CLAYTON PINOCHET, a newspaper publisher
> IDA LONG, a small, young, black woman; heir to the Pinochet
>   fortune

The Novel

The most important incident that occurs in *Your Blues Ain't Like Mine* is the murder of Armstrong Todd, an innocent black boy, by three ignorant and despicable whites. This tragedy occurs early in a novel that spans three decades. The author's primary focus is on the long-lasting results of that tragedy in the lives of the survivors.

Campbell begins her novel by tracing the events that lead up to Armstrong's death. When Lily Cox unwisely enters the pool hall owned by her husband Floyd, she makes it possible for the black bartender, Jake, to plant in Floyd's mind the idea that somehow Armstrong has directed a French phrase toward Lily. Later, when Jake makes sure that Floyd's father and brother hear about the episode, Armstrong's fate is sealed. The three Coxes find Armstrong alone, beat him, and give Floyd the honor of shooting him.

In the next two chapters, Campbell moves the scene to Chicago in order to show Delotha Todd, Armstrong's mother, as the pretty, high-spirited woman she was before she had to deal with her son's death. She feels vaguely guilty about enjoying a respite from parental responsibility. Wydell Todd is also thinking about his son, but he is too drunk to concentrate on that subject or anything else.

The next section of the novel deals with the immediate aftermath of the murder. Black customers stop patronizing Floyd's bar, thus costing the bartender his job and Floyd his business. The town's businessmen are worried primarily about the image of Hopewell. The Coxes are worried about being punished, particularly after the businessmen decide that Floyd will make a good scapegoat. Thanks in part to Lily's perjured testimony, however, Floyd is acquitted, and even though Hopewell has become polarized, the community pretends to go back to normal.

It is a tribute to Campbell's artistry that the characters she has presented in these early, fast-paced chapters are interesting enough to maintain suspense throughout the rest of the book, when the author proceeds more deliberately, often skipping a year or several years between chapters. During the longest segment of the novel, Campbell moves back and forth among the major characters, following their lives until it becomes obvious what the future holds for all of them.

Floyd Cox goes steadily downhill, dragging Lily with him. After losing his business, Floyd is forced to take menial jobs. He starts drinking, picks fights, and finally steals, thus incurring the first of several prison sentences. For a time, he enjoys the company of Floyd, Jr., who like his father blames his failures on the black race, but that association ends abruptly when Floyd discovers that his son is stealing from him in order to buy drugs. Meanwhile, Lily has endured desperate poverty during Floyd's absences and brutal abuse whenever he is present.

The other weak male in the novel, Clayton Pinochet, has always been aware of his own deficiencies, but unlike Floyd, he finally comes to terms with them. After Armstrong's death, he begins tutoring young African Americans so that they will be able to succeed. Although he cannot do anything about the abortions forced on both of the socially inferior women he loved, he does make it possible for his black mistress Marguerite to leave him and go to college. He even withdraws his objections to Ida inheriting her share of the Pinochet property.

Prompted by Armstrong's murder, Ida has made a heroic effort to get her own son out of Mississippi, only to be trapped in Hopewell by her duties to her foster father. Providence seems to take a hand in her destiny. After her foster father's death, she discovers in his papers a picture that proves her to be Stonewall Pinochet's daughter and thus heir to a portion of the Pinochet wealth.

Armstrong's death could have proven as disastrous for his parents as it did for Floyd and Lily Cox. Both of them are driven nearly mad by grief. Delotha starts a journey to Mississippi to kill her son's murderers but changes her mind; Wydell drinks until he has to be hospitalized. After Delotha rescues him, however, the two begin a new life together. They open a beauty shop, they have daughters, and finally they have another son, whom they name Wydell Henry Todd, Jr. Soon after his birth, it becomes evident how seriously Armstrong's death has damaged Delotha. Obsessed by this son, she excludes her daughters and her husband from her life, eventually driving Wydell back to alcohol. When she realizes that the son she has indulged and pampered has become involved in a street gang, she has to call upon Wydell. In the dramatic conclusion of the novel, Wydell puts away his bottle, picks up his son, and takes him to Mississippi, where he can learn about his own people and his own heritage.

The Characters

Although *Your Blues Ain't Like Mine* is a third-person narrative, Campbell does not write as an omniscient narrator. Instead, she works from within the mind of one character after another, describing events as each character perceives them and at the same time revealing the thoughts and memories of that character. From the opening scene, in which Lily wonders about her own response to the plantation workers' songs she hears in the distance, to the final one, in which Wydell realizes that he has broken through to his rebellious son, the most important actions in the novel occur inside the minds of the characters.

Each of Campbell's characters begins with an inheritance. Lily, Floyd, and Clayton, for example, are what they are partly because of their families. Because in her childhood she often saw her father beat her mother and was herself molested by an uncle, Lily assumes that men have the right to dominate women. Similarly, from his father Floyd has absorbed his definition of manhood as well as his knowledge that he does not measure up to his father's standard. Unlike Lily and Floyd, Clayton has rejected the value judgments of his family, but he, too, is ruled by them.

Campbell is not a determinist but a moralist; therefore, her characters face choices, make them, and change, for better or for worse, as the novel proceeds. Some, such as Floyd, become increasingly dominated by evil. Others, such as Ida, become increasingly heroic. Still others, the most complex, are shown vacillating, sometimes losing in their internal struggles and sometimes winning. Thus Clayton wins small victories over himself but cannot manage a major achievement, while Delotha and Wydell emerge, if not unscathed, at least with self-knowledge.

Wydell, for example, is not merely the hopeless drunk he at first seems to be. He is a complex person, governed by his fragile ego. This explains his first reaction to Armstrong's death: He sees it as an opportunity to play the role of the bereaved father. It is only gradually that Wydell comes to focus on his son, rather than on himself, and to admit that because he deserted his son he bears some responsibility for the tragedy. Later, motivated by his love for Delotha and her need for him, Wydell is for a time a hard-working man and a nurturing father. Then, when Delotha transfers her full attention to their son, Wydell transfers his affections to the bottle, just as he had done before. Wydell has learned something from Armstrong's death, however, and when his second son needs him, he responds.

Themes and Meanings

In an interview, Bebe Moore Campbell said that the real subject of *Your Blues Ain't Like Mine* was not racism but childhood, specifically the kind of childhood that produces adults so uncertain about themselves that they must strike out at others in order to prove their own worth. This comment explains why Campbell so painstakingly explores the mind of the unappealing Floyd Cox. Although his actions cannot be excused, they need to be explained if such social evils as racism are ever to be eliminated.

Floyd is a prime example of someone ruined in childhood. Not only has he absorbed his family's view of the world, which is based on hatred of blacks and envy of prosperous whites, but he has also been set apart from his family as their scapegoat, the one member of whom they are ashamed. It is not surprising that Floyd never becomes a real adult, making his own decisions and acting upon them, but merely continues to react, as a child would do. Moreover, he is so preoccupied with his own insecurities that, as his wife finally realizes, he has no room for feelings toward others.

If adults who are taught in childhood to feel inadequate do not become insensitive, unthinking bullies, like Floyd, they may become emotionally crippled in other ways. Even though they can see the imperfections in their lives, Lily and Clayton have been so trained to submission that they do not have the will to act upon their beliefs.

Although Campbell understands such characters, she does not mean to imply that destiny is determined simply by one's childhood. *Your Blues Ain't Like Mine* stresses the power of every human being to choose between good and evil. She contrasts Floyd, Jr., who follows his father's example and becomes a loud-mouthed racist, an addict, and a thief, with his sister Doreen, who rejects the passive role that the Cox family traditionally assigns to women and, unlike her brother, turns her rage toward constructive channels.

Campbell's ideas about childhood and free will are closely related to a third major theme in *Your Blues Ain't Like Mine*, the extent to which human beings embrace evil simply out of fear. It is the fear of his father's contempt that causes Floyd to commit a murder; it is the fear of being denied his income and his inheritance that causes Clayton to betray two women and his own conscience; and it is the fear of losing profits that prompts the rulers of Hopewell to maintain the repressive social order, which guarantees a reliable source of cheap labor. After Armstrong's murder, even Delotha is conquered by fear. Because she wishes to keep her second son, she spoils him and, ironically, thus makes him a likely victim of the streets.

Admittedly, life holds enough dire possibilities so that even the strongest people can find themselves in the clutches of fear. Fear, however, does not have to win. In Doreen Cox, Ida Long, and Delotha Todd, Campbell shows that human beings have as great a potential for heroism as they do for cruelty and cowardice. The presence of these characters makes *Your Blues Ain't Like Mine* essentially an optimistic book.

Critical Context

Although *Your Blues Ain't Like Mine* is Campbell's first novel, it had been preceded by two nonfiction works, one of them a highly praised memoir in which can be seen many of the themes and attitudes found in the novel. *Sweet Summer: Growing Up With and Without My Dad* (1989) is an account of the author's own childhood as the child of divorced parents, focusing especially on the happy summers she spent in North Carolina with her father. In this book, Campbell emphasized such ideas as the richness of rural traditions, the importance of family bonds, and the power of individuals, like her own paraplegic father, to rise above adversity.

When *Your Blues Ain't Like Mine* appeared three years later, a few reviewers fixed immediately on the obvious fact that the book was inspired by a real tragedy, the

1955 lynching of Emmett Till, a black boy from Chicago who died tragically in Mississippi. Taking Campbell's novel as a fictionalized version of the Till incident, one reviewer criticized both Campbell's pacing of her story and what was seen as a failure to reveal the true horror of that crime. That such a view reflects a misunderstanding of the author's intentions is proved by statements in an interview reported in *The New York Times Book Review*, in which she insists that her novel is about "childhood" rather than "color" and specifically about the way that a deficiency of love during childhood can affect a person's adult life.

Most critics praised Campbell's novel, pointing out how skillfully she moved from the point of view of one character to that of another, revealing thoughts and emotions with understanding and compassion, thus creating rounded characters rather than the flat ones so often found in stories of injustice. Her plot, it was noted, was dictated by her characters.

Although some reviewers stressed the moral lesson of the novel, that racism hurts everyone, others suggested that, in ironic contradiction to her title, Campbell wishes her readers to see that all human beings are more alike than they are different. In the words of Clyde Edgerton, himself a Southern writer of note, *Your Blues Ain't Like Mine* urges "an understanding of our own hearts, our capabilities for love, fear, hate and, finally, self-respect."

Bibliography
Chadwell, Faye A. Review of *Your Blues Ain't Like Mine*, by Bebe Moore Campbell. *Library Journal* 117 (July, 1992): 120. Admires Campbell's skill in showing the complicated social structure of a small Southern town, every member of which is touched by Armstrong's death. The work is open-ended, allowing for "recovery or recurrence."
Edgerton, Clyde. "Medicine for Broken Souls." *The New York Times Book Review*, September 20, 1992, 13. A substantial essay, in which Edgerton defines what he calls the "Baby-Boomer Cornbread Eaters," who, white and black, shared a diet dictated by poverty along with a consciousness that they were considered inferior. Campbell demonstrates the fact that these people were all victims of "the practice of arrogant power and injustice." Praises her characterization, her realistic evocation of place, and her message of hope.
Graeber, Laurel. " 'It's About Childhood.' " *The New York Times Book Review*, September 20, 1992, 13. A brief report of an interview with Campbell, in which she comments on the theme and the title of her novel as well as on her concern that black children will erroneously assume that they are doomed to be victims of society.
Kirkus Reviews. Review of *Your Blues Ain't Like Mine*, by Bebe Moore Campbell. 60 (June 15, 1992): 733-734. An unfavorable review. In her novel, Campbell moves from a rapid, ineffectual depiction of a real tragedy to "soap-opera" and "a glib picture of the New South." Accuses her of "crass exploitation" of Till's story.
See, Lisa. "Bebe Moore Campbell." *Publishers Weekly* 235 (June 30, 1989): 82-83.

A lengthy interview, conducted after the publication of *Sweet Summer*, that reveals much about the writer. Campbell discusses her views on family and on divorced parents, arguing that black divorced fathers, in particular, are often portrayed as uncaring, when in fact they can be as nurturing as her own father was. Attributes her own success to the consistent support of others, including her family, to hard work, and to prayer.

Steinberg, Sybil. Review of *Your Blues Ain't Like Mine*, by Bebe Moore Campbell. *Publishers Weekly* 239 (June 22, 1992): 44. A favorable review, comparing the author to Flannery O'Connor and Harper Lee. Notes "poetic prose, fine characterization, and the references to contemporary life that "add to the rich, textured background."

Rosemary M. Canfield Reisman

MASTERPLOTS II

AFRICAN AMERICAN
LITERATURE
SERIES

TITLE INDEX

III

TITLE INDEX

v

AUTHOR INDEX

AUTHOR INDEX

HORTON, GEORGE MOSES
  Poetry of George Moses Horton,
    The, III-1058
HUGHES, LANGSTON
  Big Sea, The, *and* I Wonder as I Wander, I-131
  Poetry of Langston Hughes, The, III-1064
  Stories of Langston Hughes, The, III-1366
HUNTER, KRISTIN
  God Bless the Child, I-511
HURSTON, ZORA NEALE
  Dust Tracks on a Road, I-390
  Jonah's Gourd Vine, II-631
  Moses, Man of the Mountain, II-823
  Seraph on the Suwanee, III-1257
  Their Eyes Were Watching God, III-1418

JACKSON, GEORGE
  Soledad Brother, III-1288
JACOBS, HARRIET
  Incidents in the Life of a Slave Girl, II-592
JAMES, C. L. R.
  Essays of C. L. R. James, The, I-412
  Minty Alley, II-811
JOHNSON, CHARLES
  Faith and the Good Thing, I-430
  Middle Passage, II-805
  Oxherding Tale, II-918
JOHNSON, JAMES WELDON
  Autobiography of an Ex-Coloured Man,
    The, I-72
JOHNSON, MARGUERITE. *See* ANGELOU,
  MAYA.
JONES, GAYL
  Corregidora, I-324
  Eva's Man, I-424
JONES, LEROI. *See* BARAKA, AMIRI.
JORDAN, JUNE
  His Own Where, II-535
  Poetry of June Jordan, The, III-1069
  Technical Difficulties, III-1412

KELLEY, WILLIAM MELVIN
  Dem, I-351
  Different Drummer, A, I-368
KENAN, RANDALL
  Let the Dead Bury Their Dead, II-699
  Visitation of Spirits, A, III-1473
KENNEDY, ADRIENNE
  Funnyhouse of a Negro, I-474
  Rat's Mass, A, III-1194
KINCAID, JAMAICA
  Annie John, I-35
  At the Bottom of the River, I-52
  Lucy, II-730

KING, CORETTA SCOTT
  My Life with Martin Luther King, Jr., II-848
KING, MARTIN LUTHER, JR.
  Speeches of Martin Luther King, Jr., The,
    III-1314
KNIGHT, ETHERIDGE
  Poetry of Etheridge Knight, The,
    III-1074
KOMUNYAKAA, YUSEF
  Poetry of Yusef Komunyakaa, The,
    III-1079

LAMMING, GEORGE
  In the Castle of My Skin, II-581
  Natives of My Person, II-881
  Season of Adventure, III-1246
LARSEN, NELLA
  Passing, II-929
  Quicksand, III-1183
LEE, ANDREA
  Sarah Phillips, III-1241
LEE, DON L. *See* MADHUBUTI, HAKI R.
LITTLE, MALCOLM. *See* MALCOLM X.
LOCKE, ALAIN LEROY
  New Negro, The, II-887
LORDE, AUDRE
  Cancer Journals, The, I-225
  Poetry of Audre Lorde, The, III-1085
LOVELACE, EARL
  Dragon Can't Dance, The, I-379
  Wine of Astonishment, The, III-1496

MCKAY, CLAUDE
  Banana Bottom, I-108
  Home to Harlem, II-540
  Poetry of Claude McKay, The,
    III-1090
MCKNIGHT, REGINALD
  I Get on the Bus, II-563
MCMILLAN, TERRY
  Disappearing Acts, I-373
  Mama, II-748
  Waiting to Exhale, III-1484
MCPHERSON, JAMES ALAN
  Stories of James Alan McPherson, The, III-1371
MADHUBUTI, HAKI R.
  Black Men, I-155
  Poetry of Haki R. Madhubuti, The,
    III-1097
MAJOR, CLARENCE
  My Amputations, II-842
  Painted Turtle, II-924
  Reflex and Bone Structure, III-1206

AUTHOR INDEX

Possessing the Secret of Joy, III-1166
Third Life of Grange Copeland, The,
  III-1429
WALKER, MARGARET
  Jubilee, II-642
WASHINGTON, BOOKER T.
  Up from Slavery, III-1467
WATKINS, GLORIA. *See* HOOKS, BELL.
WEST, CORNEL
  American Evasion of Philosophy, The, I-18
WHEATLEY, PHILLIS
  Poetry of Phillis Wheatley, The,
  III-1142
WIDEMAN, JOHN EDGAR
  Brothers and Keepers, I-206
  Homewood Trilogy, The, II-546
  Hurry Home, II-558
  Philadelphia Fire, II-935
WILLIAMS, JOHN A.
  Captain Blackman, I-238
  Man Who Cried I Am, The, II-759
WILLIAMS, PAULETTE. *See* SHANGE,
  NTOZAKE.
WILLIAMS, SHERLEY ANNE
  Dessa Rose, I-357
  Poetry of Sherley Anne Williams, The, III-1148

WILSON, AUGUST
  Fences, I-442
  Joe Turner's Come and Gone, II-625
  Ma Rainey's Black Bottom, II-736
  Piano Lesson, The, II-947
  Two Trains Running, III-1457
WILSON, HARRIET E.
  Our Nig, II-905
WRIGHT, CHARLES
  Messenger, The, II-800
WRIGHT, JAY
  Poetry of Jay Wright, The, III-1154
WRIGHT, RICHARD
  Black Boy *and* American Hunger, I-142
  Lawd Today, II-670
  Long Dream, The, II-724
  Native Son, II-875
  Outsider, The, II-911
WRIGHT, SARAH E.
  This Child's Gonna Live, III-1435

YERBY, FRANK G.
  Dahomean, The, I-341
YOUNG, AL
  Poetry of Al Young, The, III-1160
  Seduction by Light, III-1252

XI

TYPE OF WORK INDEX

MASTERPLOTS II